THE
MBA
HANDBOOK

THE MBA HANDBOOK

Academic and professional skills for mastering management

Eighth Edition

SHEILA CAMERON
The Open Universtiy Business School

PEARSON

Harlow, England • London • New York • Boston • San Francisco • Toronto • Sydney • Auckland • Singapore • Hong Kong
Tokyo • Seoul • Taipei • New Delhi • Cape Town • São Paulo • Mexico City • Madrid • Amsterdam • Munich • Paris • Milan

PEARSON EDUCATION LIMITED
Edinburgh Gate
Harlow CM20 2JE
United Kingdom
Tel: +44 (0)1279 623623
Web: www.pearson.com/uk

First edition published 1991 in Great Britain under the Pitman Publishing imprint (print)
Third edition 1996 (print)
Fourth edition 2001 (print)
Fifth edition 2005 (print)
Sixth edition 2008 (print)
Seventh edition published 2011 (print and electronic)
Eighth edition published 2016 (print and electronic)

ISBN: 978-1-292-08868-6 (print)
978-1-292-08871-6 (PDF)
978-1-292-17065-7 (ePub)

British Library Cataloguing-in-Publication Data
A catalogue record for the print edition is available from the British Library

Library of Congress Cataloging-in-Publication Data
Names: Cameron, Sheila, author.
Title: The MBA handbook : academic and professional skills for mastering
    management / Sheila Cameron,   The Open University Business School.
Description: Eighth Edition. | New York : Pearson, 2016. | Revised edition of
    the author's The MBA handbook, 2011.
Identifiers: LCCN 2016008426 (print) | LCCN 2016008690 (ebook) | ISBN
    9781292088686 (print) | ISBN 9781292088716 (PDF) | ISBN 9781292170657 (ePub)
Subjects: LCSH: Master of business administration degree. | Business
    education. | Industrial management—Study and teaching (Graduate)
Classification: LCC HF1111 .C27 2016 (print) | LCC HF1111 (ebook) | DDC
    650.071/173—dc23
LC record available at http://lccn.loc.gov/2016008426

10 9 8 7 6 5 4 3 2 1
20 19 18 17 16

Cartoons by Neill Cameron

Print edition typeset in 9/13 Stone Serif ITC Pro by Lumina Datamatics
Printed and bound in Malaysia (CTP-PJB)

NOTE THAT ANY PAGE CROSS REFERENCES REFER TO THE PRINT EDITION

BRIEF CONTENTS

PART 5 INTEGRATING YOUR SKILLS
AND GOING FORWARD

CONTENTS

PART 2 TRANSFERABLE PERSONAL SKILLS

PART 3 TRANSFERABLE LEARNING SKILLS

PART 4 SKILLS FOR ASSESSMENT

PART 5 INTEGRATING YOUR SKILLS AND GOING FORWARD

PREFACE

I originally wrote *The MBA Handbook* because I saw so many students failing to gain much value from their MBA studies because they lacked the necessary understanding of what learning at this level is about, and lacked at least some of the skills necessary for such learning. This seemed a tremendous waste of students' – and tutors' – efforts, and of students' money.

These aims have remained constant, but subsequent editions have reflected my own growing understanding of the learning process, and students' feedback on the book. There has been a constant need to update any reference to IT: within a couple of years, anything written is overtaken by developments in the field. This edition features online search and a wider range of presentation software than before. But apart from this, the book has remained essentially the same – largely because so many students profess to love it as it is. It is still a handbook rather than a textbook. While key ideas are referenced, there are far fewer references than in a standard text. The text is based as much on experience as on scholarship.

While the basic skills development content has remained essentially the same, successive editions have included more in-depth discussion of what, and how, managers on MBAs need to learn. This has been driven by the increasing financial, and other, uncertainties that managers now face. The shelf life of much of the 'traditional' MBA content is diminishing, and learning to think constructively in the face of uncertainty is becoming much more important.

Theories devised in times of stability may have limited relevance in times of rapid change. Case studies of organisations operating in a very different economic and competitive context may offer reduced insights to those managing during the next 20 or 30 years. Theory and cases can still serve as an invaluable vehicle for developing the conceptual skills needed to understand and respond to complex and uncertain situations. But the lasting benefits of MBA study will come from developing these conceptual skills, rather than from the means by which they were developed.

Continuous learning and development is part of the definition of a professional. Managers in changing times need constantly to develop their ability to think effectively when faced with new uncertainties and complexities. While MBA teaching traditionally has introduced the idea of experiential learning, and elements of reflection, these often have not been exploited fully. Increased understanding of the characteristics of professional learning, and of the role of practice in such learning, is shifting the emphasis much more towards an experimental – rather than taught – approach to theory. The experiments are experiments in thinking with a view to exploring the effects of different ways of thinking, rather than experiments as understood in the hard sciences.

Management is now increasingly seen as being about making sense of new situations, drawing on a wider range of evidence than that which can be measured objectively. This is underpinned by ideas of a constructed rather than objective 'reality'. From this perspective the process of construction is itself something to be considered and experimented with. The book seeks to develop a deeper understanding of the role of assumptions, tacit theory and/or mindset in both perception and interpretation. Such awareness forms the basis for challenges to existing thought habits, and the development of more flexible ways of thinking. Because mindsets are often shared, and when they differ they may lead to conflict rather than insight, there is an increased emphasis on collaborative learning and reflective dialogue. Managers will find this helpful at work, as well as during their course.

Another shift in emphasis in recent years concerns ethics. Many organisations now recognise that a wider range of stakeholders need to be considered than shareholders alone. Growing recognition of the impact of organisations not only on the local environment but on wider society has raised the profile of issues of sustainability, and the ethical issues presented by the need to decide between conflicting stakeholder objectives.

This edition places slightly more emphasis on personal skills, including additional discussion of emotional competencies. There is increased emphasis on teamwork, communication and virtual working. Employability features more strongly. There is less expectation that students will use the book before the course starts. It has become difficult in recent years to fit the changes into the original chapter structure. This time the decision was taken to alter the structure to fit the current content better. I apologise to lecturers who may find that some of their lecture notes will need to be changed as a result. I hope that it will be very easy to see what changes are needed, and that you will find the new structure more logical. I am hopeful that these changes will help students to benefit more fully from traditional MBA programmes, by giving them a more critical approach to theory. For students on MBAs where the emphasis is shifting towards professional and practice-based (rather than purely academic) learning, the benefit will be even greater. As ever, feedback would be welcomed.

ACKNOWLEDGEMENTS

Among the many people I should like to thank are Penelope Woolf for persuading me to write this book in the first place, and Natalia Jaszczuk for support throughout the present edition; the Open University as an institution, and close colleagues, in particular, for giving me the space to write, and my students for being an endless source of challenge, stimulus and ideas. Last, but definitely not least, I should particularly like to thank Hester, Neill and James for their research, comments, suggestions and general support throughout.

Sheila Cameron

Publisher's Acknowledgements

We are grateful to the following for permission to reproduce copyright material:

Cartoon

Cartoon on page 303 from Cartoon by Neill Cameron, www.planetdumbass.co.uk.

Figures

Figure 6.2 adapted from *Organizational Psychology: Readings on Human Behaviour in Organisations*, Prentice Hall (Kolb, D. A., Rubin, I. M., McIntyre, J. M. 1984) p. 21; Figure 6.3 adapted from *Organizational Learning: A Theory of Action Perspective*, Addison Wesley Longman (Argyris, C. and Schon, D. 1978).

PART 1
UNDERSTANDING THE TERRITORY

1

MANAGEMENT, LEADERSHIP, LEARNING AND THIS HANDBOOK

Learning outcomes

By the end of this chapter you should:

- understand some key issues facing managers and leaders today, and the central role learning plays in dealing with these

- appreciate the distinctive challenges of learning at postgraduate level, and how the book will help you meet these

- see how most of the skills needed to do well when studying management are equally important for career success as a senior manager, entrepreneur or consultant

- understand the structure of the book and how it can help you develop these key skills

- have started to think about your own learning priorities, and how best to use the book in the light of these.

Introduction

Studying for an MBA or other postgraduate (PG) management qualification is a major investment of time, money and emotional energy. Not everyone gets the return on this investment they hope for. Some students drop out, many students do not do as well as they had hoped and far too many gain a qualification but do not develop the conceptual and other skills needed for rapid success. This book is intended to help you approach your study in a way that will not only help you gain good marks but also, more importantly, develop the personal, management and leadership skills that will contribute to a successful career.

This first chapter gives a brief overview of the likely challenges postgraduate management study will pose, and prompts you to clarify your learning priorities. It explains the book's structure, and the design features that will help you to enhance your learning and your grades. It explains how to start examining your aims, assessing your learning needs and taking action in the light of this assessment. You can then continue using the book as an aid to managing you learning as you work through each chapter.

You are investing not just money, but time, emotion and energy in your studies. Fifty years ago, when MBAs were new in Europe the qualification alone would have almost guaranteed career success. Today, as you probably found when choosing a programme, you can choose between a multitude of MBAs , MAs and MScs in management-related subjects and specialisms. While a postgraduate qualification is still helpful, the letters after your name no longer guarantee success. Recruiters look for evidence of a wide range of relevant skills and experience, and unless you continue to demonstrate these skills and perform well in each role, promotion may be slow. As your career progresses your achievements will increasingly become more important than your qualification.

Your chosen programme will offer many opportunities to develop career-relevant skills, and the good news is that they will also lead to better grades. Successful learning on a management Master's degree requires many of the skills a manager needs. Sadly, too many students fail to recognise the importance of these skills so fail to exploit the opportunities to develop them. This chapter argues for the transferability of key skills, and their importance. Later chapters will discuss and develop the different skill sets you will need.

You are probably already highly skilled in some areas, but may have development needs in others. This chapter will help you identify your own learning priorities. The explanation of the book's structure and design will help you work out how best to use the book to meet these priorities.

Management and leadership issues and learning

Organisations, and therefore their managers and leaders, face greater and more varied challenges today than ever before. You will almost certainly spend some of your time studying the external factors affecting almost any organisation. These are often referred to by the acronym PEST/STEEP/PESTLE/STEEPLE, depending on how finely the factors are categorised. A look at these factors shows how rapidly they are changing, and some of the challenges they are likely to pose for managers.

Socio-demographic factors such as population movements within the EU, and illegal inward migration from impoverished or war-torn areas can affect demand for some services and supply of labour.

Technological developments have created whole new product areas and marketing possibilities, transformed management work and organisational structures, and enabled operation on a global scale.

Economic factors can have a huge impact on demand for products and availability of finance (consider the impact of the banking crisis on overdraft facilities for small businesses).

Environmental (i.e. biosphere-related) factors, such as attempts to curb carbon emissions to slow global warming, offer massive opportunities to green energy providers, and may threaten other businesses, significant weather changes and sea level rise may impact many regions and organisations.

Political factors such as the rising force of Islamist regimes, and Russia's expansionist tendencies can render supplies (e.g. of oil) and markets highly unpredictable, while trade agreements have been another major enabler of globalisation.

Legal factors, which might be seen as a subset of political, or considered in their own right, can have a profound influence on organisations affected by, for example, legislation limiting or making illegal goods, services or procedures core to their operation.

Ethical issues, such as willingness to pay bribes, may limit competitiveness in some markets, while issues such as concerns with growing inequality may affect management pay and restrict some activities.

Many of these external factors, and their impact were/will be hard to predict, and it is likely that there will be many more that we cannot at present envisage. (For example, in July 2015 the UK government 'discontinued' their *Green Deal* scheme for encouraging householders to reduce energy consumption. Individuals who had invested in gaining accreditation as assessors for this scheme, and a great many companies set up to provide the improvements funded by the scheme were taken completely by surprise by this change in government policy, which threatened their very existence.)

Organisations which can anticipate external changes, perceive their potential impact and respond appropriately are more likely to compete successfully. This means that they need to be flexible, innovative, and very sensitive to their environments. Senior managers need to constantly monitor environmental factors, selecting and interpreting the necessary information to make sense of this fluid and uncertain context. They will need to craft innovative responses, probably working closely with colleagues from many different cultures to do so. They will then need to inspire others to work towards making necessary changes. Above all, as new situations and challenges constantly present themselves, managers need continuously to *learn*.

Your programme will aim to develop the conceptual and interpersonal skills needed to cope with such challenges, but not all of these skills will be directly assessed. If you focus only on what you need to write for assignments, you will miss opportunities to develop many of the important softer skills. If you do not take the risk of challenging some of your deepest-held assumptions, and learn to hold back from 'certainties' to explore other ways of thinking you will be at risk throughout your career of leaping to the obvious – but wrong – solution. And if you do not develop the habit of reflecting on your practice, and the thinking that led to it, you will not develop the mental flexibility and professional learning skills senior managers need.

It is factors such as these that make both the challenges and the potential benefits of your study more than you probably expected. The next section explores some of the challenges of postgraduate study in more detail.

Management and study challenges addressed in the handbook

Much of the theory you learn in your studies will be in the form of sets of categories. Categorising things is one of the ways we try to make sense of them. The challenges posed by postgraduate management study can be categorised in many ways, but the following may be helpful:

- **Purely practical challenges** such as finding and managing time and energy for study, particularly if you are studying part-time and face competing pressures from job and family. There may be other practical difficulties if you have not studied for some time, or are new to the country in which you are studying

- **Moving from undergraduate to postgraduate level**, with the greater academic demands this implies. These challenges will be greater if your earlier education has been in a very different educational system

- **Specific aspects of the subject-matter**; for example, many students with an arts background are nervous about the numbers involved in studying finance, while engineers and scientists may be nervous about the ambiguities and lack of certainty in many areas of management

- **Linking theory to practice and professional development**, which is essential in professional studies where the ultimate goal is to use what you learn in a subsequent career

If you appreciate – and prepare for – these challenges you will be better able to cope with them. This section outlines these challenges and points to the parts of the book that will be particularly helpful in relation to each. As you read it, note chapters you think may be particularly helpful for you.

Practical challenges

You will achieve little in any area if you cannot plan and organise your own time and other resources, set yourself objectives, motivate yourself to get going, measure your progress and take action to correct if progress is not what you need to meet your goals. These are the basics of any management activity, and apply equally to managing yourself. As

➤ **Ch 3** well as being a pre-requisite for gaining your qualification, planning and management skills will contribute to success throughout your career.

If studying while working, the challenge of finding enough time (and energy) for study may be as great as any intellectual challenges you face. On a part-time pro- gramme you will typically need to 'find' 12 or more hours a week for course work. This poses a serious time-management challenge, if, like most part-time students, you have a family to consider, and/or are coming to terms with practical aspects of living in a new country.

If you are working while studying you will need to manage your time at work in order to protect your study time, and to manage your study time in order to gain maximum benefit from it. Time management is an obviously transferable skill: many MBA gradu- ates claim that by far the greatest benefit they gained from their studies was greatly im-

➤ **Ch 4** proved time management.

If you have a job and/or family you will also need to manage your relationships with them in relation to your study. Employers, supervisors, family and friends are all key stakeholders in your learning: they can help or hinder you greatly. They are more likely to help if they understand the benefits to be gained, and *how* they can help. Stakeholder management is another transferable skill, equally important for senior managers and the self-employed.

Managing time both at work and home will require you to manage some of the key stakeholders in your studies: your work colleagues and your family. Good managers and good leaders are very aware of the importance of stakeholders and of potential conflicts between stakeholder objectives, and take care to manage these. The skill you will need for

➤ **Ch 3** study success is highly transferable to your management role.

Managing stakeholders will involve communication skills – unless you can communi- cate freely about your needs and negotiate over any necessary compromises you will not gain their support. Because communication skills are a pre-requisite for almost any job, your programme is likely to offer many opportunities for group discussions and group project work. Learning with others, particularly through collaborative reflective dia-

➤ **Chs 6,** logue, is a vital skill for managers in a rapidly changing business world. Group projects in
9 particular will depend upon team work and communication skills.

Despite your best plans, there are likely to be times when unexpected demands and other pressures will be more than you can comfortably handle and your stress levels will rise. Techniques for managing your own stress will be important in such cases. Stress is a significant issue in many organisations. It can contribute to poor performance, absence, disciplinary action and unfair dismissal. The ability to recognise and manage your own

➤ **Ch 3** stress – and by extension stress in others – is another highly transferable skill.

Challenges of postgraduate study

Any postgraduate management qualification will seek to develop – and then use and as- sess – conceptual skills *beyond* the level of a first degree. This size of the difference will depend on your first degree. If you studied in a 'hard' science or technology area the dif- ference is likely to be greater than if you studied a social science subject, for example, unless your programme is highly quantitative. If you studied in an educational system based on learning – and remembering – 'facts' the difference will be greater still. (If you do not have a first degree, or gained it so long ago you can remember little about it, then the challenges will be greater still.)

Some educational systems are based on what is often called a 'jug and mug' model of teaching and learning. In this model 'knowledge' is transmitted by the teacher, and students' learning is tested by seeing whether they can reproduce from memory what they have been taught. Students are not required to do much thinking, and their study is firmly directed by their teachers.

At postgraduate level, certainly in management-related subjects, students are normally expected to take considerably more responsibility for choosing suitable resources to supplement lectures, and *thinking critically* about these. Senior managers are expected to take decisions based on evidence, so the ability to assess evidence and draw conclusions from it is an important transferable skill. Presenting these conclusions, and the arguments that led you to them, convincingly is another important management skill. Models and other sorts of theory are an important aid to analysing situations, but the value of theory needs to be *judged*. Many organisations have suffered because a chief executive has uncritically embraced the latest management theory or fad.

➤ Chs 6,
14, 15

Most postgraduate programmes will require you to carry out a substantial piece of independent work, in your own organisation if you are studying part time, or on a consultancy basis with a co-operative local company, or based on existing information. This will test both your self-management and project management skills and your ability to draw on existing knowledge to make sense of situations in a way that suggests future action.

➤ Chs 10,
13, 14,
15

A much wider range of work is likely to be expected for assessment at postgraduate level, not only the essays and written examinations you may be used to but also management reports, reflective writing, presentations using visual aids, and sometimes poster presentations and projects and/or business or marketing plans. Written work will need to be clearly argued from evidence, and to show that you have thought about ideas in the light of a range of theories and your own experience if relevant. Again, all these skills (with the possible exception of the essay form) are clearly relevant to management.

Challenges specific to management content

➤ Chs 10,
11, 13,
16

Different modules on your programme will inevitably present different challenges. The modules themselves will teach you how to address most of these. While this book will occasionally use some of the theory you will learn (as with STEEPLE) when it helps with understanding the skills element which this book addresses, this is not its main purpose. Instead, it addresses more general issues that no individual modules may 'own'. Thus it covers basic skills that all students are (wrongly in my experience) assumed to already have. Your own needs will be different from those of other students. Work out which 'gaps' you have already. If you feel you need to develop your writing skills, or to revise basic mathematics, or help with analysing case studies, this handbook provides it.

Linking theory to practice and professional development

An expectation of any member of a profession is that they will take responsibility for remaining up to date, and for continuously developing their skills. Some programmes have been designed to meet the requirements of one or other professional institute, and will therefore specifically address professional development issues. Even those which are not directly linked are likely to seek to develop relevant learning skills, and in particular learning by 'reflection on practice', something not addressed in may undergraduate programmes. If it is new to you, you may not at first appreciate the value of reflective learning. However, reflection on practice is an essential part of the continuous learning needed in any professional career, so it is worth doing all you can to develop the skills and the habit. You will also need to be able to evidence such learning: building a learning portfolio, with learning plans, progress reports and other evidence of learning and com-

➤ **Ch 6**   petence is likely to be useful throughout your career.

Your reflections are likely to be helped by thinking about practice in the light of management theory, and you will certainly need to engage with theory in this way if you are to gain the deeper learning expected at PG level, and which will help you to be effective at work. An important strand running through the book concerns the link between ideas, thinking and practice. The way you react to a situation will depend on what/how you think about that situation, and how you think will be influenced by underlying ideas – assumptions, beliefs or theories about the people and organisations concerned. Your studies will introduce you to a wide range of new theories. But these will only influence your

➤ **Chs 7, 9**   career if you use them to alter your own thinking and make the link to your own practice – while you are studying -past, present and/or future.

Potential benefits of postgraduate management study

You may now be realising that there is more potential benefit to your studies than you initially realised. You may also be realising that study may be more demanding than you anticipated. When you face difficulties, or start to lose motivation, it is really helpful to remind yourself of the benefits you will gain from reaching your goal. And if you know which potential benefits are most important to you, you can prioritise your efforts to be sure of achieving these.

Activity 1.1

....

Before reading further, imagine yourself five years into the future. Imagine that your career has progressed more than you could have hoped and think of all the ways your qualification, and the learning you gained on the way has helped you achieve this.

The letters after your name, while valuable, are likely to be the least important benefit. In his autobiography John Horsler (2011) describes his own MBA experience. The owner/

chairman of Adroit Holdings, Horsler was already a successful manager, and had just been head hunted as managing director for a not very profitable plc when he chose to study. Clearly, he did not need to gain a qualification to further his career, but having left school at 16 he felt that learning more about what he was actually doing would be good. He never regretted what he described as 'a life changing decision'.

John says that his studies helped him to realise just how much variation there was in different people's perceptions of any situation, and their thoughts about what they had perceived. This helped him to recognise – and use – different perspectives in order to gain a deeper understanding of the situation. Furthermore, his studies gave him the final confidence to buy a business of his own for the first time.

The following comments by past MBA students give some idea of the wide range of benefits of postgraduate study.

Quotes by past students

'I am now far more creative in the way I approach problems.'

'I am now good at seeing what we need to do to fit in with overall strategy.'

'I find I am far better at coping with complexity – I no longer try to over-simplify situations in order to make them manageable.'

'I now see that my own perspective on a situation is no more valid than the perspectives of others involved, and that I have a lot to learn from them.'

'I couldn't see the point at first, but I now think I shall always carry my "reflective notebook" with me, and also make time to reflect over the past week.'

MBAs were once available only to the elite, but are now far more widespread, and have been joined by many other management Master's degrees. This means that employers want to see more than letters after your name. They are likely to look at the reputation of the university providing your qualification, and at your achievements before and during the programme. A postgraduate management qualification may still increase your chance of being interviewed for a senior role, but what you have actually learned and achieved are increasingly important. If you are in a job, how you perform, and the impression you make on your seniors, will probably have far more impact on subsequent promotions and job applications than the qualification itself.

Sadly, many students who gain a qualification show little other benefit from their studies. This will soon become apparent to their work colleagues. Part of the reason may be that they learn the wrong things – Mintzberg (2004) suggests that being exposed to management education can leave a 'distorted impression of management. Management is a practice that has to blend a good deal of craft (experience) with a certain amount of art (insight) and some science (analysis).' An education that over-emphasises either aspect at the expense of the other can produce either technocrats or heroes. Neither is helpful. What we need, rather, is 'balanced, dedicated people who practice a style of managing that can be called "engaging". Such people believe that their purpose is to leave behind stronger organisations, not just higher share prices' (*op. cit.* p. 1). Since this was written many programmes have been redesigned to give more weight to experience, but many still pass those whose *learning* has yet to achieve the right balance, and many students do not recognise the importance of learning from experience.

Mintzberg concludes his argument by saying, 'No one can create a leader in a classroom. But existing managers can significantly improve their practice in a thoughtful classroom that makes use of those experiences'. You make use of your experiences by using ideas learned through study when reflecting on that practice.

These short quotes cover themes that will run through this book, in particular the balance between theory and practice and the need for 'thoughtfulness' (and thinking and reflection), if you are to benefit from study. One aim of this book is to help you to develop the skills for such 'thoughtfulness'. But they may also cause you to question some of your reasons for study.

Activity 1.2

Read the above quotes carefully, noting the criticisms Mintzberg makes. Consider the extent to which you agree or disagree with them, and your reasons. Discuss with others if you can.

Later chapters explore critical thinking in more detail. This activity is asking you to try thinking in this way. Being *critical* involves questioning assumptions and assertions. It involves making judgments in the light of evidence, arguments and your own experience. It requires you to question your own assumptions and ways of thinking.

You cannot properly assess the validity of Mintzberg's arguments and evidence unless you read his book. But even a superficial 'unpicking' and evaluation of the quoted statements may have started to bring to the surface some of your own beliefs about management, learning and its purpose. If you can discuss your reaction to these quotes with others you may find interesting differences of opinion – exploring these will help you identify assumptions you and they are making that you may not be aware of.

In case you are not in a position to share your views on the quotes, here are some of my reactions so that you can see how you differ from me. I chose the quote because, like Mintzberg, I feel that any postgraduate management programme needs to be built around the idea that *management is a practice* and must *draw upon management experience*. If not, they may produce graduates who are a liability rather than an asset to any organisation. Furthermore, I think he raises an important ethical issue which MBA and similar management programmes need to address: is the role of a manager merely to add value for shareholders, or do managers have social responsibilities?

Where I *disagree* is with the implication that there is a great deal wrong with all management education: Mintzberg was writing mainly about MBAs in the US in the early 2000s. Some US programmes were already very different from those he criticises, and more are now. The majority of European MBAs, and many other Master's management programmes are much less removed from practice than those Mintzberg criticised. Part of reading critically, addressed in Chapter 7, is judging the relevance to your own situation of data used to support a conclusion. Data from a different geographic context or from a time when things were rather different from today may mean that the conclusions they support may not be relevant to your own situation.

Activity 1.3

In the light of what you have read thus far, list what you see as the main benefits you might hope to gain from your studies in addition to the qualification itself. Underline any that are particularly important and keep this list safe. Revisit it from time to time, adding any additional benefits that occur to you as your studies proceed.

How to use this handbook

This handbook aims to help you complete your qualification with good grades. More importantly, it seeks to help you to gain real and lasting benefit from the learning opportunities study at this level can offer. If you take full advantage of the opportunities for deeper learning your programme offers, rather than merely learning what is needed to pass assessment, you will be transformed as a manager and leader, and your career prospects will be greatly improved.

The book will help you achieve this, but only if you use it as *a prompt to thinking* – and thinking seriously – about yourself, your strengths and weaknesses, and the way in which you habitually think about learning, and about management and leadership. You need to be prepared to challenge some of your own deeply held beliefs in ways that may redefine your sense of your own identity.

The book is designed to help everyone studying management on an MBA or other postgraduate programme, in order to develop their professional practice as a manager, and accelerate their career. As Mintzberg noted, universities and their students find it a challenge to balance the academic and the practical. You may know more about the practice of management than your teachers. (In an ideal world they would learn as much from you as you from them.) This handbook aims to guide you through both practitioner and academic aspects of learning. I hope it will also help you to engage in dialogue with work colleagues, fellow students and your lecturers about key aspects of management, helping all participants to develop their understanding of emerging issues

➤ Chs 6, 9

Note, however, that this handbook is *not* a textbook. It does not seek to give a definitive view of anything, it is not full of facts, and referencing has deliberately been kept to a minimum. Instead it draws upon more than 30 years of teaching and examining management students, primarily at MBA level, and experience as an external examiner on a wide range of postgraduate Master's programmes. This is supplemented by some of what I have read that has helped make sense of what my experience suggests helps managers learn and develop as professionals. It is designed to prompt your own thinking in directions that may help you learn – and often manage – more effectively.

You have already encountered three 'Activity' boxes. If you took time to do the activities, you are using the book as intended. If you did not, you need to go back and do Activity 1.3 at least, and seek to do all the activities in following chapters unless they are irrelevant to your own situation. These activities are designed to prompt reflection on your own management thinking, learning and practice, and help you recording your reflections and other learning. Such reflection if essential if you are to benefit from the book, and to learn vital skills from your studies. Reading the activities is not enough – you need to work through the activities and exercises provided. Skipping them may seem to save time, but it is a false economy.

It will be helpful to capture not only your responses to activities, but other ideas prompted by the book. You may like to scribble in the margins or stick in a Post-it, carry around a small notebook, create a specific file on your tablet or other portable device, or use a mix of methods for different types of thought. The important thing is that you choose an approach that is convenient and comfortable for you, and one that you can easily refer to later. You will find it really helpful to revisit your thoughts from time to time, whether for an essay or to check your progress. Sometimes it will prompt you to action you have forgotten you intended, but can now see was important. Sometimes you will be amazed (and encouraged) at how far your thoughts have developed in a short period.

➤ Chs 6, 9

Collaborative reflection is important, so when you can, discuss your thoughts with others. Collaborative reflection using dialogue is one of the best ways of becoming aware of aspects of your thinking which are shaping your conclusions and actions without your being aware of it. The book covers the skills for dialogue and group discussion which will help with this.

Because of the diverse backgrounds of MBA students, some chapters will be more important to you than others. For example, if you have a maths degree you are not going to need to read the chapter on numbers, but may find material on reflective learning, case analysis or report writing helpful.

Some skills are dealt with in a single chapter, others are revisited several times. This is because learning, particularly learning about complex issues, can be seen as a spiral process. You may need a broad grasp of several aspects of a topic as a basis for further more in-depth learning. Thus you will find that topics such as knowledge, theory and learning are revisited in several chapters.

Your first challenge in taking responsibility for your learning is to identify the chapters that are a priority for you. If you are to gain full value from your MBA, you will need to actively manage your learning. The same applies to optimising your benefit from this book.

Activity 1.4

If you have not already done so, glance at the contents pages to familiarise yourself with the scope of the book. Identify areas that you already know are high or low priorities for you. As you work through the book you will be able to check your initial assessments and identify other areas where development might help.

How the book is structured

There are two aspects to the structure, the arrangement of chapters within the book, and the features of any single chapter. The contents list will have given you an idea of the structure of the book, and its division into five parts addressing different sorts of challenges, broadly in the order you will meet them. The discussion of study challenges indicated chapters that were particularly relevant. Table 1.1 summarises the relation between structure and challenges.

Part 1	Understanding the territory	Relevant to:
Ch 1	Management, leadership, learning and this handbook	Understanding the challenges managers face Linking theory and practice Using the handbook to optimise learning
Ch 2	The challenges of MBA and postgraduate study	Understanding the design of learning programmes Appreciating the central role of reflection in professional development Setting learning objectives
Part 2	Transferable personal skills	Relevant to:
Ch 3	Managing yourself and other stakeholders	Identifying your management development needs Identifying and managing key stakeholders Managing emotion and stress Becoming more assertive
Ch 4	Managing your time	Prioritising Developing planning and organisational skills Making effective use of work and study time
Part 3	Transferable learning skills	Relevant to:
Ch 5	Managing your learning	Making practical arrangements for easier learning Planning and managing study time to achieve goals Keeping a learning log
Ch 6	Professional development	Using both learning and management theory to develop as a professional Identifying your learning style and likely challenges Engaging in dialogue for collaborative learning Developing reflective writing skills Building a portfolio

➤

Ch 7	**Critical use of ideas and information**	Finding relevant, reliable information in libraries and online Critically evaluating ideas and arguments Developing reading and note-taking skills Using bibliographic software
Ch 8	**Diagrams and other visuals**	Using diagrams to understand complex situations Choosing and using appropriate diagrams to help communicate Critically interpreting diagrams
Ch 9	**Teamwork, leadership and learning**	Developing communication skills Becoming an effective team member and leader Helping groups learn and perform more effectively Working in action learning sets and virtual teams
Ch 10	**Case studies, complex problems and consultancy**	Accepting and working with complexity Diagnosing the 'real' issues in complex cases Using concepts to make sense of complexity Developing consultancy skills
Ch 11	**Seeing stories in numbers**	Overcoming any fear of numbers Using basic calculations and graphs to understand and communicate numerical information Understanding probability and statistical significance.
Part 4	**Skills for assessment**	**Relevant to:**
Ch 12	**Understanding your assessors**	Different types of assessment, and their objectives Understanding any differences in approach between the UK and other countries where you have studied Seeing assignment s as communication Avoiding common pitfalls with assessment

1

MANAGEMENT, LEADERSHIP, LEARNING AND THIS HANDBOOK

Ch 13	**Writing to impress**	Communicating in clear written English
		Understanding questions, and academic expectations for an answer
		Building ideas into a clear essay or report structure
		Citing and referencing sources
		Protecting against plagiarism
Ch 14	**Speaking to impress**	Planning and developing a presentation to meet audience needs and expectations
		Choosing and using visual aids and presentation software
		Presenting as a group and/or online
		Handling logistics, nerves and audience questions
Ch 15	**Examinations and other forms of assessment**	Preparing for written and oral examinations
		Addressing question asked in either form of exam
		Developing a portfolio for professional assessment
Part 5	**Integrating your skills and going forward**	**Relevant to:**
Ch 16	**Projects, theses and dissertations**	Understanding key requirements for a project, thesis or dissertation
		Making best use of your tutor or supervisor, and managing any organisational expectations
		Choosing a sensible and feasible topic to research
		Finding and using literature to refine topic and chooe a suitable method of researching it further
		Analysing and drawing conclusions from evidence
		Drafting a compelling final report or thesis
Ch 17	**Managing your career**	Clarifying your career objectives and planning steps to achieve them
		Building your CV and networking
		Identifying suitable job opportunities and crafting a successful job application

Structure of each chapter

As well as the overall arrangement of chapters within the book it will help to be aware of the structure within each chapter. Many of the features of the book are outlined in the 'Guided tour' of the book on pp. xiv–xv. If you have not yet looked at this, it would be helpful to do so now.

All chapters follow a similar pattern to this first one, starting with a set of learning outcomes for the chapter followed by an introduction. Think about the outcomes first, highlighting any which are particularly important for you, and adding any others that you would like to achieve by reading the chapter. At the end of your work on the chapter, check whether these additions have also been met.

To achieve the outcomes you will need to work through any activities and exercises included in the chapter. Exercises are intended as a check on your understanding of techniques or concepts and normally will have an answer. These answers are printed at the end of the chapter in which the exercise occurs. Activities do not have answers, though the subsequent discussion in the text may draw upon what you have written. You can jot down short answers to activities on the text itself. It will be helpful to construct a file of some sort where you can put longer answers (there is more on this in Chapters 2, 7 and 8).

At the end of each chapter you will find suggested sources of *further information* or relevant interesting reading. Note that this is not a list of the references for that chapter. References for the whole book are provided at the end of the book. Note that you will find far fewer references than in most texts, as this is intended as a practical rather than scholarly handbook, and draws as much on experience as reading.

'Further information' offers a list of sources that you might find useful if you wish to read more on a particular issue. It is an idiosyncratic selection – on many topics there are dozens of possible sources. I have picked those that seemed to go beyond the chapter, but not so far beyond that they would take an unreasonable amount of your time or effort, and that seemed to me to offer reasonable advice or information. If you can find something else that suits your needs – there are always new online resources becoming available – then use that rather than feeling you need to stick to the *further information* list.

What you gain from a chapter will depend upon your current thought processes and mindset, and the issues that are of concern to you at the time you read it. If you re-read it later you will almost certainly find additional messages or points that seem to be significant. It is therefore well worth revisiting chapters *whenever* the content is relevant to an aspect of your study or relates to something in your management role that is proving even slightly problematic.

 As indicated, there is also a companion website associated with this book. You will find it at **www.pearsoned.co.uk/cameron**, and items on this website are shown in the text by the symbol shown here. There you will find a range of proformas for activities, additional exercises for some of the chapters and links to other useful sources of information.

Activity 1.5

Think in broad terms about your preparedness to study and areas that concern you. List these, noting down reasons for your concern. Do this in a form that you can file for later reference. (There will be suggestions for how you can organise such notes later.)

Now select two of the chapters that seem most relevant to your needs and spend some time skimming these. Try to assess how long they would take you to work through if you were to do all the activities thoroughly. Then think about how long you can afford to spend working on them, either before your course starts, or while you are doing coursework at the same time. Try to be realistic in your estimates. If you have focused on more chapters than you know you can find the time for (being honest), then be ruthless. Discard the least pressing. It is better to set yourself an achievable task, than to attempt too much and then become discouraged and achieve nothing. You can always revise your targets later if you are getting on more quickly than anticipated.

Decide on target completion dates for the chapters you have selected. Complete the chart below, or devise a more extended one. Be sure to note your target dates in your diary, too, to ensure that you do not forget to check your progress. You will need to bear your course timetable in mind, if you are already registered for a course, or your anticipated course start date if not.

Chapter	Target completion date	Notes
_____	_____	_____
_____	_____	_____
_____	_____	_____
_____	_____	_____
_____	_____	_____

Comment

The above activity should have introduced you to one of the key ways in which you intend to use this book, that is, to write on it! By the end of your course you should have absorbed all you need from the book, and need to make only limited reference to it thereafter. So there is no need to keep it in pristine condition. Deface it as much as you like, provided this will help you. Indeed, it will be suggested that you deface other printed materials, too (provided that they belong to you, not the library), so you might as well start now. However, some of your notes will be kept more usefully on your computer.
(An electronic version of this and other activities is available from the companion website.)

Planning your work on the handbook

As time is likely to be scarce, you need to target your efforts to meet your own specific development needs in relation to study and your career. You will probably need to re-visit this exercise throughout your studies, but a first rough pass in relation to your

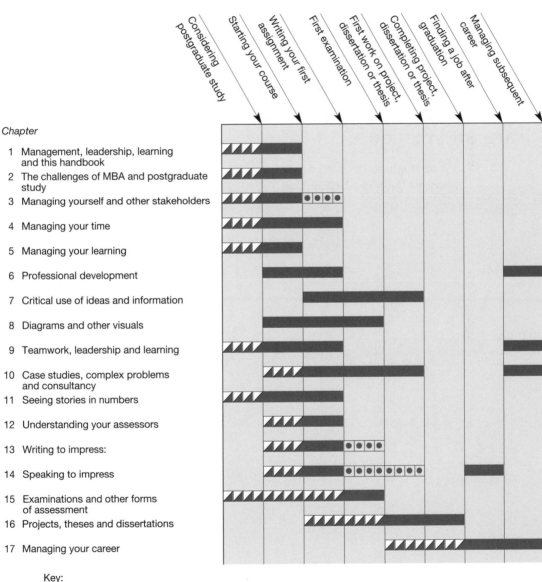

Figure 1.1 Optimal study times for handbook chapters in relation to course milestones

current study needs will start a thought process that you can continue in more detail later on. Figure 1.1 shows how work on the various chapters might relate to milestones in an MBA or similar course. You should now study this diagram, highlighting priority chapters.

You should not be locked into your plan. Course demands and other experiences (babies, house moves, promotions, mergers, etc.) will almost certainly cause you to alter your priorities and assessed needs. When this happens you should revisit and revise your plan. You may sometimes wish to look at parts of the book you decided were not important, in order to check that your decision was right. Or you may realise that a topic was introduced in an earlier chapter, and that you need to include the relevant part of that chapter. Marginal flags with chapter numbers show when this may be the case.

Further information

The whole Mintzberg introduction is available via http://www.bkconnection.com/static/Managers-Not-MBAs-EXCERPT.pdf

2
THE CHALLENGES OF MBA AND POSTGRADUATE STUDY

Learning outcomes

By the end of this chapter you should:

- understand the thinking behind the development of postgraduate management programmes

- appreciate the relevance of management theory to management practice

- be aware of the blend of learning resources you are likely to encounter and how best to use them

- appreciate the nature of professional learning and the role of reflection

- have started to reconsider your strengths and weaknesses in relation to the career you want

- have developed a hierarchy of learning objectives in the light of these

- have started to record aspects of your own learning using appropriate templates.

Introduction

This chapter addresses important aspects of the learning 'territory' you have entered, the different sorts of learning which are important for those aiming at senior management, and ideas about how this learning is best achieved. This will help you understand why your programme is designed as it is, what your assessors are likely to be looking for, and what you need to do both to satisfy them and to meet your own learning objectives (which will themselves be revisited in the latter part of the chapter. If you understand the thinking behind your programme, and its historic roots, you will learn more effectively.

In recent decades there has been a radical shift in thinking about management learning and professional practice. Part of this shift came from the recognition that management needs to be considered in context, and that the current context is fluid, complex and uncertain. Another factor has been an increased realisation that perception and sense-making are active mental processes. This shifts the emphasis away from learning about an objective reality, and towards an exploration of different and better ways of making sense of complex situations, and of constructing an inevitably subjective reality. A third factor is the growing recognition that purely academic learning is of limited value to professional managers unless it is rooted in, and constantly related to, professional practice.

This chapter starts with a brief history of senior management education over the last century, and the ongoing tensions between academic theory and management experience and practice. It explores the relationship between theory and professional learning and practice, and argues for the importance of reflection in achieving synergies between them. It suggests that a key management skill is 'sense-making' when faced with complex situations, and explores the conceptual skills which contribute to this. The discussion in this chapter forms

➤ Ch 6   necessary preparation for the discussion of professional learning skills described in Chapter 6.

If you are already an experienced manager this chapter will help you to approach your study in a way that will make it more professionally relevant. If your management experience is limited, the chapter will alert you to the value of drawing on others' experience, and seeking more of your own, as well as helping to prepare you to learn more effectively from your management experience after you qualify.

The first part of the chapter will give you the understanding needed to consider your own learning objectives in more detail, and to plan your study in the light of these. It

➤ Ch 1   will also reinforce the message in Chapter 1 about important conceptual skills for senior management, which will help you sustain your motivation for learning these, especially in the face of competing demands on your energies.

The work you will do in the second part of the chapter will extend the thinking you have already started about your own objectives, and help you use your (limited) study time to best effect in achieving your own learning and career objectives.

Educating senior managers – a short history

Many senior managers do not have any formal management qualifications – as the press is all too eager to remind us each time 'MBAs' are blamed for a business disaster. CEOs always used (and some still do to) reach their position by virtue of starting a company which grew, being born into a family which had already grown a business, or working their way up from the bottom. Do managers therefore need a formal qualification? Richard Branson left school at 16 and does not have an MBA. Bob Diamond, who resigned from Barclays Bank in the aftermath of the LIBOR scandal, has both a BA in Economics and an MBA. The annual output of MBAs and other management Master's degrees is now so high that they no longer have the elite status they once did.

Plato arguably established something close to a business school at least 2,500 years when he began to provide education/training for future leaders at his house in Academia, a suburb of Athens. However, Joseph Wharton is given the credit for the first specifically business school associated with a university (of Pennsylvania), which he founded in 1881. The Harvard MBA, which has perhaps been more influential, dates from 1908.

Harvard's MBA originally relied upon experienced and successful mangers sharing their experience with students. By the 1950s this reliance on experience and 'war stories' and lack of academic rigour led to heavy criticism of the programme. Harvard responded by making the programme much more academic, reorganising itself into traditional academic disciplines. Particular emphasis was placed on quantitative analysis and economics. Many US and some European MBAs are still heavily influenced by this model.

Teaching was heavily case study based – a method pioneered in the Harvard Law programme. Case studies served as proxy experience. Students analysed 800 or so lengthy case studies, as many as three a night, each needing two to four hours study. This introduced them to a wide variety of organisational problems and business contexts, and they learned to recognise typical organisational problems. The academic level was extremely high, and the atmosphere fiercely competitive and pressured. Books, lectures and case discussions were the main learning resources.

Only a small fraction of applicants were accepted: simply being accepted meant you had joined the elite. Surviving the pressures of the programme took toughness and ability to stand pressure. But what really made graduates attractive to employers was the high level of analytical skills the programme developed. Graduates could approach new problems in a structured and rational fashion. They had a clear grasp of finance and financial models. They could interpret business statistics and they had the confidence that came from having succeeded on a tough and elite programme. Graduates were particularly attractive to management consultancies and investment banks, their main destination.

But even the more academic MBA programmes had their critics, and such criticism has continued. For example, the press in 2009 carried dozens of articles blaming MBAs for the financial crisis. The feeling what that teaching had swung from relying too heavily on experience to becoming overly academic and removed from the realities of management. Critics question the relevance of the competencies developed in the MBA, the view of knowledge on which traditional MBA teaching was based, the exclusion of management practice and experience from the learning model, and the way that profit for shareholders is given far more weight than concern for customers and other stakeholders. The same criticisms could be levelled at other management Master's programmes.

Fifty years ago, although MBAs were already popular in the US, Master's-level management study was only just becoming available in the UK. There has been massive expansion since, peaking around 2010/2011, and then falling off somewhat by 2013. But there are still some 500 European business schools producing around 20,000 graduates a year, most of whom already have substantial management experience behind them. (This is still a small number in relation to the 150,000 or more MBA graduates annually in the US, together with increasing numbers of managers gaining specialist management qualifications.) This expansion has destroyed the 'elite' aspect of MBAs (apart from those from the very top ranking schools). As a well-known professor of organisational behaviour from Stanford, Jeffrey Pfeffer (2014) summed up the situation 'A degree has value only if the degree is scarce, and the MBA is completely unscarce.'

A significant force for change has been technological development and the 'information explosion'. Lectures, supported by books and some discussion, are no longer the only medium for learning. A major development in the 1980s was distance learning, which greatly expanded the availability of postgraduate Master's programmes. Specially written study texts largely replaced lectures, and students came together only occasionally for discussion and other group activities. This meant that student:lecturer ratios would become far larger. Students no longer needed to give up their jobs in order to study as they could do most of their work at home, at times convenient to them.

Distance-learning enthusiasts saw this approach as the first real exploitation of print for education since the time of Caxton. However, the time for the reliance on print was short-lived as the massive growth in the Internet from 1990 onwards opened up far more possibilities.

You are now likely to experience what is often called 'blended learning' where the blend may still include traditional books and some lectures, but also a much wider range of resources, including podcasts, lectures you can access online, links to other online talks and resources from other providers, virtual discussion groups which may have a global membership, and much more besides. Many of the articles and books that traditionally would have been on shelves in your library are now available online. Your university is likely to provide some sort of virtual learning environment (VLE), which will allow you to share resources with fellow students, have discussions with them, access administrative resources, submit material for assessment, and store evidence of your developing skills in an 'e-portfolio'.

The blend can be adjusted to suit particular student groups. For example, full-time students may make less use of online discussion facilities than those studying at a distance or part time, where the ability to contribute at different times may be an advantage, as well as the saving of travel time. These developments have enabled so much more variety breadth of input to programmes that in themselves they can be seen as challenging the traditional model.

The next section explores some of the challenges to traditional MBAs in more detail, and suggests an alternative view of management learning which is likely to underpin some at least of your own study.

Challenges to the traditional model

As well as considering issues about what is taught and the beliefs about learning that underlie teaching methods, this section will look at challenges to the generalist and post-experience restrictions of traditional MBAs that have led to the massive expansion of types of postgraduate management education in recent years, in particular the plethora of specialist Master's programmes on offer.

Curriculum (ir)relevance

The traditional discipline-based approach to management teaching may generate a syllabus better suited to academic interests than manager's learning priorities. For example, Pfeffer and Fong (2002) suggest that business schools differ significantly from other forms of professional education in the extent to which the curriculum is driven by academic interests rather than the concerns of the profession and the learning needs of those preparing to join it.

Rubin and Dierdorff (2009) compared MBA content with the management competencies that their earlier research had identified as being important for managers. Top among the six general competencies they identified were:

- managing decision-making processes, involving gathering information and assessing quality of things, services or people
- managing human capital, involving coaching and developing others, negotiating and handling conflict, and teambuilding.

The others were managing strategy and innovation, managing the task environment, managing administration and control, and managing logistics and technology.

Activity 2.1

Consider how important these competencies are to your own experience of management and organisations. If you are familiar with a different competence framework, consider which is most relevant to your own management experience. If Rubin and Dierdorff's framework does not seem to match your own experience, why might this be? Again, discuss with others if you can.

These are the sorts of questions that you will learn to ask about any research evidence during your studies. There are two obvious reasons: one is that these rankings are derived from 8,633 managers and represent an average, while you are a single person. There is no reason to suppose that your experience is 'average'. Second, the data relate to US managers. If you are not working in a US context, relevant factors might be different. (However, I work in the UK, and in a non-typical management role, and the framework seems, if not an exact match, sufficiently close to my own experience to act as a starting point for thought.)

Rubin and Dierdorff (*op. cit.*) analysed the curriculum offerings of 373 AACSB (Association to Advance Collegiate Schools of Business) accredited US business schools.[1] They found that the two competences most highly ranked by managers appeared fourth and fifth in terms of required course coverage, while managing logistics and technology – ranked least important by practising managers – was third on the list in terms of syllabus.

This study looked merely at syllabus content, hence at the knowledge aspect of competence. An examination of skills and behaviours developed might show even greater divergence. This is linked to the second major challenge to traditional MBAs, which concerns the nature rather than the content of learning.

Beliefs about knowledge and the 'real' world

The next challenge is a philosophical one, relating to what is meant by 'knowledge' (the area of philosophy known as epistemology). Philosophy may seem a long way from learning about management, but is actually highly relevant. (You probably will need to consider epistemology when designing research for a final dissertation, and more on this can be found in Chapter 16.)

➤ Ch 16

The traditional MBA model was based on a view that learning is a process of acquiring knowledge about the real world.[2] It sought to convey this knowledge to students, and develop the analytical skills they would need to approach problems in the real world in a rational manner, in order to maximise shareholder value.

This *realist* view leads to one particular approach to education where transmission of 'facts' predominates – the jug-mug model outlined earlier.[3] But an opposing view of knowledge is increasingly influencing business education (and much else). According to this view, we cannot 'know' about anything remotely complex in the sense that the realists believe. Instead what we *feel* we know is actually a *constructed view of a situation*, rather than a perfect reflection of the situation itself.

➤ Ch 1

From this perspective, reality as we know it exists only inside our heads. Our thought processes actively influence what we perceive and how we interpret it, creating a personal and subjective experienced reality. According to this *constructionist* view, we *perceive* only some aspects of the situation, and we *interpret* what we perceive in ways that create our own version of an experienced reality. Our 'construction tools' include past experience, learning, values, beliefs and assumptions. This means that much of what we need to learn has to do with how to construct more useful versions of situations, and with understanding other people's realities, rather than merely absorbing information about a supposedly objective and undisputed world.

Activity 2.2

Which of these two views of knowledge is closest to your own? (Your response to Activity 1.1 may provide a clue.)

If you are a realist (and this view still underpins much of hard science and engineering), you may find the notion of reality as a 'world in your head' rather disturbing at best, insane at worst. But consider the following as evidence of the unreliability and selectiveness of perception:

- optical illusions, such as a mirage (an Internet search will provide many more entertaining ones)

- experiences where you 'did not notice' or 'paid no attention to' something that later turned out to be crucial (I once nearly crashed into a car I simply did not see because I was not expecting a car to be there)

- times when you were sure that you understood a situation properly but could not persuade otherwise intelligent colleagues to see it your way.

The unreliability of perception has been known from ancient times. It was only with the rise of experimental science as a dominant approach to gaining knowledge that it has been somewhat forgotten. There are now many instruments that seek to measure a variety of dimensions of preferred ways of thinking. You may know your Myers–Briggs 'type', for example, or have experienced similar psychometric tests.[4] Such tests are used widely in selection. It is less common for the differences in the ways of thinking that they reveal to be exploited in the work context.

The importance of knowing

The view that perceptions and interpretations are the product of an active conceptual process was a core feature of a school of philosophy called *pragmatism,* developed shortly after the American Civil War. Such processes were seen as largely habitual, indeed often unconscious. They are, however, sophisticated thought routines derived from past experience and learning. Dewey (1910), a prominent pragmatist and influential educationist, developed a model of learning based on noticing when traditional thought patterns did not seem to work, thinking reflectively about why and coming up with different possible ways of thinking (hypotheses), testing these in action, and reflecting on the results of the test. This may lead to a better way of acting and/or a new useful idea. This model underpins many models such as Kolb's (1984) experiential learning cycle, which still influences management education today. These models are

➤ Ch 6   discussed later in Chapter 6.

Cook and Seely Brown (1999) have gone further. They suggest that it is *knowing* rather than knowledge that matters for professionals. Knowing is specific to a situation and embodied in action. As a manager you tend to be judged by what you *do* in response to specific situations, and what you *achieve*, rather than by what you know. (Although, of course, what you do will be influenced strongly by what you know and how you think.)

> Professional learning needs to be based upon, and entwined with, practice and reflection on that practice.

This realisation is the basis of one of the biggest shifts in management education in recent years.

Characteristics of the twenty-first century context

A different challenge concerns the nature of the 'reality' that we may or may not be able to know directly (the philosophical domain of ontology). Current thinking is that it is much messier, much more complex and uncertain, than the traditional MBA assumed. It is also much more dynamic.

Many organisations are now huge, operating around the globe in a wide range of very different cultures. Size often adds to complexity by increasing the scope for inter-relationships. Most situations involve a number of inter-related factors, and stakeholders with different priorities and needs. People's motivations vary greatly, and the different realities within their own heads contribute to the complexity. Focusing on one or two factors (as an analytical approach tends to do) and seeking 'a solution' frequently makes a situation worse rather than better: unanticipated interactions with other factors may produce disastrous results.

The context in which management is carried out is probably changing more rapidly now than at any point in the last 60 or 70 years. Traditional MBAs offered a 'toolkit' of models of reality and ways of solving specific problem types derived from *historic* case studies, successful managers' *past* experience and research on situations *in the past*. In times of change these models and tools may not fit current situations very well. An early criticism of MBAs (Mintzberg, 1992) suggested that traditional MBAs were seriously damaging US business because the process of case study analysis fostered a willingness to pronounce on complex issues from a basis of dangerous ignorance. The method favours the ambitious, glib and quick-witted, rather than those committed to the good of their organisation. A case study approach is unlikely to develop the circular diagnostic skills that managers need when faced with complex and uncertain situations.[5] Mintzberg (2004, 2009) has subsequently elaborated on this critique.

In times of rapid change a key skill for senior managers is the ability to notice key factors in a totally new situation and make useful sense of them. Relevant concepts, frameworks and models can help generate insights in such cases and also suggest possible ways forward. But by definition theories are derived from past data, so cannot be used uncritically to prescribe future action. Managers need to know how to select and assess potential ideas and models, and then use a range of models to understand the present and think creatively about the future.

➤ Ch 9

This process can often be best done with others. Indeed it forms the basis for action learning, described later in this chapter and also in Chapter 9. It is the reason that many MBA students now find themselves undertaking an action-oriented final project, rather than the traditional academic dissertation, as discussed towards the end of the book in

➤ Ch 16

Chapter 16.

With MBAs becoming increasingly common, educational institutions have sought to differentiate their offering to potential students. This has led to specialist MBAs, something which early providers, who stressed the importance of a generalist qualification, would have found unthinkable. The other major change has been the introduction of Master's programmes open to those with little or no management experience, which presents problems for those who believe, with Mintzberg, that experience is essential to management learning. Universities seek to provide relevant experience during the programme in a variety of ways, through simulations, placements and consultancy projects, for example. If your prior management experience is limited, these will provide vital learning opportunities.

The changing role of theory

Note that the term 'management theory' usually includes a wide range of concepts, frameworks and models. It is a much broader category than 'theory' in science. Traditionally theory was seen as a best explanation of observed phenomena based on the available evidence. From a realist perspective, when you learn theory you are learning about the world: the theory is a representation of reality. From a constructionist perspective, theory is rather different – a potentially useful way of looking at the world rather than in any sense definitive.

To a constructionist, theory is a starting point for thinking rather than a generator of predictions or solutions, or a constraint on what is considered. And because management contexts are so complex, and changing so fast, any theory based on evidence needs to be assessed critically for its relevance and utility in a given context. Critical thinking is a key Master's level skill, and particularly important for managers. There is more on critical thinking and the role of theory in Chapter 7.

➤ Ch 7

Increasing recognition of the importance of values

Traditional MBAs tended to assume that the purpose of an organisation (commercial organisations at least) was to maximise value for shareholders. Organisations were in competition and the market would decide the winner.

This view has been challenged from a variety of perspectives. Important critiques include that:

● markets are far more imperfect than many theoretical models assume
● an exclusive focus on shareholders ignores the claims on an organisation of a variety of other stakeholders.

Some organisations are now immensely powerful. Their budgets, and the power they can exert, may be equivalent that of some nations – according to Global Trends (2013) 40 of the 100 largest economic entities in 2012 were not countries but corporations. This gives them the power to influence markets, and to do immense damage not only to individuals but to whole populations, perhaps even to the whole planet.

The idea of *stakeholders* is an important one. It means anyone who can influence, or who is influenced by, an organisation. Key stakeholders typically include employees, who may have devoted their energies to the organisation over many years, customers and 'innocent bystanders' such as those affected by pollution caused by mineral extraction. With the increasing power of corporations, many would suggest that the claims of society as a whole need to be given more consideration. There is a growing interest in socially responsible management, driven by much wider aims than the maximisation of shareholder value.

Activity 2.3

List some of the stakeholders in your own (or any familiar) organisation and potential conflicts between their interests.

It has been argued that MBAs often produce a narrow focus on short-term profit and 'shareholder value'. This follows Friedman's (1963, 1970) clearly stated position that businesses have only one social responsibility – to use their resources (within the law) to maximise profits. You may remember this was the argument made in 2014 when organisations such as Starbucks were criticised for their creative ways of avoiding paying tax. Shareholder interests often compete with the claims of a wider range of stakeholders, or indeed with many organisations' own best long-term futures. For example, the UK budget suffers from loss of tax from major organisations. Employees suffer from zero-hours contracts. Local residents may suffer from pollution, particularly in parts of the world where there are few effective pollution controls, making it cheaper for multi-nationals to carry out 'dirty' operations there.

These are but a few of the powerful arguments for a reconsideration of 'shareholder theory', and consideration of a wider view of corporate social responsibility.

The need for continuous learning

In times of change the shelf-life of much traditional management 'knowledge' is short. Managers therefore need to go on learning throughout their careers. Continuing development is a core requirement for most, if not all, professional bodies. If you wish to be a chartered engineer, or psychologist, or retain full membership of the Chartered Management Institute (CMI), the Chartered Institute of Marketing (CIM), the Chartered Institute of Personnel and Development (CIPD) or other professional management bodies, you will need to demonstrate that you are taking steps to maintain your professional competence. If you wish to thrive as a manager, you will need to show that you can rise to new challenges as effectively as your peers (more effectively if you are seeking to be more successful in your career than they are).

Many graduates of traditional MBAs seemed to feel they 'knew it all' and did not see the need to go on learning from their subsequent experiences. Certainly, the learning approach needed to absorb and analyse voluminous case studies drawing upon learned models was not one suited to learning from life after the MBA. Other management Master's programmes, particularly those which adopt a more academic stance, may be subject to similar criticisms.

Perhaps even more than knowledge of academic theory, managers need to know how to use such theory to carry out careful diagnosis and rethinking of situations in the light of increasing understanding. They need to be able to find, evaluate and develop new ideas, models and theories, to experiment with different actions suggested by these, and learn – with others – from the experience. These are the skills that will lead to success as a senior manager.

Activity 2.4

Think about what you have read in this chapter so far. What really surprised you and why? What do you disagree with, and what in your experience supports your disagreement? What ideas struck you as having implications for your own continuing learning as a manager? Note down your answers, together with any actions needed to progress your thinking or make changes to your practice for future reference.

Reflection and professional practice

To learn from experience you need to stop and think about what you did, why you did it, how successful it was, and what needs to change. The thought process described as reflection lies at the heart of this sort of learning. Schön (1983), who was strongly influenced by Dewey's philosophy referred to earlier, wrote a highly influential book on professional development entitled *The Reflective Practitioner*. In this he emphasised the key role played by reflection on experience in professional learning. MBA programmes are now increasingly prioritising professional, rather than purely academic, development and incorporating reflective elements.

A focus on professional development stresses the importance of learning through your own management practice. Kolb (1984, p. 38) defined learning as:

> '. . . a process whereby knowledge is created through the transformation of experience.'

Typically, a professionally oriented Master's programme will include an action learning component in which you address real problems, with support from a group of fellow learners. Even if it does not, you may find it useful to form such a group, at work as well as for study. Guidelines are given in Chapter 9. Remember that learning is a key management skill. If you have no other management experience, you can practise reflective thinking about your approach to learning.

➤ Ch 9

Reflection on practice is key to action learning, as it is to any practice-based professional learning. Many managers initially are uncomfortable with the idea of reflection. For example, Jim, a senior engineer, realist and 'action man' was seriously sceptical about the idea of making time to reflect. But by the end of his first year of study he was a total convert, carrying a small notebook in which he captured thoughts as they occurred. He consolidated and added to his notes every week. He swore that this habit was one of the most valuable things he had gained from his MBA.

➤ Ch 6

There will be guidance on productive reflection in Chapter 6, but, meanwhile, you can start to practise the approach by noting down, and thinking about, your responses to activities as you work through this book. If you followed the instructions for Activity 2.1 you are already reflecting. Even if your programme does not require you to submit examples of reflective writing, and you are not a member of a professional institute, learning through reflection is a valuable skill.

Collaborative reflection and the importance of dialogue

Individual reflection, whether prompted by reading or by events at work (and ideally drawing upon both) can generate powerful learning. But collaborative learning can be even more powerful as it is far more likely to have a critical dimension than individual learning. Being critical partly involves becoming aware of assumptions and values that are driving your thinking. It is difficult to become aware of your own assumptions as they are deeply embedded, below your conscious awareness. Dialogue with others who are thinking on the basis of different assumptions can help to bring such assumptions to the surface, making it possible to check whether they are helpful.

➤ Chs 6,
     9

Dialogue is the term used for the particular type of discussion that is directed towards this purpose and is discussed in Chapters 6 and 9. Such discussions require particular skills in participants. These skills will be really important for action learning and other learning-oriented discussions on your programme. They are also important for any manager or consultant seeking to work with other stakeholders to address a complex issue in an organisation. When dialogue makes you more aware of the assumptions you – and colleagues – are making, you will often realise that they are limiting your thinking unnecessarily. Removing such assumptions may increase your team's creativity.

Keeping a learning or personal development file

➤ Ch 6

It helps to keep a file for everything related to your learning, typically called a learning file or a personal development file. This both helps you learn effectively and saves a lot of time. The activities you have done already may have generated some notes, either on the pages of the book or electronically. (If it is helpful, you can download a copy of all the activities from the companion website **www.pearsoned.co.uk/cameron** as a basis for these notes.) As you read this chapter you may have had further thoughts, perhaps about the extent to which you habitually reflect on your own practice and what this suggests for future learning. In Chapter 6 there will be more guidance on reflective writing, but meanwhile it will help to save, and start to organise, all your responses to this book. You can add to them later with responses to your courses.

How you do this is up to you. Your course may offer an e-portfolio as part of the VLE provided. Alternatively, you can create such a file on your own computer, or even rely on a trusty notebook or paper file (though this makes it harder to import relevant reflections into assignments, project report, or other documents). What matters is that it works for you, and is reasonably flexible – you may wish to reorganise things later.

In addition to specific responses to activities, key things you may want to note include:

- key points you want to remember perhaps with a reference to where you can read more on them
- ideas you have had that you want to capture and think about more when you have time
- questions you want to pursue, perhaps with further reading or talking to people
- aspects of your practice that you want to think about more and perhaps change.

➤ Ch 6

If you start to experiment with your own ways of keeping learning notes now you will have material to work with later when more formal approaches are discussed in Chapter 6.

Activity 2.5

Revisit your earlier list of potential benefits and add to it in the light of what you have read since. If you have not already started to organise your development file, do so now, and store your revised list there.

I hope your list now includes benefits such as an increased awareness of the importance of the changing wider context within which management takes place, and of the role of your own habits of thought in responding to issues. You may also have noted the benefit of an increased ability to think more clearly, from a wider perspective, and more creatively. You may have noted the way in which theory can help you think differently, or the lifelong benefit of being able to learn more effectively both from what you read and from what you experience, and to learn both on your own and through collaborative dialogue.

Setting your own learning objectives

You started to think about benefits from your studies in the last chapter. It is worth revisiting these in the light of the greater understanding of types of potential learning that you gained from the present chapter. It will be helpful to think about your own strengths and weaknesses in relation to your study and to the career you would ideally like.

Since your view of yourself is not necessarily accurate, seek evidence of strengths and weaknesses from as many sources as you can. An important aim of most Master's programmes is to develop your ability to collect evidence and draw valid conclusions from it: this is an opportunity to practise.

Despite earlier cautions about an *exclusively* rational approach to management issues, there are many times when a rational approach is highly appropriate. A classic rational management model for making changes suggests the following stages:

- decide where you are now
- decide where you want to be
- identify possible routes from the first to the second
- select the best route
- follow it
- monitor progress and adapt if necessary.

You can use this model to help you reach any action-oriented decision, including decisions about how to direct your energies during your Master's study.

In order to decide where you are now you need to look at your strengths and weaknesses in your current role.

Assessing your management strengths and weaknesses in your present role

A framework you will almost certainly encounter during your studies is SWOT, an acronym for strengths, weaknesses, opportunities and threats. This is usually applied at the organisational level, but you can also think about yourself as a potential 'product' in an employment market, using the SWOT factors. The S and W are mainly internally focused, while the O and T look at the competitive environment. The inward and outward features are, inevitably, related. Something might be a strength in one context, a weakness in another. Or something might be an opportunity for an organisation or manager with particular strengths, but not for another which lacked them.

If you are studying with a view to developing management skills, your current strengths and weaknesses form a key aspect of 'where you are now'. Your programme will stress the importance of drawing conclusions from evidence, and you should have a variety of sources of potential evidence to draw upon here – feedback from your boss, colleagues, customers, family, and people who have interviewed you, as well as your own assessments of past performance and any psychometric or other work-relevant tests you have taken. If you feel short of evidence, seek some more. Ask for specific feedback on key aspects of your practice. Find some online tests you can take (though some of these are not all that reliable – there is scope for a critical approach to any such test).

Suppose you have a niggling concern about your interpersonal skills. You don't always feel comfortable talking to people, and feel you relate less well to colleagues than others do. If so, you might, for example, specifically ask for feedback on your interpersonal skills from a boss, fellow students, friends and/or your partner. Ask them to suggest aspects of your behaviour which might affect you work relationships, and ways these might usefully be changed. You might also reflect on an interchange that went less well than you had hoped, and try to identify where it started to go wrong and what you might have done differently. These are but a few examples: it is for you to judge the best approach in your situation.

Activity 2.6

List your strengths and weaknesses in your current job, and/or other roles, drawing upon as much evidence as you can to reach your assessments. You may find it useful to capture this in the form of a table with a second column for evidence of each strength or weakness noted.

Assessing strengths and weaknesses for future roles

Here you are extending your time frame to consider, at least in part, future opportunities and threats. You could consider developments of you current role, if working, and how you would like to develop your career in the future. Evidence here may be harder to come by, but might include the person specifications for jobs that you would hope to be in a position to apply for in the next few years, observations of senior managers within your own organisation and their capabilities, competence frameworks for senior management or consultancy roles, and conversations with your mentor if you have one.[6]

It will help to start wide: abilities to see the big picture, to learn from experience, and to network might be as important as more specific skills.

Activity 2.7

Consider your ideal career path (your response to Activity 1.1 may provide a starting point) and assess your strengths and weaknesses in relation to the desired trajectory. Again, you may find it helpful to have a column for strength or weakness, and another for evidence.

From your responses to the previous two activities you can go on to develop learning aims and objectives, and consider what actions are needed to achieve these. These aims will act as a reference point throughout your study, and indeed beyond, so save them in the learning file you are starting to develop. They will help you to assess priorities, plan actions and monitor progress over the next few years. They will probably change as you learn more about management and yourself, and about the options that may be available to you. Review your aims at intervals and update your lists.

Assessing your academic background and competences

Your current learning skills are an important aspect of 'where you are now'. If you have not studied at university level recently, or indeed ever, you may find it difficult adjusting to the pace of study. You will need to develop new learning skills at the same time as you engage with course content. In this case, most of the chapters in this handbook will be a crucial resource for you.

If your first degree was in an educational system based on the jug-mug model, with 'knowledge' transmitted by a high status academic, and received and reproduced without question, you may find critical thinking and learning through dialogue particularly ➤ Chs 1, 6   challenging. Other chapters will be more or less important depending on your own academic background. Use the contents list, and Table 1.1 to work out which you most need.

Your cultural background

Management student cohorts often include a wide range of cultural backgrounds. 'Culture' includes the values, assumptions and ways of thinking and behaving that are shared by a group of people (their particular reality 'construction tools'). In addition to the more obvious national and religious cultures, there are cultures specific to organisations, social classes, professions, different management functions (finance people tend to see the world very differently from HR, for example) religions, age groups, etc.

We tend to feel comfortable with those who share our values, ways of thinking and so on. I was shocked a while ago when doing a Higher Education Funding Council for England (HEFCE) quality assessment to see a class where students sat in small groupings according to age, gender and ethnic origins. When the lecturer asked the class to break into small groups to discuss an issue, students stayed in these groupings. The tutor seemed surprised I should comment on this. Of course, students find it easiest to discuss with people like themselves.

But this was a massive wasted learning opportunity. Students could have used the discussions to become more aware of how people different from themselves saw situations, and through this to become aware of their own thinking tools and their possible limitations. By choosing the comfort of cultural homogeneity, these students were cutting themselves off from the chance to develop both greater cultural awareness, and more flexible thinking tools. If you are studying in a heterogeneous group, seize any opportunities for this kind of learning

Academic (and other status)

If you come from a culture where status is important and it would seem disrespectful to question your teachers – or even disrespectful to question fellow students, or to offer your own opinion – you will face real challenges on a programme that has embraced ideas of constructionism, action learning and collaborative dialogue (*see also* Chapters 6 and 9). To learn in the intended manner you will be expected to disagree and put forward your own ideas. Yet your very identity may be rooted in not showing 'disrespect' in this way. You may feel it would be totally inappropriate to criticise eminent professors who have published in reputable journals. Yet, on a programme based on ideas of a critical engagement with course ideas, and of learning through critical dialogue as will be discussed in Chapter 6, you will miss out if you do not participate and challenge both fellow participants and authors of concepts and models relevant to you.

➤ Chs 6, 9

A key difference you may find is the need to use your own words, quoting only sparingly from other sources, and making sure that you show clearly when you are using a direct quotation, and where it is quoted from. In some educational systems it is accepted that students will 'borrow' work from each other, or create patchwork essays from lengthy extracts from textbooks or materials online. Digital cutting and pasting is now so easy that many students are tempted to resort to it when under pressure. But using words that are not your own is called *plagiarism*, and is likely to be heavily penalised. Universities have sophisticated software to detect such 'copying', and you may get a zero mark, or fail the entire programme. It is not worth the risk. If you are tempted, or cannot see what is wrong, be sure to read more about avoiding plagiarism in Chapters 7 and 13, and study your university's plagiarism policy before submitting any written work.

➤ Chs 7, 13

Activity 2.8

If you come from a 'non-questioning' background and are studying in a context that expects students to question each other and perhaps also the faculty, consider what you might do to increase your ease with taking part and questioning, and where you might look for support in this. Note action points in your learning file.

Developing objectives

➤ **Chs 13, 16**

Most projects start with an overall aim(s), from which are derived the often shorter-term objectives and specific tasks that collectively will achieve this aim. This approach will be essential for any final dissertation or project on your course (*see* Chapter 16), but even small undertakings such as writing an assignment (covered in Chapter 13) can bene-fit from clear thinking about overall aim, and then specifying necessary objectives to achieve it. This allows you to identify and sequence specific tasks so as to achieve your overall aim within the planned timeframe.

First, therefore, reconsider your overall aim in studying.

Activity 2.9

List your current learning aims for Master's study, revising any earlier lists and prioritis-ing aims if possible. As this will be an important resource, save your list.

I hope that, having worked through the last chapter, your aims are not restricted to 'knowledge about' and include elements of improved practice and more flexible and crea-tive ways of thinking and of dealing with complexity, and that they relate to the strengths and weaknesses you evidenced above. They might also include learning to take an equal part in dialogue.

You are probably familiar with the acronym SMART for objectives – i.e. that, ideally, they should be:

- Specific
- Measurable
- Achievable
- Relevant
- Time-defined – e.g. have specified deadlines.

If things are not specific and measurable, how will you be able to assess progress? If they are not achievable, or not relevant, why bother? And if they are not time-defined, how will you know whether you are on track to achieving your overall aim?

The risk with this approach to objectives is that things which are hard to measure tend to be left out, even if they are important. Check that you have not limited your list in this way. You may need to take a more creative approach to what counts as a measure for softer objectives; for example, 'greater confidence in talking to colleagues'.

Activity 2.10

For each of the learning aims that you identified earlier, write down the objectives that you will need to meet in order to achieve that aim. You may need one or two layers of sub-objectives before you can identify specific tasks that will enable you to achieve these objectives.

If you are used to project management, these ideas will be familiar (though you may have difficulty in applying them to something as nebulous as learning). If you are not, check that your logic is correct. The tasks need to help you meet the objective to which they relate. The sub-objectives, when met, will ensure that the objective that they serve is met. And collectively, meeting the objectives will enable you to achieve the overall aim. You will find this structured approach useful in a variety of contexts and, in particular, in planning your dissertation, which will be covered in Chapter 16.

➤ Ch 16

A hierarchy of objectives

When you are sorting out your thoughts about aims and objectives, a useful technique is to represent them as an *objectives tree* or *hierarchy of objectives*. Such trees look like the familiar organisation chart, but show aims and objectives instead of management roles.[7] They are drawn from the top downwards. You start with what seems to you an important aim and put it at the top of the tree. Then you think about all the things that you need to achieve in order to realise your main aim, and put them in at the next level down. For each of these you consider necessary sub-objectives and so on downwards until you have gone as far as it makes sense to go. You may like to represent your work on Activity 2.10 as a tree.

If you were struggling with listing objectives above, try turning them into an objectives tree – you may find that this alerts you to objectives or tasks you had omitted.

Figure 2.1 shows an example of a hierarchy relating to career objectives.

Career objectives are but one subset of your objectives for your life in general, as reflected in your vision. For each of these you can construct a different tree. It is important to balance career objectives with your broader life objectives. It is very easy for career to take a higher priority than is perhaps compatible with your own and your family's longer-term happiness. The following activity can act as a reminder of this.

Activity 3.7

Draw objective trees for all the major goals in your life. Highlight any conflicts between sub-goals, either on a single tree or between trees. Think about any barriers to achieving your goals and note these. Identify areas where your studies may help you achieve your objectives. (Again, save this for future reference.)

Conflicts between objectives are common. For example, you might have one goal of getting into the squash club's first team, which would require a lot of practise and coaching, and another of obtaining your (part-time) Master's, which is also very time-consuming. If a third objective is to spend 'quality time' with your growing family, and you already have a job that requires you to put in long hours if you are to be considered for promotion, conflicts could be impossible to resolve! The guidance given in Chapter 4 on improved time management will help, but it cannot work miracles.

➤ Ch 4

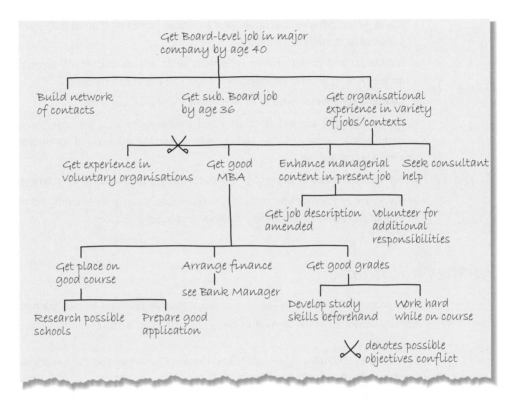

Figure 2.1 Hierarchy of career-related objectives for an intending Master's-level student

➤ **Chs 4, 5**   You will need to think about how to handle any conflicts between goals. One whole set of objectives may need to be put aside until another is achieved, but remember to retain objectives to do with health, family relationships and sanity! Once your priorities have been decided you can use Chapters 4 and 5 to help you direct your efforts effectively.

In deciding how to prioritise your efforts you will need to consider not only your professional overall objectives but also your strengths and weaknesses, in relation to both work and learning. Your prior educational experience will be a key factor.

SUMMARY

- Much management thinking is now based on a view of experienced reality as something actively constructed by each individual.

- Business contexts are complex, dynamic and uncertain. Different stakeholders will have conflicting priorities.

- The ability to make constructive sense of such contexts is a key management skill.

- Management 'theory' becomes less a reliable representation of that 'reality' and more a series of aids to sense-making.

- Individual and collaborative reflective skills are as important as analytical ones in sense-making and taking decisions based on the sense made.

- Learning objectives need to fit with wider life and career aims.

- Assessing your current strengths and weaknesses as a manager on the basis of as much evidence as possible will provide a useful starting point for deciding on learning aims and objectives.

- An objectives tree or hierarchy of objectives may be helpful in structuring objectives.

- If you are studying in an unfamiliar culture, some of your learning aims may relate to learning to operate with different social and academic rules.

Further information

Broughton, P.D. (2010) *What They Teach You at Harvard Business School*. London: Penguin.

Harvard Business Review November–December (1992) for a debate on the value of traditional MBAs.

Mintzberg, H. (2004) *Managers Not MBAs*. Harlow: FT Prentice Hall, for a more recent and extended critique of the traditional MBA.

You will also find useful information about MBAs at the following websites:

http://charteredabs.org/, the UK association of business schools. While mainly aimed at academics, you can find interesting topical material here on issues related to management teaching and learning.

www.mbaworld.com, the site for the Association of MBAs, which offers information on accredited schools if you have yet to choose an MBA.

http://www.ft.com/business-education for regular updates on issues in business education and links to useful free non-credit bearing online courses – Massive Open Online Learning Courses (MOOCs)

Notes

[1] The belief in an objective real world that derives knowledge directly by means of observation represents a philosophical position called *realism*.

[2] The term as used here refers to those who adopt the philosophical position of realism – not quite the everyday use of the word!

[3] The Myers-Briggs Type Indicator (MBTI) is a widely used psychometric instrument that classifies people into 1 of 16 'types' according to their preferred ways of thinking and acting.

[4] By this I mean a process of obtaining information, interpreting it, seeking further information in the light of that interpretation, reinterpreting the situation, seeking further information, and so on.

5 By mentor I mean someone with more experience than you and with whom you have an agree-ment that they will suport you in your development. This might be within your own organisation or more generally.

6 Terminology varies. Aims, goals and objectives sometimes appear in a different order. The key point is to move down from the general to the specific, whatever the terms you use to identify the different levels.

PART 2
TRANSFERABLE PERSONAL SKILLS

3
MANAGING YOURSELF AND OTHER STAKEHOLDERS

Learning outcomes

By the end of this chapter you should:

- have looked at your learning as a system in an environment, and considered the implications of this perspective

- have identified key stakeholders in your learning

- have assessed your personal management skills and identified those needing development

- be aware of the importance of managing stress and emotions, and of how you can identify and reduce stress levels

- be aware of the distinctions between aggression, avoidance and assertion, and have a plan for developing your own assertiveness

- understand the relationship between work context and learning, and have started to negotiate for the support and resources if appropriate

- appreciate the impact your study can have on both colleagues and family and be taking steps to gain their support.

Introduction

It may be helpful to think in terms of a learning system, with yourself at its heart, comprising a variety of inter-related components that together deliver your learning. Such a perspective highlights both inter-relationships between components, and the context or environment in which the system operates, and which can substantially affect it. Understanding context is vital in any management endeavour. Key elements in the context for your learning include the institution where you are studying, the resources and assessment structure it provides and – if you are working your organisation. Family, friends and any other demands on your time are also important. A popular approach to organisational strategy sees an organisation as succeeding through constantly monitoring its environment, and developing and making the best use of its resources and capabilities to thrive in that environment. This chapter takes a similar perspective on your personal 'learning system'. It looks at key individuals in your environment, your external stakeholders, and how to manage your relationships with them to gain their support. It also looks at you as a key internal stakeholder, and at the highly transferable personal skills you will need to survive in a challenging environment, especially managing your

➤ Chs 4, 5   stress and your emotions. (Later chapters consider planning and time management skills, and how to manage your learning more effectively.)

By the end of the chapter, you should be starting the conversations with family, close friends and any relevant work colleagues that will help you avoid divorce, dismissal or physical and mental decline in the next year or three. The chapter will also help you develop the ability to manage your stress and emotions, essential skills for study, career and life in general.

Stakeholders in your learning system

It is possible – and often useful – to view any collection of parts that work together towards a particular goal as a *system*. Systems thinking developed from the late 1950s as a counter to the simple 'cause and effect' thinking that was then dominant in much of the social sciences. It used the underlying metaphor of a biological organism, and suggested that it was helpful to look at problem situations with this metaphor in mind. The metaphor highlights the importance of context and inter-relatedness of elements and subsystems (for example, circulatory, respiratory and digestive systems). The context – often called *environment* – provides inputs (e.g. food and oxygen), receives outputs (e.g. waste and carbon dioxide), and can influence the organism in other ways (e.g. temperature, predators) and in turn is influenced by the organism/system. The metaphor and approaches based upon it have proved surprisingly useful as a basis for exploring a wide range of situations.

Check this by considering your 'personal learning system' as if it were an organism. What would it need to function, and what would it take from, and give to, its environment? Key system elements would obviously be yourself and anything else essential for your learning. The environment – things which can influence your learning and in turn

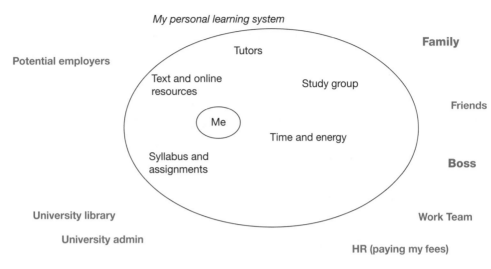

Figure 3.1 A personal learning system and environment

be influenced by it – might include your job (if you are working), sponsor (if sponsored), tutors, university systems (unless you see these as part of your learning system) and family and friends.

Figure 3.1 shows a possible personal learning system for a part-time student already in a management role. You might find it helpful to draw your own system and environment.

Organisational theorists tend now to consider a wider range of stakeholders than the shareholders that were once their main focus. A stakeholder in an organisation is anyone with a legitimate interest in that organisation: a person or group who can influence or be influenced by that organisation. Applying the idea to your learning, stakeholders are the human parts of both your learning system (internal stakeholders) and its environment (external stakeholders). Thus in your version of Figure 3.1 stakeholders in the system would be you, your resources, and perhaps study or project group members if you are working closely together. External stakeholders might include things over which you have less influence, but which are still important, such as your tutors, university, organisation and family and friends.

Organisational stakeholders will often have conflicting objectives, and managing stakeholders and the inherent conflicts is an important management skill. You can probably think of conflicts between your own stakeholders. Perhaps your organisation is sponsoring you so wants you to learn as much as possible in order to develop your leadership potential, while your immediate boss needs you to work all the hours there are in order to meet customer demands. Your partner may similarly want you to spend as much time as usual with your family, while you may need to free time for study. How well you manage such conflicts can make the difference between success and failure.

The central stakeholder in this system is you! You too are also likely to have conflicting objectives as you may have discovered from previous chapters. To internal conflicts and conflicts between different stakeholders you need first and foremost to develop your personal management skills. These skills are the basis for management of any kind, so will be invaluable throughout your career, indeed all aspects of your life. A central skill is managing your emotions, and in particular, managing your stress levels. To help you focus your efforts, first assess your current personal management skill levels.

Assessing your personal management skills

This assessment is for your own use, so be perfectly honest with yourself, and check your own assessment against feedback from others if you can (look back to answers to previous activities).

➤ **Ch 6**

Activity 3.1

Use your assessment of your current skill levels to suggest your learning priorities for this chapter and the next two. For each item give a score between 1 and 5 where 1 = never, 2 = seldom, 3 = moderately often, 4 = usually and 5 = always. (An electronic version is available on the companion website.) Reassess your skills levels at intervals to see how far you have progressed and suggest any change in priorities. You may wish to address some of these areas during your work on Chapter 6.

Planning

I ensure that I have clear and measurable objectives ❑

I work out what resources I shall need to achieve my targets, and ensure that I acquire them in good time ❑

I ensure that any preparatory activities are done in advance of the event for which they are preparation ❑

I regularly review my progress on my various tasks and projects, and take action as soon as any problem becomes apparent ❑

I take action as soon as I start to get behind on a job, and take pride in meeting deadlines ❑

Colleagues regard me as highly organised ❑

Time management

I am extremely careful about planning my time to ensure that it is used to best effect ❑

I ensure that I do not neglect what is important because of the pressures of what is urgent ❑

I work on one thing at a time rather than trying to split my efforts ❑

➤

I take steps to minimise interruptions at work ❏

I fit my work into a reasonable working day, and do not take it home with me ❏

Colleagues are surprised at how much I manage to achieve ❏

Managing emotions

I am aware of my emotions ❏

I know when my emotions are influencing my actions ❏

If I am feeling angry or upset, I stop and gain control of my feelings ❏

I notice if what I say or do affects others' emotional state ❏

I can stay calm and positive even when things get difficult ❏

I am happy to discuss my emotional state with others ❏

Managing stress levels

My job is well within my capabilities, and does not stress me ❏

I use my leisure time in ways that I find relaxing ❏

I fall asleep easily, and sleep well ❏

I eat healthily and do not drink more than I should ❏

I do not worry about something if I cannot influence it ❏

Colleagues regard me as a calm and balanced person ❏

Assertiveness

If someone tries to exploit me, I tell them what I feel about this ❏

If there is a conflict of opinion, I express my views firmly ❏

If people disagree with me, I do not get angry ❏

My needs are as important as those of other people ❏

Other people's needs are as important as my own ❏

My colleagues regard me as reasonably assertive ❏

Comment

Obviously the above gives only a very rough indication of your skills levels. But if your assessments are reasonably honest and accurate, and you score 24 or more on a section, you should be well prepared in that area. However, self-assessments are often a long way from other people's assessments so it really is worth seeing whether friends or colleagues' see you in the same light as you see yourself. File your responses as a baseline against which to assess progress. There will be similar questions on other areas, and your responses will inform your reflections on personal development in Chapter 6.

3

MANAGING YOURSELF AND OTHER STAKEHOLDERS

Managing your emotions

Emotions used to be seen as something that managers should not have – or certainly never show. Emotion, after all, interfered with rational thought. It is now recognised that it is impossible to separate thinking and emotions. Emotions, or feelings, necessarily colour our judgements – which is both good and bad. It is our feelings that motivate us, giving the 'value' to rewards or punishments.

The positive value of emotion is shown by an interesting case (Damasio, 2006) of a highly successful man who, after brain surgery for a tumour, lost his 'emotional connection'. While IQ and other tests showed his (very high) intellect was unimpaired, he could no longer function at work or in relationships. He could no longer distinguish between important and unimportant factors.

Given the centrality of emotions to decisions and actions, emotional awareness is extremely important. Under the influence of a strong emotion we might say or do things that we later regret. This is why it is important to be aware of your emotional state – and that of the person you are with – and act accordingly. It may be best to defer speech or action until you are calmer – the discussion of mindfulness later in the chapter may help achieve such calm.

➤ **Ch 9**

Goleman (1998) popularised the term 'emotional intelligence' (EI), and his work resonates with many managers. Despite academic criticism of much of his work, EI is widely seen as important for leadership and for any form of working with others (*see* Chapter 9). Goleman argues that what makes 'star performers' in an organis ation outstanding is not their academic abilities and know-how, which is taken for granted, but 'personal qualities, such as initiative and empathy, adaptability and persuasiveness' (Goleman, 1998, p. 3). He suggests an emotional competence framework made up of personal competences of self-awareness, self-regulation and motivation, and social competences comprising empathy and social skills. Questionnaires are available online to allow you to assess the full range of competences Goleman suggested (see online resources).

➤ **Ch 6**

While the framework can be criticised in many ways, including the complaint that it goes far beyond mere emotion, it provides a useful 'shopping list' (*see* Chapter 6) for analysis, highlighting some important sub-competences for professional development. Your studies will offer scope for developing these competences, and it is important that you take advantage of these in order to work and learn productively with others.

➤ **Ch 6**

Self-awareness means knowing your strengths and limitations (*see* Activity 3.1), and recognising your emotions and their effects. This will give you a strong sense of your own worth and the confidence that comes from this. A habit of regular reflection, ideally building on feedback from others, will develop your self-awareness. You can usefully reflect both on your management practice and on your learning experiences. Chapter 6 will help develop your reflective skills and self-awareness further. Confidence in your own worth is a pre-requisite for the assertiveness skills addressed shortly.

➤ **Ch 9**

Self-regulation includes self-control (self-awareness is a building block for this), and less obvious ethical issues such as honesty, integrity and taking responsibility for your own performance. It is related to elements of innovation and flexible thinking. A key theme of this book is that what you learn during your studies – provided you use it to challenge your own thinking rather than as 'facts' to be learned – can make you a more flexible and innovative thinker. Critical dialogue with diverse colleagues will help this to happen. There is more on dialogue in Chapter 9.

Motivation refers to the direction and strengths of your efforts. Goleman (*op. cit.*) suggests this involves motivation to achieve, commitment to group or organisational goals, and a willingness both to take the initiative and to persist when things go wrong. Your own motivation both in relation to study and to your present job and career path is a vital part of your study context. This is why it was addressed previously.

Empathy, the first of Goleman's social competences, is highly relevant to the ways in which management programmes are developing. He suggests that it comprises:

- understanding others
- developing others
- service orientation (i.e. sensitivity to customer needs)
- leveraging diversity
- political awareness.

I would suggest that it is the first of these elements, understanding others, which is absolutely crucial. The others in the list (and much else) depend upon it. If you do not understand someone else's way of thinking, their beliefs and values, their objectives and their sensitivities, and their emotional responses, you will be severely limited in your dealings with them. As one of my current students said to me recently, 'It was only when I received your comments on my first assignment that I realised that of course you wouldn't know about ... [this key feature of her organisation] and so a lot I said about ... [the issue] would make no sense at all to you.'

➤ **Chs 6, 9** Collaborative reflective dialogue, together with your own personal reflection (covered in Chapters 6 and 9), should help you realise just how great is the distance between the planet you live on (the world in *your* head) and other people's planets. This realisation is the foundation for both effective communication and collaborative learning.

Social skills, Goleman's final set of emotional competences are of fairly obvious importance. The abilities to influence others, communicate effectively, build relationships, manage conflict, collaborate with others and build effective teams are clearly important for mangers. Interestingly, Goleman sees *change catalyst* as a component of social skills. (If you were thinking critically about this framework you might perhaps wonder whether, from your perspective, change management was worth considering as a separate category.) Even more interestingly, Goleman lists leadership ('inspiring and guiding individuals and groups' *op. cit.* p. 27) as one of the eight social skills. It is thus an element in social competence, itself a subset of emotional intelligence. This is particularly interesting given the prominence attributed to leadership skills by some authors and recruiters.

Activity 3.2

Revisit your responses to Activity 3.1 and see whether you can add to them in the light of this competence framework for emotional intelligence. If this section has prompted thoughts relevant to your study or management development, note these in your learning file, adding any implied actions to your development action plan.

Managing stress

Managing your stress levels is one form of self-regulation. Work is a major source of stress, and stress is a major cause of absence from work, and a source of potential legal action against an employer. In 2006 the Confederation of British Industry (CBI) estimated that workplace stress was costing industry in the UK £9.6 billion a year (Frost, 2006). The Advisory, Conciliation and Arbitration Service (ACAS) (2014) cite slightly more recent Health and Safety Executive (HSE) estimates of 13.5m working days lost to stress in the UK, with average days lost per case as 31. According to the CIPD (2015) stress, continues to be a major source of absence, and may affect 20 per cent of the workforce. (The CIPD website is an excellent resource on this and related topics.)

While definitions of stress vary, they usually include an element of a negative response to perceived excessive pressures or other types of demand. These pressures might result from inadequate time or other resources, or demands beyond a person's competence level. Over time stress results in impaired health and/or performance.

> **Stress can:**
>
> - impair concentration
> - affect judgement
> - damage your health
> - impact on your team
> - damage other
>   relationships.

It is important to monitor your own stress levels. While occasional periods of high stress are almost inevitable, especially if you are studying while working, remember that sustained stress has a range of negative impacts. You need to take action to reduce stress before this happens.

Stress is subjective. You are stressed when you *feel* stressed! It is irrelevant that others might not feel stress in the same situation. There is substantial variation between individuals both in their ability to do tasks and in the level of pressure that constitutes stress. It is *your* perceived stress level that you need to manage. One of the most stressful periods in my life occurred when I started a new job: for weeks I was given nothing to do except 'familiarise' myself with a heap of files. This individual variation in what is 'appropriate' pressure makes it difficult to predict and detect stress. But the fact that it is the *perception* that matters means that it may be possible to reduce stress by changing a person's perception of a situation, without changing the demands placed upon them.

Short-term pressure may not be a problem. Sometimes it is almost welcomed as a challenge. The job becomes more exciting, and meeting the challenge can provide satisfaction. If you work through the night and meet an impossible deadline, you may feel great. If you have to do it several nights a week, you will not feel great. Similarly, if pressure increases gradually over time you may not mind at first, but there will come a point when your job is no longer an exciting challenge, but rather something to be endured. This is likely to have a negative impact on your enjoyment of life in general.

ACAS (2014) suggests that stress at work mainly arises from:

- Excessive demands (in terms of overload or difficulty)
- Lack of control over when and where to do the work
- Lack of supportive trusting relationships

- Uncertainty over what is expected of the jobholder
- Uncertainty or insecurity arising from poorly managed change.

The trouble is that one of the many bad effects of stress is to distort our judgement: there is 'no time to think', and, besides, our thought processes have become impaired. If stress levels have risen gradually, we may not realise what is happening. We go home a little later, and a little later. We cut back our running to twice a week, then once, and then miss it altogether. Our partners are no longer keen to go out to dinner with us because we are too tired to be good company.

> **Causes of stress include:**
> - sustained overload (or underload)
> - role ambiguity
> - conflict of objectives
> - emotional pressure.

The fact that stress sets in at different levels for different people makes the situation worse. If we see others thriving on more work than we are coping with ourselves, we feel that we should not be stressed. Organisations may have cultures demanding that all managers exert the same superhuman efforts as their exceptional chief executives. Admitting to what might be seen as weakness is unacceptable in many working contexts.

The first stage, as with any problem, is to look in more detail at the situation. But how can you see whether you are stressed or not, given the difficulties described? The surest guide is how you feel. Supplement this, if you can, with assessments by others close to you.

Activity 3.3

Think of the last time you felt really good about your job and/or your studies. A time when you woke each day looking forward to the challenges ahead, and arrived home at night looking forward to the leisure activities you had planned. Now think about how you felt this morning, and how you felt when you got home after work. It can't be *too* bad, or you would not have felt up to working on this chapter, but is the difference significant? If you have a partner, ask them if they think that you are under more stress than they think is ideal. Ask your colleagues if they think that you are ever irritable, or perhaps make errors of judgement because of pressure. Think about your health. Do you have a number of minor ailments, perhaps more than you used to? Headaches, respiratory and digestive disorders, sleep problems, asthma and eczema are among ailments that can be made worse by stress. What is your alcohol intake? If you need a couple of drinks when you get home to help you relax, this suggests a fairly high stress level. Can you turn off thoughts of work when you are at home? Or do you continue to toss problems around half the night? Do you tend to eat too much, or find difficulty eating enough to maintain a reasonable weight? (A questionnaire is available on the companion website.)

➤ Ch 4

Comment

*Your answers to the above questions and, if you have time, to the further questions on the companion **website**, should make it possible for you to assess your own stress level, and to be fairly honest with yourself as to whether this is something you should be tackling even before the course starts. Even if stress is high but not excessive, you should perhaps be thinking about developing techniques for handling the increased levels once your course starts.*

*If there is no problem, skip to the next chapter (remembering that this chapter exists should you need it in future). If there is a potential problem, more analysis is needed. This should focus on the **causes** of the stress levels you are experiencing, and on the possible ways open to you for **coping** with stress when it is unavoidable.*

If simple overload is a problem, work carefully through Chapter 4. More effective use of your time, together with clear thought about your objectives, should do much to reduce your problems. If it does not, you may need to discuss any overload at work with your boss, or talk to your tutors if you feel overloaded with coursework.

Role ambiguity, lack of clarity about what you are being required to do, can be a source of stress at work and in your role as student. You may need to discuss your uncertainties with your boss or tutors. There is little point in working hard at something that is not quite what is wanted of you.

A simple clash of objectives can be almost as stressful as ambiguity. You may have objectives which are themselves incompatible, or your objectives and those of the organisation or your university or your family may not be compatible (more on managing other stakeholders shortly).

Activity 3.4

Assess the major sources of stress in your recent past and present. (Use the list of sources of stress as a prompt. Online questionnaires are available too.). Divide stressors into those that you can reduce, and those that you can do nothing about. (You will probably want to list these privately.)

Reduce stress by:

- controlling workload
- resolving conflicts
- re-evaluating priorities
- accepting the inevitable
- relaxation and exercise.

Distinguishing between what you can change and what you need to cope with is an important first step. You may be familiar with the serenity prayer

 'God, grant me the serenity to accept the things I cannot change,
    The courage to change the things I can, And the wisdom to know the difference.'

(probably by Niebuhr in the early 1930s)

The next step is to find ways of reducing stressors that *can* be reduced. This will depend so much on your personal situation that discussion here would be inappropriate. In order to think as creatively as possible about options, you may find it helpful to discuss your situation with a good friend.

Once you have thought of action you could take, set yourself deadlines for actually *doing* something. Check regularly that you are keeping to your deadlines. If you have involved friends in this, they will be helpful as progress chasers. This can be an exercise in planning skills. You may wish to file your plans and record of future progress as an example.

Coping with unavoidable stress

For unavoidable stress, there are three things that may help you cope: attitude change; relaxation techniques; lifestyle changes, including exercise.

Attitude change

Accepting things that cannot be changed is essential to coping with stress. There is no point in wasting energy trying to change the immutable or fretting about it. If there is genuinely nothing you can do to reduce your workload, you need to see what else you can change, or how to remain serene in the face of impossibility.

First you need to *value yourself* sufficiently to accept your own definition of what is reasonable, even if this is at odds with what goes on around you. If work overload is damaging your health, then if you cannot change the job, you may need to say that you are not prepared to continue working at this pressure level. You may lose your job (although in Europe employers have a legal obligation not to put employees under such pressure so you could contest this). It is far more likely that, if you do not recognise your own limitations, your performance will gradually decline to the level that your job is threatened anyway, and your health will be at risk. This topic is developed further in Chapter 4.

➤ **Ch 4**

The following technique, drawn from neuro-linguistic programming (NLP) described by Andreas and Faulkner (1996), is designed to reduce negative feelings. It uses visualisation to reduce the intensity of feelings about a situation or event that has happened to you. While it may seem strange at first if NLP is new to you, it is worth a try if the 'patience to accept' is proving difficult.

Think of such a situation, trying to see it unfolding as a film, complete with images and sounds. Next, deliberately select theme music that *mismatches* the prevailing mood of the 'film' – perhaps a ridiculous or joyful tune. Replay the film in your mind with the new music sounding loud and clear. If you then revisit the images *without* the music, you are likely to find your unpleasant feelings have greatly diminished. (To neutralise them completely, repeat the exercise a few times more, each time using different, but still inappropriate, music.)

A simpler (though not at all easy) technique, drawn from cognitive therapy (see Neenan and Dryden (2004), for an introduction), may be to try to note the negative automatic thoughts (NATs) and the assumptions underlying these, which may be driving you to undervalue yourself. A NAT is something that pops unbidden into your mind – e.g. 'Colleagues are going to think I'm rubbish because I can't handle this workload.' There may be a range of further assumptions underpinning this. Some may relate to the world – 'This level of workload is reasonable.' Some may relate to deeper beliefs about yourself – 'I'm incompetent', 'I'm not worthy of this job'. Identifying and questioning these assumptions may be an important step to changing your attitudes about the situation.

Another may be to strengthen yourself by focusing not, as is common, on your weaknesses, but on your strengths. Try listing each day what you have done well. Ask your friends what they *like* about you. Keep a 'warm fuzzy file' for emails which thank you for things you have done well and other evidence of your strengths as perceived by others, and read its contents at regular intervals.[1] All this may seem fairly tangential to reducing overload and stress, but you may be surprised at its impact.

Relaxation, meditation and mindfulness

Even the simplest approach, relaxation, needs to be *learned*. You cannot suddenly relax on demand: it takes skill. You may need to practise for a while before you start to feel the full benefit.

Books, CDs or one of the countless online sources (see suggestions) can help considerably at the beginning. However, if you wish to start practising basic relaxation without further help, sit comfortably, or lie, in a quiet, dimly lit room. Make sure you are warm enough – you will cool as you relax so wear warm clothes or use a blanket if necessary. Spend a little time letting your body go soft; think of it melting into the floor like warm fudge. Relax your face muscles and, although your eyes should be shut, imagine you are looking towards a far horizon. If you find it difficult to do even this, put on some relaxing music that you enjoy. Just let everything go, breathe deeply and evenly, and enjoy the rest. Even ten minutes of this can reduce stress levels.

Relaxation is a first step to meditation. In simple meditation, the aim is to clear your mind of the 'chatter' – all those thoughts that swirl around without your intending to think them. When you are relaxed, try one of the following:

- Focus all your thoughts on your breathing, keeping this fairly slow and regular. Notice the cool in-breath, the warmer out-breath. Gently discard any other thoughts that intrude, returning to your breathing each time.

- Focus your thoughts on a visual image, such as a blue water lily or rippling water. The image must be one that you can visualise clearly and that conveys a sense of peace. Again, if thoughts come into your mind, let them float past, returning your attention gently to your chosen image.

- Focus on a simple phrase or even a single word which has a calming effect. 'I am at peace' or simply 'Peace' are examples, but choose whatever feels best to you. Repeat this in time with your breathing. As before, if thoughts arise, let them pass like clouds in the sky, returning your attention calmly to word or phrase as soon as you notice the thought.

Practise for about five minutes at a time to begin with (set the timer on your phone), gradually building up to 15 or 20 minutes. You should find that, with practise, you will be able to keep your thoughts increasingly focused on your chosen object, and that you will feel greatly refreshed at the end of the period. At the end of your time, move around gently before getting up, and rise slowly to avoid dizziness.

Mindfulness is now mainstream in medicine and increasingly in organisations. A friend who works in the Probation Service is currently on a mindfulness course with fifteen senior management colleagues. Google has put a lot of resource into mindfulness and shares some of its resources online. At a Google talk Kabat-Zinn (2007a), who pioneered mindfulness in medicine, defined mindfulness as: 'Moment to moment non-judgemental awareness.' He gives evidence of the impact of mindfulness on various physical indicators, including the immune system. A subsequent talk (Kabat-Zinn 2007b) emphasised the 'tenderness' of this awareness and described mindfulness as a means to create a place to 'rest in being, whatever you are doing', separate from the thinking and the stories you tell yourself all the time. These stories serve to make sense of things and make you feel good (or sometimes bad) about yourself, but they necessarily limit your experience, taking you away from awareness of the present. In this second video Kabat-Zinn leads a formal meditation session saying this is a good way in to mindfulness in the rest of your life.

Mindfulness Based Stress Reduction or MBSR is now a recognised therapeutic approach. If there is a difference between mindfulness and meditation – and it is not clear that there is – it is in the route taken to a similar end point. Meditation seeks to get behind the thinking 'me', often with a spiritual intent, while secular mindfulness seeks to make you more aware of the here and now, and through this go *beyond* thinking. (It is hard to describe such things – they are best found through practise.)

One advantage of 'mindfulness' as an approach is that when used for training or therapy it does not demand a Buddhist or other religious ethic or practice, and is based on research by respectable psychologists. This makes it more acceptable to organisations and health services. You can be mindful whatever is happening: there is no need to sit in a quiet place. You can do the dishes mindfully. It is a revelation to eat mindfully.

Activity 3.5

For perhaps five minutes of your next meal focus totally on the food you are eating. No radio or TV, no book, no talking to friends. Look at your food. Enjoy its appearance, its smell. Then put a small amount of food in your mouth, put down your cutlery, and shut your eyes. Feel the food with your mouth for a while, then start to chew slowly, focusing in the sensation and the taste. Chew for a while with this full attention. Only when you have swallowed, open your eyes and repeat for the next mouthful. You may be surprised at how much more you can taste, and how intense the experience.

A basic point underlying mindfulness is that we only live in the present. The past is something we have constructed out of past 'nows'. The future is an idea in our heads. So living in the now, tuning in to it, is important. You can see that as you become more aware of your whole self, and your body's reactions, you will be much more aware of your emotions. The calm that mindfulness can bring will help you to manage them.

3

MANAGING YOURSELF AND OTHER STAKEHOLDERS

Yoga, done with full awareness of your body and breathing, is a route to mindfulness as well as a preparation for meditation. Most yoga classes will end with a relaxation, so this may be one route to consider if you wish to feel less stressed. Alternatively, simply increase the time you devote to activities you find relaxing. Listening to music, reading poetry or flying kites: the possibilities are extensive. Since a major source of stress is often friction from those with whom we live, see whether a shared form of relaxation can be found. 'Relaxation' that increases friction will not reduce your stress levels. Something that is relaxing *and* companionable may reduce stress in two ways at once.

Exercise and lifestyle

Exercise works on your emotions and increases your sense of well-being, as well as making you physically fit. It is great for reducing stress. If you are not already an exercise convert, or doing a physically demanding job, think seriously about building more exercise into your routine as part of your pre-course preparation. If you have not developed the habit *before* your course starts, time pressures may make it difficult. But after a week or two you will probably find you are achieving more in less time. Any exercise, provided it raises a sweat for half an hour or so and you do it at least two or three times a week, will work.

So choose whatever exercise appeals to you. Some people *hate* running, but love swimming, squash or fast walking. Some swear by dancing (privately) to energetic music. Given the demands on your time, your chosen activity should be time-efficient. This is why jogging is so popular, it is cheap and there is no time wasted getting to the start of your exercise. You can usually find a friend, or even your partner, to run with you, too, which will prevent you skipping the run because you don't feel quite like it.

If you are new to exercise, start very gently. *Force* yourself to set exceedingly modest targets to begin with and resist any challenge to run farther or faster than before, or play squash against a better opponent than is ideal. Injury will be counter-productive, as well as the risk of building up a psychological resistance to further exercise. And always keep well within what feels good. Within a couple of weeks you may be surprised how much more you can do and enjoy, both in your exercise and your study.

Activity 3.6

If relevant, decide on a plan for introducing a modest amount of exercise into your life. Set targets and review your progress against these. Again, involve a friend or member of your family if you can, as this will increase your motivation significantly. Note progress in your learning file.

Relaxation and exercise can do much to fit you for successful study and management career. Other aspects of your life that will complement this move are sleep and diet. Again, individuals vary in the amount of sleep they need, but whatever that need is, it is important that it is met. Sustained sleep deprivation, even slight, can damage your immune system and raise your blood pressure (and have other negative effects) much as stress from work can. If you find it hard getting to sleep once in bed simply practise some relaxation or meditation first.

It is a cliché to say that 'we are what we eat', but it is easy to ignore our need for a balanced and nourishing diet, especially when under pressure – which is when it is perhaps even more important than usual! Caffeine, alcohol and fast food do not help you think and study. Water, fresh vegetables, some fruit, fish and wholegrains do. Why not eat your way to better grades?

Getting yourself into good shape and managing your stress and health will help you survive work pressures as well as the demands of study. Managing your lifestyle is another transferable skill!

Developing assertiveness skills

Look back at your assertiveness ratings in Activity 3.1. If you tend to acquiesce with the demands of others and put these above your own needs, you will have difficulty negotiating with stakeholders and gaining their support. If whenever you are asked to take on more work you say 'Oh, all right. I suppose I can do it' you will be creating pressures leading to stress. If you tend to keep quiet when you disagree with what others in your group are saying, or stop defending a particular point as soon as there is any dissent, you will probably not enjoy the group work on your course. Nor will you make a very positive contribution to it. Assertiveness is important in all aspects of life.

The cost of avoiding conflict 'at any cost' is often *high*, as you may already realise. But creating unnecessary conflict is equally unhelpful. If you tend to emphasise your demands to the point of upsetting people, you may still have a need to become more assertive. Aggression is no closer to assertiveness than is avoidance and may create as many problems. Figure 3.2 explores the relationship between avoidance, aggression and assertion.

The essence of assertion is to stand up firmly for your own rights while giving due regard to the rights of others. Avoiding conflict may 'respect the rights of others', but at the expense of your respecting your own rights. You may end up working on a weekend when you need the time to meet an assignment deadline, or overloaded with all the routine jobs while colleagues have time for new challenges which allow them to develop and be noticed. This can destroy your work satisfaction and promotion prospects, and longer term, your health.

There are other, less obvious costs to avoidance as a strategy. If your reticence means that you contribute less to work or study groups than you could, the group is missing out on your input. You may disagree with the others because you have information that no one else possesses. Or you may have understood information differently from others – and perhaps

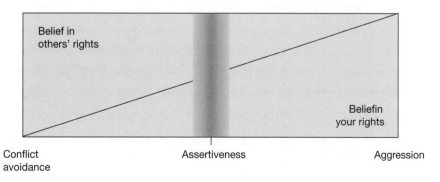

Figure 3.2 The relationship between aggression, assertiveness and avoidance

better. Even if your disagreement stems from a misunderstanding, perhaps because your background is different, it may point to an area where careful explanation is needed in any presentation. If you fail to express your disagreement, and to persist until people hear what you are saying, your potential contribution will be lost.

If your response is aggressive rather than assertive, you may be much less effective than you think. Aggression tends to arouse either matching aggression or defensiveness in others. Neither is likely to lead to constructive problem solving, nor to future positive relations between the parties concerned. If you are aggressive to a superior, he or she may be equally aggressive in response, creating a contest in which your superior is likely to emerge the victor, and to think less well of you as a result.

With subordinates aggression is more likely to cause a defensive reaction than provoke aggression. But defensiveness may mean that you never find out why the conflict really arose. There will be excuses rather than a genuine attempt at finding reasons, so things are unlikely to be better next time. Furthermore, subordinates will find their own, possibly counterproductive, ways of avoiding future conflict. Longer term, your aggression can damage their health, as well as your own.

➤ Chs 6, 9 Assertiveness is particularly important in dialogue aimed at learning (more on this in Chapters 6 and 9). This requires open and honest challenge to others' ways of thinking. The aim is not to convince others that you are right, but to find out why you think differently. If your style in a group is to dominate through aggressive behaviour, such as interruptions or sarcasm, you, and others in your group, will not be able to learn in this way. At work you may prevent the best solution from emerging if it is not the one you favour. You may also risk damaging other team members. The group may become demotivated – to the detriment of everyone's development, and hence output more generally.

Assertiveness skills can help you coach your subordinates (giving and receiving praise benefits from assertiveness skills just as much as does giving and receiving criticism). They can lead to better discussion on how to handle a crisis and help you negotiate an expansion of your role to allow you to use newly developed skills.

The benefits of assertion, rather than aggression or avoidance, go far beyond helping you to control your workload and to make a positive contribution to discussions. At home, as well as at work, assertiveness can often lead to constructive outcomes for all stakeholders, rather than conflict. Thus even if you are not working you can start to develop your skills immediately, at home, as well as when working on group exercises.

Exercise 3.1

Classify each of the following responses as aggression, assertion or avoidance:

(a) 'You always blame me when things go wrong. It was Fred who accepted the contract.'   _____

(b) 'That's all right. I'll see if I can find something for you to use as an ashtray.'   _____

(c) 'I find it very difficult to feel I am making a contribution when I am never allowed to finish any sentence.'   _____

➤

(d) 'Well I suppose I could go to the meeting, though I am a bit busy at present.' _____

(e) 'I need to work on my report this afternoon if I am to meet our agreed deadline. Do you think that the meeting is so essential that I should go despite this?' _____

(f) 'Why are you always so critical?' _____

(g) 'Never mind. If you all think the main problem is cash flow I'll go along with that.' _____

(h) 'It seems to me that we are focusing exclusively on the financial aspects of this case, and ignoring fairly important human resource implications.' _____

(i) 'You are right. The first section is unclear, though I don't think this criticism applies to the subsequent analysis. Perhaps next time we could discuss what is needed in a background section in a bit more detail before I start the report.' _____

(The correct classification is given at the end of the chapter, p. 75.)

To become more assertive:

- believe in your rights
- express these calmly but firmly
- practise using 'assertive' phrases
- prepare, if possible, for any likely conflict.

Once you appreciate that assertiveness is an adult, self-confident, rational rather than emotional, straightforward and constructive response in a situation, you are ready to start developing your skills. If you still need convincing, observe interactions around you, at work and at home, and classifying responses in the same way as you did in the above exercise. Note which are most effective.

Believing in your rights

You first need to work on your own confidence, and think about your rights in any situation. It is easy to say that assertiveness is about respecting your own rights, but too many of us undervalue those rights, and underestimate the worth of our own contributions. If you wish to become more assertive, you need to *believe* that you do have rights in a situation. Key rights are:

- **The right to ask for what you want, or to make clear what you do not want.** Your wants and needs in a situation, whether a desire for time off, for recognition for what you have achieved, or a chance to use valued skills, are valid information. If you do not make your wants clear, others may be totally unaware of them, or fail to appreciate their strength. Whether or not they are aware of them, people will find it easier to ignore your wants if you leave them unstated.

- **The right to be listened to and respected.** There is no reason why you are not worth as much as anyone else. If you are not being respected as a person, this reflects badly not on you, but on those who are failing to respect you. In any situation, a key element may be the different perspectives of stakeholders. Your contribution to this diversity is potentially valuable, even if you feel you have less experience than others. You can be more analytical about a discussion if you are coming to it fresh. You are less contaminated by shared preconceptions and assumptions. Many problems resist solution because the shared view of it is so strong that no one can see outside this. So appreciate the value of your contribution, particularly if it *is* different from those of the rest of the group. And stand up for your right to make it.

- **The right not to know, or not to understand.** You have a perfect right not to be omniscient. The real trouble comes not from ignorance, but from the desire to hide it. If you do not know something, or don't understand it, admit it and ask for help from those who do. Sometimes you may be the only one who has seen a flaw in a line of reasoning, and they may not understand either. Sometimes, once you have clarified something, you may be able to use that knowledge more effectively than those to whom it was already familiar.

- **The right to make mistakes.** There is no obligation to be infallible either, although it *is* important to learn from your mistakes. Again, it is usually far more damaging, and takes far more effort, to try to hide mistakes rather than to face up to them and learn from the experience. In some organisations mistakes are recognised as evidence that you are trying to push back the boundaries.

- **The right to change your mind.** All too often it is seen as a sign of weakness to move from a position you have adopted. But if subsequent exploration of a problem shows it in a new light progress depends upon you changing your mind. A group in which positions are defended to the death, regardless of subsequent discussion, will not be effective. Dialogue will be impossible. Sometimes the most significant contribution you can make to a group discussion is to say that you have changed your mind about something and explain why. At work you may have taken a decision in the light of imperfect knowledge (the normal condition for taking decisions), but subsequent events may have shown a better possible course of action. Again, it is a sign of strength rather than weakness to revise your decision, though information about the reasons for this will be useful to others who are involved.

Activity 3.7

During the next two weeks observe those around you. Note any situation where assertiveness might be appropriate. Think about whether those involved in the situation are acting as if they believe they have the above rights, and whether they are respecting similar rights in others. Observe your own reaction in such situations. Which of your own rights do you have the most difficulty in respecting? (It is important to be honest with yourself here.) Discuss with someone whom you trust reasons why this might be, and why the right is important. Keep any notes in your learning file.

Expressing assertiveness

Exercise 3.1 showed that the words in which you express yourself are important if you are to assert yourself effectively. As well as believing in your rights, you need to practise using assertive language.

The essence of assertiveness is clarity, objectivity (though your own wants and feelings are valid data), calmness rather than emotion, firmness, a refusal to be sidetracked and the pursuit of a positive and constructive solution rather than a victory. The words you use therefore will be characterised by at least some of the following:

● use of phrases such as 'I prefer …', 'I think …', rather than 'You …', 'He …'

● use of phrases such as '… could …', 'choose' and '… might …', rather than '… can't …', or '… shouldn't …'

● checking that you have understood before responding – 'I think your argument is …'

● asking for more detail if you are not clear – 'Could you give me another example …'

● acknowledging the other person's feelings – 'I know that you have been hoping …'

● saying what you feel – 'I feel very frustrated …'

● calm repetition, possibly using the same words each time, when it is clear that you are not being listened to

● the absence of apology (unless justified).

Activity 3.8

During the next two weeks write down the words you have used in any context where you might have been more assertive, and then 'rewrite the script' using more assertive words. If you can, act out these rewritten scenarios with the help of a friend. This should make you more comfortable with using the words, and more likely to use them in a real situation. Watch out for, and note, assertive phrases that colleagues use to good effect.

➤ **Ch 9**   **Body language** is as important as the words you use (more of this in Chapter 9). If you avoid all eye contact, speak with your hand over your mouth, cower into your chair or lean as far away from the other person as possible, you will find it harder to use assertive phrases, and their effect will be diminished even if you succeed. If you raise your voice, clench your fists, stare the other person down and get *too* close to them, the effect will be aggressive, whatever you say. So get into the habit of observing first the body language of those around you and then your own. Make sure that your body language is reinforcing your words, rather than giving a conflicting message. Stand or sit straight and fairly still, with open shoulders and head held high. Look the person in the eye as you speak. Keep at a comfortable physical distance. Friends may be able to alert you to physical habits that you could seek to change in order to *appear* more assertive.

Preparation

The final important step to assertiveness is to prepare for any anticipated conflict situation. Think about what you want to achieve and why. If you feel in danger of undervaluing your rights, discuss the situation with a supportive colleague to reinforce your beliefs. Think about the other person's likely response. If your colleague, or a friend, is willing to cooperate, act out the scenario in a range of possible ways, trying always to be calm and assertive, rather than avoiding issues or becoming aggressive.

If a situation is thrust upon you with no warning, it is often acceptable – and extremely useful – to ask for thinking time, so that you prepare yourself at least a little rather than trying to respond while in a state of mild shock. A response such as, 'This is a complete bolt from the blue. I had no idea you were feeling like this. Could you give me five minutes to think about it . . .' may lead to a much more constructive outcome to the encounter.

Assertiveness skills take time to develop. So too does the skill of knowing when to be assertive. Aggression has its (limited) place, and there will be times when avoidance will be an appropriate response. You can, however, become considerably more effective in a wide range of situations where assertiveness *is* appropriate through preparation beforehand, use of the sorts of phrases that are most effective during the encounter, and reflection as to your success afterwards, with a view to further development of your skill in this area.

The above discussion is necessarily no more than a brief introduction to the subject. If you want more help, there are many good books and some useful websites devoted to the subject. Even better, go on a good course. If you start developing your skills now, and review your progress at intervals, your job performance, your studies and your relationships outside work should all benefit.

If you have developed the ability to be assertive, you will be well on the way to being an effective negotiator, particularly in the context of the sorts of negotiations necessary to protect your time, and gain any other resources necessary to your study. The essence of successful negotiation is to understand your opponent, and their likely objectives, to be equally clear about your own objectives and to identify, if at all possible, a solution that is acceptable to you both, and as favourable to yourself as possible, within that shared area of mutual acceptability.

Managing organisational stakeholders

You need not read this section if you are studying full time without organisational sponsorship. But if you are working while studying some of your key stakeholders will be relevant organisational colleagues, probably your boss, your team, any mentor and HR or training and development staff.

If these stakeholders are supporting you, your organisation might provide:

- financial support
- protected time for study
- access to senior colleagues for discussions and/or mentoring
- organisational information for use in assignments
- an internal consultancy project if your final assignment requires this
- opportunities to practise what you learn and to gain feedback on your performance.

It is not unreasonable to seek such support. Your first aim in studying is probably to become a better manager, which will also benefit your organisation. Your second is probably to increase your potential, which, if you stay with the organisation, is again in their interests. And any organisational issues that you successfully address during your studies will have saved them a consultancy fee.

The more support you have from work, particularly in terms of time to learn and opportunities to apply that learning, the more benefit they stand to gain. Provided, of course, that you behave ethically and 'play fair' with your organisation. If they are supporting you, there is an obligation to do your best to satisfy their requirements as well as your own. To adopt a strategy of getting as much out of the organisation as you can while studying with a view to leaving as soon as possible thereafter might be ethically questionable.

Of course, you may be studying secretly, with a view to changing jobs as soon as possible. Or your study may be known, but attract no support from your employers. Key senior colleagues may see postgraduate study as irrelevant, or feel threatened by the possibility that you will become better qualified and more competent than they are. But remember the earlier point made in Chapter 2 about the need to challenge assumptions, and the role that evidence can play in this.

➤ **Ch 2**

I was phoned at work one day by a manager part-way through an MBA who had been nervous about admitting to study because he felt it might be seen as either presumptuous or threatening by his employers. But following the advice given in an earlier edition of this book, he did approach them. He was delighted (so much so that he had rung to tell me about it and to thank me) that they had not only agreed to pay his remaining fees and allow time off for study, but also given him a new project to manage that allowed him to apply his newly acquired skills. (This shows how important it is to test *assumptions* that may be holding you back! This will be covered in Chapters 6 and 9)

➤ **Chs 6, 9**

This last point indicates the importance of non-financial support for any practise-based form of learning. To apply ideas at work, you need to be in a role with scope to experiment with the way you manage and, possibly, with the way your team works. Otherwise you will not be able to make the vital connection between ideas and ways of thinking and management practice.

To negotiate optimal support from your employer you need to identify the sort of support that would be most useful to you, the sources of that support and the ways in which you are most likely to be able to influence them.

Activity 3.9

List the forms of organisational support that would be most helpful to you and prioritise these. Identify the key people you will need to influence in order to obtain these resources.

Note: support needs may change as you progress through your course. You should revisit and revise this list every few months.

In case you have not thought of all the potential sources, the commonest ones are outlined below.

Potential sources of organisational support

There are several obvious sources of organisational support, described below.

HR managers are likely to have a strong interest in management development within the organisation and should be in a position to support you in many ways, so discuss your plans and progress with them. They may be able to arrange contacts with organisational information sources, discuss possible project topics, take your part if your line manager starts to overload you once the course has started, and help you to obtain any resources you may need, or put you in touch with other past or present students. They may suggest supplementary short courses, which might help you with parts of the course you find particularly difficult.

> **Sources of organisational support:**
> - the HR or training manager
> - your own manager
> - a mentor
> - your team.

Your immediate boss is another important source of potential help. She or he can both protect you from overload and help you to see how what you are learning relates to your organisation. A perspective from slightly higher up the organisation may help you to understand better how strategy is formed in your organisation.

Regular discussions on your progress with a sympathetic boss can help your motivation and give you an opportunity to test your understanding of the organisation and key issues therein. There are several potential benefits to your boss. As well as enhancing your learning, discussions about how to apply the course should be beneficial to both of you. If your boss has a qualification, supporting you may act as a useful reminder of previous learning and a stimulus to its continued application. If not, there is scope for shared learning.

A mentor within your organisation is a third source. If you have a mentor, involve them from the start in your thinking about your Master's. If your organisation does not have a formal mentoring scheme, see whether you can set up such a relationship. Discuss this with your training manager. A mentor is a senior manager, not in your direct reporting line, committed to supporting you in your personal and career development from the perspective of their greater knowledge of the organisation (or profession). Because they cannot directly influence your progress you can discuss your personal and career development freely. Their indirect influence, through helping you understand organisational issues and think about your own may be huge. A mentor from a slightly different part of the organisation can offer a wider perspective on the organisation and increase your own understanding of organisational issues. Again, because of their relative seniority, mentors often are able to arrange access to other senior people in the organisation if you need this and they may provide information helpful for assignments.

Regular discussions can also be of benefit to the mentor, who may learn from your different perspective. Some organisations now formally recognise this two-way learning with co-mentoring schemes, where long-serving senior managers deliberately seek to benefit from the fresh perspective of recent recruits. You may find that, even if the concept is new, it is welcomed.

Your team is the final major source of organisational support. Many managers find that they can usefully reinforce their learning by involving those they work with. One of my students used his own Master's as a framework for developing the team he managed. He shared course concepts with them as he learned them and then made opportunities for all to use them. He said it was the most cost-effective form of staff development he had ever encountered!

Other more general organisational resources. There may be a range of other organisational resources you can draw upon. Are management journals or other useful publications circulated at work? If so, are you on all the mailing lists? Do you have corporate membership of professional or other institutes that offer facilities for members, such as a good management library to which you could gain access through your organisation? Are there networking opportunities you are not taking advantage of?

Activity 3.10

Draw up a plan for negotiating with key resource providers for support. Start to implement this plan once you have worked through the next chapter which addresses some of the skills required.

Put a note in your learning file to revisit this activity when you have worked on these skills.

Managing your relationships with family and friends

Because they can be a source of huge support or extremely effective saboteurs of your efforts, it is really important to gain the support of your family, or others with claims on your non-work time. Study is, for the most part, a solitary activity. You will be shutting the door, metaphorically and quite probably literally, on those who are used to enjoying your company. If this is resented, you may find the resentment expressed in a wide range of ways, all of them destructive to your study.

Examples of potential hindrances:

- 'I've asked [your best friend] to lunch on Sunday.'
- 'I've got us tickets for that show you wanted to see.'
- 'I've used my airmiles to get us a week in Hong Kong.'
- 'I've poured you a glass of wine and we can watch that video.'
- 'How many times do I have to ask you to fix that socket?'
- 'If you don't want to spend time with me I'll find someone who does. . . .'
- 'Either you stop studying or I go. . . .'

As a tutor, it is heartbreaking when someone near the end of their studies has to withdraw from the programme because it is 'my marriage or my degree'. This is usually because the student failed to have open discussions with their partner when deciding to study, and did not consider the impact on their partner of their withdrawal. It is really important to recognise, and discuss the impact your study will have upon those close to you, and the feelings they are likely to experience about it, ideally before committing to study. Partners who see it as a joint and informed decision are more likely to be committed to your success. Potential feelings include being left out of something exciting, left behind in career terms, exhausted if now carrying previously shared responsibilities for house and children, and plain lonely if you are shut up with your books or computer, or out at classes when not at work. So, start talking to your partner as soon as possible about what study will mean (or is already meaning) in terms of all the costs as well as the potential benefits.

Note that advantages that seem 'obvious' to you may be less obvious to those around you. Study can be intellectually exciting: the sense of personal growth can be exhilarating. You can make new friends who share your new enthusiasms and bond through shared adversity. Once you are enthusiastic about something it is easy to assume – wrongly – that this enthusiasm is shared by those around you.

It is easy for a partner to feel excluded and the benefits may be genuinely unequal: it is *your* career that benefits while your partner takes the major share of keeping the family going, perhaps at the cost of their own career. If this is the case, you may need both to explicitly communicate your appreciation for your partner's contribution and to negotiate some compensatory rewards – for example, promising to fund and support your partner through a relevant qualification once you have gained your own. There will also be ways of minimising some, at least, of the costs to partners; for example, by a shared approach to planning the leisure you will need to survive. This is addressed in the next chapter.

Activity 3.11

If you have not yet done so, sit down with your partner and others close to you and talk through your current thinking with respect to study – the pros and cons as you anticipate them and the different ways in which these are likely to impact, short- and long-term, on family life. Ask, without trying to 'persuade' them, for their views on the decision, what they see as important factors and what ideally they would preserve in your family life though your period of study. Try to come to a shared decision about how you can approach the requirements of study while taking their needs into full account.

Thus far the focus has been on preventing family and close friends from hindering your study. But they can provide substantial help once on your side. The importance of listening skills is addressed in Chapter 9. It can be really helpful to have a 'coach' who will simply listen as you sort out your thoughts by talking them through. If your organisation does not provide a coach, a friend, family member (or fellow student) can usefully play this role.

➤ Ch 9

A common fault in assignments is the assumption that something will be clear to the reader because it is 'obvious' to the writer. This assumption is based on another assumption: that the reader is starting from the same knowledge base and perspective as the writer. Family members and friends who know less about the organisational situation may be able to read drafts of assignments and point out where more explanation is needed, or where the logic contains implicit assumptions not likely to be shared by the reader.

Support from your wider network

Sometimes you may need to exploit contacts outside your immediate circle of family and friends. Do friends or colleagues have particular expertise (or books) that might be useful to you? Perhaps you know people who have studied a similar course before? They may be a valuable source of coaching, notes and moral support. Are others in your organisation on the same course? If so, can you meet sometimes to discuss progress?

If you work in an unusual organisation, can you arrange the cooperation of friends in more mainline contexts? It may be extremely useful to discuss with them how things work in their organisations when course ideas do not easily match your own situation. What other information sources can you access through your existing networks?

Would it be useful to extend your network, and join a professional association in order to use their resources? It is likely that there will be reduced student rates, and this may be a useful investment. Indeed, if you are seeking a professional qualification, this may be a requirement. You can learn a lot by attending local meetings of such an association, as well as extending your contacts. (Check first whether your organisation has corporate membership you could exploit.)

Managing relationships with your university

Your chosen institution is a key source of resources and support, including your tutors, other support services for students, library resources and your fellow students. Many students seriously underutilise many of these resources, perhaps because they do not realise they are there, or do not appreciate their immense potential value. When the need for support is greatest, students may feel too pressured to find out what help is available if they are not already aware of it.

Activity 3.12

Think about any known and potential support needs you have that your institution might be able to meet. Then read through the outline of the more obvious forms of support below and add to this list. Make an action plan for finding out how to access any support you might find useful. Revisit this at intervals and revise in terms of any emerging support needs.

Tutors are often willing to give occasional coaching if a particula r topic or way of working is difficult for you, perhaps because of your educational or cultural background.

Learning support staff may have expertise and a wide range of equipment and software and support available for anyone with physical or psychological needs, such as visual or hearing impairment, dyslexia or mobility problems. They may offer international students a range of courses and support to help with adjusting to a different educational culture, or developing language skills.

Library staff are expert at accessing informational resources from organisational data and statistics to books and journal articles. They may offer training in online search and bibliographic skills. Many students discover the full value of library resources only when they approach a dissertation or final project, and do not have time to develop their informational skills. Do this early on – the resources and skills to use them can be a huge asset from the start of your studies.

➤ Ch 7

IT staff may be able to help with computing problems, Internet and VLE access issues and even statistical and other useful software.

Student association staff and members may offer different sorts of support at the start of your study and at key points during it.

Fellow students on your course can be your best source of support, motivation and learning. As one of my students said at a workshop:

> There will always be times when you feel down, or it all feels too difficult. It is my study group that has kept me going when I've hit these times.'

Another, in a different and explicitly action learning set said:

> We ask each other really blunt questions, but it is OK because we are all in there to help each other. And it is really helpful as it makes you see things you had missed. You think "Why on earth didn't I see that?"

Another said:

> ➤ Ch 9
>
> I wouldn't have got through the finance part of the course if Fred [group member working in a finance role] hadn't been so patient in explaining it to me.

Managing your emotions

Earlier the chapter stressed the importance of emotions. You may experience not only stress but also extreme disappointment, happiness, anxiety and other emotions during your study. Submitting assignments related to your own role as a manager may be stressful. You may feel at times that your very identity is being challenged or found wanting. Your identity may also feel threatened if values and beliefs and assumptions which have formed part of your 'mental furniture' for much of your life are challenged. Again this can provoke anxiety and other negative emotions.

Emotional support is therefore important – as was implicit in much of the above discussion of relationships with stakeholders. The potential emotional stresses of postgraduate study, particularly if combined with work pressures, are substantial. There will be times when you will be exhausted, wonder how you can continue and doubt the wisdom of your chosen course. At such times emotional support can be invaluable to reinforce your original choice, give you back your faith in it and generally help you feel you can cope. Much of this support can come from the sources already described, family, colleagues, friends, fellow students and tutors. But if you hide your need for support (and most of us hate to admit such needs, or to discuss our emotions) you are less likely to receive it. Ongoing open communication in which you admit to any pressures and worries, and actively seek people's help can make a huge difference to the support you experience.

SUMMARY

- Stakeholders in your learning can have a significant influence on your experience of study.
- Managing these stakeholders can help you gain their support in different ways.
- Any successful management of others is based on personal management skills.

- Key transferable personal management skills include self-awareness, particularly of skills and emotions, managing stress, and assertiveness.
- Organisational support is really important and worth pursuing if at all possible.
- Family support is crucial and most likely to be obtained if planning for study is a shared enterprise, recognising the needs of all involved.

Further information

http://www.open.edu/openlearn/money-management/management/leadership-and -management/managing/systems-explained-diagramming for excellent resources on systems and diagrams (accessed 13/7/15).

For an emotional intelligence questionnaire, try http://www.silverandclaret.com/wp-content/ uploads/EI-Questionnaire.pdf (accessed 1/7/15).

For a questionnaire designed to assess student stress from life events, go to http://www .monmouth.edu/campus_life/counseling/questionnaires/stress.asp (accessed 2/7/15).

For useful resources on stress reduction, try: http://www.nhs.uk/conditions/stress-anxiety -depression/pages/ways-relieve-stress.aspx (accessed 7/1/15).

For a 12-minute guided relaxation based on tensing then relaxing, try http://www.dummies.com /how-to/content/reduce-stress-and-anxiety-a-guided-relaxation-exercise.html (accessed 7/1/15).

For a video of a session at Google led by Jon Kabat-Zinn, the originator of mindfulness, go to https://www.youtube.com/watch?v=3nwwKbM_vJc (accessed 7/1/15).

https://www.youtube.com/watch?v=rSU8ftmmhmw for lecture by J K-Z 2007 at Google on mindfulness stress reduction and healing (accessed 7/1/15).

http://yourskillfulmeans.com/ for a wide range of resources and suggestions related to mindfulness, meditation and stress reduction (accessed 7/1/15).

Note

[1] The term 'warm fuzzy' is used in Transactional Analysis to describe positive or appreciative responses from people (contrasted with 'cold pricklies').

MANAGING YOURSELF AND OTHER STAKEHOLDERS

3

4
MANAGING YOUR TIME

Learning outcomes

By the end of this chapter you should:

- have started to improve your planning skills
- have estimated the time requirements for study
- know the principles of good time management
- have identified the key objectives for study and/or job
- be allocating your time according to established priorities
- be directing your efforts towards the efficient achievement of your objectives
- have reduced ineffective use of your time by others
- be monitoring your time use and adjusting plans accordingly.

Introduction

Postgraduate study requires a lot of time – typically 1,800 hours to gain a Master's degree in management. Time-management skills are essential if you are to use study time effectively. If you are working while studying you will also need to improve your time management at work to ensure that you protect the time you need for study.

In the late 1980s a survey found that 'Eight out of ten managers work late at the office and 47 per cent take work home ... Very few were prepared to say "no" to their bosses about taking on extra work', says the survey. 'Taking work home and working late at the office are symptomatic of the late 1980s culture ... these practices are unnecessary and caused by poor time management, failure to set priorities, setting unrealistic targets – or all three.' (*Personnel Management*, January 1989, p. 9.) Things have not improved in the decades since the survey.

Bringing work home may or may not indicate poor time management: it is, however, fairly incompatible with part-time study. If you regularly work late, and/or bring work home, you will probably have difficulty meeting course requirements. Use your assertiveness skills (developed in Chapter 3) to negotiate a reduction in workload if you can.

➤ Ch 3

If no reduction is possible you may need to learn how to achieve the same results in less time, by becoming more efficient. Someone recently told me that the most valuable benefit of his part-time MBA did not stem from the course content, useful though this had been. Far more significant was the fact that combining study with work had *forced* him to practise good time management. By the end of his course the habits were so well established that he continued to manage his work time far more effectively.

This chapter will tell you little that you do not know already – you are probably well aware of ways in which you *could* make better use of your time. The problem is that breaking old habits and establishing new ones is not easy. It takes constant awareness and effort at the start, until the new habits are established. (I met someone on a time-management course a few years back who said he often attended such courses because he needed 'booster shots' at regular intervals! One is put in mind of the man who was 'an expert on giving up smoking' – having done it so many times.)

Motivation is essential. Once you know how much time you need to 'create' for study (addressed shortly), you will have established a powerful need. The sooner you start to change your habits the better. Nothing can make the process *easy*. You can expect a difficult period while you are consciously trying to do things differently, perhaps to the surprise or resentment of colleagues. If possible make the changes *before* course pressures build. Eventually you will wonder why you ever functioned in your old fashion. Assertiveness skills (developed in Chapter 3) will be an essential component.

➤ Ch 3

You are more likely to achieve significant change to your ways of working if you can work on this chapter with a small number of work or study colleagues. This will bring the experience much closer to that of going on a short course, and will strengthen your motivation to make the necessary efforts. It will also provide you with a wider range of ideas, and improve your colleagues' performance as well as your own. You may find that you can talk your employer into seeing this as an in-house development exercise, allowing you to get together during working time.

This chapter requires you to carry out a series of activities. Merely reading is not enough. The answers to the activities often will be fairly lengthy, so you may find it helpful to start a time-management section in your file for your work on the topic. Proformas are available on the **companion website**.

Planning skills

Time management demands planning skills. Planning means establishing clear and appropriate objectives, working out what is required to achieve them (activities, resources, time) and then capturing this in a plan (with specified time targets). Once you have your plan you can monitor progress against it, and adjust your efforts if necessary to stay on track if things go adrift for some reason. You were introduced to the elements of the planning process in working through Chapter 1, and they will be dealt with in more detail in Chapter 16, since planning is essential to project or dissertation success. But since planning skills will contribute to your success from the outset, start to develop them now.

➤ Chs 1, 16

Planning has long been seen as central to effective management. Fayol (1916, trans. 1949), perhaps the first management 'guru', listed *forecasting and planning* as the first elements of management. The others were *organising* the necessary resources, *commanding*, i.e. instigating the activities needed to implement the plan, *coordinating* activities to meet goals and *controlling* activity to ensure it is done properly. Subsequently, Luthans (1988), in a study of a range of managers in different settings, found planning, decision making and control to be a major part of their jobs.

Activity 4.1

Look at the person specification for your current or last role, or other set of management competencies to which you have access. Check whether planning is seen as a core competence.

Planning may already be one of your strengths. If not, and you know that sometimes waste your own (and others') efforts, and fail to achieve goals as a result, make developing your planning skills a priority. Such skills will be essential if you are trying to balance work and study demands. You will need to be very clear about your objectives, and about the activities and resources needed to achieve them, both at work and for your course. Otherwise you will find yourself with impossible clashes of demands. The following guidelines may help.

Guidelines for effective planning

➤ Ch 2

- When accepting a new task, check that you are clear as to the overall aim and the objectives (*see* Chapter 2), and know how progress will be assessed. Your organisation

➤

may already insist on SMART (i.e. specific, measurable, achievable, relevant and time-defined) objectives. If not, it is a useful mnemonic.

- For each major objective, work out the hierarchy of subordinate objectives needed (again these need to be SMART) and the actions and resources they will require if they are to be met.

- Set aside 15 minutes at the start of each day for planning. Consider the tasks that you intend to work on. Check that your objectives and success measures are clear, and that you have all the resources necessary. Prioritise tasks and plan the order for addressing them.

- Set aside 15 minutes at the end of the day to review progress on tasks, and any action needed to compensate for deviation from plans. (Note any learning points.)

- Draw up your list of intended tasks for the next day.

- Every month, set aside at least an hour for thinking about longer-term objectives, both for your job and for you personally. Check that your shorter-term goals are contributing to satisfactory progress towards longer-term goals. If not, work out what to do about this.

- Keep a work diary in which you record objectives, progress towards them, notes of any 'corrective action' needed if objectives are starting to look unlikely to be achieved, and notes on learning points.

If you can improve your planning at work before course pressures start to build, you will find it easier to plan for the increased volume and complexity of demands as you progress through your course.

Control

Plans are only of use if you follow them, monitor progress against them, and take corrective action when things go adrift – as they almost certainly sometimes will. No estimates are perfect, and things happen that you have not anticipated. When Fayol (op. cit.) was seeing control as an essential management function he was referring to all the activities involved in monitoring progress towards (time and quality) objectives, and making such adjustments as are needed to bring performance back on track for achieving the objective whenever things start to go adrift.

The key elements in any control system are therefore:

- Specific objectives

- A means of monitoring progress towards these, and towards interim goals

- Scope for taking action to reduce any discrepancy noted between values monitored and what they should be according to the plan.

When planning your study it is important to think about how to measure progress towards objectives, and to decide milestones against which progress can be monitored.

These need to be sufficiently frequent that any deviation is noted while there is still time to take corrective action.

Making time for study

The most important resources for successful study are time and the energy to use it effectively. Unless you are studying full time (in which case skip the next two sections), freeing the time needed for study is likely to be your biggest challenge. If you fail to do this, you will fail the course. If you succeed only partially, you will learn far less than you might, and gain lower grades than you are capable of. Your first step is to work out how much time you need. As with any managerial problem-solving exercise, it is important to collect evidence that will establish the nature and size of the problem facing you.

How much time do you need?

The time needed will depend on the demands of your chosen programme and on your own capacity for getting through the work at speed. This may vary, with some parts of the course proving far more time consuming than others. Some people find accounting and finance hugely time consuming, some find the 'softer' subjects take more time. Projects and dissertations are notoriously demanding of time for most people.

> **Do you have a time problem?**
>
> - How much time will you need?
> - How much time will you have?
> - Can you see how to bridge the gap?

If you have yet to start studying, make a rough estimate based on information from your institution. The demands will become clearer once you begin study. Make sure any estimate includes *all* likely activities: online collaboration; attendance at face-to-face sessions; work on study materials provided with the course; any additional required reading or use of other materials; preparation of assignments; any residential periods and any other time needed for completion of the course.

'Official' and 'real' time demands can vary significantly. I have come across several managers who have had to drop out of programmes because quoted study times were unrealistic. It is therefore worth checking the official estimates against the experience of several current or past students, and any indications you have as to whether you are a fast or slow worker.

As a rough guide, many students on full-time MBA courses claim to work for up to 70 hours a week during a one-year course (and some courses take more than a year). If studying part time these hours will probably be spread over two or more years: work out the weekly load given the duration of your planned study. The projected hours will be for the mythical 'average student'. The extent of variation from this average is demonstrated by a survey I did of distance learning students on a course that was rated as 100 study hours. The average was indeed close to this, but student estimates of the time actually taken ranged from 70 hours to 150 hours.

How close you are to 'average' will depend on how fast you can assimilate material, how quickly you can write assignments, how much of a perfectionist you are, and how much you are wanting to gain from the material itself. (You may choose to devote more time to subjects that interest you and/or are highly relevant to your current job.) If all you are trying to do is pass, you will need less time than if you are aiming for a distinction. If you are in the habit of engaging with the more serious management literature you may need less time than if you have read nothing but technical manuals for the last five years.

Using your first estimate of your time need (you can always revise this later), estimate how much time you can fairly easily free for study. This will require careful thought on your part, and checking of estimates against reality, and may take you some time.

How do you currently use your time?

Unless you are studying full time, freeing enough time for study is likely to require major reorganisation of your life. Few managers are sitting around doing nothing for 12 hours a week (a fairly typical part-time study load) waiting for something to fill that space. Some activities will need to be sacrificed altogether, some reduced, and some, perhaps, be done more efficiently, at least for the duration of your course. A few may be capable of being combined with your study. The next step requires a rough time audit to give you data on which to base decisions about what to change.

Activity 4.2

Jot down estimates of time spent per week, using the categories given as prompts. They are in no sense intended as a definitive list, and you should add any other significant categories at the end. An electronic version is available on the **companion website**.

(Ignore the two right-hand columns for now. You will need these later.)

Work	Hours	Revised hours	Planned savings
Time at work			
Time travelling to and from work			
Time spent on work brought home			
Time on physical maintenance	Hours	Revised hours	Planned savings
Sleeping			
Eating and other necessities			
Exercise			
Other			

Time on mental maintenance	Hours	Revised hours	Planned savings
Leisure (list activities)			
Meditation, etc.			

Time spent on social activities	Hours	Revised hours	Planned savings
With partner and children (if any)			
Other social activities (list)			

Time spent on 'environment' maintenance	Hours	Revised hours	Planned savings
House			
Garden			
Car			
Other maintenance (list)			

Other activities	Hours	Revised hours	Planned savings
(List any significant other use of time, e.g. TV)			

Estimates like this are notoriously unreliable, and need to be checked. So ask your partner, if you have one, to do a similar estimate of your time usage, and then compare estimates. You may find some interesting discrepancies. Then go back over your diary for the last few weeks, and see whether this is consistent with what you have written. Finally, think carefully about last week. How did you spend your time then? In what ways was this atypical? Modify your estimates in the light of these checks.

It may be worth doing a more serious reality check, choosing a typical period of time and logging your actual time usage. Watch out, however, for seasonality effects. If, for example, your course has a summer break, and you are working through these activities during the summer, ask whether your time patterns will be sufficiently representative to be worth the effort of logging.

Activity 4.3

Log your usage of time, if possible for a period of at least a week, preferably two weeks (a simple format is available on the **companion website**). Log waking time and activities until arriving at work. Log your time of leaving and activities thereafter until you go to bed. You can record either *events*, i.e. the start time of each new activity, or *time usage*. For this you will need to make an entry each hour, estimating use of time within that hour. Complete the 'revised hours' column in Activity 4.1 in line with your log, and reflect on any differences.

Stop once you feel you have sufficient information about actual time usage to progress. If your log differs significantly from your instant estimate, you might like to highlight areas of difference and reflect on these.

Comparing your revised time log with hours needed for study, will show you how big a time problem you have. Once this is established you can start to think about how you can change your time usage to free enough time.

How much time can you free?

Obvious possible cuts in existing activities include any TV watching and leisure reading. A more painful necessity for many is significant reduction in their social life. But there are some creative ways of 'freeing time' by making fairly minor changes in habits. Taking a slower but less crowded train could yield three hours a day of ideal study time for the extrovert commuter who works best with a degree of external stimulation. Leaving for work an hour early when traffic is lighter may save significant driving time, and give you ideal study conditions in an empty office. Flying time provides many students in mobile jobs with hours of potential time to work on their course materials. Replacing a meal by a (healthy) snack can be good for the figure, as well as freeing several hours per week.

Time planning needs to be realistic. People you live with need, and have a right to, some of your time and you probably need your time with them too. Otherwise, as discussed in the last chapter, you will lose their emotional, and often their practical, support. This is why it is crucial to involve those close to you in preparations for your studies. So make finding time for study a shared problem. Your family needs to feel that your solution is their solution too, and takes account of their needs as well as yours. If not, they may well indulge

➤ **Ch 3** in effective (though perhaps unconscious) sabotage of your efforts to work on your course.

Many of the world's most successful people claim to manage on four hours of sleep a night, but most people need considerably more, and will be unable to work or study successfully without it. You might experiment with *gradually* cutting back on sleep; you may find that your brain still functions and you feel well. But stop the experiment if there is any detriment. The last chapter pointed out the significant health hazards of sleep deprivation. A Master's in management is, above all, a test of endurance. It is not worth risking your ability to last the course. Note, too, that if you routinely cut sleep to a minimum, there will be less room for burning the midnight oil as an emergency measure.

What time do you need for personal maintenance?

Successful study demands good mental and physical health, and good energy levels. For this you need to protect some time at least for things that make life worth living (at least in your view). *Schedule* some relaxation and treats for yourself. These need to be actively planned. Otherwise their effect will be destroyed by guilty feelings that you should really be working. Knowing that there is a treat coming up may make it easier to stick to a piece of difficult work. The last chapter pointed out the importance of exercise and relaxation to manage stress, so make sport and active relaxation (yoga, meditation or your favourite television comedy) a positive part of your strategy for effective study. Regular exercise will help you use study time more effectively.

Activity 4.4

If you have not yet started your course, draw up the sort of timetable you will need to fit in your estimated study time. Test this for feasibility for a period of about two weeks.

➤

4

MANAGING YOUR TIME

➤ Chs 7, 11

Use your scheduled 'study time' for activities similar to study. These might consist of working through some of this handbook, doing suggested remedial work, for example on your mathematical skills, or reading and taking notes on relevant management literature. Alternatively, you could use it to get ahead on personal business such as tax, letters, to free time you would otherwise need after your course starts. If you are already studying, see whether following your study schedule improves things. You will find it useful to keep any plans and comments on their effectiveness in your study file.

Obviously, the closer your chosen activities are to the sort of study your course will demand, the more reliable the test. Getting ahead with gardening or DIY might save time later, but would not test your ability to keep to the timetable you propose. While you may be able to slap paint on walls at 1.00 am, your ability to read, absorb and evaluate management literature at that time might be much reduced.

At the end of the trial consider whether your approach to freeing time is realistic and sustainable. Discuss it with your partner to check whether they are happy with the time allotted to them. Ask whether there are other activities on your list they would like to share.

I was humbled to hear from a tutor on a Scottish island that an earlier edition of the book had 'changed the life' of one of her students. Such is the power of print. He followed the instruction above, and for the first time ever discussed with his wife whether she was happy with the time they spent together, and how they might do things together in the little time he would have free from study. As a result, they stopped spending most of their 'shared' time silently in front of the television and, despite his studies she felt they were doing far more together, and more enjoyably, than they had in years.

If the time simply is not there . . .

If the activities above suggest that you *cannot* free sufficient time for study without doing serious damage to your life, you have limited options. You can give up the idea of study, take longer gaining your qualification, or reduce the time you spend at work. Some students negotiate time off for study, or a more general reduction in workload (as discussed earlier). Others practise effective time management at work in order to achieve the same in less time. Consider whether either (or both) is possible for you.

Beware promises of time off work for study if they are not associated with reductions in workload. HR managers may make generous promises that are not honoured by those who allocate your work. Many managers find that work does not go away, but merely awaits their return from study leave. Any leave taken involves putting in substantial overtime either before or after the leave. Time off to attend classes, exams and/or residential components is essential, and time off for revision or dissertation writing time can be a great advantage. But you do need to consider whether any other promised study leave will involve you in excessive overtime to compensate.

If you can genuinely see no way of bridging a substantial time gap reconsider your study plans. Over-commitment can seriously damage your personal life, your job performance and even your health, as well as threatening success in your study. However, before you abandon your plans, check whether better time management at work could enable you to cut back on the hours you need to put in. You may be surprised at just how effective this can be.

Basic time-management principles

As indicated earlier, the principles of time management are simple and make good sense. But this does not make it easy to change ingrained habits and start putting these principles into practice!

To make changes, you will need a continual awareness of time as a scarce and non-renewable resource. It is necessary to plan all your use of time, and to monitor this usage on a continuing basis to ensure that bad habits are not creeping back.

Guidelines for good time management

- Direct your effort *appropriately*, i.e. towards the most important things
- Direct your effort *efficiently*, i.e. maximise your achievements for time and energy expended
- Stop *wasting* time.

Activity 4.5

Start your time-management file by thinking about your last full working week, and writing down answers to the questions below or use the electronic version on the **companion website**:

- Were you absolutely clear what objectives you were trying to achieve? _____.
- To what extent did you achieve them? _____
- How many hours did you work? _____
- How many of these hours were spent directly on work towards your objectives? _____
- What proportion of your desk surface was clear when you arrived at work each morning? _____
- Of the time directed towards objectives, how much was spent working as effectively as possible? _____
- What prevented full efficiency? _____
- How often were you working on something when you knew there was something more important that should have been tackled? _____

➤

- In addition to the above, think about how your time was divided, and write down estimates of the percentage of your working time devoted to different activities:

Reading _____   Writing _____

Formal meetings _____   Informal meetings _____

Travelling _____   On the phone _____

Other activities (add all those that are relevant to your job) _____

_____

_____

_____

_____

Directing your effort appropriately

To direct your effort appropriately, allocate your time according to the importance of the different tasks facing you. Spend more time on those crucial for success, less on those that are less significant, and none on work that is unnecessary. This may sound obvious, but it is surprising how often some managers work on low-priority jobs (perhaps those they enjoy) while a high-priority job is waiting. Do you supervise subordinates far more closely than might be necessary, or indeed desirable, or do work that could be delegated? Do you aim at perfection when something far less would be 'good enough'? Do you read documents in close detail when a quick scan would suffice, or attend unnecessary meetings? Do you ever take on more work when you are already fully committed?

Activity 4.6

Identify your own key job areas. Think about your job and list up to seven key objectives. If you find this difficult, refer to your job description and discuss it with your boss. Your last appraisal report might also be helpful. For each objective identify the tasks needed to achieve it. These may be ongoing or one-offs. Place your list of objectives and tasks somewhere convenient for easy reference – in your desk diary, in your newly formed time-management log, or on the wall. You will need it for future reference.

Activity 4.7

Identify your current misdirection of effort. Look back at your answers to the previous activities, and think about your time usage in relation to the objectives you have just identified as important. List those aspects of your own behaviour that contribute most strongly to misuse of time.

_____

_____

Remedial action if you suspect misdirection of your effort

The action needed will depend on what you have identified as your most pressing faults, but some or all of the following probably will be helpful.

Plan your time. When you next get to work, and daily thereafter, review your key objectives, and plan the best use of time that day to achieve progress towards these. Allow time for essential routine tasks and plan a margin for the unexpected, but aim to make some progress towards at least some key objectives each day. If you prefer to plan in the evening spend 15 minutes or so at the *end* of each day, reviewing progress and planning the next day's work, so that you can start next morning with a clear idea of what to do. Some use travelling time for review and planning. Phone apps make it very easy to set, review and revise objectives when on the move. Experiment to find the best planning routine for you, and then follow it regularly.

> **Direct your effort more appropriately:**
>
> - understand why you over-commit
> - plan more effectively
> - concentrate on important work
> - delegate
> - do things 'well enough'
> - stop doing unimportant things.

Managers commonly underestimate the time required for task completion. This often stems from a genuine and confident belief that *this* task will proceed without the delays and other glitches experienced in the past with similar work. Such optimism is typical of poor time managers. If you suspect yourself of this 'planning fallacy', log your estimates for tasks and the actual time taken for a while. Stark evidence of a mismatch may help you improve your estimating.

Delegate more. Delegation requires an initial time investment in training your subordinate(s), and a willingness to believe that you are not the only person who can do the job properly. It also requires absolute clarity on your part concerning the objectives of the work, a reasonable deadline, and suitable points at which progress should be reviewed. All this must be communicated clearly to the person who is to do the work, together with an idea of how the work relates to other departmental work and objectives. This understanding of the context in which the work is required will make the job far more meaningful for the subordinate, and will make it likely that any discretion needed will be exercised in an appropriate way.

'Busy' managers often feel they have no time to develop their subordinates. They do not *think* clearly enough about what is required to do the work well, let alone communicate this to the subordinate. As a result, the work is poorly done, the subordinate learns nothing, and the manager's view that 'It's quicker to do it myself,' or even 'I'm the only one who can do it properly,' is reinforced.

Activity 4.8

Within the next week, identify at least three areas of work that could be delegated. Plan any staff development necessary for this delegation to be successful and take steps to set this in motion. Once it is complete, start to delegate work. Ensure that objectives are understood and agree targets and review points. Leave the subordinate to get on with it between reviews. Log plans and progress in your file, and put a note in your diary for six weeks hence to review the success with which you are delegating.

Understand why you over-commit. We usually contribute to our own overload by agreeing to do more than is reasonable, either because we underestimate the demands from our current workload or those of the new task. Or we may be insecure, afraid of being left out and want to prove that we are essential to the organisation. Being busy, and involved in everything, reduces this anxiety. Sometimes the new task may simply have looked too interesting to refuse. If there is a culture within the organisation of saying 'yes' to every piece of work assigned, agreeing to over-commitment avoids adverse notice. Or sometimes it may be that non-working life offers few rewards and working long hours is preferable to facing the demands of the family, or being alone.

Whatever the reasons, over-commitment is seldom a solution. It can lead to high levels of stress, which may be physically damaging. Chronic fatigue leads to less efficient, low-quality work and missed deadlines. This negates many of the reasons for taking on the work in the first place!

Activity 4.9

Identify the reasons for your own over-commitment and make a private note of any personal weaknesses they reveal. For each of these, think of at least one step that you could take in the near future to improve the situation. Decide when you will act, note review dates in your diary and log progress in your file.

➤ Ch 3 **Practise saying 'no'**. Assertiveness skills (discussed in Chapter 3) are necessary for many of the remedial actions listed in this chapter. They are of particular importance here. You need to:

- know what is reasonable and to accept that you have a right to this
- persist calmly, and with explanations, in asserting your rights.

Calmness and persistence are likely to succeed where anger and defensiveness will not. If you do wish to accept an interesting new assignment, then you will need at the same time to say 'no' to some of your existing work, i.e. negotiate a reduction in existing load.

Activity 4.10

From now on, keep a record of all new tasks that you are asked to do. Try to refuse them unless you are not currently fully occupied or they are accompanied by a reduction in existing work. Set a suitable review date in your diary to assess progress in this.

Renounce perfection. You may take pride in being thorough and gain satisfaction from doing things as well as is possible. Sometimes it is essential to achieve a result as close to perfect as you can manage. But more often this is totally unnecessary or even unhelpful. Brief minutes of a meeting, noting action points may actually achieve more than something approaching a verbatim record, and will save other people's time, as well as your own.

➤ Ch 9 Current definitions of quality emphasise fitness for purpose, and it is worth heeding this.

Activity 4.11

Think of the last four pieces of work that you completed. Consider whether a lower standard would have been equally effective. If so, identify what was unnecessary. Was there excessive detail or better presentation than is strictly required? Set review dates in your diary at monthly intervals to assess your progress away from unnecessary perfection and log progress.

Do be careful in the above to preserve the *necessary* perfections. You must, for example, be fully prepared before conducting a disciplinary or appraisal interview, and cannot afford to skimp if you are drawing up a project contract or entering into negotiations with a trade union!

Stop doing things. Think carefully about how you described your use of time in the previous activities, particularly about the way in which you spend the largest fractions of your time, and those jobs that are routine. How many jobs could be omitted without disaster? Are you filing things that you will never need to refer to again? Are you routinely circulated with, and reading, materials from which you gain little? Are you attending meetings at which your presence contributes little? It is all too easy to accept demands on your time, particularly those that are part of the accepted routine, without ever questioning their necessity.

Activity 4.12

During the next month check at the start of each activity whether it is really necessary. Omit it if not. And take steps to avoid ever doing it in the future. Ask your secretary to bin some types of material directly or to remove your name from mailing lists. Withdraw from working groups or regular meetings, and so on. List any activities you already know to be unnecessary and add to the list as the month goes on.

Make your effort more effective:

- organise your working space
- organise your computer files
- avoid procrastination
- use prime time for prime jobs
- clarify objectives
- set deadlines
- do one thing at a time.

Effective effort

Once you are sure that you are directing your efforts towards the right things, work at making those efforts as effective as possible. One common problem is procrastination, leading to effort being wasted worrying about what things you have to do, rather than actually getting on with it. Another is lack of organisation: time is wasted looking for things, important deadlines may be missed, or delays caused by failure to do preparatory activities. You will not work effectively when you are tired or if you are frequently interrupted. Trying to do two things at once is another common problem.

Activity 4.13

List six factors that you feel contribute most to your own reduced efficiency at work.

1. _____

2. _____

3. _____

4. _____

5. _____

6. _____

Jot down ideas for addressing these in the light of the suggestions below.

Remedial action if your efforts are not fully effective

The remedial action you take will depend on your particular weaknesses, but it is likely to include at least some of the following.

Organise your working space. It is extremely hard to concentrate when surrounded by a mess, so aim to keep your desk and floor clear. Organise your computer files, back up regularly, and install a simple 'brought forward system; for example, sorting tasks into 'Do today', 'Do this week', and 'Awaiting information'. You will also need a system that easily allows you to retrieve all documents and notes you are ever likely to need when working on each of your key job areas.

The system you choose is unimportant. That you *have* a system is vital. A major component in any system will be your wastepaper baskets, real and virtual. If you are not sure where to put something and it does not need action, and does not relate to a key area of your job, you probably do not need it. So bin it. Once you *are* organised, you may be pleasantly surprised by the time you save by instant access to the information that you need, and how much better you feel, working at a clear desk (and desktop).

Stop devoting effort to *not* doing things. As my grandmother was irritatingly fond of pointing out, 'Procrastination is the thief of time.' It wastes energy in displacement activities and the work hanging over you creates a sense of doom and oppression. Even work that has been put off for excellent reasons can absorb effort, particularly if you keep thinking about it while working on something else. To avoid this, you need to decide when you *will* start the work, note this in your diary or work planner, file it and then forget about it until the scheduled time. The simple act of 'booking work in' to some future date makes it much easier not to worry about it in the meantime, as well as easier to start it when the scheduled time arrives. David Allen (2001) has made a substantial fortune largely out of this simple principle.

Procrastination is usually associated with tasks that you don't enjoy or are so big as to be rather frightening. If a task is one you are *not* looking forward to, it can help to supplement the 'booking in' by scheduling a reward for tackling it. Perhaps arrange to meet a congenial colleague for a meal when you have finished compiling budgets, or even a stiff whisky when you get home after conducting that disciplinary interview.

For large tasks, a 'divide and conquer' approach can help. Split the larger task into more manageable sub-tasks, set deadlines for these and book them in individually. You will see that this is the approach recommended in a later chapter for your dissertation. A pioneering training organisation, Time Manager International, classified such jobs as 'elephant' jobs, using the splendidly graphic albeit distasteful image of eating an elephant. This would be impossible to achieve at a single sitting, but eventually might be accomplished if you sat down to a plateful each day.

➤ Ch 17

Indeed, there is considerable value in tackling some part of larger jobs on an almost daily basis. The anticipation is far worse than the reality, and increases as time passes, until resistance to the work may become so great that 'booking in' is no longer sufficient remedy. Even a small amount of work each day or two will prevent the build-up of this negative anticipation.

Another form of 'not working', which can be a drain on energy, is 'not working at home', i.e. taking work home and then not doing it. This can blight the entire evening or weekend. If extreme circumstances force you to break this rule, 'book in' the work to a specified time slot in the evening or weekend, and do your best to forget it for the remaining time.

Use prime time for prime jobs. All time is not equal. The time between 7.00 am and 8.00 am is likely to have a *different value* from, say, that between 2.00 pm and 3.00 pm, and that between 11.00 pm and midnight. We all have daily biorhythms: alertness and energy levels fluctuate throughout the 24 hours with individual patterns varying considerably.

The value of the 'time that you have' thus depends upon *when* you have it. You may be able to increase its value by identifying your 'good' times and rescheduling more challenging tasks to take advantage of these. Block this highly valuable time out in your diary, ignore your email, close your door and redirect phone calls in order to make best use of it. You may already be aware of your own good times. If you have not yet identified your own rhythms, you might like to jot down at regular intervals how alert you are feeling, and how well you think you would be able to cope with study at that particular time. For many managers there is a tiredness factor building up as the day goes on, and superimposed upon these rhythms.

Tackle those routine activities that cannot be omitted altogether during times when you are less effective.

Activity 4.14

If you do not yet know your own prime times, start to identify them now. During the next two weeks note down all times at which you have a feeling of working really well, and those when you seem to be minimally effective. From this identify your own 'prime times'.

Make sure that you know what you are meant to be doing. Any lack of clarity means you risk misdirecting your efforts. If you are writing something, you need a clear idea of who will read it, what they need to get from it, and exactly what you wish to communicate. Before any meeting with a colleague it is essential to have worked out what you want to achieve by the meeting. It also helps to have jotted down the points that you wish to cover. Make a similar checklist before any phone call. Unless one objective is to develop your relationship with the person called, keep non-essential conversation to the minimum necessary without appearing rude.

Spend time at the start of each task thinking about your objectives, and how best to achieve them. This will enable you to plan all the resources that you need, thus saving considerable time later. You can also save time by thinking *around* the task, about the possible effects of other factors upon it, and the implications of the likely outcome of the task itself. Planning for these at the outset can reduce the chances of this job creating further work later on.

Work to deadlines. Deadlines, whether for work or study, tend to concentrate the mind wonderfully and to focus effort. Harness this effect by creating your own deadlines for any tasks that do not already have them: set interim deadlines for tasks with a long time-span. Treat these deadlines as *real*. Your time planning and 'booking in' systems will disintegrate if work spills over into time allowed for other activities. Your deadlines may need to bring some deadlines forward in order to balance workload. Few managers can write four major reports in a single week, for example. In such cases your personal deadline will be more important than the external one: if you fail to meet the first, you are likely to miss the second. You must, therefore, resist any temptation to see the more distant external deadline as a reason for taking your own shorter-term deadline less seriously.

Work on one thing at a time, aiming to finish it. Research now suggests that multi-tasking is a myth. Instead people switch rapidly between tasks, each switch taking effort. Split attention is tiring and almost never effective – the person on the phone will notice your lack of attention if you are emailing at the same time. So discipline yourself to concentrate on one thing at a time. It is a good idea to keep a notebook to hand, so that any ideas about other jobs which surface while you are working on something else are not lost. This will help you resist the temptation to drop what you are doing and start working on the job to which the idea relates. You will know that you can ignore the idea until the end of the present job without losing it.

Write 'morning pages'. The above are all fairly obvious and logical remedies, but there is one, possibly less logical, approach you may wish to try, even if studying full time. It is the technique devised by Julia Cameron as an aid to creativity (Bryan, Cameron and Allen 1998) and subsequently applied to the work context. It is very simple. Every morning you wake a little earlier and write (longhand) three A4 pages continuously. Just keep writing, putting down anything that occurs to you. It doesn't matter what. Thoughts about work (or anything else), to-do lists or whatever. It is *intended* to be messy, disorganised and chaotic. Do not stop to think. Do not show to anyone else. When you have finished, put it to one side. Do not re-read them. Or not for now. You may want, much later, to revisit them and look for patterns, or progress, but not for some months.

It is claimed (and it works for me) that the act of writing creates a safe psychological space and starts a mental process of reordering: goals and aspirations emerge from the chaos, you will find that you get more done, are more focused. Although writing these pages takes time (20–40 minutes at first, but you will speed up with practice) it also *creates* time at work and frees up a great deal of energy. The result is not instant, but should start to be felt within a week or so. If you have time, this technique is something well worth experimenting with. (It has the added bonus of giving writing practice, so that you will answer any written exam questions much more fluently!)

Reduce time wastage

Do you act as if everyone else has more right to their time than you? Keep reminding yourself that your working time is *yours*. It is your scarcest resource, and the responsibility for its effective use lies with you. Do not let others cause you to use your time in non-productive ways. It will destroy your time planning and considerably reduce your effectiveness. Meetings may be one of the greatest thieves of your time. It is a salutary experience while sitting in a meeting to calculate the cost of that meeting and consider whether it will achieve enough to justify this. If your mind is wandering sufficiently to do this calculation, the chances are that your contribution is not justified, for a start! I heard of one organisation that had a special clock for meetings. When the number and status of participants were entered, the clock showed not the time, but the cost of the meeting so far. Apparently meetings became much shorter following its introduction.

> **Reduce time wastage:**
> - cut down on formal meetings
> - keep control of your diary
> - reduce interruptions
> - shorten informal meetings.

Another source of 'stolen' time is casual conversation with people who drop in, or are encountered when you are on your way somewhere. Such informal communication can be invaluable, a part of the networking that tends to be associated with management success, or a way of showing that you value team members as individuals. But you need to ensure that only productive conversations intrude on your time. If very busy you may need to curtail even these.

Activity 4.15

During the next week, without consciously trying to reduce lost time, log all time devoted to activities not contributing to the direct achievement of your key objectives. Identify the major sources of time loss and plan action to reduce these in future. Log non-productive time for the following fortnight and file this. Aim for a steady reduction throughout the period. Thereafter, check non-productive time on occasional days, to ensure that you are not slipping back.

Remedial action if time wastage is a problem

Again, you will need to suit the remedy to the disease, but the following prescriptions are available.

Reduce meeting commitments. For all meetings you chair, think carefully about the objectives of the meeting and whether the meeting could be run differently to achieve these. Do the objectives justify meeting with this frequency and for this duration? Is the attendance of all the participants necessary? Might a virtual meeting be more cost-effective, or the matter resolved by email? If there is a better way, you will save not only your own time, but others' too. For meetings that you do not chair, ask whether your attendance is really necessary. Could someone else represent you, if representation is needed? Could you persuade the chair to schedule meetings less frequently?

➤ Ch 9

Many meetings take too long. For any meeting you attend, you should know start and finish times well in advance, the agenda, and what preparation you need to do in order to contribute effectively. The meeting should be well chaired, so everyone can make appropriate contributions and discussion should be orderly. Decisions need to be reliably recorded and someone needs to take the responsibility for ensuring that action is taken to implement decisions. If these conditions are not met, then everyone's time has probably been wasted. You could argue that you have a right to leave a meeting at its stated finish time and to stay away if papers are not sent to you in advance.

Keep control of your diary. Some electronic diaries allow others to have access to your schedule and the *right* to book time in it. You need to find out how you can retain control over your time. It may be very helpful to others to be able to set up meetings without the need to consult participants, but the right to your time should remain with you.

Activity 4.16

Review your time for the last two weeks and the next two. How much of your time is scheduled for meetings? How reasonable is this?

Reduce interruptions. As well as protecting your 'prime time' from interruptions, you may need to cut down the total volume of interruptions. By breaking into your concentration, and requiring you to spend time afterwards picking up the lost threads, interruptions can cost you far more time than their actual duration. Be polite to those who interrupt you unnecessarily, but make it clear that in future only urgent interruptions will be welcome.

You obviously will wish to remain accessible to your staff in the case of real problems, so you need to make sure that they do not feel 'distanced' by your change in practice. If they understand *why* you are trying to alter your schedule, this is less likely to happen. If you compensate by encouraging contact at times when it will not be disruptive, such as coffee breaks, or a *short* regular meeting to discuss ongoing concerns, you may even achieve better communication than previously. Perhaps your subordinates could be encouraged to apply the same principles of time management to their own jobs.

Bosses may present a greater problem, but again careful explanation of what you are trying to achieve should go a long way towards bringing about improvements.

Shorten unavoidable interruptions. You may not wish to go so far as those managers who ostentatiously start an egg-timer when a visitor walks into their office, but you should make sure that those who interrupt you for informal meetings make their objectives clear at the outset. Ask them what it is that they want to talk about and how much of your time they think they need. If you anticipate a visitor staying longer than you would wish, do not invite them to sit down. If you feel that the meeting would be more efficiently conducted if you were better prepared, arrange a time to meet later.

Putting principles into practice

The activities in this section should have started improving your time management, but it is essential that you make time *now*, not next week or even later, to plan a systematic approach to better practice. Without a deadline for completing the planning phases, and a firm commitment to meeting that deadline, you have merely given yourself something else to procrastinate about.

Your plan will depend on the particular weaknesses that you have identified and upon the demands of your job. Only you know these. Do discuss your plan with someone else if you can. Discussion with colleagues who have been working through this chapter with you, your boss, your partner and/or a coach can strengthen your commitment to your plan and increase the likelihood of your putting it into action.

If you have not done so yet, start a time management file for use at work. Create a section for each major job objective, with subsections for each task within it. You will also need an overview chart at the start, which can show all the deadlines you are working towards, and review pages for regular completion. These will help you to monitor your time usage, and its effectiveness, using the sorts of points covered in the above discussion. Aim for something simple enough to be easily used, flexible and probably portable.

An example of part of one manager's planning process for implementing the principles described is shown in Figure 4.1.

Activity 4.17

Drawing on the work you have done in all the other activities, draw up a complete action plan for improving your time management at work. You probably will need about six weeks to implement this fully, but choose a timescale to suit your circumstances. Build in review dates for all planned changes.

Whatever actions you decide upon, it is important that you adopt the following habits:

- *Think* each day, before post, telephone and unscheduled visitors start to intrude upon you, of what it is that you wish to achieve, unless you did it the night before.

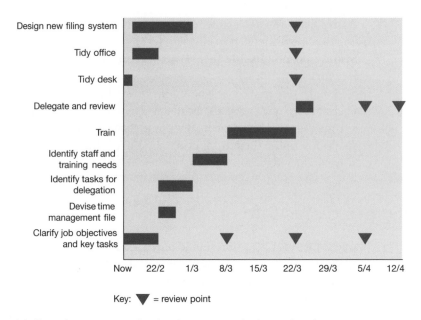

Figure 4.1 Part of one manager's planning process for improving time management

- *Check* at some point each day that you are progressing satisfactorily towards deadlines.
- *Review* your time effectiveness at intervals.
- *Alter* future plans or ways of operating if your review shows this to be necessary.

Avoid becoming so obsessive about time management that your subordinates feel that they can no longer look to you for support, or that they have no call on your time. And do not lose the informal communications that are one of the most valuable sources of information in an organisation. These can generate some of the social rewards that help make a job enjoyable, build the contacts that you may need in the future and keep team members loyal and committed to the organisation. In planning your strategy you should value these factors and make sure that you find a way of retaining them while cutting time-wasting interactions. Remember, time management is an aid to *better management*, not an end in itself.

SUMMARY

- Time is a scarce resource that must be managed.
- Good time management requires planning skills, and clear objectives.
- You may need to change what you do out of work to create study time. It helps to involve those close to you in this planning.
- You may also need to arrange for work to be reduced to allow for study and/or to manage time at work more effectively.

- Good time management requires planning time use and monitoring effectiveness of time usage.
- It may mean breaking ingrained working habits, both your own and those of your colleagues.
- It therefore requires considerable discipline, a plan devised to help you make necessary changes, and frequent reviews to assess progress.
- Working with others to develop your time management skills can generate better ideas and sustain motivation.
- Time management requires that effort is directed *appropriately* and *efficiently* and time-wasters are eliminated.
- Action needed is likely to include clarifying objectives, setting and meeting deadlines, planning to use your best time for your most demanding work, controlling interruptions, organising office, desk and diary, delegating more and avoiding needless perfection.
- Assertiveness skills are important for effective time management.
- It is important to start improving your time management *now* and to monitor your progress continually.

Further information

Allen, D. (2015) *Getting Things Done: The Art of Stress-Free Productivity* (New edn), Penguin.

Bird, P. (2010) *Improve Your Time Management: Teach Yourself*, London: Hodder & Stoughton.

Bryan, M., Cameron, J. and Allen, C. (1998) *The Artist's Way at Work: Twelve Weeks to Creative Freedom*, Pan.

Caunt, J. (2010) *Creating Success: Organise Yourself* (3rd edn). London: *The Sunday Times*.

Evans, C. (2008) *Time Management for Dummies,* Chichester: John Wiley & Sons.

Forster, M. (2006) *Do It Tomorrow: And Other Secrets of Time Management,* Hodder & Stoughton.

PART 3
TRANSFERABLE LEARNING SKILLS

5
MANAGING YOUR LEARNING

Learning outcomes

By the end of this chapter you should have:

- reviewed your practical arrangements for study

- developed an initial study plan

- started to make more effective use of your study time

- considered strategies for times when things go wrong

- started a learning log.

Introduction

Earlier chapters have focused on preparation for learning. This chapter aims to help you integrate this earlier work into an effective approach to managing your learning activities, and to produce firmer study plans. Study at Master's level is a significant project, and it will need all your planning and management skills for success.

Establishing a strong 'study habit' will free countless hours, and considerable energy for productive study. Without such a habit energy will be consumed by repeated 'shall I do it now or later' decisions. With the study habit you will simply slip into study mode at the scheduled times.

Specific learning skills are addressed in the next chapter. This chapter explores the different sorts of learning your course is likely to demand. They may need to be managed differently. This chapter and the next will together help you to become a much more effective learner both on your course and during your career. It is your ability to keep learning after you graduate that will have most impact on your career.

➤ Ch 6

Creating an effective work space

Time is *the* key resource you will need for successful learning: securing time is essential, and your work on the last chapter should have started this process. Having a suitable space or spaces in which to study is almost as important. Although much of your work is likely to be online, or stored in your computer, there will still be books you will need to refer to, and you may also keep paper notes or other materials. Keeping everything together and well organised is a key part of (study) time management. Freedom from distractions is important. Good lighting will also help.

A well designed chair and desk – or better still somewhere to stand at your laptop – will reduce physical strain. Substantial evidence is emerging of the damage that prolonged sitting can do to joints, back, and blood pressure, as well as increasing diabetes risk. If you sit most of the time at work and/or during a prolonged commute, it would be sensible to avoid adding more hours of sitting while studying. Treat your study location to as much ergonomic scrutiny as your work place. You need to guard yourself against neck or back problems or repetitive strain injury to wrists.

Once you have your space, a large study plan on the wall can be both a useful aid to monitoring progress and a prompt to action. You are seeking to form an association between going to your study location and slipping into study mode. Each time you go there and start work immediately and productively you will be reinforcing your study habit, and making it easier to start work the next time.

This approach will suit most people. But extreme extraverts may find it hard to concentrate unless there is a background level of noise and activity. If this is you, and you find it is easier to work in an Internet café or pub, then do that. One size does not fit all.

Once you have created the time to study, and a congenial place, or places (some study may be done at work, some at home), you need to ensure that you make best use of the time you have created. This chapter looks in a little more detail at study planning, and at

➤ Ch 3   the nature of the learning the study is intended to achieve.

Scheduled study times – how regular do you need to be?

If study can become a *regular* habit, it tends to be easier – it avoids internal debates on whether you work now or later. Have you have ever sat down in front of your books, got up to do something, sat down again, decided a snack might help, then a coffee, and then decided that the whole thing would be better left until tomorrow? If so, you need to develop your study habits! Otherwise an hour or more can pass, leaving you frustrated and exhausted, but having achieved nothing. With a regular study schedule it becomes automatic, after a time, to go to your study on Tuesdays, Thursdays and all of Sunday, or whatever pattern you have chosen. No decision is necessary. Family and friends know the pattern and what to expect and that you will be available to them at other times. Indeed, if family and friends helped you devise your study pattern, and feel part-ownership in your plan, they may act as 'police' rather than 'saboteurs'. If you are studying full time you may want to think about your biorhythms and schedule study and leisure time to take advantage of your prime time.

➤ Ch 4

But many people live highly irregular lives so regular study slots are seldom possible. If this is you, follow the time-management practice of 'booking in' your study time. This means that you need not worry about the work when you are not doing it because you know it is under control. And it means that when the scheduled time arrives, the decision as to whether or not to study has already been taken.

Either approach will need to be adjusted if study becomes genuinely impossible. If you have a raging temperature, the cat has just been run over, or an old friend has dropped in en route from Alaska to Zaire, then it would be unreasonably obsessive to insist on continuing to study. Lesser interruptions should, however, be resisted firmly. You will *often* feel a bit tired and disinclined to study. If you start to make such common occurrences an excuse, you will never complete your course. Similarly, you can see your next-door neighbours on another night and, if you forgot to feed the cat, it will probably not die of starvation before you finish your scheduled study session.

A schedule that you stick to under all reasonable circumstances, whether it is a regular weekly schedule or one that you draw up each week or fortnight to suit prevailing circumstances, will considerably reduce the effort required for study. Sticking to a predetermined schedule will help you avoid procrastination, which is probably the greatest threat to successful course completion.

Devising a personalised study schedule

A good schedule is one that you can stick to and that makes best use of the times when your brain is in an optimal state for learning. In drawing up your schedule make sure that you do not make unreasonable demands upon yourself. It is highly unlikely that you will be able to study effectively for six hours at the end of a demanding week at work. Shorter sessions during the week are far more likely to be effective, with longer sessions reserved for weekends or any study leave. Even then, arrange for regular short breaks to keep your mind fresh – you can use them for stretches and/or other exercise.

➤ Ch 4

When scheduling how to use a particular study session, consider whether it is 'prime time' and if so reserve it for more challenging work.

Activity 5.1

Devise a study schedule for the next month, aiming to include work on any relevant sections of this book as well as your course work. Review your success in sticking to the schedule on a weekly basis, noting any learning points from this, and planning any further action necessary.

Developing a study plan

➤ Ch 4

Your chosen study schedule provides the framework for your study plan, as it provides the 'when?' You also need to plan the 'what?'. The process involved is, unsurprisingly, very similar to that of work planning described in the last chapter. Note that since your plan depends upon specific course requirements, you cannot draw it up until you have started your course

Study planning involves deciding, for each study topic, what material you will need to cover as a bare minimum, what 'covering it' means, and how long this is likely to take. Decide, too, what additional material would be worth studying if time allows, and how much time would be required for this. You then need to plan which scheduled study sessions you will devote to which work in order to do all that is necessary before any assignment deadlines, or any deadlines that you set yourself in order to balance workloads. Your planning must include ensuring that you acquire any materials not already in your possession in time for their anticipated use.

Plan for:
- time
- materials/resources
- achievements
- motivation.

This may all sound blindingly obvious – and it is – but it is surprising how many otherwise excellent managers fail to 'manage' their studies. They seem victims of a particularly seductive optimism (a version of the planning fallacy noted earlier), a belief that somehow, shortly before a deadline, time will miraculously expand to allow the necessary work to be fitted in, and all the books they require will be sitting in the library ready for their use, despite the fact that everyone else on the course is wanting to borrow them at the same time.

➤ Ch 17

Whenever you feel this nice, warm feeling of security creeping up on you, stamp it out fast. It is particularly common for work with a distant deadline. (Chapter 17 on managing projects, theses and dissertations offers techniques for handling it.) Sit down at once and draw up a realistic schedule, making sure you have included *all* the interim tasks that will be needed in order for you to meet the deadline with a good piece of work. Remember to build sufficient slack into your plan to allow for the unexpected.

Your tutors may do much of the scheduling for you, providing a study calendar that shows exactly what you need to achieve each week. But many programmes do not do this, and if not, it is important that you make one for yourself.

Setting learning objectives for study sessions

Devising, or adapting, an overall study plan is perhaps the easy part. Planning each individual session to ensure that it is effective is harder. You need to be very clear about your objectives in covering the material. It is important to focus on what you aim to achieve in each session, rather than merely on how long you plan to spend. You are being assessed on your achievements rather than your 'effort'.

You thought earlier about your learning objectives for the qualification as a whole. These provide a context for all your study. But to manage your learning effectively you need to consider what you intend to gain from each learning activity. There are many ways in which you can learn, and many things that can be learned. Sometimes you will be aiming to learn material by rote, sometimes to respond to it critically. Sometimes you will be seeking to master a technique or develop a skill, sometimes to relate material to your own professional practice, sometimes merely to consider a theory in relation to another theory.

➤ Ch 1

Learning objectives for a session should make clear what you are seeking to learn and in how much detail. They need to be set with an understanding of how the learning relates to course aims, as well as your own objectives, and of how your learning will be assessed. Unless you have clear learning objectives you will not be able to check whether you have achieved them.

Practical scheduling considerations

When setting objectives for a session you should take account of your own body rhythms and plan your work in accordance with your personal good and bad times. Even if you can schedule most of your sessions to take advantage of 'good' times, as suggested above, there will, almost inevitably, be occasions when you have to study even though you are not at your best. In this case, as at work, you should make sure that you schedule demanding tasks for your better times, leaving more routine work for times you are not at your peak.

Consider, too, how long you can maintain your concentration without strain (typically an hour or less. You are likely to make far more effective use of your time if you schedule short (five- to seven-minute) breaks every hour or so, using this time to have a drink, move about or get some fresh air. A few brisk exercises or even a very brief walk can do wonders for concentration, as well as easing the strain caused by sitting still.

➤ Ch 4

(Chapter 4 considered energy in general. Some useful study-break options are suggested in Helpfile 5.1 at the end of this chapter.)

Activity 5.2

If you have been working on this book for at least 40 minutes, stop and try a few exercises now. Otherwise wait until you have been working for 40–60 minutes and try them then. Before you start, note any parts of your body where you are aware of tension or

➤

discomfort. Check to see whether any remains after the exercises. If so, experiment with other movements to relieve it.

Try to do exercises after each of the next five hours of study you do. Only then can you feel justified in abandoning them if they still seem not to be working.

It is important that you schedule the end of any study sessions, as well as the beginning. This allows you to enjoy the time afterwards and relax properly. If you finish your planned task in less time than you anticipated, you might even stop early.

In addition to scheduled breaks, you should stop if you are finding it totally impossible to concentrate at any point. It is a waste of time to sit in front of a page without registering it in any way. If you have clarified your study objectives, are taking notes as suggested later and having regular breaks, you should not find this problem arises, unless you are ill or overtired, have serious worries or the material is extremely badly written. Take 10 minutes to explore possible causes. If no obvious reason can be found and remedied, try some exercise or fresh air and try again. If concentration is still lacking, try a different activity. If that fails too, admit defeat and terminate your study session rather than wasting time. Log the problem in your working file. If it recurs, look for a pattern that might help you identify the reason. Before stopping, remember to reschedule the missed time.

➤ Ch 7

At this point, it is worth starting to think again about the 'what' of learning. This was briefly outlined in Chapter 2, as including language, concepts, techniques, skills and information. It also includes becoming aware of the mental models you use and then using this awareness to challenge them. They need to be challenged if you are to work with others to respond to new situations in innovative ways.

➤ Ch 2

➤ Ch 6

The next chapter will look at this aspect in more detail, considering the deeper learning involved in using theory, reflection and dialogue to develop awareness, and the increased flexibility of thinking that this can bring. Here I shall look at some of the more 'conventional' forms of learning in relation to study planning. They have different time requirements.

Study objectives may include:

- learning and practising techniques
- understanding and evaluating theories
- applying theories to analyse a situation
- learning and/or evaluating methodologies
- learning about context
- developing your ability to be critical
- reflecting on your own practice in the light of what you have read.

Learning facts

Sometimes you will need to learn facts, such as the content of a particular piece of employment legislation, or the structure of a particular framework. If so, memorising is appropriate. Normally this is best achieved through repetition, reproduction and testing, so you might recite a list or copy a model over and over again and try to reproduce it without looking and check how much you got right. Repeat at increasing intervals until you can still remember it a month after you last looked.

The majority of this sort of 'fact learning' is done in preparation for examinations: techniques are covered in Chapter 15, which is about passing exams. If your study session addresses something

➤ **Ch 15**   that eventually you will need to learn in order to reproduce for an exam, or that will make you efficient to 'know' in the sense of being able to quote at will, either memorise it at once, or make the eventual memorising easier by interacting with the material as much as possible meanwhile. Highlight key points, make notes for subsequent memorising, look for patterns, seek to understand implications for your own role, *use* the ideas to make sense of your own experience.

Some students try to learn *all* their course materials by rote – particularly if their earlier education has been within a system relying on recall of 'the facts'. But there is a big gap between rote learning and the improved thinking skills and professional practice that a postgraduate management programme seeks to develop, as the next chapter will

➤ **Chs 2, 6**   demonstrate. While some things will indeed need to be learned by heart (see Chapters 2 and 6), there are many different sorts of learning that are much more important.

Techniques

Learning to *apply techniques* will be central to some of your study. You may need to know, for example, how to calculate the weighted average cost of capital (WACC) or the net present value (NPV) of possible projects to allow you to choose between competing potential investments. In these cases, you need to know what to include in the calculation and how to do the sums. Some of this comes fairly close to rote learning. But also, you will need to *practise* doing the calculations until you know which keys to press without thinking, or how to set up a spreadsheet to do the sums for you. This may be important in some exams, and will be essential if you are taking decisions at work based on financial/accounting evienceors.

Simply learning to do a calculation will do little to help your career unless you know when to use it, and how to interpret the results. Only then will the technique help you in your role as a manager, rather than potentially misleading you. You need to know, too, what alternative approaches might be considered and when they might be preferred. All this requires that you *understand* the technique and its significance and develop skills of judgement in relation to its use.

This requires much more than learning by heart. It requires you to *think* about the technique and the meaning of what it produces, checking this against things that you already know and understand. You need to think about when it would be useful and when it might not. And of course you need to practise the technique in different contexts in order to get a 'feel' for it.

A colleague once told me that the difference between the US and the UK in their approach to management study is neatly demonstrated by the different approaches to net present value calculations. In the US approach, it is the resulting *value* that is deemed significant. In the UK it is the *process* of arriving at that value that is of interest: one could plausibly arrive at almost any desired value by making the appropriate assumptions.

This neatly illustrates the richer type of learning that your course may aim for, but also the greater time requirement it implies. When planning your study you need to be clear which level of learning is appropriate and to budget your time accordingly. Allow time not only for practising techniques until you are confident in their use and, if appropriate, for trying to *understand* their application but also for thinking about the contexts in which this would be appropriate.

Theories

Much of your course material is likely to relate to management theory. Some of your study of theories may be in order to 'know' them. This may not require all that much time. But this would have minimal impact on your professional practice. The next chapter discusses the sort of engagement with theory that will have a much more profound impact upon this, and upon your career. Here it is enough to point out that you will need to read Chapter 6 before you can plan your learning objectives in relation to theory, or decide how long it is likely to take to achieve these objectives.

➤ **Ch 6**

Methodologies

Another category of learning to which you will be exposed will be that of methodologies or ways of approaching problems. (Strictly, I should be talking about 'methods', as 'methodology' means the body of knowledge about methods, but the everyday usage of the word in the above sense is widespread, so I have reluctantly used it here.) Again, it will be far more rewarding, and interesting, and have more effect on your managerial practice (and in particular how you relate to consultants) if you go beyond rote learning of content into an understanding of why the methodology is offered, what it can and cannot do, what advantages and disadvantages it has compared with alternative approaches, and when it would be suitable.

It does not matter whether you are talking about a simple approach, such as the framework for looking at a competitive environment via analysis of social, technical, environmental and political (STEP) factors (introduced in Chapter 1), or a more complex approach such as Checkland's Soft Systems Methodology (Chapter 8). If you go beyond understanding, and start using the methodologies when you have the opportunities in your job, your learning has the potential to be an order of magnitude greater.

➤ **Chs 1, 8**

Understanding context

Gaining an understanding of *context* and its importance is crucial at Master's level. The STEP factors just referred to constitute a simple classification of potentially important factors *external* to the organisation. For departmental-level problems, the wider organisation will constitute an important *near* environment. Much of your learning will involve coming to appreciate the importance of both types of environment, understanding their likely impact and becoming more sensitive to all the relevant factors in any particular problem that you may have to face.

Rote learning will have little part to play in this. Instead, you will need to think about what is happening in the cases with which you are presented, and start to become more aware of general trends, such as political ones, that influence business. You will need to concentrate particularly upon those environmental factors to which your own organisation is especially sensitive. This sort of learning should be a continuous process, once you are sensitised to the issues involved.

Objectives for group sessions

A lot of significant learning takes place alone, and you will have control over setting learning objectives and taking actions to achieve this. However, some of your most powerful learning opportunities may take place in a group setting. Group discussions can be the vehicles for practising a variety of interpersonal skills, for developing your ability to hold productive dialogue (see Chapters 6 and 9). Here both objectives and the means of achieving these may need to be negotiated.

➤ Chs 6, 9

This is not always easy and there may be a temptation not to have the necessary discussions. Yet if you avoid setting explicit objectives, it will be hard to monitor the extent to which you are achieving them and even harder to adapt if you are not learning effectively. Even the discussion of learning objectives can generate learning so, if you are to use group sessions effectively, it is important to plan and review them just as carefully as objectives for your private study sessions.

Becoming critical

A key objective of most postgraduate programmes is the development of your critical faculties. During your career you can expect to encounter all sorts of new fads and theories. Much of what appears in the management literature is of limited usefulness. The ideas may be old ones, thinly disguised in new jargon. Or the content may be primarily the author's opinions and prejudices, even wishful thinking, rather than based upon hard evidence or sound reasoning. A great many consultants' reports will be based to some extent on the latest management theory, whatever its worth. You will need to be able to evaluate these reports, and the theory on which they are based. Some may be worthless, others highly significant.

➤ Chs 6, 7, 12

There is more on this in Chapters 6, 7 and 12. Here it is important to note that you should approach *all* your study materials critically: do not automatically assume that anything in print is worth reading or even 'true' in any general sense. There is much 'management theory' available on a variety of websites and even in reputable journals that needs to be treated with extreme caution. Claims in such papers may go beyond the evidence and /or the arguments on which they are based may be flawed. Some may present a very incomplete and slanted view of a subject. You need to develop the skill to evaluate everything you read, and come to a fair, justified judgement. Otherwise you may produce a dissertation that is itself weak, and finish the course without developing the important transferable skill of being able to critically assess academic papers and consultants' reports.

While it is hard to set objectives for becoming more critical and even harder to assess progress towards this, you could usefully reflect on the extent to which you have adopted this approach in any study session.

Keeping a learning log

Sustaining motivation is for many a major challenge. Keeping a study log can help. This might be a really simple record of what you have done and learned, but you can usefully do more than this to enhance your learning.

When you are planning any single study session, clarity about your learning objectives will help you both estimate the time needed and check that you have achieved your objectives. Setting down your objectives at the start of a session is itself potentially motivating: seeing that you have achieved them is even more so. If you can see the point of something in terms of your personal development as well, it will be far more interesting than if you are merely doing something 'because it is on the syllabus'. Recording your achievements can be very satisfying, and looking back over your achievements even more so.

There are many ways of capturing your learning and a basic *study log or learning log* is the simplest. Figure 5.1 shows an extract from a very simple log kept by a past student. This is very strictly a log or record of what has happened. While valuable in itself (particularly when carrying out research) you may wish to extend your log slightly and include a column for follow-on action suggested by your study. Figure 5.2 shows a possible format. It also includes duration of study/event in the first column. This allows you to monitor the time you are spending on each topic or course.

Recording is fairly personal: experiment until you find a format that works for you. Whatever you choose, consider making notes on the significant points absorbed, and the sources from which they were derived, any queries that arise during your study that you will need to pursue at a later date, and any interesting points you might wish to raise with your tutor or in class discussion. Make a particular note of anything that looks potentially relevant for forthcoming assignments. Comment, too, on any difficulties encountered in maintaining concentration, and on the accuracy of your time estimates, and anything else that is relevant to future planning of your study sessions.

Event and date	Reason for doing	What I learned from this
2.11.2010 Read first part of course introduction	Required reading	Key management roles, current management challengers (ICTs, globalisation, etc.) Kolb's learning cycle.
14.11.2010 Attended first tutorial	Get better idea of course (and tutor) requirements	Need to make explicit reference to key concepts in assignments, need to submit on time, word-limit penalties, value of web-groups.

Figure 5.1 Extract from student log

Date and duration	Learning objective	Learning event/material studied	key learning points	Action points

Figure 5.2 Possible format for a learning log

➤ Ch 6

Your log, together with your study plan, can help you study far more effectively. The next chapter will suggest ways in which you can go beyond this basic record and use the act of reflecting in writing as an even more powerful learning tool.

Remember to include *all* learning events in your record. These might include lectures, reading, group discussion and conversations with colleagues at work inspired by ideas you have encountered in your studies and other learning experiences at work.

Professional institutes often require you to keep a record of your continuing professional development (CPD) as a condition of membership. The Chartered Institute of Personnel and Development suggests members use the format shown in Figure 5.3 (**www.cipd.co.uk**) – though they say they are happy for any reasonable format to be used. (I've included an extract from my own record to show how this might reasonably be used.)

It may also help to write a less structured reflective piece after training or other events you attend. Reflective writing is discussed in the next chapter.

➤ Ch 6

Key dates	What did you do?	Why?	What did you learn from this?	How will you use this? Any further action?
May 05	Attended London seminar run by Bioss on their consultancy model	Wanted to see whether this model would be appropriate for inclusion in new course 'The HR Professional'	How Jaques's ideas and levels have been developed into a full consultancy model-this would be a useful example of theory-driven consultancy	Incorporate into new course unit. Need to visit Bioss website for more detail and contact them re. collaboration

Figure 5.3 Extract from the author's Personal Development Record

What do I want do learn?	What will I do to achieve this?	What resources and support will I need?	What will be my success criteria?	Target dates for review and completion
How to reflect more effectively	Experiment with the formats provided in this chapter to see what works for me Discuss with tutor whether I could get some feedback	Notebook Time Input from others in my learning set Feedback	To have actually kept journal for a month and submitted for feedback To feel I'm learning more effectively To have used output from reflectiom to drive further learning via plan Feedback from tutor to say this approach is acceptable as evidence	Review: 1/7, 8/7, 15/7 Submit 22/7

Figure 5.4 Extract from a study plan

Logs are retrospective but they are closely linked to a forward-looking study plan which will help you manage your work. Figure 5.4 shows an example. You will note that this allows you to ensure that you have assembled the resources for study and provides target dates so that you can monitor progress. When you are working on a major project or dissertation you may also need to do a more general project plan, which is covered in Chapter 17.

➤ Ch 17

Your study plan, study log and a working file will help you manage your studies. Instead of key objectives, you could use *courses* as your main dividing categories, subdivided by learning objectives and study tasks. Your study plan should schedule these tasks so as to ensure that all course deadlines are met and workloads kept even, or adjusted to other conflicting demands. Again, regular review of your effectiveness is crucial. Your study log, by recording what you have achieved, difficulties encountered and thoughts about future tactics, will enable you to gain insight into your own study skills and their development. It helps motivation because of the satisfaction derived from recording achievements on each occasion.

Guidelines for using study time effectively

To study effectively:

- Develop a strong and ideally regular study habit
- Schedule your study time in advçance
- Take your body clock into consideration when planning
- Set clear objectives for each session
- Always start work on schedule, with no procrastination
- Take scheduled study breaks, using some for exercise
- Use study planner, learning diary and plan, in a learning file to help capture learning and reflections.
- Review progress regularly and adjust plans where necessary.

If things go wrong

Failure to free time for study is a major cause of student failure. Lack of a study plan or lack of the self-discipline to follow it is the other major cause. If you have carefully worked through this chapter and the last, you should be protected from failure from these causes. But sometimes, despite your best plans, things can go wrong. Accidents, bereavement, family illness or your own, work or relationship problems, or particular difficulties with parts of the course can all threaten your success. Figure 5.5 shows some of the common causes of failure to complete a programme.

If you are constantly reviewing progress, you should be aware of the size of the problem when it arises, and whether or not plans can be revised to accommodate it. If you have built some 'slack' into your schedule by preparing work ahead of deadlines you can afford to be ill for a bit.

The first step, if you encounter a problem, is to work out, by yourself or with a supportive friend just what is going wrong, and why, and whether there is scope to put things right. If so, you need to do whatever is necessary straight away. But if you have been the victim of increasing pressure and already used up any slack, or are faced with a major emergency, you need to talk to someone, probably your tutor or study counsellor, or a student advisory service. If you followed the suggestion in the last chapter to explore the resources available when you hit problems, you will already know the right person. If not, find out quickly. The longer the situation continues, the harder it will be both to

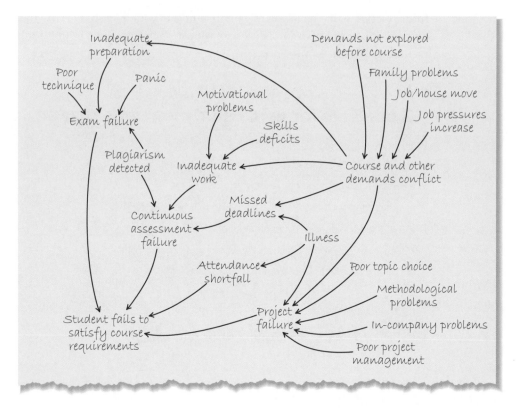

Figure 5.5 Multiple-cause diagram exploring causes of student failure

➤ Ch 4

retrieve it in study terms. And the more your stress levels rise, the harder it will be to even ask for advice or help.

Talking to a tutor or counsellor will help you distinguish between things you can do nothing about and those you can. You can then plan for the latter, and work out the best strategy given the former. You may be surprised at the amount of help and flexibility your university can help if you are facing major problems. Staff will know just how much can be done and may know of options you are unaware of. They *want* you to succeed – for financial and reputational reasons as well as sheer human feeling.

If you have to rush off to a family emergency, make sure you let tutor and/or administrative staff know what has happened and keep in touch with them while you are away. You may need evidence of your reasons, so getting letters or copies of official documents from hospital or employer or other relevant authority involved with the emergency is important.

The above fairly practical points, combined with good planning techniques similar to those that you should by now be using at work, should help you to make effective use of the study time that you have freed, perhaps at considerable sacrifice, and cope with any disasters that arise. The following chapters on more specific study skills should further enhance your effectiveness.

SUMMARY

- It is important to develop habits of time and place if at all possible: this will reduce the effort wasted by procrastination.

- Your study schedule identifies *when* you intend to work. It should be realistic and devised to make use of as much 'prime time' for study as is feasible.

- Your study *plan* shows how you intend to use the time you have scheduled and your learning objectives. It should include regular breaks within sessions.

- Your study log records what you have done and the learning objectives you have achieved.

- A professional development record is likely to be more event-focused, and may be required for professional institute membership.

- Time management techniques are as applicable to study as to work. In particular, you should actively plan your study in order to achieve objectives and meet deadlines. You should pay attention to your body rhythms and plan your non-study time too.

- Different approaches will be needed for learning facts, techniques, theories, methodologies or material intended to broaden your perspective, or heighten your awareness.

- Your study will be more effective if you adopt a critical approach and make a habit of testing ideas against your prior work experience, trying to use as many course ideas, techniques and methodologies as possible in the practice of your job.

- If things go wrong you need to assess the size and nature of the problem and take corrective action as soon as possible. If the problem is more than you can correct for, and threatens your success, seek advice from within the university or outside.

5

MANAGING YOUR LEARNING

HELPFILE 5.1
EXERCISES THAT CAN BE
USED DURING STUDY BREAKS

Remember, the point of the exercises is to make you feel good, not to cause pain. Stop at once if there is any discomfort. And if you have back or other physical problems, consult a doctor first.

Stretch

Stand with feet slightly apart, and reach as high as you can towards the ceiling. Hold this position for 10 deep breaths. Then curve to the right to give a stretch along the left side for 10 breaths, followed by 10 breaths stretching to the left.

Hang

Keeping feet in the same position, and legs straight, hang forwards from the hips, with head and arms loose. Only rest your hands on the floor if this is totally comfortable and bend your legs a little if this feels better. Aim for a slight pull behind the knees. Hold for up to 10 deep breaths then unroll upwards slowly, from the small of the back, imagining that you are putting your vertebrae back in place one by one. Engage your abdominal muscles while doing this to protect your back.

Shrug your shoulders

Do this up to 10 times, exaggerating the movement as much as possible, perhaps including a circling motion involving your elbows.

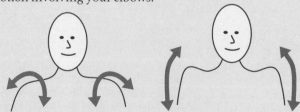

Circle your head

Drop chin on to chest, then let your head roll in a large circle towards your shoulder, backwards, over other shoulder and back to chest. Repeat in the reverse direction.

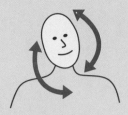

Massage your back

Lie on your back on the floor, knees drawn up loosely towards your chest, hands clasped above them. Pull your knees gently towards your chest five times, feeling your lower back pressing slightly into the floor. Then place one hand on each knee and move knees in small horizontal circles, keeping them joined, again feeling the movement of your back against the floor.

Twist your spine

Keeping knees bent, place feet flat on floor just beyond your hips. Feet should be parallel and about a shoulder-width apart. Stretch arms out to each side, along the floor. Keeping both shoulders firmly on the floor, flop both knees over to the left. Relax, breathing steadily. Then increase the twist by turning your head to look along your right arm, and letting your knees move further towards the floor, going no further than is comfortable with both shoulders still on floor. Hold for up to 10 deep breaths, and then do it in the opposite direction.

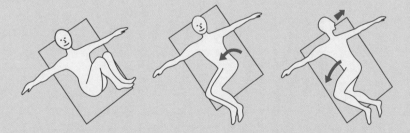

Relax

Spend about a minute lying on your back and breathing, deeply and regularly, trying to keep all your muscles relaxed and your mind as clear as possible. Get up slowly after this, taking at least five deep breaths to become vertical.

5

MANAGING YOUR LEARNING

6
PROFESSIONAL DEVELOPMENT

Learning outcomes

By the end of this chapter you should:

- understand the nature of the learning most relevant for professional development

- understand how both learning theory and management theory can help you develop as a manager

- have identified some of your own characteristics as a learner

- have identified aspects of learning that are likely to be more and less challenging for you

- have begun to experiment with different approaches to learning

- understand the role of reflection in learning and be experimenting with reflective writing.

Introduction

Most of those studying for an MBA or management-related Master's degree will be doing so for professional reasons – seeking, a successful career as manager. Such study is likely to be very different from past experiences of education, particularly if you are studying in a country with a different learning tradition from that in which your earlier education took place. It will require different learning skills. This chapter explores the nature of professional development, and management learning in particular, and how you can learn most effectively. This will help you identify what *you* need to do in order to get the most out of your studies.

'Management learning' includes different types of learning serving different purposes. Thinking has moved far beyond the 'jug–mug' idea of an expert imparting knowledge to a passive student. Competences, or the ability to *do* things, are now recognised as important and learning through reflection recognised as central to professional practice. Ideas from knowledge management suggest that managers' ability to *construct meaning* lies at the heart of both management learning and success in a complex and rapidly changing organisational world.

The chapter will draw upon some of the extensive body of theory about learning to suggest useful approaches and practices. Thus, in working through the chapter you will go through a process that will become familiar during your course – using concepts to help you make sense of a situation, and drawing on models and frameworks to suggest ways forward. This bridging of the gap between *theory* and *practice* is a key challenge for any professionally relevant study at this level.

The chapter aims to help you develop your own learning practice by adding a reflective element to the study log suggested in the previous chapter. It also seeks to introduce the idea of learning through dialogue and develop the idea of a critical approach. Collaborative reflection and dialogue about situations and actions and critical thinking skills are central to continued professional development, and are highly transferable to your career as a whole. Unless you understand this approach to learning you will not develop the learning skills you need to 'add value' to yourself during your course and your career. Without such ongoing development your career progress is likely to be limited.

What is learning?

Long, long ago I went for an interview for a job at the Civil Service College. It was a typical Civil Service panel interview, with – I think – seven panel members. About halfway through the interview, the then head of the college, a middle-aged, middle-European man, asked me rather aggressively what I thought I had learned from my experience as an Open University tutor that might be relevant to the job in question. I enthusiastically replied that the one thing I had learned was that, if you wanted to change the attitudes or behaviour of adults, learning needed to be participative. He looked at me disdainfully, and said, 'But Mrs Cameron, we are not trying to change people's attitudes or their behaviour.' At that point I stopped wanting to work there (I'm still not sure why I accepted the job!) as I couldn't see what on earth they *were* trying to do in the name of training.

In retrospect, I think that the Civil Service College took a jug–mug view of learning at the time. It had not made the shift in focus that took place from the 1980s (in the UK at least) towards management *competence*. Subsequently, there have been further shifts, including a move towards emphasising sense making and knowledge creation. Another change has been an increasing emphasis on leadership rather than management. Indeed the two are linked: key leadership competences typically include making sense of the situation, and moving from this to creating and communicating a compelling vision for others to follow.

The knowledge management argument runs thus. The role of management is changing, and changing rapidly. The world in which managers operate is fluid – prediction is difficult. Competition is often fierce. 'Information' proliferates as IT becomes ever more sophisticated. Senior managers need more than 'facts' and 'competences'. In such an environment the ability to 'make sense' of a complex and rapidly changing world, and to learn continuously from experience, is crucial. Learning is seen as going beyond the absorption of facts and theories into developing the ability to actively *construct meaning* or *make sense* of complex situations, or challenge existing ways of making sense.

Learning in this context means developing the ability to think more flexibly. It means understanding that the sense you make of a situation is a product of your existing habits of thought: others may make have different perspectives and construct different meanings. From this perspective it is clear that you can become more effective by increasing your awareness of, and challenging, your existing habits of thinking and then developing new ways of thinking, better suited to new contexts. Developing the ability to adopt a variety of perspectives on a situation and to work with others who have different perspectives will enable you to create a richer understanding of the issues you face. (If your cohort includes students from a wide range of cultural and professional backgrounds this diversity offers huge potential for developing this ability.) Your richer understanding and your relevant knowledge will help you to take more effective action to address unfamiliar issues in changing context. Such learning will involve *thinking* and *judgement* and developing your skills in each.

First, consider the possibility of the importance of perspective.

Activity 6.1

An organisation is losing money because a new product in which a great deal of investment has been made is not selling as well as forecast. Think about four or five stakeholders in this issue (e.g. marketing manager, product development manager, customer) and list possible different ways in which each might see the issue and the action necessary. Discuss your answer with others from different backgrounds if you can.

You may have listed possible views such as:

- The marketing manager might see it as a problem of product design, or faulty organisational strategy in deciding to enter this product market, or faulty pricing strategy or inadequate marketing budget.
- An HR manager might think it is mainly a problem of training the sales staff.
- The product development manager might think that it is all because of failure to invest in incorporating some new (expensive) features that he originally proposed for the product . . . and so on.

It doesn't matter if you came up with wildly different ideas – the point is that, even in a situation where people have similar or identical information about an issue (and they often do not), they may be aware of – or see as significant – different features of that situation. And, even if they originally see it in similar terms, they may see different ways of dealing with it. Even when they have seriously incomplete information about the issue, they may still be sure that 'their solution' is correct.

All of this is because our minds are really good at two things – selecting only part of a situation to attend to and 'joining the dots' (see Figure 6.1), so that this partial set of observations produces a clear and 'obvious' image of what *seems* to be reality. These are extremely useful abilities; we could not survive without them. Imagine running out of the way of a bus if you attended to everything in the situation, the people by the roadside, their clothes, the colour of the sky, and so on, before working out what to do.

We use sophisticated heuristics to achieve this 'obvious' sense of reality.[1] But the price we pay is that our view and our conclusions may be limited and/or misdirected. This is because our perceptual and thinking processes are based on *past* experience – our own and perhaps others'. When things change, our thought habits may no longer fit the situation. If we are to adapt to new situations we may need to change some of these habits of thought. This means unlearning things we may not even be aware of.

To achieve such unlearning, we need to become aware of how we are thinking – as individuals and as teams, to challenge it, and to change it if a better way of thinking can be found. If you can learn to do this during your MBA, and to go on doing it thereafter, you are likely to be far more effective than those who stay at the level of what seems to make 'obvious' sense. (This is especially important when that obvious sense clearly is not achieving the intended results.)

Three aspects of your course can help you become aware of, and then change, your ways of thinking. The first is the theory you will learn, the second is the group discussions you will take part in and the third is your attempt to relate theory to your own professional practice. The chapter will first look at types of management theory in more detail than earlier chapters. It will then look at different models of management learning and, finally, at ways in which these have influenced our understanding of what is required for professional learning. From this you will be able to see how you can manage your own learning to maximise your professional development.

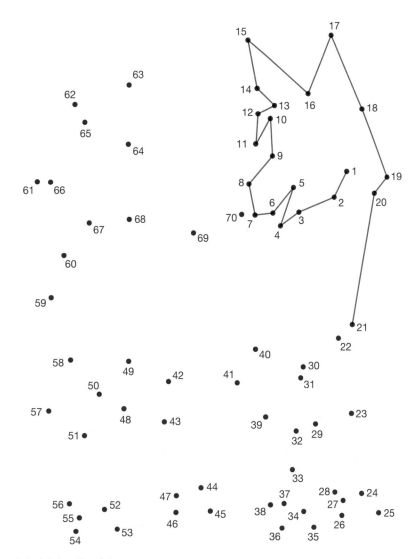

Figure 6.1 Joining the dots

What is management theory and why is it useful?

Formal theory is of more than academic interest. As Lewin (1951) – possibly translating a much earlier statement by Kant – pointed out, 'There is nothing as practical as a good theory,' (*op. cit.* p. 169). But this begs questions about both what constitutes a good theory and how to use it when you have found one.

First, it is important to note that management theory is not, for the most part, what a traditional scientist would recognise as a theory. To a scientist, 'a theory' is normally taken to indicate an organised set of propositions derived from systematic objective observations, which generates testable predictions of the impact of change in one or more variables in a situation upon other variables.

➤ Chs 2, 5   As noted in Chapters 2 and 5, the term *management theory* is used far more loosely, encompassing any description, checklist, and prescription for good practice, framework, model or predictive theory in any area related to management or managing, provided it is derived from some sort of observations or other data. 'Theory' is sometimes used even more loosely to refer to other course content (for example, techniques such as discounted cash flow).

Types of 'theory' in management

Because 'theory' is used in this more inclusive way on most management programmes, and will be used in this way throughout the book, it is worth looking at the main types of 'theory' you are likely to be studying in a little more detail, and considering the possible differences between them. I say 'possible differences' because these terms are used in different ways by different authors. Even if you find the terms used slightly differently on your course, the distinctions themselves are worth noting.

A **concept** is any abstract idea. 'Motivation' is a concept. 'Learning', 'stakeholder' and 'reflective practitioner', are concepts. Such concepts can be really helpful in making you aware of an aspect of a situation and helping you to understand it. I can still remember my excitement (it *was* a long time ago, and the term was not yet in common use) when I first came upon the idea of *hidden agendas* and started to look beyond the official objectives for meetings. Later, you will meet the idea of 'cognitive housekeeping': adding a new concept is one of the ways you can improve your 'cognitive house' and increase the flexibility of your thinking.

A **metaphor** is a familiar term used to describe something that probably is less familiar. It carries with it the suggestion that understanding the former will help you understand the latter. It will certainly enable you to *feel* as if you understand it, although this feeling may be misleading. 'Jug and mug' and 'system' are examples of metaphors. Other examples include talking about an organisation as a 'well-oiled machine' or 'a tight ship'. Metaphors can usefully highlight key features of a situation. Metaphors can also be a great aid to creativity as the associations they allow may expand your thinking. However, unconscious use of metaphor can limit thinking. The machine metaphor, for example, rather rules out consideration of growth, learning or creativity if used as the only way of thinking about the organisation.

> **Theory has the potential to:**
>
> - Convey others' thinking and experience
> - Make you more aware of particular features of a situation and provide a language for describing them
> - Act as a lens to bring selected aspects of a situation and their relationships into focus
> - Make you more aware of your own tacit theory
> - Suggest reasons for observations or likely effects of actions
> - Indicate potential good practice
> - Stimulate creative thinking.

Morgan (1986) uses the spider plant (*chlorophytum comosum*) as a striking metaphor for one form of organisational structure, where similar smaller organisations are started with only a small and temporary connection to the parent. Shortly you will encounter a 'cogs' metaphor (Figure 6.4) in the context of exploring the type of engagement you will need with your study. But metaphors are useful only as far as the similarity goes. The comforting feeling of understanding a metaphor can be a dangerous illusion if you imagine that it will fit in every way. As with models (discussed shortly), you need to remember that metaphors only partially resemble the thing to which they are applied.

Framework tends to be used to indicate a rather more organised abstraction. Frameworks are extremely common in management 'theory'. Thus, you may well encounter the 4 (or 7) Ps[2] in your marketing studies, and you have already used the SWOT[3] and SMART[4] frameworks for examining yourself and formulating your objectives. We looked at these

➤ Chs 2, 3   in detail in Chapter 2. Such frameworks tend to provide useful checklists for analysing a situation. If you wanted to look at the environment in which you were operating you might use PEST (or STEP or STEEPLE) and look at sociological, technological, environmental (in the biosphere sense), economic, political, legal and ethical factors surrounding the organisation – or a subset of these.

A **model** is a simplified representation of something, but normally goes beyond a framework in showing relationships between elements. Thus, the map of the London Underground shows the relationship between lines and stations on a line. Models in management theory usually are simplified representations of some elements and rela-

➤ Chs 8, 9   tionships in a situation. They often involve diagrams (see Chapter 8) as relationships are more easily represented diagrammatically. Again, it is important to remember that a model is a simplified representation and it should not be confused with the reality. A model of communication is used in Chapter 9. Examples of models you are likely to encounter when thinking about strategy are Porter's (1985) value chain and Grant's (1991) resources and capabilities model. A model of learning, Kolb's (1984) experiential learning cycle, has already been introduced and will be discussed in more detail shortly.

Predictive theory, the kind you would encounter in the hard sciences, exists in management but forms a small part of what is normally termed 'management theory'. Predictive theory traditionally has been seen as an organised set of assumptions which allow you to make predictions about a situation. It is normally derived from observation and its predictions are tested by further observations.

While a framework such as SWOT or PEST (or STEEPLE) alerts you to things it may be useful to consider, it does not in itself allow you to predict anything. A predictive theory such as Expectancy Theory (a brief explanation is given in the box overleaf in case you have not yet met it on your course) does allow predictions. Here it suggests that, if you reduce the value of outcomes, link them less closely to performance, or make it appear less likely that effort will produce the desired (and rewarded) performance, then less effort is likely to be made. The multi-factorial nature of management makes predictions difficult to test and the constructed nature of perceptions adds to the difficulty: this is probably why 'theory' is used more loosely in management study.

Box 6.1 Expectancy Theory [Lawler and Porter (1967)]

Expectancy theory suggests that there are three major linked elements that need to be understood in order to predict the effort that someone will put into their job. The first is the likelihood, *as they see it*, of that effort resulting in the desired performance. The second is the likelihood that, *as they see it*, this performance will result in some sort of outcome. (Outcomes might be positive or negative and intrinsic (e.g. a sense of achievement) or extrinsic (e.g. a bonus).) The third is the value *to them* of the expected outcomes. Note that all these things are *subjective.* The person concerned may over or underestimate their chances of successful performance and may misperceive the link between performance and reward. And it is the value *they* put on the outcomes that matters, not some general value – not everyone values money particularly highly.

To work out motivation, you need to multiply the two perceived probabilities by the perceived value of the outcomes likely to follow performance.

The theory predicts that motivation would be strengthened by an increase in the strength of the perceived effort–performance link. The real probability might be increased by additional training or resources, or the subjective probability might be increased by increasing someone's confidence in themselves. Motivation would also be strengthened by an increase in the perceived performance–outcome link by actually linking rewards more closely to performance or by clarifying perceptions if there is a link, but the person doesn't understand it. Motivation could also be increased by increasing the value of the outcomes to the person concerned – some organisations offer a 'menu' of incentives in recognition of variation in such values.

Another possible way of classifying theory concerns simply whether it is descriptive, prescriptive or explanatory. (Almost every model is based upon a set of categories.)

Descriptive theory does no more than provide a description of some aspect of management [for example, Mintzberg's (1973) classic observations on how senior managers actually spend their time].

Prescriptive theory goes beyond this to suggest how aspects of management *should* be carried out (for example, various 'best practice' guidelines).

Explanatory theory provides concepts, constructs or conceptual frameworks that help us think about and/or understand an aspect of management and may well generate predictions.

The value of theory

Different types of theory may have different purposes and value.

At Master's level, descriptions and prescriptions receive limited attention, although at lower levels they may be important. Prescriptions in particular are treated with suspicion, as there are few 'one size fits all' prescriptions for situations of any complexity. And at senior management levels many issues are complex.

Instead, the emphasis is on theory which will help you become more aware of relevant factors in a situation, better able to think about their implications and better able to figure out what best to do about them. Because *context* is so important, you will learn more effectively if you constantly think about the implications of different theories for the contexts and issues that you have experienced at work. If you are working while studying you will be able to do this day by day, possibly the most favourable way of learning as a manager.

To illustrate how theory may be helpful, the next section will draw upon some classic learning theory to consider how you might become a more effective learner.

Learning models and metaphors

As indicated, the body of theory on learning in general, and management learning in particular, is extensive. We shall look at three different ways of considering management learning that you may find help you understand how to approach your studies. Kolb's (1984) idea of a cycle of learning from experience is often used within professional development programmes, as is Argyris and Schön's work on single- and double-loop learning and Schön's (1983) on reflective practice. The 'cogs' metaphor was developed as a result of concerns with learning within a particular MBA programme (though experience as an external examiner suggests the issue is typical of many management Master's programmes). The exercise provides different views of what is going on when managers learn, and shows how theory can inform thinking about practical issues.

Kolb's experiential learning cycle

Kolb and Fry (1975) developed a model for a process of learning from experience, which has been widely influential in management teaching. The model was derived from earlier ideas of pragmatism, particularly those of Dewey discussed in Chapter 2, from Lewin's ideas about action research, and from Piaget's work in developmental psychology. Kolb (1984) subsequently worked out the ideas in more detail in a book.

➤ Ch 2

The model suggests that learning develops through a cycle of four discrete and sequential stages, each with an associated *learning mode. Concrete experience* is followed by attempts to make sense of that experience through *reflective observation,* followed by *abstract conceptualisation* and theorising, followed by *active experimentation* in which action suggested by the new concepts is taken to test these ideas. This generates further experience, reflection, conceptualisation, and so on, as shown in Figure 6.2. Note that, although experience is a natural starting point, you might enter the cycle at any point.

This model draws attention to a number of features of learning which it may be helpful for you to consider. First, it shows learning as very much an *active* process involving both thinking and experience: neither by itself is enough. Years ago I received an application from a manager wishing to register for all seven modules in our Diploma simultaneously, rather than over the next two years as was normal. He said that he had been managing for years, so it was almost a formality to gain the qualification. My response

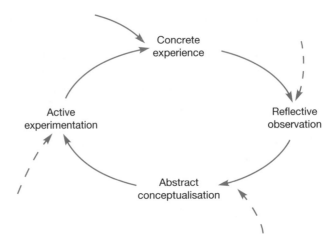

Figure 6.2 An experiential learning cycle, adapted from Kolb (1984)
Source: Adapted from Kolb, D. A., Rubin, I. M. and McIntyre, J. M. (1984).

was that, for all I knew, he had been a *bad* manager for years. Indeed, if he had not learned through reflection on that experience and experimented with different and better ways of managing he might have more to learn than less experienced managers, and find it harder to change deeply entrenched habits of thought and action.

Second, the model highlights the importance of *reflection* in the learning process. This is such an important component of professional development generally, and of many management-related programmes, that it will be dealt with in more detail shortly.

Third, as might be expected given its roots in pragmatism, the model highlights the importance of taking *action*. Learning is seen as a process involving experiment. Action is needed to test the utility of new ideas and ways of thinking.

➤ Ch 2

Learning styles

Kolb suggested that each stage involved a different mode of learning, using different skills. Indeed, active experimentation and reflective observations were diametrically opposed, as were concrete experience and abstract conceptualisation. He suggested there were four different learning styles, each associated with two of the stages in the learning cycle. People, he suggested, tend to have a preferred learning style. Table 6.1 shows these styles in relation to the stages and modes of learning.

Kolb (1976) devised a Learning Styles Inventory (LSI) to enable students or their teachers to assess their preferred learning style. Being aware of this can help you to understand aspects of the cycle which you may tend to neglect. In theory, it could also help your instructors to design learning experiences suited to the learning preferences within their class.

Table 6.1 Learning modes associated with Kolb's learning styles (indicated by shading)

Mode	Active experimentation	Concrete experiences	Reflective observation	Abstract conceptualisation
Learning styles				
Accommodative	▓	▓		
Divergent		▓	▓	
Assimilative			▓	▓
Convergent	▓			▓

The four styles are distinguished as follows.

Accommodative. Likes to follow directions, plan and seek new experiences. Prefers to solve problems in an intuitive, trial-and-error manner, opportunistic and action-driven, risk taker. Likes to work with others and draw on their information.

Divergent. Likes observing rather than acting, strong on imaginative ability and creativity. Likes social interaction and perspective taking. Good at putting the parts together to see a whole.

Assimilative. Likes concepts more than people. Good at inductive reasoning and building theoretical models.

Convergent. Good at problem solving and applying practical ideas. Prefers technical tasks and things with 'right answers' rather than dealing with uncertainties.

Activity 6.2

Which of the above four styles do you see as closest to your own learning preferences and strengths?

Honey and Mumford (1986), dissatisfied with the complexity of the Kolb styles model, derived a much simpler framework from Kolb's cycle. Again, they suggested four different learning styles, but each is linked directly to a single Kolb stage, rather than pairing them. Again, they have developed a learning-styles inventory to help people identify their own preferred learning style. (There is money to be made in such inventories.) Without using the full questionnaire, the next activity gives you a broad idea of what your learning style might be, using this classification.

Activity 6.3

Tick the statement most characteristic of your own reaction to a learning situation.

1. 'I'm game to try it, let's get started.'   ❑
2. 'I need some time to think about this.'   ❑
3. 'What are the basic assumptions?'   ❑
4. 'What's this got to do with my job?'   ❑

The following descriptions relate to the four learning styles identified by Honey and Mumford.

Activists. These are open-minded and involve themselves fully in new experiences. They are not noted for their caution, or for their tolerance of boredom. They love short-term crisis fire-fighting, and the challenge of new problems, brainstorming and finding solutions. They are weaker on implementation, consolidation and anything requiring sustained effort. They are highly sociable and like to be the centre of attention. If this sounds like you, and if you favoured statement 1, you are probably an activist.

Reflectors. These are thoughtful and cautious, preferring to consider all possible angles, and collect as many data as possible before coming to a decision. They prefer to observe others rather than take an active role themselves, and will adopt a low profile in discussions, adding their own points only when the drift of the discussion is clear. If this sounds like you, and you preferred the second statement, you are probably a reflector.

Theorists. They approach problems logically, step by step, and adapt and integrate their observations into complex but coherent theories. They like to analyse and synthesise and to establish basic assumptions, principles, theories and models. They are often detached and dedicated to rational objectivity. They are uncomfortable with anything that doesn't fit into their theoretical framework and hate subjectivity, uncertainty, lateral thinking and a flippant approach. If this sounds like you, and you chose the third statement, you may well be a theorist.

Pragmatists. These thrive on new ideas, provided they can put them into practice. They like to get on with things and are confident about trying to apply new ideas. Open-ended discussions are seen as highly frustrating 'beating about the bush'. Problems and opportunities are seen as a challenge and they are sure that there is always a better way to do anything. If this sounds like you, and you preferred the fourth statement, you could be a pragmatist.

As with most simple categorisations (and you will encounter a lot of them during your studies), both these sets of learning styles are oversimplifications. Examples of 'pure types' may exist, but you are likely to have found elements in more than one category which you felt applied to you. Honey and Mumford's analysis is useful, however, because it is clear from each of the 'styles' that every strength has associated weaknesses. By being alert to these, you can take steps to minimise the effects of weaknesses and arrange your learning activities so as to build on your strengths.

If you have *activist* tendencies, your open-mindedness, energy and creativity will be enormous assets. But you will need to find ways of sustaining your motivation during the course. You will also need to discipline yourself to plan adequately for assignments, and to ensure that you are meeting requirements fully. Your tendency will be to get excited about something and leap in without exploring all the other possibilities. You will thrive on new and diverse experiences and on short exercises such as role-playing, competitive team activities and business games. You will love learning in groups and volunteer to chair meetings, give presentations or lead discussions.

But other group members may resent your leading role and feel they are prevented from making a full contribution themselves. Lectures will strain your concentration. And you will find it hard to learn from other people's experiences. You will also be unlikely to think sufficiently about your learning objectives before a task and may be poor at assessing what you have learned afterwards. Dissertations potentially are a major problem, as they require both careful planning beforehand and sustained work thereafter to carry them through. Neither of these comes easily to an activist.

If you are a *reflector*, your strengths will be in careful analytical work and detailed, painstaking research. You will consider the full picture, never neglecting important background features. You should find a dissertation the most enjoyable part of your course, provided you do not spend too long planning, thereby leaving yourself insufficient time for data collection. You will be excellent at observing groups in action.

However, many characteristics of Master's work will be uncomfortable for you. You will hate to be asked to reach conclusions on the basis of insufficient data, will hate being forced into chairing groups or making presentations and will find the conflicting demands of work and study particularly hard to reconcile. Indeed, you may hand work in late because you spent too much time perfecting it. If you fail an exam, it will probably be because you used the time to produce excellent answers to rather fewer questions than were required.

If your strongest tendency is as a *theorist*, you will thrive on the more academic aspects of a course, such as evaluating competing theories, perhaps even coming up with improvements, organising data into neat frameworks and looking for interrelationships between factors in a situation. You may indeed prefer a more academic specialist Master's to an MBA. If your programme includes a course on Systems Thinking, you will probably enjoy this enormously. Provided objectives are clear, and the situation well structured, you will be able to handle complexity well. Concepts will excite you, whether or not they are relevant at the time.

You will be highly uncomfortable, however, if you are asked to participate in activities without the context or purpose being clear, and particularly if you have to take part in situations where emotions or feelings are significant factors. In a dissertation, your methodology section probably will be brilliant, but you may risk adopting a more complex methodology than was strictly necessary, and will find it hard to cope if you are

6

PROFESSIONAL DEVELOPMENT

forced to work with less than the perfect data you had planned. You also will be reluctant to include qualitative information. In group work you will be infuriated by the less considered approach of the activists in your group and may find it difficult to work effectively with them.

If, like many managers, you are mainly a *pragmatist* (according to this model, which does not exactly match the philosophical stance), you will find your course enormously exciting, provided you can see how to use it in your job (part-time study may suit you best, for this reason). You will enjoy any skills development parts of the course, provided you get good feedback on your performance, and will do well at learning any techniques that will help you do your job better. Part-time and distance learning are particularly suited to pragmatists because of the opportunities they offer for practising skills and applying concepts to their job as soon as they are learned.

You will be highly frustrated by any lecturers with no practical managerial experience, or indeed by any material presented without guidelines on how to put it into practice. In project work or dissertations you will leap into solving a problem, probably coming up with excellent and practicable solutions, but a lack of emphasis on the conceptual underpinning of what you are doing may cause you to receive low marks. Also, you will tend to apply solutions from one situation to another, preferring something that has been shown to work to something totally innovative. This may limit your options on occasion. Creativity usually is not your strong point in any case.

Whatever your preferred style – in either scheme – and however strong your preference, you will, on occasion, be required to take part in learning activities unsuited to your natural style. It is possible to increase your capacity to benefit from these by developing aspects of those styles that do not come easily to you. This will have potential benefits at work, as you will be better able to go through all the stages in the Kolb cycle, as well as helping with your course. A 'fully competent learner' operates comfortably at *all* stages of the cycle, and you may need to work on your less preferred styles to become one.

Activity 6.4

From the following list of activities designed to develop aspects of the different styles, choose at least six that you feel would be useful to you and practise them. Write a note in your diary one month from today to review progress.

To develop activism

1.   Do something totally out of character at least once a week (e.g. talk to total strangers, wear something outrageous, go somewhere totally new).

2.   Force yourself to fragment your day, switching deliberately from one activity to another.

3. Force yourself to be more prominent at meetings. Determine to make at least one contribution in the first 10 minutes. Volunteer for any chairing or presentational role.

4. Practise thinking aloud. When you are trying to solve a problem, bounce ideas off a colleague without thinking before you speak.

To develop reflection

1. At meetings practise observing behaviour and interactions and analysing what is happening (Chapter 11 will help).

2. Keep a diary, reflecting each evening on the day's events and what you have learned, or enter this in your development file.

3. For your next piece of written work aim for perfection, doing more drafts than normal, and polishing it as best you can.

4. Undertake to research a topic of concern at work, investigating in as much depth as possible.

5. Before actions or decisions, force yourself to draw up a list of pros and cons, looking as widely as possible for potential results and effects.

To become more of a theorist

➤ **Ch 9**

1. Spend at least 30 minutes daily reading something heavy and conceptual, trying to analyse and evaluate the arguments involved.

2. Find a complex situation at work and analyse how it developed and what might have been done differently.

3. Before acting, clarify your objectives and try to structure the situation to make the outcome more certain.

4. Look for inconsistencies, dubious assumptions and weaknesses in others' arguments.

5. Practise asking probing questions, persisting until a clear, logical answer is received.

To become more of a pragmatist

1. When discussing problems, make sure that you do not conclude before devising action plans for yourself and any others involved.

2. Put as many techniques as you can into practice (e.g. time management, forecasting, making presentations, drawing up budgets).

3. If possible, seek feedback from experts on the above task.

4. Tackle some DIY project (but not if you have already started your course!).

5. Keep a note of your progress in your file

Whatever your preferred learning style, there are advantages in making active links between your studies and your work experience, so it is well worth getting into this habit. Discussions with fellow students, colleagues and/or interested others can help here.

6

PROFESSIONAL DEVELOPMENT

You may be given the opportunity to test your learning style as part of your course. If not, and you would like to have a slightly better indication than the above can give, you can find a variety of free learning style questionnaires online (see suggested additional resources). Treat even these with some caution, as fitting complex individuals into a limited number of 'boxes' will always have limitations.

Multiple intelligences and sensory preferences

Another way of 'typing' people used when considering learning is by sensory preferences and/or different 'intelligences'. Educators have long measured IQ as an indicator of future academic performance in school children. IQ was seen as an innate trait, rather than something which could be learned. Thus it might be less susceptible to coaching than attainment tests. Although the original research was somewhat flawed, IQ tests did serve a useful purpose in the context for which they were designed. However, the idea has been seriously criticised when it comes to adult learning. You have already encountered Goleman's (1998) idea of EQ, a measure of emotional intelligence. But long before EQ was suggested, Gardner (1983) suggested that IQ was but one of a number of different 'intelligences'. He suggested these were: linguistic; logical-mathematical; spatial; bodily-kinaesthetic; musical; interpersonal and intra-personal. These last two are similar to aspects of EQ. Another intelligence, related to sensitivity to nature, was added later, while others relating to morality and spirituality have been suggested but not incorporated into the model.

Gardner's work was a useful counter to over-reliance on measures of IQ, drawing attention to many other potential contributors to success. He linked the idea of different intelligences to learning styles by suggesting that learning might be most effective if you could use your strongest intelligences in the learning process.

A simpler framework suggests that learning is more effective if linked to your preferred sensory mode – visual, auditory or kinaesthetic (VAK). Both this and Gardner's ideas have been welcomed by teachers, but there is little research evidence to suggest that using either, even if the practical issues this raises in a class situation are overcome, improves learning. You might, however, use either framework, or both, to prompt further reflection on what helps *you* to learn more effectively, and use any insights this generates to improve your study planning.

Single- and double-loop learning

Another way of thinking about management learning is in terms of the control loop. The result of action is compared with the desired result and future action adjusted to reduce any gap. Argyris and Schön (1978) called this *single-loop learning*. This action and observation of results with feedback affecting further action provides a model of the process for learning relatively simple skills.

This has similarities with Kolb's cycle, and key differences. Both involve a feedback loop, but Kolb's model is explicitly conscious. In single-loop learning, feedback and changes to behaviour might be either conscious or unconscious. You might become better at throwing a basketball through a hoop with practice without knowing quite what you were doing differently to improve your aim. You almost certainly learned to ride a bicycle through physical trial and error. On the other hand, only if you *consciously* consider your tutor's feedback on your last assignment when writing the next one, is your grade likely to improve.

Argyris and Schön contrasted this simple feedback loop with *double-loop learning*, which involves reframing the situation, consciously asking, 'What is going on here?' and looking for different ways of thinking or acting in order to get a different result. (There is also a suggestion of triple-loop or transformational learning, in which you would more radically rethink your values and even your identity.)

Double-loop learning can operate at the individual or the organisational level. In the organisational case it involves a questioning of policies, practices and norms. Senior managers need to contribute to such questioning if they are to help organisations to develop. Becoming an individual 'double-loop learner' should help you to contribute to organisational learning as the questioning habit will help in both cases. Figure 6.3 represents these different loops.

Like Kolb, Argyris and Schön suggested four steps in their double-loop learning model:

becoming aware of your own theory-in-action and the distance between this and espoused theory;

inventing new meanings;

producing new actions;

generalising results.

You can see marked correspondences, for example, between 'reflection' and 'becoming aware', and 'inventing new meanings' and theorizing. It is much closer to Kolb than is single-loop learning. Does this model add anything to Kolb, and help you to learn more effectively? For me it adds the useful distinction between theory-in-action and espoused theory, and retains the need for feedback from the single loop. Espoused theory is what you would say is driving your action if you were asked. Theory-in-action is what actually drives your sense-making and action – often called tacit theory, but some find

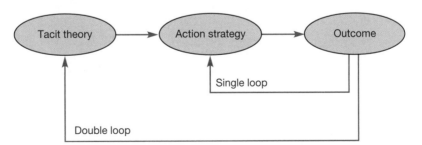

Figure 6.3 Single- and double-loop learning

Source: Adapted from Argyris, C. and Schön, D. (1978).

'theory-in-action' a more powerful term. In contrast, espoused theory is what you *say* you believe. Thus a manager might *say* that he valued his staff above all else and felt it was important always to be available to support them. He might *genuinely believe* that this was his 'theory'. Yet his staff might find it almost impossible to gain access to him and totally impossible to get him to actually listen to their concerns because he was always involved in other issues that took all his energies and attention and which, by implication, he felt were more important than his staff. In particular, I find the notion of learning as a process of becoming more aware of how you think to be particularly helpful, and closer to the model derived from philosophical pragmatism. It has radically shifted my own approach to both thinking and learning. You may find the same.

Critical engagement

The third way of looking at management learning was developed as the result of an extended action research project carried out with Open University colleagues involved in MBA teaching. This may help you understand both the issues discussed above and how theory can help you make a more useful sense of a situation. It used an action research approach, relying heavily on dialogue.

The issue addressed was our observation that too many students had completed all the taught modules in the programme, and were starting work on their final project, yet were still only at the stage of 'knowing about' theory. They had yet to make a connection between the theory and their own management practice. This final module asked them to draw upon the theory they had learned and actually *do* something to make a difference to their organisation and themselves. Far too many were unable to do this.

In working out what to do to help students 'connect' with theory at a deeper level we interviewed and engaged in dialogue with a wide range of stakeholders in the programme. We also looked at teaching and assessment materials. They led us to see that we too had a gap between our espoused theory and our theory in use. This caused us to challenge much of our existing teaching practice.

➤ **Chs 3, 8**　　One 'breakthrough' came when we drew on *systems theory* (introduced in Chapter 3 and discussed further in Chapter 8). This is a way of looking at situations in terms of systems of inter connected parts that work together, within an environment, to produce particular outcomes. (The approach can be seen as using the extended metaphor of a biological organism.) We asked ourselves whether we could gain insights by describing the issue in terms of one or more relevant systems. (Systems are in the mind, they are tools for thinking – they do not have to stick to reality.)

To spur creativity we chose to think in terms of a system that did the opposite of what we wanted, one that encouraged *instrumental learning* (discussed shortly) about management rather than seeking to challenge students' thinking about their own practice.[5] Almost immediately, we realised that we academics were a key part of such a system, as were the assignments we set students. So we stopped thinking about what was wrong with *students* that was stopping them learning as we intended, and started to look at *ourselves* and the system of which we were a key part.

Taking this perspective helped us think about the features such a hypothetical system would have, and then to see just how many of these were actually present in our own teaching and learning system. Once we 'saw' the situation in this way, we could start to think constructively about changes we could make to encourage a more *engaged* approach, one that gave far more recognition to managers' experience, and one in which faculty and managers on the programme might co-create learning in a shared enterprise (Cameron, 2010).

This was practically oriented research, aimed at improving something central to our operation. Those of us involved in the project were pretty sure action was needed, but we wanted to talk with other colleagues and gain their cooperation. We sought to communicate both our changed understanding and the urgency of doing things differently if change was to happen.

Here we found it useful to have a concept that attracted people's attention and a metaphor to convey a richer sense of its meaning. The concept was *critical engagement*. Both these words have 'good' associations for academics, and the phrase sounded both new and relevant. If we held a meeting on 'critical engagement' people came, and came with an open mind because they did not think they already knew what it meant.

Since both 'critical' and 'engagement' have many possible meanings, we wanted an easy way of conveying what we meant. A metaphor of three interlocking cogs seemed to work. One cog represented management theory, another a manager's way of thinking, and the third cog represented his or her practice. The cogs could be connected (engaged) with each other or not.

If practice and thinking were *engaged* – i.e. these two cogs were in contact with each other – changes in thinking might generate changes in practice, and changes in practice might generate changes in thinking (the basic action learning cycle). If theory and thinking were also 'engaged', changes in thinking might arise, not only from experience of practice but also from encounters with theory. Thus a new idea might shift thinking, and changes to thinking might impact on practice. Figure 6.4 is an attempt to represent this metaphor, with the cogs connected. Note that it suggests that for practice to 'move forward' it needs to be engaged with thinking. Like Kolb's, this is a cognitive model. And you need to remember, as Korzybski (1931) pointed out, 'The map is not the territory' (as drivers with SatNav systems sometimes discover).[6]

Activity 6.5

Consider how well each of the above models works for you and why. Think about a significant learning experience you have had as a manager or a learning challenge you currently face. How well does it 'fit' with each of the models above? What does thinking, in terms of each model, add to your *understanding* of learning as a manager? What does it suggest you might do to *become more effective* as a learner? Does any model have aspects that you *find unhelpful*? Can you think of *a model that would work better* for you? Note your responses in your learning file.

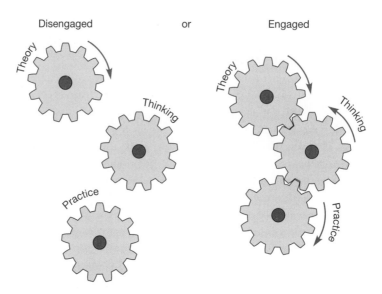

Figure 6.4 A cog's metaphor for practice-based learning

➤ Ch 5

Kolb offers a neat format for learning logs (as outlined in Chapter 5), which many managers have found gives them a starting point at least. They keep their logs in a format with a column for each stage. But others find that their experience of learning is much messier than a neat cycle, and hard to represent in a table with necessarily small cells. They may prefer the idea of simultaneous movement of 'cogs' and of their thinking 'moving', and to simply describe such movement without using a table.

Some find that the idea of 'theory-in-action' really helps them to start to uncover how they *think* by looking at what they actually *do*. This is something with which you may want to experiment for a while before deciding what works for you.

Reflection and professional learning

You can see that all three ways of looking at learning involve some sort of reflective thought processes. You may well find that your MBA requires you to submit reflective writing as part of your assessment. Many students find this difficult. This section seeks to help you overcome any resistance to the process, and begin to use reflective writing as a valuable learning tool rather than an annoying and slightly puzzling activity required by eccentric tutors.

It is clear from the earlier discussion that reflection in professional learning is linked to action. It has a retrospective component but is, at the same time, directed towards future action. And it is directed towards a different sort of learning from simply improving through practice. This kind of learning is both deeper and more personal, as it involves changing your ways of perceiving and thinking.

Deep or surface learning?

Much of the argument for reflection rests upon the idea of 'levels' or 'depths' of learning. You might, for example, learn five key theories of motivation, their authors and the textbook diagrams in order to reproduce them for an examination. This is one level of learning. But it is unlikely that it would help you much when faced with a demotivated team who are making your life as a manager very difficult. In order to tackle this, you would need to find out what was causing the demotivation, and then decide what you could reasonably do to improve the situation in the light of this analysis. This would require a much deeper understanding of motivation and of organisational contexts than the mere ability to reproduce material from the textbook would allow.

Some people make a simple distinction between deep versus surface learning. Moon (2000), who has written a lot about the role of reflection in learning, suggests a *series* of levels of learning with increasing changes to the way you perceive and think about the world. These are shown in Table 6.2. (You may be able to see links with Argyris and Schön's (1978) work described above.) A simple division between surface and deep learning would occur around level 3. The table shows how this learning might be shown in course work you submit. This may help you think about the role of reflection in work for assessment.

For senior managers in times of complexity, change and uncertainty levels 4 and 5 will be important. Many of the activities in this book are designed to deepen your course learning towards the 'working with meaning' level. This is where you are really engaging with ideas and questioning – and perhaps improving – the mental models with which you make sense of the world. This is where your 'thinking cog' is moving. Moon (2000, p. 139) describes such reflective thinking as: 'a process of "cognitive house-keeping", thinking over things until they make a better meaning, or exploring or organising the understanding towards a particular purpose or in order that it can be represented in a particular manner'.

Table 6.2 Levels of learning

Surface learning	1.	**Noticing** – represented as 'Memorised representation'
↓	2.	**Making sense** – represented as 'Reproduction of ideas, ideas not well linked'
↓	3.	**Making meaning** – represented as 'Meaningful, well integrated, ideas linked'
↓	4.	**Working with meaning** – represented as 'Meaningful, reflective, well-structured'
Deep learning	5.	**Transformative learning** – represented as 'Meaningful, reflective, restructured by learner, idiosyncratic or creative'

Source: Based on Moon (2000, p. 138).

6

PROFESSIONAL DEVELOPMENT

Activity 6.5 was intended to prompt this sort of thinking. Indeed, it went beyond the purely cognitive to link to possible action. As another example, you might get really excited about the idea of motivation, look for current papers on this, comparing what different authors said, and decide on the relative merits of the different theories you encountered, and their weaknesses, perhaps with a view to writing a new paper or changing how you sought to motivate your team.

Changing how you think is not always comfortable. Imagine that you were doing this because the team was demotivated. Imagine too that, without knowing it, your behaviour was contributing to lack of motivation. You might consider yourself an excellent manager: you are firm with your team, you stand no nonsense. Suppose that your reading showed you that there are different styles of managing, and that the rather authoritarian way you have managed all your life might not be appropriate for your current team of highly creative people tasked with finding new ways of doing things.

Setting aside long-held beliefs and assumptions can be surprisingly anxiety provoking – it can feel as if your very identity is threatened; however, it is essential if you are to start to think differently about people and their needs. Without thinking differently it will be difficult to act differently.

There can be a tremendous excitement about realising that your own thinking has been holding you back, and seeing ways forward when you had imagined yourself trapped. In an educational context, Entwistle (1996) suggests that a *surface approach* is directed merely towards meeting course requirements, often when there is a feeling of being under pressure and/or worried about the work. Study is done without regard to its purpose, beyond that of passing the course. The material is approached as a series of unrelated 'bits'; there is an emphasis on routine memorisation, without making sense of the ideas presented.

In contrast, a *deep learning approach* is driven by the desire to understand the ideas for yourself, and is associated with an active interest in the subject matter. Thus, you try to relate each new idea you come across to your previous knowledge and to any relevant experience. You look for patterns and any underlying metaphors. You look carefully and critically at the author's evidence and logic. Material approached like this is far more likely to be remembered. And if ideas are related not just to other ideas but to relevant experience, your learning is far more likely to lead to improved practice. It is thus particularly important for any study of vocational relevance.

You might think that, if you adopt a deep approach, you will inevitably get better marks than by taking a surface approach. Usually you will. And you are more likely to be able to remember what you have learned after the course and incorporate it into your practice as a manager. But it is possible to get so carried away by passion for a subject that you forget the course requirements altogether and actually do worse! It is therefore suggested that a third type of approach, the *strategic approach*, is important. This is directed towards doing as well as possible on a course, being always alert to course requirements and the need to use time and effort to best effect in meeting them. It involves balancing deep and surface learning in order to achieve this. Much of this handbook is devoted to enabling you to do just that.

This form of learning is more exciting than surface learning and has a far more profound impact upon your ability to go on learning from the many experiences you will have throughout your life. Many professional organisations now require evidence of such ongoing reflective learning and practice as a condition for continued membership. (If you already have a habit of 'reflective practice' you will need no convincing of its worth.)

Self-authoring

Kegan (1994) looked at 'levels of mind' rather than levels of learning, but made points that are closely related to some of the issues already raised in term of ways of making sense of things, and the anxiety associated with challenges to identity. He suggested that as a person matures they pass through different 'ways of knowing' or levels of mind. Like Moon, he distinguishes five levels. Each represents a more complex way of thinking than the earlier ones.

The first, typical of pre-school children, is an *impulsive* level. The second, typical until adolescence is an *instrumental* way, where thinking is driven by fitting things into categories. The third level, the *socialised* mind, is strongly influenced by what others think, and the need to fit in. Cultural influences are therefore very strong on people at this level, as is reliance on authority. People at the socialised level make loyal followers, and would feel comfortable with Entwistle's surface learning. Estimates suggest that up to 75 per cent of adults are at this level or below.

The fourth level is the self-authoring way of knowing, where almost all the remaining adults seem to operate. It is this level that the book is intended to help you reach (or exploit, if you are there already). The 'self-authoring' label refers to an individual being able to construct an identity independent of the environment, and to judge things according to their own value system. The surrounding social system is something that can be examined, rather than something driving thinking as at the previous level. So whereas 'socialising' thinkers would be afraid of thinking differently from those around, at this level they would be more likely to be afraid of being subject to other people's views. They would be concerned to meet the standards they set themselves, rather than standards set by others. Kegan describes the underlying structure of meaning- making at this level as systemic, as this is the framework within which things are interpreted.

The fifth level is rare – reached, Kegan says, by less than 1 per cent of people. People here look for problems rather than merely seeking to solve them. They can adopt different perspectives and value/belief systems simultaneously, and play them off against each other. Kegan calls this the *self-transforming* level. He emphasises that it is not necessary to reach this, or indeed the previous level, for a successful life, provided that your level is adequate for the challenges you face. But senior managers, faced with taking decisions in a complex and changing situations, and involving more than personal interests, will need the fourth and perhaps fifth levels of thinking. Only these levels allow the complexity and independence of thought and separation from the situation that are needed to respond effectively to the sort of challenges senior managers face, and the learning needed to prepare them for it.

Kegan's colleague, Baxter Magolda (2001, 2009) suggested that a normal college context often prevented students from reaching the self-authoring level by reinforcing dependence on authority. She suggests that to develop self-authoring and self-transformative ways of thinking, the learning context needs to:

- validate participants as knowers, valuing their thoughts, feelings, and thought process, and giving permission for them to develop their own ideas

- locate learning in participants' own experiences, developing the ability to see, and use, these as opportunities for learning and growth

- see learning as a mutual process where students and tutors (or mentors and mentees – see the earlier discussion of mentoring) collaborate to analyse problems and learn together

- emphasise the complexity of work and life decisions, and discourage simplistic solutions

- encourage participants to pay attention to their own thinking and develop their personal authority

- encourage the sharing of authority and expertise, and collaboration in problem solving.

I was excited when I found Baxter Magolda's work because it so clearly articulated my own views about management learning, reflected even in the first edition of this book. It always feels good to have one's existing views reinforced! Did I learn anything as a result? It did not change how I thought, but it made it easier for me to convey these thoughts to others. And having these points laid out so clearly helped me to reflect on my own or others' teaching experiences that had gone particularly well or badly, and work out why. In terms of the cognitive housekeeping analogy it provided me with a lovely new mental 'bookcase' on which I could arrange some of my existing ideas in order to browse them more easily or select some that were particularly relevant to what I was thinking about.

Although Baxter Magolda was writing for teachers, the bulleted points above may be at least as valuable for students. First, particularly if your earlier education was along more authoritarian lines, they may help you to understand the importance of reflection, discussions and dialogue with fellow students, and have a more equal dialogue with your tutors. Second, they may reinforce many of the messages in this book, particularly about complexity and the value of your own experience for learning. And third, they may give you more confidence to contribute your own opinions, particularly when they differ from the dominant view.

Baxter Magolda is not saying that you are always right! Your thinking may be based on inadequate evidence, dubious interpretations of that evidence, or faulty arguments, and may be biased by assumptions that no longer fit the situation. But she is saying that your views and experience are important, and worth discussion and examination, and that your tutors, as well as your fellow students, can learn from that examination. Resist any suggestion that you and your past are not an important component in your learning system!

The reflective process in professional learning

Schön (1983) built on his work with Argyris to develop the idea of a 'reflective practitioner', now widely accepted as key to professional development in many professions. Schön made a useful distinction between reflection *in action* and reflection *on action*. If you were struggling with the models above you may prefer the even simpler model shown to me by one of the best management teachers I have ever met, Dr Reg Butterfield. It has three stages in a cartoon cycle, as shown in Figure 6.5. (If English is not your first language, the mis-spelling is deliberate, echoing working-class speech as shown in cartoons in previous decades.)

The Butterfield cycle is both simple and memorable and includes the question at the heart of reflection, 'So what?' This is a question you need to bear in mind whenever you are reflecting (or, indeed, whenever you are using theory in analysis). For me it sums up the essence of the reflective process: something to reflect upon (the 'wot?'), consideration of the implications of this (the 'so wot?') and some element of taking this into the future (the 'wot next?').

The following guidelines may help you reflect. If your course has already given you tools for reflection, use those instead. But if it has not, and you do not quite know where to start, you may find these helpful.

When to reflect

Successful reflection depends first and foremost on making time to reflect. You should by now be managing your time better. Once you are convinced of the value of reflection, making time for it will become a priority.

Schön's distinction between reflection *in action* and *on action* suggests you need to make two sorts of time. Reflection in action means stopping briefly to think whenever you 'notice' something worthy of consideration. Perhaps a negotiation is not going as anticipated, or you start to feel uneasy about how something is developing. It can be

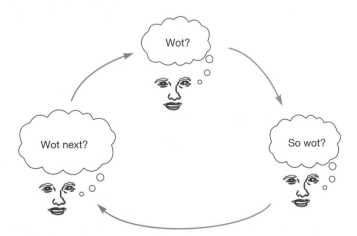

Figure 6.5 The Butterfield 'so wot?' cycle

really useful to stop and think what might be causing this feeling or result and how you might change what you are doing in the light of this. If you cannot work out what to do differently then and there, it might be worth noting it for future consideration when you have time.

Other useful times for reflection are at the beginning or end of either an activity/event or a period of time. Thus you might set aside reflective time at the start and/or end of each working day, after each significant component of your job, and before or after each study period or other learning event. An important point to note here is that, since reflection relates to both past experience and future action, you can usefully reflect before an event as well as after it. Another key point is that your reflection can be driven by new ideas – intellectual experiences perhaps – as much as by things that happen at work or in a study group. (This is one reason why using Kolb as your only model may not be enough.)

It helps to reflect as soon as possible after the event upon which you are reflecting. You need to be able to note what it was that struck you and any thoughts about 'so wot?' and 'wot next?' while you can still remember.

> The basic elements for successful reflection include:
>
> - time to reflect
> - something to reflect upon
> - a medium for capturing reflection
> - skills in reflection
> - honesty
> - feedback.

For example, on the train on the way home from a meeting, I noted in my little book (I'm a paper person):

> This felt really weird – why? Think it was mainly time travel element. Last time I was in this room was 30 years ago – when I worked for the DE just around the corner and was doing my MPhil research on Jaques and his levels! Comforting that some ideas endure, though they seem to have developed it quite a lot. The 'flow' idea from Csikszentmihali really resonates with my own experience of being over- and under-stretched. Someone mentioned this the other day as relevant to some other research. Wonder if/how it relates to coaching. Need to get his book and read more about it. If we want to demonstrate some HR consultancy underpinned by sound theory, this would be a really good example to pursue. Need to contact Bioss to see if they would be willing to provide a case study.

You can see that these notes are brief and informal, but they capture some points that I wanted to pursue.

What to reflect upon

In short, an answer to this question is: 'anything that strikes you as worth thinking about'. It might be a disaster, something that went particularly well, something that did not go as expected or something that left you feeling puzzled. If you are studying while working, you will have daily opportunities to reflect on experiences, often prompted by relevant reading you have done. Your course will also provide experiences of things relevant to work. Group tasks or projects are an obvious example.

After a group meeting you might ask yourself whether it went well and, if so, why? Was there anything that might have gone better? How did you feel during the meeting? Was this how you expected to feel? Why? How did your own behaviour influence others in the group and contribute to the progress you made? Were there ways in which you might have been a more effective team member? What might you do differently next time?

You might reflect, individually or better still as a group, upon how well the team as a whole is progressing towards its objectives and ask yourself whether there are ways in which this might be improved and how you could be more effective. Your reflections on your own and others' behaviour in the light of theory – perhaps motivation theory or what you have learned about effective group working – might also help you to realise the significance of parts of that theory that you had not appreciated before. It might make you aware of shortcomings in a particular theory in terms of its ability to cast light on your experience. You might reflect on the content of the project work in the light of theory you have been taught, which is potentially relevant to the project itself, and whether you might make fuller use of that theory or seek other theories.

Some of your reflection might be prompted by reading or lectures. After the event you can usefully deepen your learning (and make it far more likely that you will remember the material) by thinking about how what you have read or heard relates to what you already know. Does it contradict other theories or support them? Does it suggest different interpretations of data on which they are based? Does it relate to your own experience or to things you have read about business in the paper? What light does it shine upon things that you didn't fully understand before? Does it make you realise the importance of something that perhaps you previously disregarded? Does it make you doubt something that previously you had assumed might be true?

➤ Chs 7, 13 Much of this more abstract reflection on the relation between different ideas, and the extent to which they are based on firm evidence, relates to the *critical thinking,* which has already been highlighted as important. This will be discussed further in the context of critical reading and writing answers to assignments, which demonstrate critical thinking skills.

Perhaps most important of all, since your primary objective during your course is to *learn,* is to reflect upon the learning process itself. For any 'learning event', whether reading, lecture, other course work or work experience, ask yourself questions such as:

- How did that go?
- How did I feel about the experience?
- What did I learn from it?
- What did I fail to learn?
- How might I have learned more effectively?
- How have my ideas about learning changed?
- What will I do differently in future to help me learn better?

You can see the links to Activity 6.5. You might want to revisit your answers to this using these extended questions.

You can see that reflection presents the difficult task of questioning your own thought habits and thinking about *how your own thinking is affecting your actions*. Kline (1999, p. 12) asserts that 'everything that we do depends on the quality of the thinking that we do first'. How often, when a member of your team has made a big mistake, have you asked in despair, 'What on earth were you thinking?'

The task is difficult because our thought habits are both unconscious and a part of who we are. It is difficult to bring them to the surface and it may feel like a threat to our very identity to change them. However, questions such as the above can provide helpful prompts to this task. And working with a diverse group – who will have different thought habits, so different answers – can be invaluable. You are more likely to be able to 'think about your own thinking' if you are working with one or more other people who see things differently from you. This way you can start exploring both the reasons for these differences and their implications. This is part of the reason why action learning sets (dis-

➤ **Ch 9**   cussed in Chapter 9) are so powerful.

The role of feelings in reflection

You may have been surprised to see the 'How did I feel' question above but, since part of the role of reflection is to surface unconscious thought habits, feelings are an invaluable clue. They can highlight areas of concern that you have yet to put into words and may sig-

➤ **Ch 3**   nal profitable areas for reflection (as discussed in the context of emotional intelligence).

Suppose after a job interview you ask yourself, 'How did I feel?' and answer, 'Somewhat uncomfortable from the very beginning'. If you try to work out the source of this discomfort you may learn a lot. Ask yourself questions like, 'When did it start? Was it before I even walked into the room?' Such reflection might show that you felt unprepared for the interview, with obvious implications for future action. Or perhaps you weren't sure about whether this was a company you wanted to work for – maybe you have ethical concerns about their product or way of working. This might affect your choice of companies to apply to in future. Perhaps you felt 'unworthy' of the job? If so, assuming you were honest on your application and they decided to interview you, does this suggest that perhaps you undervalue yourself? Or did the discomfort start with a particular question that you were asked early on? If so, what was the question and why did it make you feel uncomfortable? I could continue, but you should see by now where exploring feelings might lead you.

Feelings can also be important when you are thinking about things you have read or that someone has said. They tend to be driven by your non-conscious, non-rational brain, which has far more processing capacity than the conscious part. Discomfort here may mean that there is a mismatch that you have yet to realise consciously. It may be that assumptions that form a central part of your way of looking at the world are being challenged. It is very easy, and feels comfortable, to dismiss such challenges as rubbish. Our very identity stems from the set of assumptions, values and beliefs about ourselves, which act as a filter through which we see and interpret what happens to us. We tend to be very protective of our identities. It can be unsettling, even painful, to have them challenged. But it is through such challenges that 'cognitive housekeeping' – or even an extension to our cognitive house – is achieved.

One of my most profoundly disturbing experiences as a very young trainer in the Civil Service occurred during an interviewing course I ran for people working in the equivalent of 'HR'. I went through some of the relevant theory and guidelines for effective interviewing and then had the course members role-play interviews. Nothing very innovative there. But a large number of the participants, mainly women in their middle years who had been interviewing for decades, burst into tears. I had not said anything about their performance. But, by reflecting on what they had done in the role-plays in the light of the material we had covered, it had dawned on them that for years they had been really bad at interviewing. Part of their identity was 'expert interviewer' and they had been sure that 'their way' was the best, indeed the only way, of going about it.

There are three morals to this story. First, they needed to change their way of *thinking* not only about what they did but also about themselves, if they were to do it better. Second, it took *honesty* with themselves to bring about this change. In order to protect themselves, they could have decided that the material I was teaching was wrong, or that any feedback they received was useless. Honesty in answering reflective questions is an essential component in learning from reflecting. The third message is that such change can be seriously painful and support may be needed. I was totally unprepared and unqualified to give such support and failed those women really badly. You are probably much younger than they were, but still need to tread carefully when exploring your own and others' assumptions, particularly about yourselves, for example during collaborative reflection.

Activity 6.6

Think about something you have read or experienced, or perhaps received feedback on, that occasioned some discomfort. Think about your feelings in more depth and try to explore why you felt like that. Now think about something that has made you feel really great when you did not expect to and carry out a similar exploration. Note any learning points from this exercise in your file.

I hope that this activity has shown you that feelings may be a pointer to something important that you might ignore if you stayed in the purely rational domain. It is important to include 'feelings' both as prompts to reflection and as an important part of your exploration. As a (painful) illustration I offer an example of my own where I was prompted to reflect.

As a member of various teams producing study materials, part of my role has been to comment on others' drafts. I noted that I gave far more comprehensive comments on others' work than they did on mine and felt good about this: for a long time I believed that I was better in this role than they. Therefore I could not understand why, when I offered my services as 'critical reader' to a new course team, they were less than enthusiastic about my offer. When I asked why, an embarrassed team member said that I was seen as 'rather negative'.

I was devastated. I had put hundreds of hours (often of unpaid overtime) into reading and commenting on these drafts. When I reflected on my colleague's comment, I realised that I had been focusing solely on the draft materials and their likely impact on students. Despite teaching my students about both motivation and how to give constructive feedback, I had totally ignored my colleagues' feelings and motivation and the likely impact of my comments upon them. There was a big gap between my espoused theory and my theory-in-action! Thereafter, I thought not only about the likely impact of the draft materials on students, but also about the impact of my comments on the colleague who had drafted them, drawing on what I had long cheerfully taught my students about giving effective feedback!

The role of theory in reflection

Kolb suggested that theory is the *product* of your own reflective observation. It is not clear merely from the cycle diagram just how important theory generated by *others'* experience and thinking can be as a prompt to reflection. In the above example, I clearly had not heeded it. The cogs metaphor suggests that theory generated by others can play an important role in learning and can prompt changes in thinking. This might be:

- at a purely 'theoretical' level, when you relate a new theory to other theories and data and evaluate the new theory in terms of these

- at a more personal level where you use taught theory to make you more aware of, and help you challenge, your own beliefs and tacit theory and change these if appropriate

- at a practical level when your changed thinking leads to a change in your professional practice.

All three are valid forms of learning, serving different purposes. Practising managers may be more interested in the second and third points.

Critical reflection on theory

Whether you are evaluating new theory against existing theory or against your own experience you are starting to make *judgements*. This brings you into the 'critical thinking' domain that is really important at Master's level. Critical evaluation of theory involves assessing theory in terms of its coherence and consistency (with the evidence from which it is derived and with other findings) and of the extent to which it adds to existing theory. It also brings in the question of key concern to pragmatists – how useful is this theory? What is its contribution to understanding the issues that confront you? Critical reading is developed further in the next chapter. Here we shall think about the qualities of the theory itself.

Criteria for theory:

- coherence
- consistency
- contribution.

Theorising, even loosely, is a process of *generalising* from experience or observations. So a fair question is whether a model, framework, or whatever, fits the observations from which it was derived and helps make sense of them. An even more important question may be the extent to which it can be generalised to other situations and, in particular, your own.

Suppose you find an interesting dissertation on talent management in Indian manufacturing industry. The author has interviewed 4 senior managers in a leading Indian company and 16 managers who report to them. He has concluded that 'lack of clarity of career paths is the key factor in loss of potential talent'. If you work in a service industry in Germany, or a joint venture in China, you might, legitimately, wonder whether this finding applies to your own context. Even in India you might wonder how fair it is to make statements on the basis of senior managers' views alone about something like this. What do leavers who represent 'potential talent' think? It may be very different from senior management's view, and more important.

Questions that will help you to approach *theory* critically are shown in the box below.

Questions that may help you think critically about a theory

What is the evidence on which this theory is based?

What explicit assumptions have been made?

Are these reasonable?

What implicit assumptions are reflected in the theory?

Can/should these be questioned?

Is the evidence provided adequate to support the generalisation?

Is the theory logically consistent with the evidence and within itself?

How does the theory relate to other theory in the area?

Are the differences justified by the evidence?

Do they add to an understanding of the subject of the theory?

➤ Ch 7

There are, of course, many other possible questions – some will be suggested in the next chapter – but these will provide a good start. Add any others that you find useful.

Your thinking will also have been influenced by a wide range of experience (in this sense there can never be a complete disconnect between practice and professional thinking) as well as any formal study. Much of this will have been incorporated into conceptual routines for perceiving situations and processing what you perceive. These routines will be largely tacit – you will be unaware you are using them.

The image of meshing your theory and (professional) thinking cogs is intended to convey the possibility of challenging how you currently think at work. Remember this is derived from experience and from others' beliefs, so *past practice* is involved as it has shaped current thinking. Societal assumptions are important too. An important question when reflecting critically concerns the extent to which ways of thinking are derived from societal assumptions (for example, there might be a widespread, albeit unacknowledged, belief that men are more effective, or their incomes more important). Such assumptions might be influencing how a situation is perceived and interpreted.

It is hard to access ways of thinking that once influenced you, but now have 'gone underground'; or become 'tacit'. Some of the following questions are to help you 'engage' with theory as a professional and reflect on current issues at work.

Questions that may help you engage with theory as a professional

Does this theory relate to contexts relevant to my own?

How does it help clarify issues that I face in my own practice?

How does it help integrate different aspects of my experience?

Does it bring into focus elements that I have tended to ignore?

Does it incorporate assumptions that could be challenged, even if they are widespread in my society?

Are there concepts and/or relationships in the theory that extend my current ways of making sense of situations?

Is there anything in it that seems to contradict my understanding of the topic addressed by the theory? If so, where is the difference, and might it be that my understanding is limited?

How does it help me to understand past experiences?

How does it help me make sense of issues currently facing me?

With practice, and the use of such questions, your 'reflection' will become a more deliberate, and much richer, process of making sense of what happens to you as a manager and in your organisation. Your learning will be much more effective when you consciously seek links between what you learn and your own practice, and ask yourself 'What was I thinking?' when things do not go as you expect or intend. Reflection will help you to consider your own impact and to become more aware of the link between your thought patterns and your actions. This will help you think – and act – more effectively.

As an established habit reflection can be a key element in your ongoing continued professional development throughout your career. This is why reflective practice is seen now by many professional institutes as essential to professional practice.

Remember, reflection is perhaps even more effective when done with others, so involve fellow students and colleagues in reflective conversations whenever you can. Look at what goes well as well as what goes badly. Try to understand what is happening

➤ **Ch 9**   and to learn from this. Be open to the idea that your own thinking and behaviour may be contributing to an issue. There is more on such dialogue in Chapter 9.

Reflective writing

➤ **Ch 5**   Good group reflection is more likely if members are good at reflecting individually. And individual reflection is itself a powerful learning tool. You may be required to demonstrate your ability to reflect in this way for assessment. (A reflective chapter is often required as part of a dissertation.) Writing can be an excellent aid to reflection as well as providing material for assignments. And it is easy. You do not need to do anything special as the example of 'train jottings' (above) shows.

Good reflective writing goes far beyond the simple study log formats introduced in the previous chapter.

Personal reflection is essentially an internal dialogue based around questions such as those outlined earlier – and honest answers to them – so you need a medium within which this personal dialogue can take place. Simple learning logs, especially if they use a tabular format, tend to be less helpful here. Many managers find that it helps to keep a separate, less structured, learning journal or diary as well. If you want to share this with colleagues for collaborative reflection, a blog can be a good medium.[7] Your university's VLE may well provide a blogging facility.

Improve your learning:

- test concepts against experience
- discuss your 'sense making' with others
- seek feedback from colleagues on how you are perceived
- reflect continually on experience
- keep a learning log
- develop less preferred learning styles (see later).

If you have now started to keep a learning, or personal development file as an aid to capturing, evidencing and managing your learning, your learning journal will form an important part of this.

Again, because reflection is personal it is worth experimenting with both the medium and the format. Many now use an app on their phone for 'in action' jottings or make a brief audio recording. Others find a small notebook works best for them. In either case, it will help to make time at intervals to read through your jottings and use them as the basis for a less hurried reflection on action. People vary in their preferred degree of structure for this. The main thing is that you find a way of using writing to help you reflect more productively, to provide some sort of useful record for future reference and to submit, if required, for assessment.

If you want some structure to help you start, you might try using very basic questions to provide the substance of each paragraph. For example:

Paragraph 1	I was struck by . . . because . . . (remember to include relevant feelings)
Paragraph 2	This relates to . . .
Paragraph 3	Thinking about it I can see that . . .
Paragraph 4	This suggests that I was thinking in terms of . . . rather than seeing the importance of . . .

6

PROFESSIONAL DEVELOPMENT

Paragraph 5   If I think about . . . it suggests that in future I might want to do . . .

Paragraph 6   I also need to find out more about . . . and/or do . . .

Activity 6.7

Reflect on a learning experience you have had recently. Write six (short) paragraphs on the topics outlined about capturing your reflections. Reflect on whether this structure feels comfortable or whether you would like to modify it in some way. Keep your reflections in a 'learning journal' section of your file.

The following is a piece of reflective writing (at the end of an MBA) on how reflection has altered the way that the manager 'makes sense' of organisational situations.

A good example . . . is that, during my project design phase, I worried about the Knowledge Inventory (KI) being the 'definitive' repository and having to be an accurate representation of our knowledge. Reflecting on this had shown it to be almost impossible and, using Pareto's 80:20 rule, attempting to make it 100 per cent definitive would take huge amounts of time compared to it being 80 per cent definitive and still very useful. My revised perspective is one of accepting a state of not exactly satisfying, but a realisation that the KI can never be 'wholly accurate', but a better representation of our organisational knowledge compared to where we are now. I now think in terms of moving a problem along a continuum towards a better state, rather than always seeking a 100 per cent solution. I consider this is linked to the over-analysis issue outlined above – previous over-analysis was the result of attempting to find the perfect solution.

The beauty of the continuum model is that it creates a sense of a timeline over which we can continue to make improvements and refinements – once again showing the iterative nature of the model of planned change. Each iteration moves us further along the continuum, progressively improving the situation.

Overall, a substantial change in my mode of engagement is that my perceptions of and reactions to problems has 'moved', and I am now almost regarding them as opportunities to apply my learning to see 'what sort of a fit' I can make, and what this application of theory is telling me about the problem.

Another example of narrative reflection, again on a final project, shows how self-perceptions can change through reflection on feedback from colleagues, interpreted in the light of concepts gained through reading.

This [project] has provided me with an opportunity to leap from a position of learning through theory and knowledge to gain significant understanding and insight into my own personal behaviour and style and that of other people.

The human interplay and how to read the power structures and influences that people, including myself have, has been a powerful learning experience. It is almost as though I have stepped outside of my skin and looked at myself through a new window.

By doing this, I could see my strengths and achievements through this [project]. I could view my weaknesses without being defensive, but examine their effect upon other people and test concepts for more effective communication.

Eight months ago, I found critical feedback very difficult to take and had become rather hung up about people thinking me 'too passionate and enthusiastic'. I could not see what they meant, after all wasn't that a good thing? I now understand that the feedback was in respect of the effects of the passion and enthusiasm, not passion and enthusiasm itself. I can see with clarity that my exuberant style can make people feel railroaded into agreeing with me and unable to stop me and raise important questions.

Last year, I truly felt let down that people had waited 40 years to tell me the truth about my style and the effect that it has, even though I had never actually asked them. Through this course, I have learned and understood that only I am responsible for my behaviour and it is my responsibility to reflect on how that impacts on other people and to make and implement plans for self-improvement.

Towards the end of the [project], I had a significant moment of dawning enlightenment. I had been through a very traumatic time at work, almost losing months of work that I was very committed to. I was working very long hours and was tired. I had a very heavy workload with tight deadlines, and felt that I may not get through this [project] which would mean I had to start again. I was not being supported by my line manager and felt very alone.

During a literature search, I found an article, just released, 'Bridging the Gap between Stewards and Creators' (Robert, Austin and Nolan 2007). The article felt as if it had been written for me and my situation. It explained so many events and suggested that the conflict and struggle that I had experienced was inevitable.

I started to understand and was able to not only live with it, but see the positives that the different style of my colleague could bring to balance my own work. I was able to think about how we might start to more fully appreciate each other and ask for help to bridge the gap between our opposite traits. Help is not something that I commonly ask for; but suddenly it seemed to be acceptable and necessary.

The more I searched though the research literature about innovation, the more I found that conflict and struggle between different personalities in the innovation process was experienced by others around the world.

It was a moment where I no longer felt ostracised or alone in my quest for innovation.

6

PROFESSIONAL DEVELOPMENT

I cannot describe the significant step change in my understanding and the ensuing calm that I have developed for dealing with situations, but feel that I must continue to develop this understanding above all else. I need to develop my 'innovator' strengths to reach their full potential, and continue to understand my own behaviour and its effects on individuals and teams. By adopting more open strategies for public (Raelin 2001), group and individual reflection in action (Johnson 1998) I will be able to build on my new understanding and continue to develop my personal effectiveness at work.

Johnson (1998) describes reflection on action as 'making the difference between having 20 years of experience, and one year's experience 20 times'. I know that I am still in the early stages of my development and that I have to develop further before I can even think of myself as having experience that builds year on year. My new understanding has caused me to reflect much further back than this [project], probably as far back as five years, finding clarity about past successes and difficulties, including times where I have had problems influencing other people or have found myself in conflict.

The penny feels like it has dropped which is a very empowering and energising experience. I now feel confident that I have just gained five years' experience, rather than one year's experience five times.

This was a major project and it has been hugely successful for the organisation. Furthermore, a whole new network of partnerships has been created and these are continuing beyond this particular initiative. The success on this project can be easily replicated and the organisational learning has been good.

More significantly, I believe that I have gained even more value from understanding myself and my impact on others. My learning from my interactions with just one person has led me to a paradigm shift in my thinking.

Although these two examples were written at a particular time, they summarise a 'reflective conversation' that took place over a year. You will find it useful to have such an ongoing conversation with yourself as your thoughts develop and also as you are able to distance yourself more from the original event and your reactions to it.

Activity 6.8

As an experiment with a different approach, construct another journal entry, this time on your learning from this chapter. Choose your medium. Label your entry 'work on Chapter 6', date it and write a fairly free-form entry. Possible questions to address, if you are unsure how to start, are:

- What is the most interesting thing I have read in this chapter and why was it interesting?

- What are the three main things I have learned from it?
- What, if anything, that I previously thought was true now seems as if it may be wrong?
- What was new or surprising in the chapter?
- Was there anything missing that I expected to find? Can I find this some other way?
- What am I still unsure about?
- What did I dislike about this chapter and why?
- Was there anything that particularly interested me? Can I find out more about this?
- What do I intend doing differently as a result of reading this chapter?
- What do I need to do to make it more likely that I will actually carry out this intention?

Keep this entry in your learning file and revisit and update it at intervals. From here on, make reflective entries for each chapter as you work through it, as part of a more general learning journal.

➤ Ch 8

The questions above suggest a journal based purely on words. However, reflection is likely to be far richer if you extend your recording to include diagrams such as mind-maps or rich pictures (*see* Chapter 8). One of the key elements in reflection is looking at relationships between things, and diagrams are normally far better for this than are words. If you are doing comparisons between different ideas, say, you may also find it useful to use a table. The golden rule is to use what works for you and what works for the particular sort of thinking that the learning event requires.

Organising your file

There have been repeated references to keeping a learning file, and by now you should have started to collect 'learning-related' items, such as answers to activities, and reflective writing in one place. It is now time to check whether this is organised in a way that suits your learning style and will be an aid to effective learning.

➤ Ch 2

Ideally this file will include a very personal section where you will store your consideration of your strengths and weaknesses and your study, career and perhaps life, objectives and chart a path towards these. You were starting this process in Chapter 2 when considering what form of study to pursue, if any. Also you will probably want to include more course-specific items, such as timetables, assignment schedules and drafts of written work for assessment.

Well-organised and maintained, your file will help you manage your studies and take a strategic view of your development, at work and through your course, relating to the longer-term path you seek to take.

Activity 6.9

Check that you now have a good basic structure for your file. Look at what it contains and what is missing. Are your answers to relevant activities organised in a way that allows you to find the one you want? Do you have sections for study planning and reflective writing? Does your file allow you to check progress towards objectives? Does it help you manage your study? Does it help sustain your motivation? If not, spend some time reorganising it to suit you better.

If you are unhappy with your file, but cannot see how to improve it, you could start with a statement of your main objectives and key stages to be reached *en route* to these. Then develop a page for each of these sub-objectives, outlining the actions that will help you achieve them. In order to plan how to reach these key milestones, you need to take an honest look at where you are now. What are your current strengths? Which skills do you need to develop? Consider the full range of skills and other abilities that are involved, not just narrow job skills. Aspects such as interpersonal awareness, social skills, flexibility, and clarity of thought, willingness to be wrong and energy levels may be important, as well as more obvious characteristics. If strengths give you a problem, think of your last four major achievements, work or otherwise, describe them and think about what abilities you demonstrated in achieving them. For weaknesses, try a similar exercise with things that have gone less than well.

As you progress, update your personal development file, amending strengths and weaknesses in the light of work experience and course learning. Once a quarter, revisit your overall objectives. You may find that you now feel that these were unnecessarily modest, or the reverse. One area of development that is important, but hard to log, is self-awareness, but your course should help by giving you feedback on various aspects of your performance. It will also help with that other notoriously difficult area of 'making sense' more effectively of situations around you.

As you log your daily learning experiences in your work diary and study log, writing comments on how your way of *making sense* of work situations has altered as a result of your study will be particularly useful. What assumptions have you become aware of? Which of these have you deemed unhelpful and changed? What additional factors /relationships have you become more aware of? What are you doing differently as a result of such changes in thinking? Your note taking should always highlight links between theory and practice and in assignments you should be actively seeking to use theory to inform your analysis. Remember to review and consolidate your reflections and other elements in your file at regular intervals.

Throughout the book the importance of linking theory to experience, and of becoming a reflective practitioner, is stressed. Start now to think about how you can develop the habit of making linkages and actively interpreting experience in the light of theory or concepts (developed by yourself or offered as part of the course). Soon this will become second nature. Ensure that you capture this experience in your file. This will mean that you gain more from your study than specific learning of course content. You will have developed the capacity to learn from everything that you do and experience, throughout your working career. This could be of far more benefit to you than anything else that you learn on the course itself.

SUMMARY

- Learning can be viewed as the active construction of meaning or 'making sense'. One can think of different levels of thinking in the sense-making process.
- Learning is usefully seen as a continuous cycle of experience, reflection on experience and the development and testing of concepts.
- Individuals have different learning styles, for example varying in their preference for activist, reflector, theorist or pragmatist learning styles. Each style has strengths and weaknesses.
- For optimal learning you need to be comfortable with all four styles in order to use the four styles in the learning cycle. Aspects of non-preferred styles can be strengthened.
- Other views of learning stress the importance of linking theory and reflection to professional practice.
- Reflective practice is now recognised as essential by many professions.
- Reflection involves a dialogue, with yourself and/or others in which you question your experiences and responses to them with a view to developing the way in which you think about them, and improving your future practice.
- Reflective writing can be a helpful learning tool.
- Keeping a work diary, a learning log and a more reflective learning journal. Combining insights from these into a personal development file will help you to learn effectively from experience and contribute substantially to career success.

6

PROFESSIONAL DEVELOPMENT

Further information

Bolton, G. (2014) *Reflective Practice: Writing and Professional Development* (4th edn), London: Sage. This is a fascinating, but moderately dense, book showing how creative writing can help with developing reflection. Although aimed mainly at teachers, it would be applicable to any professional.

Butler, G. and Hope, T. (2007) *Manage your Mind: the Mental Fitness Guide* (2nd edn), Oxford University Press.

Buzan, T. (2010) *Use Your Head*, Harlow: Pearson.

Lucas, B. (2001) *Power Up Your Mind*, Nicholas Brealey.

Moon, J.A. (2000) *Reflection in Learning and Professional Development*, RoutledgeFalmer.

Schön, D. (1983) *The Reflective Practitioner*, Basic Books Inc.

Additional resources

http://www.clinteach.com.au/assets/LEARNING-STYLES-Kolb-QUESTIONNAIRE.pdf if you wish to test your own Kolb learning style (accessed 8/7/15).

https://rapidbi.com/learningstyles/#honeymumfordlearningstyleslsq for a 'lite' version of the Honey and Mumford questionnaire (accessed 12/1/15).

http://www.bgfl.org/bgfl/custom/resources_ftp/client_ftp/ks3/ict/multiple_int/questions/questions.cfm for a test of multiple intelligences (accessed 12/1/15).

http://developmentalobserver.blog.com/2010/06/09/an-overview-of-constructive-developmental-theory-cdt/ for a clear and concise overview of Kegan's theory and self-authoring (accessed 12/1/15).

Notes

[1] An heuristic is a mental shortcut or 'rule-of thumb' that allows people to solve problems and make judgements or take decisions quickly and (normally) efficiently.

[2] Product, price, place and promotion + people, process and physical evidence.

[3] Strengths, weaknesses, opportunities and threats.

[4] Specific, measurable, achievable, relevant and time-defined objectives.

[5] Instrumental learning is learning only what is needed to do well in assessments, rather than for any wider purpose.

[6] If you have time, you might like to find out more about the thinking behind this by searching the Internet on this quotation. It may give you a deeper understanding of the role of conceptual processes.

[7] Online 'web log' entries.

7
CRITICAL USE OF IDEAS AND INFORMATION

Learning outcomes

By the end of this chapter you should be able to:

- find and select useful sources in libraries and online

- use bibliographic software to manage references

- use different reading *techniques* as appropriate, in order to make the most effective use of your time

- read critically, evaluating evidence and arguments

- take useful notes on what you have read.

Introduction

Studying for a Master's degree will almost inevitably involve many hours of reading, and reading in a particular way. This chapter looks at how you can cut down on these hours while increasing the benefit gained. This involves finding appropriate sources, reading more *efficiently* thus saving time, reading more *effectively* thus increasing benefits, and becoming more *critical*. These skills will be essential when you come to a project or dissertation, but you can usefully start to develop them from the start – they will also help with earlier assignments. Since managers also need to read a lot, and to assess the value of what they read, these skills are highly transferable to the work context.

Even if you consider yourself a proficient reader (and there is an exercise to test this) you may have scope for developing your reading skills. In particular, it may be important to learn to read more critically. Critical reading and thinking are key postgraduate skills. The chapter will also help you to make more useful notes on what you have read, and to organise your list of references for what you have read. These notes and references will help learning, writing assignments and revision. Perhaps, most importantly, they can protect you from accidental plagiarism, which at worst can cause you to be removed from the programme.

This chapter looks at reading inefficiencies and provides (online) exercises to help you improve your reading speeds if you so wish. While speed reading cannot achieve miracles (Woody Allen once stated that, after a speed-reading course, he was able 'to go through *War and Peace* in 20 minutes. It's about Russia'), it can help when first selecting materials for study, so techniques for very rapid reading are covered briefly. Usually, however, you will want to retain rather more than this from your reading. Although most reading techniques were developed for use with print, similar principles are likely to apply to e-books or other electronic text.

Mechanical reading efficiency may be helpful, but being able to read critically is perhaps even more important. The principles of critical reading can also be usefully applied to what you write in assignments, examinations and dissertation or project report. If you succeed in distancing yourself from your work sufficiently to read it from a critical stance, you are likely to see ways in which arguments or evidence can be greatly strengthened.

Efficient eye movement

Activity 7.1

Before reading further, look at your watch and note the time ____. Now read the next section quickly but carefully, without stopping, aiming to remember significant pieces of information contained in the text (there will be a short quiz on these) until you are told to look at your watch again.

Most readers are unaware of their eye movements while they read and assume that their eyes are moving steadily along each line before moving to the next. If this were the case, and if you read at one line per second, which most people who are asked assume to be a reasonable speed, you would be reading at 600–700 words per minute. At this pace, you would find you could cope easily with the volume of materials you are likely to encounter on a postgraduate programme. Eye movements when reading are far more complex, however. The eye makes a series of extremely rapid jumps along a line, with a significant pause, 0.25 to 1.5 seconds, between each jump. Furthermore, many readers do not move, albeit in this jerky fashion, straight along a line. Instead, as Figure 7.1 shows, they indulge in frequent backward eye jumps, fixating for a second, or even a third time, on a previous word and at intervals their eye may wander off the page altogether. With erratic eye movements like this, and forward jumps from word to adjacent word, many readers achieve reading speeds of only 100 words per minute. At this rate of reading the volume of work for an MBA is likely to prove an impossible task.

At the purely technical level, it is possible to achieve reading speeds of up to 1,000 words per minute by:

- reducing the number of fixations per line, stopping every three to six words rather than every one
- eliminating backward movement and wandering
- reducing the duration of each fixation.

Such improvement will require substantial concentration and considerable practice. But benefits will include: improved ability to get through your course materials; reduced eye fatigue because of the reduction in eye movements; faster reading at work, contributing to better time management. The investment will therefore pay off handsomely. Also, far from being reduced by faster reading, comprehension may be improved. The pattern of a sentence, and its meaning, may emerge much more clearly, and be more readily absorbed, if the sentence is read in phrases, rather than one word at a time. Your interest will be sustained if ideas are coming at you more quickly, and your motivation will be higher if you feel you are making rapid progress. Improved reading techniques offer a wide range of benefits.

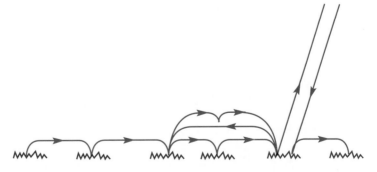

Figure. 7.1 Typical unskilled eye movements when reading

7

CRITICAL USE OF IDEAS AND INFORMATION

If practice is what is needed, why are we all reading so slowly? Surely we have been 'practising' reading most of our lives. Unfortunately, we have been practising our existing bad habits (in the process establishing them more firmly), rather than practising rapid-reading techniques. You will find that it takes much *more* effort, at least at first, to read at increased speed and improvement will be made only through the practice of exercises specifically designed for that purpose. Even when you have developed efficient reading techniques, you may still find that you have to make a point of consciously practising them at intervals, to prevent yourself from falling back into less efficient habits.

Activity 7.2

Look at your watch again and note the time ____. Now note how long it is since you last noted the time ____. There were approximately 700 words in that piece of text. Divide that figure by the number of minutes elapsed in order to find your reading speed in words per minute. Write this down ____.

Exercise 7.1

Now check your comprehension by answering the following questions, saying whether each statement is true or false, according to the preceding text. Do not glance back at the text.

	T/F
1. Poor readers fixate once per word.	_____
2. With practice, a poor reader can increase from a speed of 100 to 1,000 words per minute.	_____
3. A speed reader will fixate only once per line.	_____
4. Once you have mastered speed-reading techniques they will become second nature.	_____
5. The only drawback to rapid reading is that it tends to reduce comprehension.	_____
6. The duration of each fixation can range from as little as 0.25 of a second to as much as 1.5 seconds.	_____

Comment

Answers are at the end of the chapter. If you got more than one wrong, you should be aiming to improve your retention skills since you were specifically instructed to try to retain the information in the passage.

➤

A reading speed of 250 or more words per minute, with reasonable retention, is an adequate basis on which to start your course. If your speed was significantly less than this, or at your present speed you are not absorbing enough, you may find the following exercises useful.

If your results suggest you would benefit from exercises to increase your reading speed, a selection are provided online. Substantial improvements can be achieved by moving your eyes more efficiently, and using a pointer to pace your reading and keep you focused. But improvement does require a significant time investment in sustained practice (usually for several weeks).

Selecting reading material

Focusing your reading on what best serves your purpose is critical. The amount of guidance provided will depend upon the type programme you are on, the practice of your university and how long you have been studying. At the start, reading lists may be fairly prescriptive, and some institutions even provide substantial study notes and texts. Even then, you are likely to need to make some decisions about what to omit when short of time, or about additional reading in areas that really interest you. By the end you will probably be expected to do most of the finding and selecting for yourself. On projects and dissertations *all* students are faced with major choices of what to read and you will

➤ Ch 16   find more guidance on this in Chapter 16.

This handbook can do no more than suggest a systematic approach to an answer that will suit your particular circumstances.

Define the problem

What are your objectives? Why are you looking for texts to read? What do you *really* need to find out? Is it facts, ideas, alternative approaches, background information, or some-

➤ Chs 13,   thing else that you are seeking? Is the information a requirement for an exam, necessary
16   or potentially useful for an assignment, or to help you understand an issue that currently
➤ Ch 5   concerns you? Refer back to the discussion of the different types of learning in Chapter 5. Once you have identified the sort of thing you are looking for and what you want it to do for you, you will be better able to describe what you are looking for. These labels, refined into 'keywords', will help you search for relevant sources.

Identify options

What sources exist? What does Wikipedia say about the subject? Note: this is *not* a reference to be quoted in assignments – academics hate it because it is *not* to be trusted as a 100 per cent reliable source. But it can be an excellent starting point for getting a feel for a topic and suggesting places where you might find useful materials. Use Google Scholar or Amazon to identify recent relevant textbooks, or browse in a good bookshop. You can find out a lot without needing to buy the books. Identify those journals most likely to have papers on your topic. Look for a recent review article in one of them and note references at the end of some articles that sound relevant. Soon you should be able to identify key authors on a topic and then make a list of related issues that will help expand your list of keywords. Use Google Scholar or another academic search on your extended list.

Seek your librarian's help in identifying and searching relevant databases to which your university subscribes. Use the same keywords to search the Internet more generally. Look at reference lists in recent theses on the topic. Ask teaching staff and other students or knowledgeable colleagues for ideas. Check government publications and websites, in-company resources, etc.

TECHSkills 7.1 provides background information on other search resources and suggests how best to use them. Further guidance is given in Chapter 16.

TECHSkills 7 .1 Searching online: the basics

Given the plethora of online resources, efficient search techniques can save you many hours, and help you avoid missing important items. It may help to understand how some of the main tools can help you, what other places you can look, and the terms to use when searching.

General search engines:

You will be familiar with using Google, Yahoo!, MSN or other search engine to find information online. These search engines have a database of web pages collected by computer programmes called 'spiders' which crawl around the web following links between pages. The search engine will select what the spiders have collected, and provide links to pages which match what you asked for. Note that because they are searching their 'copy' of what they have found, some of these links may not work when you try them. Note, too, that you may get different results with different search engines and from the same engine at different times as they order results according to popularity and financial factors.

Metasearch engines:

These will search using several search engines and give you the combined result, thus partly getting around the issue of different results from different engines.

Specialist search engines:

General search engines look at everything. A more specialised search engine will look at a more specific selection. Perhaps the most useful is Google Scholar, which searches only academic sources. It also gives information on 'cited by', which shows later papers which used the work – an indication of how influential it has been, and 'related articles' which may suggest additional useful search terms if your original search has been too narrow.

Library catalogues:

You may find your university library's e-catalogue is easy to use, and your best way of finding relevant articles. However, some such catalogues are better suited to helping you find books or articles you have already identified as relevant. If this is the case, starting with Google Scholar to find a reference, and then going to your library catalogue, may be more efficient.

Specific journals:

If you are interested in a specific area (e.g. LEAN manufacturing), check your library's list of journals on this or related topics and look at recent articles on your topic of interest. The reference lists at the end of any relevant articles will suggest further things you might like to scan.

Online repositories:

Increasingly, universities offer free access to research by their staff (see, for example, the Open University's open research repository at **http://oro.open.ac.uk/.** Such repositories will be easily searchable by topic.

Author websites:

If you are interested in work by a particular author you will often find useful information on this, and perhaps links to openly available resources, from the author's personal website.

Online 'digests':

There are now many online equivalents of textbooks which can provide a good starting point. An obvious starting (though not ending) point is Wikipedia. This is unreliable in that it can be altered by anyone so may not always be accurate, so you should never rely upon it, or cite it in your writing. But entries may provide a good starting point, often covering related ideas and listing references, which can be helpful in your own search. Always check information against other sources.

More controlled versions of digests, where the provider commissions and 'publishes' content, often as a way in to paid-for training or resources are slightly more reliable. A useful example is **http://www.businessballs.com/**. Check whether tutors are happy with you citing such sources, or whether as with Wikipedia you should merely use them as background information.

Another source of useful information is professional institutes, such as the CIPD or CIMA. Their websites often have some useful and/or topical information openly available (though for more detail you may need to be a member). Such information is reliable enough to be cited, or can be used to extend or refine your search.

Online essays:

You will find a plethora of essays available, free or for a modest price. **Avoid these like the plague**. They are of variable quality, and if you are tempted to use them you will be caught: universities have software that will easily detect such plagiarism.

> **Note 1:** Whenever you find a relevant source, save the address, with a brief note of why it was useful and the date you accessed it. You will need to list the address just as you would any other reference when referring to the information in anything you write. There is guidance on software to help with this shortly.
>
> **Note 2:** When saving/copying material found online, remember to make it very clear that this is a copy, so that you do not inadvertently later use it as if it were your own, which would be plagiarism.
>
> *More advanced search skills are covered in Chapter 12.*

Identify your measures of effectiveness

Coverage relevant to your purpose is obviously crucial. Availability is important, with price and order time also significant. Reputation is crucial. The level at which something is written is also a factor to consider. You do not want something trivial, but nor should it be so specialist that it is impenetrable. It helps if something is well written. Has the author used substantial evidence or extensively surveyed published material, or is the piece written on the basis of opinion and prejudice? When was the work published? You will need to consider in each case which of these factors is most important for you. If using material 'published' electronically, be particularly cautious. It may not have been subjected to the scrutiny given to papers in refereed academic journals. Because of their potential shortcomings in terms of accuracy and evidence base, most universities will not give credit to references to Wikipedia, Businessballs and similar non-academic sites, useful as these may be as starting points to understanding an idea or topic.

Selection

Once you have identified possible sources and decided upon your selection criteria, you will be in a position to select those most likely to be helpful. If you have access to physical materials in a library, you will be able to scan them rapidly to gain an idea of their likely usefulness. However, it may well be more convenient to read electronic abstracts. These are likely to be freely available online, even for journals to which your library does not provide electronic access.

Given the wealth of writing on most management topics, you need to be very selective if you are not to be swamped by potentially relevant reading. Always ask a tutor or project supervisor for as much help as you can get in the vital area of identifying materials that are worth the effort of obtaining and reading. In evaluating possible materials, check whether the author's objectives are compatible with your own. Particularly in North America, where academic tenure depends largely on the length of a lecturer's publication list, there is enormous pressure to publish, regardless of whether the person has done any research or had any ideas worth reporting. Whole books may be written around a single, fairly basic idea, filled out with anecdotes drawn from the author's consultancy experience. These may be interesting, but may not score highly on relevant measures of effectiveness.

Going through these stages systematically should help you to make a sensible choice of materials. Having done so, you need to consider the appropriate reading speed for the materials selected.

Choosing your reading speed

The appropriate reading speed will depend upon your purpose. Sometimes you will be looking for a highly specific piece of information in a text, sometimes you just want to get a feel for an argument, sometimes you will want to think really carefully about what you are reading.

Rapid scanning, the fastest speed, will enable you to check a particular point, or identify the relevant part of a book or article. The index, plus rapid scanning of the text, will be enough. This relies on the ability of your brain to attend to only a part of what is happening. You may know the so-called cocktail party effect – the way in which someone can often hear their name being mentioned at the other side of a noisy crowded room. You can bring selective attention to bear upon written materials as well.

To do this, scan the page too rapidly to read, allowing your brain to notice the word or phrase that you are seeking. Scanning requires concentration and a determination not to be sidetracked by interesting points irrelevant to your purpose. Of course, if you *can* spare the time, such digressions can be rewarding; indeed, some would say they are what study is all about. Alas, they will often be a luxury.

Gaining an overview, takes slightly longer, but is useful when you want to grasp the overall pattern of a book, chapter or article. Focus first on any contents lists, then introductions and summaries, and main headings and subheadings, then diagrams and tables of results. Several rapid passes through the material may help you to map it better than a single, slightly slower pass. Note any specific questions you would like the material to answer, together with any aspects that arouse your curiosity more generally.

Speed reading is slightly slower still, and suitable for lengthy materials that are only slightly relevant, or for background reading to identify the author's main arguments.

Reading to increase understanding will be needed for much of your study, especially if you need to think about the extent to which ideas and arguments are based on relevant and reliable evidence and about their relation to your purpose. Although this is slower than speed reading, many speed-reading techniques will still be useful. These include eliminating redundant eye movements and more rapid reading of any non-essential parts of the texts. But where there is little redundancy and concepts require active thought, you cannot speed read. You need time to make sure you have understood the author's points. It is important to identify any unfamiliar concepts that the author uses or those where you are not sure you know what is meant. Be particularly alert to 'everyday' words or phrases that seem to be being used in a non-everyday manner. ('Critical' is one such example in this book.) If you do not understand a concept in a paper – or are unsure of the specialist sense in which a phrase is being used – you need to work on it until you do. Otherwise reading the paper will be of little use.

It takes time to consider the evidence and arguments that underpin the points and any proposed models or other theory. When reading critically it is important to assess these.

You also need time to consider what the author's points mean in the light of your own experience and professional challenges.

For this type of study you will need to take notes, both to aid comprehension and for later recall. You may want to capture your reflections, so may need to stop reading to think and write in your learning journal. You may even want to consult other sources before coming back to the main materials. You may need to practise working something out, if it is complicated, and to be sure that you understand when and how to do what you are practising. You are unlikely to be able to speed read texts on finance!

Learning by heart involves the slowest reading of all. If you need to be able to reproduce an equation, or a diagram, a set of categories, you will need time to commit it to memory. Fortunately, much of your reading will be for other purposes. Indeed, you may find that, once you have gone over all the details, relationships and possible uses, you will have *learned* the material in question in a far richer way than merely learning by heart.

If this does not happen, rote learning or mnemonics may be needed. I still recite the colours of the rainbow, on the rare occasions when this is requested, by remembering the phrase from my childhood, 'Read out your green book in verse', and go through the entire '30 days hath September …' rigmarole to feel sure that August really does have 31 days.

An alternative to devising a phrase is to make the initials into a pronounceable word or acronym. (Remember SMART objectives?) Many authors help by going out of their way to come up with things that are, in themselves, memorable. The uncharitable might say that this, rather than the merit of what it is that they are enabling you to remember, is what has made them so popular. You will, almost certainly, encounter the 7 Ss, the 4 (or more) Ps, and many more of that ilk. Rhyming is also popular. The 'form, storm, norm, perform' sequence

➤ Ch 9   is used in Chapter 9 on teamwork, and there are several other such formulations in different areas. If authors have not been so helpful, you can have fun devising your own mnemonics.

If speed of recall is important, such as when you need to know what 7×9 is in the middle of some mental arithmetic, then learning by repetition may be preferable. But mnemonics are extremely useful for information that you might not need for several months, as they will enable you to drag from the recesses of your memory material that otherwise would be inaccessible.

Guidelines for effective reading

- Establish your purpose in reading.
- Select appropriate material.
- Scan the entire text rapidly to establish structure and coverage.
- Refine your purpose – what key points/questions are of interest?
- Read relevant parts of text at fastest appropriate speed.
- Capture your understanding by diagramming structure of arguments, highlighting text and/or note taking.
- Review this against your purpose.
- File your notes carefully.

Many of these techniques can be used with online sources too, but there are a few additional things that can make screen reading more efficient. Some are obvious, some less so. Some are more time-consuming than others, and these you may wish to reserve for more important materials which you want to study in more depth.

TECHSkills 7.2 More effective reading from screen

Copy key text into a Word or similar document. You can then expand it or change the font to increase readability, cut out any ads, highlight parts of particular importance, or delete chunks that are not relevant. **Note: if saving the document ensure that you make clear it is a copy and note the URL to avoid plagiarism.**

Use your cursor as a pointer, rather than a finger.

Alternatively, switch on your highlighter and drag highlight with cursor as you read, this acts to show the line you are reading, making it easy to follow, and if you stop reading you can 'save' the highlighted version, making it easy to resume at the point you stopped.

Use your mouse to keep the line you are reading at the top of the screen to avoid eye-jumps backwards.

If the text is really hard, look around for a more readable (though equally trustworthy) source; though beware of oversimplified consultants' offerings.

7

CRITICAL USE OF IDEAS AND INFORMATION

Reading critically

The idea of questioning the material you read was introduced in the last chapter in the context of reflection on learning points from reading. There, the focus was very much on the theory itself, then on relating it to your existing mental models and experience, and assessing how it might enhance or improve your thinking or practice. This is closely related to the process of reading critically and indeed depends upon it. But here I want to look in rather more detail at a further aspect of being 'critical': considering what is written in relation to its author.

➤ Ch 6

Developing critical thinking is a key objective for postgraduate courses. And *critical* in this sense is not saying disparaging things about an author, but engaging with the materials at a 'deep' level, making sure that you understand the claims being made and the arguments and evidence that the author is using to support these claims. Having understood them, you can judge their validity and relevance to your own issues.

The author's context

An important factor to consider is the context within which the author is writing. This will determine the relevance of their data, but also will have affected how they designed their research and how they interpreted their findings. Important elements of this are the author's background, time of writing and purpose. There may be cultural, discipline-based or other assumptions which are never made explicit, but which underpin the claims made. (As a psychologist I long found papers written by those with a sociology background difficult: the agendas and the vocabulary and the assumptions made seem to me to differ radically from those with which I was familiar.) When you read critically you need to be alert to such assumptions, and be prepared to question them.

Some older books and papers offer splendid insights into enduring aspects of management, and ideas may be clearer in their original than when 'developed' by others. But some relate to contexts very different from those facing organisations today. Caution is needed when using them to help you think about the present. As a colleague said in a recent meeting, 'Porter's ideas were great for manufacturing organisations in the US in the 1980s, but may be less relevant to most organisations operating in Europe today.'

The author's purpose is also significant. Some texts are written to gain business (for example, many pieces by consultants are written to market their services or products). Some seek to influence particular people. You may have read concerns about the number of academic medical papers written by those whose research has been funded by drug companies. This is less an issue for management research but might still be a factor. Unintentional bias is hard to avoid in such cases.

The claims being made

Having considered the context in which something was written and the implication of this, the next step to becoming a critical reader is to work out the key point and claims an author is making. By *claim* I mean any idea which someone says is 'true'. Usually authors give reasons for their claims (without reasoning, claims remain assertions).

An argument is made up of a claim plus its associated reasons.

Before looking at arguments and how they are constructed, it is helpful to understand some of the terms used. In particular, I should like to look at possible differences between
➤ **Chs 2,**   some of the terms that have been used in earlier chapters, often under the broad heading
   5, 6   of 'theory'.

Management writing varies greatly. Sometimes the author is proposing a new theory,
➤ **Ch 6**   concept, model or framework (*see* Chapter 6) sometimes critiquing an existing theory, sometimes describing a case study. Some less academic publications may seem to be proposing the answer to life, the universe and everything!

Analysing the argument

In most papers you read, the author will argue from evidence (which might be other theories, research data or even armchair observations) to make a particular case. There may be a series of secondary claims needed to support the main contention. When you are reading critically, you will need to identify both primary and secondary claims and assess the strength of main and sub-arguments. As an example of this sort of approach, I'll take a classic motivation theory, Herzberg's (1966) 'Motivation-Hygiene' theory: you may encounter this at some point in your studies. (You met another theory of motivation (Expectancy Theory) in the last chapter, so can compare the two.) I shall abbreviate the
➤ **Ch 6**   argument here, for simplicity.

Box 7.1 Herzberg's (1966) Theory of Motivation

Herzberg claims that man has two sets of needs: one set concerns the need to avoid pain and the other concerns the specifically human need to grow psychologically. This claim is supported by the results of interviews with 200 engineers and accountants, described as representing a cross-section of Pittsburgh industry. Interviewees were asked to think of a time when they had felt especially good about their jobs, and then to answer questions about why they had felt like that, and its impact on their performance, personal relationships and well-being. This process was then repeated for a time when they had negative feelings about their job.

Five factors stood out as strong determinants of job satisfaction: achievement, recognition (for achievement), work itself, responsibility and advancement. Dissatisfaction was associated with company policy and administration, supervision, salary, interpersonal relations and working conditions. Thus satisfaction was associated with the person's relationship to what they do, while dissatisfaction was associated with the context within which they do it. Herzberg provided a chart showing how responses were distributed. This broadly supports the 'two factor' idea. Although most factors receive mentions in the context of both satisfaction and dissatisfaction, they appear in the 'wrong' category much less frequently than in the 'right' one.

Now look at this theory critically. Remember the original claim: there are two categories of human need operating. The evidence to support it appears plausible. Different circumstances seemed to cause feeling good about your job and feeling bad. But is the evidence adequate to support this?

In the box no detail is given about whether the 'theory' was already known to the person categorising the responses, or whether this was done blind. This is important because there is room for subconscious bias in any subjective judgements: the paper from which the box is derived (an extract from a book) did not make this clear, so I would need to go back to the original research paper to check the method. (At this point you would make an action note to do this.)

What about the sample of people interviewed? You could argue that two professional groups in a single US city is not really a representative sample, even of US employees. Would blue-collar workers respond in the same fashion? Would poor people in other countries be similarly unmoved by money? And how relevant now is research carried out more than 50 years ago?

Then what about the reasoning? Is the conclusion inevitable from this evidence? Would you get these results *only* if people had two different sets of needs, or are there other possible explanations? A widely held principle in philosophy and science, is known as 'Ockham's (or Occam's) Razor' from its originator, William of Ockham (c. 1287–1347), an English Franciscan friar. This states that if there are several explanations for an observation you should adopt the simplest. There is quite a lot of evidence to suggest that in other contexts we tend to take personal credit for good things that happen to us and blame others for the bad. Herzberg's results could be explained equally well by this human tendency. To decide which explanation was more likely you would need to find a way of testing this that did not depend upon personal reports of feelings.

Yet another 'explanation' of the findings is possible. Herzberg points out, the 'motivators' tend to be associated with performing the task, the dissatisfiers with the context in which it is performed. Would not Expectancy Theory, which was being developed at around the same time, predict exactly this? And in a way that enabled further predictions to be made about ways in which strengthening the effort–outcome link could increase motivation? A key test when you are reading critically is how much a model or theory adds to existing understanding.

This is linked to the next question, the 'So what?' Even if it adds something, how useful is this? At the time, Herzberg's theory had a profound influence on organisations. Out of it came a new approach to improving employee motivation called 'job enrichment'. Instead of offering pay rises, organisations sought to motivate staff by increasing responsibility. (This also allowed them to cut some supervisory jobs!) A whole industry grew up, offering the highly prescriptive approach Herzberg developed. (Indeed, 'increasing responsibility' is still the thrust of many job redesign exercises, although because the underpinning theory is less simplistic, the chances of success are arguably higher.)

Did it work? Sometimes it did. But in other cases the effort–performance link was already weak because the staff concerned lacked the necessary skills to do what was required of them. As Expectancy Theory would have predicted, the effects of job enrichment and giving additional responsibility were catastrophic in such cases! These catastrophes might have been prevented by a more critical reading of Herzberg before job enrichment was embarked upon.

➤ Ch 3

Mapping the argument

In looking at Herzberg's much quoted and, at the time, highly influential piece of writing, I was trying to do three things:

- identify the claim being made
- evaluate the evidence being used in support of the claim
- evaluate the reasoning used to link the evidence to the claim.

Working out the structure of an argument in a paper can be quite difficult as authors do not always distinguish arguments from assertions and opinions. It can be really helpful to draw an argument map. This is closely related to the more generalised mind map described later in this chapter. In an argument map each branch represents a single 'reason' with the twigs being the pieces of evidence that together form that reason. Figure 7.2 shows an example of an argument map. (*See* Figure 7.3 for an example of a more generic mind map.)

Branches in an argument map might be the logical links with twigs as the relevant evidence they are linking to the claim. Many different logical links are possible. Key ones are:

- A proves B
- A suggests that B is likely

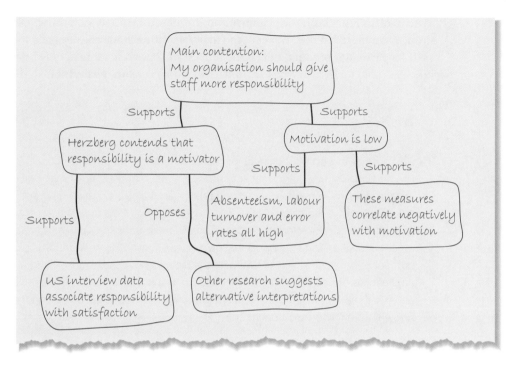

Figure 7.2 Example of an argument map

- A is consistent with B
- A suggests B is unlikely
- A is inconsistent with B
- A disproves B.

When you have a complex argument, unless there is actual proof – rare in management research – you will be faced with working out how much weight to give to the different evidence and logical links. This will depend upon the strength of the evidence itself, its consistency and the strength of the evidence–claim links.

Although we have been talking about mapping other people's arguments, the technique is invaluable when you are planning an essay or report. You will be able to see whether your reasoning is clear, and based on adequate evidence. If you are planning a research project or dissertation, it can be equally invaluable to think about your potential evidence *before* you finalise your research design and consider how – however it comes out – it relates to claims you might hope to make in your report.

➤ Chs 12, 13, 16

Software packages that allow you to map arguments can be useful for complex arguments where many reasons operate on several levels. In these cases each twig is in itself a claim, and has supporting reasons (premises), objections to reasons (rejoinders) and objections to objections (rebuttals). By teasing them apart it is possible to evaluate each chain of claim–supporting claims–evidence, by looking both at the logic involved and the evidence (and assumptions) to which this logic is applied. As in the example above, you may find that both the evidence and the reasoning leave something to be desired. If you are interested in this, you can find material online. It may be designed to support – or sell – a particular product, but in the process may provide more detailed teaching than there is room for here (try **www.austhink.com/reason/tutorials**).

Activity 7.3

Select an article from a business or management journal or professional. Try to iden-tify the principal claim and any secondary claims. If applicable, it may help to decide whether theory, framework and/or metaphor are involved. Define any new concepts. Ask 'So what'? If the claim is true, what does it imply? If the implications are important enough to justify the effort, try to tease apart the arguments involved. What claims and /or evidence are used to support the main claim(s)? What if any evidence is used to sup-port any intermediate claims? What are the logical links used? Do they add up to a valid argument, provided the evidence is sound (i.e. is the conclusion drawn the only possible one)? Is the evidence adequate? Are there any hidden assumptions being made? If so, how valid are these assumptions?

Hidden assumptions are difficult to identify, but may be absolutely critical to an argu-ment. There was a hidden assumption in the Herzberg case, as you may have seen once the alternative explanation was pointed out. This was that 'no other explanation is possi-ble'. Once this assumption was queried, other possible explanations were looked for and some found. So when a reason is offered it is always worth asking whether this reason is sufficient in itself to support the claim.

The other real difficulty in business research is the complexity of most of the issues ad-dressed and the variety of contexts in which these issues arise. This makes it very difficult both to obtain convincing evidence and to know how far to generalise from it. Even if the evidence and argument was adequate in its context, would it be reasonable, for example, to draw conclusions about all employees from two professional groupings in one city? It was clear in the example above how difficult it was to interpret the subjective responses given by the professionals concerned. There is a real dilemma faced by many authors between seemingly 'scientific' quantitative data and the richer, but harder to interpret, qualitative information. More of this in Chapter 16.

➤ **Ch 16**

Assessing value to you

You may be convinced by the author's logic and evidence but, if you want your read-ing to increase your chances of success in a career, rather than merely to contribute to good marks, you need to assess any theory's implications for your professional practice. This means engaging the 'cogs' shown in Figure 6.4. What light does it cast on your own practice or understanding of situations at work? Is it consistent with your experi-ence? Is there anything in your experience that might cause you to question its validity in your context? Maybe the particular evidence used by the author looked good, but you have access to additional and contradictory evidence. Perhaps it adds little to what you already know, or does nothing to challenge the way you already think. There is now so much written about management that you will often find that a paper seems to be're-labelling' an existing concept, without adding anything to your understanding of an issue.

There are many other useful questions to ask when reading critically, and you will find a selection given in the guidelines below. These build on earlier guidelines so there is some overlap. Add any further questions you think might be useful, aiming to develop your own set of guidelines.

Key questions when reading critically

- When/where was this written and what was the author's purpose?
- What claims is the author making?
- What new concepts are introduced, and what do they mean?
- Are they really new or merely 'rebadging' of existing ideas?
- How/when might they be useful?
- What new frameworks are introduced?
- What do they add to existing frameworks?
- How/when might they be useful? Are there limitations to their application?
- Is there any new theory introduced?
- Do the 'organised assumptions' that make up the theory 'hang together' logically?
- Does it extend an existing theory? (Sometimes quite small additions can be surprisingly useful.)
- Is it consistent with other theories that you already know? If not, what are the inconsistencies? Are they explained/justified?
- How/when might the new theory be useful? Are there limitations to its application?
- Are there ways in which this new theory might usefully be amended?
- Was the author arguing a case to which she or he was personally committed? (This can indicate potential for bias.)
- How strong is 'the argument' supporting the claim? Are there any shortcomings in the evidence or the logic, or any hidden assumptions that might be questioned?
- If there are inadequacies, is this because the paper is a shortened version of something else? If so, could you find more of the evidence by looking at other sources?
- How does this theory relate to your own management experience? If there are inconsistencies, can you find reasons for this?

Taking notes

There are several reasons why note taking is important. With borrowed books, some parts may be so important that you photocopy them, but for the rest of the book you will need something that you can refer to once it is back in the library. If you are working with your own books, or have downloaded copies of books or papers, then taking notes *while* you are studying is still helpful. In particular, it is easier to sustain your concentration if you are taking active notes, i.e. going beyond merely extracting points to copy. Such active notes can help you to sort out the essence of what an author is saying (for example, it helps to map an argument). They can capture any reflections on your work experience in the light of what you are reading (or *vice versa*). They can capture links to other reading you have done or note reading you need to do. Such notes will probably supplement the learning points in your learning log and might usefully be indexed from there.

Your notes may well be *more* helpful than the original materials: they may be easier for you to understand. Or you may have managed to represent the original materials in a way that makes more sense to you, and included relevant other material, such as cross-references to key parts of other courses that have a bearing on the point, or comments on how the material relates to your own experience. Because they are briefer than the originals, your notes may be easier to refer to and to revise from. Indeed, review and revision is one of the most important uses of notes.

The most useful type of notes will depend on the purpose for which you are taking them. Notes on borrowed materials will normally need to be more detailed than those on materials you own or can retain. For borrowed materials you may well need to copy out the most quotable phrases and diagrams, as well as any references that look potentially useful, and you may need to go into detail on the actual content.

With electronic materials there may be a strong tendency to copy huge chunks, if only because it is so easy (remember to guard against future plagiarism by making clear the extent of any copied text and noting the source as discussed shortly). Your copy will allow future reference, but you still need to be able to extract and absorb key points if you are to make effective use of the ideas and information they contain. So, even if you have saved the material intact, you need to read it carefully and take notes.

The most basic form of note taking is to highlight key points or concepts. This will in itself ensure that you are *thinking* as you read, continually striving to extract the main ideas. This form of interaction with the text helps you to absorb more, and to maintain your concentration more easily, than with passive reading. It also means that when you return to the materials you will be able to extract the key points very quickly by reading the highlighted text. If you have made brief notes in the margin to supplement the highlighting, the process will be even easier. Such notes might be brief 'labels', explanations of points that took you some time to grasp, examples from your work which exemplify the idea, or cross-references to other materials.

Highlighting and annotating is, of course, only possible if you 'own' a copy of the materials. If you are working with a PDF you may find it helps to cut and paste key parts into a Word file that you can highlight, rearrange and/or annotate.

If your course does not provide a glossary, you may wish to construct your own with definitions of key concepts. Or you might wish to produce a digest of each module, defining and explaining each major idea contained and cross-referencing or adding relevant notes from your reading. Other 'active' approaches to note taking are outlined below.

➤ Chs 13, 16

Three approaches to note taking

Cameron and Price (2009) suggest three useful approaches: pre-structured notes, thematic notes, and three-minute essays.

Pre-structured notes are organised along similar lines to a consultancy or business report, or an academic paper. They use headings such as:

- Central research question or issue
- Research methods used
- Evidence generated
- Conclusions drawn
- Strengths and weaknesses
- Your own evaluation/thoughts about the piece.

Once you become familiar with your structure both taking the notes and referring to them afterwards becomes easier.

Thematic notes are those you organise around the key themes in what you are reading – something which will only emerge once you have read – or at least scanned – it. You can incorporate relevant argument maps under each theme. Thematic note-taking is only appropriate for key resources but can aid critical reading and makes it easy to link papers from different disciplines/modules which cover similar themes.

Three-minute essays are a useful form of notes on any learning experience, and can be used in conjunction with other forms of notes. The process is very simple. At the end of the learning experience (it might be a group discussion, lecture, or a paper you read) set a timer for three minutes and simply write down what you have learned, what struck you as needing further thought, and any links to other topics or notes. Three minutes is a trivial time to invest, so it requires little discipline to get into the 'three min' habit. Yet the rewards in terms of embedding learning, as well as providing useful notes for future reference, may surprise you.

Notes in diagram form

Whatever approach you choose for your note taking, it is important to note relationships between ideas from different sources and related to different disciplines. Diagrams (discussed further in the next chapter) are invaluable for this. Most Master's courses are taught as a series of discrete modules, but the problems you encounter as a manager are unlikely to fit within such disciplinary boundaries. When you are analysing general case studies and in your final project or dissertation it may be useful to draw on ideas

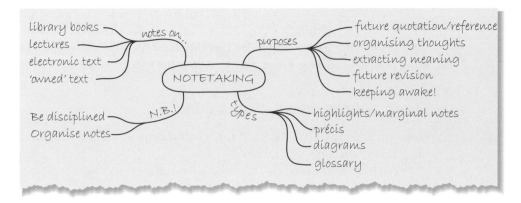

Figure 7.3 Diagrammatic notes on note taking

and techniques from a range of modules and disciplines. Integrating ideas from different sources will be much easier if you always note how different topics interrelate, or have the potential for interacting. Thematic note-taking helps with this. Whichever note form you adopt it helps to highlight such relationships. And diagrams can be particularly useful in this. Figure 7.3 gives an example of diagrammatic notes on what you are reading right now, but you can use whatever form works for you. The key thing is to use placing on the paper, and some sort of connection (lines or arrows) to how connections between ideas.

➤ **Ch 8**

Argument maps are of course one form of diagram, but many others can be used to support more 'wordy' notes, showing other relationships between components. Diagrammatic notes may also help you remember what you have read. The process of drawing a diagram forces you to *think* about the structure of text in a way that a précis of points made may not. Drawing engages a different part of your brain. The resulting picture may be much easier to remember than words. A useful type of diagram for such note taking is described in Chapter 8, together with further guidance on diagrammatic note-taking. Figure 7.3 shows what you might have produced if taking diagrammatic notes on note taking itself. This is an example of a mind map – you can obtain software to produce basic diagrams of this form very easily (some basic versions are available for free in the hope that you will like them enough to invest in more sophisticated versions).

➤ **Ch 8**

Note taking to avoid accidental plagiarism

If you read nothing else carefully, read this. Plagiarism means using other people's work without acknowledging it. If you do this in a course assignment, you are likely to be seriously penalised, perhaps even asked to leave the programme. The most obvious form of plagiarism is copying another student's work and submitting it as your own (or purchasing a pre-prepared assignment from one of the agencies which advertise this service). This is clearly dishonest and may cost you your degree.

But it is also plagiarism to include in any essay or dissertation work that you have copied from print or online sources without making very clear (by use of quotation marks and/or italics) the extent of the quotation and the author of the original. Because of the ease of copying from electronic sources, this sort of plagiarism is increasingly common. Universities now use software designed to identify not only students copying from each other but also those using text that exists online.

Some students deliberately use text from other sources because they are unsure of its meaning (or of their skill in writing English) so feel it is safer to copy someone else's words. Others may not realise that it is plagiarism to reproduce extracts from materials written by others. Some may accidentally plagiarise because of the way they have kept notes. The following guidelines on avoiding plagiarism will be referred to again in Chapter 13, but you need to understand them before you start taking notes. You will then see why it is so important to consider plagiarism (and proper referencing, discussed later) when note taking or copying text for future reference.

Guidelines on avoiding plagiarism

1. Write all assignments in your own words unless there is a particular reason why it is helpful to quote the actual words used by an author (for example, when contrasting two definitions).

2. When quoting someone else's words, make it absolutely clear which words are not your own, using quotation marks and/or italics to show the extent of the quotation.

3. When quoting exact words, you need to cite the author and date, and give the page number(s) from which the quote is taken at the end of the quotation.

4. In order to avoid plagiarism in any writing, you need to make it very clear when taking any notes/copies that they *are* copies, and where they are copied *from* (including page references for print, and URLs and date accessed for materials found online).

If you follow the guidelines above, you will be able to *deliberately* quote exactly what someone said when you are writing an essay or dissertation, correctly attributed, and with minimal effort. Equally important, you will avoid any accidental unattributed quotations, aka plagiarism, which could attract disciplinary action.

Academic referencing

The mention of citing references above assumed that you are already familiar with doing this from your undergraduate studies. If so, skip most of this section – though the TECH-Skills box on bibliographic software may be helpful if you have not yet used this.

If, however, you are not confident that you can reference sources to your tutors' satisfaction, read on. It will help you ensure that your notes capture the information you will need when writing essays and reports. Academics typically place a lot of emphasis on 'correct' referencing. This is at least partly because their careers depend on recognition for their research. 'Stealing' ideas through plagiarism is therefore a serious form of threat.

Although such theft is more likely to damage them if perpetrated by other academics, it is important that no student – who is, after all, a potential future academic – is left without an understanding of the importance of referencing and of how to do it.

The other part of the reason is that if you are reading critically you will often wish to question the evidence on which an author bases their evidence (remember the Pittsburgh accountants and engineers). If you are dubious about an argument, you may wish to go back and read the full paper from which some of the evidence is taken. It is very easy to quote selectively, indeed necessary for space reasons, but author bias can lead to selecting only the tiny part that supports an argument, and ignoring the larger part that does not. So as a critical reader you need to go back and at least scan the original source. As an interested reader you may simply want to know more.

This need to be able to refer to sources explains the need to give full details of the source, and the need for page number(s) for any direct quotes so that they too can be found. This information needs to include information on author(s), date of publication, title of publication, and publisher. Often location of publisher is also called for. And if you are referring to a chapter in a book with different contributors, or a paper in a journal, you need to refer to the title of that too, and give page numbers for the chapter or paper. Journal information needs to include volume and issue number to make it easy to find the right one.

Annoyingly, there are several 'correct' ways of doing this, depending on whom you are writing for. Many UK universities use the Harvard system, or something similar. If you are writing for a journal you may find they require a different system. It is important to find out what system your university expects – they will almost certainly provide useful guidance on using this system. (There is extensive guidance on Harvard available online). You will need to know the referencing style required, and to make sure that you capture all the information needed for this when taking notes (and write your references

➤ Ch 13   in the approved fashion at the end of essays and reports (*see* Chapter 13). The variety of 'correct' styles is now less annoying as if you use bibliographic software (see TECHSkills 7.3) as this allows you to save and retrieve references in several different styles.

'Citing' simply means giving a signpost to the source of the idea or information you are using, at the point where it is used. This is normally done by mentioning the author and date of publication in the text at the appropriate point (as with the Cameron and Price (2009) citation earlier in this section. Unless you are quoting directly (in which case you need the page number on which the quote originally appeared), this is all the information you need in the body of your report or essay. The full information (title, publisher etc.) appears at the end, in the 'References' section of your document.

TECHSkills 7.3: Bibliographic software

In the old days when your only access to journals was printed copies in libraries, writing your 'References' section at the end of an essay or report depended on the notes you had taken at the time. Anyone who was lazy about noting and then filing references when they were reading was doomed to hours of frustrating search for the full reference for the

➤

7

sources they wanted to use. Now that most reading is online the whole process can be quick and painless if you use bibliographic software. (RefWorks and EndNote are two such packages in common use at the time of writing.) So useful are these tools that your university is likely to provide such software for students.

The advantages are that you no longer need to type in a reference – the software does it for you!

As well as creating your own 'library of references' it will allow you to search them by author, topic, date, or other fields. You can insert the citation within an essay or paper, with a couple of clicks, and create a reference list at the end in an output style of your choice. Thus if your university requires Harvard style references, but the journal to which you were sending a paper based on your essay required a different style, the programme will obligingly make the changes for you.

You may, however, lose access to a university-provided system a year or two after you graduate, so would need to either sign up with the system in your own right, or export your library elsewhere if you want access to it thereafter.

Because different systems are in use, and because each is likely to provide comprehensive tutorials in how best to use it, there is little point in going into detail here. The main point is to find out what your university provides and invest time as soon as possible in learning to make efficient use of that system. If no such software is provided, consider subscribing to a system in your own right – some basic versions are available free (see electronic resources for suggestions) while others offer a free trial.

Whatever the form of your notes, disciplined filing is essential. A series of organised notes can be invaluable, while disorganised notes in randomly titled computer files, or strewn around the house, are useless. You need to keep a good index to your materials, so that you can instantly put your hands on the relevant notes for a future assignment or project. (You may be able to use elements of your learning file to help with navigation.)

Efficient reading skills and good note taking should increase the benefit from your studies many times over, a benefit that should be apparent in your assessment grades, and even more so in your subsequent career. The time needed to develop these skills is, therefore, potentially an excellent investment.

SUMMARY

- Reading efficiency and effectiveness can both normally be improved through practise.
- The decision as to what to read is important and requires you to be clear about your objectives, as well as knowing what is available.
- There are several sources of help, including lecturers, librarians and colleagues.
- Different reading speeds are appropriate for different purposes, ranging from rapid scanning to slowly working through materials.

- It is important to read critically, questioning arguments and the evidence on which they are based, as well as the additional value contributed by the author's text.
- Mapping the arguments put forward can be a useful approach when evaluating an author's claims.
- Note-taking skills are important and should reflect your purpose(s) in reading.
- Notes can usefully index other materials on the same subject, for a similar purpose or relating to a similar context.
- It is essential that your notes show clearly when something is a direct copy, and its source. Otherwise you may be end up facing disciplinary procedures for plagiarism.
- The references for what you read will be an invaluable and enduring resource. You need to store these carefully. It is well worth learning how to use bibliographic software to make this easy, and to ensure that you can access your references after graduation.

Further information

Butterworth, J. and Thwaites, G. (2005) *Thinking Skills*, Cambridge University Press. This is helpful on argument and on use of data.

Buzan, T. (2010a) *The Speed Reading Book*, Harlow: Pearson.

Buzan, T. (2010b) *Use Your Head*, Harlow: Pearson.

Buzan, T. and Griffiths, C. (2014) *Mind Maps for Business: Using the Ultimate Thinking Tool to Revolutionise How You Think* (2nd edn), Pearson.

Answers to Exercise 7.1

1. False. Poor readers fixate more than once on some words. This backtracking is a major cause of slowness and you should have remembered this.
2. True, provided it is specially designed practice.
3. False. The text claimed three to six fixations per line, although it may well be true, as later text will show. You may have *known* that the statement was really true, but it is often necessary to note what is actually in a piece of writing, even if it conflicts with what you think is true.
4. False. You would still need to practise the techniques at intervals to maintain high speeds.
5. False. Rapid reading may increase comprehension. This was another very important point.
6. True.

8

DIAGRAMS AND OTHER VISUALS

Learning outcomes

By the end of this chapter you should:

- appreciate the importance of diagrams and other visuals as an aid to understanding managerial problems

- understand how visual images can aid communication

- be using a variety of appropriate diagrams for a range of purposes

- be able to interpret critically any diagrams you encounter.

Introduction

Problematic organisational situations typically involve a large number of interrelated factors. These relationships will be at least as significant as the factors themselves. It is extremely difficult to represent such situations without the use of diagrams. (By a diagram I mean any representation where position on the page is significant and lines, and possibly symbols, are used to add further meaning.) Words are inadequate for describing multi-directional relationships. The pattern of those relationships is unlikely to emerge without the use of diagrams.

Diagramming is an essential skill for both study and employment. As you saw in the last chapter, diagrams can be used to sort out an argument, your own or one you read, and can form a useful part of the *notes* you take in lectures or on things you read. Diagrams can be used to help you *clarify your thinking*, whether you are analysing case studies or other problem situations or planning an essay. They are an invaluable *aid to communicating* your thoughts to others involved in the analysis, and your findings when you write an assignment or report on your work. Thus, they help your learning and can improve your grades.

Diagramming skills are highly transferable. You can use the techniques in project groups at work to aid problem solving and to improve the effectiveness of your written reports and oral presentations for your organisation. (You have already encountered a range of diagrams in this book, drawn in the interests of communication.) The visual presentation of numerical information in graphs and charts is dealt with in Chapter 11. This chapter concentrates on other forms of diagramming for clarifying, exploring and communicating key aspects of a situation, whether for study purposes or at work.

➤ Ch 11

The importance of visual representations

Visual representations of information or ideas have been around for some 40,000 years, as evidenced by a variety of cave paintings. The ease of producing computer graphics has led to their proliferation in the media, reports, and marketing materials and just about everywhere you turn. Search 'infographics' to see the wealth of material and software available.

Graphics speak to a different part of our brain from prose. They can create powerful emotional reactions through colour, words and pictures. It is important to be aware of this when 'reading' a graphic in order to be over-influenced by the way it is presented, and less than critical of its content. It is important to be critical because there are many ways in which diagrams can mislead us (discussed further in Chapter 11). These factors are equally important when using graphics to communicate.

There are several key reasons for using visual representation to supplement mere words. The first concerns the nature of what is being presented, and the ability to present – and absorb – more information graphically than text or the spoken word allows. Speech, especially when written, is characteristically linear. Word follows word in a one-dimensional sequence. When relationships are as important as elements (typical of most management situations) diagrams work better than words. Imagine trying to describe how to get across London on the Underground without access to the tube map. And most managerial situations are much more complex than the Underground.

Diagrams can use colour, symbols, pictures and spatial relationships to supplement words. (On the Underground map, colour is significant, as is the relationship of one station to another, though distance between them on the map is not significant.) Patterns between elements can be shown readily and understood on a diagram, though there must be an agreed convention between 'artist' and reader as to the meaning of patterns. Similarly, symbols will increase the information that can be usefully conveyed only if the meaning of those symbols is agreed beforehand.

Diagrams, whether bar or pie charts, maps, or those using other agreed conventions, can be an invaluable aid to communication, whether incorporated in reports or used as visual aids to a spoken presentation. Like other models, by simplifying they can give prominence to particular aspects you choose to highlight. Extraneous material is omitted. From a large table of figures, for example, it is possible to draw a bar chart of monthly or annual values for a key variable, so that any trend is readily apparent. This would be totally obscured by all the other figures on the table if the raw data were presented. An organisation chart can clearly represent reporting relationships which might be equally hard to understand if described in words alone, particularly if the organisation is structured on matrix lines. In all these cases, diagrams are being used to communicate something that has been worked out beforehand, and is understood by the sender, in such a way as to be easily understood by the receiver.

Simplifying situations

Diagrams can play an even more powerful role when you are trying to understand a situation or an argument, and to work out by yourself or in a group the complexity of relationships contained therein. They can be invaluable when you are trying to follow a lecture or article, helping you to tease out its structure, as well as providing a form of notes that will be useful for future reference or revision.

In case study analysis, where complexity can be considerable, diagrams can help you explore how situations arose, and represent the complex dynamic of interrelationships that will need to be taken into consideration if the likely results of a possible solution are to be anticipated. In planning a report or a presentation, you can use diagrams to clarify and structure what you want to say. When planning your dissertation you will find you can use diagrams to move from an original vague idea of your intended topic to a detailed series of questions to be answered and approaches to answering them. Other diagrams such as networks and planning charts will help you schedule your research activities and monitor progress. In group work, the construction of joint diagrams can be an excellent way of developing a shared understanding of the situation and of highlighting differences in perception between the various group members.

Diagrams can be used in a divergent or a convergent fashion. They can be used to tease out all the possible strands of a single theme or topic, as in dissertation planning, or when representing your first ideas of what *might* be relevant in a report you are going to write. Or they can be used in a more convergent way, to impose structure on something where

➤ Chs 10, 13, 14, 16

> **Diagrams can:**
> - clarify perceptions
> - develop understanding
> - emphasise relationships
> - simplify situations
> - show different perspectives
> - aid communication
> - make information more memorable.

structure is not immediately apparent, such as your first ideas on a topic, or a somewhat convoluted argument in an article.

Presentation

Diagrams can be rough working tools, in which case the rougher the better. It is much easier to discard a rough diagram as your thoughts move on than a carefully drawn artistic one. It is easier to see a rough diagram as the tentative model that it inevitably is rather than the 'true picture' a beautiful graphic can suggest.

So do not be inhibited from using diagrams because you doubt your artistic skills. When you are using diagrams for analysis, artistic skills can be a positive disadvantage, discouraging modification. Diagrams are such powerful analytical tools precisely *because* they can be regarded as tentative, disposable models. Your diagrams are a way of making explicit your current perceptions and of making it easier thereby to examine those perceptions and improve them by experimenting with variations. So the inartistic are at a considerable advantage when using diagrams for analysis. If you *are* an artist and using diagrams to help develop your thinking, you should resist the temptation to make them too beautiful!

There will, of course, be occasions when a polished finished product is called for. When you are using your diagrams for communication, you will want them to be as clear and attractive as possible. If you are writing or presenting a report to the Board, or finalising your dissertation, high-quality graphics can contribute considerably to the overall impression of the quality of your work. But the ease of using computer graphics means that clear thinking about what you want to convey is far more important than artistic skills.

Even when you are seeking to impress, it is important to remember that your aim is to give a clear and fair representation of your argument or evidence. I have had many heated discussions with graphic designers who have 'beautified' diagrams I have produced for use in texts. Their versions were indeed more attractive and professional looking than mine but, by making things symmetrical that were not intended to be, or changing the diagram so that it no longer followed an accepted convention, they had reduced the diagram's clarity and/or altered its meaning. Computer graphics present almost irresistible temptations to elaborate and beautify. Focus on using only those features that will help you convey your message accurately and in a way that your audience will find easy to understand and remember. Unnecessary detail may obscure the big picture – something

➤ Ch 14   that diagrams can most powerfully convey.

Symbols and conventions

Symbols and conventions about the meaning of symbols and how to combine them are an important part of good graphics. Symbols and conventions can be seen as a 'language' – they are the words and grammar of a particular type of diagram. An example of a convention for the London Underground map (or maps for other metros) is that stations on a line will be shown in the right order, but that the distance between them on the map does not relate to actual distance. If your reader is familiar with the convention, all that is needed is to say what convention you are using and stick to it resolutely. If no suitable convention exists, then devise one, give a clear key as to what arrows or other symbols mean in your diagrams and stick to your usage so that your reader can become familiar with it.

As an enthusiastic walker, I can just about manage to navigate using a map. I have come to 'read' it almost intuitively so that, if the hills and woods ahead don't look quite what I was expecting from the map, I start to feel uneasy and pay more attention. But imagine how impossible this would be if each map used different symbols. With a key to symbols on each map, you *could* use them. But the process would be much more laborious than with the standard convention, which allows you to become familiar with the symbols used when walking in one area and to understand them at a glance when you go elsewhere, whether to the Lake District or Land's End (or equivalent parts of the country in which you are walking).

As well as increasing the amount of information that can be communicated easily, conventions serve a further purpose for the diagrammer. In drawing a diagram, you are trying to produce a useful model of a situation. Models are characterised by being simplifications of a situation and by being capable, normally, of manipulation. The simplification is where the increase in your own understanding may first arise. The situation is almost always very complex. By using a particular diagramming convention, say one that focuses on causal links, or one that looks at flows within the situation, you are being forced into a particular kind of simplification.

It may be difficult to represent the situation in just this way and you may be tempted to take liberties with the convention. But the discipline of keeping within the rules can generate a creative tension between your understanding of the situation and the needs of the diagramming convention. This may in fact advance your understanding in a way that using the convention less rigorously would not. If you find, therefore, that the conventions described here are frustrating, stick with them despite this.

It is worth remembering that every way of seeing is a way – or indeed a multitude of ways – of *not* seeing. This is as true of diagrams as of anything. But by drawing a *series* of diagrams from different perspectives, and looking at different aspects, you can gradually accumulate understanding. If a series of conventional diagrams is not enough, you can always draw additional diagrams to a less rigorous convention. In this way you should gain full benefit from the diagrams in terms of increased understanding, as well as generating diagrams readily understood by others familiar with the convention. If you are not used to thinking spatially and doubt your drawing skills, you may need to persevere for a while before you find diagrams indispensable. But one day you will find yourself reaching for paper and pencil when you are talking to someone, or trying to sort out a problem at work, and it will seem natural to use diagrams to improve your assignments.

The magic management box

By far the most common 'diagram' you will encounter is the two-by-two matrix, as shown in Figure 8.1. The heading above refers to the fact that many authors (and particularly students writing assignments) seem to think that producing such a box is the answer to everything. Think of some catchy labels and then decide which cell your example fits and you feel you have made progress.

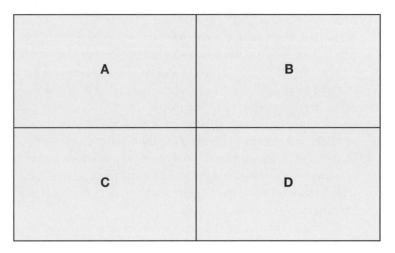

Figure 8.1 The classic box

If you are familiar with drawing graphs in maths, you will know that it is conventional to have 'zero' at the bottom left-hand corner, with numbers increasing as you go up the vertical axis for one value, and/or right along the horizontal one.

Such 'boxes' are derived from the idea of a graph, but with two interesting variations. First, rather than having a numbered scale on each axis they simply split dimensions into 'high' and 'low' or some other two-way categorisation. Second, there seems no obvious convention for deciding on the direction of the scales.

Consider two commonly used frameworks, familiar to most management students. The first is the Boston Consulting Group Matrix, or Boston Box, which you are almost certain to encounter on any introductory marketing course. This classifies a firm's products according to market growth and relative market share. As you would expect, market growth, the vertical dimension, has 'low' in the lower row, and 'high' in the higher row.

However, the horizontal dimension is not as you would expect. The left-hand column is high relative market share and the right-hand one is low. Thus products in cell A have a high share of a high growth market (they are labelled 'stArs'); those in B have a low share of a high growth market ('proBlem children'). Those in C have a high share of a low growth market ('Cash Cows'), while those in D have low share of a low growth market ('Dogs'). The mnemonic capitals and underlining may help you remember for exams.

The Boston Group suggested that an organisation needed to look at its products, drawing each as a circle that lay within the matrix. The circle need not be in the centre of the cell and its size could represent the value of sales of that product. From this it would be possible to think about current profitability, cash flows and likely future prospects. Dogs, for example, have few prospects, so should be discontinued when their contribution ceases to cover overheads, or they have other value. The matrix helped them explain this point to clients.

Another classic framework you may encounter when studying organisations relates to culture. It classifies organisational environments according to the degree of risk they present and the speed of feedback they provide (Deal and Kennedy, 1982) and suggests appropriate cultures for each box. Again, this reverses the horizontal axis. Thus, if risk is the vertical dimension, it goes from low to high, and if speed of feedback is the horizontal, it goes from quick to slow. A (quick feedback, high risk) needs what they call a 'tough guy /macho' culture, B (slow feedback, high risk) is called 'bet-your-company' where decisions *have* to be right, C (low risk, quick feedback) produces a 'work hard/play hard' culture, while D (low risk, slow feedback, characteristic of bureaucracies) is called a 'process' culture.

Activity 8.1

Label the dimensions on Figure 8.1 for a Boston Matrix and label the cells appropriately. Label the dimensions on Figure 8.2, and the cells, to construct Deal and Kennedy's culture matrix. Think about how you would position your own organisation's products (or those of an organisation you know well) on the first and its culture on the second.

It is obvious that the world is unlikely to split neatly into four discrete boxes. Markets can grow at many different rates. You might have 1 per cent or 49 per cent of a market, or any other percentage. Where do you draw the line? Sometimes, this complication is ignored and things are 'put in boxes' and everything in that box is treated according to the resulting label. But often it makes sense to locate positions anywhere on the grid to reflect just how high or how low on a dimension it is. Two-by-two box Elements are located at different points within a box to indicate their relative positions on the two axes. Either way, management writers have found this simple device, together with suitably attention-catching labels, a convenient way of communicating important points about complex ideas, and students find them a useful way of remembering the points.

When using 'magic boxes', always remember that such figures are no more than a particular way of modelling a limited aspect of reality – one way of mapping a far more

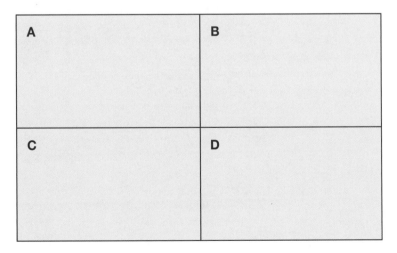

Figure 8.2 Deal and Kennedy model (blank – to be completed)

complex territory. Treat them with caution. But look for what they *can* communicate, as well as what they do not.

Brain patterns or mind maps

A highly versatile diagramming technique in the 'helping you to think' category, and one that is invaluable for note-taking, is that of mind-mapping – the brain patterns described by Tony and Barry Buzan (2010). Variants of this form of diagram appear in a variety of contexts, variously described as mind maps, spray diagrams, relevance trees and fishbone diagrams.

In constructing a mind map (the catchiest general title), you normally start in the *centre* of the page with a word or phrase indicating your main idea or central theme and then branch out, with each sub-theme taking a separate branch. These branches divide further into sub-sub-themes. Software is readily available to make it easy to draw mind maps on a PC.

Figure 8.3 shows a Buzan-type mind map for the possible uses of diagrams as described in this chapter. (Figure 7.3 was also an example of a mind map.) You can often 'illustrate' your diagram with small sketches to make it more useful/memorable. Colour may help to distinguish different types of element, too. The Buzans highlight the following advantages for this type of diagram over linear note-taking:

➤ Ch 7

- the central idea is more clearly defined;

- position indicates relative importance – items near the centre are more significant than those nearer the periphery

- proximity and connections show links between key concepts

- recall and review will, in consequence, be more rapid and more effective

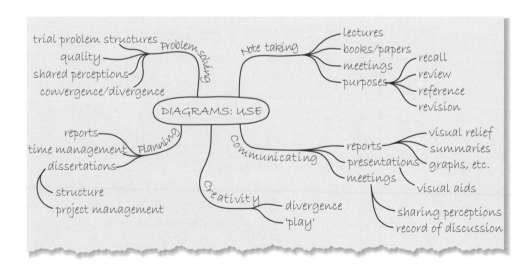

Figure 8.3 Mind map showing uses of diagrams

- the structure allows for easy addition of new information
- patterns will differ from each other, making them easier to remember
- when using the patterns creatively (divergent use), the open-ended nature of the pattern helps the brain make new connections.

The above list comprises a convincing argument for the use of such diagrams in note taking, although(if taking notes in a lecture, it may help to supplement your mind map with more narrative notes, perhaps using one page for diagrams, the facing page for narrative.) Mind maps can be just as powerful when you are planning an assignment or essay question.

An equally important use of diagrams is to clarify your thinking about a complex situation or topic. When doing this it is normally helpful to start with simple diagrams preferably with few limiting conventions. This keeps your thinking 'free' as you are starting to grapple with the problem situation. Once you have a clearer idea of the full range of potentially important factors, you can choose diagrams that focus more narrowly on specific aspects of the situation. To focus too early may lead you to ignore a whole range of relevant factors simply because they do not feature on the form of diagram you have chosen to use.

Mind maps are useful for clarifying your thinking in a variety of contexts, from early analysis of a problem situation to generating a thesis topic. Because of their deliberately divergent form, they can lead you out from a central idea into a variety of subsidiary ideas that you might not otherwise have thought of and, at the same time, can form the basis of the structure of anything you might write on the topic.

An alternative format, with many of the same advantages as mind maps, is the relevance tree. Relevance trees were developed primarily for research and development management (Jantsch, 1967) but are almost as widely applicable as mind maps, to which they are functionally equivalent. Figure 8.4 gives an example of a relevance tree for the early stages of a research project.

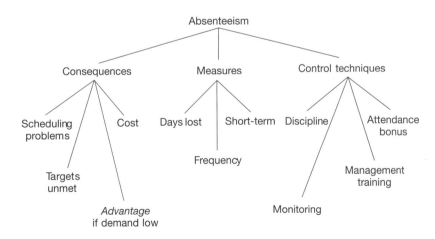

Figure 8.4 Relevance tree for the early stages of a research project

8

DIAGRAMS AND OTHER VISUALS

The main advantage of the relevance tree format is that you avoid the 'budgie syndrome' incurred by having to tilt your head at every conceivable angle to read the various twigs. Disadvantages are that the width of the page will rapidly limit the number of 'twigs' possible and that the more formal, less playful, appearance is less likely to stimulate creativity.

The fishbone diagrams widely used in the Six Sigma approach to quality and project management are similar in many ways to mind maps, but are drawn with parallel twigs and are, therefore, tidier than mind maps. Their purpose is also rather different. They are used to support a logical consideration of all the theoretically possible causes of quality problems. Each major branch represents a class of potential causes. Again, the tidiness places constraints on the branching that is possible and makes it harder to add to the diagram, thus reducing its usefulness for creative purposes. However, since it is primarily a rational tool, this may not matter. Figure 8.5 shows a diagram of this kind.

As the Buzans emphasise, 'messy-looking' diagrams are a positive advantage at the note-taking or thought-clarification stage. They can be quickly 'tidied up' into something fairly respectable once you have done the thinking. If you *are* using them as a note-taking device, this is worth doing: it is hard to sort out a lecture structure while listening to it and you will probably have needed to modify your diagram somewhat as you went along. Drawing a tidy version will have two benefits. First, the tidying-up process will consolidate your learning. Second, you will find the tidier version easier to use for reference or revision.

Even in their tidy form, such diagrams are best seen as primarily for your own consumption – an audience may not appreciate them. Once your ideas have become clearer

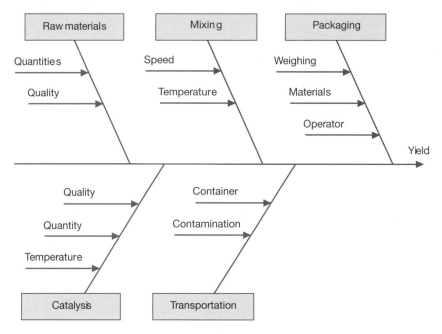

Figure 8.5 Ishikawa-type 'fishbone' diagram used in quality analysis

through drawing the diagram, most of the information can usually be translated into the major and minor headings of a report.

The Buzans do make one interesting suggestion about possible public use of this kind of diagram. In planning or problem-solving meetings points are often lost and the chair may have difficulty in keeping discussion to the point. If the person organising the meeting uses the mind map structure as a basis for running the meeting, such problems may be avoided. They suggest providing a board showing the central theme and perhaps two sub-themes for the meeting. As each member concludes a point, he or she is asked to summarise it and show how it fits onto the map on the board. This ensures that all contributions are recorded in a structured way, keeps speakers more to the point, means that a shared perception of the structure of the discussion is built up, and allows participants to have a copy of the resulting pattern to take away as a record of the meeting. Magnetic write-on shapes, or (cheaper) Post-it® notes, allow structure to be revised as the meeting develops. Conferencing systems often allow participants' PC screens to be used in a similar fashion during 'virtual' meetings.

You might like to experiment with this approach during group work on your course. Once convinced that the method works, and once you feel comfortable operating in this way, you might try it with colleagues. Remember, though, that you should gain participants' agreement to this method of working *before* the meeting, rather than spring it upon them when they arrive.

Relationship diagrams

Mind maps are useful in the early stages of your thinking about a topic. Another useful technique in the early stages of analysis is the relationship diagram. Because this, too, has few limiting conventions it is helpful while your thinking needs to stay loose. Relationship diagrams differ from mind maps in that they do not require you to start with the main idea. This can be a considerable advantage if you are not yet sure which *is* the central theme (e.g. when you first meet a case study).

The convention for a relationship diagram is to use 'words', sometimes enclosed in blobs, to denote relevant factors in a situation and 'lines' to indicate that there is some sort of relationship between them. It is as simple as that. But, by constructing such a diagram, it is possible to identify key groupings of factors, which may help you to go on and draw a mind map, a systems map or other appropriate diagram.

There are some practical considerations. Aim to minimise the crossing of lines. If not, you may end up with something that resembles a children's puzzle and is very difficult to 'read'. Do a first version without worrying about this and then draw a second version that is rearranged so that lines are clearer (some diagramming software will do this rearrangement for you). Usually crossing is minimized if closely interrelated factors are close together.

It may help to distinguish strong from weak relationships, perhaps by use of thicker lines for the former. Other than this, there are few rules, apart from the general one applying to all diagrams that, once complexity reaches such a point that clarity is lost, it

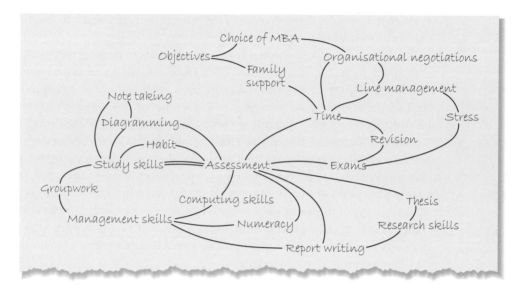

Figure 8.6 Relationship diagram drawn in the early stages of handbook planning

is worth thinking about drawing more than one diagram, rather than trying to cram too much on to a single one. Figure 8.6 shows an example of a relationship diagram drawn in the early stages of planning this book. It convinced me that my intended simple structure would not accommodate the complexity of interrelationships between the topics to be covered and that something slightly messier would be needed.

Rich pictures

➤ **Ch 6**   Systems thinking was introduced in Chapter 6 as a way of looking at complex situations using the metaphor of a biological organisation. This means looking at all (or parts) of a situation as if it were some sort of system, with all the features that a biological system would have – a set of parts, related in some way, achieving some sort of output, and operating within an environment.

Peter Checkland (1981) was an influential systems thinker who developed a *soft systems methodology* for addressing complex problems involving people. To help capture potentially relevant aspects of a situation when starting to explore the problem, he devised a graphic and amusing form of relationship diagram. This he called a 'rich picture'. It supplements the words and lines of the basic relationship diagram with cartoon-like pictorial symbols to show both the nature of the things the words represent and the relationships the lines indicate. This type of diagram is suited particularly to group work during the early stages of investigating a problem. Using large sheets of paper, such as flipcharts or wall boards, everyone can join in drawing the diagram and there is usually much discussion of the relevance of possible items and relationships. There is no fixed convention as to symbols, though crossed swords are often used to

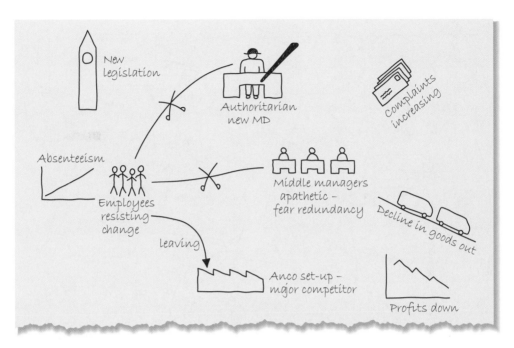

Figure 8.7 Start of rich picture constructed in the early stages of case study analysis

indicate conflict, ££s for money and sketch graphs to indicate trends. Stick men abound, with bowler hats for the managers, cloth caps for the workers. Beyond that, part of the fun is devising the symbols. Figure 8.7 shows a rich picture drawn in the early stages of a case study analysis.

Whether or not your syllabus includes a course on systems, and you learn how to use the other stages in Checkland's approach, rich pictures have many advantages. They can be a great aid to individual analysis (I know one student who, at the planning stage of his project, lined his downstairs loo with flipchart paper, laid out some pens and added to his rich picture on each visit). Drawing rich pictures in a group is even better. The pictorial element encourages participation and creativity and is *fun*. It allows you to share perceptions and develop a much fuller and more complex set of potentially important factors than either a written description or a simple relationship diagram would permit. While you may later choose to disregard some of these factors, it is always easier to narrow down than to broaden your base once you are halfway through. In general, breadth at the outset will be an advantage, though selectivity will be necessary as your analysis proceeds.

As with mind maps, rich pictures are best seen as 'for authors' eyes only'. You will risk being seen as eccentric, or worse, if you include them in a report addressed to those unfamiliar with the method, although the growth of infographics, some of which look much like rich pictures, has made them more acceptable. Figure 8.8 shows a splendid example of a rich picture successfully included in an MBA dissertation. If you have the personal presence you *may* be able to use rich pictures successfully face to face. Indeed, because

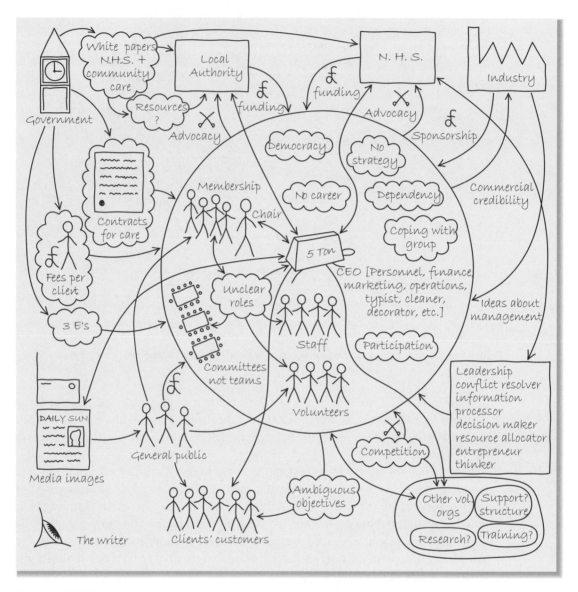

Figure 8.8 Rich picture used in a successful MBA thesis (with thanks to C. Bolton and de Montfort University)

rich pictures have so many strengths, and because they are easy to explain and use, you usually will find that you can introduce the concept to a group that has never used them before, without any need for expert guidance.

Even if you love drawing rich pictures there will still be many occasions when simple mind maps will be invaluable. Try using both when you are faced with any complex situation, at work or on your course, individually or in a group, and reflect on their relative merits.

Systems maps

In Checkland's methodology, rich pictures are a first stage in trying to identify relevant systems. Systems maps are a means of representing these. You cannot expect to gain full benefit from systems maps unless you have been exposed to basic systems concepts but, since many management courses include systems teaching, and since students find these diagrams far more difficult than the simplicity of the convention warrants, they are included here. Skip them if you do not need to use them now: you can come back to this section if they turn out to be necessary later.

Systems maps are a variant of the Venn diagrams now taught as part of primary school maths. Venn diagrams are blob diagrams where the blobs represent classes of things, so that where they overlap it shows that items are members of both sets concerned and, when one blob is totally contained within another, all members of the first set are also members of the second. Figure 8.9 shows an example. Think about what might be represented by the overlap in this case.

Although systems maps look like Venn diagrams, the convention is slightly, but significantly, different. In a systems map a blob represents a *system*, i.e. a group of components that have, in some sense, a group existence. Components in a system are interrelated to such an extent that, if a component were to leave the system, both component and system would be altered in some way. Thus, a battery full of chickens would be a system if all the parts that contributed to chicken production, such as food supplies, temperature regulation etc., were included. The mass of chickens might be seen as a component of that system, though not as a system themselves, as they do not by themselves constitute a viable unit. This is in contrast to a Venn diagram, where chickens might well constitute a class of objects deserving of a blob to themselves. (You might have white and brown blobs within this, or male and female, for example, and all might be a subset of the category 'farm animals'.)

On a systems map, any elements grouped within a blob should be a system. They could be the system you are looking at, or a subsystem of it, i.e. something that could itself be regarded as a system if the level of analysis changed, but in this case is contained within the system you are choosing to explore. The line around the blob is the system boundary, a rather more complex concept than a physical or geographical boundary. It is better thought of as a rule for deciding on inclusion, and could have a number of dimensions.

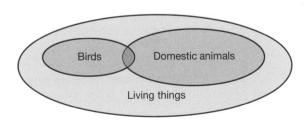

Figure 8.9 A simple Venn diagram

Figure 8.10 shows an example of a simple systems map drawn at the stage of planning a move into distance education for a business studies department. Below the first simple map (a), there is an elaboration of this (b), showing what the author felt would be needed for successful delivery of such education.

Points to note about these diagrams include:

1. As just described, they are *not* simple Venn diagrams. Many students asked to draw a map would have shown staff, buildings, students, etc. as components. Indeed, they would not be wrong; at one level this is important information. But if we look at the *system structure*, particularly subsystems and the relationships between them, a much more enlightening picture emerges. It is all too easy to draw a systems map of an

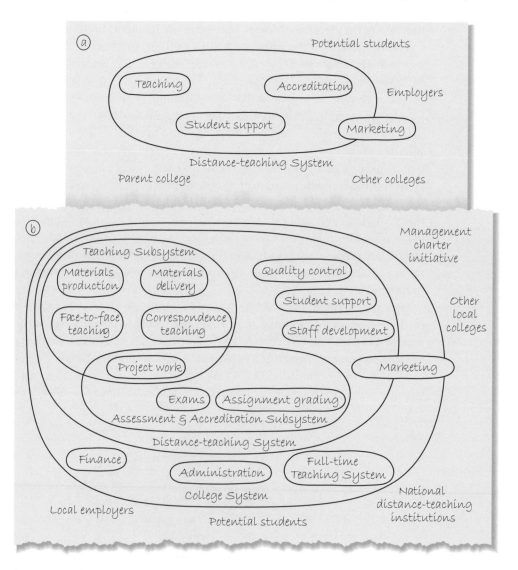

Figure 8.10 Systems maps: (a) Simple map for a distance-teaching system; (b) a more complex systems map

organisation showing every sort of employee, for example in the above case to show lecturers, administrators, students and so on, as components. But this is unlikely to add to the author's or the reader's understanding of how that organisation functions. Indeed, it may show *less* than an organisation chart. It is the effort of *imposing* a new structure, in terms of functional systems and subsystems, systems to *do* various necessary things, that aids conceptual development.

The question 'does it *do* something?' (and if so, what?) is perhaps the strongest test of whether something should be regarded as a system. Indeed, the system title should reflect what it is that the system does, and should be clearly indicated on the diagram. In deciding whether or not to include a particular component, the acid test should be 'will this system do what its title suggests without the inclusion of this component?'

2. A simple diagram usually communicates far better than a complex one. While you may wish to go far beyond even the level of complexity in the second diagram for your own purposes, for communication you should always aim to keep your diagrams as simple as possible. If complexity is essential, start with a simple diagram first, showing the basic structure, following this with more elaborate versions.

3. Overlaps are used sparingly, as they reduce clarity. Whereas on a Venn diagram you *should* overlap in the case of shared membership of sets, on a systems map there is no such compulsion. In the example given, in the case of project and assignment work, learning and assessment functions may conflict, so it is important to highlight this. Also, the fact that marketing of the courses is under the control of the wider college system is important. But the relationships between student support and teaching and assessment, or quality control and staff development, do not need to be indicated by overlaps. Because these are all shown as system components, they are, by definition, interrelated and overlaps do not need to be used to emphasise such relationships.

> **Systems maps should include:**
>
> - system boundary
> - any subsystems
> - other elements
> - factors in the environment
> - system and subsystem title(s)
> - a diagram title.

4. Anything that the system cannot control, but which can influence it and therefore needs to be taken into consideration in planning, is shown in the system *environment*, i.e. outside the boundary of the system, but still there. (If you take a stakeholder rather than purely shareholder perspective, the environment also includes anyone influenced by the system.) It is not necessary to draw a further line around the environment unless your target system can be seen as a subsystem of a relevant wider system. If so, it can usefully be shown as totally contained within the wider system. But if this is not the case, a boundary around environmental factors would be misleading as they would not themselves constitute the system it would imply.

Multiple-cause (and other causal) diagrams

All the diagram types so far described are representations of things and of the relationships between them. But when you are analysing a problem situation you usually want to understand *events* and why they happened. Multiple-cause diagrams are a powerful tool

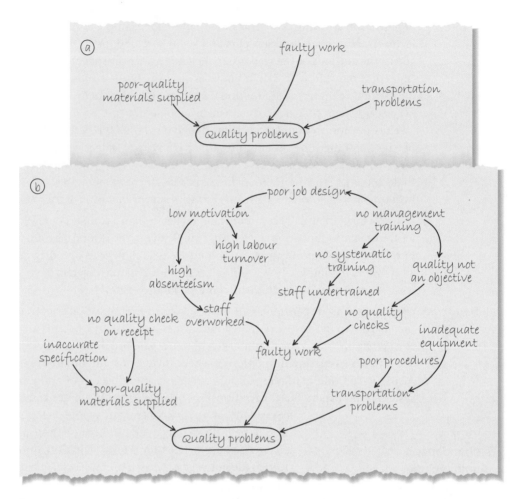

Figure 8.11 Multiple-cause diagram showing factors leading to quality problems in an organisation

for this. In drawing a multiple-cause diagram, you use phrases and arrows. Starting with the event you wish to understand, you move backwards, looking at factors contributing to that event, factors contributing to these factors, and so on. Figure 8.11 shows an example of a first analysis of factors contributing to quality problems in an organisation. It is fairly easy to draw such diagrams electronically using no more than ellipses, words and arrows.

Provided that you remember to start with the end event and work *backwards* (and it is surprising how easy it is to forget this simple point), and that you look for contributory *events* or states, not things (in the example it is not management that is the contributory factor, but its untrained state), then you should have no problems. Even weak causal factors may be worth featuring. An arrow leading from A to B need not mean that A *causes* B, merely that it is one of the factors contributing to it.

In a multiple-cause diagram you are deliberately travelling in one direction – back in time from the actual event you are seeking to understand to its contributory factors, and then back to theirs. This needs to be distinguished from the Ishikawa fishbone diagram shown earlier (Figure 8.5) and from other cause and effect diagrams.

Ishikawa diagrams, though showing potential not actual causes, are often called cause and effect diagrams. As noted, they are widely used in quality approaches such as Lean Six Sigma. (This is an approach that joins the Lean manufacturing approach directed towards improving flow and eliminating waste, and Six Sigma, which uses statistical tools to uncover root causes of quality problems as a means to reducing variation. Used together they provide a structured approach to problem solving.)

There are other cause and effect diagrams too, which may look quite like multiple cause diagrams. However, they move both forwards and back in time from the issue that concerns you, looking at future possible effects as well as past contributory factors. This can be useful if you are seeking to justify work on addressing the issue, and if you want to explore likely effects of an intervention. Because they also look back to the causes of the issue, seeking to identify root causes that need to be addressed, you may sometimes find them more useful than a multiple cause diagram. It will depend upon your purpose and upon the degree of complexity that a combined diagram generates. When you are investigating an issue it may be clearer if you focus on multiple *causes*.

Other diagramming techniques

> **Chs 16, 11**

There are many other techniques that you will encounter in your studies if you are not familiar with them already. Various forms of flow charts, algorithms or other engineering diagrams are commonly used. Systems maps may be elaborated into influence diagrams by the addition of arrows from major influences to the things influenced. You will almost certainly be taught the use of networks and bar charts for planning and project control, and Chapter 16 gives an example of their use in theses and dissertations. Chapter 11 shows how diagrams such as histograms and graphs can be used to represent numerical information. This chapter has concentrated on those diagramming types most useful for note taking, the preparation of assignments and general problem solving. Once you become competent in the diagramming types described, you will also find the use of other diagrams easier. It is partly a matter of confidence, partly the development of the habit of looking for patterns and the skill to represent these diagramatically, using space, convention and symbol to advantage. This skill applies to all types of diagram.

Diagramming hazards

> **Ch 7**

Note that many authors use diagrams poorly. A well-presented diagram can look so impressive that you fail to see that it is a logical mess. It is easy to assume that it is your fault if you feel you are missing the point. If this happens, look carefully at the diagram and apply the sort of critical thinking described in the previous chapter. What is it trying to show? What do the symbols represent? Are they being used consistently? Are any links logically sound? Are they based on evidence or merely hypothesised by the author? Is the title appropriate? The diagram may be riddled with shortcomings that obscure its meaning, or even conceal the fact that it is essentially meaningless.

Has the diagram been restricted (or indeed overcomplicated) by the drawing package used? Many diagrams in reports are thus restricted. It is easy to draw tables, or to use the basic drawing facility in Word or charting in Excel (*see* Chapters 3 and 11) or the 'ready-made' diagram shapes offered by the 'Insert' and then 'Diagram' menus. But often insight depends upon a richer or more free-form diagram. Better to scan in something more appropriate, than to be restricted to the ready-made forms.

➤ Chs 3,
11

If you get into the habit of 'critically reading' every diagram you encounter, you will gain more (or justifiably less) from the diagram than if you accept it uncritically. And you will look critically at your own diagrams, thereby developing your diagramming skills.

General diagramming guidelines

● Working diagrams should always be spaced out as much as possible. Drawing by hand may give more freedom than using computer graphics in early stages. Take large sheets of paper and use the whole sheet (a whiteboard is even better). Space will allow easy addition and modification and will make your result much clearer. When using diagrams for communication, you should also avoid cramped diagrams. Again, space will aid clarity.

● Try to avoid mixing types of diagram. Avoid events on a 'thing' diagram such as a systems map, or 'things' on a dynamic event-based diagram like multiple-cause.

● Start with simple diagrams, developing more complex ones from these only if the complexity is necessary. The simpler the diagram, the clearer will be the pattern.

● Always give each diagram a title to say clearly what kind of diagram it is and what it represents, and use a key if necessary.

● Experiment with different versions of diagrams, and different diagram types, to develop your thinking about a situation. Remember, diagrams are models, and their full value is apparent only when you play with them.

● If you are communicating diagrams electronically, remember that the whole diagram needs to be capable of being clearly read from a single screen – a diagram which needs expanding to more than a screen in order to read the words loses almost all its impact.

Activity 8.2

During the next month, each time you encounter a problem situation where the solution is not immediately obvious, try using different diagrams to clarify your thoughts. If possible ask a colleague to 'read' your diagrams back to you, i.e. to translate them back into words. When the words do not match your intent, explore the nature of the

➤

misunderstanding and think about how you could have made your diagrams clearer. Note below, or in your learning log, points learned in the process.

_____

_____

_____

Activity 8.3

Also during the next month, use mind maps when planning reports or presentations, or as a method for taking notes on any presentation you attend or article you read. Again, note any learning points below or in your log.

_____

_____

_____

Exercise 8.1

Identify as many faults as you can with the following diagrams. (Answers are given at the end of the chapter.)

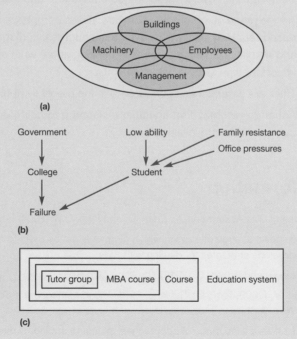

SUMMARY

- Diagrams and other visuals can communicate some forms of information better, and more memorably, than mere words.
- Because they can be non-linear, diagrams are a powerful analytical tool, better suited to representing complexity than text alone.
- Use of position, symbol and conventions allows patterns to be explored and increases the amount of information that can be handled easily.
- Diagrams can thus be a useful supplement to more linear narrative notes.
- Diagrams are also a useful vehicle for communication in team work, helping to develop shared understanding and encourage creativity.
- Carefully chosen diagrams can usefully communicate the results of your thinking to others outside the team. Good diagrams can give an impression of overall quality.
- Diagrams may be convergent or divergent, dynamic or static. It is best to avoid mixing types on a single diagram.
- Mind maps are particularly good for note taking and for exploring the structure of arguments, or developing your own structure.
- Relationship diagrams and rich pictures are also useful for early exploration of problem situations, system maps for slightly later analysis.
- Multiple-cause diagrams are particularly useful for understanding how events or states of affairs came into being.
- Sometimes it may be helpful to add effects to produce a cause and effect diagram.
- A wide range of infographic software allows complex and impressive visuals to be produced relatively easily. However, such impressive diagrams may not be better. Space and simplicity aid clarity. Clarity of thinking about what to communicate may be far more important than skills in using the software.
- Titles are essential and consistency in the use of symbols is important.
- Although you may find an initial resistance to using diagrams, with practice you will come to find them invaluable.

Further information

Bryson, J.M., Ackermann, F., Eden, C. and Finn, C.B. (2004) *Visible Thinking*, John Wiley & Sons.

This shows a range of ways in which diagrams can be used to make sense of situations and develops strategies for dealing with them.

Buzan, T. and Buzan, B. (2010) *The Mind Map Book*, Harlow: Pearson.

Pidd, M. (2009) *Tools for Thinking: Modelling in Management Science* (3rd edn), Chichester: John Wiley & Sons.

This offers a wide range of approaches, including additional diagramming conventions, for dealing with complexity.

http://www.open.edu/openlearn/money-management/management/guide-diagrams?
LKCAMPAIGN=Google_grant_GenericOU&MEDIA=olexplore&gclid=Cj0KEQjww42tBRCO-
sfEiO3DvYMBEiQAHeqMKPm6eefK2Jjy2vKRlARNNnSHictzfK_h_SX0bAurUqAaAmkQ8P8HAQ
(accessed 13.7.15). For a series of excellent podcasts on diagramming, rich pictures, systems
thinking and systems diagrams.

http://www.balancedscorecard.org/Portals/0/PDF/c-ediag.pdf (accessed 13.7.15). For a tutorial
on Ishikawa cause and effect diagrams.

http://www.crisp.se/henrik.kniberg/cause-effect-diagrams.pdf (accessed 13.7.2015). For excellent examples and explanations of cause and effect diagrams more generally in Lean thinking.

https://www.moresteam.com/toolbox/fishbone-diagram.cfm (accessed 10.1.15). For a simple
Ishikawa tutorial.

Answers to Exercise 8.1

(a) Both the system shown (assuming this is a systems map) and the diagram lack titles. This
is a serious omission. There is nothing shown outside the boundary. It is highly unlikely
that a system is not susceptible to influences outside itself. There is no attempt to break
the system down into functional subsystems, i.e. subsystems that *do* something. This is
essentially a list, not a systems diagram. It is unclear what grouping the components within a
boundary add. The overlaps add nothing but confusion.

(b) Words on a multiple-cause diagram should be *events* or *states*. Student, college and
government are *things*, not events. Arrows should mean 'this event contributes to this event'.
Office pressures don't 'cause' a student!

(c) You can see why blobs are preferable to squares. It is much easier for the eye to distinguish
them. Lots of parallel lines are very confusing. Nesting these 'systems' *might* be helpful,
though it is hard to imagine why. It would be more informative, I suspect, to look at fewer
levels of system in more detail.

9
TEAMWORK, LEADERSHIP AND LEARNING

Learning outcomes

By the end of this chapter you should:

- be developing communication skills, particularly talking and listening

- understanding the importance of learning through dialogue

- be exploring ways of learning more effectively in a group

- appreciate the value of diversity in a group

- understand the role of action learning sets

- have assessed your strengths and weaknesses both as team member and leader

- be developing team, influencing and negotiation skills

- be giving constructive evidence-based feedback to group members and learning from feedback received

- recognise and avoid the dangers of group work

- have developed your 'virtual team' skills

- recognise and avoid some of the dangers of 'virtual publication'.

Introduction

Being able to work – and learn – with others is a key management competence. Current organisational structures rely heavily on teamwork. Being able to influence a team is a key leadership skill. Building good working relationships with colleagues at all levels is important. At job interviews you will frequently be asked to demonstrate that you are an effective team member or have exercised leadership.

Your course will probably require you to learn in a group context to develop interactive skills, and because ideas and assumptions need to be challenged by others if you are to become aware of the limitations of your own thinking. These skills have importance far beyond the course. In a fluid organisational context, *learning* with others will enable you to respond to new challenges at work. In particular, action learning is widely used by organisations seeking to respond to changing situations.

Virtual groups are becoming increasingly important as organisational teams often span several continents. With distance learning, online interaction may be the norm, and many face-to-face programmes offer a virtual learning environment (VLE) where students can conveniently work together. While most of the general principles of teamwork apply equally to face-to-face and virtual working, the chapter considers additional factors that are particularly helpful for virtual working.

This chapter looks at the interpersonal skills upon which successful team working depends, the elements that contribute to effective teamwork in general, ways in which you can exercise leadership within a group or team, and skills for learning dialogue. Even if you are reasonably confident in your team-working skills, you should look at the section on dialogue. This may be less familiar to you but is particularly important for the deep learning that will give you the most lasting benefit.

➤ Ch 6

While you can benefit from studying the chapter on your own, you will find it even more helpful if you can find others willing to work on some of the activities with you.

Key communication skills

Effective team working depends on collaboration and coordination. Effective communication between team members is essential for both. You need to be able to express yourself clearly and to listen effectively to what others are saying, so that information is conveyed easily, when needed, and without distortion. But much more than factual information is communicated between team members. Part of what makes teams effective is that working with others meets social and esteem needs, increasing motivation and commitment to the team. Communication therefore also needs to relate to feelings. Members need to know when someone is feeling less than good about some aspect of team work. They then need to be able to communicate in ways that create good rather than bad feelings. Key ways of creating 'good' feelings include paying full attention to what people say and feel, taking it seriously, and showing your appreciation of them as people and of their efforts.

Words are not the only medium for communication. Paralinguistics (non-verbal elements of speech, such as speed, pitch and volume) and body language (posture, gestures and facial expressions) are also important, particularly for conveying feelings and attitudes. Furthermore, it is much easier to lie in words than in these other aspects. For example, Mehrabian (1972) found that when verbal and non-verbal messages were contradictory, only 7 per cent of the 'message' received about feelings and attitudes came from the actual words 38 per cent from the paralinguistics, and 55 per cent from facial expressions. (Note that this was a particular experimental setting and only related to feelings and attitudes – the figures are often misquoted as relating to all communication.) Our inability to lie non-verbally may partly account for the importance of authentic leadership, discussed later.

You may feel that you have been talking and listening all your life and that you have nothing more to learn. You *may* be right. But I know many people who have been *failing* to communicate fully for much of their lives without being aware of their limitations. Good communication is much harder than it sounds! Our assumptions about the world filter what we perceive in the first place and then exert a strong influence on how we interpret whatever it is that we *have* perceived. This makes *genuine* communication – i.e. for a listener to fully understand what it is that a speaker intends to communicate – extremely difficult. If you look back to the examples of reflective writing by MBA students in Chapter 6 you will be able to see how assumptions were interfering to some extent with perception. To make it worse, much of the time a 'listener' is not actually listening at all, but instead is thinking about what to say next and looking for the first opportunity to say it.

An early communication model, developed at the Bell Telephone Labs in the 1940s by Shannon (Weaver and Shannon, 1962) offers a framework for thinking about some of the potential difficulties.

Because they were concerned with telephones, the Bell Labs' engineers were thinking of mechanical encoding and decoding of sound from speech into electrical current variations and vice versa. They also thought in terms of communication as (one-way) transmission of information.

The realisation that the brain is heavily involved in perception has led to a highlighting of the importance of the encoding and decoding processes in communication. Mehrabian usefully drew attention to the importance of seeing the signal as involving not just words but non-verbal elements. But these are not the only factors affecting the

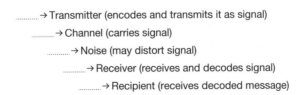

─────→ Transmitter (encodes and transmits it as signal)
   ────────→ Channel (carries signal)
      ─────────→ Noise (may distort signal)
         ──────────→ Receiver (receives and decodes signal)
            ──────────→ Recipient (receives decoded message)

Figure 9.1 Processes involved in communication (Based on Weaver and Shannon, 1964)

decoding, or interpretation of the signal(s) received, and the recipient's response to these. One aspect is context, another (or perhaps part of it) is expectations. If you expect your boss to be negative towards you, a comment genuinely intended as helpful and support-ive may be interpreted as negative and critical.

While there are some practical issues about the signal being heard and understood by your intended recipients, these are relatively simple. Far more difficult is to frame the message in a way that it will be interpreted *as you intend* by the recipient. This requires the sender to understand the assumptions and expectations of the receiver, as well as any limitations (such as language skills and vocabulary) they may have. It also helps to mon-itor their non-verbal signals as you talk, and to modify your message accordingly. This means that communication becomes two-way, even before a listener answers. Your own non-verbal signals are important too: they need to be consistent with your words or they may carry an unintended message.

Looking at communication in this way shows just how complex are the skills involved. You need sensitivity to body language, emotional self-awareness to alert you to times when you may be transmitting inconsistent messages, awareness of others, and an understanding of how they think (this is why dialogue is so important, and discussed later in the chapter). You will also find the following analysis important when you are

➤ Chs 13, 14

writing assignments and speaking in public (Chapters 13 and 14) as both are forms of communication.

What else can the simple model suggest about how to make communication more effective? Consider each element in turn.

Sender

When you are the sender, it is essential to be clear about your own objectives. What mes-sage(s) do you want to convey? Unless *you* are absolutely clear about this, you are unlikely to achieve your objective. Are you aiming to impress, inform and/or influence? Have you included the need to sustain others' commitment and motivation?

Self-awareness is important. Do you tend to make things too involved or to skip over necessary detail? Do you unintentionally antagonise people? Or do you avoid necessary conflict? The more you know about your own characteristics as sender, the more likely you are to be able to achieve your (clarified) objectives. It is worth giving this aspect of your skills serious, and honest, consideration.

Receiver

How well do you understand your listener? What are their objectives and characteris-tics? What expectations might they have of you that you need to take into consideration? What may they not know that you take for granted? How might they be feeling now, and when they receive your message? What clues are they giving you as you speak?

Non-verbals may require particular attention in a multicultural group as there are different 'non-verbal dialects'. Interpersonal distances vary. Standing near enough to someone to touch them and perhaps putting a hand on their arm might seem warm and friendly in one culture, threatening or insulting in another. If you are in a multicultural learning set this is something you can usefully explore – increased understanding can be a great asset when you need to cross cultural boundaries at work.

When you are listening, how attentively are you listening? What assumptions are *you* making about the speaker and their likely message that may be affecting how you interpret it? Becoming aware of your own limitations as a listener will help you listen better, and will help you understand the limitations of those to whom you are speaking.

Message

Once you are clear about *what* you want to communicate you can think about how to make others take it seriously. Body language will be important. If you look confident and speak firmly your message is likely to have more impact than if you are whispering and shrinking away from your listener. Can you add evidence to support your view? Can you convey your appreciation of earlier speakers by endorsing what they say before developing their ideas further?

Transmission medium/channel

When you are talking to someone face to face, you can transmit the full range of non-verbal signals, as well as the words. When working virtually, unless you have a sophisticated system, the signals may be more limited. In a text-only medium you have only the words (and any emoticons you choose to use). The section on virtual groups later in the chapter will consider strategies for overcoming such limitations.

Effective communication thus depends on understanding your own and others' ways of thinking, awareness of the importance of feelings, and sensitivity to context. The necessary focus and concentration on these aspects can be extremely difficult to sustain when you are in the middle of a heated discussion, particularly if you have not paid conscious attention to much more than the words said in the past. But Mehrabian's research suggests that you were unconsciously aware, and by raising this to conscious levels you will be able to become much more effective within groups, and a more effective leader.

It is not surprising that the Chartered Institute of Personnel and Development (CIPD) (2007) Learning and Development Survey found 'communication skills' to be the most frequently mentioned item in employer competency frameworks. By becoming a better communicator, you will become more effective in many aspects of your work. The following activity may help you decide whether you need to spend time addressing these ➤ **Ch 6** highly transferable skills.

Activity 9.1

Answer the following questions as honestly as you can in order to gain a rough indication of your current skill levels. Score each item 1 if it is usually the case, 2 if quite often, 3 if sometimes, 4 if seldom the case and 5 if almost never.

When talking with new people, much of my attention is on planning my
reply rather than really listening to what they are saying _____

People I talk to are rather boring _____

I find it quite difficult to take a full part in any group discussions _____

In a group, I don't feel that my contributions have much impact _____

I get into arguments if people don't see my point of view _____

If people give me negative feedback, I defend myself by explaining why I
acted as I did _____

I focus more on a person's words than their non-verbal signals _____

I have no hesitation in telling people they are bad at something _____

People seem not to hear what I am saying _____

I feel uncomfortable in a social or group work situation _____

I find it hard to create a good impression in an interview _____

I interrupt if something someone says prompts a really good idea _____

Total _____

Note, this is a very crude questionnaire, but it will act as a starting point for thinking about these skills. Few people, if they are strictly honest, will score much above 50. (A very high score might mean you are unaware of your shortcomings.) Above 40 is good, but shows room for improvement. If you have any doubts about your skills in this area, file your current score, and then reassess yourself at the end of the chapter and thereafter at intervals (a version of the questionnaire is available on the companion website), and develop an action plan for developing your skills.

Active listening

Although the focus is often on the sender, communication fails if there is no listening. There are many signals that suggest someone is not really listening to you. They may look around the room while you are talking, forget or misremember what you have said, or interrupt you in mid-sentence with some non-sequitur or something about themselves. Now, be honest with yourself and think about how often you give out these signals yourself! By not listening you are shutting off a potentially valuable message, and, at least as importantly, communicating lack of respect for the speaker.

Activity 9.2

Think of a recent social and/or work situation at which you were present and at which people clearly were not listening to each other. Why do people persist in such non-communication? List as many reasons as you can for the talker continuing to talk and for the listener not to listen, in the situation(s) you have just identified. If you are working through this chapter with others, compare your lists with theirs and discuss any similarities and differences.

You may have listed some or all of the following reasons for the persistent speaker's behaviour. They may:

- want to be seen by others to be talking – to create a good impression;
- fail to realise that the other person is not actually listening;
- enjoy the sound of their own voice;
- believe that the other person finds their words fascinating;
- be working out what they think by talking, even if they are having no effect on the thought processes of the other person;
- wish to stop the other person from saying something;
- talk to avoid an uncomfortable silence.

You may have come up with many of the above, plus a variety of other reasons. Some reasons represent more or less sensible behaviour, such as trying to avoid boredom or exploring your own thoughts and where they lead. Some are defensive, such as preventing the other person from saying something they do not wish to hear. Some are aggressive, such as exerting power over others. Some represent lack of perception. Some have to do with communicating something other than the message contained in the spoken words. If someone is not listening to you, it makes sense to consider why this might be – or even ask them – rather than persist. Possible reasons include:

- lack of interest in the speaker as a person or in what they are saying at the time;
- fears about how to respond getting in the way of listening;
- inability to concentrate;
- inability to understand what is being said, or to perceive the emotions leading to its expression;
- desire *not* to hear because the subject is uncomfortable, unpalatable or challenges strongly held beliefs.

In addition to the above list, there are all the possibilities for 'hearing wrongly' because what is perceived is distorted by assumptions. 'Not listening' and hearing wrongly waste both participants' time and energy, and create negative feelings between you, which

Active listening helps you:

- build relationships
- learn
- develop ideas
- develop colleagues
- work better together.

may make future relationship building difficult. The listener may miss the opportunity to learn something useful, and the speaker's self-esteem may be damaged. In group situations 'not listening' can waste the entire group's time and energies if useful contributions go un-noticed.

In contrast, active and effective listening has the power to benefit individuals, relationships and shared tasks. The first major benefit of being listened to is *satisfaction of our own social needs* – we are social animals with a need to interact with others and to feel valued by them.

A linked benefit has to do with developing *social capital*. (OECD, undated). This idea is closely related to that of *networking;* the greater the number of people with whom you have mutually trusting relationships, the greater the likelihood that you will be able to collaborate with them or exchange information or favours at some future point. Such relationships can greatly increase your success at work. Active listening can help you build your social capital.

Listening skills are essential for effective *information transfer.* We learn a great deal from conversations with other people. This is one of the reasons that networking is so important. The information could include simple facts such as a problem that customers seem to be encountering, or names of useful contacts. But more tenuous information can be just as useful. For example, really listening to someone may give you a better idea of what is important to them and of their potential to take on additional challenges. When you are interviewing you are seeking information from a candidate, so again skilled listening (as well as questioning) is essential.

A fourth category has to do with *task planning and management* for a team. Communication is clearly essential for this, whether at work or in relation to study. For shared tasks the need is obvious. For solitary ones, almost certainly you will still need to communicate – often by talking – to make sure that you understand the task fully and have the resources you need. You may, at some point, need to renegotiate deadlines or resources if circumstances change or objectives turn out to have been unrealistic.

Perhaps *the* most important benefit of good communication concerns *developing ideas*. You can help someone you are coaching or mentoring develop ideas by listening to them. And good listening is a key element in learning or problem solving as a group. While much of this can be done in a solitary fashion, a group has access to a wider range of information and perspectives, and these can stimulate thinking in new ways (particularly if the participants are skilled in dialogue).

Elements of effective listening

To communicate effectively *both* participants need to be skilled listeners. If you are listening actively and effectively you will do the following.

Suspend judgement. Probably the most important element in listening, and usually the most difficult, is keeping an open mind while you are listening. If you have already judged a situation and come to an opinion, you are likely to hear only those things that are consistent with your existing opinion.

To listen better:

- suspend judgement
- concentrate on the speaker
- watch body language
- avoid interruptions
- seek clarification
- acknowledge feelings
- allow silence
- encourage and prompt
- avoid opinions
- don't offer your 'solutions'
- show you value the speaker.

Concentrate on the speaker. You need to focus on what they are saying, and how they are saying it. You need to think critically when listening, just as much as when reading. What is new to you? Is there a logical thread? You need, too, to focus on their body language. Are there inconsistencies in the words, or between words and non-verbals? If something sounds wrong to you, is it because you and the speaker have different basic assumptions? If the speaker is giving 'facts', what is the evidence for these? Similarly, what underlies opinions? What feelings are being expressed?

Show that you value the speaker. Eye contact, smiles and an 'open' posture help (crossed arms or legs convey 'closedness'). Nods and expressions of agreement show your continuing interest. Paraphrasing what the other person has said at key points shows that content has registered with you. 'So what you are saying is . . .' or 'It sounds as if . . .' shows that something has registered and allows you to check that you are receiving the message intended, and may help the speaker to realise just what they *were* saying, and/or its implications.

Avoid interruptions. Sometimes you may be so interested that you cannot control your excitement, but interruptions usually signal 'not listening'.

Seek clarification. If you are not sure what someone means, or if it seems inconsistent with something said earlier, explore why. Use questions such as 'Do you mean . . .?' or 'How does this fit with . . .?' or 'I don't quite understand . . .'

Recognise feelings. These are important. Saying 'I can see how angry this makes you . . .' can convey that you have heard, and accepted, their feelings.

Allow silence. If the speaker is trying to say something difficult, or using talking as a way of developing their thoughts, they may need time to think. It is important not to rush in because you have been dying to say something, or you find silence uncomfortable. Instead, show by your body language that you are comfortable with the silence and allow the person the thinking time they need. (You can usually see that they are indeed thinking, as their eyes will wander round the room rather than looking at you.) A good interviewer will always allow a candidate this thinking time. In a group, try to avoid leaping in as soon as someone stops for breath rather than having come to the end of their intended contribution.

Encourage and prompt. If a speaker appears stuck, a gentle probe such as 'That's really interesting. What happened next?' or 'How did you feel about that?' or 'So what options do you think you have?' may help move their thinking on.

Avoid directing the conversation. If you are trying to learn and perhaps to help the speaker, taking charge of the conversation can suggest that you are more concerned with *your* perspective than the speaker's and will limit what you learn. (In a more formal interview to *your* agenda, you can be more directive. And in a group that is straying from the agreed task it may also be important to summarise or redirect the discussion.)

Avoid expressing your own views. If someone feels that you are making negative judgements, they will soon stop talking. Praising them may direct the course of their thinking to what you want to hear. People have a strong need to be approved. This is particularly likely if the listener has a higher status than the speaker – for example, if you are listening to someone who reports to you at work.

Be wary of suggesting solutions. If the conversation is a joint problem-solving discussion solutions may be helpful – eventually. But first, the problem needs to be explored and fully understood (*see* Figure 9.3).

Show that you value the speaker. One of the results of a 'good' exchange is increased self-esteem. Your active listening itself conveys value, but you can go further by expressing your appreciation of their input in words.

To become a better listener you may need to overturn at least some habits of a lifetime – which is extremely difficult. To make progress you need first to become much more aware of the dimensions of listening and then to start reflecting actively on how well you are listening.

Attentive or 'extreme' listening

There is a variant on active listening that can be useful in a range of situations from resolving conflict to developing your thoughts by 'thinking aloud' while someone listens. It can also give you useful 'listening' practice. This variant is *attentive listening*, and relies on attending very closely to the talker, rather than prompting, clarifying or, in any other way, directing the conversation. At its simplest, the talker talks and the listener listens, all the while looking at, and concentrating fully on, the talker. The listener does nothing but listen. I often call this 'extreme' listening because most people find this extremely difficult to do!

This technique has been developed into a technique for a wide range of applications in organisations (Kline, 1999). You can try it if a friend asks for advice on something – though explain what you are doing and gain their agreement first. You may also like to use it if you cannot reach agreement in a group. Agree to spend six minutes talking in pairs. For the first three minutes one of the pair talks, the other listens without saying anything. Then the roles are reversed for three minutes. People then take turns feeding back to the group any new thoughts prompted by either talking or listening.

Talk and text

Talking skills include simple aspects like being heard and more complex ones relating to saying things in a way that will have the intended effect. Text is both simpler and more difficult. The differences point up some of the challenges of talking. Many talking issues were implicit in the discussion of listening. You can 'send' more effectively if you:

- **ensure that people can hear what you say** – some listeners may not hear if you are too quiet, or fail to understand if you are too quick.
- **ensure that people understand you** – as well as speed (particularly important in mixed language groups) content needs to be clearly organised – unless you are talking to sort out your thinking. If your message is muddled it has little chance of communicating anything. Make sure that you have sorted out just what you want to convey before starting, and use language that your audience will understand.

- **check you are being heard and understood** – watch your listener's reactions carefully for feedback on this, and if it is not what you expect, ask questions to find out why.
- **consider your listener's objectives and likely perspective** – even when conveying straightforward information your message may be misinterpreted if you do not take this into consideration.

Good 'talkers':
- speak clearly
- check listeners' reactions
- meet listeners' needs
- listen.

Listening – and observing body language – is crucial even when you are leading an exchange. Otherwise you will not be able to monitor responses, and adapt accordingly.

Some of your 'talking' will be in virtual meetings (discussed later). If the channel is text-only (emails and/or messages posted in discussion forums) you need to choose your words with extreme care. Text cannot convey non-verbal messages, so misunderstandings are more common, particularly if the reader does not have an open mind about your likely messages.

An added hazard is that it is extremely easy to send a message to a wider audience than you intend, or for one of your recipients to broadcast the message more widely. It can be surprisingly embarrassing to find that perhaps mild criticism or humour about someone has reached that person when you did not intend it. The following guidelines may help you when you are 'speaking' via text only.

Guidelines for effective online communication

- Use a descriptive title for communications – whether email or a posting to a forum. This will allow someone to find the appropriate message when it is one among many.
- Check that you have addressed your message appropriately – including inappropriate addressees wastes their time and creates other problems.
- Avoid saying anything that could give offence if forwarded on to any other person
- Be as personal as you can, thanking people by name where appropriate – creating 'social ease' really helps communication.
- Be concise (but not terse).
- Make clear why you are communicating and what response you want/need.
- Give all the information readers need in order to respond appropriately.
- Make your message self-contained – unless earlier messages are clearly shown in a chain, quote the relevant part of whatever you are responding to.
- Word your message carefully so that points are clear and unambiguous
- Never respond while angry. It is easy to misinterpret text or overreact and start a 'flame war' in which anger rises ever higher. This does not help communication!

Dialogue

Good talking and listening skills are essential for dialogue. In this context *dialogue* does not mean words in a play or film, but indicates a particular kind of talking and listening with the aim of creating new understanding. It was developed as an educational method in ancient Greece (the word comes from the Greek *dia* 'through' and *logos*, 'word, meaning or reason'). Plato's accounts of Socrates' dialogues with various leading figures show how Socrates would use questions to expose and pull apart their assumptions and reasoning. This was not to make them look foolish but to enable them to develop an even better understanding of the subject of the dialogue.

Dialogue is invaluable for collaborative reflection and any form of action learning or action research as well as a useful learning tool for increasing shared understanding. Yankelovich (1999) distinguishes dialogue from other discussion, debate or deliberation. In all four types of communication you will need listening and talking skills. Looking at the specific characteristics of dialogue makes clear the additional skills you will need. These characteristics are shown in Box 9.1.

Dialogue is likely to be challenging. It is not easy to uncover assumptions and even more difficult to change them. They are, after all, part of who you are and you may feel

---

Box 9.1 Characteristics of Dialogue

Dialogue is purposeful

Dialogue is a form of discussion, but not all discussion is dialogue. Dialogue is distinguished by having a purpose, shared by all participants, of increasing mutual learning and understanding and an agreed approach to achieving this goal. This approach involves careful and supportive questioning of each other's ways of thinking.

Dialogue does not involve taking sides

Dialogue is different from a debate in being collaborative rather than confrontational. In a debate you do what you can to strengthen your own position and weaken that of your opponent. You want your position to win. In dialogue all participants want to learn rather than win. So they look for what is valuable in others' contributions as much as for contradictions or questionable assumptions in their own or others' thinking. Learning will come from changing the way some or all participants think, not by convincing others that that they are right.

Dialogue seeks to identify underlying assumptions

The main focus of dialogue is the way participants think, the tacit theory, mental models and assumptions that are contributing to their way of seeing and interpreting the subject of the dialogue. As discussed in Chapter 2, these help thinking most of the time and, indeed, are what make you an 'expert' in something, but they can be a hindrance if they do not fit a particular situation and can inhibit learning.

➤ Ch 2

very uncomfortable to have them questioned! This is why dialogue needs to take place in a supportive context and why it requires specific skills.

The value of diversity in dialogue

In any group diversity is an asset. Different backgrounds, expertise, perspectives and views can create a much broader understanding both of the situation itself and of ways of thinking about it. In dialogue, where you are seeking to uncover limitations in your own thinking, working with people from different backgrounds and cultures is a particular advantage. They are much less likely to share the same 'thinking tools'. Their values and assumptions will be different from yours. By engaging in dialogue with people with very different tacit models and ways of thinking from yours, you can become much more aware of your own ways of thinking. It is exploring the *differences* in perceptions and interpretations between people that make you aware of beliefs and assumptions you may not realise are shaping your thinking.

There will be many more such differences in a diverse group than when members come from similar backgrounds and therefore share similar value and assumptions. So try, wherever possible, to join with as diverse a group as possible for any dialogue aimed at a deeper learning. You will learn more about your own thinking, and increase your mental flexibility, as well as learning more about ways of thinking associated with the cultures represented in your group. Such awareness can be invaluable in a global team.

Skills for dialogue

The active listening skills just described will all be important, particularly the skills of suspending judgement, recognising feelings (which can be a clue to many things of which we are not consciously aware) and showing you value participants. You will need the ability to express yourself reasonably clearly. But you will need more than this.

Activity 9.3

Given the characteristics of dialogue outlined above, think about the skills you will need to learn in this way, and consider the extent to which you practice them in the conversations you usually have.

You may have thought of skills in different categories, but one way of grouping them is to think about skills for creating the right climate, skills for asking helpful questions and listening skills including identifying values, mental models and assumptions.

Creating a suitable climate

Many of these skills will be covered in the section on team working, which follows. It is important to create a sense of shared purpose. Those new to dialogue may take some time to fully grasp its purpose. They will be unused to the rather different process involved, with its emphasis on openness to new ways of thinking. It is particularly important to create a climate that is non-competitive and supportive, so that participants feel supported and comfortable enough to explore the way they and others think without defensiveness.

'Recognising feelings' may need to be more empathic than in normal active listening. Goleman (1998), who has done much to raise the profile of the emotional dimension of management, sees empathy as a key element in what he calls emotional intelligence, defining it as 'awareness of others' feelings needs and concerns' (*op. cit.* p. 27). This awareness will help you perceive and explore subtler emotions and concerns, thus making it possible to start to explore their roots.

➤ Ch 3

Asking helpful questions

It takes considerable skill to ask the sorts of questions that will uncover things in someone's thinking of which they are unaware. This skill will depend on the ability to stand back from your own feelings and views about the situation in order to explore how someone else is thinking to reach their view. Similarly, you need to be willing to let others help you explore your own way of thinking. Thinking of questions that uncover the deeper assumptions, values, mental models and/or tacit theory that may be shaping our thinking is not easy. Values and assumptions may have been developed long ago, influenced by culture and a wide range of experiences. Kline (1999) identified three types of assumptions commonly found when coaching executives:

- assumptions about how the world is;
- assumptions about how the world should be;
- assumptions about the person talking.

Many of the supposed 'facts' about a situation may be assumptions and some 'facts' may not be recognised as relevant. Listening with an open, non-judgemental mind will help you to ask questions which may identify or clarify relevant assumptions.

To summarise, effective dialogue needs more than listening and team work skills. You also need to be skilled in creating a climate in which people feel equals and in which they feel safe. You need to be able to help the group reach shared understanding and agreement about the purpose of the dialogue. Listening with empathy will be important. And you will need to know how to ask the 'powerful' questions that can help people to uncover and question their assumptions. Through all this, empathy and picking up on emotional cues will be important. Skills for dialogue will be particularly important in *action learning*, described in a later section.

Effective teams

A *group* can be any set of people that interact more or less frequently, more or less formally, and with goals that may be unclear to the members. A *team* is usually seen as a particular sort of group – one that has a specific membership and has been formed to achieve specific goals. This team/group distinction is not one that is universally made, and indeed many of the points about team work will apply equally to looser groups, such as a group of students who are asked, during a single class, to discuss a particular case. However, teams that work together over a longer period to carry out an assigned task are more important in a work context, and it is this sort of teamwork that this chapter primarily addresses.

The basic talking and listening skills discussed above form the foundation of effective teamwork. But an effective team also needs all members to understand, agree and be committed to achieving the task for which the group was formed. Members need to feel enabled and motivated to contribute to their full ability and have between them the necessary abilities and other resources to achieve the task. They need to feel comfortable working together and work in an efficient manner to achieve the task. There will be active management of the work undertaken and regular interactions between members. Both task and process management will be important, as will the formation of the group. There will also be hazards to be avoided. I'll look at these issues in turn.

Task and process

Teams can be formed for many purposes. These days teams may seldom meet face to face; indeed, members may be on different continents, linked by video and/or computer conferences. Fortunately, the same basic principles apply to both face-to-face and remote group work, although the latter may need attention to the narrower communication channel.

Activity 9.4

Think about a group that you have belonged to recently, that you enjoyed belonging to and felt was effective, and another that was much less satisfactory. Try to think of at least three ways in which the groups concerned differed and list these below.

'Good' group

_____

_____

_____

_____

'Bad' group

_____

_____

_____

_____

Comment

There could have been many reasons why your identified groups differed. Size might have been a factor, the compatibility of the individuals concerned, the quality of leadership, or clarity of task, any number of different factors. But it is likely that, ultimately, the factors you listed affected you either because they interfered with the group's achievement of its task, or because somehow they stopped the group working well together. Perhaps members were not in sympathy with each other, did not feel valued by the group, or even true members of it, and so did not work together effectively. If so, the process was wrong, with consequent detrimental effect on the task.

For a group to work as a *team*, that is, to achieve synergy and to be in a sense *greater* than the sum of its parts, the social needs of members must be met. (In this context 'social' does not mean pleasant, if aimless, chatter over coffee, but the satisfaction gained from feeling that you are making a contribution to a group task, and that you and your contribution are recognised and valued by other group members.)

Unmet social needs can drive people to act in non-helpful ways. You probably have encountered colleagues at work who insist on talking for a far longer than the value of their contribution warrants. The less the group appreciates their input (and the signals can be crystal clear) the more determined they are to monopolise the floor, taking satisfaction either from the sound of their own voice or from annoying their colleagues. Action in pursuit of one's own needs can disrupt group process. Therefore behaviour that recognises and supports the social and esteem needs of others tends to help group process.

As with any task, the group is likely to need to:

- define the problem;
- clarify and agree objectives;
- generate possible options;
- evaluate options and select one.

The group may sometimes need to go on to:

- implement that option;
- monitor implementation.

Managing the *task* requires that each of the above stages is gone through systematically. The first two stages are, of course, crucial. Unless all members are committed to an agreed set of objectives, they will not function as a team. Nor will they be motivated to progress the task. (Naturally, if the agreed problem definition is *wrong*, effort will be misdirected.)

But it is equally important that the group *process* is managed well. If it is not, motivation is unlikely to be sustained and many members may be unwilling or unable to make their full potential contribution to the task. When working remotely it is easy to forget process issues, but they are even more important when members do not physically meet.

Many classifications of group behaviour have been proposed; doubtless you will encounter several during your studies. The following is not intended as definitive in any way, though it is fairly widely used. Take it as a starting point, if you like, for developing your own classification, if you wish to explore this area thoroughly.

Behaviours seen in groups and teams

Behaviours serving task needs

These are as follows:

- **clarifying objectives** – essential if work is to be effectively directed;
- **seeking information from others** – they may be part of the team because of their knowledge or particular perspective;

- **giving relevant information** – you too may have been included for your information;
- **proposing ideas and actions** – necessary if the team is to have any impact;
- **developing ideas or proposals suggested by others** – vital if synergy is to be achieved;
- **disagreeing** – it is important to express any disagreement you may have, rather than keeping quiet to avoid conflict or because you feel you must be wrong;
- **summarising progress so far** – helpful if discussion is tending to become repetitive and needs to move on, and helpful in giving members a sense of achievement;
- **evaluating progress against objectives** – again gives a sense of achievement and additionally shows what still needs to be achieved;
- **timekeeping** – essential if there is a deadline, but useful in all circumstances;
- **assigning responsibilities for action** – decisions are more likely to result in action if someone is identified as having responsibility for that action;
- **setting up a review mechanism** – it is important to check that implementation is progressing as intended and to take corrective action if not.

Behaviours serving process needs

These are as follows:

- **encouraging members to contribute** – particularly important if some find it difficult to speak in a group;
- **rewarding individual contributions** – praise or agreement will make someone feel good about belonging and wanting to contribute further;
- **checking that you have understood** – it is important to do this before expressing disagreement, as your disagreement may stem from assumptions that are affecting your interpretation of what has been said – indeed, when you understand them you may actually agree with what the person intended;
- **resolving conflicts in a positive way**, without either party feeling rejected – this is helped by valuing disagreement because it serves to highlight important differences in information or interpretation;
- **changing your own position** – it is helpful to be open to different ways of seeing things in the light of discussion and to be prepared to question your own views and alter them if convinced;
- **controlling 'over-contributors'** – it may be necessary to ask some people to put a point aside or let others express their views but, again, this should if possible be done in a positive way;
- **praising team progress** – again, members will feel motivated by realising how they are progressing towards achieving objectives;
- **discouraging unhelpful behaviours** – *see* below.

Behaviours interfering with task or process needs

These are as follows:

- **contributing too much** – or otherwise seeking attention;
- **reacting emotionally** – rather than considering points raised calmly and rationally;
- **defending** one's own position excessively;
- **attacking the position of others by ridicule, or other unreasoned statement** (e.g. 'You always make impractical suggestions') – such attacks are normally directed at the person not their point;
- **interrupting or 'talking over' another group member** – this stops them making their intended contribution;
- **derailing a discussion** by raising a totally different point or even a totally irrelevant red herring when discussion is in full and productive flow;
- **holding private conversations** during the meeting;
- **not listening** – failing to concentrate on others' contributions so that ground has to be covered more than once;
- **using excessive humour** – while some humour can defuse difficult exchanges, too much can interfere with the task;
- **withdrawing** ostentatiously from the group (the pushed-back chair, crossed arms and determined silence . . .) – this can make other members feel uncomfortable.

Try observing some meetings, whether at work or on your course, with these behaviours in mind, recording your observations. The simplest method is merely to chart interactions. In meetings members often address their remarks to individuals, rather than to the whole group. One aspect of process can be recorded by mapping these interactions. Figure 9.2 gives an example. Each arrowhead represents a separate interaction. Arrowheads to the centre mean remarks addressed to the group as a whole.

If you wish to get more sophisticated, you can categorise the behaviours involved and record each instance against the person generating it. There are too many categories in

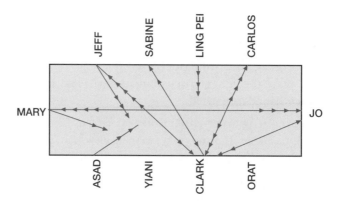

Figure 9.2 One way of recording group interaction

	JEFF	SABINE	LING PEI	ASAD	YIANI	CLARK	JO
Clarifying objectives							✓✓✓✓
Giving/seeking info.						✓✓✓✓✓	
Proposing/developing			✓✓✓	✓✓✓		✓✓✓✓	
Summarising	✓						✓✓✓✓✓
Timekeeping	✓✓✓						✓
Encouraging/rewarding							
Conflict reduction		✓✓✓✓					✓✓✓
Gatekeeping							✓✓✓✓✓
Interrupting/overtaking			✓✓✓✓ ✓✓✓	✓✓✓✓✓✓		✓✓✓✓	
Attack/defence			✓✓	✓✓✓			
Changing the subject					✓✓		
Excessive humour		✓✓				✓✓	
Withdrawal		✓			✓		

Figure 9.3 Example of a simplified form used in recording behaviours in a group

the list above for easy recording. The specimen chart in Figure 9.3 gives an example of a possible recording form (a version is available on the companion **website**). With either approach it is worth looking at those who contribute little and asking whether this level of contribution is appropriate. With the second method you will be able to see whether there is a lot of interrupting by other members, perhaps causing a more diffident member to cease in mid-contribution. You can also see whether the unhelpful behaviours are contributed by a limited number of members, or more widely distributed. If you notice a change in the proportion of unhelpful behaviours at some point, you may also be able to think back and consider what could have caused this.

A simpler recording method focuses on capturing how the task is progressing through the main stages of the problem-solving paradigm, logging the time at which each stage is started and completed. There is unlikely to be a single pass through. Stages are often 'revisited' several times, sometimes effectively, because understanding has deepened, sometimes merely because of poor task management. You may find that some stages are omitted altogether, or undertaken surprisingly late. I have often observed student groups who, after much heat and little progress, ask each other plaintively, often in the last 10 minutes of an exercise, 'What are we really meant to be doing?'

At work you will often see similar failures to agree the task and clarify objectives properly. Early in my career I was at a large meeting to discuss the commissioning of research

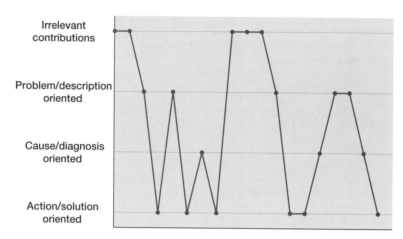

Figure 9.4 Kepner–Tregoe-type chart of discussion flow

by a government department. Some participants were fairly senior civil servants, others more junior specialist advisers. Many proposals were discussed in great depth, and with impressive intellectual skill. After about two hours, frustrated at sitting in silence, I finally summoned up the courage to ask how much money remained in the research budget. Without knowing this, I could not really contribute to the discussion. (I assumed everyone but me already knew.) After some rather embarrassed debate, it emerged that almost none of the budget remained: it had all been committed many months previously!

Kepner and Tregoe (1965) found similar results in their classic work, *The Rational Manager*. They charted the progress of discussions on problems and found patterns similar to that shown in Figure 9.4. You can see how little attention is given to diagnosis and how 'disorderly' is the flow of discussion.

While I hope that your observations will show nothing as dramatic as this, it can be enlightening when you are in a group to see which stages of the approach are habitually rushed, which laboured over, and how many loops indulged in, and to relate this to the quality of decision reached. From your various observations, you should become much more sensitive to the dynamics within groups, and to how these could possibly be altered for the better in order to arrive at better outputs.

Choosing team members

You may find yourself assigned to a group, in which case you will have to work within the constraints imposed by your particular group's composition. But if you do have a choice, or indeed are putting together a team at work, there are several factors you may wish to consider.

Team size

Size can have a powerful influence on effectiveness. The optimum size will depend on the task, but four to eight usually will be the best range. A larger group gives you potentially greater resources of knowledge and experience to draw upon and allows for division of labour on large tasks. However, the compensating drawback is that, the larger the group, the smaller the scope for individual participation. Larger groups can also present logistical problems as it may be difficult to find meeting times convenient for all members. More formal approaches tend to be necessary in order to manage a larger group. Parkinson (1958), in addition to formulating his famous 'law', suggested that maximum inefficiency was reached in a group of 21, as once this size was reached, a group member had to stand to be heard and, once on his feet, found the temptation to make a speech irresistible.

Expertise

The range of expertise contained within the team is important. While you may find it comfortable to work with a group of similar background, and therefore similar perspective, to your own, many tasks demand a range of expertise, as indeed do many tasks at work. Teams with complementary skills tend to be more effective. Aim to include as many different management disciplines as possible and ensure that those essential to the problem are represented.

Shared objectives

This one is really important. Being graded on work you have done as part of a team with different goals and priorities from your own can be deeply frustrating. It is important to realise that people seek management qualifications for many different reasons. When it comes to objectives, and how hard you are prepared to work to achieve them, similarity rather than variety is desirable. If you are highly ambitious and aiming to do as well as possible in the course, you will find it frustrating to be in a group whose main concern is to do the minimum necessary to pass. If you have taken the perfectly valid decision to be in the latter category, you will find a bunch of high-fliers equally unrewarding to work with.

Group type

People tend to prefer to play a limited number of roles within a group. Belbin (1981, 1993) suggested that, for a group to be productive, nine team role types need to be present. Different individuals will be stronger in some roles, weaker in others.

The best teams consist of a mixture of such preferences. It is helpful, therefore, that, as with expertise, you aim for a variety of preferred group types if possible. At the start of your course you are unlikely to know other course members well enough to be aware of their preferred role type in groups and their strengths and weaknesses in this way. You may, however, have the opportunity during your studies to take various psychometric tests in order to become aware of your own characteristics. If so, the results can be helpful. The behaviour categories listed below can, in theory, be performed by any group member, but there will be a strong tendency for people to revert to their preferred roles if they are not concentrating on deliberately adopting less preferred ones.

The types (or roles) Belbin suggested for effective group functioning are:

- **Coordinator.** The coordinator clarifies goals and promotes decision making, is a good communicator and social leader and a good chairperson. Coordinators may, however, be seen as somewhat manipulative and too prone to let others do the work.
- **Plant.** The plant comes up with original ideas, is imaginative and usually very intelligent. But others may see plants as careless of detail and prone to resent criticism.
- **Shaper.** Shapers are task minded and dynamic and stimulate others to act. But they may be impulsive, impatient and intolerant of vagueness.
- **Monitor–evaluator.** These assess the qualities of ideas or proposals, being good at dispassionate, critical analysis. They may, however, be seen as lacking warmth and imagination and have a damping effect on others' enthusiasm.
- **Resource investigators.** These are good at bringing in resources and ideas from outside. They tend to be extroverted and relaxed, but not overly original. The team usually will have to pick up their contributions and run with them, as their enthusiasm wanes rapidly.
- **Team worker.** Such people are very important in holding the team together through focus on the process side. Sensitive, good at listening and at defusing friction, they may be indecisive and too keen to avoid conflict.
- **Implementer.** Their strength is in practical organisation and turning ideas into manageable tasks. They bring method to the team's activities, but may be inflexible, and resist changes to plans.
- **Completer–finisher.** They are good at checking details and chasing deadlines, so are essential for group performance, although they may make themselves unpopular in the process.
- **Specialist.** Specialists provide rare skills and expertise and are focused and self-motivated. But they may see only a narrow segment of the situation and lack communication skills.

Although the above may read like a list of stereotypes, it is based firmly upon Belbin's work with groups within organisations, and his finding that groups with a mix of roles consistently performed better than groups that were more homogeneous (in role terms). Although Belbin's work is still widely used, there are now many other 'typing' products commercially available – these typically have their own psychometric instruments to classify people into a roughly similar set of types.

Thinking in terms of (fairly persistent) personality types may make you feel doomed to failure if you cannot form your team with the 'right' mix. Thinking in terms of behaviours and preferred roles, allows you to see scope for people being willing to take on less preferred roles, and to develop useful behaviours. Observations such as those in Figure 9.3 can help you identify what changes are needed for the team to become more effective.

Team development

It is rare for a team to be effective from the moment of its formation. Members are unsure of each other at first and do not know what will turn out to be acceptable and unacceptable behaviour within the group. How formal will it be? Will disagreement be acceptable? Is everyone going to be far better informed, more confident, more experienced and a great deal more intelligent than they are? Different groups have different 'norms' of acceptable behaviour. And members fit into groups in different ways, playing different roles and having different status, depending upon the circumstances. A popular (because easy to remember?) description of the stages of group formation was formulated by Tuckman in 1965. It suggests that groups go through four stages.

- **Forming.** This is when individuals try to establish their identity within the group. Behaviour is often tentative at this stage and extreme politeness may prevail. A leadership pattern may emerge.

- **Storming.** All the positions established at the earlier stage are now challenged. There may be considerable conflict. Personal agendas emerge. Status battles may ensue. A group can disintegrate at this stage. Alternatively, if the conflict is constructive, it can generate greater cohesion, a realistic commitment to objectives and trust.

- **Norming.** This is when the group develops norms for how it will operate. Acceptable behaviour within the group is established.

- **Performing.** Only when the earlier stages have been passed through is the group in a position to operate effectively.

'Adjourning' is sometimes added as a fifth category to highlight the need for attention to be paid to the way in which a team is disbanded. If members have worked closely together there may be feelings of sadness or dissatisfaction if this stage is ignored.

If members are aware of the need for the earlier stages, they are less likely to be disturbed or discouraged by them than if they expect instant 'performing'. Instead, they will pay attention to managing the group process through the early stages, so that conflicts are used constructively, appropriate norms emerge and the performing stage is reached as painlessly as possible.

The need for a chair

Many groups that have a struggled with an exercise say 'If only we'd had a chair'. The advantage of having an agreed chair is that someone has the *designated responsibility* for achieving progress towards objectives. Members accept that it is the chair's job to manage both task and process issues, and behaviour directed towards achieving this will be accepted by the group. The chair has the *right* to silence an over-verbose member, to push people towards expressing agreement with what seems to be emerging as the group view, to instruct individuals to carry out follow-up work, etc.

With a skilled chair who is good at both task and process issues, a group can be highly effective. Indeed, with a newly formed and temporary group, which will not have time to go through the processes of group formation, a designated chair is essential. This is also the case for most groups larger than about eight and any formally constituted group. However, as with most benefits, there are associated costs. While a good chair can be a tremendous asset, a poor one can be an equally powerful liability. Because it is the *chair's* responsibility to manage the group, members take no responsibility for this themselves. Few chairs are equally good at managing task and process (indeed, you will note that Belbin saw the chair's role as primarily coordination, rather than the combination of many of his roles commonly expected).

Some chairs are singularly poor at *both* aspects. They may lack the necessary interpersonal skills, and/or they use the position to satisfy their own social needs for attention and the exercise of power. I have known chairs who monopolise the meeting, driving their own preferred conclusions through, regardless of the views of other group members. Under such a 'tyrant chair', group members rapidly cease to feel any commitment to the group and see no point in trying to make a contribution. Instead, they gain what little satisfaction they can from criticising the chair behind his or her back, or may cease to attend altogether.

Other chairs are 'willing but weak': they would *like* to help the group to be effective but lack the necessary skills. They may want to control the over-wordy, but be unable to do so. They may not have sufficient grasp of the arguments flying around to be able to summarise effectively. Under such a chair, members will be equally frustrated, if less angry.

In either of the above cases, group members usually see the group's failures as the *chair's* responsibility. They will not see that they have failed to assert their own rights as group members to effective chairmanship. Nor will they recognise their own responsibilities for managing aspects of task or process clearly beyond the reach of the chair.

If a group genuinely chooses a chair because they think the person is capable of filling the role, then problems are likely to be few and those that arise can be discussed openly because the chair knows that she or he has the group's support.

Hardest is the case when a chair is forced upon a group, perhaps by virtue of seniority. This used to be standard practice in the Civil Service and it was clear that chairmanship skills were *not* necessary for promotion. With an imposed chair, group members feel far more inhibited about taking on aspects of the role that the chair cannot handle. Yet, there is no real reason why they should not assume these roles. If done with tact and skill this can be a great relief, both to the chair and to the other group members, and can turn an ineffective group into one that feels it is getting somewhere.

If the chair is self-assumed, the situation may be very difficult to resolve. Members sometimes volunteer to chair because they believe (rightly or wrongly) that they have the necessary skills. More often it is because they are very task-oriented and want to start getting on with the job, rather than wasting time talking about how to tackle it. The highly task-focused person is often weak on process. Sometimes a volunteer chair may simply be an incipient tyrant, with strong needs to dominate and equally strong, though not necessarily right, views on what 'the answer' is. Such a chair will not allow group members to play a role in managing the group, or indeed any role at all other than that of audience.

In such circumstances, group members will have the choice of allowing the chair his or her head, or voicing their unhappiness and expressing the need for a change of style.

In a learning situation, a poor chair need not be a liability. If you know you need to develop your chairing skills, and are open with the group about your limitations, you and they may learn much from your efforts. With their help, and with feedback on your performance, you can learn a lot. By offering your weakness as material for analysis, you can help the whole group to learn from how you handle the role, as well as give them practice in giving feedback. Because you have admitted to your shortcomings before you start and have asked for help, the group will be happy to take some of the responsibility for ensuring that the task is progressed.

Because of the risks associated with vesting all the management roles in one individual, some working groups choose to share roles between members. With a small, long-established team, well into the performing stage, this may be done informally. Provided all members take responsibility for achieving the objectives and contributing to process, this may work very well. Less assured groups, or those with a complex task, may prefer more formal allocation of roles, with individuals agreeing to take the main responsibility for timekeeping, for making sure that everyone has a chance to contribute, or for summarising at intervals or checking against objectives.

If your course involves much group work, or if you join an informal study group, you may be able to experiment with different ways of working, sometimes with a chair, sometimes allocating different roles to members, sometimes trying to be completely informal about it. Eventually you should be able to choose the best approach for any given task and set of members; both will be important considerations.

Practical aspects of team effectiveness

There are some very practical factors that can have a marked influence on how well a team works.

Seating arrangements are critical. Members tend to interact with those with whom they can have eye contact. With a rectangular arrangement they will therefore talk to those opposite, rather than adjacent to them. Circular arrangements are often, therefore, to be preferred (unless you wish to *discourage* interaction between certain members).

Physical comfort can help. If a room is stuffy or cold, or members are hungry or thirsty, the quality of the meeting is likely to suffer. Indeed, chairs have been known to gain agreement to unpopular decisions by making sure that they are low on the agenda and are discussed at 1.20 pm, when the strongest concern is with getting lunch before the canteen closes, rather than fighting a particular decision.

Stamina is limited. Full involvement in teamwork requires intense and sustained concentration. After about two hours, sometimes less, effectiveness is likely to diminish if there is no break for relaxation. It is important, therefore, to have an agreed end time for the meeting and to have a number of interim deadlines so that the business is progressed at a rate that will allow this end time to be adhered to. With practice it will become clear how much can be attempted within a two-hour (or other length) meeting.

Phasing activities to fit a meeting's natural cycle also helps. Just as a group goes through a series of stages over time, any single meeting has a number of identifiable stages, which need to be understood if the meeting is to be fully effective. The first is *nurturing*, making people feel welcome and valued. Offering coffee and encouraging members to talk to each other, having greeted them on arrival, can help this stage. Then there is the *energising* phase, when members gradually get 'up to speed'. It is inappropriate to tackle major tasks in this phase, though fairly routine items on which easy decisions are possible can speed the energising process. *Peak activity* occurs in the next stage, when major work should be undertaken. The final stage is *relaxation*, when the group unwinds and achieves a feeling of completeness, having finished. It is important not to omit this stage, or members will feel slightly dissatisfied and the sense of achievement generated in the earlier stage can be somewhat diminished.

> **Meetings go through stages of:**
>
> - nurturing
> - energising
> - peak activity
> - relaxation.

If you are setting an agenda for a meeting, you should bear in mind the stages highlighted in the margin when doing so. If you are working in a case study syndicate, it can still be helpful to steer the group towards finding small but useful activities that can act as energisers, and trying to manage to include a relaxation phase at the end.

The dangers of group work

Can a team work *too* well? This may seem a silly question, but it is important to be aware of just how powerful an effect a group can have on its members. Being approved of by the group may come to be enormously important, while being rejected by them may be psychologically damaging or, at best, very painful. If the team is firmly agreed on something, members feel that it *must* therefore be true. These aspects of membership lead to some of the potentially unproductive outcomes of teams.

The first such negative outcome is called *groupthink*. The apparent unanimity of the group's view may convince any disagreeing member that they must be mistaken, and even if not, they may not express their view for fear of rejection. Thus the group disregards any external evidence of poor performance, and rejects any member rash enough to suggest a problem – along with their message. Therefore a problem may grow far beyond the point at which disaster could be averted. You can see this in some company Boards who refuse to acknowledge impending failure and in other task groups. If you find yourself as a sole dissenting member on a study project, you may like to ask others whether groupthink might be operating.

> **Beware:**
>
> - groupthink
> - scapegoating.

Similarly, if Board members are aware of the possibility of groupthink, they *may* be better able to resist it, despite the difficulty of this.

Another hazard is *scapegoating*. If a group performs poorly it will seek an individual to act as scapegoat and accept all the blame for the failure. ('Blame the chair' is a mild version of this game, 'blame the tutor' another.) This can be a painful experience for the scapegoat and removes from the group any perceived responsibility for what happened, costing them an important learning opportunity. Valuable learning comes when members reflect on how *the group* and the way it was working contributed to what happened, and what might have been done differently, and better.

Becoming a skilled team member

To work on your personal effectiveness, you need to know your own strengths and weaknesses.

Activity 9.5

Think about your own behaviour in the last two meetings you took part in at work or on your course, either as chair or member. Use the behaviour categories listed previously as a basis for identifying your own strengths and weaknesses in groups, and list these below.

Strengths

_____

_____

_____

Weaknesses

_____

_____

_____

If possible, check your perceptions with those of someone you trust. Ask them to observe you in a meeting soon, and give you feedback on aspects of your behaviour which they feel contributed to the meeting, and aspects which reduced your effectiveness. Indeed, if you are in a group of students who work reasonably well together, members might agree to nominate an observer for each meeting for a while, so that you all get feedback on your behaviour and can support each other in increasing your personal effectiveness, as well as the effectiveness of the group as a whole.

Knowing your strengths and weaknesses helps you to work out ways of improving. Simple changes to the way you phrase your contribution might help. Perhaps you have strengths, for example, in summarising, which you are not exploiting fully.

Many people, whether as chair or as member, are less effective than they might be because they are insufficiently assertive. Either they do not realise the difference between assertiveness and aggression and avoid the former for fear of the latter, or they have never developed assertiveness skills, so the phrases that would help do not come readily to their

➤ Ch 3

tongues. They may, simply, never have thought about their rights in a meeting. If you recognise yourself in this description, and have not already done so, work through the section on assertiveness skills in Chapter 3.

Giving and receiving feedback on effectiveness

Skills in giving and receiving feedback are essential for your own learning and the learning of your fellow students or work colleagues. It is very easy to give feedback in a 'holier than thou' fashion, which carries the message that the observer is infinitely superior to the observed and in possession of secret knowledge of all the observed's faults. As many of us feel vulnerable in social interactions, such feedback can be highly destructive. The group needs an agreement beforehand on how it wants feedback given and a commitment to supporting its members in their efforts to improve in the light of feedback. With such agreement feedback can provide one of the most important developmental aspects of your whole course. Few jobs allow scope for detailed feedback on this important area of performance. This is odd when you consider the enormous potential for organisational damage caused by poorly managed meetings and task groups.

To provide personal feedback that is positive rather than causing psychological damage takes skill and sensitivity. To develop the skill you need to receive feedback on how you give feedback. You may come across as less supportive, and more critical, even more superior than you think.

It is easy to focus review and feedback on what is *not* working. While it is obviously important to identify such things, and to do something about them, it is equally important to look at what *is* working well. Indeed, there are many (particularly in the positive psychology movement) who would argue that you are likely to learn far more by focusing on what is positive. If, at the end of a meeting, for example, you review the progress you have made as a group and highlight achievements, the group will feel 'rewarded' and be motivated to future effort. Members will be more likely to use any behaviours identified as contributing to that success in future. And if there are a few 'areas for improvement', they will find it easier to recognise these if they are starting from a position of feeling good about themselves.

> **Good feedback:**
>
> - focuses on behaviour not person
> - emphasises the good more than the bad
> - is constructive
> - is collegial not superior.

Giving feedback is a skill and you cannot learn it from a book. That is why it is important to obtain feedback on your feedback. The following points should be remembered:

- Feedback is less threatening if it focuses on the behaviour shown, not on the person behaving: 'That remark about . . . might have been interpreted as an attack on . . .', rather than 'You were very aggressive'.

- Feedback should focus on good aspects even more than bad ones. This will reinforce strengths as well as making the recipient feel strong enough to face up to a limited number of weaknesses without becoming instantly defensive.

- Feedback that is given as between equals tends to be more acceptable, especially feedback that you give to fellow students. If you are giving feedback to a subordinate, you may draw on greater experience or knowledge, but it is normally best if the feedback is based clearly on such things, rather than mere position.

At the end of each meeting there should be, in addition to a review of individual effectiveness, a short period devoted to thinking about group effectiveness, which may prove useful in pointing out areas of potential improvement.

Guidelines for effective teams

- Select members with appropriate skills, knowledge and, if possible, a mix of preferred team roles.
- Ensure that all members understand and accept the objectives.
- Pay attention to both task and process.
- Accept that feelings may run high during early 'storming'.
- Value all contributions.
- Review both task progress and group process at regular intervals.
- Reward success.

Leadership and influencing skills

Employers increasingly look for leadership potential or ability when recruiting or considering candidates for promotion. Leadership is often defined as the exercise of influence, rather than authority derived from position. So you do not have to be acting as chair to practise leadership in a group. Taking the lead in a group without a formal chair can develop your confidence. And if you know how to behave so that others will want to follow your lead, it will also help you show leadership in work and other contexts.

A vast amount has been written on leadership but there is still substantial confusion as to what constitutes leadership and how it differs from management. The distinction highlighted earlier is often adopted – that management stems from position and has to do with conformity and control, while leadership comes from other sources and has to do with making people want to follow a particular direction, or make a particular change. However, sometimes management and leadership are used interchangeably, with all senior managers being labelled 'leaders'.

So what skills does leadership demand? Goleman (1998) claims that emotional intelligence (EI) is central to leadership. (Note that, clearly, he is taking 'leaders' to mean senior managers here, but the points are more generally applicable.) He identifies five components of EI at work:

- **Self-awareness** – the ability to recognise your own emotions and drives and their impact on others and to be honest with oneself and others.
- **Self-regulation** – the ability to control impulses and moods, to suspend judgement, to think before acting.

- **Self-motivation** – a passion for the work itself and energy and enthusiasm to pursue goals.

- **Empathy** – the ability to treat people according to *their* emotional reactions (rather than your own).

- **Social skills** – proficiency in managing relationships and building networks.

➤ Chs 1, 6

➤ Ch 10

You should by now be developing most of these competences. Reflective learning (as outlined in Chapter 6) should be increasing your self-awareness and, if you are including reflection on feelings, will also impact upon self-regulation. Your work on study planning and on motivation will help with self-motivation more generally. So too will ongoing emphasis on the need for clarity of objectives. This chapter and the previous one, together with the feedback you manage to gather on your own impact, will help with developing communication and other social skills – indeed, you should be able to see close parallels between Goleman's factors and the characteristics needed for effective talking and listening described earlier.

If you have the emotional sensitivity Goleman describes, you will be well on the way to being able to influence people and make them want to follow your lead. I would argue that understanding their motivation is also important for this and being able to make them feel good about the group task. (The process-oriented group behaviours are a big help here, while being able to listen attentively and/or actively, as appropriate, will help greatly in both one-to-one situations and groups.)

Authentic leadership has been argued as important by a number of writers on leadership, including Cashman (1998) and Avolio and Gardner (2005). This is a combination of the self-awareness that Goleman lists and a willingness to be honest with other group members about your own feelings, possible inadequacies and mistakes. This kind of honesty can help to build trust with other team members. If a leader is not being authentic, members will pick up on inconsistencies between messages at different times, or between words and other signals, and feel uneasy, and unable to trust.

As well as building trusting relationships, honesty about your shortcomings and your worries about being able to do a task well enough, or to meet deadlines, allows the group as a whole to exercise control and modify plans and actions in response to any problems.

But there are other dimensions to leadership too, which concern the task and the environment. In the sorts of groups that you will be part of as a student, using the task behaviours listed earlier will help you to exercise an influence on a group. At work, the other factors which will enhance your influencing ability include relevant expertise, confidence, and the ability to see clearly what needs doing and communicate this to others. As you become more senior, the ability to understand the wider environment, anticipate changes in it, and appreciate their implications will become increasingly important.

➤ Ch 10

Chapter 10 will be particularly relevant here, though of course most of your Master's studies will be directed towards making you good at this.

Activity 9.6

Consider the extent to which you currently influence a team of which you are a member. What are your 'leadership strengths'? List those factors that you think are helping you to exercise leadership – perhaps you are good at making others feel part of the team and wanting to contribute to the task, or good at organising meetings. Make an action plan to become even more effective through these strengths. Look at any possible reasons for your influence being less than it might be. (Feedback from fellow team members can be really useful here.) Make an action plan to develop your skills in these areas too.

Negotiation skills

Authority will enable you to influence people because of your position. Leadership skills allow you to influence them by engaging their motivation for the task. The third way of affecting an outcome is through bargaining.

Negotiation is a process of seeking agreement when there are incompatible objectives and some compromise is needed. For example, in a classic wage negotiation the employers might want to agree a 1per cent increase, and the union might want a 7 per cent increase. The union might, however, be secretly willing to accept an increase as low as 3 per cent, but anything less would be totally unacceptable. The employers might secretly be willing to pay up to 4.5 per cent, but absolutely no more. Each would have their aim and their sticking point or 'no deal' position at which they would walk away from the table. The space for compromise exists between each party's sticking point. The point at which agreement is reached will depend upon the general interpersonal and specific negotiating skills of each party, their attitudes, motivation and preparation.

Figure 9.5 shows the 'space' within which this compromise can be reached.

Sometimes there is no gap – in the wages case the lowest increase the union would accept might be higher than the employers could afford, and thus above their sticking point. In such a case, negotiation is unlikely to produce an agreement and power will ultimately determine the result.

Fisher and Ury (1983) in a classic book on negotiation called this sort of negotiation 'positional bargaining' and suggested it was inefficient. People tended to focus on their own requirements, and to stick stubbornly to their position, without seeking to

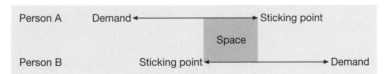

Figure 9.5 'Space' for a negotiated agreement

understand the other party's needs, or look for more creative solutions. Successful negotiations may not give each party everything they want, but they should end up with people feeling that the resolution was fair, and that their needs in the situation were respected. Fisher and Ury suggested a set of principles for successful negotiation. These are relevant to a wide range of negotiations, covering cases far more complex than simple wage bargaining.

To see how this might work in a non-wage situation, imagine that a very good friend has just announced he is getting married in five weeks. This is a weekend when you are scheduled to work. Your new boss says it is not his problem, and refuses to give you the time off. This could end badly – perhaps you take the time off anyway and lose your job without a reference. Both you and your boss would then end up with bigger problems. On the other hand, you might realise that your already highly stressed boss simply cannot face the extra stress of finding someone to change at short notice. If so, you might find someone willing to swap weekends before approaching your boss, and perhaps also offer to cover at Easter, when no-one wants to work. This way both of you would be able to achieve important objectives, an example of a creative approach to what is essentially a shared problem.

The role of informal groups

Not all teams at work will be constituted formally. Informal groups are often ignored, yet may provide valuable support and form the basis for influencing many aspects of the organisation. Well-managed groups can generate powerful learning experiences, as well as being a source of support, information and expertise on your course. If you would like more opportunities for group work than your course offers, consider how you might create your own opportunities.

Distance-learning students have long been exploiting the possibilities of self-organised study groups, and students on executive and full-time programmes are also discovering their value. Some groups operate very formally, with a coordinator, regular meetings, agendas circulated beforehand and minutes afterwards. Others are much less formal, meeting at café, pub or people's homes or online, weekly or monthly, or merely ringing each other for support or encouragement when they feel the need. Even a group of two, you and a 'study-buddy', can enhance your learning.

Both formal and informal groups can be a rich source of ideas, help and moral support. If you have yet to try such a group, it is worth finding one or two others with whom you could meet, either physically or virtually, and experience what such a group can offer.

When several people from the same organisation are enrolled on a course, they can form their own group, perhaps meeting for lunch or after work. Part of some meetings can be devoted to discussing how to apply course ideas to their own organisation. Indeed, this is such a powerful way of 'tailoring' a course to a specific organisation's needs that many employers deliberately arrange such meetings, perhaps with an in-house mentor or trainer as facilitator. (If you can see scope for this, you might suggest it to your organisation. That way you may be able to have your self-help group meetings in working hours!)

The following guidelines for study groups are derived from Open University guidance, but apply to most informal collaborative learning situations.

Guidelines for running study groups

- Nominate a meeting coordinator. This need not be permanent – the role may rotate, but someone needs to take the initiative for the first few meetings.

- Decide where and when to meet, and for how long, and ensure that everyone knows how to get there.

- Decide on an agenda. This need not be formal, but everyone needs to know the purpose of the meeting, what they should bring and what preparation, if any, would be useful beforehand. Possible topics include discussion of the next assignment, comparing members' experience of organisational practice on a particular issue, role plays and so on. Start with fairly simple objectives for your first few meetings.

- Remember the nurturing; arrange a comfortable meeting place, where refreshments are available (not possible for remote meetings).

- Check your objectives at the start of the meeting and review the extent to which they have been met at the end. Consider whether this has implications for the way future meetings will run.

- Bear in mind all the information in this chapter about effective group working.

- Fix your next meeting before you leave.

- Share phone numbers and email addresses so that interactions can go on outside meetings.

Action learning sets

Action learning was developed initially by Revans (1980) in the 1940s, very much in the tradition of philosophical pragmatism. It is now used by many organisations as an aid to organisational learning and increased effectiveness. Action learning is focused on real problems or issues, and uses dialogue to understand these and suggest actions to bring about improvements. It is distinguished from a purely problem-solving approach in that the dialogue that is needed to produce a shared view about future action is itself a mechanism for learning, involving sharing of ideas, testing of assumptions and clarifying of interpretations.

➤ Ch 6   Action learning thus incorporates many of the things discussed above and in Chapter 6 on learning. As with Kolb's approach it is an experimental and iterative process. It can be used on a small scale, or can form the basis for an *action research* initiative.

Action learning is **a group approach**, based on a **shared desire for learning** using **dialogue** to generate **insights** which are then tested through **action**. The **results of action** are brought back to the group for **further discussion**.

Action research progresses by means of a cycle of diagnosis and investigation, action planning, action and evaluation of that action, with a reflective component at each stage. Coghlan and Brannick (2009) suggest that it helps to think of an experiential learning cycle superimposed upon each of these four stages. While it is possible that you might choose to do an action research project for your dissertation, the need to involve organisational colleagues as co-researchers, to go through several cycles and to reflect intensively throughout may make it too challenging for a Master's level project. Furthermore, outcomes are difficult to predict at the outset, making it hard to write a conventional proposal for such research (Cameron and Price, 2009). The rest of this discussion will therefore focus on action learning.

Action learning sets consist of a small set of people who agree to meet regularly for mutual learning focused on real issues and actions taken to address them. A set can be as small as three or as big as seven or eight. Meetings (which might be virtual) focus on a specific issue. Initial dialogue is directed towards gaining a deeper understanding of the issue by sharing perspectives and information and challenging assumptions. Action to address the issue is taken in the light of this and the group then reflects collectively on its impact, seeking to deepen their understanding as a result of the impact of the action, as well as to take further steps to address the issue.

Organisational action learning sets often use an external facilitator to create a climate supportive of the type of dialogue needed for this form of learning, and help the process more generally. Sofo et al. (2010) suggest that this is very much a coaching role, aimed at encouraging dialogue rather than discussion, listening rather than speaking and a deeper creativity in problem solving. They contend that the three most critical elements in action learning are:

- reflective questions
- learning at individual, team and organisational levels
- an action learning coach to ensure that process is smooth, that there is a climate conducive to learning and reflective clarity. (The coach would intervene only when necessary to optimise both learning and progress towards action.)

Sofo et al. (2010) describe an example of action learning at the American Red Cross focused on an issue relating to disaster response. The coach in that case used two sets of questions that you may also find useful. After the first 15 minutes she asked questions along the lines of:

- How are we doing as a group?
- What have we done well so far?
- What could we do better from now on?

She also asked each member to write down what they now believed was the real problem.

During the last 10 minutes of the meeting she asked questions along the lines of:

- What did we do best as a team?
- What leadership skills did we demonstrate?
- How could we apply what we learned during this session to other parts of the American Red Cross?

In an informal action learning set to help you benefit from your course, you are unlikely to have the luxury of a coach or facilitator. But it is an ideal opportunity to take turns at practising this role because the role is important. You will find that it all too easy for your meetings to turn into discussion or debate rather than dialogue. Tasking someone with facilitating the meeting and ensuring that the conditions for dialogue are maintained can keep the group in the 'dialogue domain'.

In an informal action learning set formed of fellow students your real-life issues will all be different so a process of taking turns will be needed, with all or part of a session devoted specifically to one member's issue.

As facilitator your role would include managing the dialogue on this issue by helping people to stay focused on *understanding* the issue rather than leaping to suggested solutions, by noticing clues to assumptions and asking questions about these to help uncover them, and helping the process in any other way that you can. You might also pay attention to the extent to which relevant course theory is being used to help increase understanding and challenge assumptions. If the session is going to include discussion of more than one person's issue, you would also ensure that the time was split fairly. Your role would *not* include playing a part in the discussion: it would overload your brain to do this *and* pay sufficient attention to the process.

Activity 9.7

If you are working while studying, find two or more fellow students willing to experiment with an action learning approach and agree one or two meeting dates. Select a facilitator for the first meeting and agree who will present a real issue that they are facing at work. Run the meeting along the lines outlined above and collectively reflect at the end on its value. If the meeting helped you all to learn, then consider how it might work even better and set another meeting date. Whatever your feelings, reflect individually on the experience in your learning diary, noting implications for future learning at work or on your course.

Virtual teams

Action learning sets or other learning groups can work well online, offering the opportunity to develop virtual team skills. These have become increasingly important with globalisation, and teams spanning several continents. With geographically dispersed teams, high travel costs, too much time, energy and money preclude frequent face-to-face meetings. (Travel also adds greatly to an organisation's carbon footprint.)

Dispersed teams therefore use a wide range of systems to 'meet' virtually. Video conferencing is now widespread and larger organisations may use highly sophisticated telepresence systems that use a variety of techniques (such as matching furniture and wallpaper and life-size images) to trick the mind of participants so it almost feels as if that distant participants are just across the table. In such cases, virtual teams cease to be very different from face-to-face ones. Such systems are, however, expensive, and the kit is normally located in major office locations. However, Skype and Lync offer cheaper/free video conferencing via laptops and audio conferences can be arranged by phone or online. Text-only conferences are now a part of normal life, and your university's VLE is likely to offer a facility for these. (If you are on a distance learning programme you will probably already familiar with virtual classrooms and discussion forums.)

Virtual meetings

Online 'meetings' rely on the same group skills as any other meetings, but some aspects may require more care because of the nature of the medium. You need to understand not only the technical aspects of doing whatever your chosen system allows but also the ways in which you can improve effectiveness by modifying aspects of your behaviour to suit the context.

Because such a wide variety of systems for virtual working exist, you need first to identify the relevant parameters:

- Is the 'meeting' synchronous or asynchronous?
- Is the medium text, audio and/or vision?
- Does the system include features to help with managing process?
- What limitations does the system have?

The effectiveness of any virtual 'meeting' will depend on the general task and process skills of participants, the suitability of the channel and system to the task of the meeting, and the degree to which participants have the skills needed to exploit the strengths of the system they are using and minimise its disadvantages. Table 9.1 shows some of the systems you are likely to encounter, and factors to consider when using them. You will almost certainly have experience with using some of these, so can check your own experience against the table.

Significant factors when choosing a system are cost, convenience and effectiveness. When *using* a system the main challenge is coping with 'channel' limitations, and for asynchronous systems, maintaining momentum. While sophisticated video systems can be treated almost a face-to-face meetings, simpler systems progressively lose body language and paralinguistics.

As *all* the systems in Table 9.1 have the advantage of not needing travel with attendant cost savings, this is not mentioned on the table. Similarly all *real-time* systems require people to be free at the same time, which may present diary problems and be difficult in some time zones.

Table 9.1 Strengths and weaknesses of some commonly used virtual meeting systems.

System and Features	Strengths	Potential Limitations
1. Text based asynchronous forum (such as university conferencing system, chat room, blog or Facebook group).	Cheap. Can allow discussion to be organised into separate 'threads' for different topics. May suit those with stronger written than spoken English. History of contributions is clear and can be stored. Messages can have documents or other files attached, and can include links to relevant websites.	Text is relatively impoverished as a communication channel – it carries the same risks of misunderstanding etc. as email, so a facilitator/moderator who can delete unhelpful posts, and more things to better threads, and summarise at intervals is a good idea. (A blog will normally be 'owned' by someone with this role.)
2. Audio conferences via phone system or Internet.	Relatively cheap. Real time so can conclude meeting quickly, and participants can 'spark off' each other. Conveys 'paralinguistics' so richer than mere words.	People need to be free at same time. May be hard to know who is speaking. System may cut out all save loudest speaker if people talk at once.
3. Simple video conferences e.g. via Skype, or Microsoft's Lync,.	Can be very cheap or free. May allow screen sharing. Allows body language as well as tone of voice and words.	Some systems can be expensive. Low-grade video can be a distraction rather than a help.
4. Virtual classrooms – may include a video component but this makes high bandwidth demands.	Designed to replicate key features of a classroom, allowing the tutor to put up slides, write on whiteboard, set instant tests to check understanding, and divide students into breakout rooms for small group work. Students can put up a hand to indicate they want to talk (or in a small group just say something), can move work on a whiteboard back into main forum for plenary, and 'vote' to show views or understanding. Sessions can be recorded for absentees or revision.	The more complex the system, the more the tutor may need to focus on system aspects. A helper can free the tutor to concentrate on the task and process. Students may need time to become comfortable with the mechanics of the system.
5. Virtual meeting systems designed to make people in different locations feel as if they are all in the same room.	Can simulate a shared location so effectively that people really feel as if they are in the same room, and can hold a meeting as easily as if they were genuinely face to face.	Very expensive! May need technical back-up. Usually linked to specific locations, e.g. head offices on different continents.

Asynchronous systems allow people to contribute at times that are convenient to them (helpful for a time that spans different time zones). Asynchronous systems allow participants to take time to consider all previous contributions in relation to theit own thoughts before responding, so can allow more considered, reflective contributions. The corresponding cost is that asynchronous work needs a period of time, and unless this is strictly limited, the discussion may lose momentum. Asynchronous work is not usually suited to anything needing an urgent response. Again these common features are not shown on the table, but need to be remembered if you are comparing systems.

Even with an asynchronous system it can help to set aside some short periods when people will all try to log on at once and respond quickly to each other – this can be a useful antidote to the more disconnected and 'measured' asynchronous communication.

Working collaboratively on a shared document

You may find virtual meetings extremely useful as a study group, or when working on a group project when it is hard to get together. They can help you agree on how to progress the project, allocate tasks and discuss progress. If you need to produce a shared report, you have a number of options for collaborating. You can do this via email, sharing and commenting on drafts, or by attaching drafts in an online text-based forum, with the message explaining why a draft is as it is, what needs still to be done, and/or explaining edits to a previous draft.

An alternative approach is to set up a wiki. Messages in a forum or blog cannot usually be edited (apart from being deleted by the moderator). A wiki uses software that makes it very easy for collaborative working, as all participants can add to or amend a document that has been posted. It also allows a series of pages to be linked. This allows for rapid production of a document by a group – 'Wiki' comes from the Hawaiian word for fast. Your university will probably provide you with wiki facilities.

With a wiki system people can write and/or change parts of the document until everyone is happy. (The best known user of such software is Wikipedia. The collaborative authorship is what makes academics wary of using Wikipedia as a main source. But its collaborative nature can give it a richness that is valuable when you are starting to explore a topic, provided you use it critically, and as a signpost to more reliable sources.)

As with emails, there are dangers associated with the ease with which electronic documents can be 'published'. While you are working in a shared private area such as that provided by a university VLE, and provided all with access agree not to copy material elsewhere you should be safe. But as soon as you post a document in a public space it becomes a 'publication' and subject to copyright legislation. You would then need permission from the owner of the copyright to include any direct quotes from that material. The same applies to any images you have copied from online sources, unless there was a specific notice with the image giving permission to publish it. Even then, there may be conditions you would need to observe.

Once a document becomes public, with your name attached, it may be found by potential employers. This could be an advantage if it were an excellent piece of work, but you might not want a less than excellent document, or one presenting a view which might be contentious, to be freely available.

Challenges of online collaboration

Despite the availability of a wide range of software for online collaboration, some aspects still present particular challenges. It may be harder for members to be clear on, and committed to, the team objectives, yet this is as important as with face-to-face teams, as is the need to continue to feel involved. You cannot make someone feel better with a smile or tone of voice if using a text-based system.

If you are conferencing in real time while sharing screens, you will need to work hard at ensuring that 'airtime' is shared fairly. Gatekeeping is essential, and even if you do not have a formal chair you will almost certainly need to designate someone to manage the turn-taking element. In an asynchronous conference this is less of a problem, but it is easy for people to feel 'distanced' and withdraw, so particular attention needs to be paid to process and making people feel involved.

When working remotely the early stages of teambuilding may need particular attention. Clarifying objectives, deciding on the roles members will play and agreeing ways of working may take more effort. It is harder to thrash out complex issues and explore areas of disagreement remotely. Nor is it easy to develop the sense of membership and mutual support essential for effective team working.

Ideally virtual teams will go through these early and crucial stages face to face. Once members feel they 'know' each other it is much easier to sustain subsequent progress while working remotely. If this is not possible, care needs to be paid to achieving this online. Familiarity with remote working also makes things easier. If you get the chance to practise your virtual team skills during your course make the most of it. It will develop skills that are highly attractive to many employers, and that may make you a much more effective manager and leader in a global organization.

You are probably already making extensive use of social networking, blogs and chat rooms, but could usefully reflect on how best to harness and adapt your skills, together with your general team skills, to a more task oriented online context. Key challenges are outlined below.

Establishing a sense of membership. If your group will be working together in text-only meetings on a significant project, meet face to face at least once if you can. If this is not possible, then try to create a virtual social space in which you can get to know the other team members. Post a more detailed résumé than you otherwise might, and start the discussion by posting messages that are about yourself and your current concerns. Make clear, too, what you can bring to the discussion by way of knowledge, experience and perspective. If there will be constraints on your availability, it is worth highlighting these, too. For a student group you might want to strengthen your online identity by signing your messages in a memorable way, e.g. 'Finnish Frederika', and adopting a particular font for your messages (though make sure that it is easy to read and will not be a distraction).

To help others feel part of the group, respond to their contributions in a personal way and one that will make them feel comfortable about membership and valued as an individual, e.g. 'Great to have a perspective from Finland, Frederika. There must be some major differences in perspective on [this issue] so your view will be really interesting. I went to Helsinki a couple of years ago – loved the food!'

Establishing rules of engagement (norming). It is important to establish how the group will operate, how much time people might expect to put into the exercise, how often they are expected to log on, how contributions are going to be summarised or otherwise organised, whether there will be different sub-areas for different sub-groups or tasks, whether there is someone who will be taking responsibility for managing such aspects and for archiving or editing contributions.

Agreeing objectives. It is really important that the group agrees what it is trying to achieve and objectives need to be SMART so that progress can be checked. It is worth setting aside a specific time period at the beginning with the aim of ensuring that everyone agrees and has expressed commitment to the objectives.

Planning how to achieve these objectives. Because of the asynchronous nature of interaction in many virtual groups, particular attention needs to be paid to defining specific tasks, allocating responsibilities for any sub-group working and setting clear target dates for sharing of sub-group outputs. Time management is extremely important when working asynchronously. The plan needs to take into account members' availability and frequency of logging on. It is all too easy for substantial time to pass with no progress because key individuals are not contributing quickly enough and frequent milestones can reduce the risk of this.

Contributing effectively. One of the advantages of asynchronous working is that you have time to think before responding. Unfortunately not everyone takes advantage of this. Online discussions that are interspersed with short messages that do not actually make sense because they are too brief, do not make clear what they refer to, or ignore much of what has gone before can be very hard indeed to follow. A message like 'Don't agree with Fred' is unlikely to be helpful if Fred was making three points, two of which build on a series of thoughtful previous messages. The guidelines for effective online communication are as important here as when emailing.

You do not have to display the wisdom of Solomon to make a useful contribution. Nor do you need to be *right*. So don't let this caution prevent you from contributing at all. But do try to ensure that you have read the full argument as it has developed thus far and thought about it before responding. Make it clear what you are responding to – replying to the most recent message in the string, with the same heading, will help (provided you first read the earlier messages in the string). Quote any particular points that you wish to respond to. Make clear the evidence or reasoning that underlies your response. Ensure that you have expressed your thoughts clearly (another advantage over real place meetings is that you can 'say' something, think about it and 'say it differently' before sending). And remember the process issues – 'Fred, I think you've made a really interesting point here, and it has made me think about my own assumption that [. . .] But your suggestion that [. . .] is inevitably the case doesn't fit with my current experience. In my company we [. . .] I'd really like to know from others whether my company is unique in this, or if you have similar experiences.'

I hope that this example shows how you can value a contribution – and its contributor – while still disagreeing with content. It also ends with a question to other team members, which may make it easier for them to join the discussion.

It may be helpful, when appropriate, to give the URL of relevant evidence so that others can check your interpretation. Another useful feature of online working is that you can share materials very easily, so take advantage of this by attaching copies of relevant articles, or of your notes upon them, drafts of reports, or any other resources that may help your colleagues. If file titles are clear, and there is a brief explanation of the reason for an attachment, colleagues can decide whether or not to download it. (Without a clear explanation there is a risk of 'death by information', which can reduce the effectiveness of an online team.)

When you want to start a new point, start a new 'string' with a different (and descriptive) message heading to avoid confusion and to make it easier for a moderator or discussion leader to summarise the messages relevant to a particular point.

Monitoring progress and 'adjusting' effort. It can be depressing to feel you are the only person contributing to a 'discussion'. The group needs to agree how progress will be monitored and non-contributors 'encouraged' to play their part. While it may be fine for a member to read a general discussion and contribute but rarely (this is common in real space groups too), it may seriously reduce the quality of output for collaborative work towards a specific task. Summarising discussion at intervals and assessing how far there is still to go in order to complete the task can be invaluable in saving other people's time and in motivating the group as a whole.

Working in real time. Even if a conference is mainly asynchronous, it can be helpful to set some time windows during which everyone tries to be online at the same time. This can speed up decision taking greatly and is one way of 'energising' a discussion that is not moving along fast. It can be particularly useful when finalising one task and agreeing how best to more forwards to the next.

The following guidelines summarise points of good practice when interacting asynchronously.

Guidelines for asychronous virtual working

- Meet face to face if at all possible, in order to get to know group members and start to build trust.

- If you cannot meet, allow some 'social' time in the conferences for people to feel comfortable together.

- At the same time, post résumés so that people can check who you are if they forget. Include a photo if you can.

- Obtain members' explicit agreement on what is needed to achieve the group task and on the most effective way of operating (times of logging on, deadlines for contributions and so on).

- Break tasks down into constituent parts with deadlines and be absolutely clear who is responsible for doing what.

- Ensure that someone accepts responsibility for reminding people of incipient deadlines.

- Be particularly careful to give feedback in a constructive and supportive way, and pay attention to making people feel their contributions are valued.

- Summarise discussion at regular intervals and check on progress.
- Set aside some short periods when everyone will try to log on at once and respond quickly to each other – this can be a useful antidote to the more disconnected and 'measured' asynchronous communication.

Synchronous virtual working

The immediacy of synchronous working may outweigh the potential disadvantages of time zones and diary coordination. If your system allows a group to talk while sharing screens, 'meetings' can proceed almost as if you were in real space, even without a sophisticated telepresence system – virtual classrooms replicate key features of a lecture theatre, for example. But managing contributions can be a real challenge in less sophisticated systems. Attention needs to be paid to ensuring that 'airtime' is fairly shared: gatekeeping is essential. Even if it seems to create a more stilted 'conversation' it may help to give one member particular responsibility for signalling who is to speak next.

In any form of group work you need a progress (and process) check at regular intervals. To avoid groupthink you need to be brutally honest about how well the group is progressing. If there are problems it may take considerable skill and process management to get back on track and to turn this into a positive learning experience for members. If you can learn how to do this you will be even more valuable as a team member at work and better able to exercise effective leadership.

SUMMARY

- Effective communication and talking and listening skills form a basic building block for working in a team (as well as being important in many other contexts). Such skills are far from universal. They are required to a high level for learning dialogue.
- Particular care is needed when communicating in text only, as non-verbal signals are missing creating scope for unintended negative messages to be received.
- Teams need agreed objectives and to pay attention to both task and process if members are to feel motivated and enabled to contribute fully.
- Teams will work best if they include the necessary range of expertise, and members able to take on the full range of team roles and offer a wide range of perspectives.
- A good chair can manage both task and process issues, but all these need not be the chair's responsibility and not all groups need chairs.
- Groups normally go through stages of 'forming', 'storming' and 'norming' before 'performing', and a single meeting will need to go through a cycle of 'nurturing', 'energising', 'peak performance' and 'relaxation'.
- Important behaviours in teams include clarification, information giving and seeking, proposing, summarising, evaluating, timekeeping and identifying further action for *task*

management and agreeing, encouraging, praising and resolving conflicts for managing *process*.

- Observation and feedback can give valuable insights to members on their individual effectiveness and help the group to consider how to become more effective.

- Key tasks for leaders include identifying requirements, task management, and process management and, in particular, making individuals feel valued and motivated. 'Emotional intelligence' and conceptual skills for problem identification and clarification contribute to effective leadership.

- Groups need to guard against negative features, such as groupthink and scapegoating.

- Action learning sets are a particular form of group that use reflection, dialogue and action to develop understanding and address issues. Such sets need an internal or external facilitator.

- Virtual groups need to pay even more attention to task and process management than face-to-face ones.

Further information

Barker, A. (2002) *How to Manage Meetings*, reissued 2007 as part of the *Sunday Times* 'Creating Success' series.

Belbin, R.M. (2010) *Team Roles at Work (2nd edn)*, Routledge.

Harvard Business Review (2014) *Running Meetings*, HBR Press.

Lepsinger, R. and DeRosa, D. (2010) *Virtual Team Success: A Practical Guide for Working and Leading from a Distance*, Hoboken, NJ: John Wiley & Sons. Useful if you want to know more about virtual working in a job context.

Maginn, M. (2004) *Making Teams Work*, McGraw-Hill.

Schein, E. H. (2013) *Humble Inquiry: The Gentle Art of Asking Instead of Telling*, San Francisco, CA: Berrett-Koehler. Excellent on effective questioning – check out the generous excerpt available at http://www.bkconnection.com/static/Humble_Inquiry_EXCERPT.pdf (accessed 13.1.15).

West, M.A. (2012) *Effective Teamwork*, Blackwell.

9

TEAMWORK, LEADERSHIP AND LEARNING

10
CASE STUDIES, COMPLEX PROBLEMS AND CONSULTANCY

Learning outcomes

By the end of this chapter you should:

- understand the strengths and weaknesses of case studies as a vehicle for learning

- be prepared for the main difficulties encountered in working with cases

- be able to approach case study analysis in a systematic and effective way

- appreciate the importance of the 'diagnosis' stage

- be aware of the need to use a range of models to handle complexity

- appreciate the relevance of case study work to consultancy

- understand how learning from case studies can inform projects and dissertations.

Introduction

The central role of case study analysis in traditional MBA programmes was discussed earlier. First used at the Harvard Business School in 1869, case studies are still widely used in postgraduate management study as vehicles for both learning and assessment. Managers need more than familiarity with a range of concepts, theories, frameworks and techniques. They also need the ability to apply these techniques to the complex and 'messy' situations that make up the stuff of management. Successful application depends upon appreciating the *context* of the application and being able to unravel the complexities in the situation. Case studies, which are representations of organisational situations, provide that context and usually a degree of complexity too.

By working through a number of cases you will become better able to recognise types of problem situation, more skilled at extracting key features in these and better able to work out root causes and possible actions. This process of diagnosis is absolutely crucial and often underemphasised in real life. There are never 'right answers' to organisational problems but, through cases, you may become better able to understand the nature of the problem and avoid the 'obvious', but totally wrong, solution! If you carry out a work-based project at the end of your programme this will be important. Making things worse will not help your career.

➤ Ch 2   You may remember the criticisms of the case study method mentioned in Chapter 2. It was suggested that it contributed to superficiality and a belief in 'solutions' that was positively dangerous for managers. Concerns were also noted that the idea of building a 'vocabulary of solutions' based on past experience might not be as helpful in times of rapid change as it was in more stable times. If you focus on diagnosis and asking productive questions and appreciate that case studies – and any 'solutions' to them – are inevitably simplified, you may avoid these criticisms. If you do, you can gain a lot from thinking about ideas in the context of case studies.

As well as providing the context for you to use concepts from the course, cases offer the opportunity to practise a wide range of transferable skills. These include reading and note taking, diagramming, analysing information, coping with complexity and ambiguity, working in groups, time management and written and oral presentation. They also place more of the responsibility for learning on the student than do lectures or seminars.

Given this, it is not surprising that case study work poses considerable challenges. This chapter is directed at helping you make full use of the learning opportunities that case studies present. It will also help you to do well in case-based assessment and prepare you for some of the issues you will face in a work-based project, on your course, or later as a consultant. It first outlines key features of case-based learning and then offers a method for approaching cases. Although you cannot apply the method in full until you have studied the concepts to use in analysing the case, a quasi-case concerning problems facing a student is available at the companion **website**. This will allow you to practise analysis using concepts introduced in this handbook.

Your course may include a group consultancy project or you may be involved as an internal consultant at work. If so, case study work will have developed invaluable analytical and critical skills, the ability to cope with complexity and a broader understanding of a wide range of organisational contexts. The skills addressed in this chapter are highly transferable.

The place of case studies

Looking at how (and why) cases are used goes a long way to explaining their popularity, as well as some of the criticisms. More importantly, if you understand *why* you are being asked to work in a particular way, you are more likely to benefit from that work.

The case method

In the case method of teaching you are presented with information about an organisational situation, often a mix of written description of the situation, 'exhibits', and some quantitative information. Some cases are very brief – a few pages outlining events in the organisation and what was problematic, together with, say, financial information in the form of tables. Others are more extensive and include 'original' information such as press cuttings, copies of internal memos, survey reports – the possibilities are endless. There may be video or audio material, perhaps including interviews with key protagonists. Some cases run to 60 or 80 pages, others very short. Indeed, you may be given very little, and instead be asked to assemble your own materials about a specified organisation from the wealth of information available online.

> **Case studies:**
>
> - are interesting
> - introduce 'real' situations
> - allow *use* of concepts and techniques
> - give practice in handling complexity
> - develop team and communication skills.

Whatever the nature of the case with which you are presented, you will be required to 'analyse' it. This means working out what seems to be happening and why. You might be asked merely to explain a situation, you might be asked to evaluate actions that have already been taken or to consider possible future actions and compare the likely effectiveness of these. In doing so, you will be expected to use ideas that you have been taught in your courses, thus exploring the usefulness of theories and techniques in different contexts and gaining practice in linking idea to situation.

You may be asked to analyse the case single-handedly (particularly for a written assignment or exam, where your analytical skills and conceptual grasp are being tested). More commonly, the case will act as a focus for group learning, so that you can practise team working and dialogue, as well as case-study-specific skills. In group case analysis typically you will be asked to stand up and present your analysis and conclusions to the rest of the class (whether face to face or in a VLE). The following discussion assumes a

➤ **Ch 14**   group context, but most of it will be relevant to individual case study analysis.

Intended learning

Cases use a different style of learning from other methods, thus adding to the variety of the learning experience. They present a version of 'reality' that gives a sense of access to privileged information and to what may go on in an organisation that students with limited organisational experience may find particularly useful. However, early encounters with cases can be stressful.

When faced with a case study, a typical first reaction is panic – 'Help! What am I supposed to do with this?' followed closely by the feeling of drowning in a sea of so-called information. This 'information' may tell you nothing you really want to know. By now you may be barely speaking to some of your group, who are not pulling their weight, and wanting to inflict serious physical damage on others who seem to be deliberately obstructing your work. The whole thing may seem a total waste of time.

Case study work is useful *precisely because of* its capacity to generate this frustration. If you are studying in order to become more effective as a manager and accelerate your career, rather than merely to acquire letters after your name, you need to develop the relevant skills. Many of these skills will be conceptual ones, and of a fairly high order at that. Others will be interpersonal skills.

Managers are constantly faced with new and complex situations. Many interrelated factors may be involved and colleagues may have different views both on what is happening and on what should happen. Some important factors may be unknown, perhaps unknowable until it is too late. Ready-made answers seldom work. Someone may sound impressive when they say, 'We had this problem at X and solved it by doing Y, so we should do Y,' but this claim needs to be treated critically. The chances are that at X there were key differences: what worked there will not work here. Indeed, they may not really have had 'the same' problem at all.

In many situations it is difficult to know just what the problem *is*. Frequently a situation will be construed as a particular type of problem when deeper investigation identifies something completely different. One of the most valuable skills a manager can have is the ability to diagnose a situation, identifying the underlying factors that are creating symptoms of a problem. To take appropriate action as a manager or consultant faced with a complex, unfamiliar and uncertain problem situation, you need to be able to:

- identify stakeholders in the problem situation and their different perspectives;
- understand the wider context within which the situation is located – how it links to other problems (and other non-problems), what is changing outside the area of immediate concern that may impact upon it, what constraints will be imposed by the context;
- figure out what information you have, or can obtain, that will cast light on the situation, and assess how reliable this information is likely to be (sifting through potentially irrelevant case study information is good practice for this);
- become aware of assumptions you and others may be making about the situation – these may have created false diagnoses or be limiting perceived options;
- Feel comfortable with ambiguities and uncertainties;
- live with these until you genuinely 'make sense of' and understand the problem situation, diagnosing what is 'really' happening and all the contributory factors and causal relationships involved, their inter-relationships, and/or the likely effects of possible actions;
- given this understanding, work out the best course of action;

- check with others and convince anyone who needs to be convinced that this action is indeed appropriate;
- ensure that all involved in this action are committed to it, and enabled to implement it.

Case study work should help you to become better at these aspects of dealing with complexity, both on your course and at work. The next section looks at perhaps the hardest aspect of this, something that will affect most of your Master's studies and your career success. This is overcoming your natural reluctance to deal with complexity and uncertainty.

Dealing with complexity

Case studies are not reality – more of their limitations in this respect shortly. But they are a pretty good halfway house. They are complicated and hard to make sense of. The difficulties they present allow you to develop the conceptual skills that feature in the list above. Of these, that loosely called 'making sense' is perhaps the hardest of all. Working out what the issues are, when faced with a seeming 'mess' of information, feelings, different perspectives and interpretations of 'the problem', presents major challenges. The same is true of working out the causal factors and relationships involved.

Good problem solving depends upon adequate diagnosis. Whether you are following the rational problem solving model or taking a more creative or organic approach, you need to understand what is creating the difficulties experienced. 'Define the problem' may seem an obvious and simple first step, but it can be the hardest thing of all if there is any degree of complexity involved.

Nobody likes complexity and uncertainty. We have developed lots of ways to avoid it by simplifying, making assumptions and moving immediately to solutions. Kepner and Tregoe (1965) identified this tendency when they observed problem-solving groups and found that they acted highly irrationally, leaping to discussing solutions before exploring the nature of the problem. Figure 9.3 showed an example of the sort of discussion they observed.

➤ Ch 9

There are probably good evolutionary reasons for this rush to solution: if a lion is prowling outside, or a flood rushing upon you, deep explorations of causes are unlikely to help you survive. But instant solutions do not make for good decisions when faced with the complexities encountered at work. One of the reasons that consultants sometimes have a bad name is that many of them have a single 'product' or approach that they apply to almost every problem. If they have been selected carefully for relevant expertise, this may not matter. But if the problem for which they are called in is not one to which their stock solution is appropriate, they may cost the company significantly more than their (considerable) fees.

The frustrations you encounter in dealing with the complexities of cases on your course should contribute to making you more effective as a consultant, whether on a course consultancy project or in real life. You will learn the importance of holding back and exploring all the themes in a problem. You will see how applying as wide a range as possible of concepts and theories highlights different aspects of the situation leading to a broader and deeper understanding. Once you start to listen with an open mind, you will realise that team members who disagree with you may do so because they are adopting a different perspective from your own, and making different assumptions. Their perspective may highlight features in the situation you had not appreciated, or cause you to value differently ones you *had* identified. It may also make you aware of some of your own assumptions and how they are affecting your perception and interpretation of factors in the situation. This is why dialogue is so important a skill.

 ➤ Ch 9

Critical application of ideas

Much of the academic content of your course will consist of ideas intended to *help* you make sense of organisational complexities. Case studies give you something to make sense *of*! One skill not explicitly mentioned above is choosing suitable frameworks and ideas to help with this (although it is implicit in 'making sense'). The ideas taught in your course will not in any sense be 'solutions'. But, by using them in a situation, you may find that they lead you to explore important elements, which then suggest what is needed to improve things. This point was nicely made by one of my students who said:

> 'What is different about this course is that all my previous management training has purported to give answers: this one is giving me the questions.'

Different ideas are of more or less use in different situations. You need to be able to work out which will be useful in any particular situation and then to derive benefit from using them. A framework is useful in a particular context if it prompts you to ask questions that generate useful information about the situation and/or helps you to make sense of the answers and other evidence generated. You are likely to be faced with new theories and concepts throughout your life and will need to be able to critically evaluate these, too. Are they logically consistent? Are they based on reasonable evidence? When are they likely to be useful? How? When are they likely to be of little value? Working critically with theories in the context of case studies will equip you to evaluate new ideas throughout your career.

By now you should see the importance of those features of case study work that are most likely to drive you to despair – complexity, uncertainty, information unreliability and/or overload, and 'woolliness' of what you are being asked to do. These are precisely the features of real working life that are most difficult to cope with as a manager. It is these aspects of cases that will help you develop the necessary conceptual skills. A consultancy and/or work based project will allow you to apply them to real issues.

Groups, assumptions and communication

As well as developing your conceptual skills, case study work offers the opportunity to practise the communication, team and negotiation skills you need when dealing with complex problem situations in reality.

Communication skills will be practised in two ways. Obviously you will need to communicate with members of your team while working on the case. Usually there will be a great deal of heated discussion about interpretations and significance of information and the virtue of different courses of action. Your ability to make your points in a way that others can understand, and to argue clearly and coherently, will be important. The skills addressed in the previous chapter will be vital. Furthermore, through presenting your analysis and conclusions, orally and/or in a written report, you will develop the communication skills that you would need if you were to gain approval for a particular proposal. (These skills will be addressed in subsequent chapters.)

➤ **Chs 9, 13, 14**

Some of your fiercest debates are likely to stem from different underlying assumptions and values, whether about the specific case situation, organisations in general or life as a whole. These offer great potential for learning through dialogue, provided you treat them as such and use the relevant skills, resisting the temptation to focus entirely on the task. Such dialogue will produce invaluable learning in its own right, as well as leading to a better task outcome. Without understanding the range of possible perspectives on a situation you may misdiagnose the situation, fail to understand important factors involved and recommend 'solutions' that make things worse rather than better.

➤ **Ch 9**

Contextual awareness

There is one more area of potential learning. The importance of context was stressed above and the context is an important part of any case. Managers often focus on internal aspects of a situation, when the significance of these depends upon things *outside* the organisation. Your analysis of any particular case will develop your understanding of the importance of specific contextual features. By studying a large number of cases you will also develop an appreciation of the range of internal and external contexts that exist and their characteristics. It will not give you the same understanding as you would gain from working in a wide range of different organisations, but that option is not open to everyone and takes time even for those who can do it. Cases are a shortcut to broadening your understanding of the world of business, of the sorts of situations that can be problematic, the kinds of factors likely to be relevant to these and the wide range of possible options that might be considered.

Limitations of cases

The above may have suggested that cases are the perfect route to management learning. It is important, however, to be aware of their very real limitations. The most obvious is that cases are simplifications. They have been filtered by the case author, who chose what to include and what to exclude and how to describe what was included. The greatest challenge to managers in real life often comes from the parts that are 'simplified out' of a case. The messy interactions between people, resistance to change, power and its manifestations, the amount of time needed for communication – the list of such things is endless. But, if you become better at dealing with those aspects that frequently feature in cases, you should have more time and energy to deal with these other, trickier aspects.

10

CASE STUDIES, COMPLEX PROBLEMS AND CONSULTANCY

'Filtering' by the author can also be frustrating because, inevitably, you will find that there is no information on things that you feel are important. You are then forced to base your analysis on assumptions about key aspects. Alternatively, you may be swamped with an oversupply of data (though remember that developing the skill to select relevant information from such a mass is important in real life). Such frustrations, while annoying, can actually enhance your learning, so are not therefore really limitations of the approach.

More worrying is the way in which cases are sometimes taken as a 'model' of how things should be done (and the common practice of giving 'solutions' may enhance this). Such equating of the case with reality is positively dangerous. Case descriptions are biased snapshots of a point in time, or perhaps a period up to such a point. The bias may lead you to a particular interpretation that would not have been valid even in that situation, and may be even less so in seemingly similar situations.

The 'historic' nature of cases adds to the problem of using cases as 'models'. Success may be widely publicised at the time, but may prove transitory. It is fairly tempting to analyse the factors contributing to a favourable situation and assume that you have found a universal recipe for success. But what is successful one year may fail the next. I was once involved in a marketing course where every 'exemplary' firm we filmed for the accompanying video was in serious, and public, trouble, even before the first students saw the video! We had not chosen our companies particularly badly. Clutterbuck (1990) also observed a high failure rate following recognition of an organisation's success. Clutterbuck and Kernaghan's (1990) study of organisational failure included a throw-away comment in the foreword to the effect that, within three years of an earlier study of successful companies (Goldsmith and Clutterbuck 1984), one-third of the companies from which the authors developed their formula for success were in severe difficulty. Any 'answers' or 'recipes' you are tempted to derive from case studies should therefore be treated with extreme caution!

One of the reasons tutors like teaching with cases is that they are often in possession of the 'solution' and can reinforce their credibility with students by offering it to students at the end. But the above shows the dangerous nature of 'solutions' that may be offered. First, even if the solution consists of what the organisation actually decided, you cannot to know if it was the right decision. This is the difficulty with complex situations. There are so many things you do not know. In real life a decision may have rapid disastrous consequences that suggest that the decision was *wrong*. But this does not mean that, given the information and probabilities facing the organisation at the time, it was wrongly taken! Normally the outcomes are more ambiguous: the changed situations may be deemed better by some, acceptable by others and not as good as the original by a few. In such cases it is very difficult to evaluate the decision. Since so many organisational situations are of this kind, it can be argued that a further limitation of case studies is that they can give students the idea that it is appropriate to seek 'the solution' to a messy organisational problem.

There is increasing concern, too, with the idea that academic lecturers have 'the answers' while students, many of whom are practising managers, sometimes at senior levels, are there to learn them. If this perspective is adopted with experienced managers, then the wealth of relevant experience and observations that they could, potentially, contribute to group learning may be lost. If case discussion is seen as a vehicle for such sharing, and for productive dialogue about ways of thinking, it can be a powerful learning experience. If it is seen as a search for 'the answer to the case', learning will be limited.

A final potential limitation of case learning is that not all tutors have the necessary skills to use them effectively. Although students do a lot of the work themselves, and need to accept the responsibility for managing their work and their learning, tutors can make a huge difference. To help students learn from cases, a tutor constantly needs to be able to 'diagnose' progress and give inconspicuous direction, and then to draw all the potential learning points out of student experience. The following method for coping with cases will help you to maximise your learning whatever the degree of support on offer.

Coping with cases

By now it should be clear that analysing any substantial case is likely to present a wide range of challenges. These include:

- rapid reading;
- managing and interpreting large amounts of information;
- living with ambiguity;
- working effectively in a team;
- using abstract ideas to help with analysis and synthesis of something approximating messy reality;
- coping with time pressures;
- presenting information orally and in writing;
- managing your own learning, to a greater or lesser extent.

The links to most of the chapters in this book are fairly obvious. Most will help you in case study work. This chapter looks at two aspects of cases not dealt with elsewhere, the emotional dimension and the problem of where and how to start when faced with a forbiddingly complex situation.

Earlier it was hinted that case study work can generate a high level of negative feelings, often caused by a sense of failure. This may be because you feel you have 'got nowhere' with the case. If so, the 'method' offered shortly should help. Or you may feel you have done less well than other groups, of having 'lost' some kind of contest. Because the emotional dimension of learning is often underrated, you need to be aware of the possibility of such feelings and to understand where they come from. You should then be able to avoid them and instead see failure as a valuable learning opportunity.

Failure and dissatisfaction

Most managers seeking a qualification seem to have a high need to achieve and are also fairly competitive. Many also feel that getting things 'right' constitutes achievement,

10

CASE STUDIES, COMPLEX PROBLEMS AND CONSULTANCY

and giving a more impressive presentation than another group constitutes 'winning'. But note the caution given earlier about whether 'right' answers *can* exist for complex cases and think about why you are working with a case. It is *not* (except perhaps in an examination) to come to a right answer. It *is* to develop all the skills listed earlier: the case is a vehicle for *learning*. And learning requires practice, feedback and reflection.

So, use case studies to experiment with different ways of using course ideas to sort out a case. And remember that your learning comes not only from your own group's experience, but also from seeing what others achieved that perhaps you did not. You need to reflect on what worked and on what didn't work for the group, and on why others may have reached different conclusions.

A sense of failure can get in the way of learning. Defensiveness sets in. 'Scapegoating' can occur, with one group member (or perhaps the tutor) blamed for the 'failure'. This will prevent any learning. Alternatively, the group may indulge in a kind of 'groupthink', deciding that they *did* do brilliantly, despite what people said about their analysis – others just did not understand its merits! It is important that you are alert to the possibility of these responses. And, if you start reacting in these ways, or see the group reacting thus, try to stand back and ask the following questions:

- What were we doing anyway – why does it *matter* to be best?
- How can we learn from what we have done?

If you can address these questions with your group, you will be able to transform your experience of the exercise and also the extent to which you learn from it. What you ini-

➤ Ch 9 tially felt to be a failure can become a very real learning success.

A method for approaching cases

There are three strands to the method for approaching cases. The first strand concerns practical aspects of managing the task and materials facing you. The second is more conceptual and concerns the best way to deal with complex problems. The early, diagnostic stages of analysis are discussed below: they are absolutely vital. Resist any temptation to skimp them and get on to the 'real work'. The real work is in understanding the situation fully enough that recommendations you would not have thought of at the start become obvious! The third strand is that of working effectively in a group. This was dealt with in

➤ Ch 9 Chapter 9, so is not discussed in detail here, but you need to be fully aware of the task and process management aspects of team work and refer to that chapter where necessary.

The stages below are important in almost any group work on a case.

1. Preparation

One practical issue concerns the sheer volume of many cases. If you are issued with a case in advance of the session at which it will be discussed, avoid the temptation to put it to one side and forget it. Plan enough time to familiarise yourself with the case and its contents. Allow time for a solo pass through at least the 'understanding' and 'scanning' stages described below. If you do not do this, your learning, and that of fellow group members, will suffer and they may see you as a passenger and resent this.

2. Understanding the task

One of the first things you need to do is understand what is being asked of you. Are you supposed to adopt a particular perspective or slant your analysis towards a particular 'client'? What sort of outcome is being asked for? Is it an evaluation of something that has happened or recommendations as to what *should* happen? If the latter, how far down the path to a detailed action plan are you expected to go? Are there particular parts of the course you are supposed to draw on, or particular techniques you must use? What form of presentation is asked for? Are there constraints on this – word or time limits, for example? How long do you have to work on the case?

➤ Ch 13   If you are unsure about the meaning of words in the question, consult the glossary at the end of Chapter 13 (Helpfile 13.1). If you are still unsure, or other aspects of the brief are unclear to you, talk to the person who assigned you the case. Misunderstandings about what you are expected to do are in no-one's interests. Once you are working in a group, you need to check whether your understanding of the task matches that of others in the group: it is essential that you reach a shared (and correct) understanding of the task.

3. Scanning the case

Once you know what you are meant to be doing, you need to get a 'feel' for the situation in the case. Scan the case, trying to get a general idea of what it is about and the sort of information with which you are presented. If any questions occur to you at this stage, points 'jump out' as significant, or course concepts seem relevant, jot them down when you get to the end.

➤ Ch 7   Having done this, go through the case slightly more slowly, using a highlighter or taking notes of points that seem important. If there are sets of figures, try to see what they might mean in general terms. (Effective reading techniques, covered in Chapter 7, will be invaluable in case study work.)

4. Description – exploring the situation and identifying themes

As you scan you will inevitably start to impose structure on the situation, judging some things more important than others. But try to do this as little as possible. It is far easier to narrow your scope later than to widen your perspective once you have imposed limits. If you are by now working as a group, you will find rich pictures (*see* Chapter 8) to be really useful in helping you to come to a shared perception of what is going on. (Relationship diagrams do this too, but tend to be less fun, and you will learn more if you are enjoying it.)

➤ Ch 8   Try to identify and represent *everything* that could possibly be relevant to the situation. From these you will be able to construct the web of interrelated issues that cause

Useful pre-diagnostic questions:

- Who thinks there is a problem, and why?
- What is the evidence upon which they are basing this opinion?
- What is (or is not) happening and when and where?
- What related things are not problematic and why not?
- What is the wider context within which the situation exists?
- Who, or what, can influence the problem situation?
- What other stakeholders are there?
- What constraints restrict the 'solution space'?

the situation to be worthy of analysis. Make sure that you look at factors outside the immediate problem context, as these may be significant. If different views emerge, try to find out the reason for differences. Have some people seen things in the case that others have missed? Or do they bring different sets of assumptions to the group? Either may be important.

Once you can agree on a fairly broad representation of the situation, look for 'themes' – linked sets of factors that seem to contribute to one aspect of the situation. For example, there might be one strand to do with perceived poor quality, another to do with changes in competitor behaviour. Within each such strand there might be groups of sub-issues.

At this stage you are looking for a useful way of *describing* the situation. If you are looking at a problem situation, it may help to think of what you are doing as analogous to a lawyer interviewing a client, or a doctor asking a patient, 'What seems to be the trouble?' Note the word 'seems'. You are looking for presenting symptoms. What is actually happening? You have not yet worked out what *is* the problem. Much less are you ready to think about solutions! Beware of falling into that common trap.

Finding out what is happening may involve some fairly deep digging into the information provided. Are there any trends in figures? Graphs may help show these. Avoid digging too deep, however. Until you have moved into the next stage, and worked out *why* things are happening, too much detail can cloud the issue. Furthermore, you may spend time on things that subsequent diag-

➤ Ch 11

nosis shows to be marginal. A degree of moving back and forth between this stage and the next (diagnosis) may be necessary. This is called *iteration*, and you may need to backtrack in this way at any stage. As you find out more information about the problem, your ideas of important factors and relationships will become clearer. You will be able to see where you need to look more deeply to clarify your ideas about what is actually happening. Some of your investigative work may take considerable time and effort. You may need to plan how to divide it between sub-groups and how and when to share their findings.

5. Diagnosis – working out why things are as they are

As noted earlier, proper diagnosis is the real challenge. The diagnosis stage is probably the one to which you should devote most of your effort, though its success will depend upon the adequacy of the previous stages – an unclear task can thwart you, as can an imperfect or overly narrow grasp of the situation or issue.

Now you need to start imposing structure on the mass of information in the case. There are several approaches to structuring, the most important being to use course ideas and frameworks. One useful way to bring these in is to take each of the themes or strands you have identified and brainstorm potentially relevant course concepts. This will provide a useful reference list in the heat of later moments.

Another way of forcing you to look at concepts from an early stage (and of ensuring that you look at all the layers of the problem) is to structure issues vertically, from those concerning individual employees, through the group or section, to the organisation as a whole and, finally, to its wider environment. You can thus produce a matrix of main issues and their related problems and think about relevant concepts for each 'layer'. You may wish to add a final column for implications and/or recommended actions but, if you do so, this should not be filled in until later (a version is available on the companion **website**). (*See* Figure 10.1.)

This approach can be somewhat mechanistic – an apparent attraction if you are faced with a big and messy problem. The danger is that it may lead to a somewhat superficial investigation of causes because of the limitations of space on the matrix and premature categorisation. However, it can act as a useful prompt to look at all these layers. Do not, though, try to fit everything into cells on a tidy matrix like that in Figure 10.1. For example, you may be offered several frameworks for looking at the wider environment – the classic one is 'STEP' (or STEEP, PEST, STEEPV, PESTLE . . .). This highlights key aspects of the environment (sociological, technological, economic, (green) environment, human values and political/legal and perhaps ethical factors) that may be significant. It acts as a useful checklist for exploration, but you would be hard pressed to fit it into a matrix like that above.

	Issues	Concepts	Implications/actions
Individuals			
Groups			
Organisations			
Wider environment			

Figure 10.1 'Layer matrix' for case study analysis

Another classic framework you will almost certainly encounter is Porter's (1980) model of the five forces driving industry competition. This would cause you to look at the threats posed by new entrants to the market and of substitute products, the bargaining power of suppliers and buyers, and the degree of rivalry among existing firms. Again, this might be a useful way of looking at one aspect of a situation, but would be hard to fit into the simple matrix in Figure 10.1.

➤ **Ch 8** One useful strand of your diagnosis is to explore how a situation arose. What were the contributory factors? Drawing a multiple-cause diagram (*see* Chapter 8) is an excellent aid to this and such diagrams are invaluable for diagnosis. They help you to broaden your thinking away from 'obvious' diagnoses and into the layers of interrelated causes that are a feature of most organisational situations. By working back through these you can identify the *root causes* (those that do not themselves have causes) that need to be addressed if the issue is to be resolved.

If you are trying to explore relationships between parts of an existing problem situation, try using relationship diagrams or systems maps. Both can help you to gain a clearer view of the situation from different perspectives.

The more diagrams you draw and the more frameworks you can use to provide 'shopping lists' of things to explore, the richer will be your diagnosis. This will minimise the risk of jumping to premature and simplistic conclusions. So deliberately use as many 'tools' in your diagnosis as possible, and force yourself to confront at least some of the complexities in the situation.

➤ **Ch 6** Use the predictive power of theories, too. For example, if the case involves poor motivation you could draw upon Expectancy Theory (described in Chapter 6). This suggests that motivation depends upon the perceived links between effort, performance and reward. Using this model would lead you to look at these *links*, paying particular attention to where they may be weak, and at the *values* staff place on the rewards associated with performance. The theory would predict that the problem would lie in weakness in one or more of these areas.

Remember to go back to the case information and look more carefully at things that become important as your diagnosis proceeds. You will need to produce *evidence* to support your diagnosis. (Evidence-based practice is now seen as important in a wide range of professions and you will need to think carefully about evidence in any project or dissertation you are required to produce.)

Use the data provided. What *information* can you derive from the data? Are there any apparent trends? Where are they leading? Are there discontinuities in trends? If so, what are they associated with? Are some figures out of line with others, for example are your selling expenses out of line with those of your competitors, or is one product line contributing much more (or less) than others? You may need to do some calculations in order to turn data into information which answers the sorts of questions you are asking. The data will seldom be given in the form you want!

Throughout your diagnosis make a deliberate attempt to sort out evidence from assumptions, and to ask both how sure you are that your assumptions are correct and how important it is to your diagnosis that they are. If others in the group have different assumptions, this is easy. If you are all sharing similar assumptions, it is harder to identify and then question them.

Above all, try to avoid thinking about 'solutions' at this stage. As your ideas evolve it is good, even necessary, to move between this stage and the third and fourth stages of tackling cases (scanning the case and describing it). But to move on to solutions before you are sure what the problem really is risks a 'solution' to something that is not the problem and that may even exacerbate it.

6. Production of a problem statement

It is very helpful at this stage to produce a written statement of your perception of the key problems. This will act as a reference point during future discussions. It will also form a basis for improved statements of problems if your understanding of the situation deepens during subsequent discussions, and will be useful in preparing your subsequent presentation. It is surprising how often in the heat of discussions you can forget what it is you are trying to achieve and wander off in some different direction. Even if this is a productive redirection, which has come about because your perceptions have become clearer, it can be confusing if not everyone knows what the redirection is. If it is an inadvertent redirection, the scope for misplaced effort is enormous. A clearly written problem statement can be an excellent way of avoiding this.

In consultancy projects it is even more vital to produce an agreed statement of the problem to be addressed and of the way in which it is to be approached. Without an agreed project proposal, a consultant may at some point find it difficult to gain necessary access to information, or may be criticised for failing to achieve something that was not part of the agreed brief. An agreed statement can protect against both these problems. The same issue is equally important in projects with an organisational client, while a more academic dissertation will need a research question to be agreed (*see* Chapter 16).

➤ Ch 16

If you have more than one problem, it is helpful to prioritise them. If you have time to tackle only some, it would be sensible to focus on those with highest priority. Useful criteria for selection include:

- **importance** – what will happen if the problem is not addressed?
- **urgency** – how quickly must this problem be solved?
- **hierarchical position** – to what extent is this problem the cause of other problems?
- **solvability** – can you do anything about it anyway?

7. Deciding on criteria for a solution

It may seem out of order to consider how you will choose between solutions before you have thought of any, but there is a serious reason for this. It derives from the power and attractiveness of solutions and the need to counteract this. Once you have thought of

➤ Ch 16

even one solution, there is a danger of becoming wedded to a particular idea and slanting your criteria for choice in favour of this particular one. This point is discussed further in Chapter 16, in the context of dissertations and theses, where similar considerations apply.

It is, therefore, safer to think about criteria for solutions as soon as you are clear about the problem structure. In one sense criteria follow from this. If the deepest problem identified is to do with culture, for example, then solutions must be likely to influence this for the better. But if there are also financial problems then there will be criteria associated with these as well. Indeed, whatever the problem, financial criteria are likely to be important.

If you list the characteristics of a 'good' solution at this stage, you will have a set of yardsticks against which to measure your options, yardsticks that relate to your identification of organisational needs, not merely to your particular set of options. As well as identifying the positive aspects to be sought from a solution – the ability to reduce costs, to generate capital, or whatever – it is also worth looking at the constraints that will limit the possible option range. Is there an absolute budget for a project? Are there national union agreements that must be honoured? Are there legal constraints? By identifying these as well, you will have mapped out the field within which solutions *must* lie, as well as the part of the field in which it is most *desirable* that they fall.

8. Generating alternatives

Once you have a clear idea of your objectives, have decided upon the problem areas that you wish to address and are reasonably sure you have analysed their root causes, you can start to think about possible ways forward. What are the options? You will again need to draw heavily on course concepts to suggest better ways of operating. Other useful sources of ideas might be information you have gained from other case studies, from reading the business press or from each other's past experience. This last source is perhaps your richest resource of all and, in your discussions, you should always be aware of what other members have to offer and ensure that their contributions are encouraged where they can be of value. However, it is crucial to link experience to the concepts and theories you are using.

You may also find it helpful to use creativity techniques: the broader the range of options you generate, the better. You are probably familiar with brainstorming already. This is one of the longest-established techniques habitually used by managers. Although you may be using it at work already, and will almost certainly cover it at some point in your course, a very brief description is included here in case you are not familiar with the approach and need it soon. If you have been taught other creativity techniques, use these too.

Brainstorming

Brainstorming is often used loosely to refer to any attempt at coming up with ideas. However, it was designed originally as a specific method for disabling the censors that habitually operate within our subconscious, suppressing ideas unworthy of attention before they ever surface. The method aims to create a climate within which silliness and unserious behaviour are the norm, thus freeing participants to voice those normally suppressed ideas. Among these may be the germ of a totally new approach that offers a way out of an existing deadlock. Furthermore, one person's silly idea may spark off a new train of thought in another person, which may itself lead somewhere.

Thus, in running brainstorming sessions, you try to create a climate of fun and to free people from their inhibitions. You also aim to capture and display *all* ideas voiced so that they can act as a stimulus to further thought, as well as being available for further consideration after the exercise.

To reduce inhibitions, the group must agree to voice *no* criticism of any idea expressed and contribute *all* ideas that occur to them, no matter how bizarre. The weirdest ideas may be the most valuable. To get the group into the mood, start the session by spending a few minutes brainstorming a manifestly silly topic, such as what to do with a dead parrot or how to terminate an endless visit from your in-laws.

To ensure that all ideas are captured and displayed, it is normal to work in a room with writing surfaces all around, whether whiteboards or sheets of flipchart paper stuck to the walls. One of the group members writes down all the ideas as they are called out, using writing large enough to be read easily by everybody.

The group then agrees on the topic to brainstorm and starts shouting ideas. The only allowable criticism is that of people voicing criticism! The group continues until it runs out of steam. Only then is any attempt made to evaluate the collected ideas. This is often done by a smaller group, who may group ideas, look for totally impossible ones and see how they might be made possible, or merely look for the best among the bunch. Your group could decide on the best way of handling ideas, given the task in hand.

Other techniques

Some idea-generation techniques try to ensure that all group members make a contribution; sometimes quieter members say little in brainstorming. Nominal Group Technique, for example, involves a rather bureaucratic taking of turns in contributing ideas and voting on the best. This is not likely to reduce inhibitions all that much, however, and may be stressful for some,

Post-its® which allow the writing of ideas then sticking them up, rather than calling them out, may also help quieter people to contribute more fully. They also have the virtue of allowing points to be rearranged so that related points can be clustered. (On a practical note, if sticking to flipchart paper so that you can take them away, you need to check that they stick firmly. Often they will fall off. So, as soon as you are happy with positions, it is worth taking a photo or making them more secure with sticky tape.)

Other approaches make conscious use of analogy and metaphor or forced associations, perhaps to random objects provided by a facilitator, or words selected at random from a dictionary. Thus, you might think of the problem 'as if' it were something else, or consciously look for similarities and differences between your problem and something completely different as a way of stimulating your thoughts out of their habitual channels.

However you choose to become creative, it is important that you do generate a sufficiently broad range of options. You are unlikely to walk out of a chain store with an exclusive designer suit; your chosen option can never be better than the best among those you generate.

You may need to go through successive cycles of divergence and convergence in generating options. The first pass may generate a huge variety of widely different possibilities. After focusing on one broad class, you can be creative again in deciding on options within that class, narrow down, and broaden out at the next level and so on. This is a common way of approaching product design, but is also applicable to the design of organisational solutions, though with the proviso that the interrelatedness of organisational problems sometimes may mean that the extremes of focusing, which this method produces, can be insufficiently holistic.

Figure 10.2 shows how the method can be thought of as the generation of part of a tree, along which you travel by way of ever smaller branches and twigs. It is important if you are using this method that you ensure that each set of branches or twigs consists of mutually exclusive options, or that you consider any overlaps very carefully. If not, by choosing one path you may be neglecting whole areas that feature elsewhere and that might be highly relevant.

9. Evaluating options and selecting the most appropriate

If the solution tree approach described above is adopted, you will already be exercising choice at the generation of options stage. With other methods usually there should be a variety of options generated, as few problems have a single possible solution. The next

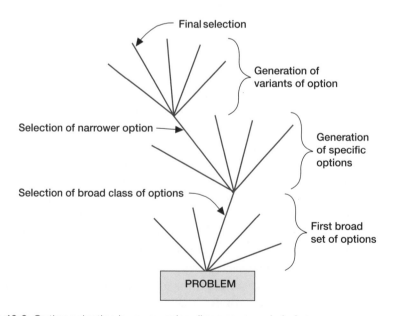

Figure 10.2 Option selection by successive divergence and choice

stage is, therefore, to evaluate the options, in order to see which option, or combination of options, is likely to be most effective.

In evaluating options you will need to consider their likely effect, not only on the focal problem, but on the situation, and indeed the organisation, as a whole. If these relationships are not understood, and the possible implications of each option thoroughly teased out, there is a risk that the cure will be worse than the disease. Since forecasts are always guesses, it is important to have an idea of how likely your forecast outcomes are. And, as before, it is important to know how sensitive your forecasts are to your assumptions.

Once you have teased out the likely effects of your options, you can test these against the criteria you decided upon earlier. If there is a single criterion, the process is relatively simple. If there are several criteria that you feel to be important, then you may wish to weight these, giving more emphasis to the most important criteria. If you are using quantitative criteria, then it may be sensible to multiply scores on each criterion by the weighting factor and derive an overall weighted score. If more qualitative factors are important (and qualitative factors should never be excluded merely because they are harder to deal with in analysis), you will need to find some other way of handling the different aspects of your predicted outcomes. One fairly robust technique is to construct the sort of table found in *Which?* magazine, where goods are rated on a number of criteria, being given dots, rather than a number score. Figure 10.3 gives an example of this technique. This allows an 'at a glance' evaluation to be made of the table. The use of dots rather than numbers avoids giving a spurious impression of accuracy. This tabular approach is just as effective with policy options as it is with washing machines.

10. Designing an implementation strategy

In real consultancy you would be thinking about implementation issues as you worked through your analysis, even if this was not strictly within your remit. In case study analysis within a course, you may not be required to consider this aspect since you are unlikely to be in a position to implement recommendations. Nevertheless,

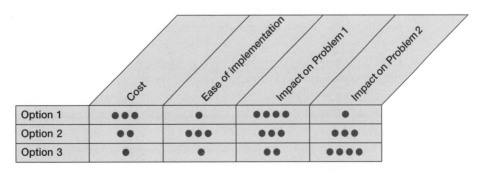

Figure 10.3 Schematic for a 'Which?'-type approach to option comparison

it is important that recommendations appear implementable and you may well be asked to produce an action plan as part of your assignment. Successful action is much more likely in real life if implementation has been considered from the earliest stages. Whether or not you are strictly required to make recommendations for implementation of your chosen option(s) it is, therefore, worth at least thinking about how they might be implemented.

For successful implementation in general, it is important that those who will be affected feel involved in the decision to make changes, rather than the changes being something wished upon them from on high. This is not just good PR. Those involved are likely to have genuinely useful contributions to make to the decisions, as they will have relevant knowledge and understanding not available elsewhere. In a real project you might set up consultative mechanisms to achieve participation. With a case study clearly you cannot do this, but it is still worth thinking about who would be involved and what contribution they might make were this possible.

➤ **Ch 16**   The other vital element is extremely careful planning (*see* Chapter 16), with all necessary steps taken into consideration. It is no use planning a highly sophisticated new information system and forgetting to plan for the considerable staff development needed to make it work. This would have to involve not only those inputting data, but also those intended to benefit from the outputs, and is absolutely essential if the system is to be of any real value. Such planning *can* be done in the context of a case study and, if you are required to do it, should be given due emphasis. It is all too easy to see the decision itself as the important thing and not to plan time to allow for thought as to how this decision can be made effective. Critical path analysis may well be helpful, but the real work will lie in thinking about the decision in relation to the organisation. What are its different implications for all those involved? This will enable you to identify the steps that will be needed to ensure that positive effects are fully achieved and as many of the negative ones avoided as possible.

11. Presenting your findings

In presenting your findings you will want to convince your audience that you have thoroughly understood the problem, obtained all the necessary information to reach a decision, analysed this information in a sensible fashion and drawn the conclusions that are to be trusted. These conclusions should be presented clearly, so that your audience is convinced that your recommendations should be followed.

➤ **Ch 14**   For class-based discussions, it is likely that you will need to make an oral presentation. Chapter 14 deals with the basics of making an effective presentation to a group. You should work your way through this before making (or critiquing) your first case study presentation, unless you know you are already an expert in this field.

In real-life consultancy, you may often be called upon to make a presentation, but you will *always* need to make a written report on your findings. If you are analysing the case for assessment, then, too, you will need to produce a written version of your findings.

➤ **Chs 13, 15**   Chapter 13 deals with written reports, and Chapter 15 touches on case study-based answers in examinations. You should refer to these as appropriate.

Guidelines for case study analysis

- Clarify task requirements.
- Skim-read.
- Read more slowly, highlighting issues.
- Explore the case and its context, identifying themes.
- Formulate problem statements.
- Identify solution criteria and constraints.
- Identify tasks and allocate to individuals or sub-groups.
- Analyse, using course concepts to help find root problems.
- Work out recommendations.
- Craft analysis and recommendations into a clear presentation.

Exercise 10.1

Work through the 'What Should Chris do?' case on the companion **website**. Note, answers are posted on the **website** rather than at the end of the chapter, but do not look at them until you have worked through the case.

From cases to consultancy

As already indicated, analysing a case requires many of the same skills as consultancy. You can practise these skills by acting as an internal consultant on small projects. Analyse aspects of your own organisation as if it were a case, seeking to use a range of concepts and techniques to cast light on situations and suggest how they might be improved. Distance learning students may find that they are often set assignments requiring them to carry out such internal analyses.

Once you have become confident with analysing complexity in cases and at work, you may wish to go on to practise acting as an external consultant. Since many Master's students work as consultants for some or all of their subsequent career, many programmes include a consultancy or other work-based project to give students at least a little practice in this area. You will need, however, to go on and develop a wider range of skills if you are to become fully effective. The complexities of an unfamiliar real situation will be far greater than those represented in a case. And you will need to seek out most of the information you need, rather than being provided with it. There will, too, be the dimension of liaising with your client and ensuring that you understand his or her objectives for the project and that you retain your client's trust throughout.

➤ **Ch 16**   (This aspect is a feature of many projects so is discussed further in Chapter 16.) You will need a high level of interpersonal skills to maintain a good relationship with the client organisation. And if you plan to live by consultancy, you will need marketing and other skills.

SUMMARY

- Case studies are a vehicle for practising the application of skills, knowledge and techniques learned in courses to quasi-real situations. They also, importantly, develop the ability to deal with complexity and uncertainty.

- Cases can also increase awareness of the business context in which students are likely to eventually operate.

- Group interaction, time-management and presentation skills can be developed at the same time as conceptual/analytical skills.

- In case study work students usually are given more responsibility for managing their own learning than they are used to, which may cause difficulties.

- Further difficulties arise because tasks may be somewhat unclear and because case studies frequently contain an overabundance of information. Group dynamics may also hinder progress.

- It is essential to devote sufficient attention to diagnosing the real causes of a situation, resisting the universal tendency to leap to solutions rather than explore the complexity of the problem.

- The complexities within a case can be usefully approached by the use of relevant course concepts, together with an overall structure based upon a national approach to problem solving: explore situation; define problems; decide criteria; generate options; evaluate options; present recommendations.

- Case study analysis is useful preparation for consultancy work, and any work-based project or dissertation, but it is important to remember that real life is more complex than cases and seldom allows clear 'solutions'. Consultants also need to employ a far wider range of skills.

Further information

Butterworth, J. and Thwaites, G. (2013) *Thinking Skills: Critical Thinking and Problem Solving*, (2nd edn), Cambridge University Press. Good on both arguments and the use of data.

Clutterbuck, D. (1990) *The Phoenix Factor: Lessons for Success from Management Failure*, Weidenfeld & Nicholson.

Easton, G. (1992) *Learning from Case Studies* (2nd edn), Prentice Hall. This gives much more detailed guidance on case study analysis than is possible here.

Kneeland, S. (2008) *Thinking Straight*, Pathways.

Pidd, M. (2009) *Tools for Thinking: Modelling in Management Science* (3rd edn), Chichester: John Wiley & Sons ltd.

http://www.open.edu/openlearn/education/extending-and-developing-your-thinking-skills /content-section-0 (accessed 14.1.15). For a free course on thinking skills.

10

CASE STUDIES, COMPLEX PROBLEMS AND CONSULTANCY

11

SEEING STORIES IN NUMBERS

Learning outcomes

By the end of this chapter you should:

- recognise some of the main uses of mathematical tools for management

- understand possible reasons for any resistance to mathematics

- understand the basic 'language' of simple maths

- be able to perform simple calculations with confidence, using calculator or spreadsheet

- be able to communicate data graphically

- understand basic concepts of probability

- be able to interpret the statistical significance of findings.

Introduction

One of the reasons employers seek those with MBAs or other degrees with a finance element is their assumed ability to make sense of financial information and other quantitative business information and statistics. Management decisions need to be based on evidence, and much of this evidence is presented as numbers. If you can 'read' these numbers, and understand the 'story' they tell, you will be at an enormous informational advantage over those who cannot. Far too many even senior managers are nervous of numbers, and all too ready to believe what they are *told* the numbers mean. If you can ask relevant questions, pinpoint fatal flaws and spot trends or imminent threats that no one else sees, your contribution will be invaluable. All too often I have seen strategy based on managers' misguided conclusions, or consultants' reports that looked 'scientific' when in fact the data and the arguments based upon this evidence were seriously flawed. If you can see such flaws, and can go further, taking raw data and turning it into useful information which you then communicate to colleagues, you will have a powerful weapon at your disposal. Being comfortable with numbers, being able to extract meaning from them and being able to communicate that meaning are essential managerial skills.

Most management-related Master's programmes aim to develop students' ability to turn numbers into information: they do not always succeed. Sometimes this is because they assume a basic level of numerical competence that not all students possess. Such students struggle with finance and other quantitative aspects of the programme. While they may pass modules, they often do not develop the skills that will contribute to organisational success. This chapter is intended for anyone who is unsure whether they have this basic level of skill, or who is 'terrified of maths'. It aims to set mathematics in context and to show that playing with numbers can be easy, even fun, rather than tedious or difficult. It shows you how you can extract meaning from numbers and communicate this, whether graphically or otherwise. It shows you how statistical techniques can help you assess how significant the messages are. And it covers basic mathematical skills so that you can use simple equations and spreadsheets to help you answer questions. These skills will in themselves be of use at work, but they will also enable you to learn far more from quantitative parts of your course

If you are already confident of your mathematical ability and comfortable with basic statistics, you do not need this chapter (though you might like to check your assessment of this by working through Exercise 11.1 below). Use your time on other topics with which you are less happy. If you were good at maths at school, but have since forgotten most of it, a quick scan of the chapter will refresh your memory and remove any anxiety.

If you are seriously worried, use this chapter to develop your skills and help to build your confidence. I have tried to mix 'easy' material with the more difficult. If things start to get difficult, continue. Things will shortly get easier again. You will find some very basic 'remedial' maths in the Helpfile at the end of the chapter: it may be helpful to work through this early on.

Most people find pages of numbers remarkably hard to 'read'. Graphs or other pictorial representations of numbers make it easy to see 'patterns' and are easily generated from spreadsheets. Even if some of the 'harder' maths in the chapter is more than you want to engage with, you should still work on the parts that help you turn numbers into diagrams. You will find this invaluable if you are trying to make a point in a presentation, a report or a meeting. The picture will communicate the 'message' that the numbers contain. Graphs can also mislead, and you need to be aware of *how* this can happen and able to spot it when it does. If you understand how to represent numbers pictorially, using techniques such as bar charts or the sort of graph you drew at school, you will be well on the way making some sense of numbers and communicating this sense.

If you are very worried about your number skills, you might like to scan the chapter fairly quickly, selecting only those parts that seem easy to study in detail. It is better to take something simple and master it than to avoid it altogether out of fear. Some parts are *really* easy. Mastering them will build your confidence. At a second pass you may find some of the rest is easier too.

Diagnosing your current skill level

The first thing that you need to feel comfortable with is the set of symbols that constitute the 'code' of mathematics. Use Exercise 11.1 to check your memory of the basics. The result is private so it doesn't matter if you only get a few questions right. It is important to work through the whole exercise, doing as much as you can, *and writing down your own answers* before you look at the answers at the end of the chapter. If you find it difficult or impossible, don't worry. Turn to the end of the chapter, pour yourself a drink and/or do some deep breathing, and work your way through the Helpfile, 'Cracking the code'. You should find that it is really quite simple and that, by the time you have worked through the chapter, you can return to the exercise and complete it with relative ease. If you feel in need of more practice, further exercises can be found in sources such as Morris (2008), suggested at the end of the chapter, and on the companion website.

Exercise 11.1

(a) Write the following as decimals:

$\frac{3}{4}$ $\frac{6}{7}$ $1\frac{1}{3}$ $1\frac{5}{7}$ $\frac{9}{11}$ $\frac{6}{8}$

_____   _____   _____   _____   _____   _____

(b) Write the following as percentages:

2 $\frac{3}{4}$ $1\frac{1}{3}$ $\frac{10}{11}$ $\frac{1}{4}$ $\frac{2}{3}$

_____   _____   _____   _____   _____   _____

(c) What is the value of:

2^3 14^2 3^4 $3^2 \times 3^2$ 12^3 1^4 6^0

_____   _____   _____   _____   _____   _____   _____

(d) Write as a power of a single number:

$2^2 \times 2^5$ $\quad$ $3^4 \div 3^2$ $\quad$ $10^3 \times 10^5 \div 10^8$ $\quad$ $17^5 \times 17^3$ $\quad$ $21^{21} \div 21^3$ $\quad$ $x^3 \times x^2$ $\quad$ $xy \div x^2$ $\quad$ $z^2x \times z^2y$

—— $\quad$ —— $\quad$ —— $\qquad$ —— $\quad$ —— $\quad$ —— $\quad$ ——

(e) Use your calculator to work out the following writing your answers using only two places of decimals:

$\sqrt{16}$ $\qquad$ $\sqrt{144}$ $\qquad$ $\sqrt{36}$ $\qquad$ $\sqrt{38}$ $\qquad$ $\sqrt{2}$ $\qquad$ $\sqrt{10}$

—— $\qquad$ —— $\qquad$ —— $\qquad$ —— $\qquad$ —— $\qquad$ ——

(f) Write as a power of a number (or letter):

$\sqrt{2^{16}}$ $\qquad$ $\sqrt[4]{10^4}$ $\qquad$ $\sqrt[3]{3^2}$ $\qquad$ $\sqrt[4]{x^2y^2}$ $\qquad$ $\sqrt[7]{z^{14}}$

—— $\qquad$ —— $\qquad$ —— $\qquad$ ——

(g) If $x_1\, x_2\, x_3, \ldots x_r$ represent the numbers 1, 2, 3, $\ldots r$, what is the value of $\sum_{r=1}^{3} x_r$?

_____

(h) Represent the following information graphically (use a separate piece of paper, if not drawing from a spreadsheet):

Sales volume:	0	1000	2000	3000	4000
Production cost ($):	5000	10 000	15 000	20 000	25 000
Sales revenue ($):	0	7500	15 000	22 500	30 000

(i) Which of the following are true?

i. $7 \neq 7$ $\quad$ ii. $3 \geq 1$ $\quad$ iii. $5 > -5$ $\quad$ iv. $3 < -5$ $\quad$ v. $x^2 > x$ when $x = 1$

—— $\quad$ —— $\quad$ —— $\quad$ —— $\quad$ ——

(j) Write the following without the bracket:

$2(x + y)$ $\qquad$ $3(x - y^2)$ $\qquad$ $-3(x - y)$ $\qquad$ $(x - y) - (x - y)$ $\qquad$ $(x - y) - (x - 2y)$

—— $\qquad$ —— $\qquad$ —— $\qquad$ ———— $\qquad$ ————

(k) Which of the following is true?

i. A result with $p > 0.05$ is more significant than one where $p < 0.05$.

ii. Statistical tests can tell you if your predictions are correct.

(l) Work out:

$5 + 2 \times 4$ $\qquad$ $3 \times 6 - 5 + 4$ $\qquad$ $x + x \times x \div y$ $\qquad$ $1.2 \times 3.4 - 1.2 \div 6.1$

—— $\qquad$ —— $\qquad$ —— $\qquad$ ——

Additional exercises are given on the companion website.

Causes of difficulty

Often, worries about mathematics are unfounded. Perhaps this exercise was easier than anticipated; if so, you may wish to reconsider whether you need to study this chapter at all. But if you found most of the above questions difficult, it is worth thinking about *why*.

A few people suffer from the number equivalent of dyslexia, known as *dyscalculia*. Far more are simply the victims of poor teaching. Children are really good at working out 'fair shares' or how long it will take to save up for something. Yet somewhere along their educational road, this becomes 'mathematics' and 'difficult', even frightening. If you have an emotional reaction to numbers, and feel panic setting in at the sight of an equation, you will need to address it. It is a very real reaction and one that will interfere with your learning. Try taking deep breaths, consciously relaxing, or even a modest intake of alcohol before working with the difficult bits. Do as much practice of simple 'sums' as you can and move on to harder things only when you feel confident. Success will reduce the fear. And keep reminding yourself of how your work as a manager would be improved by feeling more comfortable with numbers and basic mathematics.

Activity 11.1

Think about the numbers that have passed across your desk/screen during the last week or month. Give yourself a score out of 10 for the extent to which you felt confident that you could understand, interpret and use these numbers. ☐

List uses you might have made of them if you had been happier in dealing with them.

_____

_____

I have been faced recently with current and past student registration figures, the results of a market research survey, financial models showing likely income from a new programme at different fee levels and different student numbers, budget figures for the last (and previous) financial year, and assorted statistics at the end of research papers. I wanted answers to questions such as, 'Is it worth our while, financially, to develop the new programme?', 'Are we currently operating as effectively as in recent years?', 'Do these results support the author's theory?' Your own list is likely to be somewhat different. But you may have referred to similar needs to calculate the value of something you wish to know, to work out whether variations in your findings are likely to be meaningful, or referred to the need to answer 'what if?' questions.

Activity 11.2

Think about your experience with maths at school. How do you think your teacher rated your ability?

_____

_____

11

SEEING STORIES IN NUMBERS

Highlight any of the following that you felt confident about doing when at school:

> simple arithmetic; simple algebra; plotting graphs; working out averages; working with fractions; differential equations; basic statistics and probability tests.

Underline any that you think you have forgotten by now and double-underline any you never knew.

The above two activities, together with Exercise 11.1, should have helped you get a feel for the size of the task facing you in coming to terms with the basic maths you will need to use to benefit from your course. Use the information to work out how much time you will need to devote to this topic, amending your study plan if necessary.

Activity 11.3

If you are working while studying, aim to become more aware of the potential uses of numbers and of mathematics at work. Construct a section in your learning log in which you note all the 'numbers', statistics and equations (which may be built into spreadsheets), that pass across your desk and/or are available to you (perhaps on an intranet) when making decisions. Include any numbers for which you do not at present see a use and explore the uses to which they are put by others. This will help you make sense of your coursework and alert you to techniques that are in common use in your own organisation and information sources you could learn to use better. (If not working, use a management periodical, *The Economist*, Financial Times and/or similar as a basis for thinking about this.)

Assess your own abilities in making effective use of the information and develop an action plan for developing any necessary skills.

I hope that by now you can see the importance of devoting time to developing your numeric skills. These will enable you to make better use of numerical information at work, as well as to gain good marks on your course.

Descriptive equations

Difficulties may be caused by the use of equations for purely descriptive purposes. Mathematical expressions used in this purely descriptive way are not intended to provide 'solutions', or answers to specific questions, but rather to clarify (the charitable view), or spuriously impress (a more cynical interpretation). After a complex description, an equation will appear. Sometimes the equation may be even more complex than the description, involving lots of mathematical symbols and lots of different letters, the meanings of which have to be explained in a lengthy key. Unless the equation is the first step in constructing a model, or does indeed clarify the argument, you can probably ignore it.

Rather than putting down the paper with a feeling of failure, see what you can derive from the text alone, as Roger Penrose, a mathematics professor at the University of Oxford, suggests:

> . . . a procedure that I normally adopt myself when such an offending line presents itself. The procedure is, more or less, to ignore that line completely and to skip to the next actual line of text! Well, not exactly this; one should spare the poor formula a perusing, rather than a comprehending glance, and then press onwards.
>
> (Note at the start of *The Emperor's New Mind*, Oxford University Press, 1989.)

Lucy Kellaway (2000) expresses her view of such things in another formula, which you may enjoy!

$$F + M = P*R \text{ } where \text{ } F = formula, \text{ } M = management, \text{ } P = pretentious \text{ } and \text{ } R = rubbish!$$

I'll leave you to ponder the meaning of the * in the above. It does make the point that there are a lot of spurious equations around in the literature. (Though of course there are some extremely useful ones too.)

Modelling

While I have much sympathy with Kellaway's view, once you go beyond purely descriptive uses, equations can, properly used, provide an invaluable *modelling* tool.

A model is something that has enough key aspects of the real thing to allow you to answer questions about it, but more easily or economically than by experimenting with the thing itself. Thus an architect might construct small simplified models of alternative designs (easily done on a computer) that allow a client to gain an impression of each in order to make a choice.

Similarly, a manager might 'model' a situation by using equations representing relationships between key variables. Such a model might allow you to work out the expected return on different mixes of products, at different prices, different fixed and variable costs and/or with different levels of sales, the impact on profitability of different levels of absenteeism, or perhaps the expected returns on different investments given prevailing interest rates (or with a range of possible interest rate changes over the period for which money will need to be borrowed). The equation will not tell you what sales figures will be, nor what will happen to interest rates, but it will tell you the likely *results* of different values of these, *provided*, and this is important, that you have chosen an appropriate equation to model the relationships between the factors in question.

If you want to work out the cost of compound interest on a loan of €266 000, borrowed at an annual interest rate of 8 per cent over 5 years, you will need only slightly more complex techniques, which will be introduced later. If you want to work out the optimum product mix under varying conditions of labour demand, materials costs, profit margin, etc. you will need more complex techniques still. Mathematics can provide whatever degree of complexity you are likely to want, though for complex uses it may not be cost-effective to learn the techniques yourself. If a problem requires PhD-level expertise in Linear Programming, it is probably better to hire an expert, rather than try to master the higher reaches of the subject yourself. It *will*, however, help considerably if you know enough to have a broad understanding of what he or she is doing.

Understanding probability and statistics

Before going further, there is one idea that you need to understand because it underpins much of the chapter. This is the idea of *probability*, that is, of the likelihood of something happening. (If you gamble, you probably have a fairly clear idea of this anyway.) If something is certain to happen, it is said to have a probability of 1. If it is impossible, it has a probability of 0. Thus, if I have a bag of white balls, and I put my hand in and pull one out, there is a probability of 1 ($p = 1$) that it will be white, and of 0 that it will be black. If the bag (and we assume that it is an opaque bag, I am choosing by feel alone, and all the balls feel the same) contains two balls, one black, one white, the probability of choosing the white one is 0.5. The probability of choosing the black one is the same. If there are four balls, three white, you can probably guess the probability of each – for white $p = 0.75$, for black, $p = 0.25$. Lots of the numbers you deal with in management *could* have been influenced by chance. And this is where statistics comes in.

'Statistics' means both '*sets of data*' and also '*the branch of mathematics concerned with making inferences from such data*'. When Disraeli referred to 'lies, damned lies and statistics' he was, presumably, referring to the invalid inferences that may be drawn, and indeed are still frequently drawn, from sets of numbers. Statistics in the second sense deals in *probabilities*.

Imagine, for example, that two selection methods are compared. Of the 200 candidates selected by one method, 150 are rated as excellent by their bosses 5 years later, 10 are satisfactory and the rest have left. Of 100 selected by another method, 50 are rated as excellent, 25 as satisfactory, 2 as unsatisfactory and the rest have left. We have no reason to believe that the two groups were treated any differently once they joined the organisation, or that the pool of applicants was any different in either case.

Most people would be fairly ready to believe, from the above figures, that the first selection method was better. But it is not something about which we can be *certain*. Odd things can sometimes happen purely by chance.

Suppose you spend a day tossing coins and carefully noting in a small notebook the result of each throw. By evening you will have many sheets of paper covered with rows of things like HHTHTTHTTT . . . There will have been some stretches when you had a run of heads and other stretches when you got mostly tails. Of course most of the time they will be fairly mixed but, if you picked two sheets at random, you might, purely by chance, get one with far more heads than tails and another where the reverse was true. Someone not knowing your method of generating the results might be convinced that the two pages referred to quite different situations.

Selection of potential employees is not an exact science. We can expect a degree of random variation to enter into it, even if it is not as random as tossing a coin. Has this random variation accounted for the difference in the results of the two selection methods?

It is hard to answer that question because we are very bad at assessing probabilities unaided. How likely do you think it is, for example, that in a class of 32 schoolchildren at least 2 will share a birthday? How likely is it that if you toss a coin just six times you will get either six heads or six tails?

In fact, the chances of shared birthdays are about three to one, i.e. it is three times as likely that there is a shared birthday as that there is not. And, although if you got HHHHHH, many people would accuse you of using a weighted coin, the chance is as high as 1 in 32. So, if your class all tossed six pennies, you would not be at all surprised if one of them *did* get six alike.

If straightforward things like this are hard to assess, it is clear we need techniques for assessing the probabilities of more complicated results, so that we know how much significance to attach to them. How likely is it is that the differences between the two selection methods described above were caused purely by chance? A vast battery of statistical techniques exists and you will, almost certainly, be introduced to some of them during your course. Later in the chapter some of the simpler ideas of distribution, probability and correlation are introduced.

It is worth noting, however, the one lesson that has stayed with me since studying statistics as an undergraduate. Even if you know something about statistics, check any research plans with a competent statistician who can advise you on the size of sample you need and on the sorts of statistical tests you should use to decide whether your results are significant. (This will be particularly important when planning data collection for your dissertation. Many students ignore this advice and their results are worth very little in consequence, despite their hard work.)

Much organisational research pays scant regard to statistical considerations and therefore produces results of dubious validity. When these results are treated as sound, they may result in unwise decisions. Probability and statistics can never tell you what *will* happen. But they can tell you how likely various outcomes are under different assumptions about the environment. Before getting on to this, however, there are simpler ways of making sets of numbers 'speak'.

Making data more meaningful

Much of the data with which you will be faced, whether at work or generated by your research for a dissertation, will be in the form of strings or tables of numbers. Most of us find it difficult to make any sort of sense of a large set of numbers. Bar charts, graphs and other graphical representations allow patterns in those figures to be seen at a glance – these will be covered soon.

Measures of the centre

> **You can describe a set of numbers using:**
> - mean – the average – the sum of values divided by the number of values
> - median – the middle value if values are ranked according to size
> - mode – the value that occurs most often.

First, let us look at ways of summarising a set of numbers without graphs. The one you are likely to be familiar with is the *average* figure for a group. Suppose as chair of an Exam Board I noted that two markers had given the following scores:

Marker 1: 20, 70, 80, 83, 50, 55, 75, 60, 61, 30, 95, 55, 54, 51, 40, 57, 69, 70, 75, 81.

Marker 2: 40, 43, 47, 60, 49, 55, 51, 60, 63, 49, 42, 70, 75, 50, 46, 41, 49, 67, 60, 42.

It is hard to compare 2 sets of figures and would be even harder if you have 10 markers, each marking 150 scripts, as I often did. In order to start to draw conclusions, you need to organise the figures in some way. The simplest is to provide a summary of the scores, by giving the *average*, or *mean* score. To do this, you add the marks awarded by each marker and then divide by the number of scripts marked.

Exercise 11.2

Find the mean score for each marker above using a calculator:

Marker 1 _____   Marker 2 _____

Sometimes, if the distribution is a bit odd, a mean score can be misleading and you will find some other measure of the 'middle' of the group useful. (Imagine how uninformative the 'average income' on an island inhabited by 50 subsistence farmers and a multi-billionaire would be.) One of the two other most commonly used values is the *median*, which gives you the size of the middle value if you order all the measurements by size and then take the value of the measurement which is in the middle of the list. Thus the median value of 1, 1, 4, 5, 7, 10, 10, 10, 11 is 7. There are 4 values bigger than this and 4 smaller. The other measure is the *mode*, or the value that occurs most often. The mode for the list above is 10. You can see how either median or mode would paint a better picture of the islanders' income than the mean in the example above.

Exercise 11.3

Find the mean, median and mode for each of the following sets of values:

(a) 5, 5, 3, 2, 6, 7, 9, 11, 1   mean _____   median _____   mode _____

(b) 1, 3, 1, 10, 13, 2, 7, 8, 4   mean _____   median _____   mode _____

➤

> To get a better 'feel' for the effect of different sorts of distributions on these measures of central tendency, experiment with writing lists where mean, median and mode all have different values. Try to construct at least one list where the differences are substantial (no answer is given for this part).

Range

The mean (or median or mode) may be all you need to know, but you can see that you lose a lot of information by merely giving the average. One group has a much wider spread of scores than the other and the average gives no indication of this. One simple way of adding this information is to supplement the mean with information about the *range*, the spread from the highest value to the lowest. In the earlier example, the range for Marker 1 would be 20–95, for Marker 2, 40–75. You can see that Marker 2's scores are more bunched together.

Interquartile range

The range can be misleading if you have a maverick outlying score. Suppose you were looking at absenteeism in two departments. Most sick absences might be for two or three days. But one department might have someone who was terminally ill and had been unable to work for months. This would make both the mean and the range in that department far higher than the figure for the other department. For this reason a measure called the *interquartile range* is sometimes used. You remember that, in order to work out the median, you ordered the data and counted up until you reached the middle value. Quartiles are worked out similarly but, having ordered the data, you count up to the quarter point and the three-quarter point. The interquartile range is the distance between these two points, that is, the range within which the middle half of your observations lie.

Exercise 11.4

Work out the interquartile range for Markers 1 and 2 above.

By extension, if you have large sets of data, it can be helpful to identify deciles or even percentiles. The bottom 5th percentile would represent the 5 per cent of the population with the smallest values – for example, ergonomists typically ignore the top and bottom 5th percentile. Thus, if (like me) you are shorter than 95 per cent of the population, you may find work surfaces too high in kitchens, or have difficulty reaching the control pedals in a car.

Spreadsheets are a useful way of dealing with large sets of data. They calculate means and other values at the touch of a button. If you are not yet familiar with using them the following may help. They can both perform just about any calculation you want, and show results in number and/or graphical form. Microsoft Office uses Excel, and the following description applies to this software. You can find a wealth of free online tutorials in Excel and other common spreadsheet software (some suggestions are given online) which will explain things far more clearly than any basic explanation in simple text can do. Your university may also offer spreadsheet training. Spreadsheets are such an invaluable tool in business that time invested in developing your skills in this area will be well spent.

TECHSkills 11.1 Using spreadsheets

A spreadsheet is an arrangement of 'cells', i.e. spaces, arranged in rows and columns. You can enter text and/or numbers into any cell. You can also enter equations (more on equations shortly) to calculate values from the contents of other cells. Obviously you need to specify which cells are to provide the terms in the equation. In Figure 11.1 the first column shows registration figures for the previous and current years for different courses. The appropriate equation is entered into the shaded cells (see how the cells are identified by column letter and row number). When you enter figures into the boxes, or change existing figures, the spreadsheet does all the necessary calculations.

You can enter text into any box to provide 'labels' (such as 'Last year', 'Accounting', or 'Total' that will make clear what the numbers mean. Obviously you will not use these cells in any formula: they are there for clarity.

To summarise, cells can be used for **titles**, for the table as a whole, or a row or column, for **numbers**, representing data, or for an equation or **formula** (see shaded cells) used to calculate new values.

Once a spreadsheet has been set up with the correct formulae you can use it with different sets of numbers. For example, in 12 months you could delete last year's figures and replace by this year's and then enter the new figures in the 'this year' column. Similarly, you could add rows for additional courses you had introduced, and then simply enter their numbers.

Even with something as simple as the data in Figure 5.2, you can see the potential for saving time and reducing errors. For more complex data sets and formulae the time

		A	B	C	D
	1		**Last year**	**This year**	**Percentages**
	2	Accounting	100	109	=(C2/B2)*100
	3	Business studies	230	218	=(C3/B3)*100
	4	Computing	200	242	=(C4/B4)*100
	5	Design	50	46	=(C5/B5)*100
	6	**Total**	=B2+B3+B4+B5	=C2+C3+C4+C5	=(B6/A6)*100

Figure 11.1 Example of a spreadsheet

saved can be amazing. You will find spreadsheets useful in finance courses and for any project where you are collecting data and wish to relate different values to each other.

There are many shortcuts provided by the software. For example, the need to total a column or row is so common that Excel provides an Autosum function, which allows you to instruct a total to appear at a single mouse click (the equation for a sum is shown in Fig 11.1 is an example of how to sum without using this function). It is also extremely straightforward to calculate percentages, ignore negative values, round numbers to a given level, provide an average, or compute the rate of return on an investment, if you know present and future value. The 'chart wizard' produces a range of graphs from your data – another extremely useful feature.

Distributions and histograms

Mean and range together tell you something about the data, but there may be other important features not conveyed. Suppose Marker 1 gave one student 20, one 80 and all the rest 50, whereas Marker 2 gave half the students 20 and all the rest 80. In this case, mean and range would be the same for both groups, yet if you described the markers only in terms of means or ranges you would be failing to communicate the fact that the scores were actually very different. For a start, Marker 2 is failing half the scripts, whereas all save one of the scripts seen by Marker 1 are gaining a pass. In many cases it is helpful to see how scores (or values) are distributed within different groups. You can get an idea of this at a glance from the numbers given in the example above, as I have deliberately exaggerated the distribution. But suppose the differences, though real, were less extreme, and that each marker had dealt with 500 scripts. You would not be able to see the *distribution* of the scores at a glance and would need the figures to be summarised in a way that showed the pattern more clearly.

A primitive and simple technique, the tally, can be very useful. To produce a tally, you divide your measures into a number of categories. Here 5 categories might be chosen: say 0–20, 21–40, 41–60, 61–80 and 81–100. If you had a larger number of scripts you could afford to use smaller bands. Then for each score you put a tally mark in the appropriate band, as below. (Adding the fifth mark as a diagonal slash across means the groups of five stand out more clearly and makes adding up afterwards much easier.)

Marker 1	
81–100	///
61–80	~~////~~ //
41–60	~~////~~ //
21–40	//
0–20	/

Exercise 11.5

Complete the tally for the actual marks given earlier by Marker 2 (no answer given):

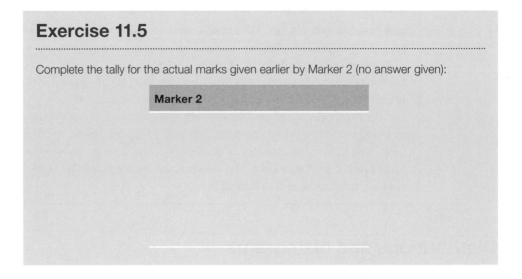

Often, instead of tally marks, a bar of an appropriate length is drawn. These bar charts, which show how often different values occur, are called *histograms*. As the categories on a histogram should cover all possibilities, with one category starting as the other finishes, the bars usually are drawn as adjacent. They can be drawn horizontally or vertically. Figure 11.2 shows a vertical histogram for Marker 2's scores.

These diagrams are an extraordinarily useful way of summarising data. They are easy to draw, whether by hand or by computer, and give a clear picture of how results are distributed. The only thing you need to beware of is the occasional practice of using categories of different size. In the tally example given, each band was 20 marks. But if you wanted, for example, to amalgamate 0–20 and 21–40, to give a band twice as wide, you would need to adjust the height so that the *area* of the bar still corresponded to the number of instances. When 'reading' bar charts, remember this – looking at the height if categories are not of equal width potentially is misleading.

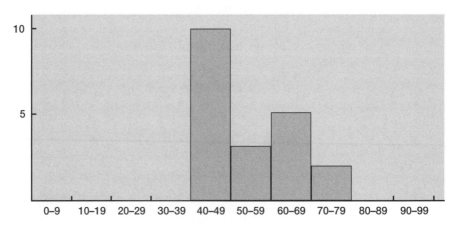

Figure 11.2 Histogram for Marker 2 scores

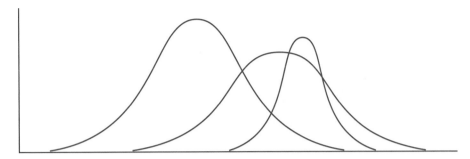

Figure 11.3 Examples of normal distributions

Normal distributions

One distribution is of particular interest. This is called the 'normal distribution' or, because of its shape, a bell curve. Figure 11.3 shows some examples of normal curves with different central points and different spreads. The normal curve is a theoretical one but, for many different variables, if you were to take a large sample and plot them in infinitely narrow bars, you would come up with a curve like this. Imagine that you measured the IQ scores of 20 000 people and drew a histogram with bars only one mark wide. You would get something very close indeed to a normal curve. Many variables are distributed 'normally'. The height of adult men (or women) would show a similar pattern, or even the weight of loaves of machine-produced bread. Perhaps more importantly, as many statistical tests depend upon this, the arithmetic means of large samples from a single population are normally distributed.

You can see that the normal distributions shown vary in their means and their ranges, but are all symmetrical. This means that, for any normal distribution, the mean, median and mode will be the same. If you know the mean of the distribution, you know a lot about it. If you also know its 'spread', you know all there is to know. This 'spread' is described by something called a *standard deviation*.

Standard deviation

If you have done any statistics at all, you will have heard of standard deviations. They are used widely in a variety of situations as an indication of how figures are distributed. A median, or the interquartile range, will tell you where a certain proportion of your values lie – that was how you worked them out! If you have a normal curve, the standard distribution will also tell you how much of the distribution lies within a certain part of the curve. (For a normal distribution, 68 per cent of values will lie within one standard deviation of the mean and 95 per cent within two standard deviations.)

Figure 11.4 shows this graphically.

It is not particularly difficult to work out a standard deviation. Your spreadsheet will probably have a function for both sample and population standard deviations, but it is worth understanding the process. The following box shows the necessary stages.

To calculate a standard deviation:

- find the average or mean value of your observations ($\bar{x}$);
- work out the difference between each value and this mean;
- square all of these differences (this means that the values are all positive);
- add all these squares together;
- find the mean value of the square (called 'variance') by dividing the sum of squares by n where n is the number of observations;
- take the square root of this average – this is the standard deviation.

Using an equation to express this (and it shows that even a slightly nasty looking equation *can* be useful – it is easier to remember than the set of instructions above):

$$\text{Standard deviation} = \sqrt{\frac{\sum (x - \bar{x})^2}{n}}$$

Or by working out the bracket and cancelling the 'n's that result:

$$\sqrt{\frac{\sum x^2}{n} - \bar{x}^2}$$

The second way of writing this is much easier to work out when you want to insert your values of x and n.

This gives you the standard deviation of a whole population. But usually you will have measured only a smallish sample of that population and this formula will give you a smaller value on such a sample than you would have obtained if using the whole population. If you have a small sample, a better estimate of the standard deviation of the 'parent' population is obtained by dividing by $(n-1)$ rather than n. For a large sample the difference will be insignificant – dividing by 89 rather than 90 will make little

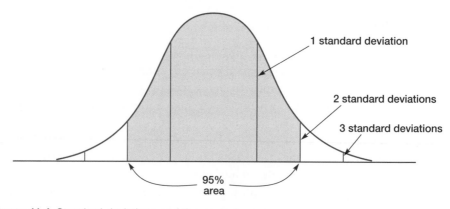

Figure 11.4 Standard deviations and the normal curve

difference. For a sample of 9, dividing by 8 rather than 9, say, will make a noticeable difference.

Note that, while each of the above ways of representing data (means, medians, range, standard deviation and so on) tells you *something* about how sets of data compare, you need to be very careful about drawing conclusions about the *significance* of differences between the sets, and even more careful about the reasons for these differences. And this is where you start to need statistical techniques.

Statistical significance

In Exercise 11.2 you found that Marker 1 awarded a higher average score but that this could be the result of a variety of things. It might be merely random variation. On the next set of scripts there might be no difference, or the difference might be in the opposite direction, even if all other things were equal. Statistical tests can tell me the probability of the difference being due to chance alone. Some of the figures that pass across my desk are printouts telling me means and standard deviations of different markers, whether they are marking low or high, and whether this difference is significant.

Beware, though. Even if tests strongly suggest that there *is* a significant difference in marks awarded, they will not tell me whether it is the marker or the students marked that are different. While it is indeed possible that Marker 1 was more generous than Marker 2, this is not necessarily the case. The probability generated by statistical tests may tell me that it is highly unlikely that such a difference arose by chance. But it won't tell me what the non-chance factor was. At my own exam boards I need to know whether there are obvious reasons for differences between markers' scores before drawing such a conclusion. Perhaps one marker has marked a high proportion of scripts from overseas exam centres where many of the students may have English as a third or fourth language, and do less well in exams because of this.

Even if I am fairly sure that there are no obvious reasons for expecting a difference in the students, and the statistics suggest a real difference, they do not *prove* Marker 1 was applying different standards. Normally, if a result is such as would arise only one time in 20, the result is described as 'significant' ($p < 0.05$). If it were to be expected only once in a hundred times, the difference would be deemed 'highly significant' ($p < 0.01$). But note that, even if the difference is highly significant, the statistics have not 'proved' anything. They make it a reasonable assumption and I normally would adjust the 'severe' marker's score accordingly. But I need to remember that, roughly once every hundred times, my 'reasonable assumption' will be wrong!

Some of the significance of the standard deviation now becomes clear. You can see that the points indicated by the 2nd and 3rd standard deviation distances in Figure 11.4 relate directly to significance. For a normal distribution, points lying more than 2 standard deviations from the mean are 'significantly different' and those more than 3 standard deviations away are highly significantly so. (This is assuming you are testing for any difference. Results would be twice as significant if there were only one direction in which a difference, if it existed, could be expected.)

Bar and column charts

In case your nerves are slightly frayed by now, let us take a step away from continuous curves and back to bars. A histogram is a special form of a bar chart. Bar charts have many uses beyond depicting frequency and, because of this, are one of the standard diagram forms easily produced from a spreadsheet. (Since spreadsheets will oblige with either horizontal or vertical 'bars' it is now common to distinguish between the two. Excel calls the vertical ones 'columns' rather than bars, and this chapter will follow this convention, although traditionally 'bar' was used for either layout.) If you have a number of sets of data on different features of something, bars are helpful. You might have annual rainfall and average temperature for major cities around the world, or various production figures for a number of different plants. You cannot draw graphs of rainfall or production because there is no particular way of ordering the different sets of data. Lima could come before London because it was earlier in the alphabet or, with other South American cities, before or after Europe, or wherever you choose to put it. The bars or columns are drawn as separate from each other, although, if there are several bars for each town, plant or whatever, these bars may be drawn as touching each other, and separate from the other sets of information. The goal is clarity. It would be misleading to imply continuity of data in the same way that it exists on a histogram. Several different types of information can be shown clearly on the same chart by using different colours or shades and a key to show what these represent. Figure 11.5 shows an example of a column chart.

It can be a tremendous advantage to use different scales to increase clarity. For example, if all the values you are plotting lie between 90 and 95, differences will be barely

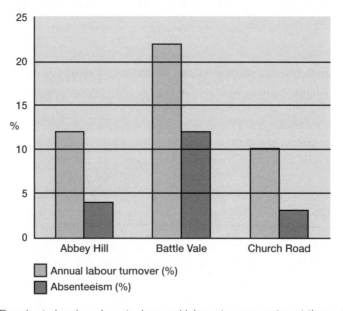

Figure 11.5 Bar chart showing absenteeism and labour turnover rates at three sites

Exercise 11.6

Represent the following information on a bar chart, either drawing this by hand or using a spreadsheet to generate it (see TECHSkills 11.1):

Business school	% entrants with degrees	% women
Aston	62	13
Bradford	88	19
City	88	30
Cranfield	82	11
Durham	71	32
LBS	97	22

(The above figures are for 1983, and taken from Hussey, 1988. Sadly, the percentage of women does not seem to have risen as much as one might hope, given that research suggests that an MBA has a bigger impact upon a woman's future salary than upon a man's.)

Note: Because of the difference in range of the two sets of figures you may find it helpful to use two scales, one covering the full range for the percentage with degrees, one covering a much smaller range, therefore allowing a wider spread within that range for the percentage of women. Experiment to see what gives you the clearest picture.

perceptible on a 1–100 scale but, if you use the same distance to represent from 90 to 95, the variations will be much more apparent. Be careful though. Once you stop using 0 as the bottom of your scale, a bar that is twice as high as another no longer means that the value is twice as much.

Sometimes it is necessary to use each interval on the scale to represent an increase in size gained not by adding, but by multiplying. This is known as a *logarithmic* or *exponential* scale. It allows you to represent a much wider range of values on a single scale than would be possible with an interval scale, yet still to see how things at the small end relate to each other. You will see an example of such a scale when you come to the next diagram.

You will see that great care is needed in interpreting bar or column charts, as the use of different scales can be misleading if the differences and their implications are not clearly understood. Using different scales may make your diagrams much clearer but, if the reader is careless in reading them, you may not communicate. If you are using other than a normal interval scale starting at zero, you may wish to point this out in

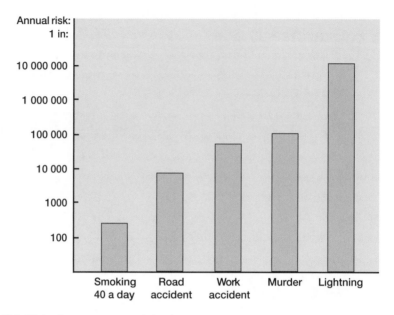

Figure 11.6 Risk of some causes of death

your text to be doubly safe. Sometimes scales seem to have been chosen almost with the intention of misleading. Look at the chart in Figure 11.6, which is similar to one that appeared in a reputable scientific periodical. What, at first glance, is most likely to kill you?

It is only when you stop to think that surely lightning *can't* be so much more danger-ous than smoking that you realise that the scale is dealing in risks, expressed in such a way that unlikely things get a taller bar than likely things. Think: a 1 in 10 chance is much *bigger* than a 1 in 100 chance, yet it comes lower on the scale.

Sometimes bars are used to show proportions. In this case the height of each bar will be 100, with a part of each bar devoted to the different quantities that go to make up that whole. Again, you will need to differentiate the parts with colour or shading. For example, a survey of a small village over a number of years might show the proportion of owner occupation rising. This could be represented as in Figure 11.7.

You cannot tell from the chart how *many* of any type of dwelling existed in any year, as you could from the type of bar chart described before. In fact the village was growing quite significantly over the period in question, but there is no way of telling this from Figure 11.6. All that you can say is how the total in any one year was divided between the three categories. You need to be very careful not to draw conclusions about whether actual *numbers* in any category are increasing or decreasing. Although the proportion of privately rented accommodation decreases, the overall growth in housing provision might well mean that the actual numbers of privately rented dwellings are increasing, albeit more slowly than the overall rate of increase. Again, you need to be careful when reading the diagram.

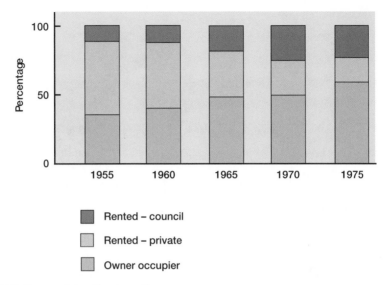

Figure 11.7 Types of dwelling in a village

Pie charts

Once spreadsheets made their production easy, it became more common to show proportions of a total in different categories as slices of circles not rectangles, hence the *pie chart*. Colours and '3D' (see Figure 11.8) meant such charts *looked more attractive and sophisticated* than simple bar charts. They are easy to understand, even by those who are uneasy about fractions. While some people might struggle to explain how proportions of ⅙, ⅓ and ½ relate to each other, it is immediately obvious with a pie chart.

However, pie charts become less useful when there are many 'slices'. We are not very good at judging fine differences between angles by eye and it can be quite hard to tell whether some of the 'slices' are bigger than others. The picture can be further confused by the 3D effect, which actually distorts the relative areas. Figure 11.9 shows how confusing this can be, particularly in '3D'. When there are more than four or five 'slices', you may find using a bar chart is much clearer. When drawing pie charts for smaller sets of numbers always use flat circles.

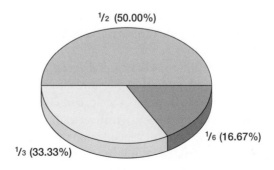

Figure 11.8 A very simple pie chart

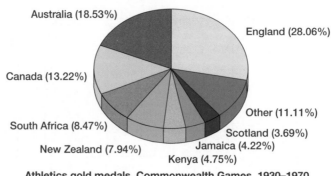

Athletics gold medals, Commonwealth Games, 1930–1970

Figure 11.9 A pie chart with too many slices

Exercise 11.7

Convince yourself of the advantage of bar charts for many categories by representing the pie chart (in Figure 11.9) in bar chart form. You will see how much easier it is to compare the size of the different parts.

Note that, while bar charts can be used to show either a range of values, or, by fixing the height of the bar at 100 per cent, to show proportions, a pie chart can be used *only* for proportions. It is totally invalid to use it to show, say, sales figures for a number of years.

Graphs

One common way of showing how two variables are related is to draw a graph. The basic principles of coordinate geometry allow you to plot a point using two 'coordinates'. You will be familiar with this if you use maps. Suppose I am organising a group walk in the country. Rather than rely on verbal directions on how to get to the meeting point, I will send people the map grid reference, in this case 'Landranger 175 GR 772817'. Walkers can look along the map for the 77 line on the grid and follow it up until it meets the 81 line running across. The point they need is a bit to the right and rather more up from this.

On a map the dimensions are purely geographical: E ↔ W and N ↔ S. You are more likely to be interested in rather different variables and in a series of points rather than a single one. Again each 'axis' – the horizontal line and the vertical line – has meaning, but the dimensions might be anything. Height, weight, number of observations, value of sales, or temperature – it will depend upon the data. For example, you might be interested in how costs are related to volume of production. If so, you would want to plot the cost for each production level.

Cartoon by Neill Cameron, www.planetdumbass.co.uk

Your first decision is which axis to use for which. Note that costs would *depend* in some way upon number of units produced. At school, you probably talked about an '*x*' axis and a '*y*' axis. Typically, the independent variable is referred to as '*x*' and is plotted along the horizontal or '*x*' axis and the dependent variable is plotted along the '*y*' or vertical axis. (Note this is easy to remember if you think '*x* is "a cross"'.) So, if cost depends upon production, it is dependent and needs to be plotted on the *y* or vertical axis. You also need to think about appropriate scales for each axis, so that the 'picture' is as clear as possible.

Exercise 11.8

Plot the graphs representing each of the following sets of figures (try it by hand as well as using a spreadsheet):

(a)	Month:	Jan	Feb	Mar	Apr	May	Jun	Jul	Aug
	Sales (€K):	57	60	99	95	110	90	95	79
(b)	Production	<100	100+	200+	300+	400+	500+	600+	700+
	Cost/unit (€)	2.5	2.25	2.0	1.5	1.25	1.0	1.0	1.0

In Exercise 11.8, you could see clearly how production costs were related to the volume of production. In this case the relationship was not linear, i.e. in the form of a straight line. Presumably there were minor economies of scale over the first part of the range (a slightly more significant one at the 300 point than the rest, perhaps by using a different machine). Beyond 500 there seemed to be no further room for improvement, at least within the range considered.

Note that, in plotting a graph, you need a *scale* for each axis, in contrast to a bar chart where the order of the bars does *not* matter, say rainfall in various capital cities, and you have a scale along one axis (say, cm) but not along the other axis. There, you merely have a number of labelled points or bands. (Sometimes you will see the top of such bars joined together to give a *graph* but this is not really valid. A graph should always represent the relationship between *two* variables.)

Of course, as with bar charts, you can show several things on a single graph. You can see from Figure 11.10 that a rough visual comparison can be made of the two sets of figures shown. This would be much more difficult if you were working just from the sets of raw figures.

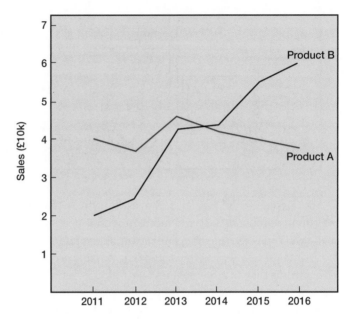

Figure 11.10 Graph showing sales for two products

Graphs and equations

A graph is a good way of showing how two different things are related. The figures in Exercise 11.8 presumably were worked out from knowledge of the different costs involved. Sometimes you may have this knowledge in the form of an equation. Suppose that you know that cost of production consists of a fixed element and a variable element, or

$$C = F + nV$$

where C is total production cost, F is the fixed cost (for example, workshop rental), n the number of units produced and V the variable cost (for example, labour and materials) per unit produced. You might also know that you can sell a unit for £P. If so, you could express sales revenue (S) as

$$S = nP$$

Do not worry if you are puzzled by these equations. Read fairly quickly to get the general sense. There is more on equations later. You can revisit this section once you have read that.

Exercise 11.9

If fixed costs are £50 per week, variable costs £1 per unit, and units sell for £2, plot the lines showing how both costs and income increase as production increases. From this, deduce the number of units that must be produced and sold if you are not to lose money on the enterprise!

Exercise 11.9 should have shown several things. First, note that the equation is an example in the classic form $y = nx + c$, where y is the *'dependent'* variable. It is called this because it depends on the value of another variable, or the *'independent'* variable, i.e. the one that you choose to fix at some value in order to see what effect this has on the dependent variable. Thus to plot this graph you would work out the value of y for each value of x, make a mark for each pair of x, y values and join the dots.

If you do this, you will note that $y = nx + c$ is a straight line: this is because it does not include squares or higher powers of x or y. (If y had been a function of x^2 then the line would have been curved. Try plotting $y = x^2 + 1$ for values of x from -4 to $+4$ to prove it!) Thus every change in x will produce a proportional change in y. The slope of the graph will depend upon the number in front of x. If this is a 2, then for every unit increase in x, y will increase by 2 units, and so on. You can find out the value of the constant term, c, by looking at where the line cuts the 'y' or vertical axis. (Look at the graph in the answers to Exercise 11.1 for another example, and check that your $y = x^2 + 1$ curve indeed cuts the y axis at 1.)

It should now be clearer how you can use graphs to answer questions. From the graph in Exercise 11.9 you could work out the level of sales beyond which (assuming you sell all you make) you will go into profit. (This point is known as 'breakeven'.) This was the reverse of finding where to meet for the walk! To find the value of x you drew a vertical line down from that point until it met the x axis and, to find the corresponding y value, you drew a horizontal line from the point across to the y axis. Reading off the values gave you the solution.

Exercise 11.10

Plot the graphs for the following two equations for values of x from 23 to 13:

(a) $y = 2x^2 - 1$
(b) $y = 4x + 3$
(c) Use the graph to identify possible values of x and y if both equations apply.

Fitting lines to data points

In the examples in Exercise 11.10 you knew the equation. Often you may have merely a collection of observed pairs of values (say, essay marks and exam scores for a group of students, or value of sales made and number of outlets visited by the salesman that month). In this case you can still plot the values, but it might not make a lot of sense to join up the dots – if you have a lot of values, there might be a mass of zig-zags. But look at the pattern made by the dots themselves. Sometimes you may see a clear pattern emerging. If so, you will want to know whether there is indeed a relationship (correlation) between the variables and, if so, what that relationship is, what is the best line you can draw to represent the set of points and what is the strength of this relationship. The stronger the relationship between the two variables, the easier it will be to fit the line to the data visually.

Exercise 11.11

Draw the line that you think best fits the data in the scattergraphs below:

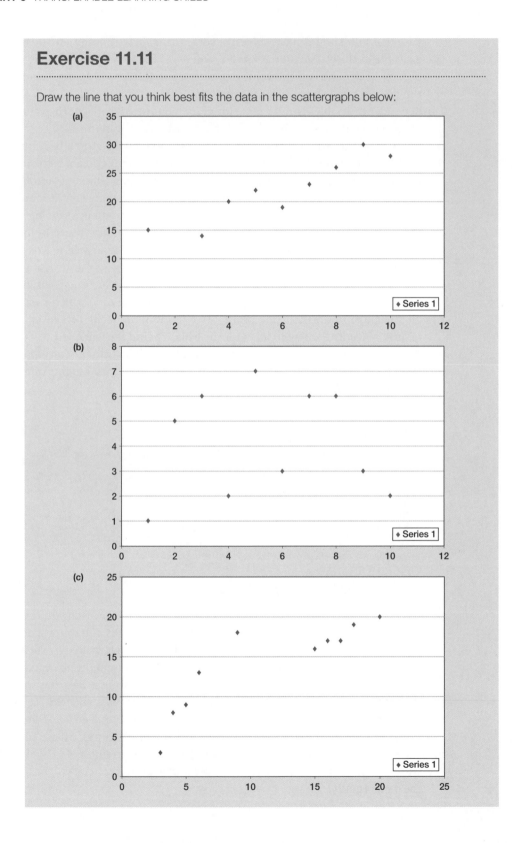

You probably experienced a lot of uncertainty when trying to fit a line to the set of points in scattergraph (b) above. But because this is a very common problem, a statistical technique has been developed that will allow you to assess both the strength of the relationship and the line of 'best fit'. Note that this works only for straight lines of the form $y = nx + c$. If the dots look as if they would better fit a 'U' shape or some other non-straight line, then the approach is not appropriate. Scattergraph (c) above is a case in point. While it is fairly easy to fit a line to the whole set of points, visual inspection suggests that two different lines would give a much better fit.

Linear regression

The mathematical technique for fitting lines is called '*linear regression*'. You could, with patience, draw a series of possible lines and work out how best each fitted the points by working out the sum of the (vertical) distances from each point to your line (*see* Figure 11.10). (These distances between actual value and the value on the curve you have fitted are called residuals.) Or better, as when working out the standard deviation, you could get rid of the problem that some distances are negative by working out the sum of the *squares* of the distances. Your best line would be the one for which the sum of these squares of residuals was least.

Fortunately, given that this trial and error process normally would be tedious in the extreme, it is possible to work out what line is best from the numbers themselves. Each 'dot' on your scattergraph can be thought of as having an '*x*' and a '*y*' value. Thus continuous assessment might be thought of as *x* and exam score as *y*, and the line you are trying to draw would represent the best equation of the form 'exam score = function of continuous assessment + constant'. (In my experience, exam scores tend to be 15 per cent lower, so there would be a negative constant.)

If you ever want to work out a regression line, use the procedure outlined in the box below. This may seem a long process, but is much quicker and more reliable than trial and error! (*Note: See* the Helpfile if the Σ and $\bar{x}$ symbols puzzle you.) Using Excel is even better.

Process for working out a regression line of the form $y = a + bx$:

- work out the average value of $x (\bar{x})$ (i.e. x multiplied by mean x)
- work out the average value of $y (\bar{y})$ (i.e. y multiplied by mean y)
- for each point, work out $(x - \bar{x})$ – call this diff$x$, and $(y - \bar{y})$ call this diff$y$, and multiply them together to give diff$x$.diff$y$
- add together all the (diff$x$.diff$y$)s to give Σ (diff$x$.diff$y$)
- square each (diff$x$) and add these squares together to give (Σ (diff$x$)^2)
- divide Σ (diff$x$.diff$y$) by Σ (diff$x$)^2; this gives you 'b'
- $a = \bar{y} - b\bar{x}$

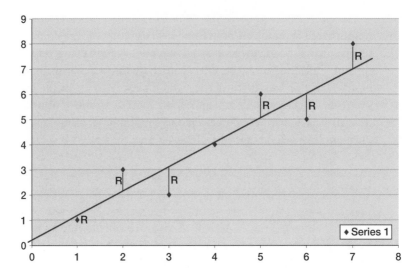

Figure 11.11 A fitted line showing residuals

If you find it easier to work from a formula:

$$\text{If } y = a + bx$$

then

$$b = \frac{\Sigma(x - \bar{x})(y - \bar{y})}{\Sigma(x - \bar{x})^2}$$

Do remember, though, that this makes sense only if the data points look as if a straight line would be the best fit to the data. If, when you plot them, the scattergraph you get suggests a curve of some point, you will need different techniques to work out the best fit.

Correlation coefficients

Once you have found a line of best fit, you may well want to know how strong the relationship between the two variables actually is. Is the correlation significant? For example, you might have figures for advertising spend and sales at different points in time. Or the figures might be for outlets visited and sales as described above.

Clearly, if the points were pretty close to your line of best fit (i.e. the residuals were small), you might be confident that the two things were related. A *correlation coefficient* (denoted by *r*) indicates the strength of the relationship. It is a way of describing how much of the variation in your data is explained by your regression line. Or conversely, how much is unexplained – how big are the residuals? Or, to get away from the positive /negative problem, how big is the sum of the squares of the residuals? (Now you can see why '*r*' may have been chosen to represent it.) If the coefficient is 11, the points are perfectly related. As *x* increases, *y* increases and all points lie exactly on the line. If *r* is 21

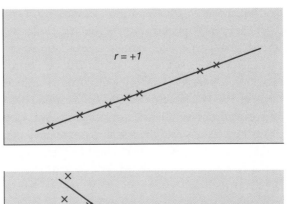

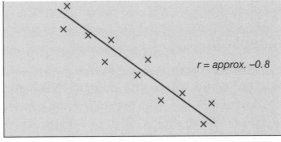

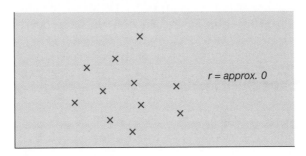

Figure 11.12 Approximate correlation coefficients for different data sets

then again the relationship is perfect but, as x increases, y decreases. Figure 11.12 shows approximate values of r for different sets of data.

The formula for calculating r looks very similar to that for b above – indeed, the top, or numerator, is the same. But the denominator is the square root of what you get when you multiply $\Sigma(x - \bar{x})^2$ by $\Sigma(y - \bar{y})^2$. There is a nice symmetry here.

Thus:

$$r = \frac{\Sigma(x - \bar{x})(y - \bar{y})}{\sqrt{\Sigma(x - \bar{x})^2 \Sigma(y - \bar{y})^2}}$$

However, Excel has a built-in correlation function, so you should not need to work this out for yourself.

The size of r does not in itself tell you how significant the relationship is. The more data points you have, the more significant is a correlation of a certain size. There are statistical tables in which you can look up the minimum size of *r* needed for different levels of significance for the number of observations you have. But remember, even if you have decided to call one variable a dependent variable, a correlation between this and the independent variable is not evidence of *causality*. There might be a third variable that influenced both the things you were looking at. Or there might be a causal relationship, but in the opposite direction from that you imagine – instead of A causing B as you assume, B might be causing A.

The correlation coefficient described above was worked out by Pearson, and assumes you are using a real measurement scale to get your values, for example number of visits and volume of business. But often in management research you may only be able to rank things rather than measure them. If so, you will need different, 'non-parametric' statistics.

Forecasting

But to return to something simpler and more obvious. Graphs frequently are used to show trends over time. Indeed, graphs (and regression lines) can be used to provide simple forecasts. By continuing the graph in the direction it seems to be heading, you can estimate future values. As most graphs will show a degree of variation about what seems to be the general direction, you will need to beware of continuing just in the direction of the last section of the graph, as a slightly odd last value might mislead you significantly – this is where regression lines help. But try to forecast the future direction of the following graphs by eye.

Exercise 11.12

Extend, or *extrapolate from*, the following graphs to provide an estimate of future trends, putting a dot where you think the next point is most likely to be:

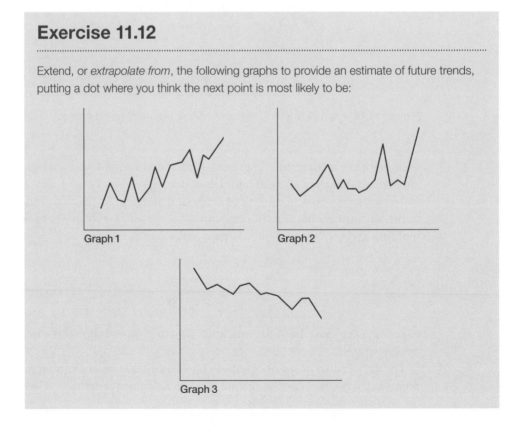

Graph 1

Graph 2

Graph 3

In the discussion above the main emphasis has been on showing data in a way that makes visual sense. These techniques are likely to be extremely useful to you. But it was also clear that, to extract the full sense, you may well need to supplement them by doing simple sums, or working with equations.

Estimating

A calculator or spreadsheet makes calculations easier, but you may inadvertently key in a wrong number or symbol. To avoid this, check by repeating the calculation, and check further by working out a rough answer in your head. The technique for doing this is called *estimating*. For example, if you are adding up 10 numbers in the range 700 to 900, you can estimate that the answer will be somewhere about 8000. If it is more than 9000, or less than 7000, you have done something wrong. Whatever the calculation that you are doing, it is worth getting a ballpark figure in your head, so that you know if some extra noughts have crept in somewhere, or you have pressed a + somewhere instead of a −.

Exercise 11.13

Estimate the value of the following before doing the calculation on your calculator:

	Estimate	Answer
(a) 2734 + 5955	_____	_____
(b) 40 569 ÷ 9	_____	_____
(c) 25% of 39 400 113	_____	_____
(d) 95 + 15% of 113	_____	_____

Rounding

To estimate, you are probably working to the nearest hundred or thousand to get a rough idea of what the answer will be. This technique, called *rounding*, is very important. You will remember that, when you used your calculator to work out 1⅔ it filled up its display with '6's. You will seldom wish to work to so many places of decimals. Total accuracy often is not particularly important. To work to lots of places of decimals is not only inconvenient: it implies a spurious accuracy, casting doubt on your grasp of what your results really mean.

Suppose that your project involved using a questionnaire to obtain a measure of job satisfaction. Respondents were asked to rate a number of aspects of their jobs on a scale from 1 to 5. If you wanted to work with average scores in this case it would be totally absurd to give these to much more than one decimal place, as the ratings themselves are subjective and the scale crude.

When rounding, you increase the last number you are using by 1 if the first number you are discarding is greater than 5; leaving it alone if the number you are discarding is less than 5. Opinions vary as to whether you should round up or down if it is 5.

It doesn't really matter which you do but, whichever you prefer, you should do this consistently. Thus, 1.5326719 would be 1.5 to one decimal place, or 1.533 to three decimal places.

Exercise 11.14

Round the following to two places of decimals:

1.6324   3.9995   7164.2294   51.1111   1.6556

_____   _____   _____   _____   _____

You will see from this exercise that rounding to, say, two decimal places does not provide a consistent level of accuracy. A better measure is the number of *significant figures* in the answer, i.e. the number of digits between the first digit, which isn't zero, and the number that you round (inclusive). Thus 7 268 893.4 is 7 269 000 to four significant figures, and 0.006038215 is 0.00604 to three significant figures.

When you are including sets of figures in reports, think carefully about the number of significant figures needed to convey your message with most force and clarity. Too many digits can obscure the picture; too few might be misleading.

Fractions, percentages and ratios

While you probably studied fractions at school, you may have paid less attention to ratios. You will encounter a number of key ratios in your accounting and business policy courses and will need to be happy with the concept. Ratios are a sort of fraction and fractions will also appear in other contexts, so a quick revision of how to deal with fractions is appropriate. The need for fractions will have emerged already if you have worked through 'division' in the Helpfile. Fractions can be expressed in three forms: as one number divided by another; as a decimal or as a percentage.

Exercise 11.15

To refresh your memory, try the following. Your garage is offering tyres at 80% of their original selling price. You decide to buy 2, which normally would cost £100. You also have a company card, entitling you to a 5% reduction on anything you buy. What should you end up paying, and should you ask for your 5% discount before or after the promotional discount is deducted?

Fractions

With a calculator it is easy to turn fractions into decimals and then to work with them just like any other number. Unfortunately we cannot leave it at that, as many of the equations you will encounter will include letters and your calculator cannot decimalise those. There are other times when you will not *wish* to turn a fraction into a decimal. Therefore, you need to know a few basic rules for dealing with fractions. Sometimes they will make a calculation so easy that you can dispense with your calculator anyway.

> **Rule 1** You can multiply or divide top and bottom of a fraction by the same thing, be it number, letter or mixture, without changing the value of the fraction.

Imagine cutting a cake into 2, 4, 6, 10 or 12 pieces. What would be half the cake in each case? Clearly, $\frac{1}{2} = \frac{2}{4} = \frac{3}{6} = \frac{5}{10} = \frac{6}{12}$

$$\text{Similarly, } \frac{2(3 + y)}{3(3 + y)} = \frac{2}{3}$$

as you can divide top and bottom by $3 + y$. This operation is called *cancelling* and is very useful in simplifying fractions, so that a sum becomes easier to do.

Exercise 11.16

Simplify the following fractions by dividing top and bottom by the same thing, i.e. a factor common to both:

(a) $\frac{20}{30}$ _____

(b) $\frac{75}{100}$ _____

(c) $\frac{6}{9}$ _____

(d) $\frac{22}{11}$ _____

(e) $\frac{16}{12}$ _____

(f) $\dfrac{3x}{4x}$ _____

(g) $\dfrac{4(x + 1)}{8(x + 1)}$ _____

> **Rule 2** To multiply a series of fractions you multiply all the numbers (or letters or brackets) on top to get the 'thing on top' (the *numerator*) in your answer, and multiply all the things underneath to get the *denominator* or 'the thing on the bottom' in your answer.

Thus, $\frac{2}{3} \times \frac{4}{5} = \frac{8}{15}$, and $\frac{1}{2} \times \frac{3}{4} = \frac{3}{8}$. You can now see how cancelling comes in very handy. You can cancel out numbers, letters or whole brackets that appear on both top and bottom in a string of things to be multiplied, even if they do not appear in the same fraction. Thus $\frac{1}{2} \times \frac{4}{5}$ can be written as $\frac{2}{5}$, for you can divide both the 2 on the bottom and the 4 on the top by 2.

Exercise 11.17

Multiply the following sets of fractions, using cancelling to make the sum easier:

(a) $\frac{2}{3} \times \frac{3}{4} \times \frac{4}{5} \times \frac{1}{2}$ _____

(b) $\frac{1}{(n+1)} \times \frac{(n+1)}{3}$ _____

(c) $\frac{1}{xy} \times \frac{x}{(1+y)}$ _____

(d) $\frac{1}{2} \times \frac{50}{100}$ _____

(e) $\frac{2y}{14} \times \frac{7}{xy}$ _____

(f) $\frac{2}{15} \times \frac{3x}{4y} \times \frac{y(y+1)}{x}$ _____

(g) $\frac{y}{x} \times \frac{7}{y} \times \frac{x^2 y}{14}$ _____

Note that, whether or not the bottom line of a fraction is written with a bracket round it, you must treat it as if it had one. It would be quite correct to write $1+y$ in (c) above, i.e. without a bracket, but you could not divide it by any y that might be in the top line, as this would not go into the whole phrase '$1+y$'.

Following this same rule, you can see that to square a fraction you square the number on the top and the number on the bottom to get numerator and denominator. Thus $\frac{1}{2}$ squared is $\frac{1}{4}$, $\frac{2}{3}$ cubed would be $\frac{2 \times 2 \times 2}{3 \times 3 \times 3}$ or $\frac{2^3}{3^3}$ or $\frac{8}{27}$. You can either write the index number against top and bottom figures in a fraction you wish to raise to a certain power, or put a bracket around the whole fraction and write the index number against the top of the closing bracket. Thus the fifth power of $\frac{2}{7}$ could be written as $(\frac{2}{7})^5$, or the nth power of $\frac{x}{y}$ as $(\frac{x}{y})^n$

Exercise 11.18

Write out the value of $(\frac{x}{y})^n$:

(a) where x is 1, y is 2 and n is 3

(b) when x is 2, y is 6 and n is 2

> **Rule 3** To divide something by a fraction you turn the fraction upside down and multiply by the inversion.

Well, obviously you have to do *something* different: $4 \div 2$ *can't* be the same as $4 \div \frac{1}{2}$. And it makes a sort of sense. If $4 \div 2$ means dividing it into two equal parts, then $4 \div \frac{1}{2}$ could be seen as dividing it into half a part. You would get 8 halfpenny pieces (if they still existed) from 4 pence, but only two 2p pieces.

$$\text{So } 4 \div \tfrac{1}{3} \text{ becomes } 12, \; \tfrac{1}{2} \div \tfrac{3}{4} = \tfrac{4}{6}, \; \frac{2(x+1)}{3} \div \frac{2}{x+1} = \frac{(x+1)^2}{3} \text{ etc.}$$

Because you are converting a division into a multiplication by inverting it, you can string together multiplications and divisions without problem, provided you remember to write all the divisions upside down and then multiply. So:

$$\tfrac{1}{2} \times \tfrac{3}{4} \div \tfrac{5}{7} \times \tfrac{1}{14} \div \tfrac{3}{5} \text{ can be written as}$$
$$\tfrac{1}{2} \times \tfrac{3}{4} \times \tfrac{7}{5} \times \tfrac{1}{14} \times \tfrac{5}{3} \text{ which cancels down to } \tfrac{1}{16}.$$

Similarly,

$$\frac{(x+y)}{(2y+3)} \times \frac{3}{x} \div \frac{2(x+y)}{(2y+5)} \text{ becomes } \frac{(x+y)}{(2y+3)} \times \frac{3}{x} \times \frac{2(y+5)}{(2x+y)}$$

which, as you can divide both top and bottom by $(x+y)$, cancels down to

$$\frac{3(2y+5)}{2x(2y+3)}$$

Exercise 11.19

Work out the following combined multiplications and divisions. Leave the brackets in as was done in the example above. Don't worry that we have not yet learned how to multiply them out.

(a) $\dfrac{1}{2} \times \dfrac{2(x+y)}{3} \div \dfrac{3(x+y)}{2}$ _____

(b) $\dfrac{x}{y} \times \dfrac{y}{x} \div \dfrac{x}{y} \div \dfrac{2}{3}$ _____

(c) $4 \div (x+1) \times \dfrac{3}{4} \div \dfrac{(x+2)}{(x+4)}$ _____

(d) $\dfrac{3}{4} \div \dfrac{3}{5} \div \dfrac{x(x+1)}{(y+1)}$ _____

(e) $1\tfrac{1}{2} \times \dfrac{3}{4} \div \dfrac{y}{x}$ _____

> **Rule 4** You can add or subtract only fractions that share a common denominator.

Percentages

Go back to your cake. It makes sense to *talk* about $\frac{1}{2}+\frac{1}{3}$, but would be clumsy to include this expression in, say, a string of multiplications. You cannot say that $\frac{1}{2}+\frac{2}{3}$ is $\frac{2}{2}+\frac{2}{3}$ or $\frac{2}{5}$, because it isn't. In order to write the addition as something with a single number on top and bottom, we need to turn each fraction into the same sort of thing. $\frac{1}{2}$ can be written as $\frac{3}{6}$ and $\frac{1}{3}$ as $\frac{2}{6}$. These we *can* add, to give $\frac{5}{6}$. Similarly, $\frac{1}{2}-\frac{1}{3}$ could have been described as $\frac{3}{6}-\frac{2}{6}$ or $\frac{1}{6}$. You can do the same if you have letters in your fractions. If you wish to add $\frac{3}{5}$ and $\frac{5x}{y}$ you can turn both into fractions with $5y$ on the y bottom line, by multiplying top and bottom of the first one by y, and top and bottom of the second by 5. This will give you the sum $\frac{3y}{5y}+\frac{25x}{5y}$ or $\frac{(3y+25x)}{5y}$. When dealing in percentages you are reducing everything to hundredths, so you have a common denominator and can add and subtract.

Note that you *cannot* cancel between different terms in an addition in the same way that you could for a multiplication. Note also that you cannot cancel between *part* of the numerator and the denominator. You cannot get rid of either the 5 or the y in the answer above by dividing the $3y$ by y or the $25x$ by 5. You have to be able to divide every term on the top line by something on the bottom line to cancel. Thus, if the top line had been $5y+25x$, you would have been able to cancel out the 5 in the bottom line, as the top could have been written as $5(y+5x)$ and the 5 could have been cancelled with the 5 on the bottom line.

Exercise 11.20

Write the following as single fractions:

(a) $\frac{3}{4}+\frac{7}{8}$ ________

(b) $\frac{3}{x}+\frac{4}{y}$ ________

(c) $\frac{5x}{y}-\frac{2(x+1)}{y}$ ________

(d) $\frac{2}{3}+\frac{3x}{5}$ ________

(e) 50% of $\frac{3}{4}$ ________

(f) $\frac{y(5x+1)}{x}+\frac{xy}{(5x+1)}$ ________

(g) $\frac{5}{(x-1)}-\frac{3}{(x-2)}$ ________

Ratios

Now that you have the basic rules for dealing with fractions at your fingertips, whether these fractions are expressed in letters, numbers or a mixture, we can move on to ratios, which are a form of fraction.

You use ratios when you are more interested in the relative sizes of things than in the absolute differences between them. To say that Part A costs 20p more than Part B may be more or less impressive depending on how much they both cost. If Part A costs £200.20, the difference is less striking than if Part A costs 40p. In the second instance it costs 100% more than Part B, or 200% as much, whereas in the first instance it is 0.1% more, or 100.1% of the Part B price.

Ratios are obtained by dividing one thing by another. Thus, in the above, with Part A at 40p, the ratio of the cost of Part A to Part B is 2 : 1, or ²⁄₁, depending on how you prefer to write it. You obtain the ratio of A to B by dividing A by B. Thus the ratio of Part B's cost to Part A's is 1 : 2, or ½. The thing you are finding the ratio *of* is written first, or on top. The thing you are finding the ratio of it *to* is written second, or underneath. So, if there are 500 students on a course and 10 tutors, the staff : student ratio is 1 : 50 or ¹⁄₅₀. The advantage of the fraction way of writing it, rather than the colon, is that you can then include the ratio in an equation if you want to, and deal with it like any other fraction. Since percentages are just another way of writing fractions, you can, of course, express ratios in percentages, too.

11

SEEING STORIES IN NUMBERS

Exercise 11.21

Imagine your departmental budget is £40 000, of which £12 800 is spent on advertising.

(a) What percentage of your budget is spent on advertising?

_____

(b) What is the ratio of your advertising budget to your total budget?

_____

(c) What is the ratio of your advertising budget to your budget for everything else?

_____

Any accounting and finance course will introduce you to many ratios. This is because ratios deal in relative values rather than absolutes and so allow you to make meaningful comparisons between operations of different size. Certain key ratios are used to compare an organisation's performance from year to year and to identify emerging trends.

A key financial ratio that you will encounter is 'Return on Capital Employed' (ROCE), sometimes known as 'Return on Investment' (ROI). While an MBA course will take you through the process of working out which figures should be used in calculating this ratio, you can practise working with ratios by calculating ROCE in a variety of cases.

$$\text{ROCE (or ROI)} = \frac{\text{Operating profit (pre-interest and tax)}}{\text{Capital employed}}$$

Exercise 11.22

Calculate ROCE (as a percentage) in the following cases (figures in £000):

	Operating profit	Capital employed	ROCE
(a)	500	4000	
(b)	164	83	
(c)	4.3	13	
(d)	(10)	256	

Because capital employed may vary, it is common to calculate an average value, using net assets at the year start and end.

Exercise 11.23

Calculate ROCE as a percentage, using average investment:

	Operating profit	Assets at year start	Assets at year end	Mean investment	ROCE
(a)	45	335	300		
(b)	330	120	160		
(c)	2200	7800	8000		
(d)	(55)	5600	5500		

Profit margin (the ratio of profit before interest and tax to sales) is clearly a major factor in determining ROCE. The other important factor is asset turnover. Asset turnover is a measure of how well the fixed assets and working capital of the firm are utilised. Profit margin multiplied by asset turnover gives ROCE.

Exercise 11.24

Asset turnover must be the ratio of *what* to net assets? (That is, if asset turnover is x: net assets, what is x?)

Another important ratio that can be used for practising working out ratios is liquidity, which shows the extent to which short-term claims by creditors are covered by assets that are likely to be converted into cash within the same timescale. One measure of this, called the 'Current Ratio', is the ratio of current assets : current liabilities. It is more likely to be given as a decimal number than as a percentage.

Exercise 11.25

Calculate the current ratio in the following cases (figures are in £000):

	Current assets	Current liabilities	Current ratio
(a)	10000	5000	_____
(b)	40	35	_____
(c)	2	3	_____
(d)	3500	2000	_____

You will learn many more ratios and how to interpret them on your course. Sometimes you will be faced with whole pages of figures from which you will be required to derive the ratios before interpreting them. This may, at first sight, seem forbidding but, in most cases, as the above exercises go some way to show, all you will need by way of mathematical skill is the ability to add, subtract, multiply and divide appropriate numbers, using a calculator or spreadsheet. The greater problem is to keep a clear head! The sums are not very important. What *is* important is to be able to look at the figures and see what they *mean*. Where do things seem to be changing, or where do there seem to be potential problems? And then you have to think about possible explanations for what you have observed and what these mean. These explanations often may be found by using other numbers, but it is a logical, not a mathematical, exercise.

Using Equations

In earlier examples you were using equations to find values, simply by substituting numbers for letters. But equations can allow you to do more than this. Take the simple (?) example of compound interest. Suppose you borrow £1000 for 5 years, at 15% interest p.a. and, instead of paying the interest, add it to the amount you owe. Thus, at the end of the first year, the amount you owe will be £1000 plus 15% of £1000. That is, the debt at the end of year 1 (call it D_1) will be $1.15 \times$ the sum borrowed.

Your debt at the end of year 2 will be $1.15 \times D_1$ or $1.15 \times 1.15 \times$ the original £1000.

Exercise 11.26

Use your calculator to find the debt at the end of year two. Then calculate the debt at the end of year three.

Year two_____ Year three_____

Now you can see why it is useful to replace numbers by letters. It enables us to write a general, all-purpose formula for how to calculate the amount owed, without specifying the actual figures. We can say that, after any number of years, call it n, the balance outstanding will be $(1.15)n \times £1000$. If you want the debt after 10 years, it will be $(1.15)^{10} \times £1000$, and so on. You could do this repeatedly, but you would soon appreciate the value of a spreadsheet!

We can make the formula more general by using a different letter, say A, for the amount originally borrowed, and even more general by using a further letter, say r, for the percentage interest rate. Thus, if we use D_n to indicate the debt at the end of year n, we have a completely general formula:

$$D_n = A(1 + r)^n$$

Using this formula we can work out the debt for any sum, interest rate, sum borrowed and any length of time, merely by replacing the letters by the numbers that we wish to use in a particular case, and then working out the answer.

Exercise 11.27

Work out the amount that will be owed:
(a) at the end of one year on a loan of £2000 at 13%   _____
(b) at the end of two years on a loan of £1500 at 25%   _____
(c) at the end of five years on a loan of £10 000 at 15%   _____

In this instance we are dealing with the simple case of substituting values in the formula to work out the amount owing after a given period with compound interest. It is simply a question of plugging in the right numbers, as the quantity you wanted, D_n, was sitting neatly by itself on one side of the '=' sign. Often it will be less simple. The value you want, traditionally referred to as x, may be mixed up in the middle of an equation and you may need to move terms around to get it to itself. Or worse still, you may want to find several terms (x, y and z?) which are all mixed up in the same equation, in which case you will need to work with several equations at once to find solutions.

Another common calculation you will need to do is, in a sense, the reverse of compound interest. Suppose you are considering an investment, say buying a machine.

You are assuming that this machine will generate a certain amount of income over a number of years. Is it worth investing? Presumably only if the income gained is more than what you would get by investing the same amount in an investment of equivalent risk over the same period. You can see from the way that compound interest grows that future income has to be quite a lot if it is to be more than your investment would generate, particularly if interest rates are high. To bring future income in different years back to a common 'present value' you divide the projected income for each year n by $(1+r)^n$ and add all these values together. (The discount rate, r, will reflect prevailing interest rates and the risk involved.) The *net present value* is what is left when you subtract the original investment from the sum of these 'present values'. If positive, you might well decide to invest.

Note that, although classical algebra traditionally dealt in 'x's and 'y's, you can use any letters you choose, and usually you will find it much easier to choose a letter that relates in some way to what it describes, as when we chose D for debt and r for rate in the example above. This makes it much easier to remember what the equation is all about and which term relates to which. Indeed, if you are struggling with an equation where the author has steadfastly refused to do this, sometimes you can make more sense of it by translating the 'x's and 'y's into letters that have a more obvious meaning. (If you are quoting a standard equation in an assignment or examination, you should, however, always use the 'official' letters.)

With some equations you will be able to find an answer. In other cases, you may have sets of variables and formulae where there is no answer as such, but where you can learn techniques that will allow you to maximise, or optimise, results. You will learn these when you study courses on Operations Research. Key among these techniques are use of the calculus (differential equations), discovered in the seventeenth century, and linear programming techniques, which date from the Second World War.

Don't panic. Differential calculus will be introduced (briefly) later in the chapter. The main point to note here is how easily you can move terms around in a fairly simple equation. Since the principle is the same, you should now be able to approach the more complex manipulations, which doubtless you will be taught, with more confidence.

An equation can best be visualised as two sets of things that are in balance. For example, look at Figure 11.13.

In Figure 11.13 x and $y + 1$ can be weighed in the pans and found equal, and we can thus write $x = y + 1$. Visualising it in this way makes it very easy to see what you can and cannot do to an equation. Clearly you could add the same quantity to each side, and the scales would still balance. Thus, in the above case, you could write $x + 1 = y + 1 + 1$, or $y + 2$, and it would still be correct. Similarly, $x + z = y + z + 1$ would also be true. You could also take the same quantity away from each side and leave the scales in balance. Thus you could write $x - 1 = y$, or $x - y = 1$.

You could multiply the two sides by the same thing, too. Doubling each side would still produce balance, as would trebling, or anything else. So $2x = 2(y + 1)$, $10x = 10(y + 1)$,

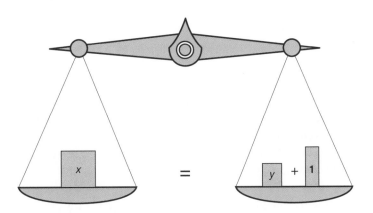

Figure 11.13 An equation as a balance

or $zx = z(y + 1)$. By the same token, you can divide each side by the same thing. Taking half of what is in each pan will still balance the scales, as will dividing by anything else. Thus:

$$\frac{x}{2} = \frac{(y + 1)}{2} \quad \text{and} \quad \frac{x}{z} = \frac{(y + 1)}{z} \quad \text{and} \quad \frac{x}{y + 1} = 1$$

Indeed, whatever you do, as long as you do it equally to both sides, you will be left with a valid equation. What you cannot do is to do something to one side, and do it to only part of the other side. Multiplying all of the right-hand side by a quantity, but multiplying only some of the left, would not be valid. Thus you could not write $2x = 2y + 1$ in the above example. (To remember this, you will need to put brackets round each side of the equation if you start multiplying or dividing.)

This is the main rule for manipulating equations. Once you have grasped it, you will be well away. Thus, suppose that you were working with the debt example we used earlier, but you knew the amount owed at the end of the period and the interest rate at which the money had been borrowed. What you did not know, and wanted to find out, was the original debt. Suppose that, after four years at 20 per cent the debt was £4147. You *could* experiment by trying different original loans and working out the debt in each case. When you got too big a debt you could try a smaller loan; if that came out too small, you could try a bigger one, getting closer to your £4147 debt each time. Alternatively, you could rearrange the equation so that the term you wanted, A, was on the left of the '=', all by itself, and then work out the figure you wanted directly. You do this by using the fact that you can do something to both sides of the equation without affecting its validity.

The original equation was:

$$D_n = A(1 + r)^n$$

Don't worry that this is much more complicated looking than the $x = y + 1$ type of example used above. The principle is exactly the same. In this case, we want to stop the A from being multiplied by $(1 + r)^n$. If you had $2A$ and wanted to have only A you would divide by 2. It is exactly the same here. If we divide $A(1 + r)^n$ by $(1 + r)^n$, then the $(1 + r)^n$'s cancel out, and leave us with A. But remember, if we did something to one side of the equation, we had to do it to the other, so we must divide the D^n by $(1 + r)^n$ as well. Thus we get the equally valid equation:

$$A = \frac{D_n}{(1 + r)^n}$$

This is a much more useful arrangement of the equation if A is what we are looking for. We know the values of D_n and r and n, so can put these into the equation, giving $A = £4147 \div (1.2)^4$, which your calculator should tell you is near enough £2000. This should be a much quicker, as well as more accurate, way of getting the answer than the trial and error method. (Note, however, that there will be occasions when trial and error is your only option, so do not underestimate that method's potential!)

To use a different equation, suppose you wanted to find x, and you knew $y = 7 + 3x + \frac{1}{y}$. You will remember from earlier that the first thing you could do would be to subtract $7 + \frac{1}{y}$ from each side of the equation, leaving you with $y - 7 - \frac{1}{y} = 3x$. Then, since we usually write what we are trying to find on the left of the '=' sign, we could swap the sides over to give $3x = y - 7 - \frac{1}{y}$. We then need to get rid of the 3, so we divide both sides by 3, giving us:

$$x = \frac{(y - 7 - \frac{1}{y})}{3}$$

If this was to be included in a longer equation, and there might be some chance of further cancelling, we might wish to sort out the rather messy $(y - 7 - \frac{1}{y})$ into a single fraction. To do this we need to express it all in 'y'ths, that is, as something over y. Just as 2 is $\frac{4}{2}$, so y can be written as $\frac{y^2}{y}$ and 7 as $\frac{7y}{y}$, so the whole phrase inside the bracket could just as well have been written as $x = \frac{(y^2 - 7y - 1)}{y}$, or the whole equation written as:

$$x = \frac{(y^2 - 7y - 1)}{3y}$$

If you know y, it is now easy to work out the value of x. For example,

$$\text{if } y = 2, \ x = \frac{(4 - 14 - 1)}{6}, \text{ or } -\frac{11}{6}$$

Exercise 11.28

Rearrange the following equations to get x on the left, then work out the values of x if:

		Value of x if:		
		(i) $y = 2$	(ii) $y = -3$	(iii) $y = 0$
(a)	$2y = x + 5$	$x = $ _____	_____	_____	_____
(b)	$y + 1 = 3x - 2$	$x = $ _____	_____	_____	_____
(c)	$y + 2x = y - x + 12$	$x = $ _____	_____	_____	_____
(d)	$\frac{y}{4} + \frac{x}{2} + 3$	$x = $ _____	_____	_____	_____
(e)	$xy = 3$	$x = $ _____	_____	_____	_____
(f)	$\frac{x}{y} = y + \frac{1}{2}$	$x = $ _____	_____	_____	_____
(g)	$\dfrac{y}{(x + 3)} = 4$	$x = $ _____	_____	_____	_____
(h)	$\dfrac{x}{(y + 2y + 1)} = y + 4$	$x = $ _____	_____	_____	_____

Working with brackets

In the above, you have needed to use brackets often because this is a way of reminding you either that everything on the top and everything on the bottom of a fraction must be multiplied or divided by the same thing if the fraction is to stay the same, or that everything on each side of an equation must be treated in the same way if the equation is to remain valid. In the exercise above, you could work with the brackets by substituting numbers and then working out the value of the bracket before dealing with it further, but sometimes you will need to work with brackets when you cannot do this. You have already seen that a simple multiplication, say $2(a + b)$, means multiplying *everything* in the bracket, here by 2, giving you $2a + 2b$ in this case. If you want to multiply *two* brackets, you need to multiply everything in the first bracket by everything in the second. Thus

$$(a + b)(c + d) \text{ will give you } ac + ad + bc + bd$$

Note that if two brackets are written side by side it means they are to be multiplied. There is no need to use a 'x' sign to show this. Work out the value of the above where $a = 1$, $b = 2$, $c = 3$ and $d = 4$, and then check that this is the same as if you multiplied 3 by 7.

Exercise 11.29

Work out the value of:

(a) $2a(3b + 2c)$ _____

(b) $\dfrac{x(6y - 4z)}{2}$ _____

(c) $3r(s + 2t) + 3s(2r + t)$ _____

(d) $(2x + y)(y + 2)$ _____

(e) $\dfrac{(3z + 4y)(2y + z)}{2(4y + 2z)(a + b)}$ _____

Differential calculus

I mentioned that this was one of the things you might need during your course, and it is one of the most alarming looking. However, as with much of maths, the basic operations are pretty simple. If your nerves can stand it, it is worth having a brief look before leaving this chapter. You may well have studied calculus at school and brief revision will bring it back.

Think back to earlier work on drawing graphs and on using equations to answer questions. You used a plot of an equation to discover a breakeven point, and you used intersections between two curves to find possible solutions to *simultaneous* equations, where you needed both equations to be able to answer a question. (*See* Answer to Exercise 11.10.)

The differential calculus is another approach to using equations to provide answers to questions. In particular, it allows you to work out the rate at which a value is changing at a certain point on a curve and the point where the value is highest (or lowest).

For straight lines, the rate of change is constant but, for curved lines, the rate is changing all the time. This rate is shown by the *tangent* to the curve, the line that just touches the curve at that point, and reflects the direction of the curve at the point of contact. (If drawing a tangent of a circle, you would draw the radius at that point, i.e. the line from the centre of the circle to the point where the tangent is being drawn. The tangent would be at 90° to that radius, i.e. at right angles to it. If you are drawing a tangent by eye, it can be useful first to try to draw the line that cuts your curve at right angles.)

If you were to plot average day length per week for every week of the year, you would find that it would start to increase from the winter solstice and continue increasing until the summer solstice when it would decline. And the line would not go straight up and then straight down, but would be in the shape of a wave. It would be flat at the solstices, and then gradually start to curve up. The line would be at its steepest at the equinoxes before it started to flatten off towards the next solstice. The angle of the line would reflect the rate of change in day length. (If your diary shows sunset and sunrise, try this for yourself.) At the highest and lowest points on the curve, the curve effectively would be horizontal.

The process of *differentiation* allows you to work out the rate of change of a curved line at any point. Where this rate is zero, the line is changing direction, passing from negative to positive or vice versa. So a zero rate of change will mean the point is a maximum or minimum value. Rather than going into the theory, and in keeping with the approach throughout the chapter, the box that follows gives a purely pragmatic approach to differentiation. It will get you started and allow you to work out simple things. For anything complex, you need another book.

Idiots' guide to differentiation

- The slope of a line plotting values of some variable y against known values of x is called (usually) 'dee why by dee ex' and written (usually) '*dy/dx*'. The process of working it out is called 'differentiation of y with respect to x'.

- If y is some function of a power of x, the *dy/dx* will be a function of one power lower of x. Thus if y is a function of x^2, *dy/dx* will be a function of x. If y is a function of x cubed, *dy/dx* will be a function of x squared.

- This function includes the *number* of the power of the x in the original equation. Thus if $y = x^2$, *dy/dx* $= 2x$. If $y = 4x^3$, *dy/dx* $= 12x^2$.

- If you have several different powers of x in one equation, you apply the same rule to each term. Thus if $y = x^4 + 2x^3$, *dy/dx* $= 4x^3 + 6x^2$.

- Remember that x is really x^1, so if $y = x$, *dy/dx* $= 1$. And if $y = 7x$, *dy/dx* $= 7$.

- Remember, too, that x^0 is 1, so any constant terms in your equation, i.e. any terms that do not depend on x, can be thought of as an 'x to the nought' term, and will be multiplied by zero when you differentiate. They therefore vanish. The fixed costs on your breakeven chart are a constant. If you were to differentiate that line they would vanish. And, indeed, they do not affect the slope of the total costs line.

- To find the maximum or minimum of a curve, work out *dy/dx* and then find the value(s) of x for which this is zero.

- Although it is traditional to use y and x, obviously you can differentiate an equation expressed in any letters, as long as one letter expresses the value of the equation expressed in terms of the other letter. (If a term appears on both sides you will need to sort out the equation before you can differentiate.)

- You can work out a second-order derivative by differentiating dy/dx. This would give you the rate at which the rate of change was changing. It is usually called d^2y/dx^2.

- Similarly, higher-order derivatives are possible.

- Integration reverses the process. But remember that constants vanish when you differentiate, so you cannot reconstitute the original equation. There will be an unknown constant that you cannot specify, so you will need to insert a letter to indicate this. Thus the 'integral' of $2x^2$ (i.e. $\int 2x^2$) will be $\frac{2}{3}x^3 + K$.

- The integral of a curve at a given point indicates the area under the curve to the left of that point. Thus the integral at x on a frequency graph of heights of males in a population would tell you what proportion of the population was 'x' or shorter.

Statistical software

Spreadsheets have huge advantages as will by now be clear. Once you have entered your data, and the equations you want to apply to different parts of the data, the numbers or graphs or charts will appear as if by magic. You can change or add figures, or change an equation slightly, and new results will appear. Excel has been criticised for sacrificing accuracy for speed of calculation, but if may well be adequate for student research purposes. Furthermore, most employers value Excel or other spreadsheet skills, so it is well worth investing time in learning how to use the software.

Excel also has a number of basic statistical functions, which may be sufficient for your needs (although some caution is needed). Using one of the many specialist statistical packages available will allow you to carry out more complex statistical analysis. However, such packages can be expensive, need time to learn to use them, and will only be worth this investment if you have a sound basic understanding of statistics and need the more complex analysis. SPSS, SAS and Minitab are commonly used, and your university may have a licence for one of these, and provide the necessary training. However, such packages are not needed for most Master's level research. For a survey-based review of use of Excel and non-spreadsheet-based statistical packages used on public policy courses (and some lovely examples of column charts used to show proportions) see Adams, Infeld and Wulff (undated, but post 2011).

Further skills development

The above treatment has, I hope, given you an idea of some of the things you can usefully do, once you are more familiar with numbers and basic mathematical techniques, and introduced the basics of the subject. There is no real substitute for practice if you are to become familiar with the techniques involved. Additional exercises can be found on the companion website. Alternatively, make up further equations for yourself and try using equations you have made up to solve problems. What equation can you construct to tell you how far a car will go on *g* gallons of petrol if it does 56 mpg? How many miles to the litre will it do if there are 4½ litres to the gallon? There are any number of such small equations that you can construct. Or you can find a range of free numeracy and basic maths tutorials online, or use a book such those suggested below. Check that your chosen book provides answers, as you will need feedback on your work. If you do feel particularly weak in this area, and you have time to spare before starting your course, this is one form of preparation that will pay huge dividends. Good luck!

SUMMARY

- Simple techniques such as bar charts, pie charts or graphs can enable you to represent sets of data in such a way as to make them more meaningful, allowing visual comparison between sets of figures, or the estimation of trends.
- Ratios, fractions or percentages can be used to indicate how parts relate to each other, or to the whole.
- Ratios are particularly important in accounting and finance.
- Ratios or fractions can be multiplied by multiplying numerators to give the new numerator, and multiplying denominators to give the new denominator. They are unchanged if top and bottom are multiplied by the same thing. They can be added or subtracted only if the denominator is the same in all cases.
- Equations can be used to find unknown values, or to provide a general formula from which values can be calculated in specific cases.
- Equations can be simplified, or rearranged, using the basic rule that an equation remains valid no matter what you do to one side, provided you do the same thing to all of the other side as well.
- Statistical techniques can be used to provide estimates of the probability of sets of results arising because of random variation, rather than because of a systematic difference. They will tell you only the probability of something, not whether it is true or not.
- Graphs can be drawn to show patterns and to answer questions.
- Differential calculus can help to answer questions about rates of change, maximal and minimal points on a graph and areas under a curve.
- Spreadsheets can make it very easy to calculate dependent variables, once you have set up the table.
- Spreadsheets also make it very easy to produce graphical representations of data.

Further information

Adams, W.C., Infeld, D.L and Wulff, C.M. (undated), *Statistical Software for Students: Academic Practices and Employer Expectations*, cached version available directly via Google.

11

SEEING STORIES IN NUMBERS

Crosby, A.W. (1997) *The Measure of Reality*, Cambridge University Press. This will not teach you any techniques but is fascinating background reading, with discussion of the role of numbers and measurement in a wider historical context. Thus it covers not only mathematics and bookkeeping but also music and painting over the period 1250–1600.

GMAC (2015) *The Official Guide for GMAT Quantitative Review 2016.* John Wiley & Sons. This gives you a large number of test items from the GMAT test, with answers.

Graham, L. and Sargent, D. (1981) *Countdown to Mathematics*, Vol. 1, Harlow: Pearson Education. This covers much the same ground at greater length and provides many more examples for you to work through, with answers.

Huff, D. (1991) *How to Lie with Statistics*, Penguin.

Jacques, I. (2013) *Mathematics for Economics and Business* (7th edn), Harlow: Pearson.

Moroney, M.J. (1951) *Facts from Figures*, Penguin. This is a classic, but accessible, introduction to statistics.

Morris, C. (2008) *Quantitative Approaches in Business Studies* (7th edn), FT Prentice Hall.

Morris, C. and Thanassoulis, E. (2007) *Essential Mathematics: For Business and Management*, Palgrave Macmillan.

Oakshott, L. (2009) *Essential Quantitative Methods for Business, Management and Finance*, Palgrave Macmillan.

Rowntree, D. (1987) *Statistics Without Tears: An Introduction for Non-Mathematicians*, Penguin.

Smith, H. and Bride, M. (2010) *Great at My Job but Crap at Numbers*. London: Teach Yourself. A great title, and conveys the unfrightening tone of the book.

Stutely, R. (2005) *The Definitive Guide to Managing the Numbers*, FT Prentice Hall.

Useful information on spreadsheets and finance for those who are worried about this part of a programme.

Wheelan, C. (2013) *Naked Statistics: Stripping the Dread from the Data*. London: W.W. Norton & Co Ltd.

Additional resources

http://www.open.edu/openlearn/free-courses (accessed 17.1.15). For a range of relevant (and other interesting) free short courses.

https://www.youtube.com/watch?v=cipckeeozBE (accessed 17.1.15). For one of a whole series of very basic tutorials on mathematical operations which would usefully supplement the Helpfile.

https://www.youtube.com/watch?v=8L1OVkw2ZQ8 (accessed 17.1.15). For good introduction to Excel spreadsheets (the first in a series).

https://www.youtube.com/watch?v=J4zq3R8b5dQ (accessed 17.1.15). For an alternative series of tutorials.

Morris, C. and Thanassoulis, E. (2007) *Essential Mathematics: For Business and Management*, Palgrave Macmillan. This also gives straightforward explanations of the topics covered here, together with statistics and calculus relevant to Chapter 11.

HELPFILE 11.1
CRACKING THE CODE

This section takes you, very gently I promise, through the basic symbols you may find in mathematical equations.

You will know that in 5 + 3 the '+' is telling you to take the *sum* of 3 and 5, or what you get when you add them together. If you had trouble doing the sum, or would have done if it had larger numbers, you can get the answer easily from your calculator, by pressing the obvious buttons. Here you would need 5, +, 3, =. Note that, for additions, the order of the terms does not matter. 5 + 3 is the same as 3 + 5.

You will also know already that 5 − 3, or 5 minus 3, means what you get when you take 3 away from 5. Again, you can easily do subtractions by pressing the obvious calculator buttons. Note that subtractions are more complicated than additions in two ways. First, the order *does* matter. 5 − 3 is *not* the same as 3 − 5. If you have £3000 in the bank and take out £5000 you are *not* in the same situation as if you have £5000 and take out £3000! In the second case you will have £2000 left and your bank manager will be happy. In the first case, you will have an overdraft of £2000 and, unless you cleared this with the bank first, they probably will *not* be happy. You will have –£2000. This may be written as (£2000) in some sets of accounts.

Second, there is the interesting question of what to do when you want to take away an amount that is already negative, i.e. has a − sign in front of it. To 'take away' your overdraft, someone would have to *give* you £2000 and, indeed, to take away a number that is already negative you *add* that number. Thus 5 − (3) is 5 + 3, or 8. Note that basic calculators can't do this for you; you have to apply this rule of signs yourself before you press the buttons.

This indicates multiplication. 5 × 3 means 5 lots of 3, or 15. Again, the obvious calculator buttons will produce the answer if you have forgotten your tables. And, as with addition, order does not matter. When dealing with negative numbers, you need to count the number of '−' signs in the string of numbers you are multiplying. If you have one, or indeed any odd number of minuses, the answer will be negative. For example, if you owe 5 weeks' garage rent at £3 per week, you have $5 \times (-3)$ or −£15.

If you are multiplying two negative quantities, or any even number of negatives, the answer will be positive. A cheap calculator will not be able to handle a string of mixed signs in a multiplication. When you put in a − it will start to subtract. So you will have to treat the numbers as positive and, again, add the right sign yourself, once you get the answer.

Part of the reason for difficulty in working with mixtures of signs on a calculator is that in a string of things to add, subtract, multiply and divide, the signs have different *strengths*. If you see $5 + 3 \times 2$, this means that you should work out the 3×2 *first*, before adding the 5. Thus you get 11 *not* 16. Multiplication and division signs are stronger than addition and subtraction signs, so must be worked on first. Sophisticated calculators are programmed with this rule, but cheap ones are not.

This indicates division. $5 \div 3$ means what you get when you divide 5 into 3 equal portions. If the second number goes into the first with no problems, for example in the case of $6 \div 3$ where the answer is 2, life is simple. If it does not, because the first number is not capable of being produced by multiplying the second number by a whole number, you start getting into *fractions*. If I produce five cakes, my three children will know that they will get fewer than two each, because there are fewer than six cakes, and more than 1½. To be sure they are happy, I could divide each cake into three equal parts and give them a part of each cake. The *fraction* of each cake that they would get would be ⅓.

Figure 11.14 shows how one share is 5 times 1/3, which could be assembled into 1⅔ cakes. You could write the 1⅔ as ⅝ if you liked. You will see in a minute why this can sometimes be useful.

This is a decimal point. You will be used to seeing figures written in decimals. 1.5 means 1½. The decimal point divides the whole number from the fraction. Adding fractions can be quite difficult but, if they are expressed as decimals, the sum can be done easily.

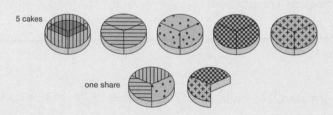

Figure 11.14 When you have five cakes and three children

Press 5, ÷, 3, = on your calculator to see what 1⅔ is in decimal notation. The same sort of system works to the right of the decimal point as to the left. You will know that the first place to the left of the decimal point represents units, the next tens, the next hundreds, and so on. As you move one place to the left, you multiply by 10. Once you move to the right of the decimal point, exactly the same applies. But, because you are now travelling right instead of left, each shift away from the decimal point means a *division* by 10. Thus 1.5 means 1 and ⁵⁄₁₀, 1.05 means 1 and ⁵⁄₁₀₀, etc.

It is very easy to work with decimals on a calculator, as they work in exactly the same way as whole numbers. As long as you remember to insert a decimal point at the right place in each number, the calculator will do the rest. You merely have to remember that your calculator will not be able to cope with a mixture of additions and multiplications if it is a cheap one, and you will have to work out the multiplications or divisions first, before inserting the result into the sum you give to the machine. If you are working in decimals without your calculator, you must remember to line up the decimal points. Thus, in adding 101.75 and 1.003, you will get:

$$
\begin{array}{r}
101.75\,+ \\
\underline{1.003} \\
102.753
\end{array}
$$

In this way, you are adding units to units, ⅒ths to ⅒ths, and so on.

If you want to add a string of fractions on a cheap calculator, you will again start to confuse it. To get around this, use the memory. Each time you work out a fraction as a decimal, add it into the memory. The button usually says $\boxed{\text{M+}}$ for this. If one of the fractions is to be subtracted, press the $\boxed{\text{M−}}$ button. When you have finished, you can access the result with the memory recall, probably the $\boxed{\text{MR}}$, button.

$$\boxed{\%}$$

Percentage or per cent. This is a fraction expressed in ⅒₀ths. Thus 1 is ¹⁰⁰⁄₁₀₀ths or 100%, half is ⁵⁰⁄₁₀₀ths or 50%, etc. This is very similar to working in the first two numbers to the right of the decimal point and has the same advantages as does using decimals. It is very hard to see how ¹¹⁄₁₃, ²⁷⁄₃₁ and ⁵⁄₇ relate to each other. If you express them as percentages it is very easy to see which is biggest, or to add or subtract them. Use your calculator to find out what a variety of fractions are in percentages. You probably will be able to do this by pressing, say, $\boxed{1}$, $\boxed{÷}$, $\boxed{4}$, $\boxed{\%}$ to get ¼ as a percentage. Start with something you know first, like ½, to check that these are the right buttons.

$$\boxed{=}$$

You will have been happily using the $\boxed{=}$, or 'equals' button on your calculator if you have been trying out simple sums as suggested above. Equations always contain an equals sign. It means that everything to one side of it is the same as everything to the other side. More of this later.

$$\boxed{2}$$

The power of two, or squared. Little numbers up in the air to the right of a number or letter mean that it has been multiplied by itself, the number of terms in the multiplication being given by the number. Thus 2^2 means 2×2, and 3^2 means 3×3. We call this 'squared', or 'to the power 2'. If the little number is a 3 we call it 'cubed' or 'to the power 3'. 4^3 is $4 \times 4 \times 4$. 10^3 is 1000. After this we run out of special terms and are reduced to speaking of 'to the power 7' or whatever. What do you think you get when you multiply two powers of a single number? Try it with $10^2 \times 10^3$. You will find you get 100 000, or 10^5. This always works. You simply can add the powers together if you are multiplying two powers of a single number. Remember this, as it has all sorts of uses. By the same token, you can *divide* a power of a number by another power of that number by subtracting the second index from the first. Thus $2^3 \div 2^2 = 2$, or $10^{12} \div 10^8 = 10^4$.

There are two funny indices, the power 0 and the power 1. Try to work out what these must mean, remembering that to *multiply* powers you *add* the indices. Raising a number to the power 1 must therefore mean using the number as it stands. 5^3 must be the product of 5^1 and 5^2. But you know that 5×5^2 is 5^3, so 5^1 must be 5.

By the same token, $5^0 \times 5^2$ should be 5^2. But the only thing that you can multiply 5^2 by to get 5^2 is 1, so 5^0, or indeed anything to the power nought, must be 1.

Square root. This is the number which, multiplied by itself, gives you the number you first thought of. Thus $\sqrt{9}$ is the number which, when squared, gives the answer 9, i.e. 3. Press $\boxed{8}$, $\boxed{1}$, $\boxed{\sqrt{}}$ on your calculator to find the square root of 81. You should be able to work out what the index number, or power, of a square root is. Stop for a minute and try.

If you are stuck, remember that to multiply two powers you *add* the index numbers. And the index for a number itself is 1. This will work only if each index is ½. Thus $\sqrt{4} \times \sqrt{4} = 4^{1/2} \times 4^{1/2}$.

Just as you can find squares, cubes, fourth powers, etc. so you can find cube roots, fourth roots, etc. Cube roots are written as $\sqrt[3]{x}$ or $x^{1/3}$, fourth roots as $\sqrt[4]{x}$ or $x^{1/4}$, etc. Work out $\sqrt[4]{16}$ on your calculator.

You will not have found a $\sqrt[4]{}$ key, but you knew that a fourth root is the square root of a square root, so if you could not do the sum in your head, you could press $\boxed{1}$, $\boxed{6}$, $\boxed{\sqrt{}}$, $\boxed{\sqrt{}}$, giving the answer 2.

If you still feel a bit bemused, you will find it helpful to find squares, square roots, cubes and fourth powers of a variety of numbers, writing down each number with its square or whatever, until you get the feel for how such numbers relate. You can check your squares by finding their square roots to see that these are what they ought to be or your square roots by multiplying them by themselves.

This exhausts the signs on a cheap calculator. Scientific calculators have a much wider range of keys, offering all sorts of facilities, including the ability to do calculations involving mixed additions and multiplications without getting muddled. Even better are the financial calculators, which allow you to derive values for things like net present value at the press of a button, instead of sweating blood working these out by hand as did earlier generations of students. Doubtless you will want to invest in one of these calculators once you start your MBA accounting courses but, while you are just gaining confidence, you might actually be better off with a simple cheap calculator: there is less to confuse you.

Other mathematical signs you will encounter frequently include the following.

$$\boxed{x}$$

x or indeed any other letter. This is referred to as a variable and appears in an equation to indicate something that can take a number of values, or whose value you do not know. Although some people are put off by the appearance of a letter in an equation, in fact you treat it just like a number and can move it around in the same way. Of course, if you want, say, to multiply it by 2, you can't write in a new number, but you can work with, say, $2x$, quite happily. Indeed, it is often very much simpler to play with letters in an equation than with numbers, which explains their popularity. When we deal with equations in more detail you will see why.

$$\boxed{\bar{x}}$$

This means the mean value of x, the value gained by adding all values of x and dividing by the number of such values.

$$\boxed{\Sigma}$$

The Greek letter sigma, used to indicate the sum of. Often you will see something of the form $\sum_{n=1}^{r} x_n$. This indicates that there are a series of values of x, which have been called for convenience x_1, x_2, x_3, all the way up to x_r. You are to add all these values for x_1 through to x_r. Thus, you could express a year's sales figures as the sum of the monthly totals, x_1 to x_{12}, written as $\sum_{n=1}^{12} x_n$ or the second quarter's total as $\sum_{n=4}^{6} x_n$.

The notation may look clumsy and forbidding, but is often an economical way of expressing something in an equation.

$\int (\dots) \, dx$ denotes integration with respect to x. (The symbol for an integration is an s, because integration is, essentially, summation.)

$$\boxed{f}$$

This means 'function'. If we say $y = f(x)$ we mean that y varies in some way as x varies, or it is a *function* of x. It could be $2x$, or $x + 10\,000$, or anything else involving x. You could, for example, write $v = f(l,b)$ to indicate that the volume (v) of a room depends upon its length (l) and breadth (b). (It also depends on its height, which you are choosing not to mention.) This is one of the favourites among those who like to repeat their text in equation form. Unless they specify what the function *is*, their complicated-looking expressions are unlikely to communicate more than their verbal description.

This simply means 'not equal to'. If you write $x \neq y$, you are saying that x *cannot* take the same value as y.

This means 'less than'. If $x < y$, then x is less than y.

This means 'greater than'. If $x > y$, then x is greater than y. It is easy to remember which is which, as in both signs the wider part of the wedge is pointing to the larger number.

This means 'less than or equal to'. If $x \leq y$, then x cannot be greater than y, though it could be the same value, or smaller.

Obviously this means 'greater than, or equal to'.

Brackets. These are very important in equations. If things are in a bracket, it means that they must be treated as a whole. $2(7 + 6x + y)$ means that you must multiply *everything in the bracket* by 2, for example. Here you would get $14 + 12x + 2y$. Also, $(5 + 3) \times 2$ tells you to do the addition first.

ANSWERS TO EXERCISES

Exercise 11.1

(a) 0.75, 0.8571428, 1.3333333, 1.7142857, 0.8181818, 0.75.

(b) 200%, 75%, 133%, 91%, 25%, 67% (taking the nearest whole percentage as the answer).

(c) 8, 196, 81, 81, 1728, 1, 1.

(d) 2^7, 3^2, 10^0, 17^8, 21^{18}, x^5, x^{y-2}, $z^2(x + y)$.

(e) 4, 12, 6, 6.16, 1.41, 3.16 (giving answers to two decimal places).

(f) 2^8, 10^1, $3^{2/3}x^1y^1c$ (or xy), z^2.

(g) 6.

(h)

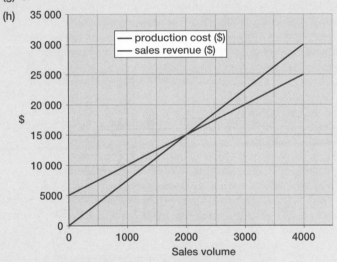

(i) ii, iii.

(j) $2x + 2y$, $3x - 3y^2$, $3y - 3x$, 0, y.

(k) neither.

(l) 13, 17, $x + \dfrac{x^2}{y}$, to two places of decimals.

If you had more than one or two (careless) mistakes you should take time to work through relevant parts of the Helpfile. You will also know which parts of the chapter will need most attention.

Exercise 11.2

61.55, 52.95.

Exercise 11.3

(a) mean 5.44, median 5, mode 5.

(b) mean 5.44, median 4, mode 1.

Exercise 11.4

Marker 1, ranked scores: 20, 30, 40, 50, 51, 54, 55, 55, 57, 60, 61, 69, 70, 70, 75, 75, 80, 81, 83, 95

Marker 2, ranked scores: 40, 41, 42, 42, 43, 46, 47, 49, 49, 49, 50, 51, 55, 60, 60, 60, 63, 67, 70, 75.

Note: when there is no single mid-point, you usually average the two mid-points (highlighted above) to give a median or quartile value. Thus the interquartile range for Marker 1 is 52.5–75 and for Marker 2 is 42.5–60.

Exercise 11.6

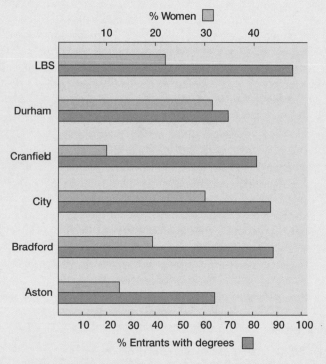

The chart shows one possibility. But it does give a false impression of the percentage of women, so you might have preferred to use the same scale for both. It would depend on whether you were interested primarily in the differences in each type of percentage *between* the schools, or the differences between the two percentages in each case.

Exercise 11.7

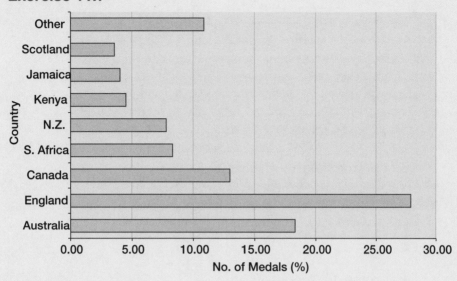

Exercise 11.8

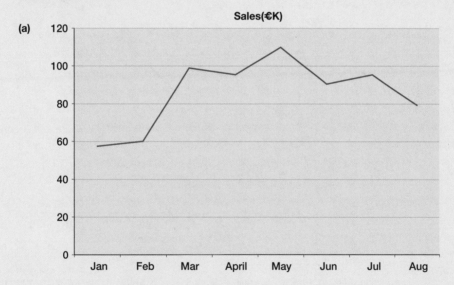

(b)

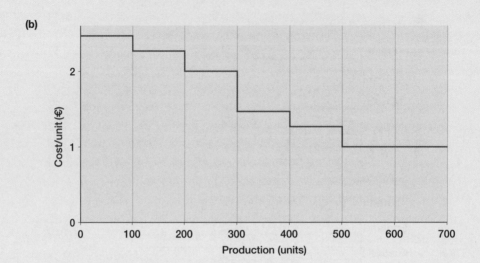

Exercise 11.9

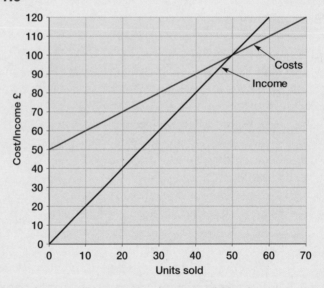

You can see from this that you will break even when you sell 50 units.

(If you sell n units, income is $2n$, while costs are $n + 50$. Thus, you break even when n is such that $2n = n + 50$. Subtracting n from each side of the equation shows that this must be when $n = 50$.)

Exercise 11.10

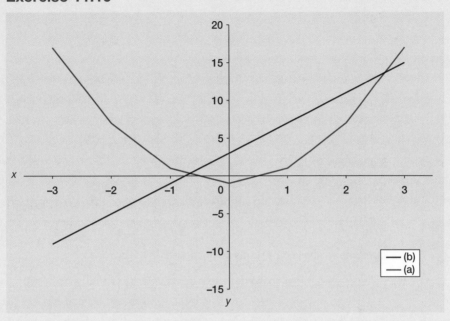

You can see that there are two solutions, one somewhere near $x = -0.7$ and $y = 0.5$, and another around $x = 2.7$ and $y = 13.5$. (Note: line (a) ideally would be a smooth curve, getting smoother the more values of x – i.e. intermediate fractions – you plotted.)

Exercise 11.11

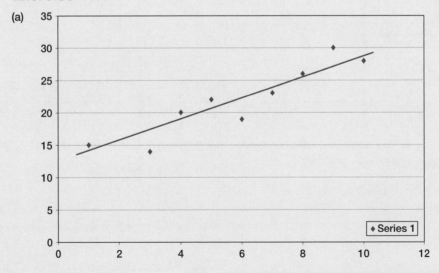

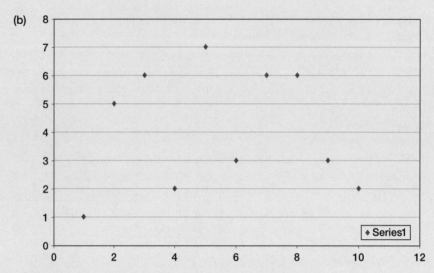

No line is shown: these data points do not appear to lie on a line.

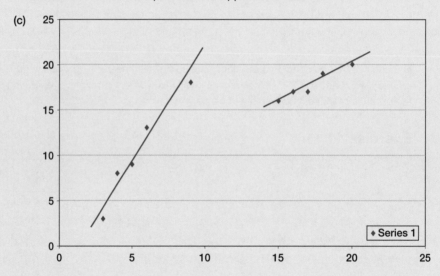

While a single line **could** be fitted to these points, visual inspection suggests two lines are more appropriate, as shown.

Exercise 11.12

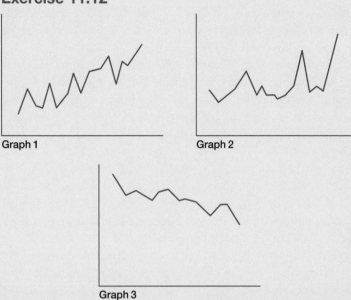

Graph 1   Graph 2

Graph 3

The shading in the graphs shows the broad areas that are reasonable. If the end of your line lies outside this area, you should ask yourself whether you have been unduly influenced by recent variations in the graph.

Exercise 11.13

(a) My rough guess was 8600. Actual figure, 8689.

(b) My rough guess was 4100. Actual figure, 4507.7.

(c) My guess was 10 000 000. Actual figure, 9 850 028.3.

(d) My guess was 107. Actual figure, 111.95.

Perhaps your guesses were better!

Exercise 11.14

1.63, 4.00, 7164.23, 51.11, 1.66.

Exercise 11.15

£76. It doesn't matter which way round the discounts are calculated. You pay £0.95 × 0.80 × 100 (or £0.80 × 0.95 × 100) and it makes no difference what order numbers appear in a multiplication.

Exercise 11.16

(a) ⅔

(b) ¾

(c) ⅔

(d) 2

(e) ⁴⁄₃ or 1⅓

(f) ¾

(g) ½

Exercise 11.17

(a) ⅕

(b) ⅓

(c) $\dfrac{1}{y(1 + y)}$

(d) ¼

(e) $\dfrac{1}{x}$

(f) $\dfrac{(y + 1)}{10}$

(g) $\dfrac{xy}{2}$

Exercise 11.18

(a) ⅛

(b) ⅑

Exercise 11.19

(a) ²⁄₉

(b) $\dfrac{3y}{2x}$

(c) $\dfrac{3(x + 4)}{(x + 1)(x + 2)}$

(d) $\dfrac{5(y + 1)}{4x(x + 1)}$

(e) $\dfrac{9x}{8y}$

Exercise 11.20

(a) ¹³⁄₈ or 1⅝

(b) $\dfrac{(3x + 4x)}{xy}$

(c) $\dfrac{(3x - 1)}{y}$

(d) $\dfrac{(9x + 10)}{15}$

(e) ⅜

(f) $\dfrac{y(5x + 1)^2 + x2y}{x(5x + 1)}$ or $\dfrac{6x^2y + 10xy + 1}{x(5x + 1)}$

(g) $\dfrac{5(x - 2) - 3(x - 1)}{(x - 1)(x - 2)}$ or $\dfrac{(2x - 7)}{(x - 1)(x - 2)}$

Exercise 11.21

(a) 32%

(b) 32:100 or $^{32}/_{100}$ (or 0.32:1)

(c) 47% or 0.47:1 (or 128:272)

Exercise 11.22

(a) 12.5%

(b) 198%

(c) 33.1%

(d) (4%) – a negative return

Exercise 11.23

	Mean investment	ROCE
(a)	317.5	14%
(b)	140	236%
(c)	7900	28%
(d)	5550	(1%)

Exercise 11.24

Sales.

Exercise 11.25

(a) 2

(b) 1.14

(c) 0.67

(d) 1.75

Exercise 11.26

$D_2 = £1322.50$, $D_3 = £1520.87$

Exercise 11.27

(a) £2260

(b) £2343.75

(c) £20 113.57

Exercise 11.28

(a) $x = 2y - 5$ (i) −1   (ii) −11   (iii) −5

(b) $x = \dfrac{(y + 3)}{3}$ (i) ⅔   (ii) 0   (iii) 1

(c) $x = 4$ (i) 4   (ii) 4   (iii) 4

(d) $x = \dfrac{y}{2} - 6$ (i) −5   (ii) −7½ (or −¹⁵⁄₂)   (iii) −6

(e) $x = \dfrac{3}{y}$ (i) ½   (ii) −1   (iii) infinity (or undefined)

(f) $x = y^2 + ½y$ or $y(y + ½)$ (i) 5   (ii) 7½   (iii) 0

(g) $x = \dfrac{y}{4} - 3$ (i) −2½   (ii) −3¾   (iii) −3

(h) $x = (y + 4)(3y + 1)$ (i) 42   (ii) −8   (iii) 4

Exercise 11.29

(a) $6ab + 4ac$

(b) $3xy - 2xz$

(c) $3rs + 6rt + 6rs + 3st$, or $9rs + 6rt + 3st$

(d) $2xy + 4x + y^2 + 2y$

(e) $\dfrac{(3z + 4y)}{4(a + b)}$ (note it was possible to divide top and bottom by $2y + z$)

Exercise 11.30

		A	B	C	D
1			**Last year**	**This year**	**Percentages**
2		Accounting	100	109	109
3		Business studies	230	218	94.78261
4		Computing	200	242	121
5		Design	50	46	92
6		**Total**	580	615	106.0345

PART 4
SKILLS FOR ASSESSMENT

12
UNDERSTANDING YOUR ASSESSORS

Learning outcomes

By the end of this chapter you should:

- understand the objectives of your assessors in setting assignments

- be aware of the different types of assessment that may be used

- understand the basic principles of communication in the context of assessment

- appreciate some of the key differences between UK assessment systems and those in some other countries.

Introduction

Thus far you have concentrated on developing a range of skills that will help you to benefit from your studies and that will transfer easily to work. Learning to be better at your job is arguably the most important outcome of your studies. But you will also want to pass your courses, and get high marks – gaining a qualification was probably your initial, and most powerful, motive! While you are unlikely to pass a course if you learn nothing, learning itself does not ensure a pass. You have to *demonstrate* to your examiners that you have learned what they intended.

The next few chapters should help you to gain grades at least as high as your learning deserves. For this you need to understand the viewpoint of those who are assessing you, and the characteristics of the types of assessment they set. You also need to develop some fairly specific skills in being assessed in an academic context, although even these may be relevant in some work situations as well.

This chapter covers the purposes of assessment, the particular challenge of work-based assignments, and the general principles of communication that underlie all types of assessment. It looks briefly at the particular challenges faced by graduates from abroad studying at Master's level in the UK. The next chapter deals with written assignments, the following one with making a presentation and the last chapter in this section looks at a range of other ways in which you may be examined or assessed.

Challenges for students from different educational backgrounds

Many students find submitting work for assessment is stressful. Some feel a failure if they get less than 100 per cent and dread writing for fear of a lower mark. Some find it hard to start writing because they cannot even work out what is required. Some are really worried about their ability to write understandable English.

The first fear may be genuine, but is based on questionable assumptions which will be addressed shortly. The second will be helped, I hope, by this chapter. The third fear may or may not be justified. While some students' language skills are so poor that they would benefit most from taking time out to improve their English before resuming their studies, they are in a minority in most universities. Most of those who have told me they worry about their language are more than able to communicate clearly even from the start, and improve greatly during their course.

There are Helpfiles at the end of this chapter and the next that may help a little with language use in assignments, but if you are really struggling with the language, seek help from your university as this book is no substitute for some language tuition.

If your worries stem from not understanding the approach to either learning or assessment that is required of you, read on. This chapter may help. Such worries may be rooted in differences in educational cultures between a home country and where you are now studying, or differences between your undergraduate discipline and management.

Some cultures, and some undergraduate subjects, do not take the critical approach you are likely to encounter on your current programme.

The idea of critical reading was introduced in Chapter 7. Master's-level study in the UK typically requires substantial independent study and independent thinking about what you read. This may be a shock if you come from a country where very little independence of thought is required and the main test is of memory. If you studied under such a system, you may find assessment in a country like the UK very difficult at first. British students with a science, maths or engineering background may have similar difficulties at first.

Another potential area of difference is the attitude to 'cutting and pasting' materials from elsewhere in your assignments. If this was acceptable in your undergraduate studies, please make sure you have thoroughly read and understood the UK's attitude to plagiarism, explained in Chapter 7.

➤ Ch 7

This chapter is written from a UK perspective and should give you an understanding of the way that assessors' minds in management related subjects are likely to work in that country and what they are likely to be looking for. Read this and the following chapter carefully. Also, you will probably need to refer frequently to the glossary of terms used in assessment at the end of Chapter 13 (Helpfile 13.1). If you can, take advantage of your tutors' willingness to explain things. If you do poorly in the first pieces of work you submit, try very hard to get detailed feedback on how you need to change your approach.

➤ Ch 13

Above all, do not feel ashamed if you find this way of working difficult and your grades are at first not what you would hope. You are undertaking something extremely challenging in studying in an unfamiliar system and/or subject. So be open about your difficulties and seek help, whenever and wherever possible. Throughout the course you are likely to find that, if you make your needs known, you can get the support you need from fellow students, tutors and others within the university community. The effort will be worthwhile. Your understanding at the end of the course will have grown far more than that of local students. And you will, at the same time, have made a significant contribution to their understanding of the wider context of management.

There is a more general point here about disappointment with grades, and how to handle it. Your grades may be lower because of language issues, or because you are struggling with a very different discipline. They may also be lower because it is very hard to get high marks in management subjects (unless they are highly quantitative) in the UK. Most universities regard 70 as pretty good, 80 as outstanding. If you come from a system (such as the US) where anything less than 90 is a disaster, it may take a while to adjust. Familiarise yourself with the meaning attached to marks at your institution, and find out if you can how marks tend to be distributed within the range used. Find out what counts as a merit and a distinction. And try to feel appropriately good about the marks you receive!

The 'language of assessment' extends to the weight carried by deadlines. In some educational cultures these may be merely indicative. In many UK universities an assignment submitted after the deadline will receive no marks at all, unless an extension was agreed in advance, or there is an evidenced reason why this could not be done. More on this later. Meanwhile, if you understand the context in which you are being assessed, the process is likely to be less stressful and you are likely to produce work which gains good marks.

Assessment in context

Assessment is a complex area, with many influences acting upon it. How you are assessed will depend upon the nature of the programme in which you are involved, its objectives and the views about learning that underpin its design. The approach to assessment may also depend upon where the institution is trying to 'position itself' in the management education market.

Critics of current forms of management education see assessment as a vehicle for policing both tutors and students in a system that demands a high level of conformity from both. From a less critical viewpoint, assessment is both a vehicle for learning and a necessary means of demonstrating that standards are being maintained.

Institutional objectives for assessment

In choosing a course you probably wanted a respected qualification. You would not want to work hard for a degree from an institution seen as third rate. Reputations of academic institutions depend upon 'standards' being visibly maintained. Institutions do not wish their graduates to bring the institution into disrepute by their subsequent incompetence or ignorance. Their first objective for assessment is, therefore, to ensure that their graduates have reached a standard worthy of the qualification awarded.

Second, this concern with standards must be *perceived* by others. Academics want colleagues elsewhere to respect the place where they work. More importantly, institutions want to gain, or keep, a 'seal of approval' from one of the major accrediting bodies: AMBA, EQUIS and the AACSB are the main bodies for MBAs and similar degrees. Some more specialist degrees have both academic accreditation and recognition by a relevant professional institution. Accreditation has become more important with the explosion in postgraduate management education. Accrediting bodies typically require a rigorous structure of assessment, including unseen examinations, with a system of external examiners to maintain comparability between institutions.

There is a third, and perhaps even more important, objective for assessment. Properly designed it can be an 'engine of learning', driving students to exert effort that they would not otherwise exert, providing both carrots (the glow of satisfaction from a good grade) and sticks (the risk of not being allowed to proceed towards a qualification). Well-designed assessment will direct that effort into activities that will enhance learning and increase understanding. If students are given detailed feedback on their efforts they will gain understanding of their strengths and weaknesses and will be able to do better in future.

You may curse the assignment that keeps you up until after midnight to meet a deadline, but the pressure may have been necessary to get you to do the work at all. You may hate getting a fail grade on the first piece of work you submit, but will thank it later, when you have remedied whatever weakness caused it, and gone on to do far better next time. (I received one thank-you email which started, 'You may not remember me, but [three years ago] you gave me 38 on my first assignment. I've just got a distinction on my final MBA course . . .')

What is assessed

Traditionally, examinations were the most important form of assessment. When teaching is seen as transmitting knowledge, they are an efficient way of testing that students can remember key information, concepts, techniques and theories. This is a common feature of many educational systems. Exams are also good at assessing the ability to construct, under pressure, a reasoned argument from evidence. This may have been less important in your undergraduate studies. Whether intentionally or not, written communication skills are also assessed.

Exams were traditionally supplemented by a thesis or dissertation, which allowed research skills and a higher level of analytical skills to be assessed, as well as presenting a greater test of writing skills and other challenges, including more independent learning and time- and project-management.

➤ **Chs 1, 6, 7**
Both these forms of assessment are still widely used today (and have subsequent chapters devoted to them). But as programmes have moved away from the 'jug and mug' approach towards developing a much wider range of conceptual and other skills as outlined in earlier chapters additional ways of assessing students have been developed. Thus you may be required (if studying while working) to apply what you have learned to situations you encounter at work to increase your understanding of the issues or to question and perhaps change your own management practice. Indeed, many programmes ask for an internal consultancy project rather than a more academic dissertation or thesis as the final piece of assessment. Assignments based on your own organisation present very specific challenges, dealt with in the next section. Some full-time programmes may arrange for group consultancy projects in collaborating organisations.

➤ **Chs 1, 6, 7**

➤ **Ch 16**
A range of other assessments are also used. You may be set other group assignments, perhaps 'meeting' electronically to work on these, and be assessed either on your particular contribution to the effort or as a whole group with a single mark. Your competence as a manager may be assessed via a portfolio of work-based evidence. Some assessment may be computer-based, with automatic scoring of multiple-choice questions. In some cases you may be asked to assess your own or other students' work, since this may help develop important judgmental skills.

Thus, 'what is assessed' is changing in two ways. The range of skills that business schools seek to teach, and which therefore needs to be assessed, is widening. The range of ways in which schools attempt to assess these skills is changing in consequence.

Work-based and practice-based assessment

➤ **Ch 7**
If studying part time, particularly on an MBA, you may well find yourself faced with work- or practice-based assignments. These allow assessors to test not only your familiarity with concepts and models taught in the course, but your ability to *apply* these concepts appropriately and constructively to a real situation. This requires a higher level of skill than the writing of an academic essay. Many of these concepts are remarkably simple in themselves. But *using* these concepts to make sense of a complex and confusing situation, and to come to creative conclusions as to what to do about it, may be a real challenge.

Sometimes assessment will require you to reflect on your own practice in the light of the theory you have met, and to submit an account of your attempts at becoming more effective. Such assessment is likely to include a large reflective element, as in such cases you are seeking to 'engage' all three cogs – theory, thinking and practice. You may also be asked to use supporting evidence, to ensure that your efforts are not driven purely by your limited perception of a situation.

➤ Chs 6, 7

In either of these forms of assessment a key part of that challenge is being sufficiently selective.

The need for selectivity

In compiling a case study (even one that seems huge), the author will not have written down more than a fraction of what *could* have been written. Points will have been selected to be relevant to the intended analysis. In a work- or practice-based assignment, you need to be similarly selective. And you may feel you are floundering in a sea of potentially relevant, though perhaps not easily accessible, information. Furthermore, you may be involved emotionally. There may be things you simply do not 'see' because you take them for granted, or because it is more comfortable *not* to see them. It is very difficult to stand back and think dispassionately about something in which you are deeply involved. You may be uncertain about what to consider and what to ignore. 'Hard' information from company records may turn out to be surprisingly unreliable. 'Softer' information from interviews or other sources may be biased or present problems of interpretation.

Another problem with own-organisation work is that it is harder to think up creative options than for a case study. In the case study you will be blessedly unaware of most of the constraints that would apply in reality. In your own organisation you are likely to be all too aware of what has already been tried and failed, or is considered as quite out of the question by significant members of the organisation. Yet, your assessors will still be looking for the ability to come up with feasible options.

Most management courses at Master's level are concerned with developing strategic skills in a manager. A prerequisite for successful strategy is sensitivity to the wider environment. Your assessors will, therefore, require you to demonstrate the ability to look beyond organisational boundaries. You may need to adopt the perspective of a more senior manager in the organisation using information about the environment to inform decision taking. If so, it may help if you check out your perceptions with someone at that level of seniority. If you are doing an in-company project, you may need to find someone in such a position who is prepared to be your 'client'. In either case you will develop skills for operating on a different level.

Work-based assignments, especially projects or dissertations, may be longer term than much of the older style of assessment. This, together with the conflicts generated by part-time study, means that you will need highly developed time-management skills.

The shift in emphasis from examinations to assessment based on work-relevant skills demands an even broader range of skills than your assessors may have intended. Convincing your assessors that you can *apply* your learning appropriately to tackle managerial problems in a creative and sound way requires many skills of vital importance to a manager, even if these skills are not directly assessed.

Common causes of failure

You considered some of the threats to success in Chapter 5, with an emphasis on failure to plan and manage your studies as a cause you could usefully address from the start. Outright failure is relatively uncommon on many management-related Master's programmes, but rather more students withdraw without completing their degree. Such withdrawal is another form of failing to meet your original objectives. Now that you have worked through more of the book you are better placed to address some of the other causes.

Activity 12.1

Look back at Figure 5.5. Add to it any additional factors that you feel might threaten your own course completion. Highlight any of the factors (on the original diagram or added by you) that you feel might be particularly relevant to you.

The factors on the diagram, and presumably any you have added, can be divided into those you can do nothing about, those that, with the aid of this book or other assistance, you *might* be able to influence in the fairly short term, and those where any remedy will be longer term. (Remember the serenity prayer from Chapter 3.) The main focus of this chapter will be on internal causes. Planning and management skills were dealt with earlier. This chapter addresses other internal factors. However, as it is vital to act quickly in the face of external threats, that point is briefly made again here.

External factors

In the 'probably unavoidable' category are illness, sudden totally unanticipated change in job demands, redundancy and relationship breakdowns. In some of these cases your studies may themselves be a causal factor. Chapter 5 highlighted the need for immediate action to inform appropriate members of your college in such cases. If warned of problems *before* deadlines are missed, tutors are far more likely to be sympathetic and may be able to suggest steps that will help you continue with your studies.

Some 'avoidable' events you may choose *not* to avoid. If you are working while studying, promotion or finding a better job (and studying increases your chances of these, long before gaining your qualification), can create huge stress. Moving house, getting married, or adding to your family are stressors for any student. If you seriously wish to complete your course, and especially if you want to do well on it, you should think very carefully before risking making life more difficult for yourself. Obviously, you may still wish to go ahead, but do not underestimate the increase in pressure that will result.

As with other threats to your success, seek advice straight away if such events cause you to struggle. The longer you delay, the fewer the options that may be open to you. And keep your tutors informed of the situation. If you have worked out a coping strategy with them, they will want to know that this is the right one and that you are (or indeed are not) in control of the situation.

Skill deficits

One of the commonest causes of failure is the inability to 'answer the question'. By this, I mean the particular question asked, all parts of that question and the right number of questions. This can be a problem with any assignment, and can be catastrophic under the pressure of exams. If you have developed critical reading skills, such misinterpretation is less likely. You can further increase your chances of answering what is intended by fol-

➤ Ch 15   lowing the advice in this section, and in Chapter 15.

Time-management, communication, achieving a good balance between theory and 'reality' and dealing with numbers, are all skills that are needed to do well in assessment, and all can be developed. There are suggestions on all these areas within this book. If you are worried about your writing ability or other personal skills, devote some time to developing these as soon as possible.

> **To minimise the effect of problems:**
>
> - keep ahead of schedule
> - seek advice at once
> - work out coping strategies
> - keep tutor informed
> - manage your stress.

If you are studying at postgraduate level on the strength of your managerial experience rather than your educational qualifications, you may be worried about your ability to cope. You may find that you are worrying unnecessarily: your tutors' expectations may be far lower than you think. If your concerns are justified, this book may help a lot. (If you are finding that you are struggling, your university may offer 'remedial' courses, or some may be available locally that could help you develop the necessary skills.)

In the unlikely event that you do get fail grades and cannot find a way of improving them, it is important to see these grades for what they are – simply a failure on academic assessment criteria. They probably say nothing about you as a person, or your skill as

a manager. Many institutions are still a long way from being able to assess professional competence reliably. I have known several excellent managers fail courses, even in areas of their own special expertise. Competent HR managers have failed human resource management courses; good senior marketing managers have failed marketing courses.

Rather than being poor managers, they had problems in areas specific to Master's-level assessment, whether exam technique, or developing an argument from evidence and theory, or communicating this argument clearly in writing. In the first area, there is clearly no relationship between this and on-the-job performance. The inability to argue from evidence might be a serious skill deficit in many jobs, but not every managerial role demands it, so it may not be interfering with their current job performance.

Some of these managers successfully transferred to more practically-oriented or lower-level programmes. This allowed them to develop assessment-related skills at a more leisurely pace before they resumed (successfully) their postgraduate study. Others decided that gaining a Master's was not that important, and there was no need to feel a sense of personal failure. Instead, they focused on what they had *gained* from their studies – which was sometimes more than had been learned by those who passed.

So do not let fear of failure cause you to drop out silently if the course turns out to be tougher than expected. Instead, discuss any such fears with your tutors and, if appropriate, with your employer. Once you know all the options open to you it will be easier to see what is the best course of action for *you*, the one that will have the greatest beneficial effect on your personal development as a manager. Dropping out may be the best option for you. But often it is not.

Dissertations/projects/theses

Figure 5.5 showed dissertations as particularly high-risk, with many different factors capable of contributing to failure to complete or pass. Even students who have coped well with the earlier part of the course may find difficulty with the greater freedom and longer timescales involved and the need for a high level of independence in directing their work.

Projects based on in-company research are singularly vulnerable to external threats: changes within the company concerned, which are outside your control, may threaten your planned project. In the extreme case you can lose your job halfway through your research, thereby losing access to further data. Equally devastating to the project, if not to yourself, is the discovery that the part of the organisation you are researching is under threat, or about to close. Other threats occur if your in-company 'client' leaves and is replaced by someone antagonistic to the project, or if your project topic suddenly becomes highly sensitive.

➤ Ch 16   The risk of many of these happening may be minimised by careful topic selection. This is dealt with in Chapter 16. If, despite care at this stage, things go wrong, then you should follow the earlier advice of seeking guidance from your tutor or supervisor at once.

Motivation

The remaining major cause of failure is loss of motivation. You might find that it requires far more effort than you expected to get the grades you want, or find it increasingly difficult to give up your free time. Once the immediate excitement of starting the course has worn off, there may seem to be few rewards along what is a very long path.

Full-time students can find their motivation is flagging at times, but it is generally less of a problem for them. They are eating, sleeping (if not a lot) and breathing their MBA or other course, surrounded and supported by other students and faculty. Much of their learning takes place through group work. The course is shorter. The conflicts are simpler, usually between work and sleep, not between work, job and family.

Part-time students are faced with a longer course of study, much of which may be done in isolation. There will be pressures and conflicts every day, these being subject to unpredictable variation. If these pressures mean that you cannot study as much as you anticipated and that you are getting lower grades than you hoped, these grades will be disincentives to further work, rather than rewards.

The three main sources of motivational 'recharging' are your teachers, fellow students and yourself. Institutions vary enormously in the amount of support and contact they offer students, and in the extent to which contact with fellow students is encouraged or even possible. As both types of contact can be great boosts to enthusiasm, ensure that you take full advantage of what *is* available. Make the effort to attend any face-to-face sessions. Even if they are not compulsory and the quality of the lecturer's input is variable: there are other benefits in terms of contact with your fellow students. If you are dissatisfied, and feel you are not learning as intended, and others feel the same, you should make your feelings known. Voting with your feet will not bring about improvements. You (or your employers) will have paid a considerable sum for your course, and can reasonably expect value for money. If you are dissatisfied with *any* aspect of your programme, make that dissatisfaction known. This will allow the institution to do something to improve the situation.

> **Motivational resources:**
>
> - your teachers
> - fellow students
> - yourself.

Some colleges are still poor at training lecturers and monitoring the quality of their work. Unless students complain, there will be no way for a problem to come to light.

If your institution provides you with a personal counsellor or academic adviser (terms vary), then this person can help with motivational, as well as other, problems. You should feel no inhibitions about seeking help. This will not be held against you, nor affect your grades other than positively. If you encounter real problems this adviser can argue for these being taken into consideration when your final marks are decided.

Support from peers

➤ **Ch 9**

If at all possible, try to develop informal contacts with other students. Informal study groups, often called 'self-help' groups, (discussed in Chapter 9) are one of the most powerful antidotes to 'motivation droop'. If you have not yet experimented with informal group support, revisit the guidelines given. Group members can not only provide motivational support but also contribute specialist knowledge and perspectives from different cultural and organisational experience.

It can be reassuring to find that, when you experience difficulty with a part of the course, you are not alone. A commiseration session when the going gets tough can be highly encouraging, as well as cathartic. And members of your group may do much to help you stay on the course if things get so tough that you are thinking of dropping out.

If there are no other students locally, you may be able to gain some of the benefits by starting a discussion group with interested colleagues at work. They will gain second-hand benefit from your studies, while giving you valuable motivational support and offering opportunities for action learning. If you are being supported by your employer, your training manager may be interested in setting up such a group, as a way of increasing the return on their investment in your course fees. If not, you might be able to make informal arrangements with other managers with whom you feel comfortable.

Self-help

The final source of help for drooping motivation lies within you. This may sound about as helpful as the suggestion to a depressive that he 'snap out of it', or advice to use your bootstraps for self-elevation, but it *is* feasible. The algorithm shown in Figure 12.1 summarises the procedure involved. The item 'Analyse possibilities for improving situation' is the key.

Obviously, the way you go about improving your motivation will depend on the underlying problem. Common problems are:

Problem: You have been working far too hard, allowing no time for exercise or relaxation, and are physically and mentally jaded.

Remedy: Build in 'treats' and schedule time off, some of it for enjoyable exercise.

Problem: You have received lower grades than you had hoped and your ego feels somewhat bruised.

Remedy: Reassess your objectives. If passing is your main objective, middling grades will get you the qualification just as well as high ones. Consider what else you were achieving in that period that was competing with your studies for your time. Applaud yourself for the full range of your achievements during the period.

Problem: Your studies seem to stretch forward into the distant and dismal future, and you really don't know whether you are making any progress.

Remedy: Assess progress to date. Look at early assignments and see how much better you could do now. Review your study log/personal development file if you have been keeping one. (If not, start such a log.) Set interim targets for the course.

Problem: You can't see what the course has to do with your job.

Remedy: Talk to your tutor and your training officer, mentor or superior in your organisation. Make active efforts to find links. Talk to other students to see whether they have the same feeling.

Problem: You are being sabotaged by resistance, overt or covert, from colleagues or family.

Remedy: Consider whether you are collaborating in the sabotage. If so, think again about why you want a Master's degree and be firmer about sticking to your goals. Discuss the problem in a positive way with the sources of the resistance. People may be unaware of it or of the strength of their feelings. You may be equally unaware of the demands you are making on them or of other changes in your attitudes.

Motivational problems are among the hardest to solve but, provided your original objectives are still valid, it should be possible to regenerate at least some of your original enthusiasm.

12

UNDERSTANDING YOUR ASSESSORS

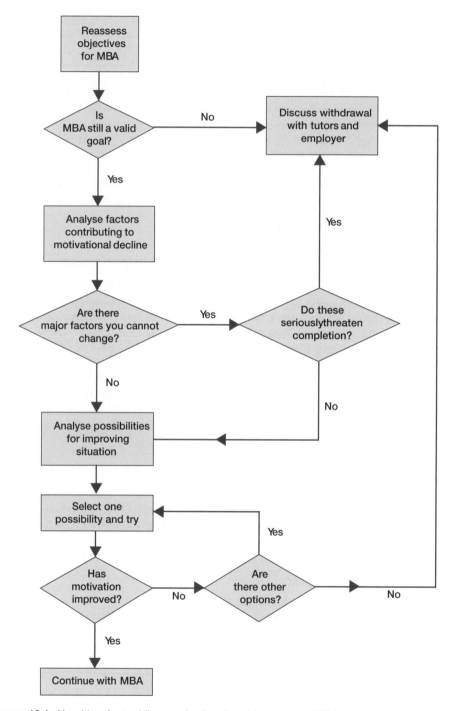

Figure 12.1 Algorithm for tackling motivational problems on an MBA (or other course)

Assessment as communication

In writing an assignment or examination, or making a presentation on your work, the effectiveness with which you communicate will affect your grade in two ways. First, because communication is an important aspect of management, you will be penalised if you show weakness in this area. Second, your tutor can give marks only for what you succeed in communicating. If you fail to demonstrate the extent of your knowledge and understanding because of communication problems, you will not gain marks for it. You therefore need to understand the principles governing any form of communication (dis

➤ Ch 9 cussed in Chapter 9) and to develop those communication skills most relevant to postgraduate management assignments

No assessor will be unduly concerned with your literary skills. Examiners are not looking for an ability to use a wide vocabulary or complex grammatical forms, or to evoke depths and nuances of emotion in your reader. And, if it is clear that English is not your first language, tutors normally will be very tolerant of spelling and grammar faults. But your language must allow you to put across the message that you intend, in a manner suitable to your target audience. As when talking, the message needs to be clear in the first place – if your thinking is muddled, your communication is unlikely to be clear. But if your thinking is clear, and you can express it in plain English, supplemented by whatever visual aids will

➤ Ch 13 strengthen your message, you will do well. This point is developed in the next chapter.

Activity 12.2

Think of the last time that you were unhappy with the effectiveness of a communication you sent or received. Jot down the aspects that contributed to your lack of satisfaction.

_____

_____

_____

_____

_____

_____

The chances are that your dissatisfaction concerned either the *substance* of the communication, or the *manner* in which it was communicated. This distinction is worth bearing in mind. It is also worth remembering that there are two distinct parties to any communication the sender or originator of the message, and the receiver or intended audience. These, and other elements in the classic communication model, were shown in

➤ Ch 9 Figure 9.1, which you could usefully revisit at this point.

12

UNDERSTANDING YOUR ASSESSORS

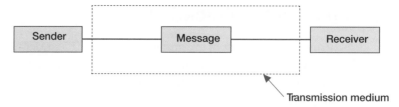

Figure 12.2 The elements of communication

Again, this model provides a useful shopping list, drawing attention to potentially relevant aspects of the situation. It does not tell you what to do about them, but it can act as a starting point for generating relevant questions. Some examples follow.

Sender

It is essential to think carefully about your objectives. Unless *you* are clear about these, they are unlikely to be achieved. Your main objective is to do what your assessor wants. What is your assessor looking to 'receive'? For this you need to understand *their* objectives for the assignment, awareness of your own strengths and weaknesses as a communicator is also important as this will allow you to pay particular attention to exploiting your strengths while finding ways of overcoming your weaknesses. Do you tend to overcomplicate matters, make unsupported assertions, or assume knowledge in your reader that you are expected to convey. Are you particularly good at explaining the meaning of figures, making implications of a situation clear? Do you find it difficult to reference all your sources? Once you know your own strengths and weaknesses – feedback on assignments should rapidly develop that knowledge – you can use that information to make your communication more effective.

Receiver

What are the receiver's objectives? This is crucial. Read assignment briefs carefully and check anything that you do not understand (the glossary of terms used at the end of the next chapter may help). As at work, think what will be most effective for your receivers. If you are asked for a report, then use that format (explained in the next chapter). If there is scope for a multi-media submission, perhaps including video clips or pictures of evidence, then be creative. At work there may be an organisational style of report writing your boss will expect you to follow. Similarly, different lecturers will have preferences for one style over another. Is there a constraint on the length of a communication? Many busy managers refuse to look at anything that cannot convince them in a one-page summary that it is worth their time. Assignments typically have word limits. When talking, take into consideration that some audiences may have very short attention spans.

The message

Is what you have to communicate simple information or is it an interpretation of information? If the latter, how compelling is that interpretation? Do the facts 'speak for themselves'? If so, how many of the facts are necessary to achieve this effect? How important is quantitative information as part of the message? Can it be presented in a way that increases its significance? Are relationships a key part of the message? In this case diagrams will probably be necessary.

In any course assessment you need to remember that the overall message must be that you have absorbed relevant concepts, techniques and information and can use these appropriately to perform well as a manager, or at least to take sensible decisions in a real or simulated managerial situation. Check that you have made your use of course concepts sufficiently explicit, and attributed them, citing references for your sources.

The channel

For course assessments, the communication channel will normally be prescribed: a written document of a certain length; an oral presentation with visual aids; or a written or viva voce examination. These may sometimes be supplemented by examples of work you have produced in your job (*see* Chapters 6 and 15). For such portfolios the prescription may be more general. (In communication at work, the range of options for the channel may be much greater, ranging from informal discussions, through email to formal meetings and reports.

➤ Chs 6, 15

Whatever your choice, you will need to bear the characteristics of your chosen channel in mind. It is worth recalling that, however they are transmitted, messages tend to lose something in the transmission. You probably played 'Chinese whispers' as a child. Any ambiguity in the message received (due in that case to the difficulty of hearing the whisper) will be acted upon by predispositions in the receiver, with additional distortion at each link in the chain. (If you take ambiguous notes, and then incorporate them into an unclear argument in an essay you may approach this effect!) Distortions can occur in assignments and exams because of poor English, careless drafting, bad handwriting in exams, or simple lack of clarity in expression. These all increase the scope for subjectivity in marking, as the lecturer may guess at your meaning. In such cases presentation of work can have an undue influence.

The same ambiguity in a correctly typed, well-laid-out piece of work might be interpreted much more charitably than if the work looks scruffy, with the marker feeling sure that the student *really* knew something but hasn't made it quite clear.

It is essential to be aware of the ease of losses in transmission and to adopt strategies for avoiding these. For example, underlining key words, including diagrams of key relationships and making a clear *brief* statement of a complex point before you immerse yourself in the full complexity can all help to reduce such losses for written messages. Signposting the structure of your argument at the outset in a report's introduction and contents page, and then using descriptive headings for sections of the report is really helpful. In essays clear messages in the text may serve the purpose of headings. Supplementing verbal messages with visual materials can also help. In a presentation these may be transient, for example displayed slides, or permanent handouts.

If you are aware of the elements that must be considered if you are to communicate successfully, and if you are absolutely clear about your objectives and those of your audience before you start, and if you *plan* your assignments with as much attention to these

➤ Chs 13, 14 factors as to the specific points required in each assessment, you should find that your grades are much improved. Following the same principles in work communications will be equally helpful. Informal spoken and email communications have been discussed already (Chapter 9). The next two chapters address points specific to more formal written and oral communication.

SUMMARY

- When setting assignments, your assessors are concerned with maintaining academic and other standards, and with encouraging learning.

- They want to be convinced that you have absorbed, and can appropriately use, information, skills and techniques taught on the course.

- This means that you will need to do more than merely reproduce things from memory, even if this was the focus of assessment on your first degree.

- They want to know that you can identify significant factors in a situation or its environment and use what you have learned to address managerial problems, generating and evaluating a sufficiently broad range of options and making sensible recommendations.

- They want to be assured that you can communicate your arguments in a clear and convincing fashion, using appropriate communication forms.

- Above all, they do not want to give you a qualification if they feel that your academic (and perhaps also management) competence at the end of the course is so low as to cast doubt on the credibility of their teaching, or of the qualification in general.

- Dropping out is often more common than failing assessment.

- If problems do occur, whether because of external factors or your own capabilities, discuss these with your tutor as soon as they arise. If relevant, discuss them with your superior or training manager, too.

- If you feel demotivated, analyse the reasons and seek all the support you can, from your tutors, your organisation and, most importantly, from fellow students.

- If you fail on assessment or cannot avoid withdrawing from the course, remind yourself that the reasons are probably specific to the course and/or its assessment. This may have nothing to do with your managerial abilities or potential.

- Plan all your assessed work from the perspective of seeking to communicate successfully, bearing in mind your own objectives and characteristics, those of your audience, the characteristics of the message intended and the channel by which it is to be communicated.

13
WRITING TO IMPRESS

Learning outcomes

By the end of this chapter you should:

- appreciate the importance of clear written communications and be improving your own

- understand the importance of clarifying requirements for an assessment

- protect yourself from any charge of plagiarism

- know how to generate a range of initial ideas and develop these into an initial outline structure for your report

- be able to expand your outline into a first draft, using clear English, supported by numbers and diagrams where appropriate

- be able to develop your first draft into a well-presented final draft

- be addressing any spelling and grammar problems.

Introduction

Written communication skills contribute significantly to career success. What you write may be widely circulated. A good report is likely to impress both superiors and clients. Much of your assessment is likely to be based upon what you write, so developing your writing skills can significantly improve your grades.

To do well in written assignments you need first to understand precisely what is being asked. Then you need to construct an answer that is well structured, clearly argued, covers the necessary ground and is in an appropriate style and format. Reports are still the most common form for substantial management and consultants' communications, and some of your assignments will probably need to be produced in this format. Even where a report is not asked for, you are likely to find that a similar, clear structure will greatly improve your work.

> **Assignments need to fully address the question and be:**
>
> - in appropriate style and format within any specified word limit
> - well structured
> - clearly argued
> - evidenced
> - based on theory
> - your own work.

This chapter covers the interpretation of questions. It deals with assignment planning, written communication in general and the use of a report format. For those finding written assignments particularly challenging there are several supplementary Helpfiles at the end of the chapter. A glossary of terms commonly used in assignments is given as Helpfile 13.1. Helpfile 13.2 covers the basics of spelling and Helpfile 13.3 punctuation and grammar. Helpfile 13.4 is specifically for non-native English speakers. Turn to the appropriate Helpfile if you know that your grammar or spelling is prone to 'wobble', if tutors or other readers complain that they are not sure what you mean, or if your grades on written assignments seem lower than you feel you deserve.

Many other chapters – indeed most of this book – will also help you do well in written assignments, and other writing. Particularly relevant are chapters on use of diagrams, on working with case studies, and on understanding your assessors' objectives. For group assignments the chapter on working in teams will be relevant. For substantial reports, in the context of dissertations or projects, you will also need Chapter 16.

➤ Chs 8, 9, 10, 12, 16

Assignment planning

As you will now be fully aware, successful planning depends on clear objectives. To plan, you need to be clear about the administrative side of what is required: for example, the submission deadline, the word limit, the required format. But there is a more substantive side to requirements. What actually is it that you are asked to write? What is the question that you are to address? Success demands that you identify both these aspects of your objectives and then plan carefully to ensure that you have the time, resources and so on needed to meet them. Guidelines for such planning are outlined below and discussed in more detail in the text that follows.

➤ Ch 4

Assignment planning guidelines

- Identify 'administrative' requirements.
- 'Deconstruct' the question to identify precisely what is required.
- Identify 'strands' or themes.
- Identify theory/concepts relevant to themes.
- Work out a structure for answer.
- Plan time and other resources.
- Identify interim targets/review points.
- Follow your plan!

Requirements and constraints

Far too many marks are lost because of failure to submit work on time, to keep within word limits, writing an essay when a report is asked for, or submitting work to the wrong place.

So make sure that you have identified all such requirements. *Note assignment deadlines in your diary, or electronic or wall calendar to ensure that you do not forget them.* Then plan the actions needed to meet them. Such planning will be equally important for written assignments at work, so it is a good habit/skill to develop. Remember the 'planning fallacy': projects tend to take longer than you think. Allow more time in your plan to allow for this.

➤ Ch 4

Content planning

The first stage here is again to fully understand what is required. It is not always immediately obvious what a question is asking. What *seems* obvious may be only a small part of what is required. You need to 'deconstruct' the question carefully, making sure you have identified *all* its constituent parts *and* worked out precisely what is required in answer to each part. Consider the following question:

As part of a review of your organisation's management and use of information, and the effectiveness of technology use in this, you have been asked to write a report for your boss to pass on to consultants investigating the issue. Your report should describe your own use, as a manager, of information, and evaluate your organisation's system in terms of meeting your needs.

This is a messy one. First there is a format requirement – a report is asked for. This means noting the recipient – here your boss (and then the external consultant) – and writing in a way that is appropriate for them. (More detail on report formats is given shortly.) It would be tactless, to say the least, to fill your report with complaints about your boss's failure to tell you anything, even if you needed to outline information that would make it easier for you to be effective!

But there are other potential traps that are far more dangerous than failing to use the specified report format. The first is the clear specification of perspective. Students were asked to write about their *own* use of information. Many wrote about the organisation in general, without mentioning how they fitted into it, or giving any idea of what information they used. Second, the main thrust of the question was about management and *use* of information, not about technology. Technology was clearly seen by the question-setter as part of a wider 'information system'. Yet many students wrote exclusively about technology. Not surprisingly, there was little evaluation. (*See* Helpfile 13.1 at the end of this chapter if you would not have been sure what the word meant in this context.) If students did, exceptionally, evaluate something, they tended not to do this from their perspective as a manager. As a consequence, many students were surprised at the low marks they received.

So how might they have done better at identifying what was required? Deconstructing the question they would have realised that the first part – *As part of a review of your organisation's management and use of information, and the effectiveness of technology use within this* – gave important contextual information, but was not the essence of the 'instruction'. Note, though, the strong hint here that a wider *information system* was being considered, with the technology involved being seen as only a part of this wider system.

What students were actually required to do was, using report format, *describe their use of information* and *evaluate their organisation's [information] system* from the perspective of their own use of, and therefore need for, information.

Several other parts are implicit. You cannot easily evaluate something without making clear just what it is that you are evaluating and against what criteria you are evaluating it. So, in order to evaluate your organisation's information system, you need to say what it *is*. Some sort of definition or other representation is called for. Later in the instructions students were recommended to use diagrams where possible, and this is an instance where a systems diagram would be very useful. Then specified criteria are needed against which it can be evaluated. Clearly these needed to be derived from the manager's own information use and needs.

If students had tried to take the question apart in this way – to 'deconstruct' it – before planning their answers, they would not so cheerfully have submitted detailed descriptions of organisational IT systems, with virtually no comment as to their appropriateness. Of course it was important to include consideration of IT as part of 'the system', but a wider perspective and evaluation clearly was called for.

To take another, rather simpler example, again of an assignment that I have recently marked:

Evaluate your organisation's approach to recruitment and selection.

Activity 13.1

Before reading further, take a couple of minutes to think about the parts of which this question is made. You might like to sketch these out in the form of a mind map on a separate piece of paper. Don't worry about the fact that you have not yet studied the course for which this was an assignment. Aim at a level of detail similar to that in the example above.

Again, this was a question where many students missed much of the point. They *described* – often at great length – the detail of their organisation's procedures, though often only those for selection. But for good marks, far more was expected. The question was designed to test the students' ability to relate the theory that they had been taught on this topic to their own situation. To answer it well, students needed to demonstrate that they understood what recruitment and selection were intended to achieve and the distinction between the two terms. (Evaluation implies testing against some sort of standard.) They needed to relate this to the organisation's overall objectives and its staffing plan. They then needed to describe key features of their organisation's policy and practice in this area, evaluating these against relevant legislation and prescriptions of good practice taught in the course. It was important to show an awareness both of the difficulties of implementing that good practice in the real context and of the problems likely to arise from ignoring it.

There are, thus, many invisible parts to a seemingly simple question. All too often, students seized on the opportunity to describe their organisation's practice at inordinate length, even down to the names of those who sent out invitations to candidates or who were on interview panels. This more than used up the allowed word limit. Inevitably, amid all this detail there was no reference at all to the effectiveness of this practice in organisational terms, nor to any considerations of equal opportunities legislation, nor indeed to anything else that their course had covered.

As a marker, I was not particularly interested in the intricacies of the particular organisation. Privately, of course, these glimpses of organisational life were fascinating, but students' awareness of such detail was not what was being assessed: there were no marks to be gained from mere description. Where the marks *would* have been available, should the students have chosen to seek them, was in a demonstration of their *understanding* of the relevant course concepts.

To show this understanding, they needed to use the concepts to describe and evaluate organisational practice. If the students in question had taken more trouble to clarify what was really required, and had understood their audience's objectives more clearly, they would not have fallen into this trap. Their marks might then have been a pleasant surprise, rather than the reverse. Use the glossary in Helpfile 13.1 at the end of this chapter to help you work out what an assignment requires. If at any point you are unsure, or seem to be interpreting an assignment differently from other students, check your

13

WRITING TO IMPRESS

understanding with the tutor who set it. Misunderstanding the task is in no one's interest, so most tutors will welcome such checks.

Of course, the need to clarify requirements is not limited to course assignments. Communication depends upon an understanding of the characteristics of the receiver, as previous chapters discussed. Any business document must be written with a clear understanding of your audience's objectives, as well as your own. Often these are not what they may appear at first sight. So explore the context of a request for a report, if you possibly can. Although the request may come from your boss, he or she may be planning to circulate your report, under your name or theirs, to a much wider audience. Knowing this, and understanding the debates to which your report is intended to contribute, you can direct your efforts far more effectively. Time spent clarifying requirements is seldom wasted; indeed it may *prevent* considerable subsequent waste of time and effort.

➤ Chs 9, 12

Once you have a clear understanding of your remit, including any elements not explicit in the original, write down the expanded version. You will need to check progress against objectives at intervals during your work. You do not wish to forget elements that you have so carefully worked to establish.

Identify themes and relevant concepts

When you 'deconstruct' a question some themes will be starting to emerge already. You probably found this in the previous activity. Your next stage is to develop these further and identify any you have missed. Once you have themes, you will have 'hooks' on which to hang concepts. But, also, concepts can suggest themes, so at this stage it is worth being fairly open to ideas about both. Individual brainstorming is a good way of coming up with a wide range of possible candidates for inclusion.

If you have been given a group assignment, you should have been working as a group on agreeing objectives and then brainstorming together. Even for an individual assignment brainstorming with others, perhaps your self-help group, can generate many more ideas than you generate on your own. Bouncing ideas off other people, and exploring the differences between your views in a constructive way, will also make you more aware of some of your own assumptions and prejudices. Thus, a group can help you to take a broader view of the situation than if you are limited to your own perspective. For work-based assignments, collaboration with colleagues has obvious potential benefit. They will probably hold essential information to which you will need access, and their (different) perspectives are an important part of the situation.

Whatever your approach, make sure that you look at the whole situation, including its context, rather than focusing narrowly on 'the problem'. It is usually easier to narrow down from a broad base than to expand on a narrow one. Breadth of approach – though not superficiality – is one of the benefits of postgraduate study.

It is important to look as broadly as possible at relevant course concepts. These are just as important as candidates for inclusion as are aspects of the situation under consideration. Many of the frameworks and theories that you will be taught in your course will provide the basis of a 'shopping list' of potential factors, and of significant relations between them, for inclusion in your analysis. These might include the 'four (or seven) Ps' (or 'Cs')·in marketing, or the STEP (STEEP, STEEPLE or PESTLE) framework for analysing the competitive environment and business planning, or Expectancy Theory if the topic concerns motivation.

Ideally, your jottings should be in a form that you can manipulate when moving on to the next stage of trying to impose structure. Computers make this easy: you can rearrange your headings by cutting and pasting or use mind-mapping software. Restickable notes or cards, which you can move around a large sheet of paper, are good low-tech alternatives – some people find that more tangible approaches work better at the early draft stage. This is particularly the case if you are planning a group assignment. Whatever you choose, your aim at this stage should be to assemble your jottings in such a way that you can absorb them all easily and build up a picture of what is potentially relevant. You can then try various arrangements of this picture to see which way it makes most sense.

> **Chs 8, 10, 12**

This is very similar, if not identical, to the approach suggested for the early stages of case study analysis and similar diagramming techniques. When the basic structure of what is required is fairly obvious, mind maps are particularly useful. They will enable you to develop this structure by drawing sub-themes out of main ones. Thus, your structure generates further ideas, rather than being imposed, perhaps uncomfortably, upon those ideas once they have been produced.

There is a slight danger of mind maps limiting you for questions where structure is *not* self-evident. If you become prematurely wedded to the first set of major branches that come to mind, the whole of your subsequent work may be locked into an inappropriate structure. You need to draw different mind maps, experimenting with different structures, until you find what seems best. Unless you can cheerfully throw a large proportion of your diagrams into the bin, it might be better to reserve mind maps for the next stage.

Rich pictures are much safer. Because they look childish you are less likely to take them seriously. But you may have difficulty in representing many course concepts in this format and need to resort to rather more words than would be ideal. Provided you retain the advantage of being able to absorb your whole picture more or less at a glance, this should not be too much of a disadvantage. Figure 13.1 shows three extracts from early notes for an assignment in which first-year MBA students were asked to assess the effectiveness of their organisation's human resource policy. (I apologise for the over-emphasis on this type of assignment, but it is likely to be easily understandable, whatever you are planning to study, and even if you have not yet started your course.) These diagrams are simply examples of possible approaches. They are in no sense models for a good answer.

Define or refine structure

How far a structure is already apparent to you will depend on the nature of the question (some make the necessary structure fairly clear) and on the diagramming or other jotting methods you have used thus far. If you used mind maps, structure should be fairly clear already. If you used notes or rich pictures, then you will now need to start looking for

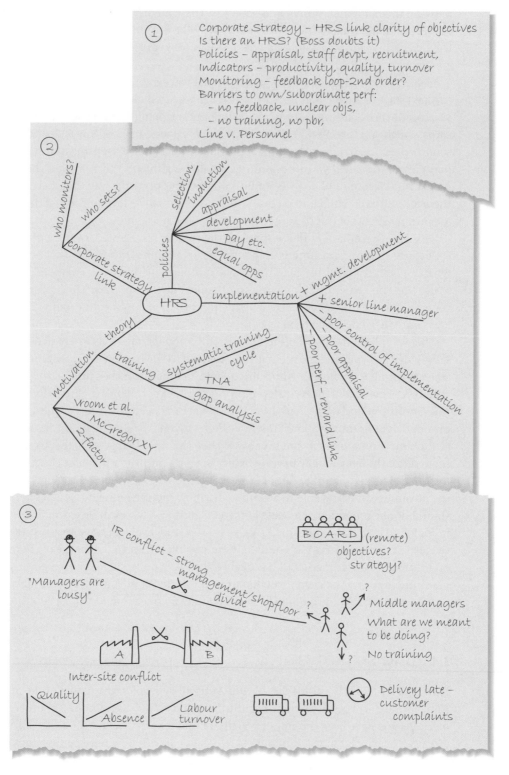

Figure 13.1 Three specimens of early student assignment notes: 1. Brain dump approach; 2. Mind mapping; 3. Rich picture

groupings of factors. You may choose to group according to problem themes, by chronology, according to factors such as geography or department involved, or by organisational level. Your structure may relate to explicitly stated separate question parts, or could be according to conceptual frameworks suggested in your course.

As well as these groupings, if the assignment is based around a problem situation, you normally will find the standard problem solving approach suggests a useful framework. You should by now have a feel for the stages (and note that you may be asked for only some of these), but to remind you they are:

- Describe the situation, including relevant elements of context, and indicate why it presents problems – this equates to exploring the 'symptoms' of a problem.
- Analyse the problem, using course concepts to help understand (or diagnose) the root causes of problems.
- Decide on measures of effectiveness: what are the criteria for a good solution; what constraints exist.
- Identify and describe the range of possible solutions.
- Compare likely costs and benefits in terms of your measures of effectiveness.
- Recommend, with arguments to support your recommendations, your preferred solutions (some organisations prefer a more action-oriented variant on this).
- Propose action.
- Say why the existing situation cannot continue.
- Describe anticipated costs and benefits of proposed action to convince the audience of its merit.
- Outline a plan for implementing the action.
- Conclude with the inevitability of pursuing the proposed action.

Such an approach is excellent for producing action if the problem has been correctly diagnosed. But it does not make it easy to incorporate the diagnosis and analysis that your tutors are likely to be looking for in assignments. You may find the simpler approach suggested earlier of identifying requirements, identifying themes and concepts, and then using these to describe and diagnose the situation works better for you. Either approach provides a framework for arguments. These arguments are at the heart of what you are aiming at.

It may help to think of yourself as a lawyer, making a case for the 'guilt' of aspects of the present situation, and then defending your recommendations, or as a doctor making a diagnosis, convincing the patient that the diagnosis is correct, and recommending treatment. Within either framework you can work through the evidence presented by the situation, using relevant concepts as an aid to interpreting these.

Of course, at this preparatory stage your arguments will be tentative and skeletal, as you will not have gathered the evidence to support them. Indeed, if a lot of research is needed, as in major projects, you may be looking for no more at this stage than themes to pursue. But it is well worth starting to think about structure long before you have all the evidence you need. You may find that the argument mapping techniques introduced earlier are useful.

➤ Ch 7

There is a serious danger, especially with work-based assignments, of falling into the 'trees hiding the wood' trap. A rough idea of structure before you leap into the details will guard against this. At the same time, it will enable you to be more selective in your information gathering. This is *not* an invitation to limit yourself to information supporting your argument. This would produce a biased case and unreliable recommendations. But you should direct your effort towards gathering information relevant to your identified themes, rather than collecting a mountain of data in the hope that it might come in useful. There is a powerful reluctance in most of us to discard something on which we have expended effort. Often you will *need* to do this in order to sharpen your focus, but there is sense in minimising the necessity.

Check against requirements

Once you have devised an adequate outline structure, your planning stage is well under way. At this point you should check back against the objectives as clarified earlier. Does your proposed structure seem appropriate given the requirements for the assignment? Be as critical as you can in this evaluation. If there are weaknesses in your structure, it may be disappointing to have to rethink it. But it is far better to identify problems at this stage and revise your structure than to have to rewrite a substantial report halfway through. Very occasionally this will be necessary, because new information or blinding insight will so alter your perceptions that you can see an infinitely better way of proceeding. But it should not be necessary simply because you were insufficiently critical of your own work at an early stage.

Plan the timing of your work

➤ Ch 16
There is a more detailed treatment of project planning in Chapter 16. For dissertations it constitutes a major consideration. Refer to this if you think planning is a weak point or if you are uncertain as to your ability to meet deadlines. Otherwise, merely bear in mind that you must plan for 'dead time', such as waiting for replies to letters or getting hold of references to books or articles you do not have in your possession. And do not underestimate the time taken to write at least two drafts of your report, preferably more. (Redrafting takes significant time, but can hugely improve the quality of your work if you are prepared to approach your latest draft as a (ruthlessly) 'critical bystander'.)

Once you have submitted a number of assignments, you will be better able to make accurate estimates of time requirements. Until you have this experience, allow a large contingency factor. To make sure that you keep to your plan, set yourself clear interim
➤ Ch 4
targets for all, save the shortest pieces of work, and treat these as real deadlines.

Time planning and keeping to your plans is crucial. Many undergraduates survive by working all night when an assignment is due. As a practising manager you cannot afford this luxury. Furthermore, Master's-level assignments are often so substantial that a single night would not suffice. You will find that your job will develop a nasty habit of peaking in its demands just when you were planning a major assignment effort. This will not be a catastrophe if you have planned for any known workload peaks, and have allowed slack time for just such contingencies and reserved it for genuine emergencies.

'I work best under pressure' is no excuse for relying on last-minute efforts. You will always be under pressure, particularly if studying part time. Your aim is to prevent this pressure from becoming impossible, by careful planning and good time management.

Developing your material

Once you have a skeleton structure and know how much time you have available, you should have a clear idea of how to start developing the substance of your assignment. Remember, however, that your structure was intended to provide a firm base for *starting*, not something you are locked into. It may well need to be amended considerably in the light of the evidence you collect and/or the way your thoughts about the situation develop as you work on your assignment.

If you do find that you need to change your approach, your initial planning was not wasted. Instead, this planning has started a process of conceptual development that is now leading you away from the obvious and into a more creative or penetrating perspective on the situation in question. So celebrate any such changes. Treat your initial structure as a working tool that you can deliberately modify (though not inadvertently ignore) when this will lead to better work.

The following guidelines, though by no means exhaustive, may be helpful in your work. The rest of the chapter expands upon them.

Guidelines for assignments

- Develop clear arguments.
- Use theory where possible.
- Seek evidence as widely as possible.
- Use diagrams where appropriate.
- Avoid assertions and opinions.
- Avoid plagiarism.
- Start drafting as soon as possible.
- Redraft for clarity and conciseness.
- Always cite sources and list references.

In preparing the substance of your report, you need to be sure that all your arguments will be substantiated. Avoid assertions (e.g. 'So-and-so is true', or 'everybody knows that . . .') or opinions (e.g. 'I think . . .'). No matter how confidently you state these, they are unlikely to impress tutors – or senior managers at work. Sadly, as a marker (or indeed as your manager), I am not interested in your opinions just because they are yours. You might or might not know what you are talking about. I want to know how you reached that opinion, what it is

➤ Ch 9 that the facts and the theory suggest. So your position needs to be supported by reasoning, based on evidence or accepted theories, or preferably both. Argument mapping is really helpful at this stage.

Your report is intended to convey a position. You have taken relevant information, using course ideas to suggest what information is relevant, and, to make sense of that information, you have organised this information and these arguments so that a picture emerges, conclusions become obvious and it is relatively easy to develop a set of recommendations from these. At no point should your reader be wondering why you have said something, or whether what you said can be believed. And, especially, your conclusions should not come as a surprise. You should be building towards these throughout your report or essay.

Avoid plagiarism

➤ Chs 7, 12 Plagiarism has been mentioned several times already, and will be again, but it is so important whenever you are submitting work for assessment that is mentioned here as well. So remember: any assignment needs to be entirely *your own* rather than including passages written by others without acknowledging their original authors.

There are many possible causes for non-deliberate plagiarism.

- ***Ignorance of your university's plagiarism policy*** is one – it may be very different from that in places you previously studied. Make sure you fully understand the policy and its importance.

- ***Ignorance of how to show quotes*** is another reason. Make sure you make it very clear, with quotation marks and/or italics, which words are a quote, and cite the source.

➤ Ch 7 - ***Careless note-taking*** is another. Chapter 7 explained the need to avoid accidental plagiarism caused by quoting from your notes when your notes included quotes or extracts from other people's work, and you had not made this clear when note taking.

- ***Careless sharing of work*** may also bring charges of plagiarism against you, even though someone else was being dishonest by 'stealing' your work.

It is important to guard yourself against all such forms of 'accidental' plagiarism. Make sure you fully understand the concept and its importance. You may not realise, for example, that you are deemed to be 'copying' if any material you use is *essentially* the same as the original and you do not make it very clear whose materials you are adapting. Re-ordering paragraphs or changing a few words is not enough to render the material your own. You still need to show the extent of the adapted material, say clearly (in an in-text citation) where you found the original, and reference the source fully at the end, in the style your university requires.

If there are similarities between your work and someone else's it will prompt a university investigation. It may be hard for you to prove that yours was the original, and if you cannot, you may both be penalised. Guard against this by never showing other students your draft assignments, never leaving them lying around, and never posting them online where others might access them. It can be extremely useful to discuss approaches to assignments with others in your study group, or to talk about a case study and discuss how different concepts might be relevant. But unless you are submitting a group assignment, limit your sharing to discussion. Never share drafts, in order to protect yourself. Seek feedback on your drafting from friends, colleagues or family, but not from those who are submitting the same assignment themselves.

Reasons for deliberate plagiarism include:

- *Laziness* and an unwillingness to do the necessary work.
- *Stress* – a student simply does not have time to complete an assignment so copies as a 'short cut'. Extreme stress affects the ability to think properly, and when stressed students sometime do things they would not normally consider.
- *Insecurity* about language ability or understanding. Students may feel that it is safer to copy than try to write their own materials, or that they have no option because they really don't understand something.
- *Belief that grades matter most,* and anything is OK as long as they can get away with it.

Plagiarism is NOT worth it. Submitting material written by other people as if it were your own is dishonest, and deservedly attracts severe penalties. No matter what pressures you are under, copying others' work is not worth the risk, even if you are comfortable with the dishonesty involved. University software will catch you.

Plagiarising, or copying, is *never* acceptable in the UK. Take the following steps to avoid it. Wherever possible, use your own words. So, if you are explaining a concept encountered on your course, rephrase it in your own words; this demonstrates understanding. *Always* give a reference to the person who originated the concept (see below). If you want to quote exact words, which is perfectly acceptable in moderation, indeed sometimes necessary to make a point, use either quotation marks or italics to distinguish that which is in someone else's words and give a *full* reference, including the page quoted from. If you want to use words found on the Web, again, show that they are a quotation and give your source. Never 'borrow' things that other students have written. (The exception, of course, is a group project, but even then you may be asked to make clear which group member is responsible for what contribution.)

> **Remember:** Using others' words, without saying that you are doing so, counts as plagiarism. You can be severely penalised for this, perhaps even asked to leave!

If you are unsure of your ability to write good English, the temptation to reproduce, rather than rephrase, may be strong. Resist it at all costs. You will learn little and may pay a heavy price if you are discovered. Discovery is becoming more common as many universities now use sophisticated software to detect plagiarism.

Seek your evidence as widely as possible

Obviously, the relevant evidence will be determined by the question. For work-based assignments you may use evidence from within your own organisation. Discussions with colleagues can provide both information and insights. An important aspect of many

13

WRITING TO IMPRESS

problem situations is that key people in that situation may see the problem very differently. Such differences of perspective may be a significant element in a problem.

Subordinates may be happy to cooperate in your work. Indeed, you may be able to make it into a developmental experience for them. This will also serve to reduce any resentment that may be developing towards your course. Superiors or mentors can help through discussions, suggesting further sources of information or commenting on ideas and drafts. Being involved will enable them to use your assignments as a form of in-house consultancy, and may stimulate their own thinking. By making sure that your learning experience is as rich as possible, they will also be increasing the return on their investment in your course. (If you wish to convince them further that such help is a good idea, you might point out that good 'customised' company MBAs or other programmes tend to be much more expensive than an off-the-shelf model. By supporting you in your work-based assignments they are, in a sense, doing their own customising, in a way that is both cheap and highly effective.)

Other evidence you might use in an organisation-based assignment could include: results of interviews with key company personnel; company data; records from your own part of the organisation; survey data collected in-company by other consultants; external information such as published market intelligence, government statistics or trade surveys. Relevant literature on the topic culled from management journals, books or even newspapers will also be needed in most cases, together with any course material or lecture notes relevant to the assignment.

➤ Ch 16

Remember that evidence is usually less than perfectly reliable and you should assess the extent of the unreliability of all the evidence on which you draw. There is more on this in Chapter 16. Look at this if you are planning an assignment based on evidence you need to gather from your company or the environment.

Use theory as much as possible

Some assignments may be purely theoretical while others may ask you to use theory to analyse a case study. In either case, theory use should be explicit. However, if you are writing an in-company report, you will normally need to be careful to use this theory *inconspicuously*. You will thus gain its benefits in making a complicated situation clearer, but will avoid antagonising your readers. Work colleagues may feel threatened if your arguments assume theory or knowledge that they lack. Always bear in mind the characteristics of 'receivers' of communications and their needs. Colleagues may feel genuinely irritated by unnecessary jargon, or profess such irritation as a form of defence if threatened.

When writing assignments mainly for course assessment, you need to be less restrained. Remember that the point of your programme is to equip you with a set of conceptual tools and techniques, and the ability to apply these in a variety of organisational situations. Such application should help you cut through complexity and reach valid conclusions as to the best of the strategic alternatives available and how to implement it. Theory which might irritate superiors at work is likely to be just what your tutors are looking for. They need it to check that you have absorbed and can use theory appropriately. Thus, theory will almost certainly need to be *explicit* in any report you write for your course.

By the end of your course, theory should have become second nature and *implicit* in everything you do. You are most likely to achieve this if you take the opportunity to experiment with different ways of using the conceptual tools and of obtaining feedback from your tutors on this via your use of these tools in assessment. Many of the marks for assignments may well be allocated to correct use of appropriate theory, so what is good for your learning will also be good for your grades. Part of your preparation for an assignment therefore will be to explore potentially relevant theories and concepts and experiment with them to determine their usefulness in your particular context.

Be critical

Remember that critical thinking is a key skill at Master's level. You need to consider the limitations of any theory you draw upon in its own terms (how strong is the evidence on which it is based, how sound are any assumptions made, how robust are the arguments that develop the theory from the evidence, what does it add to pre-existing theory, might the author's position have contributed to bias?). You also need to consider its relevance to the context in which you are using it. Were the original data relevant to your own situation or separated in time, location, culture, type of organisation or other significant way

➤ Ch 7   from the issue you are addressing? Revisit the guidelines in Chapter 7 on being critical before writing an assignment.

When you are writing, make clear that you have considered these factors and show how they have influenced your considerations. You need to ensure that your own arguments are clear and sound and that you make explicit your own assumptions.

Use diagrams where possible

When analysing a problem situation to see how it arose, *multiple-cause* diagrams can be invaluable and can often be usefully incorporated in your report. By working back from the event or situation of interest, through contributory factors and factors contributing to those and so on, multiple-cause diagrams can communicate a clear understanding of the web of relationships between events which led up to, and sustain, a problem situation. This allows your reader to see the relevance of a much wider range of possible inter-

➤ Ch 8   ventions than are immediately obvious.

Showing important interrelationships will help your reader to see why you have avoided some recommendations. It will be clear that they risk producing unintended consequences worse than the original problem. (These are not as uncommon in real life as you might think!) *Relationship* diagrams will help you to achieve the same benefits for more static situations. Don't forget the basic organisation tree, or organigram, familiar to everyone. It can represent one form of relationship very clearly. And, of course, *mind maps* and related diagrams have fairly obvious uses, both as frameworks for generating evidence, and for organising evidence into coherent arguments once generated.

Organise the materials you generate as you go along

Organise materials
better by:

- planning the materials
  you will need
- logging progress in
  acquiring them
- checking progress
  against deadlines
- organising materials as
  you collect them
- clearly distinguishing
  'quotations'
- filing full references.

If your materials are disorganised, you will spend a lot of time later trying to sort them out, or to find documents that you know are 'somewhere'. Your outline structure will provide a framework for this but it is useful, additionally, to keep a log of what you have collected and how you have filed it, and of what is still outstanding, so that you can assess progress at a glance. Such a log serves the important function of giving you a feeling that you are making progress, thus keeping your motivation high, even if the assignment is a long one.

It is particularly important to note references for each idea or piece of evidence you might use. (If you are using bibliographic software, compiling a final reference list will then be easy.) It is all too tempting to omit this. There is a strong temptation to 'do all the references properly at the writing-up stage'. (How could you possibly forget where you got something from? Believe me, it is easy to forget. I have wasted *countless* hours in looking for articles or quotations that were not in the publication I 'remembered'. Indeed, some sources seemed to have mysteriously ceased to exist since I last read them!)

➤ Ch 7

As well as noting academic references, record all possible details about interviews, letters sent, group discussions held, sources of company data, etc. You need to know the mailing list for different letters, or the participants in a particular discussion, not to have to reconstruct these from memory.

Start drafting as soon as possible

➤ Ch 16

This need is discussed more fully in Chapter 16 but, briefly, the sooner you start to draft, the clearer you will become about your remaining information needs. Moving on to the evidence-gathering stage often throws up deficiencies in your structure. Similarly, drafting can make you more aware of gaps in evidence. It is, therefore, a mistake to wait until all your evidence is complete before starting your first draft. You should be starting a skeleton draft at the planning stage, developing it as your thoughts become clearer and you gather more evidence. Decisions on major subheadings should be possible by the time you have half your evidence, even for a major assignment requiring substantial research.

Drafting written assignments

Getting started should present few problems if you have followed the guidance offered so far. By setting interim deadlines, and starting rough drafting while still collecting evidence, you should be starting your first full-length draft with plenty of time in hand, a clear idea of what you are going to write and adequate material to hand.

➤ Ch 4

The dreaded 'writer's block' should, therefore, be no threat. Indeed, if you have been developing your time-management skills at work and in your studies, even the more common, though potentially equally damaging, vice of procrastination should be much diminished.

Drafting guidelines

- Prepare outline structure at outset.
- Refine structure when possible.
- Set manageable interim targets.
- Start a rough draft very early indeed.
- If stuck, do other study for a (short) while.
- If still stuck, consider discarding recent work and changing direction.
- If still stuck, seek tutor's help.
- Check progress against targets.
- Complete draft in time to revisit and redraft.

You may occasionally find it difficult to start or difficult to restart after a break in your work. Thoughts about the absolute necessity of fixing the roof, cleaning the oven, digging the potatoes or any other preferred displacement activity, may start to surface and claim priority over starting work on your draft. If so, you have two weapons at your disposal.

First, remind yourself that this is only an early draft. It is not the finished product; it does not have to be perfect, Ernest Hemmingway, who wrote some of the most polished prose of the last century, said 'The first draft of anything is shit.' Nor do you have to start at the beginning and work through to the end. Many people find writing much more stressful than they should because they try to get it right first time, rather than seeing drafting as a process of successive refinements.

Sometimes you will find out what you want to write only by starting. What emerges may be quite a surprise (Some people write whole novels on this 'discovery' basis.). But once something has emerged, however scrappily, there is something to work with. You can redraft it, perhaps several times, into a much, much better piece. However, unless you *allow* yourself to produce something that you know to be imperfect as a starting point, the process will not be able to take place. If you know yourself to be a perfectionist, remind yourself constantly that imperfection is a necessary part of the process. A sculptor may saw wood into roughly the right shape before starting detailed carving. Those first rough cuts, unimpressive in themselves, were a necessary first step to a masterpiece.

If you are having difficulty, try starting with the part of the report with which you feel most comfortable. Introductions are never the best place to start in any case, as it is impossible to introduce a report until you know what that report contains. So start with your evidence or even your conclusions, if that suits you better. This is only a first draft, and you can modify your initial sections to take account of the content of earlier parts of the report once you get to your second draft.

Sometimes, anxiety about the size of the task can cause a block. If so, draw on time-management techniques and set very easy targets at first, perhaps drafting any two pages (or even one) at a specific time. Once you have those two pages, force yourself to stop and indulge in some detailed planning of what parts you will write when. Starting with easy targets will establish the habit of writing. Each time you complete a writing task, you should find that the resistance to starting work is less next time, until you find you are actually *enjoying* the chance to get back to work. This momentum will be sustained only if you treat your report as an 'elephant' and write a little of it every day. If the prospect of a mere two pages is enough to induce caffeine poisoning, set an even easier task aiming simply to overcome resistance to writing. Start with something pleasurable, such as writing a letter to an old friend, or rude thoughts about your course, before moving on to drafting a page of the assignment. (It is highly unlikely that you will need such tough measures if you have worked through the handbook thus far.)

If you suddenly become stuck in mid-draft, do not start wandering around the Internet or playing computer games. Instead, stop what you are doing. Work instead on a different part of the report, or even some other coursework. But make a point of coming back the next day, or soon after that, to the place at which you blocked and try to discover the cause of your difficulty. You will often find that the problem has arisen because you took a wrong turning earlier in your report, but are unwilling to face up to this because it will mean scrapping some of the work you have done. Go back to the last point at which you are totally happy with your draft and think about how you need to modify it thereafter. You probably know already, if you are honest with yourself!

Be concise

In preparing your final draft two or even three redrafts improve most work. Pay particular attention to whether you could say the same thing in fewer words. Many assignments have word limits. If you are unnecessarily 'wordy', you will not fit the necessary content into the limit and will lose marks as result. I frequently find myself writing comments like 'you need to discuss this in more depth' on assignments that are up to – or even over – the word limit. The student will respond 'but I didn't have room'. Cutting out unnecessary verbiage would have given them plenty of room. There is more on writing clear English later, but concise expression is really important. Be ruthless and cut out all phrases that do not add meaning or weight to your arguments. If you develop the habit of writing to the point in your assignments, it will stand you in good stead when writing exam answers under pressure, and in meetings at work.

Activity 13.2

The following is an example of a (weak) student's 'diagnosis' of a rather complex situation. The student is a professional, an employee of a company providing services via a customer (Y) to a consumer (X) with whom the student is in near daily contact. Read it, and then provide a more concise version. Note any other comments that you might wish to offer the student.

> What is clear from my diagnosis is that whilst I could certainly apply the rules and procedures regarding specifications and costs for a project that seemed appropriate to me, as within my job description I have the right and authority to do so, I do not have the means to enforce them against [X], other than advising [Y] of any variance and that [X] was responsible for it. This could be very damaging to the current relationship between me and [X], but also possibly between [Y] and the firm I work for given that I would be seen to be 'pointing fingers' and demonstrating a lack of control, which would not instill confidence in our performance as a company, and risk us losing the contract, as well as the tendency it would have to make my company doubt my competence. This calls for definition of the Terms of Engagement, an immediate short-term intervention that would assist everyone involved in understanding exactly what I am responsible for, and how far my authority extends. This brings me back to my original idea of using the agreement of a strategy as a dialogue in which all the stakeholders with a perspective can engage to understand the other's perspective. This does of course rely on each stakeholder attempting to understand the other's point of view! I think that this is highly unlikely to ever happen given the personalities concerned. Reflection on this, as well as the time taken to reach the current position in the project, has made me question who is to be persuaded as part of this strategy, me or [X].

Comment

This is an extremely difficult task, not least because the student is not at all clear what evidence has been gathered to underpin this 'diagnosis', nor what theory had been used to drive whatever data collection and interpretation had been undertaken. (This was an example of a report receiving a fail grade.) It is harder because the overall meaning is very hard to deduce. My best attempt is below. Maybe yours is better. (Note that it is very easy to be critical of someone else's writing. The real challenge is to be equally harsh on your own.)

> *I am authorised to specify and define budgets for projects according to set procedures, but lack the authority to ensure that [X] will observe these. I can only advise [Y] of any subsequent variance against budget and the reasons. However, to blame [X] explicitly could damage the working relationship between us, highlight my own lack of control and threaten the company's credibility with [Y].*

> *A better approach might be to define and agree 'Terms of Engagement' that clarified [X's] and my own responsibilities. Ideally this would take place through a dialogue between the stakeholders on our overall strategy and how best to achieve it, given our different perspectives.*

> *Reflection on progress thus far has made me question the validity of my own assumptions about the problem, and suggested that I may actually be a part of it.*

This uses only 50 per cent of the words of the original. I leave you to judge whether it conveys more or less meaning, and whether your own redrafting is better. I hope that your redraft retained or enhanced the impact of the stunning insight in the final point.

13

WRITING TO IMPRESS

Using report format

Reports should normally include:

- title page, with descriptive title, author, addressee and date
- acknowledgements (if appropriate)
- summary
- contents list (of any length)
- introduction
- main and subsidiary sections, appropriately titled and numbered
- conclusions
- recommendations
- references (or bibliography)
- appendices (if needed).

If you are not used to report writing, you may feel inhibited by the need to write a 'report'. Perhaps you feel that there is some mystique to report format, some secret formula that you do not know. There are two reasons for the using report formats. The first is the logical necessity to structure your arguments; the second is that the structure is intended to help your readers find their way around what may be a substantial document. Knowing the general order to expect can help.

Some organisations seek to maximise this effect by having a standard format for all company reports. If this is the case in your own organisation, make sure that you have a copy of the rules, or one or two reports to act as models, before you start writing a report for work. On your course your lecturers may also have clear (and possibly different) ideas about the structure required and, obviously, if your report is for assessment purposes, you should meet *their* requirements.

The following discussion covers what might be seen as the broad range of normal practice. Follow this in the absence of organisational or business school guidelines or prescriptions. Normally a report includes a summary, a title page giving report title, date, addressee and sender, a list of contents, an introduction, a main body which may be divided into numbered sections and subsections, conclusions, recommendations, references and appendices. The function of each will be discussed in turn.

Title page

Any report is written – and read – in a specific context. It is vital, therefore, that at the start of the report you make clear who has originated the report, to whom it is addressed, and the date. The report also needs a title, and normally this should be as descriptive as possible. This information is frequently presented on a title page, giving a professional look from the start. An example is given in Figure 13.2 – in this case students were asked to write the report as if addressed to their superior.

In deciding upon a title for a report at work, think about how it will be used. Is the title going to appear in any listings of reports? If so it will need to indicate the sort of report and coverage in a way that will enable a potential reader, browsing through the list, to know whether your report is worth obtaining. Are there other reports on similar topics in your organisation? If so, you will need a title that distinguishes your report from theirs.

Date is a vital part of the context of a report. Information usually has a short shelf-life. It may be important for people to know whether your report was written before or after some major event having impact on your topic, or before or after another report. It is,

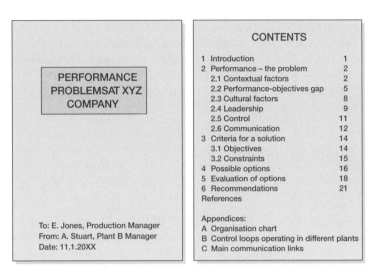

Figure 13.2 Example of student title and contents pages

therefore, essential that all reports be clearly dated, usually on the front page, as this may be the first thing a reader will wish to know.

In indicating addressee and sender, it is usually worth indicating a person's title, if this is relevant to their part in the report. Thus, you might be a senior marketing manager but have generated the report in your capacity as chair of a working party on restructuring the organisation's marketing capacity. In that case, it would be the latter title that would be important and it should be included with your job title, if that is important too.

Contents list

The contents list should show your major and minor section headings, preferably numbered, and appendices. Figure 13.2 shows a contents page for a student assignment in report format.

You will see that the contents list provides readers with a clear indication of the structure of the report to follow, as well as acting as an index for anyone wishing to refer directly to a specific part of the report, rather than read the work in its entirety. The numbering system shows clearly what is a major (e.g. 2) or minor (e.g. 2.1, 2.2) heading. Shorter reports usually will not need further division. If you need sub-subsections for a longer report, you could use a further level of numbering (e.g. 2.1.1, 2.1.2). Some organisations number paragraphs, rather than pages. This allows easy reference to any paragraph but has the disadvantage of confusing any system for numbering major and minor sections. Since the latter is such a powerful guide to structure, reserve paragraph numbering for reports where it is the required 'house style' or where frequent references to specific paragraphs are likely to be necessary.

Section and subsection titles should be as descriptive as their short length allows. This both helps the reader to follow the structure and allows easy reference to sections of most interest.

13

WRITING TO IMPRESS

Appendices are usually numbered in a different way from parts of the report proper – you can use letters or roman numerals. Again, descriptive titles are useful.

It is helpful to give page numbers as an aid to this index function, although with a short report it is not essential.

The summary is normally regarded as outside the report and does not therefore feature on the contents list.

Acknowledgements

If you have written a substantial report, perhaps on your main project, you may want to acknowledge any significant help you have had, perhaps from a supervisor or client organisation. Think carefully about the purpose of this part of your report. It can give supportive family members great pleasure to be acknowledged. You may feel strongly about references to divine help. Neither is likely to lose you marks. Failure to acknowledge your supervisor, while mentioning your goldfish, may, however, subconsciously influence the marking process. Failure to acknowledge contributions of key members of a client organisation may have an equally negative effect.

Summary

For any lengthy document a summary or abstract is useful. This can be at the end of the report, or at the front, before any contents page. For a shorter report there may be no separate summary, the introduction serving both to introduce the report and summarise key points. Many organisations insist on a one-page summary at the very front, arguing that this allows a busy manager to decide whether to invest time in reading the full report. A similar summary is often required for a thesis or dissertation.

Putting the summary at the beginning allows a potential reader to decide whether the report is worth reading in full, and also acts as orientation for those who read on. It is much easier to make sense of a complicated argument if you know the overall shape of the report in advance. Putting the summary at the end reflects its purpose of reinforcing key points of the document just read, and probably stems from the fact that it is likely to be the last thing you write. For assignments, the summary normally should be a summary of the whole report, rather than just of recommendations. You should, therefore, include a brief statement of the original problem and of the main arguments or evidence that have led you to your conclusions. In assignments with a tight word limit a good summary (which normally would not be counted against the word limit) means that the introduction has less to do, and therefore needs fewer words.

Introduction

This is a crucial part of your report. Although an initial summary, and your contents page, will have started the process of reader orientation, the introduction is where such orientation is mainly achieved. If you are not prefacing your report with a summary, your introduction will be particularly crucial. Your reader usually will come to the report with a number of questions:

- Why is this topic important?
- What was the remit of the report writer?
- What is the main argument in this report?
- On what evidence is this argument based?
- How is the argument structured?
- What are the implications of the argument?

If your introduction can answer these questions, at least in outline, your reader will be in a much better position – and more motivated – to read the subsequent report with interest, and will follow your developing argument with greater ease. Of course, if you have included an initial summary, some of these questions will have been answered already and you can mainly concentrate in your introduction on the significance of the topic and the aims of the work reported.

It is a great pity, given the above, that many students use their 'introduction', whether in assignments or examinations, to do no more than restate the set question. It is important that the remit be established, but restating the question serves little purpose. Usually you will have 'deconstructed' a question to discover the various parts implicit in it or otherwise developed your understanding of the question. At the very least, this expanded version should be included in your introduction. Preferably your introduction should go beyond this, as suggested above.

Unfortunately, the only extension of the introduction is often the inclusion of background information. Some contextual information is usually needed to establish the significance of the topic. But the introduction should not be seen as 'introduction and background'. Any detailed background information likely to be *of interest* to readers should form a separate section, preferably in an appendix. Only *essential* background information should appear in your main report. If this is extensive it may be better in a separate section. Only if brief is it suited to the introduction.

Main section(s)

As already suggested, you will normally need several major subsections within your main section and these may be further subdivided. The main sections often can be mapped moderately closely on to the stages of the standard problem-solving approach. Thus, you might include a more detailed exploration of the background to the problem (this is *not* the same as background information on the organisation), the relationship between the problem and other factors, constraints and so on, as suggested earlier in the chapter. Sub-topics within each main topic (the twigs on the branches, if you used a mind map) usually also need to have (sub)headings. Subheading numbers will relate to the major heading, as in Figure 13.2. Take care that headings and subheadings clearly indicate the content of each major and minor section.

Think carefully about what is best in the main text, what best in an appendix. Normally your aim is to make your main text as clear, compelling and interesting as you can for your readers, to increase the chance that they will understand and accept your arguments. It is these considerations that should influence your decision on what to include. Appendices should be seen as supplementary support – 'optional extras' – rather than essential to your argument. The main report should be capable of standing alone, if the reader chooses not to look at the appendices.

Diagrams frequently serve the function of supporting or clarifying your text and should therefore be included at the appropriate point. These can both reinforce your arguments and make the text look less dense and forbidding, thus sustaining your readers' interest. It is also extremely inconvenient for the reader to have to alternate between text and appendices in order to follow an argument.

Diagrams that *should* be relegated to the appendix include any extremely detailed diagrams which only the most dedicated or critical reader would wish to refer to, and any working diagrams produced in the thought process, if it is appropriate to include these at all. Your tutor *might* be interested in the thinking working diagrams show. Your organisation would not. When you *do* append diagrams, you should always refer to them, and to where they may be found, at the appropriate point in your text. There is nothing more irritating to the reader than to spend a long time thinking about a point, or wanting more evidence on it, only to find, 30 pages later, that the material is in fact there.

Similar arguments apply to tables or diagrammatic representations of evidence such as graphs or bar charts. Where they are an important part of your argument, they should be in the text. The appendix should include the more extensive information summarised in your in-text tables or charts and any detailed mathematical argument. Those sceptical about your arguments can refer to the full information on which they are based, while those who are happy to accept your condensed representation of the data will be able to follow the main thread of your argument without interruption.

To summarise, your main section should be self-standing, capable of being understood without reference to appendices. However, those not prepared to take your summaries of evidence at face value will find supporting detail in the appendices.

Within the main body of your text, if the report is a long one, you can orient the reader at intervals by including a short introduction to each main section. The structure of the report as a whole should follow the 'Say what you are going to say, say it, then say what you've said' principle. The same form can be followed usefully within each major section.

Throughout the main body of your report you should be aiming to develop arguments, based on evidence, which build up to your eventual conclusions. It is worth checking at intervals that this is what is happening. If you cannot summarise each section in these terms, you should think again about what you have written. It may be that some of the evidence that you have included does not contribute to your argument, or that part of your argument lacks supporting evidence.

Note: while 'Introduction' and 'Recommendations' are reasonable section headings, 'Main section' is not. In this part of the report your headings will be chosen to describe the particular themes you have decided to cover in your report (*see* Figure 13.2 for an example).

Conclusions

Your conclusions section should follow naturally from what you have written thus far. There should be no new material introduced at this stage, but rather a drawing together of the arguments you have developed earlier so that their implications can be spelled out. Students often have difficulty in distinguishing between conclusions and recommendations and, indeed, the distinction can be a fine one. It may help to think of the conclusions as being more to do with logic, while the recommendations deal with the implementation of these conclusions, as suited to the context. Thus, in an essay you might have 'conclusions' but not recommendations. In a report with a tight word limit and a requirement to 'recommend . . .' you might omit conclusions and include brief logical justification for your recommendations within the recommendations section.

Recommendations

Like the summary, recommendations can be at the beginning or the end. The more action oriented prefer them at the front. This suits the manager who says, 'Tell me what you want me to do, and then convince me'. There is a lot of sense to this in many work contexts. Your evaluation of an argument is much helped by the knowledge of the end to which that argument is leading. On the other hand, recommendations cannot be made until the logical process of analysis and conclusion has been gone through, so there are equally powerful arguments for recommendations appearing at the end. Most academic assignments will expect recommendations – if required at all – to appear at the end.

Perhaps the best compromise is to have an introductory summary which includes a brief statement of recommendations and then to have the fuller statement of recommendations, together with any additional arguments needed to justify them, at the end. But always ask your 'client' about their preferred position, unless the brief makes this clear.

Your recommendations should be clearly prioritised and the priorities justified. Those evaluating your report will be checking that these priorities are appropriate and that the recommendations are consistent with prevailing conditions in the organisation and its environment. For example, recommendations that call for a massive investment at a time when the organisation has cash flow problems and is already having difficulty in raising money will not be highly regarded. Similarly, if recommendations give a high priority to an interesting but not essential development, and a lower priority to something needed to ensure the continued survival of the organisation, there is likely to be little respect for the writer of the report.

> **Recommendations . . .**
> - should flow obviously from analysis
> - should be clear proposals for action
> - should be sensible and realistic.

References and/or bibiliography

You should normally include a list of *references* at the end of an essay or report (but before appendices). This list gives full details of all sources you have specifically referred to in the report. A *bibliography* includes not only sources that have been specifically mentioned but also those that have influenced your writing in a more general way, or are otherwise relevant to the topic covered. Whether or not you include a full bibliography will depend upon the circumstances. For most reports, references are all that is required. For a thesis, a fuller bibliography may be appropriate. Check with your tutors.

➤ Ch 7   So why is referencing deemed so important? Chapter 7 discussed this. Some of your evidence will be in the form of secondary data, information collected by others. You will also be drawing (I hope) on concepts that have been introduced in your courses. In both cases, your readers might wish to reassure themselves that you are making appropriate use of information or theory. To do so, they would want to look at the information themselves, to check that you are not misquoting it, or using it out of context, or go back to the author responsible for the theory you used, to see that you have really represented the concepts correctly.

More positively, your reader might be so fired with enthusiasm by your report as to be inspired to research the topic further, taking up where you left off. In either case, the reader needs to be able to find your sources. You need, therefore, to have made very clear in your text what source you are using at any point, and to include a list, usually at the end, with the full reference to the material in question.

Harvard style referencing

Most UK academic institutions recommend use of the Harvard referencing system or something based on it. This is the system adopted in this book, so you can use it as a model. If, following this system, when you cite (i.e. mention) an author in the text, you would say 'Handy (1985)' while in your references you would say:

Handy, C.B. (1985) *Understanding Organisations* (3rd edn), Penguin.

The full Harvard style also gives place (in this case Harmondsworth) of publication before publisher. Since many books are published internationally it may help to know which 'version' you are using. But place information is normally less valuable than other aspects, and with e-books is arguably even less helpful, so is sometimes omitted. There are other styles of giving references, so check which is required when you are writing for assessment or for publication. You will see that the *title* of the publication (e.g. book or journal) is distinguished by the use of italics. If you are quoting a journal article, then usually the article title is given in quotation marks and the journal title is *italicised*. In the latter case you will also need to show volume and issue numbers of the journal, and the page numbers on which the article appears. Thus:

Hendry, C. and Pettigrew, A. (1986) 'The practice of strategic human resource management', *Personnel Review,* 15, 5, pp. 3–8.

If you are referring to more than one publication by an author in a single year, you normally distinguish these by the use of letters, e.g. Handy (1985a), and Handy (1985b).

For direct quotations, for example, when you want to reproduce a whole paragraph from one of your sources, you should always include reference, normally at the end of the quotation, to the page from which the quotation is taken.

Where you have quoted from materials found on the Internet you should include the copyright statement of the relevant Web page or website, and any citation instructions, and note the date on which you last visited the Web page. For example,

> https://www.staffs.ac.uk/assets/harvard_quick_guide_tcm44-47797.pdf
> (accessed 3.8.15) provides guidance on Harvard style referencing

Appendices

Appendices (sometimes called annexes) are where you include supporting information and/or evidence for those wishing for more detail, or those wanting more information before they are prepared to be convinced by your argument. Thus, you might append a copy of a questionnaire, an interview schedule, the monthly production figures for all departments and sites that you have summarised in tabular form in your text, or detailed organisation charts for the organisation you are studying, rather than put all this in the text.

Appendices are sometimes used by students as a way of getting round the word limit, as it is generally assumed that appendices do not count against this. While this may be true – and you would need to check with your tutor – it is not a good stratagem. Material essential to your argument should not be in an appendix. If including it in your text makes you go over the limit, see whether you can be more focused and/or concise. If feel this is impossible, consider narrowing the scope of your report.

Remember to refer to relevant appendices at the appropriate point in your text so that the reader knows that supporting material is available, and where to find it.

Writing essays

You are more likely to have written essays than reports – they are common in school and undergraduate assessment, so only brief notes are offered here. An essay can be seen as a report without the trimmings. You have a title at the start, and references at the end, but none of the other trappings. But despite the absence of headings an essay in many ways resembles a report. Like an essay, it should be self-standing. It still needs an introduction to orient the reader, even if this is not headed as such. You are still required to be methodical and analytical, and to evaluate the topic set, coming to a clear conclusion as a result of theory, evidence and arguments. For more academic essays you are expected to express an academic opinion as a result of your analysis.

Your tutor will be looking for clear expression, evidence, sound arguments and use of theory whether you are writing an essay or a report. They will be looking for a balanced consideration of evidence and/or arguments for and against a particular stance – 'On the one hand . . .,, on the other . . . on balance . . .' Some business school tutors are happy with headings in an essay, in which case the report/essay distinction becomes very blurred indeed. Even if not, thinking in terms of the explicit report structure, while using a more implicit structure in your essay, can improve your writing.

If you are unsure about essay writing, there is a wealth of guidance online. Some suggestions are provided on the book website.

Whichever form you are using, essay or report, clear expression, therefore using English clearly, is important.

Writing clear English

Many students who are native English speakers lose marks because they cannot write clearly enough for their marker to understand what they are trying to say. Grammatical and spelling errors may be serious enough to cost marks. Students for whom English is a second or subsequent language often (though not always) have greater problems. It is always worth paying attention to your use of language. If you worry about your English, study the following section carefully. The credibility of any report you write at work will be reduced by poor expression. Grammatical or spelling mistakes may create doubt as to your competence in other areas. Lack of clarity in the way you write implies a lack of clarity in the way you think. Neither will improve your promotion prospects.

Clearly, this chapter cannot teach you the full complexities of the English language, especially if you are not a native speaker. Helpfile 13.4 at the end of this chapter will help, but if your English is weak you should probably take a language course before starting postgraduate study in English, or as soon as possible if you have already started. Poor language skills cause many overseas students to fail, so it is important to address any shortcomings soon. (Ask your institution what level you should score on a standard test if you are worried.) But if the problem is minor, the following basic guidelines and short explanations of how punctuation can be used may help. Helpfiles 13.2 and 13.3 will help too – they include a list of words commonly misspelled or misused in management assignments. This may be enough for you if English is your first language.

The following guidelines should help you to improve the style of your assignments or other reports, at least in terms of increasing the clarity of your communication.

Go for simplicity

While it is possible, if you are thoroughly confident in your use of English, and can keep control of a whole sequence of subordinate clauses, some of which may describe elements of the main clause, others of which may describe phrases that are already subordinate clauses themselves, without forgetting which verb belongs to which clause, or omitting verbs altogether, to construct a sentence that is grammatically correct, the overall effect is usually far from satisfactory, as the reader soon starts to lose track of the main idea, which may have been introduced several lines earlier, and by the end of the sentence it is extremely likely that he or she will have lost the thread altogether. Is that clear? Probably not! I think the last sentence/paragraph was grammatically correct, but you probably had to read the sentence several times to get the meaning. Yet, many students approach such complexity in their assignment and often they do not keep their grammar under control when doing so.

Imagine how much harder the sentence above would have been if it had used long words! If you have a predilection for multisyllabic words, habitually utilising these in preference to equivalent, albeit briefer terms, possibly intending significantly to enhance the impressiveness of your communication by demonstrating the extensiveness of your vocabulary, the capacity for obfuscation is multiplied significantly. So don't indulge yourself! Use short words and short sentences. Your meaning will almost certainly be far clearer.

If you want to gain a rough assessment of your likely clarity in terms of how you score on these two aspects, there is a measure called the *Fog Index*, which you can calculate. You can insert text into an online calculator to find the index, or work it out yourself. Select at least six sentences at random from your work – the longer the extract, the more reliable the index.

Decide in advance *which* sentences, e.g. second, fifteenth, twenty-eighth, or by throwing a die to generate random numbers. If you look at the text while selecting, the process will not be random. Count the number of words in the selected sentences and the number that have three or more syllables. Express this as a percentage. Divide your total number of words by the number of sentences you have used. Add this average length to the percentage of long words and multiply by 0.4. If your answer is greater than 12, your writing is 'foggy'. (If you want to work out the Fog Index for a shorter passage, use the whole passage and divide by however many sentences it contains. If you do not trust your sums, and do not want to use an online calculator, your word processor can probably show readability statistics – look online for guidance on enabling this facility.

13

WRITING TO IMPRESS

Exercise 13.1

Calculate the Fog Index of the first two paragraphs after the heading 'Writing clear English', and compare it with the index for the first two paragraphs under 'Go for simplicity' using all the text, rather than a sample, in each case.

Check your calculation against the answer at the end of the chapter.

Activity 13.3

Find a piece of writing that you did recently and calculate your own Fog Index. Check it occasionally in future work.

> **Improve clarity with:**
> - shorter words
> - shorter sentences
> - shorter paragraphs
> - one idea per paragraph.

Shorter sentences almost certainly will make your writing clearer. Activity 13.3 probably demonstrated this. You will be far less likely to violate grammatical rules; shorter sentences are much easier to control. With a long sentence you may inadvertently omit a verb, either from the main part of the sentence or from one of the clauses within it. Or you may use a singular form of verb when it should be plural, or vice versa, because you have forgotten the actual subject of the verb. In a short sentence such an error would be glaringly obvious.

There are clear arguments for keeping words and sentences short. You should also avoid over-lengthy paragraphs. Paragraphs serve to break a piece of writing into units which the reader can absorb at one go. Ideally, a paragraph will be 75–100 words long. More importantly, it will relate to a single topic or idea. Combining disjointed ideas into a single paragraph will confuse your reader, who will be expecting, and therefore unsuccessfully seeking, connections between them.

Be careful, however. If paragraphs are too short, it can make your writing seem disjointed. Check whether the paragraph needs to be expanded, or whether other short paragraphs are in fact devoted to the same idea and could therefore be combined. If not, do not worry too much. The occasional short paragraph will do no harm. Indeed, it can be used to emphasise a point. But, if your entire report consists of very short paragraphs, you may not be developing your ideas sufficiently.

If paragraphs are too long, text can seem forbidding and dense and the reader may find it heavy going. See whether you can split very long paragraphs into shorter ones. The carving-up process requires you to think carefully about the points you are making within that section of text. This may generate significant improvements to your draft. When you think about what you were *really* trying to say, you often find ways of saying it better.

I once spent a year as sub-editor of a student newspaper and most of my job consisted of carving large paragraphs into smaller ones. A report can stand much longer paragraphs than a newspaper, but that year gave me a ruthlessness that I lacked before and that has stood me in good stead ever since.

However you split your paragraphs, it is a good idea to link them so as to avoid disjointedness. The first part of the previous sentence constitutes just such a link (see how many more you can identify in previous paragraphs). It relates the idea of linking back to the earlier idea of splitting. Linking needs a light hand. You do not wish to spend half of each paragraph covering ground covered just before.

A floating 'this' is not a link – avoid it. I mean the 'This means . . .', or 'This is . . .' type of link, where it is totally unclear whether the 'this' is the whole previous paragraph, the last sentence or the subject (or even the object) of the last sentence. Whether you use 'this' to link sentences or paragraphs, you should always check that it is firmly 'anchored', i.e. that it is absolutely clear to the reader what 'this' is, with no ambiguity possible.

I have a strong suspicion that students are often tempted to use long words, sentences or even paragraphs because they feel that this is the expected academic style. Others think that a simple idea may be made more impressive in this way. There is also a feeling that jargon is necessary. Sadly, these feelings are well grounded. I once read about a depressing piece of research which showed that the same paper given to academic audiences was rated much more highly when the presenter used a high Fog Index delivery rather than a low one.

However, you may, in the course of your studies, conclude that many of the 'difficult' papers you read in journals are expressing remarkably simple, even unoriginal, ideas, once you manage to penetrate the language in which they are written. It is part of the academic culture to write in a 'learned' style. You will also be expected to use 'jargon', to the extent that it expresses course concepts directly relevant to the assignment set.

However, most management-related Master's courses aim to develop written communication skills relevant to work. If your course has this goal, you will not need an overly academic style for assignments. (Such a style would be a liability at work.) I am not suggesting that you use only words of one syllable and sentences of no more than five words and exclude *all* jargon. But try to use the simplest language consistent with expressing your ideas adequately to a particular audience, and use only those jargon words that are necessary to demonstrate your ability to apply course concepts to problem situations. Almost all tutors, and most managers, will be more impressed by clarity than by unnecessary complexity.

Even with short sentences you may be prone to grammatical errors. If you suspect this to be the case, work your way through Helpfile 13.3 at the end of this chapter. This covers punctuation and its role in generating grammatically correct sentences, together with other common grammatical mistakes.

Avoid sensational or emotive language

While you want what you write to be as interesting as possible, it is best to avoid sounding like a cheap newspaper. For example, if you had surveyed the observance of health and safety guidelines in an organisation and found many shortcomings, it would be in order to describe the situation as 'worrying', 'thoroughly unsatisfactory' or 'in breach of legislation'. It would not be appropriate to talk of 'a downright disgrace', 'a thoroughly immoral situation', or 'another example of capitalist managers exploiting the oppressed workers'. It is possible to make your meaning perfectly clear while using slight restraint in your language. Indeed, you may make your point more forcibly in this way, as you will avoid reducing your credibility through inappropriate language.

Use the first person with care

You will need to check the expectations of your audience here. For example, I have used the first person in this book. The views in it are personal and I wanted to avoid sounding too distant. 'The author' sounds pretentious to me. In any case, much of the text is intended to replace the tutor to whom you may not have ready access, offering the same sort of support. It is not intended as academically authoritative and suggestions are offered for you to use as you please. 'I' therefore seemed more appropriate. But your tutor may consider that writing in the first person is inappropriate in assignments (other than for reflective writing). And it may be totally inappropriate in organisational reports. Only use 'I' when you are sure this is acceptable.

Check what you have written

Better still, if your spelling or grammar 'wobbles' on occasion, get someone else to check it for you. Your main sources of help are:

- **A dictionary** – keep it on your desk and consult it whenever in the slightest doubt.
- **The spell and grammar checker on your word processor** – this will draw your attention to non-existent spellings and mistypes but, unfortunately, will not be smart enough to spot your mistake if your misspelling has generated a valid word, such as 'there' when you meant 'their'. Because of this difficulty a list of common misspellings (common in student assignments at least) is given in Helpfile 13.2 at the end of this chapter. This focuses on words where the misspelling is a valid (if unintended) word and therefore unlikely to be picked up by the spellchecker.
- **Anyone willing to help** – it is always a good idea to ask someone else to read an important draft, no matter how good your English. This will enable you to check that your intended meaning is clear throughout, and to see what reaction it produces. Again, make it clear that you would welcome, rather than be offended by, corrections to grammar or spelling, and do not become defensive if corrections are offered.

The power of English

The clarity of your English depends partly on its correctness. And clarity will have a major impact on *all* your written communications. It will help you get good grades for assignments, will make a marked difference to your exam scores and will influence the way people react to reports that you write at work. While content is important, it is not sufficient. The way in which that content is expressed will influence both how much of it is actually communicated and the way in which readers react to it. This is why your writing skills are so important.

Try the following exercise. It may suggest that you could benefit from Helpfiles 13.2 and 13.3 at the end of this chapter and you could then try the additional exercises on the companion website, to see whether your grasp of grammar and spelling has improved. During your course, pay careful attention to feedback from tutors on your writing style. Look for other sources of feedback on your writing, too, both during your course and thereafter, and try, where possible, to critique your own work.

Exercise 13.2

Improve the following text:

The problem in many organisations where labour turnover and absenteeism are high are that their is low moral and the affect of this makes workers less happy. This makes recruiting expences high, looses valuable skills from the organisation, and the staff remaining, who's moral then drops further. This is a viscious circle centred about a deepseeted problem. Yet, the managements' disinterest often means that there staff are caught in this trap for year's. This insures a constant decline in affectiveness. Personal departments are powerless to, if senior management support is absent. There as frustrated as everyone else are – and everyone knows what that means!

While it is easy to make mistakes, it is not difficult to improve the clarity, and correctness, of your writing. If you bear in mind the points covered in this chapter, refer to the Helpfiles where necessary, and always read what you have written, the production of written work for assessment can be a stimulating challenge. It need not be stressful, a chore to be postponed, and something that gives you little satisfaction and low grades, although for too many students this is sadly the case. Instead, each assignment can be both a vehicle for learning and an enjoyable and satisfying task.

Writing for the screen

I am not suggesting a change of career here, but universities often expect you to submit your assignments electronically. Everything in this chapter applies to assignments submitted in any medium, but there are a few additional points that can improve assignments submitted – and marked – electronically.

I speak with a certain amount of feeling, having marked – from the screen – many assignments of (with appendices) up to 70 pages long. (I care about both the forests that would be sacrificed to making print copies and the cost of paper and ink.) Your tutor's perspective may be similar to mine. When preparing such assignments think about making it easy for your tutor!

Seven 'secrets' of successful e-submission

1. **Be compatible** – with the system and your tutor's computer. Even if the system seems absurdly archaic, obey instructions about acceptable formats. Many universities do not have state-of-the-art machines or the very latest software. (A student recently submitted a beautiful-looking report, but the words in all the diagrams – which were essential to understanding her argument – appeared in what looked like Korean script on my machine. I could not give credit for what I could not read.)

2. **Observe size limits** – the system may reject large files over the specified maximum. Scanned materials, high resolution photos or lengthy and/or highly formatted appendices may bring you near the limit, and tutors' comments might take you beyond this, meaning the marked assignment will be rejected. So keep your file size well within the prescribed limit.

3. **Be legible** – or rather pity the tutor's eyesight. While electronic submission spares tutors from deciphering handwriting, reading from a screen is not always that much easier. A sans serif font like Arial or Calibri is much clearer on a screen than a fancier

one like Times New Roman. (Avoid really fancy ones at all costs, no matter how pretty they are!) Font sizes below 11 may be difficult for anyone with less than perfect vision, though this varies a little with font.

4. **Take care with your summary** – It is particularly difficult to grasp a long report when reading it one screen at a time. A good summary, giving the big picture of the whole report, is an invaluable aid.

5. **Leave good margins** – tutors may want to use the Word 'insert comment' facility for comments specific to a particular art of your assignment. This will then appear in the margin at an appropriate point without affecting your pagination. If your margins are miniscule, this doesn't work so well. Some tutors may intersperse their comments with your text, or not make specific comments at all, but you should at least give them the chance!

6. **Make 'navigation' easy** – in a paper assignment it is relatively easy to flip back and forth between a point in a report and the relevant appendix. With an electronic assignment this is harder, unless you use hypertext to allow linking. To the tutor this can be a godsend, allowing easy navigation to appendices or other sources.

7. **Read your tutor's comments!!!!!** – not all tutors comment extensively, if at all, but, if they do, their comments are intended to be helpful. I was once devastated to learn after I had marked her final assignment that one student – a weak student whose work had prompted comments almost as long as her original – had been unaware that I was commenting at all. She had not bothered to look at the assignment again and had read none of the comments that had taken me hours to produce.

SUMMARY

- Written assignments need to be planned carefully, with the requirements of the intended audience fully considered.

- You need to be extremely careful to avoid plagiarism, using your own words rather than 'borrowing' those of others, unless you give them due credit.

- Seemingly simple questions need to be broken down into their constituent, if implicit, parts.

- Diagrams can be useful in the early stages of planning content and structure.

- Plans need to be checked against requirements at regular intervals.

- Time management is essential if deadlines are to be met.

- Assignments may be asked for in a variety of formats. Clear structure and judicious use of subheadings almost always will improve clarity, even if a 'report' is not required.

- A report should be seen as essentially an argument based on evidence. This evidence includes information about a situation and relevant theory. Your goal is to get your readers to accept your argument and consequent recommendations.

- The drafting process should be started as soon as possible rather than left until evidence collection is complete. Several drafts will be needed, so early drafts can be amended in the light of subsequent findings.

- Report formats typically include: a title page with sender, addressee and date, as well as title; a summary; a list of contents; an introduction; the main body of the report, broken into major and minor subsections; conclusions; recommendations; a reference list; and any necessary appendices. Organisational house styles may vary.

- Whatever the format, an appropriate style and correct use of English will enhance the clarity of your arguments. Simplicity of language is usually an advantage, and spelling and punctuation are important.

- Where possible, diagrams and results important to your argument should be included in the text. More detailed supporting evidence should be included as appendices.

- If you are asked to submit your assignments electronically, pay particular attention to appropriate presentation for reading from screen.

13

WRITING TO IMPRESS

Further information

Atkinson, I. (2011) *FT Essential Guide to Business Writing: How to Engage, Persuade, and Sell*, Pearson.

Blamires, H. (2000) *The Penguin Guide to Plain English*, Penguin.

Bowden, J. (2011) *Writing a Report* (9th edn), Howtobooks.

Burchfield, R.W. (ed.) (2004) *Fowler's Modern English Usage* (3rd edn), Oxford University Press. A classic – Fowler's first edition appeared in 1926 – a sort of enlarged dictionary with hints on how to pronounce and use the words included. A mine of information.

Butterworth, J. and Thwaites, G. (2005) *Thinking Skills*, Cambridge University Press.

Forsyth, P. (2010) *Creating Success: How to Write Reports and Proposals*, London: The Sunday Times.

Fowler, A. (2006) *How to Write*, Oxford University Press. May help you improve the clarity of your writing in general.

Gowers, E. (1954) *The Complete Plain Words*, HMSO. Now available in Penguin. This is the classic work on use of English. It has been regularly updated, even since the author's death, and is well worth acquiring.

Gowers, E. (2014) *The Complete Plain Words*, HMSO - 232 Celsius, Kindle edition.

Gravett, S. (2003) *The Right Way to Write Reports*, Elliot Right Way Books.

Truss, L. (2003) *Eats, Shoots & Leaves: The Zero Tolerance Approach to Punctuation*, Profile Books. Provides an amusing defence of appropriate punctuation.

http://gunning-fog-index.com/fog.cgi (accessed 18.5.15). To calculate the fog index of any text.

http://www.usingenglish.com/glossary/fog-index.html (accessed 18.5.15). On fog index in general.

http://www.gcflearnfree.org/word2010 (accessed 18.5.15). For a series of tutorials on using Word 10 – but there are many others, and many tutorials for other common word-processing programmes.

http://www.open.edu/openlearn/education/english-skills-learning/content-section-overview (accessed 16.1.15). For one of several free OpenLearn course in English for students.

http://www.virtualschool.edu/mon/SocialConstruction/Logic.html (accessed 3.8.15).

You may find this helpful for constructing arguments and for spotting different examples of false logic.

http://learnonline.canberra.edu.au/mod/book/view.php?id=178430 (accessed 18.5.15). For guidance on essays.

HELPFILE 13.1
GLOSSARY OF TERMS USED IN EXAMINATION AND ASSESSMENT QUESTIONS

If you are not used to answering assignment questions in social science subjects, the following interpretation of terms commonly used may help you to be sure that you are meeting the requirements of the question.

Analyse

This means to examine part by part. Thus, if you are asked to analyse a problem situation, you would be looking for the roots of the problem, rather than merely describing the symptoms that are presented. Normally you would be expected to draw heavily on ideas and frameworks in the course being assessed in order to identify the root causes. The analysis may be the basis for suggesting possible ways forward and deciding between them.

Comment

This terse instruction may appear after a quotation or other statement. You are required to respond in a way that shows that you understand the topic to which the statement refers. Thus, you might need to define any terms contained, explain the significance of the statement and possibly evaluate it (*see* below), or state the extent to which you agree and disagree, and give your reasons for this.

Compare

This means look for both similarities and differences between the (usually) two things mentioned. It is very easy to forget one or the other, and safest always to think of 'compare' as shorthand for 'compare and contrast'. Normally you would be expected to describe the similarities and differences and perhaps come down in favour of one or the other. Sometimes it is possible to do this comparison using a table, with one column for each of the things being compared, perhaps with a third column for comments.

Contrast

This is a subset of compare. You are expected to focus only on the differences between the things mentioned.

Critically appraise/evaluate

This means to discuss the strengths and weaknesses of a proposition or theory (*see* 'criticise' and 'evaluate' below – you will need to incorporate elements of both) in terms of its logic and the evidence on which it is based, and would need to identify any hidden assumptions.

Criticise

This means to judge the merit of a statement or theory, making clear the basis for your judgement. This might be in terms of the evidence on which a theory is based, the internal consistency of that theory, or the theoretical, logical or factual underpinning of an opinion.

Define

This means to state precisely the meaning of a concept. Normally this will be a definition that you have been given in your course. Sometimes there may be competing definitions, in which case you may need to give both (or all, if more than two), and discuss the differences between them. Often you will be asked to include examples of the thing to be defined but, even if not, doing so may help to establish that you understand the meaning of the term in question.

Describe

This means give a detailed account of the thing referred to, again with a view to establishing that you know what is being referred to, and understand its significance. Diagrams often can help you to describe something and should be included if they add something to the words.

Discuss

This means to extract the different themes in a subject and to describe and evaluate them. What are the key factors/aspects? What are the arguments in favour of and against each aspect? What evidence is there in support and against? What is the significance of each aspect?

Evaluate

This means to say what something is worth. If a theory were to be evaluated, you would look at the evidence supporting the theory, and the usefulness of that theory to managers. Often you will need to first establish the criteria against which something is to be evaluated.

Explain

This can mean to make something clear or to give reasons for something, depending on the context. Frequently you would need to do both to answer a question. Remember that your explanation, as with all assessment, is intended to demonstrate your understanding of the concept to your assessor.

Identify

This normally means you are to decide what the important factors are and describe them briefly.

Illustrate

This sometimes means use a diagram or other graphic aid but, more frequently, means give examples to show that you know what you are talking about.

Interpret

This normally means make sense of something, make it clear, usually giving your judgement of the significance of the thing to be interpreted. You might be asked to interpret a set of figures or a graph, in which case you would need to describe in words the significant features, or 'messages' contained therein.

List

This needs to be treated with caution. Strictly it means to give single words or phrases. But sometimes the assessor really means you to give a brief description rather than merely a single phrase. If in doubt with written assignments, ask. If in an exam, make a reasoned guess from the number of marks allocated to this part of the question.

Outline

This means give a brief description of key features of whatever.

Reflect on . . .

Or provide a reflective account of . . . This is asking for a personal account of your thoughts and/or experience and a reasoned description of the process by which your thought processes changed and/or you came to act differently.

. . . ?

By this I mean those questions that seem to invite the answer 'Yes' or 'No', e.g... 'Do you agree?' or 'Are budgets an adequate control mechanism?' It is very rare for the assessor to require a simple yes or no. It is far more likely that you are expected to discuss the statement and evaluate it.

HELPFILE 13.2
SPELLING
(THE RIGHT WORD)

Because spellcheckers and dictionaries exist, I make no attempt here to list all the words that appear misspelled on assignments. Instead I concentrate on those that occur wrongly so often that the student clearly has no doubts about their correctness, and that are valid words in themselves. They would, therefore, not be picked up by a spellchecker and presumably do not cause the student to reach for the dictionary. I am assuming that you *do* use the spellchecker! It is an easy and vital tool, even if sometimes irritating.

advice–advise

The noun has a 'c', the verb an 's'. It is clear from the pronunciation which is which in this case, though people still make mistakes. You can use this pair as a model to help you decide in the case of other pairs, e.g. practice–practise, where the pronunciation is no help. Or use 'ice is a noun' to help you remember.

affect–effect

To 'affect' something is to change it, or to have an *effect* on it. As a noun, 'affect' is used by psychologists to mean mood. As a verb, 'to effect' something means to bring it about. Thus, 'In order to affect the way recruiters treat minority groups, it may be necessary to effect new legislation. The effect of the legislation should be to make discrimination illegal.'

councillor–counsellor

'Councillors' are elected local authority representatives (among other things). It is 'counsellors' who give advice, or counsel.

disinterested–uninterested

'Disinterested' means impartial or unbiased. If you mean someone shows no interest in something, you need 'uninterested'. This mistake is *extremely* common, but highly irritating to more sensitive readers.

ensure–insure

To 'ensure' means to make sure. 'Insure' means to take out an insurance policy.

hear–here

'Hear' has to do with ears, 'here' means in this place (Beatles fans may fondly remember 'Here, there and everywhere . . .').

imply–infer

'Imply' means to hint at. The speaker or writer implies. 'Infer' means to draw a conclusion, or inference, from something, and is done by the reader or listener.

i.e.–e.g.–etc.

The abbreviation 'i.e.' means 'that is', i.e. another way of saying the same thing. The abbreviation 'e.g.' means 'for example', so it is only a part of the same thing. If you mean 'and so on', you should use 'etc.'. But it is sloppy to use etc. more than sparingly. It can suggest that you haven't bothered to think an argument through. There is a fairly common school of thought (especially among editors) that none of these abbreviations should be used unless absolutely necessary.

it's–its

This is by far the commonest mistake I encounter. More than half of students seem to get it wrong. 'It's' is short for 'it is' – the apostrophe stands for the missing letter. 'Its' means 'belonging to it'. The confusion arises because in old English the possessive form used to be 'John his coat', or whatever. So when this was shortened to John's coat, the apostrophe was representing the missing letters. But now it just means belonging to and its origins are forgotten. Check that you are in the minority who can use 'its' and 'it's' correctly.

lead–led

The metal is 'lead' (as in lead pipes), so too is the *present* tense of the verb, as in 'I lead the parade every day'. 'Led' is the past – 'Yesterday I led it, as usual'.

loose–lose

'Loose' means 'to unfasten' or 'not tight'. 'Lose' refers to misplacing something or not coming first in a race.

moral–morale

This is another *extremely* common confusion. When you are talking about job satisfaction, you mean 'morale'. Every time 'moral' is used in this context it conjures up visions of defrauding the customer, or carryings-on behind the filing cabinets.

oral–aural–verbal

'Oral' has to do with the mouth, so refers to speaking (or taking medicine); 'aural' has to do with the ears; while 'verbal' means to do with words, which might be written or spoken. (Apparently ear drops labelled 'to be taken aurally' are often misapplied.)

personal–personnel

'Personal' means 'belonging to you', or 'private': if you mean 'employees', you need 'personnel'.

principal–principle

'Principal' means most important, or the head of something. 'Principle' means an idea or truth. Or if you are into morality, it can refer to a code of conduct. So 'The principal consideration is . . .' or 'the Principal of the College . . .', but 'An important principle when marking assignments is . . .'.

stationery–stationary

You buy envelopes – stationery – at a stationers. A car can be stationary.

their–there–they're–theirs

'There' is the place. (Remember 'Here, there and everywhere . . .'.) 'Their' indicates possession. 'They're' is short for 'they are', with the apostrophe indicating the missing letters again. Note, too, no apostrophe in 'theirs' (as in 'the car was theirs').

to–too–two

The only times you *don't* use 'to' is if you mean excessive ('too'), or the number ('two'). So 'Two of us are going to be too late'.

were–we're–where

'Were' is the past tense, 'we're' is the shortened version of 'we are', 'where' is the place (think of it as getting the answer 'there', which is only one letter different). So 'Over there, where we were, we're almost there'.

who's–whose

Another muddling case, like 'its', where the apostrophe indicates omission not possession. So 'who's' is short for 'who is', and 'whose' means 'belonging to whom'.

your–you're

And again, 'you're' means 'you are', while 'your' indicates 'belonging to you'.

You will see that, by remembering the simple rule that an apostrophe stands for letters left out, you can cure many of the misspellings. For the rest, you will either need to learn the correct spellings by rote, or use mnemonics. For all other words that cause you doubt, use your dictionary. If you find it embarrassing to consult one openly, get an electronic one!

HELPFILE 13.3
PUNCTUATION
AND GRAMMAR

Once your spelling is under control, the only thing left to worry about is getting the punctuation right. Punctuation can totally change the meaning of a sentence. Grammar checks on your word processor are some help here, but the following comments might also be useful. If you keep your sentences short, you will need very few types of punctuation, but are likely to want to use at least the following.

Apostrophes (')

As already indicated, these indicate where a word has been shortened by omitting letters, e.g. 'didn't'. An apostrophe is also used to indicate possession, when *s* is added to a normal word, as in 'a dog's breakfast'. For plurals, when an *s* is there already, the apostrophe is added *after* the *s*, as in 'eight weeks' work'. Note that for odd plurals, where you *do* need still to add an *s* to indicate possession, as in men's, or women's, then the apostrophe is *before* the added *s*. Remember that, where there is a special word to indicate the possessive, there is no need for an apostrophe. After all, you would never write hi's, so should not use one with its, yours, theirs, hers. Despite this, the use of *it's* to mean the possessive is probably the commonest grammatical mistake seen in assignments. Remember, 'it's' means 'it is'. The apostrophe is standing for a missing letter.

Brackets

These are used to separate off something that is an addition or insertion (such as an aside that casts light on what you have said). When they occur as the last part of a sentence, close the bracket *before* the full stop. (When a bracket encloses a complete sentence you should put the full stop before the bracket.)

Capital letters

These are used at the start of each sentence, or for names of people (John Smith), places (Paris), months (May), or adjectives derived from these (Elizabethan, French, Parisian), and for the first and major words in a title (The MBA Handbook).

Colon (:)

This can be used to introduce a list, as in the example above, or in a way similar to a semi-colon to link two clauses that could stand as sentences in their own right. You would tend to prefer the colon if the second clause explained the first, if you wanted to highlight a strong contrast between them, or if you wanted to draw particular attention to the connection between them. For example, 'He had no trouble getting on to the course: his father was head of department.'

Commas (,)

These are used to split up parts of a sentence to make the meaning clearer and allow the reader to draw mental breath. They may split strings of nouns, such as 'MBA students need time, self-discipline, organisation and motivation'. You could have added a comma before the '*and*'. In a longer list this would be preferable, for a short one it is less important.

Commas may split other lists, such as adverbs or verbs. For example, 'You need to work quickly, efficiently, thoroughly, and with extreme concentration', or 'You will need to think, plan, set deadlines, and monitor your progress'.

Commas are essential to split up more complex sentences with several parts. I shall not give an example, as this book is full of them: my husband says I have an unfortunate tendency towards baroque sentence construction!

When using commas it is essential to check that you have not inadvertently split a verb from its subject. You must not, for example, write 'The courses I am studying, include accountancy and marketing'. In this case *courses* is the subject and *include* its verb. Similarly, avoid writing 'Panda eats, shoots and leaves'. (But do read Truss (2003) for more about commas.)

Dashes (– . . . –)

These can be used instead of brackets to separate off the same sort of thing, or used singly to indicate a break in the train of thought – those occasions when inspiration strikes in mid-sentence.

Exclamation marks (!)

These can be used (sparingly) to denote excitement, amazement or to indicate humour or sarcasm.

Full stops (.)

You will need one of these at the end of each of your (short) sentences. Check that your sentence is complete before putting the full stop. It might be a single word, such as 'No'.

But if the sentence is longer, check that it makes complete sense. Usually it will do this only if it has at least one verb (a 'doing' word, like 'write' and 'go') and a noun (person or thing) to do whatever it is. If the verb needs an object, i.e. is done *to* something, then the object must be in the sentence too. If you do indulge in long and complicated sentences, check that each verb has subjects and objects as required.

A full stop is also used to indicate an abbreviation, as in Co., though is not needed if the abbreviation includes the last letter of the shortened word, as in Dr or many other titles. Remember the earlier caution about the use of abbreviations, however.

A series of three full stops, '. . .' can be used to indicate either that you are breaking off before finishing something or that you are omitting a section of a quotation. (This is called an 'ellipsis'.)

Inverted commas (". . ."), or ('. . .')

Use these whenever you are quoting, whether speech or a section of text. You can use single or double inverted commas (if there is a rule, few people are aware of it), but you should be consistent. Sometimes you may have a quote within a quote. For example, a passage of text you are quoting may itself include a quotation. If so, use double quotation marks to distinguish this if you normally use single, or vice versa. Quotation marks may also be used to denote titles of books or articles, although it is equally common to underline these or use italics to distinguish them.

Other common mistakes

The first is mixing singular verbs with plural subjects, or vice versa. So you should say 'one of the students *was* (not 'were') late', and 'the group *was* annoyed'. 'Data' is strictly a plural, but these days it is acceptable among all but extreme purists to refer to it in the singular, 'data is available . . .'. To say 'a data' still grates, and should be avoided. Talk about a piece of information if you don't like to use 'datum', the correct singular.

Question marks (?)

These are used instead of a full stop at the end of any sentence that asks a direct question, such as 'What are your objectives in seeking to gain an MBA?' But they are not needed if the question is reported, such as, 'Many students wonder why they are working for an MBA'.

Semi-colon (;)

This is a weaker form of a full stop. It is used to separate things that could be separate sentences, but that are closely linked, thus making the writing less abrupt. Always check before using a semi-colon that what follows it could stand as a sentence in its own right; if it does not, you probably should have used a comma. You also use semi-colons to separate the items in a list, when you started the list with a colon. You can use it before the final item in the list, even if this follows 'and'. You will need many resources for successful study: access to a good library; a place to work in peace; sufficient time; sympathetic family; and a supportive employer.

Another fault is using incorrect prepositions. It should be 'different *from*', not *to* (though 'to' is seen increasingly), and 'centre *on*', not *round*.

Confusing 'shall' and 'will' is also common. You should say 'I shall', or 'we shall' when talking normally about the future. 'Will' is used only to denote strong determination. Thus: 'I shall sit my exam next month. I will work very hard beforehand.'

You should also avoid confusing 'can' and 'may'. 'Can' refers to being able to, 'may' to being permitted to. I *can* swim, as placed in water I shall not drown. I *may* swim here, because it is a public beach. 'May' can also mean that something is moderately likely to happen. It may rain tomorrow. 'Might' means less likely, but still possible. There might be a flood, but I should be very surprised.

Confusing 'due to' and 'owing to' is also frequent. 'Owing to' means because of, and usually comes at the start of a sentence. 'Due to' means caused by, and usually comes after the verb 'to be'. Owing to confusion over meanings, words are often used incorrectly. Often this is due to poor teaching of English at school.

13

WRITING TO IMPRESS

HELPFILE 13.4
IF ENGLISH IS NOT YOUR NATIVE LANGUAGE

If you are about to study in English for the first time, you may be worried about your abilities. This worry is reasonable, but may not be justified. Many students who are non-native English speakers write far better English than my native speakers! However, even if your chosen institution does not insist upon it, it is worth taking one of the standard English tests available to check that you are likely to be able to cope with Master's-level study in the language.

Three areas of competence will be important:

- **Reading** – you will need to read, and understand, a considerable volume of fairly difficult materials.
- **Speaking** – you will need to be able to follow, and contribute to, group discussions.
- **Writing** – you will need to be able to express yourself in written English in assignments and, under pressure, in examinations.

I shall focus here on written English, although improving this will impact upon speaking and writing too, and one of the ways of improving your writing is to read as extensively as possible. For more detailed treatment of these points, see Giles and Hedge (1994), from which much of what follows is drawn.

To improve your written English you need to improve your vocabulary and your grammar.

Vocabulary

Although students often worry about vocabulary, the problem is seldom that the students do not use a wide enough range of words. More often, the words are used in a way that leaves their meaning ambiguous. Part of the reason for this lies in the difference between *active* and *passive* vocabulary. Words that you understand when read in context, but that you do not readily use, are part of your passive vocabulary. Those you use easily are active. (A similar distinction applies to grammatical structures.) It is likely that you will need to extend and consolidate your active, and perhaps also your passive, vocabulary.

To focus your efforts you need to concentrate on frequency, speciality and utility of words. Clearly, words that you encounter frequently in your reading and in lectures are ones that you need to know, and probably need to be able to use easily. Log any such words where you are unsure of the meaning, check with dictionaries and native speakers to be sure that you do understand, note down and learn them!

Words that appear in assignments are of particular importance. You must be absolutely sure that you understand what the assignment requires. The glossary in Helpfile 13.1 is a good starting point, but always check you understand the meaning of every word in an assignment. And make sure that you *learn* the meaning of such words. They may well appear in examinations.

Beware of terms that resemble words in your own language. For example, the common word 'sensible' in English now means 'showing good sense' (as in 'sensible shoes', i.e. ones that are comfortable for walking in). Yet, the similar-looking Spanish or Italian '*sensible*' means 'sensitive', a meaning which the English word lost shortly after the time of Jane Austen. If something is not making sense it may be because you are assuming an equivalence that no longer exists.

Dictionaries are not a lot of help, however, for colloquial English. Some assignment writers revel in using such terms, perhaps in the interests of making a scenario sound 'real'. For example, a recent reference to 'mothballing' a factory (closing it down, but in a way that it can be opened later if there is a need for it) – puzzled one of my (French) students. If the dictionary offers no meaning that makes sense, you have no option but to ask a native English speaker for help.

Many of the words or phrases you encounter will be specialist terms. Some will have originated in the study of management or related subjects, but most will be everyday words that are given a specific meaning when combined (such as transaction costs or value chain). Normal dictionaries are of limited use here – but you should be given definitions for such terms, and you will be on an equal footing with other students, as such specialist terms will be new to them too. You may well not know the equivalent term in your own language (though if you have a management text from home you should be able to find it easily).

To extend your vocabulary, Giles and Hedge suggest the following:

- Write down words and phrases rather than merely repeating them in your head – this will help them stick in your memory.

- Try to learn vocabulary in context, so write new words and phrases into a sentence to learn the way they are used.

- Try to group new words with other words that frequently occur with them – for example 'personnel' might be grouped with: personnel manager; personnel department; military personnel; 'all personnel should receive health and safety training'.

- Set aside regular 'slots' in your study schedule for learning vocabulary. Don't make these too long. Little and often is more effective.

- Work out a system for recording your new vocabulary – for example 'groupings' could be shown diagrammatically on cards, to be easily carried around.

- Read for language acquisition – this is different from reading for information (also important). Identify problematic words, check the meaning and, if they seem important (in terms of frequency or utility), ensure that you have a correct definition and start a 'grouping' card for them.

- If your course has not yet started, use an introductory management text, together with an interesting book by a 'guru' and the *Financial Times* and/or *The Economist* as the basis for your 'reading for language acquisition'.

Grammar

English grammar is complex and somewhat beyond the scope of this book. It is poorly understood by many in the UK who were educated in the 1970s and 1980s, when in state schools grammar was seldom taught. Hints are given earlier in the chapter. Study these. If possible, ask someone who is good at English to read your assignments before you submit them. Where they think grammar could be improved, make sure that they explain (if they can) what is wrong and why, so that you understand how to improve things. And ask tutors for as much feedback as possible. Some are reluctant to correct grammar for fear of seeming petty, but will do so if you show that you genuinely want their help.

If you are uncertain about your grammar, it is particularly important to keep the structure of your sentences simple.

ANSWERS TO EXERCISES

Exercise 13.1

(If my counting is right)

Writing clear English:

Words: 151

Words of three or more syllables: 16

Percentage of such words: 10.6 (a)

Sentences: 10

Average sentence length: 15.1 (b)

Fog Index $= 0.4(a + b) = 10.3$ (OK)

Go for simplicity:

Words: 232

Words of three or more syllables: 45

Percentage of such words: 19.4 (a)

Sentences: 7

Average sentence length: 33.1 (b)

Fog Index $= 0.4(a + b) = 21$ (not OK).

Exercise 13.2

The problem in many organisations where labour turnover and absenteeism are high *is* (subject is 'the problem') that *there* is low *morale*. (This sentence is easily split here.) The *effect* of this is to make workers less happy. (You could argue that this is merely repeating the morale sentence . . .) *High labour turnover* (otherwise it is not at all clear what 'this' is) makes recruiting *expenses* (I know this word wasn't included in Helpfile 13.2: Spelling, but that doesn't mean you shouldn't look it up in a dictionary if unsure) high, *loses* valuable skills from the *organization* (either this American spelling, or the English *organisation* is acceptable in most cases, but be consistent) and *puts pressure on* (otherwise this part of the sentence lacks a verb) the staff remaining. (Another place where the sentence can be split but, if you chose not to, I hope you wrote *whose*.) Their *morale* then drops further. This is a *vicious* (dictionary again) circle, centred *on* (*stemming from*, or *caused by* would be better) a *deep seated* (*deeply rooted* better?) problem. Yet the *management's* (presumably only one management is being discussed in each case) *lack of interest* (surely they are hardly unbiased in this, merely unaware) means that their staff are caught in this trap *for years* (nothing belongs to the years). This *ensures* a constant decline in *effectiveness. Personnel* departments are powerless *too* (or perhaps *to act*, depending on the intended meaning), if senior management support is absent. *They're* (but *They are* would be much better) as frustrated as everyone else *is*. (Omit the rest, as the style is inappropriate, and in any case it adds nothing.)

It still is hardly incisive, or elegant, but it is better . . .

14
SPEAKING TO IMPRESS

Learning outcomes

By the end of this chapter you should:

- feel more comfortable about public speaking
- understand how to make your presentation effective
- be able to avoid faults that commonly reduce effectiveness
- be able to structure a presentation
- know how to use visual aids effectively
- appreciate the uses and limitations of common presentation software
- be confident in handling questions
- be able to control 'nerves'
- be able to design and deliver part of a group presentation
- know how to produce a good 'poster' presentation.

Introduction

So far you have worked on skills for talking informally or in a working group. But most managers will need to make more formal presentations, whether to their team, clients or customers, or to external stakeholders. Such presentations, like reports, can be high-risk, high-visibility activities. Success, and failure, can have a significant effect on your career. Some managers rise to the challenge and thoroughly enjoy speaking in public. Others suffer agonies beforehand, and worry afterwards that they did themselves less than justice.

Your course is likely to offer opportunities to develop your presentational skills, through presentations on your own, or your group's work. You may be marked on such presentations. Even if not, the skills involved are so important that it is worth putting some effort into developing them. Even if you already make frequent presentations at work there may still be scope for improvement. If public speaking is new to you, and anxiety provoking, relax. It is not difficult to become reasonably competent and confident, and you will both enjoy and learn more from group exercises if you develop the necessary skills.

Many conferences arrange 'poster presentations' in addition to the main spoken presentations. Some courses also offer this opportunity. A poster presentation to a suitable group is an excellent way of letting them know of your work. Many of the rules of oral presentation apply, but there are additional considerations.

This book may not turn you into a *brilliant* presenter though if you have unrecognised talent in this area it may help you realise and then exploit it. If you lack any special talent, becoming *good* at presenting should still be well within your reach. Although *bad* presentations abound (you may have experienced many such) the basic principles of effective presentation are remarkably simple. By following them, you should be able to create a professional impression, and to communicate whatever you wish to your audience. This ability will serve you well on your course and in your job. (It is also handy at weddings and on other occasions where a 'speech' is demanded of you.)

The risks of presenting

Like a written report, a spoken presentation needs to communicate in an ordered way. Spoken presentations carry additional risks because speaking to an audience takes place in real time. Once you have said something, you cannot try a different version, or backtrack to 'redraft' something that doesn't quite flow. You cannot afford to 'block'. And you have an audience there who may let you know (quite forcibly) if they do not like what you are saying. If someone starts to read a report that turns out to be inappropriate, they can put it down and waste no more time on it. If they are captive in the middle of a row in a roomful of people, they are more or less forced to hear the presentation through. They may well feel strongly resentful if it turns out to be a waste of time.

Activity 14.1

Think of an unsatisfactory presentation that you have attended recently. (Lectures are fair game here!) List the factors contributing to your dissatisfaction.

_____

_____

_____

_____

You may have listed factors selected from the following list: the speaker was inaudible; slides were illegible; the speaker's voice was a hypnotic monotone which had the entire audience asleep; the entire address was read; content was so muddled that it was impossible to follow; the speaker jumbled his or her notes, and spent most of the time trying to sort them; the presenter read out the slides, adding nothing to them; the presentation added nothing to what you already knew; you didn't _want_ to know the content; the room was hot, cold, stuffy or otherwise uncomfortable. The possible list is almost endless, but the above are disturbingly common faults.

I still remember being subjected, at a society's national conference, to a speaker who gave as his speech a word for word replay of a paper of his that had appeared in the last issue of the society's own journal. (I know this because I was reading the journal during the train journey there.) This speaker had been flown 4,000 miles, at considerable expense, to give this presentation. At another conference the speaker _read_ his speech to a hundred people, all of whom had been handed copies beforehand. He was drowned out at regular intervals as the audience turned pages in unison.

The working hours lost through audiences sitting through inappropriate or ineffective presentations must be beyond counting. Yet by attention to the principles of communication already covered, and to the additional factors peculiar to public speaking, all this could be avoided.

➤ Chs 9, 13

As ever, it is essential to be absolutely clear about your objectives, and to have researched these to make sure that they are appropriate to your intended audience. If you are trying to do the wrong thing, it matters little how well you do it.

Once you have avoided the risk of shooting at the wrong target, you can think about your aim. Your delivery must be appropriate to your audience's knowledge and abilities. Your own manner is critical. You must avoid distracting or antagonising your audience by your mannerisms or style of delivery. Instead, use your manner to make your message carry a force beyond that possible with the written word. Pace your delivery so that your audience can easily absorb what you say. If you go slowly through the obvious, your audience will start to yawn. If you rush through complex arguments, those still awake will be totally confused. So adjust your speed to the difficulty of what you are communicating.

Presentational problems:

- content inappropriate to audience
- pace inappropriate to difficulty
- poor delivery
- location uncomfortable /difficult for audience
- poor visibility of visual aids.

Presentational strengths:

- clear structure
- appropriate content
- interesting delivery
- good illustrations of points
- audibility and visibility
- awareness of audience reaction
- keeping to time.

See how you can minimise any problems presented by the location itself. There may be acoustic problems that work against you. See whether by changing the seating pattern or talking more loudly than usual you can make sure that everyone can hear you.

Visual aids can be a problem. Is someone else controlling the slides? If so, make sure you can easily let them know when to move on. Is the room too bright for people to see the screen? Draw curtains or blinds. Is there too much text on the slide to be legible (make sure beforehand that this is not the case). Where do you need to stand to make sure that you do not obscure some, or all, of the projector beam?

Presentations are scary because it is *you*, in real time, in front of an audience. But this is a significant opportunity in that it allows for audience interaction. Once you have written a report it stays written, even if it does not suit the audience. A live audience can give you many cues as to how well your presentation is going. Are they asking stimulating questions or aggressive ones? Are they leaning back with their arms folded, clearly disengage, or forwards, hanging on your every word? Are they *awake*? Instant feedback from such cues allows you to adjust your presentation.

Audience interaction can become totally disruptive, making it impossible for you to present in a structured manner unless it is controlled. Carefully handled, though, it can make the whole event really stimulating for all concerned.

The rest of this chapter is devoted to showing you what is necessary if you are to avoid the risks presentations involve, and make the most of the opportunities that they offer.

Structure

➤ Ch 13

Remember that you are making a presentation for a *purpose*. There is something you want to say, and that the audience needs/wants (you think) to hear. You have a story to tell, and want to tell it effectively. Because an audience cannot turn back the page and check what you wrote earlier, it is very easy for them to lose the thread of your spoken argument. Structure is, therefore, even more important in presentations than it is in written reports, and needs to be emphasised at frequent intervals. The old advice of 'Tell them what you are going to say, say it, and then tell them what you have said' still holds good. Note the parallel, in a written report, of using an introductory summary, the main report, and then conclusions. It is possible to break these three broad sections down further.

Introductory section

Introduce yourself, explain your objectives, say how long you will be talking for, indicate the main points you will be making and how you will structure these. Make clear the ground rules concerning questions (for example, you may be happy to be interrupted with requests for clarification, but would prefer to take more substantial questions at the end).

Main section

Just as when writing a report, you need to clarify the problem situation that you are addressing: what are the significant factors in both situation and environment, and the evidence that change is needed? What was your remit, and how did you go about the work on which you are reporting? Describe the measures of effectiveness to be used in evaluating options, and how options score on these measures. Make clear what you are recommending.

When presenting orally, you will need to give additional pointers to internal structure within your main section. When you have finished dealing with one point, signal this by a brief summary of the point just made. Then give a short statement of the point you are about to start on. Visual aids can be useful for this.

Conclusion

Summarise your key points, again using visual aids if appropriate, emphasise your recommendation or conclusion, thank your audience for their patience, and invite questions.

You will find that a simple and clear structure makes audiences much better able to follow a talk.

Delivery technique

Whenever you encounter a particularly good speaker, study their technique. What is it that makes them so effective? Is there anything that would benefit your own delivery? If you have yet to meet a great speaker, explore TED talks, and select speakers that seem to you to be particularly good. As well as anything you learn from them, follow these commonsense principles.

Aim to form a relationship with your audience

When you introduce yourself try to sound human rather than too impersonal. Look at members of the audience. Check at intervals that you are on the right lines. Was that point clear? Can everybody see this slide? Treat questions with courtesy, and thank people for the points they make. Any attempt to make a member of the audience look inadequate will rapidly produce antagonism.

Make it easy for people to hear and understand

Speak clearly, without gabbling, and vary your tone. Avoid dropping your voice at the end of each sentence. Don't turn your back on your audience while you are speaking (blackboards are a hazard here). Use short sentences and straightforward language, using jargon only when absolutely necessary. Use the sorts of words and phrases you use for speaking, not those you would use in writing (the large difference between the two explains why it is often so difficult to follow a speaker who is reading).

Try to be interesting

Use visual aids (more on these shortly) to sustain interest, and vary your pace. Relevant jokes can be effective if used sparingly. Avoid jokes completely if you have any doubts at all about your skill in telling them. Bad jokes *may* have a place in an after dinner/best man's speech, but they are seldom useful in a course or work presentation.

Use detail sparingly

It is far harder to take in a mass of detail from a spoken presentation than from a written report. If detail is important, have a written handout for distribution before or after (*not* during) your presentation, to be used in much the same way as an appendix to a report. Handouts distributed *during* your talk will lose you your audience. It doesn't matter how many times you tell them not to read a handout until later: the temptation will be irresistible. If you do not believe this, try it once, on an occasion when it isn't all that important to hold your audience.

Keep any notes brief

It is reassuring to have notes, especially if you are nervous. Then you know that there is no risk of your 'drying up' completely. But keep them brief, and number them clearly so that if you *do* drop them in your anxiety, or they mysteriously rearrange themselves, you can reorder them easily. Cards are easiest to handle. Resist the temptation to squeeze as much on to each card as is physically possible. You need to be able to refer to your notes at a glance. You do not want to spend minutes peering at them to find where you are.

Mark where you need the next visual aid. Otherwise it is all too easy to leave one out. If someone else is presenting slides, you will then get out of synch. Some speakers like to use slides in lieu of notes. While this is frowned upon by purists, and certainly is not very creative, it can help clarify structure for the audience, *provided* key points only are included, and thought is given to ensuring that they are useful to audience as well as the speaker. However, such a presentation is likely to be very dull, and you risk talking to your computer screen rather than your audience, so this is not a great strategy.

If you are afraid of 'freezing' completely, it may help to write out your entire speech. But keep it in your briefcase, or lay it on the table near you. Its mere existence (together with the other preparation you have done) will make it highly unlikely that you will need it!

Watch the body language

If your audience looks puzzled, you may not be explaining enough. Drooping eyelids may mean that you are going too slowly because the audience knows the material already, or that your voice is too monotonous. If feet or fingers are tapping with restrained force, you are being highly irritating. If you do not know why people are starting to show such signals, *ask* your audience. And adapt your presentation accordingly. This is much safer than assuming you know the reason and making things even worse.

You need to consider your own body language, as well as that of your audience. Are you distracting them by expansive gestures or over-exuberant pacing the floor? Are you showing signs of nervousness (thus reducing the authority of your presentation) by fiddling with hair, clothes, or contents of your pockets? You can reduce the chances of this by minimising the opportunities – tie back hair you might otherwise be fingering, don't wear jewellery, remove jangly objects from your pockets. If you worry that this may be a weakness of yours, ask a friend to signal you if you are starting to distract your audience.

Don't try to fool people

It seldom works. If you know there is a weakness in your case, admit to it, rather than hoping that nobody will notice. (But do make sure that you have minimised such weaknesses by adequate preparation.)

Allow time for questions

Don't regard this as time that you are free to use by over-running your intended time. Not keeping to your allotted time is a sure sign of ineffectiveness. It is fine to extend into question time if your audience genuinely wishes this, but you should be disciplined about your contribution. Above all, you should avoid over-running the stated time for the session as a whole. Audiences plan their time, and do not like to have these plans disrupted.

Visual aids

From anyone but a highly gifted speaker, a lengthy presentation that consists of straight unbroken talk is hard to take. To maintain your audience's interest, some sort of variety is needed. If you are presenting a group's work, then it may be possible for different members to be responsible for different parts of the presentation. Visual aids, skilfully used, can provide this.

Also, there are some things that can be conveyed far better visually than by words alone. Relationships can be more clearly diagrammed, trends clearly shown via graphs and video clips can convey a variety of things that words cannot. Slides are not the only visual aids that can help. An object waved in front of the audience can make a powerful point. A faulty item will say a lot about quality. A pile of thick reports and a sheaf of computer print-out will help you convince people that there is too much data and not enough information. A well-chosen video clip can convey a lot in a short space of time.

> **Visual aids can:**
> - reinforce key points
> - clarify meaning
> - aid retention
> - keep your audience awake.

If your presentation is a lengthy one, say in excess of half an hour, then it is worth varying your aids. For example, in a presentation to potential sponsors about an MBA programme, I might want to give a feel for how distance learning actually works. A set of graphs and bullet points cannot do this. Examples of course video sequences, printed course units, and tutorial programmes and student assignments (with in-depth tutor comments) not only communicate important points, but also varies the pace and maintains interest.

You might want to use a mix of diagrams, some on prepared slides; others drawn on a board or flipchart at an appropriate point in your talk. This would vary the pace. Handouts that you *do* want people to look at while you talk, such as a detailed table that you wish to discuss at length, can usefully be distributed as people take their seats. Video clips could further shift the pace.

It may sound obvious, but it is important that people can *see* your visuals. Even experienced speakers frequently get this wrong. The two commonest problems are barriers between some of the audience and the visual aid, and lack of clarity in the aid itself. Avoid being a barrier yourself. The speaker who obscures half the screen is all too common. Pillars and equipment may be a problem. You may need to ask people to move to where they can see, at least while you are using the screen. This is not ideal, but better than their sitting in comfortable blindness.

Overloading slides is a far more common problem. Some speakers still project whole tables of figures or pages of text from a book or report, without a hope of any of the audience being able to read them. Check that your slides can be read from the back of the room by someone who needs a new pair of glasses. Any important words or numbers need to be *big*, so you will not be able to use many on a single slide. Colour can reduce contrast – check this is not the case. Beware, too, of the main forms of colour blindness, primarily difficulties in distinguishing red/green or blue/yellow.

Presentation software (discussed shortly) makes it so easy to create visuals that there may be a strong temptation to use far too many. If you do, your audience may retain nothing but a blurred impression of an endless series of images which they have had no time to absorb. Their attention will have been on the screen, not on what you said. It is now so easy to add photos and video clips into your presentation that the temptation to over-complicate is almost irresistible. Some of these visuals can be hugely powerful, many are purely decorative. Reject the latter.

Select only those visual aids that will reinforce your key points – for a short presentation this may be very few. It is hard to look and listen at the same time, particularly to different words. So be selective. Use visuals only when they add value to your presentation, and choose the minimum content to achieve the impact you require.

Using presentation software

The first widely available presentation software was PowerPoint, and many still find this adequate. However, there are now many other presentation packages available and it is worth becoming familiar with some of the options.

Any presentation software, once you have mastered the basics, allows you to produce professional-looking slides which can be easily revised at the last minute to include the latest information, or tailored to a particular audience. You can easily incorporate relevant tables and graphics (though *see* the caution above on complexity and overload) or other images. Your presentation is easily portable on a data stick or downloaded on arrival. You can produce a handout of your slides, with room for notes if you wish, at the press of a button.

Popular presentation software can do far more than you are likely to need, but note the caution above – few of these elaborations help. Fancy backgrounds distract, and reduce, clarity. Animations may look impressive, but are similarly distracting. Zooming in and out of frames may cause motion sickness. While it is sometimes extremely useful to build up a picture a bit at a time, you should restrict use of the facility to such times. Otherwise it will merely distract. Remember, your main aim in any presentation is unlikely to be to demonstrate your facility with the latest software. It is more likely to be communicating a particular message, or bringing your audience to a particular point of view. If you are using PowerPoint, note that it can easily constrain your presentation to an endless series of bullet points. As Naughton (2003) pointed out, it was conceived in a software sales environment. So it tends to turn everything into a sales pitch. There was a version of the Gettysburg address doing the email rounds a while ago that demonstrated this limitation (*see* **www.norvig.com/Gettysburg**). Tufte, a Yale professor and expert on visual communication, argues that PowerPoint's ready-made templates tend to weaken verbal and spatial reasoning and corrupt statistical analysis. He attributes the loss of the space shuttle Columbia to a slide that led NASA to overlook the destructive potential of the crucial loose tile (see 'PowerPoint does rocket science', from Tufte's website **www.edwardtufte.com**). His analysis may also add to your understanding of the idea of argument mapping outlined in Chapter 7.

PowerPoint is no longer the only presentation software in common use TECHSkills 14.1 outlines some of the issues to consider when choosing and using such software.

TECHSkills 14.1 Choosing and using presentation software

It is now normal to use presentation software. While PowerPoint is still perhaps the most widely used, as it comes as part of Microsoft Office, there are several other popular options. PowerPoint is basically designed to deliver a series of slides, stored on your own device – though easily loaded onto a data stick for portability, or stored a cloud for access from anywhere with Internet access. Similar tools include Apple's Keynote, and for those with a gmail or Google account, the web driven Google Drive slides – which since they exist on the Google cloud can be shared with 'friends'.

A popular alternative for those who find PowerPoint or comparable systems too linear is Prezi. Instead of a series of discrete slides, Prezi allows you to assemble your presentation on something akin to a giant board, constructing frames at different places and then zooming in and out from the big picture to individual frames as you give your presentation. The 'track' of the focus is pre-programmed – you decide on the order the frames will appear beforehand, just as you decide on the order of your slides in PowerPoint, but what the audience sees is much more dynamic and visually interesting that a series of discrete PowerPoint slides.

Prezi provides a much wider range of templates, too, and makes it easy to use frames for pictures, video clips or other non-textual material to add variety, and to resize, move or rotate frames. The ability to see the 'big picture' is the visual equivalent of the summary in a report, and zooming out at intervals enable the structure of the presentation to be clear. A basic version of Prezi is (at the time of writing) free and there are many free tutorials online (see online resources for suggestions). This basic version should be adequate for your use until presentations become a key part of your job, at which point their hope is that you will purchase the more advanced system, which offers far more features.

If you want something even more different from PowerPoint, 'Powtoon' is another popular system. This allows you to create animated presentations, and if you love graphics you may enjoy playing with it.

As well as software that helps you directly create the visual aspect of your presentation, there are programmes such as 'SlideDog', which help you create the equivalent of a playlist of videos, documents or other things you might want to use in a presentation, and then link them to Prezi or other presentation software.

In recent years the range of options has increased hugely, and your choice of presentation software becomes correspondingly harder. What is best for you will depend on answers to a number of questions:

- What packages do you already have? (For example, PowerPoint comes as part of Microsoft Office, and your university might provide other options.)

- Do you want to be able to access your presentation remotely?

- How important is it to create a good impression with your *visual aids* rather than your presentation as a whole?

- How much time (and money) do you want to spend on acquiring new software and the skills to use it? (Though as noted, there are often free basic versions available usually offering only a limited number of features, and therefore perhaps less learning time.)

You will find online reviews of the main presentation software packages, and may like to check some of these out (see online resources for a suggestion). Check who is writing the review. If it written by the company selling one of the packages being reviewed you might expect a degree of bias!

Choose your visual aids according to your audience, your resources, and your message. Hand-drawn flipchart pages have their place in 'transient' presentations, for example on group work, where all you are seeking is to convey your thought processes to fellow students. But they would be inappropriate for a formal presentation to a client.

If you have no access to presentation software (or hardware) or want to vary your pace, prepared flipchart sheets, or ones drawn as you talk, can achieve this. Again, principles of simplicity and clarity apply. If you want to draw any diagrams as you go along, remember to leave blank sheets at appropriate points. An accomplice is useful if you are forced to use a flipchart. Turning the sheets quickly and elegantly is difficult: if you do it yourself it is bound to interrupt your flow.

Handling questions

Questions can be enormously helpful – or can wreck a presentation entirely. Normally it is safest to restrict questions *during* your presentation to those seeking clarification, saving more substantive questions to the end. Otherwise you risk being sidetracked from your main argument, losing direction and running over time. If you say you will save a question until the end, make sure you do this in a positive, courteous way. A questioner who feels 'put down' may go on to be disruptive. If holding a question until the end, either make a note of it, so that you do not forget to deal with it later, or ask the questioner to ask it again at the end.

The most important thing is to understand what is being asked. This is not as easy as it sounds. Careful listening is difficult when you are nervous, and questioners often ask multiple questions, or express themselves less than clearly. It is worth noting down the key parts of the question as it is asked, so that when you come to the end of dealing with the first part you are spared the sickening realisation that there was more, but you have totally forgotten what it was. If you are uncertain as to the meaning of the question, clarify it with the questioner. Normally this will be taken as a serious attempt at meeting his or her needs, rather than evidence of your stupidity.

If a question challenges what you have said, resist the temptation to become defensive, or to attack the questioner. Take the contrasting point of view seriously. Unless you are completely sure that the questioner has misunderstood you or is misinformed, look for ways in which you can use it to *develop* your position. If they have misunderstood, and simple repetition or correction will not resolve the difference quickly, it is better to offer to discuss it in greater depth *after* the presentation, rather than get into an argument which few of the audience will find interesting.

People ask questions for many reasons, and you are likely to encounter some questions intended to display the questioner's own expertise rather than add to your presentation. Where this is the case, the simplest method is to praise the questioner's knowledge or understanding, agree with as much of the 'question' as you can, and thank the person for their contribution.

Where questions are pointing to a genuine weakness in your presentation, it is usually better to acknowledge, indeed share, the concern, rather than pretend that the problem is less than the questioner rightly thinks. It may, in this case, be helpful to ask the questioner, or other member of the audience, for suggestions as to how the problem might be resolved. You will need, at the same time, to ensure that a small problem is not allowed to grow out of proportion to your main argument.

Dealing with nerves

Most people are nervous the first few times they have to talk in front of a group of people. Good speakers are always slightly nervous. This gives an edge to their performance, while complacency can lead to flatness and boredom all round. But you need to reduce nervousness to a level that will enhance rather than detract from your performance. The factors that can help you here are practice, exposure to other similar situations, relaxation techniques and thorough preparation.

If you are in the minority who are terrified of public speaking take every chance at work, in your leisure activities or on the course, to talk in front of people. It really does get easier the more you do it.

➤ Ch 3 Relaxation techniques were discussed in Chapter 3. They can be enormously helpful immediately prior to a presentation. A *small* drink or medication may help, if the latter, experiment beforehand to ensure that your medication makes you better – rather than less – able to perform. Drugs can have variable effects, and are best avoided if at all possible.

Most important, though, is to be confident that you are well prepared. Knowing exactly what you are trying to convey and how you are going to tackle it, that you have thoroughly researched the topic of your presentation and have supporting evidence and examples at your fingertips, are the best possible antidotes to nerves. Look at the presentation not as a problem occasion but as an opportunity for doing something really interesting and worthwhile, as a challenge rather than a threat. If it is to fellow students it is an opportunity to develop skills, and any shortcomings will constitute a learning opportunity, for you, and for your audience.

> **Increase your confidence in presenting by:**
>
> - frequent practice
> - relaxation techniques
> - thorough preparation.

To get you over a possible initial onrush of nerves, make sure that you have memorised your introductory remarks. Take a sip of water and a deep breath, go through your introduction, and by then you should be calm enough to enjoy yourself.

Preparation

This is the key to successful presentations. You can *never* afford to cut corners here. It is essential to have researched not just what you are talking about but also your audience and the requirements for the presentation. That way you can be sure that you are aiming in the right direction. It is vital to have thought carefully about what to include and how to structure it, and about how best to add force to your arguments. It is important to have prepared the most professional-looking visual aids that circumstances allow. And it will help you to settle into your presentation if, as just suggested, you have learned at least the start of your introduction by heart.

Helpful preparation goes beyond this. It is important to rehearse your arguments many times, so that you feel confident in expressing them. Some of this can be done piecemeal. You can work on sections while jogging, or *sotto voce* in the dentist's waiting room. But for an important presentation you *must* allow at least one full-scale rehearsal in conditions as close as possible to the actual presentation.

Arrange furniture to resemble the area from which you will be speaking. Visualise the audience layout. Position a dummy flipchart/screen (or whatever aids you will be using) as they will be placed on the day, and go through the motions of using them. Look at your non-existent audience, introduce yourself to them, and go through your entire presentation exactly as you plan to do it in reality. Only thus can you be sure that your proposed presentation will fit the time available.

If at all possible, find an audience. Family, friends, colleagues or fellow students might oblige. Ask for their comments. Failing that, recording your presentation allows you to be your own audience. This could give you insight into strengths and weaknesses of your proposed presentation. Extensive preparation such as this may seem like overkill: indeed, for small informal presentations it is probably unnecessary. But for an important formal presentation, particularly if you do not have a lot of experience, the effort will be justified.

Another important part of preparation involves arriving at the location early enough to check *everything*. Are seats positioned so that people will be able to see all they need? Is the data projector set up and working and focused? Does your presentation work on the computer provided, if you have not brought your own? (This can be a real problem if you are using a laptop that 'speaks a different language' because you have travelled.) If you need to access online materials, is the Internet connection working? Are any flipcharts correctly positioned, and are there enough working pens? 'If anything *can* go wrong it *will*' applies as much to presentations as to anything else. It is unwise to leave anything to chance.

Finally, though this is often omitted, it is worth coming to an arrangement, perhaps on a reciprocal basis, with a colleague or fellow student, whereby they will give you honest feedback on your performance. Preferably you should schedule this for soon, though not immediately, after the presentation. Immediately after the event you may be in a state unsuited to the receipt of constructive criticism.

Virtual presentations and podcasts

Virtual presentations are becoming increasingly common for reasons similar to those driving growth in virtual meetings. Again they may be take place in real time, with scope for some at least of the scattered audience to email or phone in questions. Such presentations are often recorded to allow access by people not available at the time of the podcast, or there may be no live version, only a recording. Such presentations may be 'broadcast' through a conferencing system or made available (for example, via Dropbox or Google Drive) for people to access on demand.

If you are studying online using a 'virtual classroom' you may be asked to make presentations on group work within this system. If not, you may well need to make virtual presentations at some point in your career, so can usefully think about any modifications that may be needed. If you are presenting privately, the general principles above may be enough, although it is worth using any 'voting' or other option to check understanding as you go along.

If you are 'broadcasting' your presentation on a public platform you will need to think about copyright implications. Video clips, music, quotations and images copied from elsewhere are all likely to be subject to copyright legislation, so should not be used without permission. Some music exists which is not copyrighted, but you need to hunt for it. Podcasting is an excellent form of advertising if you eventually choose to set up your own business. A wealth of podcasting tips are available online should you wish to develop your skills in this direction.

Group presentations

If you have worked on something as a group you may be asked to make a group presentation. This can pose a number of difficult questions about who should do what. Do you want the best presenter in the group to present the whole thing, with other members in supporting roles? Or should the person who understands the project best take the lead, even if they are not the best presenter? Or do you want to share the presentation between you all, each presenting a part? The first option may produce a slick, but possibly superficial presentation, the second a more in-depth but less polished one. The third choice is normally preferred. It shares both the workload and the learning opportunities.

If you choose to share the load, this needs to be managed like any other group task. Agree your overall objective, and then work out the tasks needed to achieve this. Allocate responsibilities for the different tasks. Work out how much communication is needed between group members to ensure that their work is coordinated, and plan for the necessary conversations or other contacts.

Set a timetable for tasks, and agree a way of checking that you are on target. Agree what someone needs to do if they find they cannot keep to their schedule – who should they tell, and how soon. It happens all too often that disaster (or incompetence) strikes one or two team members and they fail to deliver. If other members find this out at the last minute it can be highly stressful for them. If they had known earlier, they might have found it easier to cope. This is why interim deadlines – and checks that they have been met – are essential.

Work out the overall style and structure of the presentation as a group so that everyone is happy with it and can shape their individual contribution to fit. Not only content, but visual aids and any parts of a handout need to be consistent with each other. You are aiming for a presentation as smooth as if it were presented by a single person, but with the advantage of variety of presenters, and perhaps of being able to draw on different expertise at appropriate points in the presentation.

As well as other coordination mechanisms it is good to schedule two run throughs as a group. The first will be the equivalent of the first draft of a report – fairly rough but sufficiently detailed that you can see where it works and where some further adjustments are needed. This meeting needs to be enough in advance of the presentation to allow for the necessary adjustments and more detailed work to be done. At least one other practice run once contributions are in near final state is also needed. This also needs to be sufficiently ahead of the presentation to allow time for final adjustments and improvements.

Both meetings (and more if you have time) can usefully consider content of each part (evidence, arguments and visuals), 'flow' between them, timings, and the impact of the presentation as a whole. Group members can also usefully coach each other on how to present more effectively (provided this is done carefully, and in a supportive fashion, using feedback skills discussed earlier). It can also be helpful if they try to listen with a naïve mind, forgetting what they already know, and looking for questions that an audience member might still have at the end of each section.

At the second meeting it will be vital to check that each contribution fits within its agreed time allocation so that the presentation finishes on time. Presentations which over-run the allowed time may be penalised or even stopped in mid flow. As it is hard to keep track of time while speaking, someone needs to take responsibility for issuing a 'one minute warning' for each section (using an agreed signal), and each group member needs to commit to finishing within a minute if they receive this signal.

With a committed and supportive group, preparing a group presentation can be an enjoyable challenge and a valuable learning experience. The learning will be even greater if you reflect together after each meeting, considering not only progress on the task, but how effectively you have worked together, and whether there are any process lessons to be learned. After the presentation, you can again usefully learn through reflection on not only your own presentation but those by other groups. Remember the need to avoid groupthink and scapegoating in this reflection, particularly if you are slightly disappointed with aspects of your presentation. You may feel more comfortable if you can blame someone else for whatever did not go to plan, but you will learn far less if you do not face up honestly to any potential scope for improvement. While doing this, remember the importance of reflecting on what went *well*, and on learning from this too. Celebrate anything that was particularly good, and things that represented a personal achievement (for example, when someone who is terrified of speaking actually stands up and makes a contribution).

➤ Ch 9

14

SPEAKING TO IMPRESS

Poster presentations

Thus far the chapter has addressed formal presentations to a (normally) seated audience. At conferences it is common to supplement the formal presentation programme with less formal poster presentations. You may, as part of your course, be asked to prepare such a presentation. Typically, a large area will be made available for such presentations, and each presenter will be allocated wall space for a poster. The audience will wander round the room, looking at the various displays and stopping to discuss those of particular interest with the 'presenter', who will be standing by the poster ready to answer questions.

This allows conference members access to a much greater number of presenters than would otherwise be the case, and is often used to allow students to present their research. If you are doing a dissertation, you may have the opportunity to take part in a poster session at an external conference. This sort of presentation is also sometimes used in organisational contexts, for example at meetings between members of different project groups, so it is worth extending your presentation skills to include this format. In either case the poster presentation tends to be aimed primarily at peers.

Poster presentations present their own communication challenges to the presenter. The 'talking' part tends to be less intimidating: you are talking to people individually or in very small groups. On the other hand, these conversations are equivalent to the 'questions' part of a formal presentation, which is, in many respects, the most challenging as much of the control passes to the questioner.

The real challenge for most, however, is in poster design. Typically, you will have a space 1 m high, and 1.5–1.75 m wide. This space has to work hard for you. Obviously, (as with any communication) your first task is to clarify your objectives. What do you want it to achieve? Clearly this will depend on what you are presenting, and where. Are you simply aiming to inform as many participants as possible? If so, what are the key points you are trying to get across? Are you trying to sell yourself or your research and, if so, to whom? Are you aiming to engage colleagues in conversation? If so, what would you particularly like to talk with them about? Are you seeking like-minded people from other universities with whom to network? If so, what would be most likely to interest such people? This is not an exhaustive list. It merely indicates the sort of objectives you might have. You need to be absolutely clear of your objectives on each occasion.

Posters aim to:

- attract
- inform
- start conversations
- advertise your work
- summarise achievements.

Clarity is paramount because 1.5 sq m is not very big, and anything within this space has to be visible from at least 1.5 m away. So every word needs to count, and you need to use pictures (or graphs or whatever) as much as possible. Aim to 'show' rather than 'tell'. A good rule of thumb is 20 per cent text, 40 per cent graphics and 40 per cent space. This last 40 per cent is not a 'waste of precious space'. You could cram more into it, but the overall effect would be crowded and hard to read. It would probably have far less impact than a well laid-out 60 per cent of the space, with the white areas serving to increase the overall appearance and clarity of text and images you have included.

Given this limitation on what you can effectively include, there are some important questions to answer.

- What are your (very few) key points?

- How can you convey these graphically?

- How can you lay these out on a poster so that they will communicate to someone walking past at a distance of up to 2 m?

Remember, you may be in competition with many other posters, and participants will not look in any detail at more than a small proportion of these. You will not have time to talk to everybody, even if you attract them. So how can you ensure that you engage those people with whom you are likely to have the most profitable conversations, prime them to ask the most useful questions, and leave a favourable impression both of you personally and of the work that you have done?

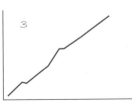

Figure 14.1 Possible layouts for poster presentations

If you Google 'poster presentations', you will find a wealth of information on how to lay out posters for maximum impact. The essential messages are:

- You need to say who you are, where you come from, and the topic covered by your poster – IN VERY LARGE WRITING.

- You need to have a clear 'path' through the poster so that people can follow the narrative easily.

- You cannot afford to waste a single word – '**Findings**' or '**methodology**' do not convey much information by themselves. But something like '**80% misunderstand age legislation**' carries a message. Think newspaper headlines here. Writ large, and with bar charts or other simple graphics to support them.

- You need a way of continuing the exchange when you have 'engaged' someone's interest. At very least show your email address clearly on the poster. Even better, have a handout expanding on key points, with your email on it. Safest of all, particularly if your key aim is to network, is to have people write *their* emails (or better, give you their cards, or you write down their email for them). You can then email a more substantial document – the text behind the headlines – a couple of days later, with a note saying how much you enjoyed talking to them. They may well forget to contact you, or lose your email once they get home. (This may be the start of a productive networking relationship as discussed in Chapter 17.)

➤ Ch 17

Figure 14.1 shows two possible layouts for poster presentations for a standard research presentation. You may be able to be far more creative – but do remember the need for it to be clearly visible from 1.5–2 m away. Messy and cluttered does not, on the whole, attract.

This chapter has introduced the basic requirements for effective verbal and poster presentations. You can use knowledge of these, together with practice, and reflection on that practice, to develop your presentation skills. If presentation skills are crucial to your job, you may need more help than this chapter can give. Try everything suggested, and get feedback from colleagues. If you feel you still have a development need, consider asking your employer whether you could go on one of the many excellent short courses on the topic. There, with intensive video feedback and tutor support, you should be able to develop your skills to a high level. If no course is possible, explore the many online tutorials freely available, and study some of the excellent speakers on TED talks.

SUMMARY

- Effective presentations depend on thorough preparation.
- You need to be clear about what you are trying to do, and what your audience needs.
- Structure is even more important than with written reports.
- Good visual aids are easy to produce and are very effective.
- Presentation software may be a great asset, but you need to be careful it does not 'drive' your presentation in ways that are unhelpful. PowerPoint may allow less freedom than other software but has advantages of availability and familiarity.

- Audibility, visibility and ability to pace your delivery to suit your audience and content are very important.
- Group presentations need careful planning and task and process management.
- Poster presentations present additional challenges of optimising use of limited space.
- Questions can be an asset but must not be allowed to be disruptive in a face-to-face presentation.

Further information

Bradbury, A. (2010) *Creating Success: Successful Presentation Skills* (4th edn), Kogan Page.

Conradi, M. and Hall, R. (2001) *That Presentation Sensation*, FT Prentice Hall.

Davies, G. (2010) *The Presentation Coach: Bare Knuckle Brilliance for Every Presenter*, Chichester: Capstone Publishing Ltd.

Gray, J. (2010) *How Leaders Speak: Essential Rules for Engaging and Inspiring Others*, Toronto: Dundurn.

Leech, T. (2001) *Say It Like Shakespeare*, McGraw-Hill. This gives an interestingly different slant on presenting.

Naughton, J. (2003) 'How PowerPoint can fatally weaken your argument', *The Observer*, 21 December.

http://www.ncsu.edu/project/posters/NewSite/ (accessed 4.8.15). There are many useful websites on poster presentations, but try this one which offers extensive guidance and examples.

http://www.edwardtufte.com/bboard/q-and-a-fetch-msg?msg_id=0001yB (accessed 14.1.15). For Tufte's discussion of the role of PowerPoint in the Challenger disaster.

www.norvig.com/Gettysburg (accessed 14.1.15). For the slide version of the Gettysburg address

http://guides.nyu.edu/posters (accessed 14.1.15). There are many useful websites but try this one.

http://www.customshow.com/best-powerpoint-alternatives-presentation-programs/ (accessed 14.1.15). For a review of alternatives to PowerPoint and explanation of how SlideDog works – but better still, look for a range of up-to-date alternatives to this (assuming you are reading the book a year or two after publication).

https://www.youtube.com/playlist?list=PL09A34EF19596B7BB (accessed 14.1.15). For a series of tutorials on using Prezi.

15

EXAMINATIONS AND OTHER FORMS OF ASSESSMENT

Learning outcomes

By the end of this chapter you should:

- understand the range of assessments you may encounter, and their different purposes

- appreciate your assessors' objectives in each case

- realise the importance of preparation for any major assessment

- be able to plan and manage appropriate preparation for any given form

- know how to manage stress before and during the assessment

- recognise the best questions to answer in a written examination with choice

- understand the necessity for time management during the exam

- be able to answer written or oral questions fully and effectively

- be starting to assemble material for a portfolio

Introduction

You have already considered key elements in continuous assessment, written assignments and prepared oral presentations. Building a skills portfolio was suggested in Chapter 6, but not developed fully. This chapter addresses 'one-off' assessment, in the form of written examinations, oral '*viva voce*' examinations, and other forms of 'time defined' activity for assessment, and develops the idea of a portfolio further. Examinations, together with a written dissertation, were once the main way of deciding whether a student had reached the standard required for a course. In the jug–mug model it was a way of seeing whether the mug was full enough!

➤ Ch 16

As thinking about learning has moved away from this model, written examinations have become less central to postgraduate assessment. Continuous assessment marks have gained importance, applied projects are at least as common as academic dissertations (see the next chapter), and more practically oriented programmes may also require submission of a portfolio of evidence of learning.

However, many accrediting bodies still see written examinations as a way of maintaining academic standards, and from a university's perspective they are a relatively cheap way of achieving 'standards' objectives. It is much easier, for example, to check that it is the student who is answering the questions, rather than their friend, colleague, paid assistant or mother! You may therefore be faced with written examinations at some points in your study, and if you are it is important that you know how to pass them without undue stress.

While this chapter may seem to have nothing to do with work, this is far from the case. An interview is very similar to a *viva voce*, as indeed is an interrogation by (discussion with?) senior managers to whom you have presented a report as part of your job. Your manager may ask you to write a paper at work with very little notice. This may feel very similar to sitting an examination. Many larger organisations use assessment centres to assess candidates for senior roles or fast-track career paths. These centres assess relevant competences using a range of activities typically including group problem solving, individual written work, psychometric tests and interviews. Thus they have some elements similar to written examinations, some to a *viva*, and many which will resemble group activities from your course. If you seek membership of a professional body they are very likely to ask you to submit a portfolio of evidence of your competence. The 'being assessed' skills addressed in this chapter are therefore highly transferable to the work situation, and relevant throughout your career.

This chapter looks at what assessors are looking for in the different approaches to assessment covered, at reasons people sometimes fail, at skills you can usefully develop and at other steps you can take to ensure that you succeed.

Objectives of different 'examinations'

In any form of examination or assessment your aim is to communicate to your assessors that you have the knowledge or competences that they are looking for. Looking at the objectives of the forms of assessment covered in this chapter gives a clue to what assessors are looking for. In most cases they are assessing one or more of the following, in a way that makes it difficult if not impossible for the candidate to cheat.

- knowledge
- understanding
- reasoning skills
- problem-solving ability
- application of these skills in different contexts
- communication skills (spoken or written)
- interpersonal skills (including leadership)

The form of assessment used will depend on which of the above are most important to the assessors, as well as on practical considerations.

➤ Ch 13   ***Written examinations*** are good at testing written communication (Chapter 13 is highly relevant here), knowledge, understanding and reasoning. If based on a scenario or case study (longer ones may be given out in advance of the exam) they can test application of knowledge. Indirectly, as significant revision is usually required, they test personal management skills. With robust photo-id and invigilation systems they ensure that they are assessing the student. They are ostensibly objective and fair if scripts are marked anonymously and there is 'blind' second marking, where the second marker does not know what the other marker has given. The method is widely understood and respected. Although markers might disagree, they are reasonably cheap in terms of labour and administration costs.

Viva voce or oral examinations are the earliest assessment form of all assessment. The format is simple. One or more examiners ask questions, and the candidate answers. Although usually face to face, vivas can be conducted remotely, by phone or video link. Like written examinations a viva, unless conducted by phone, can provide an 'identity check', verifying that the student shows similar knowledge and understanding to that shown by other work. This can be particularly important in distance learning, where tutors may have less contact with students. Vivas are also often used with portfolios and dissertations, where again the student is working largely independently and scope for 'help' from others may be considerable.

➤ Chs 9, 14   Like a written examination, a viva can assess knowledge, understanding, reasoning and application of ideas and techniques, and communication skills, although written rather than spoken (So refer to Chapters 9 and 14 if faced with a viva). A viva offers assessors the flexibility to tailor questions to particular competences, or particular worries they may have about a candidate. Thus a viva might be used if a student was ill during an exam, so had not been able to perform to their normal standards, or to check whether a student knows and/or did more than their dissertation or project report suggests. Vivas are also sometimes used to determine the final mark of students on pass/fail or distinction borderlines. Because vivas have so many disparate purposes it is important to work out the objectives of any particular viva in advance, and anticipate some of the questions. For example, if it concerns a dissertation, are there weak points in your dissertation? If so, spend some time thinking about what the weakness is, and what you could have done that would have been better. This is far more likely to impress examiners than an attempt to hide a weakness, or offer a justification for it. Remember the examiners' objective of not letting someone loose on the world that might bring the qualification into disrepute. There is a general management principle that it is OK to make mistakes as long as you never repeat them. The examiners want to be reassured that you have learned from any mistakes.

Assessment centres are used when assessors want to judge a wider range of competences than written or viva examinations allow. They are sometimes used in universities, but because of their cost are more normally used by larger organisations to select high potential, or senior staff, assess candidates for promotion or identify development needs. Groups of candidates will carry out a series of activities, some group, some individual, which simulate different aspects of working life. Activities can include group problem-solving exercises or case discussions and individual 'in-tray' activities similar to those a manager might face on a daily basis. Management games, fact-finding exercises, analysis and presentation (akin to a case study) and simulated (and real) interviews are also used. Trained assessors rate participants against set criteria. Decisions are taken and feedback given on the basis of these ratings. A similar simulation-based approach may be used by colleges to provide 'evidence' for a portfolio for students that are not in jobs, which would allow them to demonstrate some of the required competences.

Portfolio assessment is another expensive form of assessment – for both the candidate, who will spend many hours assembling the portfolio, and the assessor, who can spend hours working through a single portfolio. For the candidate there are learning and motivational benefits that may justify the time. For the assessor, there are few compensatory benefits. Full portfolio assessment is less common now than when it first became popular, but elements remain. For example, you may need similar principles when evidencing your continuing development for a professional institute. Like assessment centres, portfolios allow assessment of job-related competences. Unlike them it is not 'short duration', but done over a period. Indeed, you should already have collected considerable potential portfolio evidence. However, organising your evidence into a portfolio that addresses a specific competence framework, and preparing for a viva on it may be condensed into a much shorter period and presents many of the same challenges as an exam, so the chapter addresses this aspect.

Those assessing a portfolio will normally be looking for relevant, convincing and relatively current evidence of each competence in a specified framework. Two key implications for candidates are immediately apparent. First, you need to make a clear case for having met each competence – it is not enough to assume that it will be obvious to the assessor why a piece of evidence is there, or why it shows a particular competence. Second, if you can make the assessor's job easier, you may be viewed more favourably.

It may help to think in terms of 'making a case', just as you might when writing a report. The argument may be very simple, but it is essential and needs to tell a clear story. While the evidence is crucial, without the story and links out to each 'exhibit', the evidence itself is worthless. Often a single piece of evidence can demonstrate several competencies – life is much more 'joined-up' than analytical frameworks suggest. This means you can cut down on the volume of your portfolio, provided that each time you refer to a piece of evidence you provide a clear explanation of why it demonstrates the competence it is being linked to at that point.

Types of written examination

Probably still the commonest form of written examination is an unseen paper of two or three hours' duration, which you are required to answer without access to books or notes. Traditionally, such exams were handwritten, but verification software is making it possible for students to answer on a computer. In either case, such exams require you to draw upon your memory of what was in the course. This can seem quite daunting if you have not sat such an exam for some years, and you may worry about whether your memory is as good as it once was. If you prepare as suggested shortly, you should have fewer problems than you fear.

Three other forms of written examination are reasonably common. These are computer-marked papers, 'open-book' exams and exams based on case studies issued in advance of the exam. Each presents hazards that may not be apparent at first sight. They are therefore discussed briefly here.

Computer-marked exams are more popular at lower levels of study, but sometimes used at Master's level. They are good at checking factual recall and, if carefully constructed, can test understanding and logic. They are also very cheap to administer and mark.

There are two key points to note if you want to do well. First, 'wrong' answers may be penalised. If this is the case, it may be safer to miss a question than to guess. Find out what rules are being operated in your case, and adjust your strategy accordingly.

Second, questions may be fairly complicated, and possible answers cunningly chosen to catch you out if you have not fully appreciated what is being asked. (If you have a certain kind of twisted mind, it can be great fun setting such questions!) You therefore need to read questions very carefully indeed, making sure you understand the significance of every word, and to think carefully before answering. The 'obvious' answer may be wrong.

If you are not given lots of practice in the sorts of questions you are likely to encounter, try to get hold of past questions and spend some time trying to work out how the examiner's mind was working.

Open-book exams allow you to bring course materials and notes into the examination, or access them online. This may seem infinitely preferable to relying on memory, but beware the following:

1. Any time spent searching in your materials will mean less time for writing. To avoid this, you still need to be extremely familiar with the course content, so that you need to make minimal reference to materials. It can also help to have a note of where key diagrams or equations can be found.

2. Anything you merely copy from elsewhere will gain you zero marks, so you need to keep quotations to an absolute minimum, giving brief summaries of key points, perhaps with references, rather than extended quotes or reproductions of diagrams. Reserve the bulk of your time for actually *answering* questions, as outlined in the remainder of the

chapter. If you have not sat an open-book exam before, it is particularly important to do a practice exam under normal time constraints and conditions. This will help you become more aware of how easy it is to fall into the traps outlined, and be more aware of how to avoid them.

3. A good index, prepared with the exam in mind, is essential for an open-book exam. Even then, aim to make minimal use of the book, reserving most of the time for writing.

4. Remember that open-book exams do *not* reduce the need for revision. While it may be useful to refer to the book for a detailed formula which you will then *use*, the normal time constraints of an exam will mean any other use of books will be severely restricted.

Seen case studies exams provide you with a case study in advance of the exam, to enable you to study it. You are not, however, usually given the questions that will constitute the exam. You may or may not be able to bring the case into the exam. If you are, there may be limits placed on the amount of annotation allowed. It is important to find out what will be allowed, and work out how best to exploit this. It is possible to write quite a lot in margins, and underlining can be crucial. Cross-references to ideas or other relevant cases could be added.

Whether or not you can take anything in to the exam, spend as much time as possible familiarising yourself with the detail of the case, analysing it, thinking about which course concepts are relevant, predicting possible questions and trying to answer these. You may be able to work with others on case discussion. If so, exploit this. It is probably worth setting each other unseen questions and then marking each other's efforts. This can give you useful insight into the examiner's mind, and into what is meant by 'exam technique', as well as showing aspects of the case that you may not have fully appreciated.

Common causes of failure

Because it is so important to pass most exams, it is worth looking at the most common causes of failure. That way you can identify factors likely to put your own success at risk, and work to minimise their effect.

Stress

Most students find being examined, by whatever means, is stressful. Stress in the run up to the exam may cost you sleep or make you ill. In extreme cases it can cause students to drop out before the exam. Some stress during the exam helps, but extreme stress can completely destroy your capacity for coherent thought. Understanding and addressing this stress can help. Figure 15.1 shows common causes of exam stress. Consider which, if any, apply to you.

If your serenity prayer has been granted, you will be able to distinguish between those stress factor that are unavoidable, those that could have been avoided if action were taken early enough (time management, language problems and difficulties with the course) and those relating to the exam itself (unfamiliarity and stress management).

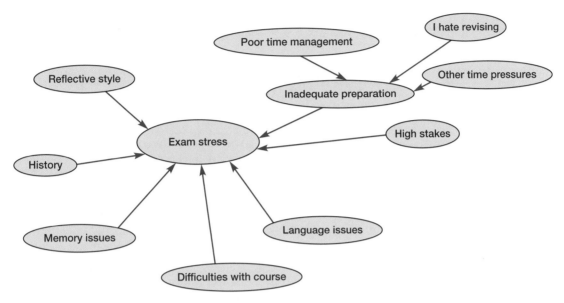

Figure 15.1 Factors causing exam stress

➤ Ch 3 Earlier chapters may have helped you avoid the first two categories. The following text suggests approaches to factors which can cause stress and/or reduce your risk of failure. Some of these are remarkably simple to remedy, others far more difficult. For clarity, the guidance is slanted towards written exams, but very similar principles apply for other forms of assessment.

Not knowing enough

This is the reason students *imagine* to be most likely to cause them to fail, whether because of memory difficulties, or because they had difficulty in understanding the course. The latter reason can be a genuine – arguably deserved – cause of failure. If you don't understand a module, and/or have learned nothing from it, you should not pass it! By the time of the exam this will be an 'unavoidable' cause of failure. However, the study skills developed through this book, together with the courage to seek help when needed, should mean that this cause was avoided long before the exam.

It is fairly uncommon for lack of knowledge alone to be responsible for failure. Usually it is possible to pass an examination with very limited knowledge, certainly knowing far less than the whole of a course being examined. But you will only scrape a pass if what you *do* know is relevant and put to good use. Conversely, you may 'know' a great deal – in the sense of being able to reproduce it – but gain few marks if you do not understand what it means, why it is important, how to use it, and importantly, how to show your knowledge when answering an exam question. If you devise a revision plan, as suggested later, use your time-management skills to ensure that you follow it, and follow the guidance

➤ Ch 13 on answering questions in Chapter 13, there should be little chance of your entering an exam not knowing or not understanding enough to pass.

Poor time management

Time management during revision is important. Time management during the exam is perhaps even more important, as it is by far the commonest apparent cause of failure. In most exams you will be expected to answer a set number of questions. The marking scheme will allocate marks accordingly, and your scriptmarkers will abide by this scheme. The familiar 80:20 rule applies. You can expect to get 80 per cent of the marks with only 20 per cent of the effort that full marks would require. So the pursuit of perfection is a certain route to failure. It is essential that you spend a reasonable time answering each question required. Even if you feel you know nothing about your last choice, still spend time on it. You are likely, despite your ignorance, to gain more marks by attempting it than by spending the time polishing another answer. *Never* inadvertently leave yourself no time to answer one or more questions. Always work out how much time you can afford for each question, and keep a close watch on the clock to ensure that each question gets its fair share. Heavily weighted questions should, of course, receive a time allocation in proportion to the marks they are worth.

> **Common causes of failure include:**
> - poor time management
> - answering too few questions
> - missing out parts of questions
> - not actually answering the question
> - not using course ideas.

Suppose you have to answer four equally weighted questions, each worth up to 25 marks of your final score. It will be fairly easy to get 30 per cent (i.e. 7.5 marks toward your overall score), even on a question about which you are very unhappy. If you do not attempt it, you will get zero. The same time spent working on another question *might* have raised what was already a 65 per cent to a 73 per cent (i.e. add two marks to your overall score) but would be highly unlikely to bring it up to 95. If your overall performance is marginal, the difference between the 7.5 marks gained by the first strategy, and the additional 2 marks by the second strategy, might easily make all the difference between pass and fail.

In working out your time budget, allow sufficient time for reading the paper and thinking about which questions to answer. Also you will need time to plan your answer. Writing time is therefore very restricted. Do not expect to be able to write a lot. And do *not* feel you have to go beyond your time budget because your answer does not look long enough. Some of the highest marks go to short answers, *provided* they are concise, relevant and well structured.

(In a viva, or indeed any interview, it is equally important to devote most of your answer to the central question, rather than talking at length about something peripheral to this.)

Failing to answer the question asked

Of course, those whose time management is awry will fail to answer one or more questions. But there is another significant group of students who allow sufficient time for a question, but then proceed to write an answer to something completely different. Examiners will usually be marking to a scheme that allocates so many marks to each sub-part of a question, so an answer bearing little relation to what was expected will gain few marks. The only exception to this is when a student has found an original, but still valid, interpretation of the question. Then, if the marker is sufficiently alert to realise that this *is* valid, it may be marked on its merits. There is no guarantee, however, that such an answer will be accepted, so aiming for originality is a risky strategy, and you need to put effort into justifying it and explaining why you are not taking the 'obvious' approach.

It is absolutely crucial that you spend some time making sure that you understand what the question is asking for, and identifying all the different parts that may be hidden within a seemingly straightforward question. This is not always easy under exam conditions. It is worth checking, too, that you are not straying away from the question during the course of your answer. Re-read the question at intervals while you are writing your answer, to make sure that you are not drifting away from the main point, or omitting important sub-points. You may find it helpful to refer to the glossary of terms commonly used in exam and assignment questions given in Helpfile 13.1 (at the end of Chapter 13).

➤ Ch 13

Panic

A tiny minority of students are so stressed that they find themselves in a state of total panic in the exam. This may result in part from a history of doing poorly in exams, or having had undue pressure put upon you to do brilliantly. If you are prone to this, you should consult your doctor well in advance, so that the problem may be both registered and addressed. You should also devote time to learning breathing and relaxation exercises, and practise these as much as possible before the exam. Such exercises are also helpful if you do not suffer from outright panic, but are still nervous enough in the exam for it to affect your performance.

Illegible script

This is a problem where exams are handwritten. Writing by hand is a dying art – you may not have written (with pen and paper) anything longer than about five lines since you left school. As a result, your arm may tire quickly, and your writing become hard to read. Markers may be faced with 100 or more scripts to mark in a very short period. If they can barely read your writing, they may miss many of the points you thought you had made. You will receive disappointing marks in consequence. If your writing problem has a medical cause, consult your tutor to see whether it would be possible for you to type or dictate your answer. If your writing is simply difficult to read, it is well worth practising writing legibly at speed, well in advance of your first exam. Perhaps you can keep your reflective journal on paper rather than use a keyboard.

Other problems

You may anticipate other problems, or encounter them unexpectedly. Perhaps you fall ill shortly before an exam, or a major traffic incident makes you late. Perhaps you have major problems at work or home during the revision period. If so, as with problems affecting continuous assessment, it is imperative that you let your tutor or someone else in authority know about the problems, and their impact on your exam performance as soon as at all possible. Most institutions will make allowances for problems *if they know about them*. They cannot do this if they are unaware that anything is wrong. And they may need evidence of the problem in order to make allowances. (Print off evidence of traffic problems, or get copies of hospital certificates or letter from your doctor.)

➤ Ch 12

While there are many potential problems, it is important not to get these out of perspective. Each is unlikely, and may never happen to you. It is merely important to know what you should do in the unlikely event that disaster strikes. Most Master's students pass their exams. With only a little attention to the rest of this chapter you should be able to end up in that large majority.

Exam preparation

> **To prepare effectively:**
> - identify what is required
> - plan your revision time
> - revise actively
>   - summarise
>   - diagram
>   - test knowledge
>   - practise answers
> - keep fit.

In one sense, your exam preparation starts when you begin to study the course. If your note taking was done with revision requirements in mind, then subsequent preparation will be much easier. However, at some point prior to the exam you will wish to focus more specifically on revision, and on developing a strategy for gaining good marks in your exam. As with many of the techniques suggested in this book, the action required is simple and straightforward. But it does require time and planning, and the discipline to start working towards the exam early, well in advance of it being sufficiently imminent to cause anxiety.

You probably will find that you use your time more effectively if you go through the following stages as you start your exam preparation.

Identify requirements

It will not surprise you that, as with any other project, you need to know as much as possible about what is required. The earlier section on objectives of assessment is relevant. It should also be possible to obtain past exam papers and analyse these for the sorts of topic covered and the type of question asked. Try to put yourself in the examiner's position. It is not easy to think of suitable questions that can be answered in 45 minutes (or whatever the time allocation) under exam conditions. It is even harder to devise questions that will allow students to show that they know, understand and can use parts of the course covered. Some topics will be much easier to write questions on than others. These naturally will predominate. Other topics are so central to understanding a subject that they are almost certain to be needed.

Look at the format of the paper. How many questions are there to choose from? How many topics does this mean you can afford not to revise? With a little research you should be able to identify those areas of the course that it would be dangerous not to know, those that look useful and those that look less important. You should also have a clear idea of the absolute minimum you must know to have even a chance of passing, the amount that would be fairly safe and what would give you a comfortable margin of error.

Find out from your tutors what *level* of knowledge is needed. Is it fine detail or broad principles? It is a waste of time learning the finer details of employment legislation if all you are required to know is the broad categories covered. But if you *will* be required to know precisely under what conditions a claim of unfair dismissal can be brought, then broad principles will not be enough. Find out, too, the balance of theory to practice that is required. Many of these finer points will vary from course to course, so you will need to gain information on each course for which there is an examination.

Make sure that you know what, if anything, you can take into the exam room. For some courses you are allowed to bring your notes or a limited amount of printed information. Check whether any case studies issued in advance of the exam should be brought in. If so, their margins may be usable for other notes too – check whether this is allowed. Programmable calculators provide interesting possibilities; again, institutions have different policies as to whether these are allowable. Palmtops are unlikely to be allowed. If the course has totally open-book exams, check you have read the caveats earlier in the chapter. Such examinations are dangerous if you are unused to them.

Prepare a revision plan

This is possible once you are clear about requirements. Decide how much of each course you wish to cover in depth, which parts you will give slightly less attention to, and what, if anything, you are going to omit. Think about the time you realistically have available for your preparation, and allow a contingency factor for the disasters that are all too common at critical points like exam time. Think about *how* you wish to work. Do you want to go through the course once, or several times? How *will* you go through it? Clearly you do not have time to read all the books again. Will some parts take longer than others because they do not come easily to you? If you have got into the habit of planning your work earlier in the course, this stage should be almost second nature to you now.

Prepare a chart, showing when you will work on each part of the course. Remember to allow time at the end for overall preparation, and practising with past papers. And do not rely on the night before the exam. That is better used for purposes other than revision. Your chart should have spaces for you to tick off each piece of work completed. Although this is not strictly necessary, you will find that it helps motivation enormously. Sustaining motivation may be important if you are starting to revise well in advance of the exam.

Revise actively

Once you have allocated your time for preparation, use this time so as to gain maximum benefit. Merely reading through your books and notes in a passive way is unlikely to be of value. As you tackle each topic, you need to bear in mind the following questions:

- What do I need to *learn* (e.g. definitions, equations and diagrams)?
- What do I need to *know* and *understand* (e.g. principles and techniques)?
- What do I need to be able to *do* with the above?

Your exploration of requirements should have put you in a position to answer these questions.

Keep these questions in mind as you work through your materials. You may find it helpful to keep two sorts of notes, those on facts you must learn, including key references, and those on more general points. Even if you followed the advice of taking your course notes with revision in mind, you should still take notes as part of your exam preparation. Condensing your original notes, perhaps progressively, is an excellent way of absorbing material.

I have seen some excellent one-page summaries of entire courses, and students often circulate these to friends or the whole group. Recipients express almost ecstatic gratitude, but beware. This may be misplaced. They do not realise that such summaries are an invaluable culmination of hours of revision, but are *not* a substitute for it. Their value is greatest for the person who produced the summary and depends upon having gone through the production process. Their value as an alternative to doing the revision is extremely limited.

So produce your own summary. While doing this, aim to interact with the materials in as many ways as possible. Draw diagrams of text. Describe course diagrams in words. Try to represent relationships with equations or diagrams. List possible uses of different techniques. Figure 15.2 shows an example of some notes that have incorporated some of these different things.

Some of your summarising can be done as a kind of test, without looking at materials. You can then go back and see whether there is anything significant that you have left out, or anything you have misremembered. You can also test yourself by inventing possible exam questions when you have finished a summary, and then (after a decent interval) trying to answer them. Use past exam papers, too, sketching out skeleton answers. Practise going through the following routine:

➤ Chs 12, 13

- Analyse the question to see what it is *really* asking, underlining key words (*see* Chapters 12 and 13).
- Identify key parts of the course that are relevant.
- Identify relevant concepts, techniques, theories and examples from that part of the course.
- Sketch out the way in which these could be used to answer the question.

Aim to do this fairly quickly. This is both less boring, and valuable practice in organising your thoughts rapidly. Then go back to your course materials to check that you have not omitted other relevant ideas or examples, and that those that you *thought* were relevant do indeed contribute what you thought they would. By *working* on materials in this way, you will find that revision is not boring, and that you will retain material much better.

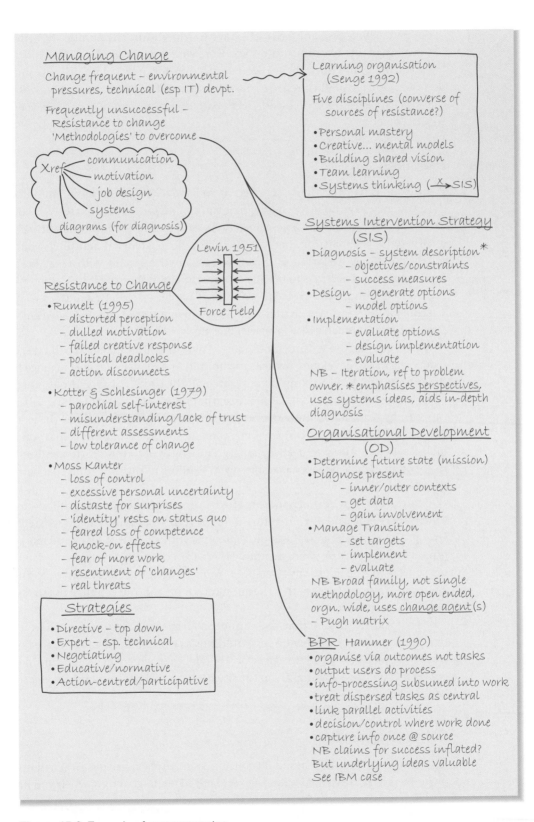

Figure 15.2 Example of summary notes

Of course, you probably will still have to *learn* a limited number of things using old-fashioned rote learning, unless you were wise enough to identify such things during your course and learn them as you went along. It can be helpful to write such things on index cards so that they are easily portable, and to carry them about with you so that you can learn them on buses, in the bath or whenever else your brain is not otherwise occupied.

Practise

If the exam is handwritten you are going to have to sit, pen in hand, for much longer than you may have done for so long that you can no longer do this freely. If you are out of the habit of writing with a pen, it really is worth spending some time getting back into it. Otherwise you may find that there is an unwelcome block that inhibits your answering the questions. So start by practising writing anything at all, with a pen! Keep a diary, send old-style paper *letters* to friends, or experiment with using Julia Cameron's 'morning pages' technique as suggested earlier (*see* Chapter 4). Do a first draft of your written assignments by hand. Any of these activities will reopen the channel between brain and pen, and make it much easier to answer questions in an exam.

➤ Ch 4

If you can, practise writing for the sort of length of time an exam will take. This will reduce the risk of developing writer's cramp, and make you better able to judge how your time is going without looking at your watch all the time. This practice is probably best combined with the next sort of practice, that of answering real exam questions. You can start by working on individual questions, some of which could be those for which you sketched out answers earlier. Some, though, should be questions that you have not looked at before. Allow yourself an appropriate length of time for each question. Build up to answering whole papers if possible, again working to the time limit that will apply in the exam.

This exercise will be much more useful if you can get feedback on your performance. Ideally, persuade one of your tutors to mark your work and tell you where you went wrong. Alternatives include swapping attempts with a fellow student and marking each other's work, or putting your attempt away for a few days, then trying to work out a marking scheme for the questions attempted. You will need to be very careful to allocate an appropriate ration to *each* part of the question attempted. You can then use the scheme to mark your own work.

Even if you are short of time and cannot do all the practice you would like, it is essential that you write one paper under conditions as close to those of the real exam as you can manage. Not only will this give you a good idea of what you can do within the time, but it will habituate you slightly to the situation, so that the nervousness you suffer will be reduced.

Other preparation

Your remaining preparation should concern more physical matters. You will need a supply of pens that are easy to write with and not likely to go wrong when you most need them. You will probably find pencil and colours useful too, and a ruler and rubber. Check out the calculator situation. Find out whether there is anything else you will need in the exam and make sure it is ready. Remember to take any identification that is required. And if you are allowed to take in refreshments, consider whether a flask of coffee and a snack might revive you during a long exam.

Make sure you know exactly when and where an exam is to be held: double-check this. You might be sure and *wrong*. A friend recently arrived late and breathless at an exam, having run two miles across town from the hall where he had sat *other* exams. Another, relying on information from his girlfriend, arrived in the afternoon to sit that morning's exam.

Some of your preparation should concern getting yourself in shape for the exam. Working all the hours there are for the weeks before the exam and keeping yourself going on black coffee is not the way to enter the exam with a functioning brain. The additional stress of being in the exam room may then be enough to completely disintegrate you. Very occasionally students will work so hard before the exam that they are barely able to write their names on the paper. This is a tragic waste of effort. It is far better to enter the exam slightly underprepared, but with your brain fresh enough to make good use of what

➤ Ch 3   you do know. Remember, exercise is a good way of reducing stress.

So include exercise in your revision plan, and make sure that the night before the exam you get some more exercise, do something relaxing and go to bed early rather than indulging in last-minute cramming. I remember feeling terribly guilty just before my finals, when, while out on a long walk, I met one of my tutors. Much to my surprise, rather than condemning my laziness, she praised my common sense. I have since come to see that she was right. Exams are not about suffering, but about how best to prepare your whole self to achieve a desired level of performance.

After all this, it remains only to get to the examination in good time. This means allowing for the worst that the road or rail system can do to you, and for fog, flat tyres, train delays, etc. In other words, allow plenty of time, and then some. It can do dreadful things to your concentration if you rush into the exam at the last possible minute, knowing that you have left your car on a double yellow line, and still sweating from the exertion of running to the exam hall.

During the examination

If you have followed your revision plan, and prepared yourself adequately for the exam, you should be keyed up enough to give your best performance but not over-anxious. The following guidelines for the day itself may help you keep stress levels to the optimum.

Use time before the exam to relax

If you arrived early, as suggested, go for a walk, or get a coffee or tea. Try consciously to relax. Visualise yourself sitting calmly, feeling clear-headed and in control, writing fluently and confidently.

Read the paper carefully

If you have a choice, much will depend on your choosing the best questions. You will need to read the paper carefully and think about how you might answer each question before making your choice. If there is a compulsory question, you may prefer to answer that first, and then take a coffee break while you think about the rest of the paper. Or you may feel that reading the whole paper may give you ideas about how to answer the compulsory part. Much will depend on the nature of the paper. It is often useful to highlight the separate parts of compound questions, to ensure that you answer every part.

Work out your time allocation for each question and monitor time usage

You *must* be disciplined about this. The results of poor time budgeting, and missing or skimping whole questions can be catastrophic. Note the time at which you will cease working on one question and move to the next, and keep to these times. Allocate time within questions according to the likely marks allocated to the different question parts. You can work these timings out before the examination if the format is known. When doing your calculations remember to allow some time for reading the paper. Sometimes you will see a question with different weightings attached to each part. Ration your time accordingly. If some questions carry a heavier weighting than others, allocate time accordingly. During the exam make sure that you move to the next question on schedule. If this does not allow you to finish an answer, jot down key points still to make and leave space. You can come back later if you save time on another question. This is a safer strategy (80:20 rule) than aiming to finish but getting behind schedule.

Read each selected question very carefully

It is essential that you understand exactly how the examiner wants the question approached. Do not choose a question simply because you know a lot about that topic in general. Students often give the impression that they have learned a topic (X), and then taken the question as 'Write down everything you can remember about X'. They often fail. To get marks, you need to *understand*, and then *answer*, the specific question asked. Consider the following question (it may be nothing like the sort of questions you will encounter, but the principles remain the same).

 To what extent do accounting techniques provide adequate control mechanisms for an organisation?

This is a seemingly simple question, but consider how much is potentially contained within it. What sort of control mechanisms does an organisation *need*, and what does control *mean* in this context? What is the nature of accounting-based controls? (You would need to give some examples to demonstrate your point.) What, therefore, are their strengths in terms of organisational control? What are their weaknesses? What sorts of problems might arise if control depended solely on accounting techniques?

You can see that a student who wrote down all the accounting techniques he or she knew, complete with all the equations, would gain few marks. They would have demonstrated that they knew all the techniques. They would not have shown that they understood their implications, or anything about the context in which they were used. Since this was what the question was all about, their mark would be low.

In choosing questions to answer, it is more important that you understand what the question is driving at than that you can remember all the details of that topic. If the question relating to your pet topic puzzles you, resist the temptation to answer it anyway, unless there is nothing else on the paper that you understand. Avoid what seem to be totally open-ended questions in favour of those that are themselves clearly structured, thus indicating the structure expected in your answer. The former question type may *look* as if it doesn't matter how you approach it, but it is in fact dangerous to assume this. The examiner may have very clear ideas about what is required. Look at the companion **website** for additional questions to 'deconstruct'.

Spend time planning your answer

It is usually essential to spend time thinking about how you will tackle your answer. Mind maps can be very useful here, as they will build on whatever structure is suggested by the question to provide a skeleton for your answer. By following this structure, you will be able to write coherently, and to the point. Time spent planning and making notes is seldom wasted. You may have less time to write your answer, but that time will be used far more efficiently. (There was a student who wrote three pages of notes and half a page of answer, but that is the only time I have known someone suffer from spending too much time planning. He appealed against his fail grade claiming that he had put a note on the exam paper explaining to the examiner that he had run out of time, and that his failure to answer the questions should not therefore be held against him!)

If you are running short of time, never cross out your notes until you are sure that you have covered everything in them. It is safer not to cross them out at all. Make notes on a separate page, clearly labelled 'Notes' and leave them there. Examiners are supposed to ignore any work that has been crossed through. However, if they are desperately seeking the extra mark you need to pass, they *may* be more charitably inclined if it is clear from your notes that you had a good grasp of the issue and merely ran out of time.

Use a clear structure

As in written assignments, subheadings make the structure of your argument clearer. This is particularly important if your *writing* is hard to read. Diagrams are also often useful. Be careful though. This is an area where pursuit of perfection is particularly dangerous. Drawing a beautiful diagram can take ages. Aim for quick clarity rather than anything too artistic. Your examiner will expect no more.

If a question asks for a particular form of answer such as a report, make it look right ▶ Ch 13 (follow the guidance in Chapter 13). And if it asks for calculations, show your working as well as the result. In this way you will pick up marks for doing it in the right way, even if stress causes you to make an error.

Check at intervals that you are still on track

This applies not only to your time usage, but also to the way that you are answering each question. Once you have worked out what the question is asking, you need to check at intervals that you are still answering this. It is all too easy to get carried away by your flow, and wander off the point. Re-reading the question at intervals to check that you are still on target is essential. A skeleton answer prepared at the answer planning stage helps prevent such wandering, as well as increasing your chance of answering *all* of the question.

Remember what you are trying to do

Above all, in writing your answers follow the same rules as for continuous assessment. Remember that you are trying to show that you *know*, *understand* and can *apply* the concepts taught in the course. Avoid unjustified assertions, go for reasoned argument instead. Build your argument from evidence and texts you have studied. Quote key authors when using concepts, preferably with a date. And even when an essay is required, rather than a report, use *introduction* and *conclusions* sections in your answer, and use other subheadings where they help make your structure clear.

If, despite your best intentions, your time management goes awry, force yourself to stop the question you are working on, even if not complete, in order to spend 15 minutes jotting down notes on the question you have not had time to answer. Again, it is important to give examiners something on which to exercise their charity, if you need this.

Above all, don't worry too much about examinations. As was said earlier, the great majority of students pass, so, even if you do not take the advice in this chapter, your chances are pretty good, and better if you don't lose sleep worrying. If you do plan your preparation, and follow a sensible strategy during the exam, you should be almost certain of success.

> **To do well in exams:**
> - budget time carefully
> - choose questions you understand
> - identify all parts of a question
> - plan your answer
> - use diagrams where possible
> - move to next answer on schedule.

SUMMARY

- Examinations test a narrow range of skills but have many practical advantages.
- *Viva voces* offer more flexibility, but are more expensive.
- Assessment centres and portfolio assessment allow job-related competences to be assessed, but are much more expensive.
- Work out your possessive objectives for any assessment and prepare accordingly.

- It is important to plan your exam preparation, starting well in advance of the exam date.

- This preparation should be aimed at ensuring that you are physically, as well as academically, in good shape for the exam.

- Active revision is far more effective than passive.

- Use past exam papers if at all possible.

- During the exam it is important to budget time carefully, to read questions thoroughly and attempt only those that you are sure you understand. You should check at intervals that your answer is still relevant.

- If you *do* encounter problems that interfere with your preparation or examination performance, let your college know at once.

- Take heart from the fact that most students at this level pass their exams.

Further information

http://www.prospects.ac.uk/interview_tips_assessment_centres.htm (accessed 15.1.15). For guidance on what to expect, and how to prepare for an assessment centre.

https://intranet.birmingham.ac.uk/as/employability/careers/apply/assessment-centres/index.aspx (accessed 15.1.15). For guidance Birmingham University offers its students on assessment centres – check out what your own university offers.

http://www.kent.ac.uk/careers/cv/portfolios.htm (accessed 15.1.15). For interesting ideas on multimedia portfolios geared towards impressing an employer.

PART 5
INTEGRATING YOUR SKILLS AND GOING FORWARD

16
PROJECTS, THESES AND DISSERTATIONS

Learning outcomes

By the end of this chapter you should:

- understand the key role of project and dissertation work in management learning

- be able to consider relevant factors and choose an appropriate topic

- be aware of the steps needed to get an organisational project accepted by a client and secure the necessary resources and commitment

- appreciate the concerns a tutor may have about a dissertation proposal

- know how to draw effectively upon existing thinking on your topic

- understand the importance of thorough diagnosis

- appreciate the importance of choosing an appropriate research method

- appreciate the advantages and disadvantages of different types of information and ways of collecting these

- know how to draw up an initial research plan and write a convincing research proposal

- understand the distinctive requirements of dissertation reports.

Introduction

At Master's-level you can expect to be asked for a substantial project, thesis or dissertation as your final piece of work. You may encounter smaller projects throughout the course. Your final dissertation or project will draw on much of what you have learned in your course, and allow you to develop skills and academic ideas that particularly interest you. You will be working largely independently. This final piece of work forms a bridge between formal study and the sort of learning and problem solving you will be doing after qualifying. If your career is in management or consultancy, you are likely to undertake many projects, singly or in a team. Many may involve some sort of investigation to gather evidence to inform a decision about what to do. The skills you develop on your final course project will be invaluable.

If you are headed for an academic route, general research skills will be needed during your PhD research, and the discussion of issues related to working with a client will also be relevant to any applied research

Good real-life management decisions are based on a thorough understanding of the issue in question, and on adequate evidence, properly interpreted. When working with case studies you were 'spoon-fed': information was sifted and filtered by the case author, and there were usually only a few possible routes to follow. Real life is far more complex. It may be difficult to decide which avenue to follow, and which questions to answer in pursuit of improvements. I t may not be obvious at first what information would be helpful, and once you have decided, there may be challenges in obtaining it. You will need to liaise with those providing information and other resources. You will need to interpret your information and draw conclusions in full awareness of the wider context. And crucially, you will need to manage your time carefully in order to achieve all this and to write a substantial report at the end. Your critical thinking, interpersonal and personal skills will all be needed, as well as your understanding of relevant theories.

Your final project or dissertation can be the highlight of your studies, allowing you to explore a real and fascinating problem, and increase your employability by developing specialist expertise. Or it can be a source of endless worry and potential cause of failure. This chapter aims to ensure that it is the former, by helping you to select an appropriate topic and approach, to manage your project work effectively and to write your report in an appropriate and timely way. It will also help you with smaller scale projects and with managing projects at work.

While all three words are sometimes used interchangeably, 'project' more commonly refers to work with a practical application, 'thesis' to longer and more academic research-oriented work, and 'dissertation' to something in between. This chapter is aimed at projects and dissertations, and since the points made will refer to both, uses the terms fairly interchangeably. In management subjects, project work is an important way of allowing you to demonstrate deep learning, and the ability to relate what you have learned to real problem situations. This chapter will address some of the challenges of application of theory to real contexts.

As well as allowing you to use concepts and skills developed during your studies and show 'deep learning', a dissertation offers you the chance to work on a topic dear to your

➤ Ch 9
heart. Potential benefits are high: you may gain useful insights into your own organisational context. To do so will require you to demonstrate both interpersonal skills (vital to any consultancy work) and investigative skills.

This handbook cannot cover either research methodology or statistics in any depth. Your course will probably have modules which do this. If not, further reading is suggested. This chapter highlights areas that students typically find problematic, and suggests steps you can take to minimise the risks, and maximise the potential benefits attached to your project.

There are many potential benefits of a work-based project. Successfully addressing a long-standing organisational problem can bring you to the favourable attention of senior managers. If you are acting as consultant to another organisation, you may be offered further consultancy, or a job. Above all, you will develop a wide range of skills (personal, interpersonal and investigative) that will be invaluable throughout your career. But work-based projects also present context-specific risks. Things may change in your target organisation and/or with the sponsor of your project, which may result in withdrawal of cooperation. It is important to be aware of such risks when choosing a project, and to take steps to manage them, as well as choosing a project that will develop your skills to the full.

A dissertation based on secondary sources may present fewer challenges in terms of managing a client and/or others in an organisation, but will require a similar level of self-management skills, it may be harder to find a suitable topic as there is almost too much choice, and your critical thinking skills may be even more important than with a work-based project.

Many of the key steps in a project need to be addressed well in advance of the research itself. Choice of topic, negotiations with your organisation and/or supervisor and careful planning are critical, and if at all possible should be commenced at least six months in advance of the 'official' dissertation period.

Characteristics of management research

Research is a process of finding things out in a purposeful and systematic fashion, in order to increase knowledge. It may be more or less practically oriented. Again, terms may be used interchangeably, but it may help to refer to more practically oriented research as business research, and that with a stronger theoretical emphasis as management research. Cameron and Price (2009) describe practical business research as

> any systematic attempt at collecting and interpreting data and evidence in order to inform thinking, decisions and/or actions in relation to an issue of interest to an organization and/or its stakeholders. (p. 4)

Saunders *et al.* (2009) suggest that management research:

- is *transdisciplinary*, i.e. it draws on a range of disciplines to generate insights that could not be gained by separate use of these disciplines;

- is intended to have *practical use*, thus either needs to point to some form of action or to take account of the practical consequences of the findings;

- involves a *reflexive* process whereby theory and practice inform each other. Thus, the problems addressed should grow out of this interaction between theory and practice;

- requires organisational sponsors of research to be convinced both of the potential use of findings and that the demands of cooperation are likely to be justified.

Your own research is likely to fall into one of three categories:

- A project addressing a real organisational problem – typical of part-time MBA or other Master's programmes. This allows students to do their research within their own organisation, often on a topic closely related to their own responsibilities, adopting an internal consultant role. Such research might evaluate some aspect of an organisation's performance in the light of theory, or address a practical organisational problem, culminating in a set of recommendations in a report to that company. Some projects may go as far as implementing recommendations.

- A consultancy-type project – more common on full-time programmes, either as part of a work placement or for a local organisation that supports your institution by offering project facilities. Aims might be similar to those of the previous category, and indeed in some own-organisation projects you may be acting as an internal consultant to another part of the organisation.

- An experimental or library-based dissertation of more academic interest, and not requiring liaison with an organisation – typical of specialist Master's programmes or full-time programmes without opportunities for consultancy or placements.

If your research addresses an issue in a real organisation, all of the characteristics suggested by Saunders *et al.* have implications for your choice of topic, and for what you need to do to carry out research successfully. In particular, they emphasise the need for sufficiently broad topic choice, and for significant interaction with your client organisation. The discussion that follows is directed primarily towards such research. If you are carrying out a more academic management-related project you may still find the issues relevant. Whether you are an MBA student addressing a very practical problem, or on a specialist programme and researching a narrower issue in a more academic fashion, you normally will need to find the right balance of theory and practice to satisfy course requirements. Neither pure theory nor theoretic problem solving is likely to be satisfactory.

Finally, there is clearly a range of practical issues to be considered in terms of gaining organisational and institutional support for your research. This raises the important issue of stakeholders in your research.

Stakeholders in your dissertation

There are at least four important stakeholders in your dissertation, as shown in Figure 16.1. (If you are doing a group project, then fellow group members will constitute a fifth important category.)

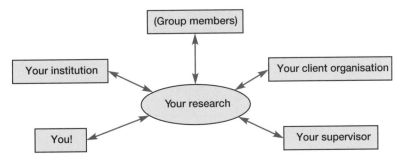

Figure 16.1 Stakeholders in a dissertation

As with any complex situation, it is worth exploring the different perspectives and objectives of these stakeholders. If you understand these objectives, and possible conflicts between them, you are most likely to be able to minimise such conflict, and maximise your chances of meeting requirements.

Your institution

Your institution is a major stakeholder in your research. A project or dissertation plays a key role in meeting the educational aims of your programme. Your work is likely to be viewed by external examiners and other quality assessors, and it may contribute to ongoing research within the department. There will be published requirements for the dissertation. You will find it much easier to meet these requirements if you understand the reasons for them.

Institutions vary in their priorities, so find out as much as you can about your chosen institution's aims and objectives as soon as possible. Generally, educational aims include developing the following skills and abilities in students:

- the ability to carry out investigative work in organisations and arrive at valid results;
- the consultancy skills expected of MBA holders (including building and maintaining a good relationship with a client);
- the ability to manage a substantial piece of work with only minimal guidance;
- analytical skills;
- report-writing skills;
- the ability to integrate and apply what has been learned on a variety of courses;
- the ability to find relevant literature beyond that included in past courses, and to use this to good effect;
- the ability to assess the value and limitations of information in deciding on future courses of action;
- the ability to approach real problems at a strategic level;
- the ability to reflect on the investigative process and on the student's own strengths and weaknesses during this, and learn from it;
- research skills that will enable students to progress to a PhD if they so require.

Institutions will have the related aims of generating high-quality projects so that they can convince quality assessors of the excellence of their teaching, and satisfy sponsoring organisations. To meet the educational objectives of most programmes the chosen topic will need to be broad enough to allow interesting analysis and use of a wide range of theory.

The client organisation

Assuming that you are able to find an in-company project, the objectives of your client organisation – and of the individual 'organisational client' with whom you deal – will be important. Many of these will be specific to the topic you finally choose, but there are some non-topic-specific considerations also.

Activity 16.1

Consider what objectives the organisation might have for your project, regardless of the topic chosen. List these here:

_____

_____

_____

_____

_____

Comment

If researching your own organisation, your list might, for example, have included a desire to involve certain people in an initiative for developmental purposes, or even to test your own capabilities in a particular direction. Other objectives might be to minimise use of company time, to be seen to be supporting management development, to support some other company initiative, and to minimise the risk of upsetting anybody. Whether the likely objectives are overt or fairly well hidden, you are more likely to be able to come to a mutually acceptable topic if you are alert to these factors.

If your client organisation is used to sponsoring projects of this kind, they may well have goals that are easily met by your research project. But, if they do not have such experience, you may need to be very careful to ensure that their objectives are consistent with those of the other stakeholders. This is discussed in more detail later in the chapter.

You!

Ideally, your client company will be giving you considerable support in your project. Even so, the main effort will, necessarily, be your own. Too often students settle on a project topic on the 'Well, I've got to do *something*' principle, and then spend a depressing six months or more working on something that does not interest them at all. Before considering topic choice in more detail, it is worth thinking about how a well-chosen project could serve your own objectives. These might include, for example:

- a desire eventually to specialise in a particular area;
- a desire to work in a particular part of the organisation;
- the wish to incorporate a leisure interest more closely into work.

More project-specific objectives might include the desire to address a problem that impacts directly upon your own work.

16

Activity 16.2

List any personal objectives that your project might be made to serve:

_____
_____
_____
_____
_____

Group members

If you are doing a group project, then it is important to think about the objectives of all group members and, if possible, ensure that you are working with fellow team members who share your objectives. It is important that they want to do as well as you do, and are prepared to put in similar levels of effort. (It is highly frustrating to feel that you are the only one in the group who is prepared to do any work! On the other hand, it may feel uncomfortable to realise that everyone else is contributing far more than you.)

As well as ensuring that your personal objectives are consistent with those of other team members, you need to pay particular attention to making sure that all group members are absolutely clear and agreed concerning the *project* objectives. This agreement will need constant communication and checking to ensure that you keep working towards the same aims. And, of course, you will need to apply all your team-working skills (*see* Chapter 9). Indeed, group projects are an excellent way of developing such skills. And because it is a more complex activity, project management (*see* later) will require even more attention than it does for individual projects.

➤ Ch 9

Your supervisor

Although you are expected to work fairly independently at this stage in your studies, almost certainly you will be allocated a supervisor for your project. This role is interpreted differently by different institutions, and by different supervisors and those supervised within them. But, in all cases, your supervisor's objectives are for you to pass! And they will do what they can to achieve this. In the best case, your supervisor can be an invaluable source of expertise, guidance, support and encouragement, and make a major contribution to your eventual success. But this depends upon your developing a good relationship with your supervisor and maintaining that contact and relationship until your dissertation has been submitted. Even if you are completing your research after you have finished the taught part of your course and have gone elsewhere, continued contact is important. Phone, email or Skype (or similar) make virtual meetings feasible, wherever you are.

Some institutions (wisely) *require* you to meet your supervisor a certain number of times, and to agree certain key points such as project proposal, data plan, report outline and at least one draft chapter. Even if this is not required, you might discuss whether you and your supervisor could usefully aim to reach such agreements, and set target dates for these. Such milestones are an important part of project management

Contact is only the start. It is important that you take feedback seriously. Supervisors can draw on extensive experience to judge the feasibility of a topic, and the work it will involve, and can tell when your (slow?) progress is starting to ring alarm bells. If they express reservations about your choice or your drafts, *take heed.* I have examined too many dissertations where students have either not been required to have these contacts with supervisors, or have ignored advice they have received. The results have been heartbreaking for all concerned. The dissertations have looked beautiful; they were nicely bound and demonstrated excellent presentation and graphic skills. They have been dedicated to the family and friends who clearly had made considerable sacrifices to sustain the student through the enormous labour involved. But all this effort and sacrifice was wasted because the students had not listened to their supervisors, and all their work had produced a dissertation that deservedly failed.

Project topics were not realistic: one student was seeking to improve the social and economic position and health of women in her home country – aiming to achieve in six months something the government and a number of charities had failed to do for many years. Data are often wildly inadequate: one student had interviewed six friends and drawn sweeping conclusions about a completely different group of managers from those the friends represented. Research questions were ignored: one student had become carried away by the economic history of his country, totally failing to address the strategic issues for finance institutions – the alleged topic of the dissertation. Other students make no use of theory or relevant research: one described a (painful) change initiative in his organisation in full and fascinating detail, but with no analysis or even mention of theory. The style of writing was often quite inappropriate, either overly complex in an attempt at sounding learned, or too chatty. Sometimes the writing was not even the student's own: one had incorporated huge sections of text copied from the Internet, without acknowledging he was not the author. (He was facing disciplinary action for plagiarism – *see* Chapters 7 and 13.)

➤ Chs 7,
13

In each case the failure will have caused the student and his or her family immense distress. Yet, this could have been avoided if the student had sought and heeded their supervisor's advice throughout the process, and made use of supervisor comments on draft material.

So, if it is at all possible:

- Agree key milestones with your supervisor, even if this is not required by your institution.
- Check your progress at each of these stages: repeated checks are important because, if you become deeply involved in a project for its own sake, you may well start to meet your personal objectives at the expense of meeting academic requirements.
- Take your supervisor's feedback very seriously – if you disagree, try to work out why you find it difficult to accept.
- If disagreements cannot be resolved, or for some reason you cannot get the level of support that it is reasonable to expect from a supervisor, see whether it is possible to change supervisors. This should not be done lightly, but occasionally may be the only way to get the help that you can reasonably expect.

The importance of topic

Research can usefully be thought of in terms of a question that you are trying to answer on the basis of evidence. When thinking about possible topics, it is helpful to formulate your ideas as questions. You are seeking a question that is *worth* answering, that you *can* answer within the constraints of resources (primarily time, money and access), and that will enable you to *meet dissertation requirements*.

Choose carefully. It is almost impossible to do a good dissertation on an unsuitable topic (though perfectly possible to do a bad one on a suitable topic). You can often refine your topic as your thinking develops, but major change becomes increasingly difficult as your work progresses. It is therefore vital that you start with a suitable topic area, and refine fairly quickly it into something that your supervisor agrees will allow you to do a good dissertation. Allow plenty of time to consider possible projects – it is a wise investment. Sometimes you may need to revise or totally revisit your choice after you have started work on it. Initial investigations might radically change your thinking about what is required. Redirection early on, even a drastic change, might save you hundreds of hours of depressing work on a poorly chosen topic. There is nothing more depressing than realising that the best you can hope for, given the direction you have chosen, is a barely adequate result. In considering possible topics, there will be several factors you will need to evaluate.

> **An ideal project:**
> - interests you
> - is of use to your client (if work based)
> - meets academic requirements
> - is feasible
> - will be valuable *whatever* you find
> - offers learning opportunities
> - is low risk.

Interest

Perhaps the most important criterion is that the topic be of interest to yourself and, if relevant, to your client organisation. You will be putting considerable and extended effort into the project. The organisation may also be bearing not only the significant cost of any working time employees (including you) devote to it, but also additional costs such as travel, printing, phone calls, postage, information searches, etc. It is an added bonus if your investigation has a potentially wider interest, so that you can increase your profile by publishing your results in a relevant journal or magazine.

If you and your organisation (and that usually means an individual within the organisation with the status to act as client for the research) are not equally interested in the topic, there are likely to be problems. If it is *your* interest that is weak, you will find it hard to sustain your motivation to do the necessary work. If your *client* is not interested, then he or she may not provide you with the support you need, whether this is in terms of refining your project plans, facilitating access to information needed or sponsoring your final report so that it is taken seriously at an appropriate level within the organisation.

So if you are not genuinely interested in a possible topic, or if you detect a lack of real interest on the part of your likely client, keep seeking alternative topics until you find one of real interest to you both.

Scope

It is also important that your chosen topic is potentially broad enough and deep enough for you to exhibit the range of skills your institution will expect. Because you will be expected to develop general research skills, you will be expected to consider different research methods or approaches, selecting an appropriate one and justifying your choice in your final report.

On a more specialist Master's course, a fairly narrow topic, studied in considerable depth, may be required. For an MBA you normally will be expected to take a reasonably broad perspective and to show the strategic awareness that the programme is supposed to develop. You will need to research your topic in such a way as to demonstrate an awareness of the organisational context in which the problem is situated. Your topic will therefore need to be broad enough to allow you to demonstrate both methodological awareness and strategic thinking.

Thus, if your employer asked you to find alternative suppliers of packaging materials and recommend the cheapest, this would not be a suitable research topic. If you had been asked, however, to review the effectiveness of the packaging operation as a whole, and make recommendations as to ways in which it might be redesigned so as to better serve organisational objectives, there would be much more scope. There would be real questions about what constituted measures of effectiveness in this case, and about suitable investigative methods and sources of information. There would need to be a clear understanding of the operation of the rest of the organisation, and its requirements if appropriate recommendations were to be made. Aspects of studies on accounting, operations management, human resource management and other ideas such as benchmarking could be used to inform the research.

You need to be careful when talking of your 'project' at work. Tutors' and employers' definitions of 'project' may be a long way apart. Your employer may imagine that a course project is the same as other 'projects' in the organisation – that is, any piece of practical work to be done to meet organisational objectives. You may need to spend some time making clear that there are educational objectives to be met too, and explaining these, before you, your college and your organisation can come to a mutually acceptable topic. ('Dissertation' might avoid this potential confusion, but you might need to work to convince your employer that a dissertation could have practical use.)

Symmetry of research outcomes

This is a less obvious, but important, criterion. It means that your research results should be interesting no matter how they turn out. Research to 'prove a point' should be avoided. First, you are likely to bias the result in your attempt to get the answer you want. There is surprisingly large scope for the unconscious introduction of bias into research. Careful design is needed to minimise this, as biased results are naturally worthless. Second, if you succeed in designing your research so that bias is eliminated, and then do *not* prove your point, the result will be of little interest.

To take an unlikely example, you might have a hunch that, contrary to popular wisdom (and research), gaining an MBA does not improve career prospects. You might carefully design a research study, comparing career patterns of matched groups of managers, the only difference being that one group gained an MBA five years ago and the other didn't. If, as a result, you found that an MBA did nothing to improve career prospects, or positively harmed them, this would be interesting. If you found, however, that those with MBAs did progress faster, the general response might be 'So what?' Demonstrating the obvious has little value on the whole, unless it is an assumption that has *never* been put to the test.

Because overturning received wisdom can be a highly desirable, newsworthy and publishable outcome, you may wish to take risks of this kind. If so, do it with due consideration, and build in enough additional information collection that your resulting thesis will be of interest, even if the original assumption was wrong. In this case, what aspects of the MBA were helpful? Which types of career progression were most common or fastest? Is there variation between different types of organisation or different jobs? Is there an age or gender effect? Does the effect depend upon whether senior staff in the organisation themselves have an MBA? Supplementary questions of this kind could provide the material for an acceptable thesis, even if the main question was a risky one and did not turn out as you expected. Of course, it is better to select a main question where any answer will be interesting.

Feasibility

This is obviously a critical consideration for any proposed project. Attempting the impossible shows lack of judgement, and is a recipe for stress and disappointment. Remember the planning fallacy – it is particularly applicable to projects. Most students have a highly optimistic idea of what is possible within the time and resource constraints of a Master's dissertation. If ever you have the slightest suspicion that your ideas might be slightly ambitious, stop at once. They are probably wildly unrealistic! All projects have a way of expanding to fill at least twice the time allotted to them. Set modest objectives and allow large margins for the unexpected.

As well as checking feasibility in terms of the time you have, you need to check your proposal against other resource constraints. These include finance and availability of information. If your project looks as if it will incur costs which neither you nor your sponsor is prepared to bear, then it is unlikely to be feasible unless some other sources of finance can be found. Feasibility may also be threatened if your project depends on:

- access to classified, or even sensitive, information;
- information that cannot be obtained without a major investment by either you or others;
- the cooperation of those outside the organisation who are highly unlikely to see any reason for cooperating;
- cooperation of those within the organisation who are unwilling for political or other reasons to support the research.

Risks

The scope for things to go wrong is closely related to aspects of feasibility and this 'catastrophe factor' should be just as carefully considered. A major risk is that considerable change may take place in your client organisation (and indeed in your own life) during the project. It is important to consider how vulnerable your potential project is to such changes. It is of course impossible to find a totally risk-free project. If you are promoted into a job on the other side of the world, or indeed, if you are made redundant, you may have more pressing concerns than whether you will still have access to the information you need to complete your dissertation. You cannot guard against the wide range of possible, but highly improbable catastrophes that just *might* happen. But you can think about those things that are fairly *likely* to happen within any organisation, and which can seriously impede a project. These include political or personnel change, increase or decrease in workload, and restructuring. You should attempt to assess the probability of such events within your organisation and their likely effect on any proposed topic. Only then can you decide whether the risk is an acceptable one.

If the risks are high, could they be reduced by reformulating the topic? You cannot prevent a department being shut down at 24 hours' notice when you are in the midst of collecting information on it. But you can reduce the chances of such disruption by avoiding as a subject for your research any part of the organisation under serious threat.

'Real time' projects, involving ongoing implementation of change or of evaluation of such change as it happens, are particularly vulnerable. Any change to the timescale of the subject of the research can have disastrous effects on a tight project plan. And if the project starts to go wrong, people may start to withhold information. It is far safer to select a topic where data sources already exist. You can then draw upon these within a timescale to suit your project requirements.

Politically sensitive projects are particularly dangerous. If the political climate within the organisation shifts, you may find that cooperation is withdrawn and confidentiality restraints are placed upon your eventual report.

The above list of factors, which should influence your choice of topic, will be common to most situations, and should be supplemented by any criteria deriving from your personal list of objectives above.

Activity 16.3

List any personal criteria that are important to you in your choice of topic:

_____

_____

_____

_____

_____

➤ Ch 10

It may seem premature to be thinking about criteria for evaluating project topics before generating possibilities to evaluate, but there is sound methodological sense in this. The argument was outlined in Chapter 10, and restated briefly here. If you think about possible options first, and then think about ways of evaluating them, your choice of criteria may be influenced by the characteristics of the option which you at first sight prefer. The unwitting bias that results removes the advantage of taking a systematic approach to the choice of option. Many problem-solving methodologies therefore explicitly recommend that measures of effectiveness are specified *before* options are generated, and this is the approach suggested here. Follow the same pattern in your research if your chosen topic involves recommending a small number of options chosen from a wider range.

Learning opportunities

Project work offers invaluable opportunities for many different types of learning and skill development. Some aspects – time and project management – will be common to all topics. But some topics may offer particular opportunities for you to develop skills that you know would be helpful to your chosen career path. It is worth thinking about how to maximise your personal development through choice of a project that will 'stretch' you in the required directions, or cause you to learn things that are particularly relevant to your hoped-for career. One student was particularly interested in ideas about the role of reflection in authentic leadership and wanted to see how far they were being used in leadership development. He had read several papers on this and the field really interested him. Through his professional network he found organisations willing to let him interview staff. As a result of his work he developed considerable expertise in the area, published a couple of papers with his supervisor, and went on to set up a successful leadership development consultancy.

Generating possible topics

Like this student, you may already have a burning desire to investigate a particular topic, and regard your dissertation as a heaven-sent opportunity to indulge this wish. So why would you want to generate possible topics? You may find that it is far from a waste of time. Indeed, a strong determination to address a pet topic can be positively dangerous. While it is certainly important that a topic interests you, it is equally important that it is of interest to your client, that it will meet your institution's requirements, and that it is feasible within the constraints operating. Your enthusiasm for a topic may blind you to its shortcomings in these areas, or cause you to underestimate their importance. By forcing yourself to take the generation of alternative topics seriously, and to evaluate your preferred topic against these, you may become more aware of potential hazards. You can then find ways of improving your preferred topic by modifying it to incorporate elements of other options.

Many students, however, have no idea at all of what they want to research, and despair sets in at the prospect of having to find a suitable topic. Perhaps you feel your organisation offers no suitable opportunities, or that your boss is antagonistic to the whole thing or no topic has particularly interested you. Perhaps you still do not really have a clear idea of what is required. If any of these apply, you may be strongly tempted to put off all thought of the project for as long as possible. Perhaps inspiration will occur at some future point?

Such inspiration, while not impossible, is highly unlikely. It is much more likely that you will run out of time to choose, and have no clearer idea, and no time for proper thought or discussion with your supervisor and/or organisation. You may then seize any topic suggested, and it is highly likely that it will suit neither your own nor your client's interest. You may then have difficulties throughout your research.

> **Sources of ideas:**
>
> - own interests
> - client concerns
> - current work problems
> - past dissertations
> - media
> - academic literature
> - brainstorming
> - ideas notebook.

If, therefore, you have no idea about possible project topics, do not procrastinate. Instead, start work *at least six months* in advance, if you can. You need extra time for this stage! Ask everyone you can think of for help in finding a topic.

In any problem situation, your chosen solution will be no better than the best option generated. (It can, of course, be worse, if you choose the wrong one!) Your aim at this stage should, therefore, be to generate as wide a range of possibilities as you can. There are several different things that can help in this. Brainstorming and

➤ Ch 10   other creativity techniques were introduced in Chapter 10, and you may have learned more about them during your course. If so, use them!

You can brainstorm possible topics with fellow students, colleagues at work, or, ideally, with both. As each group is likely to produce very different options, this will give you more ideas. From the lists you can select any item that seems to have in it the germ of a possible project and discuss the most likely with your possible client, perhaps using the successive branching and narrowing approach shown in Figure 10.2.

Activity 16.4

List the most promising topic areas generated by your brainstorming or other creativity techniques:

_____

_____

_____

_____

_____

Past dissertations are an immensely rich source of possible ideas. Your library probably has many of these which you can access. They form excellent material on which you can practise your scanning and rapid reading techniques. The best ones will give you an idea of how much can be achieved in a dissertation. You may find this inspiring or profoundly depressing! The weaker ones will demonstrate the minimum that is acceptable. If the first category depressed you, this should make you feel better. However, it should not make you complacent. The minimum may be surprisingly low in some institutions, but it would be dangerous to aim for this lowest acceptable level. There may have been extenuating circumstances, or the student may have been extremely lucky to have passed. But knowing the range of acceptable standards may make the project less threatening: many students find dissertation work unnecessarily stressful because they are aiming for a standard more appropriate to a PhD than a Master's.

Looking at past dissertation titles and their abstracts should give you a field of possibilities from which it is possible to select a small number of suitable areas for subsequent development, to be added to those drawn from your brainstorming.

Activity 16.5

Draw a mind map or other diagram to represent the field of recent dissertation topics, showing broad areas and sub-areas into which these can be classified.

Activity 16.6

List dissertation titles that suggest projects that might be possible within your own context:

_____

_____

_____

_____

_____

Existing dissertations can also be used to provide an alternative slant to your search by giving you insight into what it is that makes a project interesting for you.

Activity 16.7

Select dissertations that do not strike you as potentially applicable in your own context, but that still look extremely interesting. Analyse these to see whether they have any features in common, or in other ways indicate what your definition of 'interesting' implies. List these features:

_____

_____

_____

_____

_____

Finding a client

For in-company projects on part-time programmes you will normally be expected to find a client within your own organisation. This can present problems if you are between jobs, or likely to change jobs before the end of the project, or your organisation is about to undergo major change. If, for any of these reasons, you think that you do not have an obvious organisation to work with, discuss alternatives with your tutors immediately. They may be able to suggest an organisation willing to host a project, or help you to explore possible avenues you have not thus far considered. Some students do projects with voluntary organisations, others gain access to organisations they have worked with in the past, or have had contact with in other ways. Some choose a topic for which they can 'capture' the necessary data before reorganisation or job change makes access impossible. Others may gain permission for a project not based on a specific organisation.

Once you have identified your client *organisation*, the next set of activities involves mapping the organisation and potential areas that a project might address and finding a 'client' or sponsor within the organisation. The ideal internal client understands what you need, is supportive of your studies, has some good ideas about potential projects within his or her area of control, is open-minded about how things might turn out, has access to the internal resources you are likely to need, and is someone with whom you feel you can communicate relatively easily.

If you are not the first student to have done a project in your organisation, you may find considerable in-company expertise in the selection of suitable topics. Previous clients of the research and past students will both be good sources, and constitute a valuable resource that you should exploit to the full. If you are breaking new ground and therefore lack this resource, you will need to explain dissertation requirements very carefully to those who will need to approve your plans and to any others whose cooperation will be important.

There are obvious advantages in discussing possible topics with potential clients as soon as possible. They are, after all, key stakeholders, with considerable relevant knowledge. They may be able to suggest topics that are of particular interest to them. If potential clients feel that they were largely responsible for the choice of topic, they will have a much stronger commitment to making the project a success because of their feelings of ownership.

There are, however, risks associated with client-selected projects. These need to be recognised and steps taken to minimise them. Some risks stem from the very strong organisational meanings attached to 'project', or 'research', meanings which may be very different from those of your tutors. You may, therefore, have topics pressed upon you that offer too little or perhaps too much scope for meeting dissertation requirements. You may have topics offered with a ready-made solution to which the client is strongly attached. Apart from the high risk that the 'obvious' solution is not the right one, in such cases the client is unlikely to support the diagnostic work that may be required by your course. This is why it is essential that these requirements are made absolutely clear at the outset of discussions, and that your client understands that the topic chosen must be acceptable to you and your project supervisor.

These initial discussions are absolutely crucial to future success. As with any consultancy, building a good relationship with your client is essential. Your client needs to have confidence in your ability to produce something useful without causing any negative effects. You can help to build this confidence by preparing carefully for every meeting with your client, having a clear idea of what it is that you would like to achieve in the meeting, and using your talking and listening skills to the full. You need to be able to have an open and honest conversation about what you need, and to air any concerns either of you may have. If these are addressed at the outset, they can usually be resolved to both of your satisfaction. If they are hidden, only to emerge later, resolution can be difficult or even impossible.

➤ **Ch 9**

Many of your discussions will be with superiors, or with an in-company mentor if you have one, or with your training department. However, do discuss your search for a topic with colleagues at the same level as yourself and subordinates. They may be able to suggest additional possible topics, and can usefully comment on ideas you already have. The following activities are relevant if you are planning to do a project in your own organisation.

16

PROJECTS, THESES AND DISSERTATIONS

Activity 16.8

List three problems of which you have been aware during the last six months, either within your own part of the organisation, or elsewhere:

_____

_____

_____

_____

_____

_____

➤

Use separate pieces of paper to construct multiple-cause diagrams showing contributory factors in each case. Identify common themes between problems, and main causes within each. For each cause or theme, construct a mind map expanding the cause into as many areas as possible. List any project areas suggested by this mapping exercise:

_____

_____

_____

Activity 16.9

Similarly, think of three changes, either within the organisation or to its environment, that you think will affect the way your job will, or should, be done in the next 12 months. List these:

_____

_____

_____

Activity 16.10

Again, use a mind map to explore related areas for each potential change, and consider whether any of these areas or groups of areas might prove a useful starting point for research. List any which have potential:

_____

_____

_____

➤ Ch 8

An example of a mind map and subsequent thoughts on a possible project concerning a perceived absenteeism problem is shown in Figure 16.2. (Figure 8.4 showed how the related form of diagram, a relevance tree, could be used in much the same way.)

It is worth keeping an ideas notebook throughout your studies, jotting down topics and questions that you find particularly interesting. These might occur during lectures, while you are reading, or when doing assignments. This notebook can then provide another starting point for topic generation. It can be particularly helpful if you are doing a more academic dissertation.

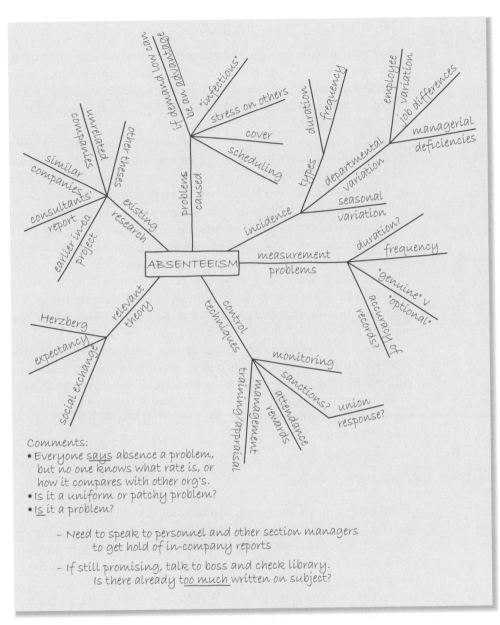

Figure 16.2 Student's mind map and subsequent thoughts on a possible absenteeism topic

Once you have selected a range of possible topic areas, you need to select a small number for further exploration. As your first attempt to assess possibilities against these criteria will necessarily be fairly rough and ready, you should be able to keep anything up to seven possibilities 'live' at this stage. (For work based projects the number will depend to some extent on organisational circumstances.)

The importance of diagnosis

It may seem premature to talk about diagnosis before you have chosen a topic. But, if you are hoping that your project will address a particular organisational issue it is important to understand the importance of diagnosis to the project as a whole, to start the diagnostic process very early, and to continue to refine your diagnosis (or if necessary change it) until you are well into your investigation.

➤ Ch 10   The diagnostic process has already been discussed in relation to addressing problem situations in case studies in Chapter 10. For real organisational problems, with their complexities and unknowns, the diagnostic challenges may be much greater, and the process is likely to take longer. It is all too easy to accept other people's assessment of 'the problem', rather than do the investigation and analysis needed to find the real cause that an intervention needs to address. You need to carry out at least a quick and dirty diagnosis early in your discussions of possible topics with a client. Multiple-cause diagrams such as you drew in Activity 16.8 to suggest potential project areas might be useful here. Doing this diagnosis with the client helps them to understand the process, will give you valuable information and helps build their involvement and commitment. If doing an initial diagnosis this way you need to make clear that further diagnosis will be needed as the project progresses, and that things may change as a result.

Apart from being central to the process of solving complex problems, the diagnostic process is often what allows you to develop and display the conceptual skills and application of theory that projects and dissertations are intended to address. Furthermore, much of the information you will need to collect may be directed towards understanding the nature of the situation. Often, once the situation is fully understood, available options may be fairly clear.

Topic selection

It will be becoming clear by now that topic selection is an iterative process, i.e. one that goes round in circles, progressing a little each time. Until you have invested considerable time and effort in developing your ideas your topic will remain somewhat provisional. For a project on a work-based problem, this means going some way towards doing some diagnosis and planning your research before being sure that this is a suitable topic. If you need to rethink your topic you may feel you have wasted a lot of time and effort. A 'quick and dirty' early assessment may be enough to identify topics as *likely* to turn out to be unsuitable. Even if not, and you do need a major redirection, you will usually have learned a lot from your earlier efforts, and the redirected investigation will benefit.

It makes sense to do a very broad-brush evaluation of a number of projects in parallel, before proceeding to a more detailed evaluation of a smaller number. Part of this evaluation may be a very hasty provisional diagnosis. After this you will be in a better position to select the option with which to proceed. If you run with enough options at each stage you will have a reasonable chance of at least one looking promising by the end of the more detailed pass. Then, even if a number of possibilities turn out to be unsuitable, you will have made progress at each stage.

Figure 16.3 shows a basic algorithm for project choice. This shows the process as a series of yes/no decisions for a single topic, which, together with a process of refinement

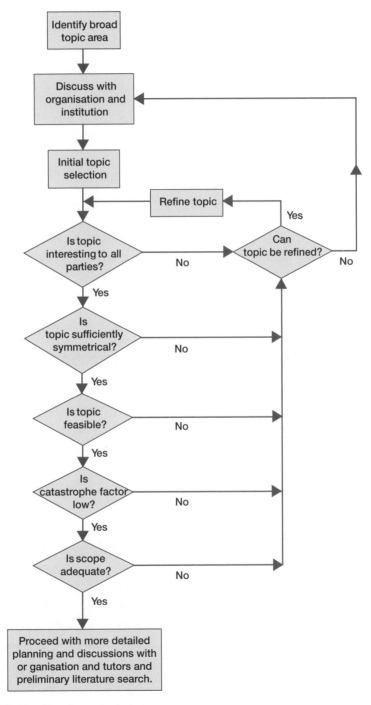

Figure 16.3 Algorithm for project choice

if possible, will enable a single topic to be developed into something that is at least a possibility, or else to be rejected.

If using the suggested broad-brush, multi-topic approach, you would need to use the algorithm on each topic, but of course several topics could be discussed in a single meeting with a potential client.

An alternative approach, or one that could be used to select from those topics that survived the algorithmic approach, would be to construct a *Which?*-type diagram (*see* Figure 16.4), in which you list possible topics and rate them, say from one to five, on each of the criteria that you are using, totalling the points for each option. If you are using such a table *without* using the algorithm first, then you would need a symbol for 'fails to meet criterion', say X. Any option with one or more Xs would be rejected, regardless of its 'point' rating.

➤ Ch 10

Two high-risk factors are real-time dependence and political sensitivity. If a topic depends upon something happening in real time, avoid it if there is any risk at all that time slippage might occur. It is far, far safer to investigate a situation that already exists.

Political sensitivities are harder to spot. Political structures within an organisation may not be immediately obvious, and may change. Think carefully about whether your potential findings could be perceived as a threat by anyone. If so, could this result in difficulties being put in your way at some point during your investigation? Are there any stakeholders with the power to block access to information or resources, or even to close down your project? If so, you need to be sure of their support, or at least neutrality.

For your second, slightly less 'quick and dirty' pass you will need to put much more detailed thought into planning. It is only once you have started to develop an idea into a research project that you will be able to see how feasible it is likely to be, given the constraints under which you will be working.

At this stage you will need to be clear, for each possible topic, who would be your client within the organisation. You will need to have detailed discussions with each client, in order to clarify their objectives for the research, and the resources and other support that they could make available to you for your research.

Criteria	Topic 1	Topic 2	Topic 3	Etc.	
Project interests me	●●	●●●●	●●●●●		
Client supports project	●●●	●●	●●●		
Adequate breadth of topic	●●	●●●	●●●●●		
Availability of resources	●●●●	●●	●●●		
Absence of political sensitivity	●	●●●	✕		
Low reliance on real-time events	●	●●●	●		
Etc.					

Figure 16.4 Example of part of a '*Which?*'-type project evaluation table

You will also need to have thought fairly seriously about your research method. It can be extremely helpful to have a draft written brief from your client at this stage. But make it very clear, if so, that you are still refining plans and may need to amend the brief (by mutual agreement) before it is finalised. If you are working with more than one possibility, this will be more obvious.

Once your client's objectives are clearly understood, check these with your project supervisor to ensure that a brief of this kind would also allow you to meet institutional objectives. You can then analyse the possible topics in more depth. A useful framework for this analysis is to aim to produce an outline proposal for each possible topic. This would need to be a rough draft of the proposal you might write for your chosen topic but with less detail. The features are described in the next section. Quick and dirty proposals like this can be really good at highlighting risks or difficulties so can help you choose the best topic from your shortlist. To decide upon a final topic in which to invest your hundreds of hours of work you need to have a good idea already about how the possibilities are likely to compare on the issues your proposal will cover, as discussed below.

'Originality' is seldom an issue with projects at this level. While good research *is* original in the sense of covering new theoretical or experimental ground – and a PhD thesis would be expected to show considerable originality – this criterion is less important for Master's research. Obviously, you would not meet your stakeholders' objectives merely by repeating research already carried out or plagiarising someone else's discussion of methodology, but theoretical originality is not usually required. The narrow constraints under which you will be operating make it unlikely (though not impossible) that you will be able to devise and demonstrate some totally new management theory. An MBA or specialist management-related project is much better seen as showing creative use of existing theory and techniques to solve a real organisational problem, and this chapter is slanted towards this type of research. A more academic dissertation might address an outstanding question in the literature by drawing together secondary sources not previously related in this way.

▶ Ch 13

If your final choice of option seems rather less than theoretically revolutionary, but your supervisor is happy with it, relax. You are more likely to succeed by attempting something feasible, than by being over-ambitious. There will be sufficient challenge in applying existing theory to produce a valid answer to a real problem.

Responsibilities and ethics

Research is carried out with the intention of making a difference to something, but it can have unintentional, as well as intended impacts. Think back to your earlier consideration of stakeholders in your research. Whenever you do something that can affect others, ethical issues arise. Your own set of values about what is right and wrong will be relevant, as well as the values of those around you. When you are in a position of unequal power for some reason, these issues become more obvious – the greater the power imbalance, the greater the capacity to do harm. (If you saw two children tussling on the school playground you might not be too concerned. If one was twice the size of the other, you would probably feel it was very wrong.)

You may not think that you have much influence when doing a project, but you usually have. This section is intended to sharpen your awareness of your obligations and responsibilities. As your university will probably require you to obtain approval for your research from its research ethics committee, you need to consider potential ethical issues before finalising your proposal.

One way of thinking about your obligations and responsibilities is to classify them. For example, you might think in terms of the following types of obligation:

- Legal – a society's laws apply when you are doing research as much as at any other time.

- Professional – professional institutions, including those relating to both management and consultancy provide ethical guidelines which members are expected to follow.

- Your university's research ethics policy – you will normally need to demonstrate that you comply with this by filling in the relevant ethics approval form, so it is worth familiarising yourself with the policy at an early stage.

- Cultural – while legal obligations are explicit, cultural norms set implicit rules, a particular problem if you are working within more than one culture.

- Personal – your own internalised set of values and ideas of right and wrong – the sorts of values which are important and relevant to research in a Western culture include honesty (to yourself and others), respect, loyalty, trust and doing no harm to others.

In any project as well as making sure that you are acting legally and complying with all relevant policies and codes, it is important to think about how your values translate into good research practice. A useful approach here is to consider your potential influence on the stakeholders in your project (see Figure 16.1), and any way in which it might do them harm.

Activity 16.11

Think about *all* the stakeholders in the project(s) you are considering. Consider what responsibilities you might have to each, and any potential for doing harm, and write these down. (If you are doing a group project, compare your list with those of team members.) You may also like to compare your list with Table 16.1. Don't look at this until after you have thought seriously about your own project. Every project is different, so your list may justifiably bear little relation to the table. However, if this is the case, think carefully about any differences in case they suggest additions or alterations to your own view. Many of the stakeholders shown are relevant to a significant proportion of projects.

You may have found it difficult to see yourself as having power, but the mere association with a university, and the use of the word 'research' may cause some people to revere your education, and incline them to believe anything you say. (Consultants, especially those charging high fees, have similar 'expert' power.) You will also be in possession of 'privileged' information, given in confidence. It is surprisingly easy to pass on something interesting without thinking, or realising that your listener might be able to identify an employee even if you have been careful not to mention their name.

You might cause damage:

- to your tutor's reputation if you hand in incompetent work;
- to the reputation of your university if you are not seen to be acting responsibly and professionally;
- to interviewees if you pass on something they said in confidence;
- to an organisational client if you make recommendations that go beyond what your evidence supports, and they follow them in good faith;
- to other researchers if you misrepresent your findings at a conference or in a publication, or fail to give them credit for their ideas.

You may have thought about responsibilities to clients and those providing information for their research, but Table 16.1 includes stakeholders you may not have thought of – fellow group members, your family and friends, and most importantly, yourself! The table makes general points. Once you have a project in mind you can usefully consider specific stakeholders in that project, their stake in the project, potential risks, and actions you need to take to minimise risk.

In planning your research and data collection you need to consider the potential impact of your research, particularly on your subjects in order to complete an ethics form for your organisation and/or university ethics committee. Honesty, openness, lack of coercion and confidentiality are key ethical issues, as is privacy, if you are proposing to initiate contact with individuals. Your research should not cause harm or distress to anyone involved, or embarrassment of any kind to subjects or stakeholders. Pressure should not be exerted to gain participation or access to information. Concealing the purpose of the research as a whole, or of a specific interview or observation, may not be ethical. Breaking a promise of confidentiality certainly is *not* ethical. If you have promised that respondents or organisations will not be identifiable from your report, then you need to be absolutely certain that no clues to their identity are left. And if you have made other promises, such as to provide a copy of the ultimate findings, you need to follow through on this.

It is in everyone's interests that you behave ethically at all times, and with courtesy and professionalism. Your institution may rely on support from the sponsoring organisation in other ways. Your organisational sponsor needs to feel confident that your findings can be relied upon. Those in the organisation who are cooperating in providing information need to feel that they can trust you to treat their answers in ways that confidence will not be reached and harm come to them. Above all your own professionalism (and any professional institution to which you belong) rests on ethical behaviour.

Table 16.1 General ethical issues relating to stakeholders in a project

Potential Stakeholder	Responsibilities	Implications
You!	To do no harm to your health, state of mind, reputation or your future.	Avoid anything likely to be highly stressful, conflict with your values, or require every waking minute to complete.
Family and friends	To spare some time/energy for their needs. If a family firm is your client, client issue need to be considered too.	As above! Plus remember that they do have needs, and maintain communication with them even if you are stressed out etc.
Fellow group members	To contribute fully to the shared work, and support the team as a whole.	Be on time for meetings, do work as promised, and to schedule, support other group members if they encounter difficulties, show your appreciation of their contributions
Tutor	To do a worthwhile project to a competent standard.	Meet and submit work as agreed. Consider and act on feedback and suggestions. Put in the time and effort to do the best work of which you are capable.
Wider university	To bring credit rather than disrepute to the university	Consider the potential for bad publicity from anything you do (or say) and act carefully in the light of this.
Client	To act professionally, do nothing to damage their reputation, treat them with respect and deliver something of value.	Be careful to make your own – and the project's – limitations clear, do not agree to anything about which you have misgivings, let them know as soon as anything goes adrift so that you can agree corrective action together.
Subjects	To use their time to good effect, cause them no harm, honour any promises.	Ensure that subjects know what they are agreeing to. Be punctual and use no more time than you have said for interviews etc., observe total confidentiality over anything said in interview, give copy of results if promised.
Other researchers	To use their work in full understanding. To make sure that anything you publish makes only justified claims.	Report your work honestly. Reference sources of ideas and data.

Your formal proposal(s)

Once you are reasonably confident in your choice you will normally be required to submit a formal proposal. This allows your supervisor to check that you are setting out on a path that is likely to lead to a successful dissertation. It also serves (perhaps slightly modified) as an agreement between you and your organisational client. This formal agreement may provide necessary protection if circumstances or personnel change. The content of these proposals should be broadly similar, but you might want to provide a slightly different version for each purpose.

Your tutor will want your proposal to convince them that the project is worth doing (for you and for the client), that you are going about it in a sensible way, that you are aware of – and will be using – relevant theory, and that it is feasible within the time and resources available.

When agreeing a project brief with a client it is important to make absolutely clear – and gain agreement to – what it is that you will deliver and when, and the resources and any other support that the client is agreeing to provide.

When I am the client myself I also want to be convinced that the potential consultant has the *ability* to deliver a result that will meet my needs, so when drafting the brief think about how you can build confidence with the way the brief is presented.

Look at your institution's requirements first. Supervisors typically ask for proposals 1000–1500 words long, but make sure that you know and observe your own institution's word limit.

The proposal for your supervisor should aim to cover:

- **Issue description** – you need to give the background to the issue and its context, and establish its significance.
- **Project aim** – you need to make clear the purpose of the project, its scope and its limitations – this is where thinking in terms of research questions is a useful start to developing more concrete and SMART project objectives.
- **Value to the organisation** – it is important to establish the potential the project has to help the organisation.
- **Value to the researcher** – it is important that any project that forms part of an MBA or similar also offers scope for professional development.
- **Likely project design** – you need to show that the research methods you propose are appropriate and that timescale and the skills likely to be employed are feasible.
- **Data requirements** – you need to establish the information that will be needed, how this will be obtained and what analysis will be carried out.
- **Theoretical relevance** – a practically oriented MBA project needs to show that it has benefited from relevant theory; a more academic dissertation may need to show not only in-depth familiarity with relevant theory but some way of testing it.

Normally there will be some scope to alter and develop this proposal with your supervisor as the project develops, but you should not depart from it – or from your client brief – without discussion and approval.

This reinforces the importance of topic selection. Much of your early work will have involved detailed consideration of possible topics and methods of carrying out the research to answer whatever question the topic poses and exploring sources of possibly relevant data. But, unless you have thought in some detail about these topics at the

16

PROJECTS, THESES AND DISSERTATIONS

selection stage, your proposal may be rejected. Worse, it may be accepted only for you to hit an unexpected block in mid-project.

Once you have a project proposal that is acceptable to your supervisor and your client (and of interest to yourself), but before your proposal has been formally accepted by your university, formalise your agreement with your organisational client. Written agreement to the brief, with its clear statement of commitments on both sides, may seem unnecessarily legalistic, but can provide vital future protection. Your client may be wholeheartedly behind your proposal, but there is no guarantee that your client will remain in a position to support you throughout your project. Personnel move, and your client's replacement might be less sympathetic to your aims, or other organisational circumstances may change.

A written agreement will not prevent such problems but can strengthen your case for continued support. It also protects you against any claims that your research is in some sense a failure because it fails to meet the objectives of the complainant. If these were not part of your written agreement, and you have delivered everything that was, you have useful evidence that you have not failed. Even if you hit no such snags, the agreed brief will serve as a useful reference point for yourself, a standard against which you can test any necessary modifications to your plans.

Literature search

Whatever the type of project you are doing, you are likely to need to make *several* searches of relevant literature. The first, fairly superficial search will have helped you identify potential topics. A second search will have informed your selection from among these. As you start to define your topic more narrowly you will need to do more focused, 'in-depth' searches. You will need first to clarify your research question. Then you will need to work out how to approach your own research (this is likely to include searching the literature on both the topic and research methodology). Finally, it is important to set your research in context when writing your report – your investigation needs to be interpreted in the light of what others have done and found in the area.

How far you need to go will depend upon the type of project you are undertaking. The closer you move to the 'academic' end of the spectrum, the more substantial will be the expected literature review part of your dissertation. Similarly, more in-depth discussion will be expected of how your findings relate to this literature. How far you *can* go will depend upon the resources at your disposal.

➤ Ch 7   You should by now be developing the relevant skills (discussed in Chapter 7) in order to do well in your assignments. (If not, you will need to revisit that chapter and work carefully through the relevant sections, including those on referencing and bibliographic software.) Now you will be applying these skills at a higher level: there will be less guidance on what to look for and where, and you will need to be far more critical in your reading. There will usually be thousands more potential sources than you will have time to use, so choosing those most useful for your purpose will be crucial, and justifying that choice in your report will also be important.

Parameters and keywords

Chapter 7 introduced the idea of keywords, but now they are likely to become more important. First, decide on some parameters to help define your search area. You will probably need to know:

- the broad subject area, e.g. marketing, motivation, health and safety legislation;
- the language of your search. Note that American and English are different languages! Many words are either completely different (car/automobile) or spelt differently (behaviour/behavior). This is important in electronic searching;
- the business sector in which you are interested, e.g. manufacturing, not-for-profit, defence;
- how far back you want to search, e.g. five years;
- the type of literature you want to search, e.g. refereed journals only, government publications.

These parameters will help you generate a list of *keywords* to drive your search. These are the words you will look up in indexes, or use with an online search engine. Think about the sorts of words that authors might have used in the title of the kind of article you want to read, together with the names of significant researchers in the area. A recent review article can be really helpful here, as can the bibliography of a past dissertation in a similar area. Ask your tutors for suggestions. See if Wikipedia can suggest relevant words. Try brainstorming possible keywords or phrases with fellow students or colleagues. Once you have one word or phrase you can use that to generate other possible terms. Suppose you have used a keyword and found a useful-sounding item on the database. If you then display the full entry, it normally will show you 'subject headings' or 'descriptors', or some other term relating to the index terms used. Among these may well be other potentially useful keywords. Looking at the references at the end of the paper may suggest others.

➤ Ch 8   Another good technique is to construct a relevance tree (*see* Figure 8.4). As you draw this, teasing out possible sub-areas, you will be able to think about which are most likely to become the main focus of your research. It can help to distinguish the 'immediate' from the 'important', and note the latter as something to work on later.

You can use such a relevance tree as a working document. As you read, you will inevitably refine your thinking about your topic. Update your relevance tree to reflect different ways of looking at the subject that emerge, or new issues that emerge as potentially important.

Types of sources

Sources can be thought of as primary, secondary or tertiary. A primary source is one where a work (or set of data) appears for the first time. Primary sources include reports, conference proceedings, theses, some government publications, company reports, and unpublished manuscripts such as letters or committee papers. They may be difficult to locate, and not all dissertations will need to make use of them.

Secondary sources are more accessible, and likely to form an important part of the literature you search. Journals, particularly academic refereed journals (print or electronic), which offer a degree of 'quality assurance', are likely to be crucial. Books, professional journals, and government publications are other good secondary sources. When you are starting your literature search, recent review articles considering a number of papers in your topic may be particularly helpful in highlighting outstanding questions or discrepancies you might explore. Although such reviews are derived from secondary sources they are normally considered as secondary sources themselves.

Tertiary sources, primarily indexes, abstracts and catalogues, are designed to help you locate other sources, or to give you an introduction or overview of a topic. These are likely to be your starting point, via your library and/or the Internet.

Using tertiary sources

Indexes. Enter a keyword (subject or author name) and the index will suggest relevant journal articles or other sources, depending on what is indexed, giving you the full reference for each. As well as book indexes and indexes to academic journals, there are online indexes to newspapers and business reports which you may find useful, together with searchable archives of newspapers.

Abstracts are indexes that give you not only the reference, but also a brief outline of the content of the article. This may enable you to decide that you do not need to look at the full article!

Citation indexes are particularly useful if you find a relevant article and want to know how the ideas in it have developed since. A citation index will tell you all the subsequent articles that have referred to that original. (The reference list at the end of the original will give you all the papers that the author used, so between the two you should have good coverage right up to the present.) Google Scholar gives a 'cited by *nnn*' number under each entry, which gives an idea of how influential a paper has been. Clicking on this will give details of all these citations. Looking at their titles and perhaps their own 'cited by' lists can further expand your stock of potential keywords.

Link terms and logic

These link terms, derived from Boolean logic, allow you to narrow your search.[1] Google uses AND, OR and NOT – it is important to use capitals. (Some systems use '+' and '–' to indicate the same thing, or some other convention.) Figure 16.5 is a pictorial representation of the relationship between these terms. Thus, to take the example shown in Figure 16.5, you could ask for 'pay AND appraisal' and be offered only references containing both terms, a much shorter list than either 'pay' or 'appraisal' alone. Pay OR appraisal would generate the longest list (Google assumes you mean 'AND' if you mention two words, so you do not need to specify.) Asking for 'appraisal NOT financial' might spare you hundreds of references on financial appraisal, but still give you a lot of other kinds of appraisal. You might wish to use OR if alternative terms are used for the topic in question, e.g. 'downsizing OR redundancy'.

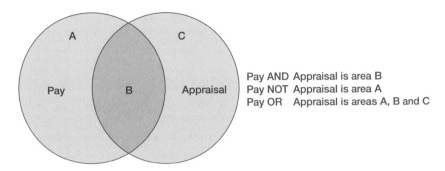

Figure 16.5 The Boolean logic of searches

If you want to search for a particular phrase put the whole phrase in quotes e.g. 'downsizing during the 2009 recession'.

If you want to search on several terms but some terms are more important than others, put the more important part of the instruction in brackets. Thus, if your main interest was in downsizing and recession and the 2009 aspect was interesting but less important (downsizing AND recession) AND 2009.

A general online search can throw up a large proportion of commercial sites, mostly of little value for academic purposes. Google Scholar, your library's databases, or indexes and abstracts can be a more efficient route. They were designed with academic user needs in mind, and tend to include only reputable sources.

As well as indexes to academic journals there are online indexes to newspapers and business reports that you may find useful, together with searchable archives of newspapers.

Catalogues, whether provided by libraries, publishers or booksellers, can be extremely useful. Examples include the British Library Public Catalogue, Pearson's own website, and Amazon's UK and US sites. (Sample URLs are given at the end of the chapter. For a fuller list, *see* Saunders *et al.,* 2009.)

Using what you have found

In order to make good use of what you have found, both immediately and later when writing your report, you need to keep your immediate purpose clearly in mind, as well as potential future uses of that source. Key points to remember from Chapter 7 include the need to:

➤ Ch 7

- take careful notes, indicating any direct quotations to avoid plagiarism – notes should include ideas prompted by sources, possible relationships to other ideas and/or sources and any questions suggested by your reading;

- organise your notes and copies of documents in a way that will allow easy reference later on, even if your topic focus shifts;

- keep full details of references with all notes and copies;

- use bibliographic software to allow for easy organisation and access.

An overall early aim when reviewing literature is to establish current understanding of an area, showing why your research question is worthy of attention. Later you will be searching for anything that casts light on the question and enables you to focus on what is particularly important.

You may consider your literature search as something you need as a chapter for your final report. While this is one use, it is far from the only one. You will need to go back to the literature time and time again to help you with every stage of your research. And while the 'literature search' chapter will indeed be a significant use, you will probably need to refer to parts of the literature in most chapters. Such references will be particularly important in your discussion and conclusions sections. Here you will be aiming to show the significance of your own findings in relation to those of others, and may be able to draw on other authors in support of your recommendations. Being aware of these uses while you read will enable you to take more useful notes.

You may find it helpful to use the following checklist for evaluating your review (derived from Saunders *et al.*, 2009).

Literature review evaluation checklist

• Does your review start at a more general level before narrowing down?	❏
• Is it clear how the research covered relates to your research question and objectives?	❏
• Have you covered the main relevant theories?	❏
• Have you covered at least a representative sample of the relevant literature on the topic?	❏
• Have you highlighted issues where your project will provide new insights?	❏
• Have you included up-to-date literature?	❏
• Is your evaluation of the literature objective and balanced?	❏
• Have you clearly justified your own ideas?	❏
• Is the review coherent and cohesive?	❏
• Does it lead clearly into subsequent sections of your report?	❏

Avoiding plagiarism

➤ Chs 7, 13

The importance of avoiding plagiarism was stressed in Chapters 7 and 13, but it seems particularly common in project reports and dissertations. It is tragic when otherwise successful students fail to gain their Master's because they are found guilty of deliberate – or even inadvertent – plagiarism. So remember: plagiarism is any attempt to pass off the writing of others as your own. In academic circles this is seen as theft of intellectual property and deceit, and is severely penalised. Even when paraphrasing you need to be very careful to make a sufficient change and to refer to your source. If you have any doubts about what is and is not plagiarism, revisit the relevant chapters, consult your university's guidance, and look at the suggested online tutorial resource. Any plagiarism is likely to be detected by university software, and heavily penalised.

So draw together and critique several authors, rather than relying on a single text. Use your own words, and try to develop new points. Mere reproduction or rephrasing of other people's words does not demonstrate understanding, and certainly does not display the critical and evaluative skills that dissertations are designed to test.

Primary data collection

Before thinking about research methods it helps to have an understanding of some of the commonest approaches to collecting primary data. Three approaches are popular with Master's students, though there are others. You will need to read a text devoted to management research, or follow a research methods course to find more about these. As part of a 'quick and dirty' iteration, it helps to consider some of the practical issues involved in gathering your own data. I shall look at interviews, questionnaires and focus groups as these are frequently used in the context of a dissertation. Note, however, that these may not be appropriate, or only marginally so, for your own chosen topic.

Interviewing for information

➤ Ch 9

One of the most popular ways of collecting information is to conduct a series of interviews. This requires you to use the talking and listening skills developed earlier, but you need additionally to know a little about the potential hazards of collecting data in this way.

Interviewing may seem simple. You merely ask some questions, either standard questions decided beforehand or even anything that occurs to you on the spur of the moment. Provided these fall under a set of fairly broad headings, this can be called a 'semi-structured' interview. You record the results, analyse them and you have the answer to your research question. Sadly, this approach may not produce useful data. You can learn a great deal from merely talking to people, provided you listen carefully. But it is difficult to put together what each person tells you and make collective sense of it. There is also a possibility that interviewees will misunderstand your questions, or tell you only what they think you want to hear. Even if their answers are valid, you may misunderstand them. Even worse, you may *hear* only what you want to hear, that which fits in with your preconceptions and biases.

Skilful interviewing rests not only on basic talking and listening skills but also on the ability to:

- formulate unambiguous questions that do not indicate, even subtly, the 'right' answer;
- avoid giving any other hints as to what you want;

16

PROJECTS, THESES AND DISSERTATIONS

- use a style that encourages a person to answer questions freely and to the best of their ability;
- probe and clarify if the answer is not sufficiently full or clear;
- record interviewees' answers accurately for subsequent analysis;
- analyse them in a way that allows you to draw justifiable conclusions.

As ever, you also need to be absolutely clear about what it is that you want to know. And you need to have thought about the number of people to ask and how to choose them, given the question that your project is trying to answer.

Interview types

Before you can decide who, and how many to interview, you need to think about the type of interview that best suits your purpose:

- **Structured** interviews are those where you work out a set of questions before you start and ask each interviewee exactly the same questions, in the same order, and even in the same tone of voice, so as not to introduce accidental bias to your results.
- **Semi-structured** interviews are those where you 'know what you want to know', that is, you have a set of themes, issues or topics that you want to explore. But you 'go with the flow' to some extent, approaching these issues in an order that seems appropriate, given the way the conversation is going, dropping issues that seem inappropriate with a particular respondent and adding others that the conversation suggests may be important.
- **Unstructured** or in-depth interviews are even more informal and non-standardised. The interviewee is given free rein to talk about a topic in depth.

The appropriate type of interview will depend both on what you are trying to find out and on where you are in your investigation. At an early stage, while your thoughts are developing, unstructured interviews are useful for finding issues that seem to be important to the people concerned and relationships that seem to exist between these issues. Having this information could help you to formulate a set of questions for a structured interview. While you can gain strong impressions from such interviews, and they may uncover whole areas you had not seen as relevant, they are very difficult to analyse in any systematic way.

If you want to be able to describe tendencies or patterns in a group of responses, structured interviews tend to be preferred. They allow you to compare the responses of different groups to the same questions and explore whether responses to one set of questions are related to responses to others. Analysis is usually easy: there is normally only a limited range of answers to any of these questions. You may be able to code answers into predetermined categories while the person is talking. Several people can do the interviewing and their sets of answers are easily amalgamated. A structured interview is really a questionnaire that is administered face to face. It has all the advantages of a questionnaire (*see* the next section, where question design is discussed). Additionally you get a higher response rate, and can persist in getting answers to *all* the questions. (Online or postal questionnaires are often ignored, or only partially answered.) For example, a senior manager may agree to be interviewed, but might throw away a questionnaire.

Despite the rather cynical comment earlier, semi-structured interviews can be extremely useful. For example, if you are trying to find out *why* a structured interview gives you certain patterns, you are likely to need a semi-structured interview. Suppose you had used a questionnaire to find out how satisfied people were with their jobs and whether they had applied for jobs elsewhere. You might have found that in most departments people were satisfied, but in two they were not. In one of these unhappy departments everyone was applying for jobs elsewhere, in the other they were not. To find out both why they were unhappy and why they were behaving differently with respect to other jobs, a semi-structured interview could be useful. It gives you the flexibility to probe for more information until you understand what is going on. You may also pick up on non-verbal cues that suggest the need for probing (though be careful if a person starts to look uncomfortable).

Types of question

The exact way in which you phrase your question can have a significant effect on the answers you are given by the interviewee. For semi-structured and unstructured interviews you will need to rely on three main types of question: open, probing and closed.

Open questions

Open questions allow the interviewee to decide what it is important to include in an answer. Questions that are *too* open can produce long and sometimes irrelevant answers. 'What do you think about the recent redundancies?' might produce anything from a rant about the government to a sob story about a mate with a big family who has been made redundant and is almost suicidal. Neither might help you answer your research question.

'What methods have your organisation used to make people redundant?' would produce a more focused answer (assuming that it was methods that interested you). 'What', 'who', 'when', 'where', 'why' and 'how' are among the words useful for open questions.

> **For effective interviewing:**
>
> - use active listening
> - set the scene carefully
> - ask simple, neutral questions
> - probe if necessary
> - minimise closed questions
> - close the interview carefully
> - record data immediately.

Closed questions

Closed questions are those that tend to generate a 'yes' or 'no' answer: for example, 'Were recent redundancies handled well?' This type of question might be very useful either as a starting point, or as a follow-up to clarify your understanding. 'So on balance do you think that the methods chosen were appropriate?' could be useful as a check on your understanding of part of an answer to a more open question. Use such questions sparingly, though. If you use closed questions too early you risk closing a topic before you have found out what you want. If you use them too often your interviewee will tend to give shorter and shorter answers.

Probing

Probing questions are used to explore answers in more depth. If you want to know more than the interviewee has given in an answer, you can say something like: 'That's interesting. Could you tell me more about the reasons for ...?' or '... why the relationship between ...?' or whatever it is that you wish to be expanded. Probes are very useful if you realise that you have inadvertently asked a closed question!

Once you have selected your respondents, gained their agreement, know what you want to find out, and the sorts of questions you need to ask, there are some basic points to note. These will help you to generate valid data.

Guidelines for interviewing

- Practise active listening and observe body language.

- Manage the start of the interview very carefully – it is crucial to its success. You need to make the person feel comfortable. Thank them for their help and explain again the purpose of the interview and how long it is likely to take. You need to stress confidentiality, making clear whether anyone else will have access to the results of the interview. It usually helps to make clear that the interviewee will not be identifiable in the final report (unless of course they have agreed to be identified). You need to indicate what will happen to the results of your investigation. It is helpful, too, to give an idea of the sort of responses you want (e.g. brief or more discursive, immediate or considered). And you need to explain how you are recording answers (normally notes or tape recorder) and make sure that the person is happy with this.

- Keep questions as short and as simple as possible. If you roll three complex questions into one, it will be hard for your interviewee to make sense of what is required. It will also be hard for you to make sense of what they say! Also, if your question is rambling, your respondents will tend to follow your lead and speak at great length without saying very much. This makes both recording and analysis difficult.

- Use language that your interviewee will understand. It is pointless to use jargon or over-intellectual language with people who are unused to such words.

- Ask neutral questions. It is extremely easy to bias answers by using negatively or positively loaded words in describing some of the options.

- Use closed questions sparingly, only when you mean to.

- Start with questions that the interviewee will find easy, interesting and non-threatening. This will allow them to settle and to feel comfortable with you. Later in the interview you can ask more challenging questions, or touch on sensitive issues, with a good chance of getting a valid response. These sensitive questions might elicit very little early in an interview.

- Conclude by thanking the interviewee and giving them the chance to raise any concerns they may have as a result of the interview.

● Record your data as soon as possible after the interview. If you have made notes, sort them out and do any necessary classifying of responses while the interview is still fresh. If you are making audio recordings, do not let these accumulate. Transcribing/analysing takes ages and is usually best done as you go along. You may wish to modify later interviews in the light of early responses (though take care not to make later answers impossible to compare with earlier ones). It is therefore important that as soon as you finish, you think about how the interview has gone. Note any problems and new thoughts that it prompted that seem important, particularly if you are near the start of your interviewing programme. A research diary is useful for this.

(This is available on the companion **website**.)

16

Focus groups

Thus far the discussion has covered interviews with individuals. If you want to gather information from a group of people, focus groups are helpful. Many organisations (including political parties) and their marketers use this technique, particularly as a way of finding out what is important to customers or potential customers.

To hold a focus group, assemble a small group (usually 6–10 people) whose views are relevant to your research. The group is asked to discuss your chosen topic. The aim is to allow group members to develop their own ideas through unstructured interaction. This can throw up ideas that the research has not considered, and show that other issues are more, or less, important than anticipated.

As the researcher, you facilitate the group. This should be a fairly passive role once the topic has been introduced. You are trying merely to encourage interaction within the group, not to steer it. If the discussion flags, you can ask supplementary questions such as 'What about …?' If one person dominates, you may need to gently subdue them. If some people do not contribute you may need to encourage them. If the discussion veers totally off the point, you may need to gently redirect it, but resist acting as chair. If you steer the discussion too firmly this will seriously reduce your chances of finding out anything that you do not already know. In industry, focus groups are often run by trained psychologists, but the group-working skills you developed in Chapter 9 should help you to make a reasonable job of it.

➤ Ch 9

You will need to keep a careful record of the discussion for later analysis. A video or audio recording is ideal, supplemented with written notes, or the notes may be enough. If at all possible, find someone to help you with this. It is very hard to take adequate notes while doing a good job of facilitation.

Focus groups can be extremely useful at the start of a project, when you are trying to identify important issues or research questions. But they have the same drawback as informal interviews. The sample is likely to be too small for reliable conclusions. The process of making sense of what was said is also highly subjective, with the researcher struggling to extract meaning from a fairly free-ranging discussion. Normally you will need to build on your focus group findings with a more systematic investigation.

Questionnaires

Surveys requiring respondents to complete a questionnaire are a popular way of collecting information for all sorts of purposes. You may have received various 'market research' questionnaires through the post or been sent a questionnaire after you bought something or made use of a service. While you can include open-ended questions, you cannot probe or clarify open responses, which can make their analysis quite difficult. The main strength of questionnaires is that they allow you to identify and describe the extent of variation in answers on particular topics and to look for relationships between positions on one set of questions and positions on another. Thus, you could use a survey to establish factual things like the educational qualifications of users of a particular sports facility, or frequency of usage, or attitudinal aspects such as their satisfaction with the various sports on offer. You could also look for relationships, such as between level of education and preferred sport and/or satisfaction levels.

Questionnaire design is crucial, particularly if the respondents are supposed to fill in the questionnaire themselves. (Sometimes questionnaires are administered over the phone or face to face in a structured interview.) You need to have a very clear idea of what you need to know, to ask it in a totally unambiguous way and to make clear how the respondent is to reply.

Activity 16.12

Imagine that you work in a medical centre and you want to collect information from patients on their alcohol usage. Think about the way in which you and people you know might respond to the following questions and how much information this is likely to give you. If possible, ask a few people, using only one of the questions below, followed by informal discussion to check what it means, then ask others all three, in the order shown.

A. Does alcohol play a part in your life?   _____

B. Would you describe yourself as a light, moderate or heavy drinker?   _____

C. How many drinks do you have a week on average? (Count a half pint
    of beer, one small glass of wine or a single of spirits as '1')   _____

| 0–1 | 2–3 | 4–7 | 8–14 | 15–21 | 22–35 | 36–42 | 43+ |

You need to be very careful in interpreting answers, as your follow-up discussion may have shown. Question A (taken from a real questionnaire) presumably elicited both 'yes' and 'no' from people with very similar levels of drinking. B may well have elicited some 'light' responses from people who consume rather more than those who see themselves as 'moderate' drinkers – they may be comparing themselves to very different sets of friends. The range of possible drinking levels given in C may make it easier for people to admit to drinking, say, 22 units than if the scale had stopped at 22+. In the first case they would appear well within the range on offer, in the second at the extreme. For areas that are often under-reported, like drinking and smoking levels, this may be an important consideration.

You can now see why it is important to *pilot* a questionnaire with a small number of people – try it out and then look at the answers that are given. Do some questions produce the same answer from everybody? If so, they may not be generating much information. Are some questions often omitted? This may be because people do not realise that they must turn the page, the question looks like part of the instruction, or because it is not clear what the question means or how to answer it. Talk to those who filled out the questionnaire about whether they had difficulty with any of the questions and probe the meaning of their answers to check that you will be interpreting them correctly. Check, too, that your layout and the way the questions are to be answered make it as easy as possible to analyse the results.

Response rates

It is really important to get a reasonable response rate. What constitutes reasonable will depend on the size of your sample, the complexity of the analysis you want to do and the randomness or otherwise of the 'sample within a sample', those people who *do* fill in the questionnaire.

Activity 16.13

Suppose that you send a questionnaire to 100 people. You write a pleasant covering letter, explaining what you are doing and why, as well as why their participation is important. You stress that responses will be treated confidentially. But you still receive only 10 replies.

Draw on your own experience of questionnaires to suggest reasons for people not replying, and consider what this means about the usefulness of the 10 you get back. Think too about how you might be able to increase the response rate. If possible, discuss this in a group, drawing on your own responses to questionnaires you have received.

You probably came up with reasons such as 'questionnaire looked too long and time consuming', 'first few questions were difficult/intrusive/boring/incomprehensible so didn't go further', 'why should I pay for a stamp to give them information?', 'meant to but somehow didn't get around to it' and so on. The best way of increasing the response rate will depend on the reasons – a well-designed, appealing questionnaire will address the first two, use of email or a stamped addressed envelope the third. Small incentives such as a prize for the lucky reply and a better prize if the questionnaire is returned within seven days will address two reasons, and reminders are also helpful.

It is vital that you *do* ensure a better response rate than this. If you send out 100 questionnaires and get 10 back, you will have very little data to analyse. Worse, you will not know if the 10 were reasonably typical of the 100, or the only 10 who were different in some significant way. For example, it might be that the only people who reply to a questionnaire about the quality of nursing care during a recent hospital stay are the tiny minority who had a really bad experience and are still angry enough to want to tell someone about this when the questionnaire arrives. If you assumed they were typical, you could be seriously misled about the quality of care that most patients at the hospital receive.

If you use questionnaires, you are facing a minefield. Plan to spend some time reading about questionnaire design and sampling, or consult an expert, before designing your questionnaire, and never use a questionnaire without first piloting it. Try it out on several people and afterwards ask them to interpret their answers, and comment on any uncertainties or difficulties they had in answering any questions.

Research methodology and approach

Many dissertations have a 'methodology' section. Strictly speaking, 'methodology' is the theory of how research should be undertaken. It includes the theoretical and philosophical assumptions on which the research is based and what these assumptions mean for choice of approach. Thus, a full 'methodology' section would discuss your beliefs about the nature of reality (ontology) and about how knowledge is generated (epistemology). It would argue your position on the extent to which researchers are impartial observers of 'fact' or seeking to make sense of a socially constructed reality in which they themselves participate. You would also need to discuss your position on the use of *deductive* testing of a hypothesis in a highly structured and 'scientific' way, as opposed to *inductive* building of theory from observations in a more flexible way. The latter approach would probably use qualitative data and recognise that, as observer, you are yourself part of the research process.

The extent to which you will need to discuss such issues will depend partly upon where your research lies on the academic–applied continuum. While it is always worth spending time thinking about your own position on these issues, sometimes a fairly straightforward justification of 'methods', rather than discussion of 'methodology', will suffice.

The words ontology and epistemology have a similar effect on most students that the sight of an equation has on a number-phobe. The brain closes down, and the student resorts to quoting large chunks of a research methods text, strewn with words they clearly do not understand. Helpfile 13.1 gives brief guidance on use of these terms if you feel you need it. It is important that any discussion of 'methodology' leads logically to choice of a method appropriate to your topic.

You need to develop a clear research strategy which will enable you to achieve your research objectives. Your chosen approach, or mix of approaches, needs to provide a believable, i.e. reliable and valid, answer to your research question, within the constraints operating.

Some questions can be answered from existing literature; some may need you to collect your own data. This may be by planning experiments or, more commonly, by conducting some sort of survey, whether by interview or questionnaire, or exploring a specific case, either to test theory or to generate new ideas. The discussion in the previous section should have given you an idea of what this can involve. Whatever method you decide upon will raise further questions. For example, if you are planning a questionnaire, issues will include: how many people you need to gain information from; which kind of people need to be represented; whether to use a paper or electronic questionnaire; which questions to include and how to achieve a high response rate. Indeed you might also ask yourself if you need a less structured approach using interviews or focus groups before you can design your questionnaire.

You need to justify your chosen approaches in terms of their appropriateness to your chosen research question, showing how they will produce reliable and valid data that will allow you to come up with a valid answer to your question. Thinking about the data you need to generate is therefore a vital early stage.

Data planning

Detailed and realistic project planning is essential, and should begin as soon as you are happy with your project choice, certainly well before you are due to commence your research. This is because you cannot fully assess the feasibility of your proposal until you have a detailed plan of what will be involved. Only then can you start to put timescales to these activities.

➤ **Ch 4**

No matter how carefully you thought it through, your detailed planning may reveal snags in your proposal such that you need a third cycle of project choice, perhaps moving to your second or third choice of option if your first looks problematic. Most snags at this stage can be handled by modifications to the proposal rather than a total redirection, but if redirection is called for, you need plenty of time to develop a new project. If you try to do this well into your research time, you risk disaster. If you are doing detailed planning early in the process, well before data collection is scheduled, even a major redirection can be successfully managed.

Before you can draw up bar charts or other detailed schedules, you will need to think in considerable detail about your data requirements. For most projects, the bulk of the 'work' consists of data collection and analysis. In conducting your research you will be aiming to collect evidence on the basis of which you can draw convincing conclusions. If your information is deficient, if you do not have enough, if it is not the information you actually need to address your particular issue, or if your information is biased or inaccurate, any subsequent analysis and conclusions will be worthless.

Obviously, the data you need will depend upon your chosen topic. By this stage you will probably have studied a research methods course, including learning how to go about detailed analysis of data requirements for a statistically valid or otherwise trustworthy result. However, you may not learn these things until you are starting your research, and therefore too late to allow early detailed planning that depends on an understanding of data needs. This section therefore indicates the sorts of issues that are important. Suggestions are given for further reading to help you make a more detailed study of data requirements and possibilities in the absence, or in advance, of a research methods module.

Two important distinctions in considering the data you will need concern primary versus secondary and quantitative versus qualitative data.

Primary data are those that you collect yourself. This might be by direct observation, interview, application of a questionnaire or by other means. Primary data can be tailored to your particular requirements. You can design a questionnaire to give you answers to precisely the question of concern to you, administer it to an appropriate sample and know exactly under what conditions it was administered. You know how accurate the data are, and should have a clear idea of any ways in which inaccuracies might have crept in. Unfortunately, you pay a significant price for all these advantages. Collecting valid data tends to be very time consuming, and may cost money too.

You can see that here is a close parallel, even overlap here with the idea of primary versus secondary sources. However, there is also a distinction. Note that a primary source might provide you with secondary data!

Secondary data are those collected by others. These might be the results of surveys carried out by others, government statistics, in-company statistics or records, etc. By using secondary data you will have access to far more information than you could possibly collect yourself, and you can get it more quickly. But you may not know how much reliance to place upon the data, particularly if they were gathered for purposes very different from your own. Even data that might be expected to be perfectly straightforward and reliable, such as a section's weekly production figures, may have been manipulated by those responsible for their compilation. Local managers often produce such figures as will keep senior management off the back of the section head. The overall total might be right, but it is fairly common for some output from a good week to be 'stockpiled', and used to raise output figures in poor weeks. If your purpose was to explore correlates of variations in output, the figures would be of little use. It is important to be aware of the possible limitations of any data that you have not collected yourself, and to check, if at all possible, what factors may have influenced the figures. You also need to bear possible unreliabilities in mind when drawing conclusions.

When talking of data it is often *quantitative data*, data involving numbers that readily springs to mind. But important factors in a situation may be very hard to quantify. Attitudes and feelings may be important. Variations in perceptions – for example, the different ways in which different groups of participants in a situation would map the relevant (for them) factors in a situation, may be highly significant. Because techniques for structuring such *qualitative* information, and deciding on the reliance to be placed upon it, are still less widely known than the techniques of basic parametric statistics used with quantitative data, such factors may be omitted altogether. If not, numbers may be attributed to them, and totally invalid ways of interpreting those numbers attempted.

This may be clearer if you think in terms of a common classification of research data.

Textual data refers to words, for example quotations from an article or transcript of an interview. Such data can be a splendid source of ideas and create a vivid picture for the recipient. An interviewee might tell you in all too graphic terms precisely what is wrong with his or her boss, the organisation, or anything about which you choose to ask. He or she might describe precisely what should be done to solve the organisation's problems. But it is very difficult to know what reliance to place upon this information.

Does this interviewee have some axe to grind? How common is this perception? There *are* occasions when such text can itself provide the basis for a more quantitative analysis, for example in examining the commonest sequences of moves in a large sample of transcripts of negotiations, but this involves fairly specialist techniques. If you are planning to make heavy use of textual data, you should consult your thesis supervisor to make sure that you will be using them in a way that will be acceptable to the institution. Some of the qualitative data you will need may well be of a textual kind, until you find some way of at least partially quantifying the information.

Where you stand on qualitative versus quantitative approaches will depend on your assumptions about the nature of management and how knowledge about it is generated. But you need to be aware that, while quantitative data can be more 'reliable' and may be more generalisable, this is not always the case. Quantitative data are often *less* informative and may generate fewer insights than qualitative.

If using quantitative data you need to be aware that there are different sorts and that what you can do with your 'numbers' will depend on their nature. Otherwise you may claim 'answers' that the data cannot, by their nature, support.

Nominal or *categorical data* refers to data where some classification has been made, e.g. into country of origin, or type of first degree held by graduate managers. It is possible to count the members of each category but, even if the categories are identified by numbers, for example you might label the category 'chemists' as 1, 'biologists' as 2, etc., it is impossible to relate categories mathematically. Two chemists would in no meaningful sense equal one biologist! Some of the qualitative information you seek may be capable of being categorised in a nominal fashion.

Ordinal or *ranked data* are those where it is possible to make some comparisons between different categories. Interviewers might, for example, categorise applicants into highly suitable, probably good, acceptable, would need significant training, and non-appointable. If highly suitable was 5 and non-appointable 1, then showing the distribution between the rankings at different appointment panels would carry some information. But you could not suggest that the difference between a '5' candidate and a '4' candidate was in any sense 'equal' to the difference between a '1' and a '2', nor that a '4' was twice as good as a '2'. Equally, it would be invalid to use any sort of statistics that assumed that this was what the numbers meant.

Interval data are those where it *is* possible to assume that differences between numbers mean something. The difference between 25 degrees Celsius and 35 degrees Celsius is the same as that between 45 degrees and 55. But there is no real zero on this scale. It was mere convenience that determined that the freezing point of water should be designated zero. So 40 degrees is not twice as hot as 20 degrees. Questionnaire scores on attitude questionnaires might, for example, be capable of being treated as interval data, though more usually they would be ordinal.

Ratio data are those where not only are intervals meaningful, but there is a real zero as well, so that ratios also make sense. Forty people out of work is twice as many as 20. An inflation rate of 12 per cent is three times that of 4 per cent, and it is meaningful to make such a statement. Ratio data are the only ones on which you can use any mathematical technique you wish. Even with ratio data you may not be able to use all statistical techniques, however, as some are more sensitive than others to the distribution of values you are likely to find in the sample you are looking at. With statistics, if you are not an expert, it makes excellent sense to discuss your plans with someone who is!

Whatever the type of data you are planning to collect, you need to feel confident that the data will be accurate, relevant and reliable.

How adequate are the data?

Would a different observer obtain the same result? Indeed, would you get the same result if you repeated the exercise? If there could be a bias, in which direction are the results likely to be influenced? Are all relevant incidents (e.g. accidents) being recorded? If not, are omissions random, or most likely to occur in one particular direction? Do the data come from a sample that represents the group about which conclusions will be drawn?

Does the sample used warrant the conclusions drawn from it?

Refer to your statistics course notes to decide what size of sample you need if you are planning quantitative data. Remember that you may well end up with fewer data than you initially think. The return rate on questionnaires usually falls far short of 100 per cent. Interviews may be cancelled at short notice, and so on. Allow for a reasonable rate of attrition, and plan your data collection so that your sample, even after this, is large enough.

It is also important that your sample is *representative.* You would be unwise to predict the election results on the basis of a survey of home-owners, for example. Yet, students all too frequently survey one very narrow section of their organisation and, on the basis of their findings, go on to make sweeping recommendations concerning the entire organisation, sometimes an entire industry. The dissertation that ended with recommendations for restructuring a whole industry on the basis of unstructured interviews with six people in a single organisation showed such staggering ignorance of the rules for drawing conclusions from evidence that whatever its other merits, it needed to fail.

Do the data actually measure what they purport to measure?

If you have devised a questionnaire, does it really measure what you think it does? How can you check? Are in-company data to be taken at face value? If at all possible, talk to those responsible for putting the figures together. I still remember the difference between the wage clerks and management as to how a bonus scheme actually worked at one of the sites I visited in the course of a research project. I was attempting to answer what I thought was a simple question as to how much people were paid. Supervisors told me that there was a bonus scheme rewarding good performance. The clerks involved insisted that, the better you worked, the less you were actually paid. Further investigation suggested that the clerks were right! So try to find some way of checking any information you gather, no matter how plausible it seems. For example, if you ask interviewees to describe an organisation's appraisal scheme, they may all tell you that appraisals are carried out annually.

Ask them to show you their last appraisal report, or to tell you the date at which their last appraisal interview was carried out, and a very different picture may emerge.

In considering your data requirements, you will need to bear all the above factors in mind, and relate them to the particular question that you are trying to answer. This is difficult, so take advantage of all the help you can get. Test your ideas on your project supervisor, fellow students who understand statistics or those within your organisation in a position to know what information may be available and how it might be obtained.

Project management

> ➤ Ch 4

Project management skills are essential, and highly transferable. Planning was addressed in Chapter 4. A detailed project plan will be the key element in your project management, providing the standard against which you monitor your progress from the time the plan is drawn to the time you submit your completed dissertation. Many dissertations go wrong because of faulty control, which could easily have been prevented by simple project management techniques. If you draw up a fairly tight schedule of tasks, you will avoid the 'I don't know where to start, so I won't' syndrome that afflicts some students.

Your plan should provide you with a series of planned completion dates for the various tasks involved. These milestones will highlight any time slippage while you still have time to get back on track (ask your tutor for advice if necessary). Many students *not* using project management techniques realise they have a problem only when it is far too late to do anything about it. Interim target dates also play a major role in sustaining your motivation: each target met will be a source of satisfaction. If your only target date is your final submission deadline, it is all too easy to feel that you are making no progress at all on the project, and to become demotivated in consequence. This is a splendid example of a vicious circle, with failure as the most likely outcome.

Identifying necessary activities

> ➤ Ch 2

Once you have clarified the aims of your research through discussions with your client and supervisor, and thought in detail about your likely data requirements, you can think about the activities that will be needed in order to acquire and analyse the data, and draw up a schedule to allow you to complete your dissertation within the time allowed.

It may help to start with your research question or other specification of your aim, and work out a hierarchy of objectives to answer or achieve this (*see* Chapter 2). You can then draw up a list of the activities necessary to achieve each objective. You then need to think about the order in which these will need to be carried out. For example, if your plans include the design and use of a questionnaire, then necessary activities will include informal discussions with a small number of people in order to refine your ideas about the design of the questionnaire, and drafting a first version of this. Piloting the draft on a small sample will provide a check that there are no ambiguities, that the questions are interpreted as you intended (you can check this by interviewing the people involved after they have filled in the questionnaire), and that the thing can be completed within a reasonable time. After this you can revise and distribute the questionnaire. You cannot analyse responses until questionnaires have been completed and returned, but may be able to start entering data before you have them all. It may be necessary to send out reminders to increase the response rate, and this will need to be done early enough that you have time to enter any data from those who respond to the reminder.

Long before sending out questionnaires you need to decide on the size of sample needed and how this should be selected. Once this has been decided, you may need to gain organisational approval to your approaching the sample. Then you will probably wish to notify your sample in some way that your research is under way and explain its purpose so that you are more likely to get questionnaires returned and completed in an honest way. You will need to set up some mechanism for distributing and collecting questionnaires, you will need to have your final version duplicated in sufficient quantities, and so on.

Critical path analysis

You can see from the above that there may be fairly complicated sequencing problems. A useful technique for sorting these out is constructing *network diagrams*. By the time you come to do your project you will probably have covered these in your course, but, in case not Figure 16.6 shows an example of a network. (This is hand drawn, but software is easily available to enable you to construct such diagrams, identify critical paths, and schedule activities efficiently.)

In Figure 16.6, activities are identified by a number (a key – not shown – will show what each number represents). You read the diagram from left to right. The duration of the activity is shown not by the length of the arrow, but by the number in the semi-circle hanging below the line. The dotted lines are dummy activities, a device used to show that a separate chain of activities will also need to have been completed prior to the start of the next activity. Thus they normally do not have a duration. You can see, therefore, that in the case of Figure 16.6 you cannot do the activity numbered 8 until you have done 7 and 16, and you cannot do 7 until you have done 5, 6 and 10. You can also see that it will

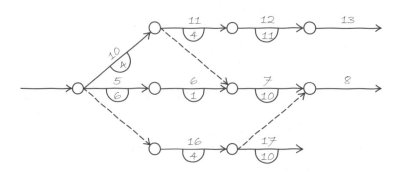

Figure 16.6 Part of a hand-drawn network

be at least 17 days (if the units of time are days) before you can start 8 and longer if you have not been able to do activities 10 and 16 in parallel.

Note that, although this is an example of a common way of drawing network diagrams, there are variants. If you have been taught a different convention, use that. The important thing is to use your chosen convention consistently so that the meaning of the diagram is clear.

The value of your diagram will depend on the accuracy of your estimates of the time that activities will take to complete. Estimating can be quite difficult. Ask for advice, and then add a margin for error! The golden rule of projects is that things always take longer than you think. Make sure that you have allowed for 'dead time' – for example, the time between sending out a questionnaire and gaining a response, or between writing to an organisation and being granted access.

Aim to schedule activities in parallel to exploit this dead time. To plan the best use of your time you need to make use of the ideas of 'critical path' and 'float'. The critical path is the minimum time a project can take, i.e. the longest path through the network. It is critical because any delays on this path will delay the project. Activities on non-critical paths could be delayed if necessary. This scope for delaying is called 'float'. To calculate it you work backwards, from right to left, subtracting activity durations from the time of the event they feed into. Thus, it would not matter if you took 10 days for activity 16, provided you started it at least 10 days before activity 8 was due. (You can identify the float in Figure 1.1 by the dotted boxes.)

➤ Ch 1

Drawing up a realistic schedule

Once you have drawn up a network, you need to think, too, about the time you have available. If you are working, you need to make reasonable allowance for times when you know that you will be unusually busy in your job, and set yourself a lighter project workload at these points to compensate. Build in some slack for unexpected conflicting demands, too. If your initial schedule cannot be made to allow for such slack, then you should revise your objectives to something more modest.

If using planning software, you will be able to print out charts and revisions with relative ease. If scheduling 'by hand', it is still worth the effort of drawing a chart as it provides a visible prompt to activity, and an overview of the pattern of your activities. It shows where slippage is possible and where it is critical that it does not occur. As it is almost inevitable that you will need to reschedule, and to add in activities that you omitted first time, it is worth leaving room at the end for extra activities, and then running off a number of blanks before you add the bars. This will make rescheduling less of a chore. Or use a whiteboard. It is important that you can draw up new schedules without wasting time when the need arises. It is not efficient to work from an out-of-date schedule, or one altered beyond the point of legibility.

Figure 16.7 shows an example of part of a hand-drawn schedule. Note that scope for slippage is indicated by the dotted areas after the bars. This should not, however, be taken as a licence to use the slack whenever you feel a little tired. The knock-on effects of this in terms of unreasonably high workloads in subsequent weeks would make a nonsense of all

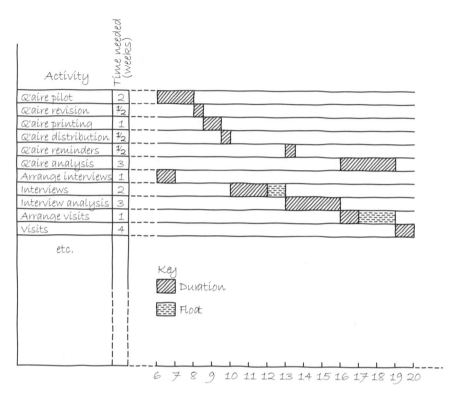

Figure 16.7 Part of a hand-drawn schedule for project planning

your planning and seriously threaten your success. Even deliberate slack should be saved for genuine emergencies rather than minor reluctance to work. If you use up your slack early in the project because of slight illness or mild overload at work, there will be none left when the real disaster hits you later on.

Once you have a schedule that seems realistic to you and covers all that you think will be necessary, with sufficient slack for the unforeseen, you have your main project control tool. All that you need to do now is to *use* it.

It may be helpful to highlight particularly important milestones in your research, and the dates by which these must be reached. If possible, agree to meet with your supervisor at, or a little before, appropriate milestones. You may have already passed some – topic choice, project approval and completion of planning! Others may be completion of your literature search, collection of information, completion of analysis, deadline for first draft of parts of your thesis, full first draft and final submission deadline. Highlight these points on your chart. (Some students show *only* these activities on their project plans, but such a lack of detail makes the plan virtually useless. I hope that the above discussion and activity led you to draw up a far more detailed chart.)

Now make a large version of your chart and put it above your desk. Put, a copy in your learning file and on whatever mobile device you use for scheduling other parts of your life.

Activity 16.14

Work out a bar chart for your proposed project. Once it is complete, perform the following checks:

1. Starting at the end, check that you have included all the activities that must take place prior to the end activity. Work back through the chart checking that for each activity all the necessary preceding activities are represented.

2. Check that you have indeed scheduled these preceding activities before the activities that require their prior completion.

3. Check that you have built any necessary waiting time (e.g. for return of questionnaires, duplication or data processing by others) into your schedule.

4. Check the workload for each week to ensure that the total is never excessive.

5. Check that your schedule is compatible with expected peaks in job or other conflicting demands.

6. Look at all activities where the float, or capacity for slippage, is small or non-existent, and check that your time estimates for these activities are realistic.

Comment

If the above activity gives you any cause for concern, you should consult with your client and your project supervisor about ways in which the scope of the project could be reduced slightly, to make it more likely that you will be able to complete it successfully within the constraints operating.

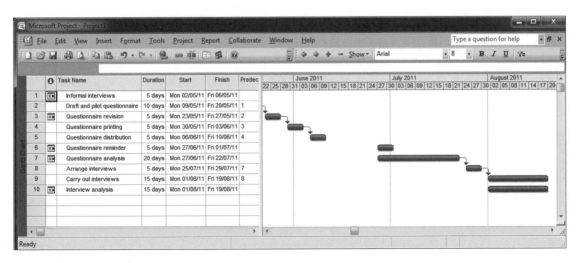

Figure 16.8 Part of a software-generated schedule for project planning

Make sure that key dates or activities are in your diary. Refer to your chart at least once a week to ensure that you are on, or ahead of, target. It can be very satisfying to colour in activities as they are completed.

If you do encounter an unexpected block, then use your chart to see where you could get ahead to compensate, so that the time scheduled for project work during the period you are blocked is still put to effective use.

Managing group projects

➤ Ch 9

Group work was discussed in Chapter 9. It is vital, with group projects, to set milestones for each member's work, and to meet regularly to review progress. It is almost inevitable that one member of the group will find it difficult to meet deadlines, whether because of unanticipated problems outside the course, or because a task turns out to be harder than expected, or just because they find it difficult to work to a schedule. The group needs to know as soon as slippage starts, so they can decide how to manage the situation so that the final deadline can be met.

Because some people are optimistic, assuming that undone work will be magically easier 'tomorrow', it is prudent to require members to circulate copies of what they have achieved at regular intervals, rather than relying on reports of 'progress'. (Call me cynical, but I find this is essential for team projects at work, as well!) If slippage is occurring on a critical path or towards the end of the project and there is not much float left, prompt corrective action will be needed. All this will be easier if the group has been communicating frequently throughout, members understand each other's strengths, weaknesses and situations, and an open and supportive way of working closely together has been developed.

Example of student experience on a group consultancy project

This project gave me experience of working with a real-life client, gathering relevant information and managing both the client relationship and the project team. I learned a lot about group dynamics, as this was the first time we had needed to work as a team on a major project of real importance. There was a lot of conflict, some of it because aims were different. One person only wanted to pass, four wanted distinctions (though one of them didn't seem to want to do any work to achieve it).

So only three of us were making a real contribution, which put a lot of pressure on us, and this got worse when one of us had to go home for her mother's funeral just as we were preparing the report and presentation. No one seemed prepared to take the initiative, so in the end I felt I had to try to 'lead' the group. I became rather autocratic, and allocated work to each member, making clear that it was their responsibility to do it by the deadline. This upset the more 'relaxed' members, and I had to put up with some very negative

➤

comments, but they did make some sort of attempt to do the work, even if it needed to be 'improved' after.

Things that contributed overall to our success were regular meetings, taking decisions by consensus, keeping minutes of meetings, having a range of specialisms in the team, trying to accommodate external pressures on members, and defining tasks and responsibilities very clearly.

The whole experience was a real roller-coaster ride: sometimes the pressure was enormous. But I now feel much more confident of my leadership abilities, and have decided to become a consultant. I have already developed an action plan for further development of the necessary skills. And yes, we did get our distinction!

Beginning to draft

One activity that can usefully be started far earlier than most imagine is the first draft of parts of your dissertation. It may seem absurd to start this while data collection is only just beginning and you have little idea of what your conclusions will be. But, if you write a skeleton draft, using guesses at what results might be, you may discover a need for additional data: perhaps by drafting you realise that, even if results *do* turn out as expected, they will support only a weak argument. By trying to construct that argument it becomes clear where additional pieces of information would strengthen your case. If you realise this while still at the data collection stage you can alter your plans to produce a much better piece of research. By the time you are officially 'writing up', it is usually too late to collect additional evidence.

Thus, the project choice phase is not the only one that should be seen as an iterative process. As with any complex problem-solving activity, a constant process of thought, experiment and refining your thought is necessary. This point is made explicit in many of the systems methodologies, some of which you may be taught during your course. The process also reflects the Kolb learning cycle introduced in Chapter 6. We cannot make sense of complexity all at once. But we can make a little sense of it, work with our new ideas, see ways in which they can be improved, try the new ideas, see further weaknesses and ways forward, and so on. Thus, step by step, we come to an improved understanding.

➤ **Ch 6**

A Master's-level project almost certainly will fall into this category of making progressive sense of complexity. So be prepared to go back and slightly revise earlier thoughts whenever things feel 'not quite right'. It is usually by such apparently backward steps that true progress is made. Similarly, you should try to make experimental steps forward, for example, by trying an early draft, or analysing dummy material, to check out your ideas while there is still time for change.

Many problem-solving methodologies recommend several loops around the whole problem-solving cycle before a satisfactory solution is likely to be reached. You are likely to be operating under such tight time constraints that repeated iterations will not be possible, but you can approximate to this by doing 'quick and dirty' mini-studies to check on your intended directions, and by the sorts of jumps ahead suggested.

Keeping a project log

As well as marking progress on your plan you should keep a more detailed record of progress in the form of a project log or research diary. In this you should record all project activity, times taken, details of what happened, snags encountered and insights gained. This can be enormously helpful to you when you come to write up your work. It can be surprising how easily things that seemed burned into your memory at the time fade into oblivion. Your log can be a source of observations made at the time and eminently quotable at appropriate points in your dissertation. Furthermore, many students are asked to submit their reflections on lessons learned, and comments on how, with hindsight, the project could have been improved. This is intended to demonstrate that you have indeed learned something about the process of this kind of research, and how to be critical of such investigations. (It can also be a valuable source of necessary marks for the student for whom everything has gone wrong and a resource if you have a viva on your project.) Your project log will be invaluable in writing a 'reflections' section. You may keep reflections on your project separate from your main learning journal or as an identifiable part of it.

With your schedule and record of progress you will have every chance of keeping on target, and of avoiding the stress or distress that many less organised students experience. But things can still go wrong. You may encounter unexpected resistance at work, the organisation may hit a crisis, or you may have to face major problems at home. If anything like this happens, shout for help at once. Discuss your best course of action with your project supervisor, and keep him or her continually informed of the situation. Keep your client informed too. It is not a sign of weakness to admit to things turning out differently from anticipated. The weakness lies in refusing to admit that this has happened until it is too late for plans to be revised or other remedial action taken. A small amount of optimism may be justified. Things *may* look better tomorrow. But if they are still looking equally dire the next week, tell your supervisor without further delay!

Writing up

Many students dread writing their dissertation. They cannot imagine writing anything that long, and feel increasingly oppressed as the deadline comes ever closer. As with topic choice, some therefore procrastinate, putting off starting as much as they dare (which is often far too much). Because they have left it too late, some parts are ill thought out, there is no time to obtain feedback on draft material from the supervisor or to revise parts that don't seem to work. The resulting dissertation is equally depressing to student, supervisor, client and examiner.

If you have followed the suggested practice of writing skeleton drafts at an early stage, and are reasonably competent at basic word-processing, the drafting process can be relatively painless. The knack is not to try to get it perfect at the first draft, but to allow time for redrafting. Revisions are easily made, your skeleton drafts can be amended and made use of, your references will be easily accessible and if you are using spreadsheets or a statistical package for your data analysis, figures and graphs can easily be integrated into your report.

➤ Ch 13 Your dissertation will need to follow the basic principles of report writing covered in Chapter 13. You may find it helpful to refer back to this. The section that follows discusses additional drafting points specific to dissertations and theses.

Who is the audience?

The first, and crucial, point is to find out the required audience for your report, and their requirements. Are you expected to submit a report addressed to your client, to the academic examiner, or in some way to blur the issue and write a sort of multi-purpose report? This latter approach would need to steer a delicate course between 'useful ideas' and 'jargon'. Your organisation, after all, primarily will want to know what to do about something that is bothering them. They are not really concerned about the extent to which you have adopted a position that could be described as 'weak logical positivist', or how appropriate a 'grounded theory' approach is to the problem. But for most dissertations you would need to convince your examiners that you *do* understand such methodological considerations, and that you have thoroughly searched the relevant literature to find theories, techniques and data relevant to your chosen problem.

Analysis will present fewer conflicts. Both audiences are likely to need convincing that your analytical techniques are appropriate to the type of data you have collected and to the questions in which you are interested, and that you have used them correctly. Both will want to know that the data you have collected form an adequate basis for the conclusions that you are drawing. And both will require that your presentation is clear, your arguments are logical, and your recommendations sensible, unambiguous and ordered according to reasonable priorities.

Probably both will also appreciate suggestions as to future steps to be taken in order to implement your recommendations, though your examiners are likely to be the only ones concerned with your reflections on the progress of the project and the lessons that you learned.

The report you submit for grading is written for the prime benefit of your examiners. If they do not require the submission of a client report, then you should probably consider 'versioning' your report for company use. With a word processor this is a minor task, and well worth the slight effort if you wish your recommendations to be acted on by the organisation, and your own image to be enhanced. (If you are writing a more specialist and academic dissertation, you may instead wish to version it for publication.)

The following broad framework is likely to be appropriate for your examiners:

Title page

1–2 page summary – *you may be required to submit this separately, rather than binding it with the report if hard copy is required*

Preface and acknowledgements

List of contents that follow – *(i.e. do not include previous elements in your contents list, but do include everything in bold italics hereafter). Numbering should usually reflect major and minor sections, e.g. 4, 4.1, 4.2, etc.*

List of tables, figures, etc. – *or list these at the end of contents list*

Numbered sub-titled sections – *normally these should include an introduction, an initial statement of project aims, a short statement of major findings and recommendations, and then detailed descriptions of relevant literature, chosen research approach (with justification), data collected, analysis, conclusions and probably reflections*

List of references

Additional bibliography – *if needed*

Appendices

Style should be clear, without unnecessary jargon, but using academic concepts where appropriate. Avoid being over-colloquial, and do not make unsupported assertions. It should be very clear how results are derived, and any shortcomings in the data should be discussed. A short introduction to each section can help make the structure of your arguments clearer to your reader, and the inclusion of relevant diagrams and tables (unless these are very complicated) will help your reader by clarifying points and by breaking up the text. Very detailed or complex information should be included as an appendix. It would interrupt your argument if it was in the main text.

If you can afford it, use good quality paper for hard-copy submission, as it improves the overall impression given by the report. Think carefully about things like font and size if submitting electronically so markers can read your work without eye strain. Pay attention to diagrams. Good diagrams can add to appearance and convey a lot of information without using word count. For hard-copy submission make sure that you know what type of binding is required. If none is specified, think carefully about the most appropriate and durable way of binding your dissertation.

Do check your spelling and grammar. It is surprising how many times the PC's warning wiggles are ignored. Repeated spelling mistakes detract from the overall impression created and, in extreme cases, a dissertation can be referred for corrections. Check, too, that you have not made mistakes when typing numbers, as errors here are more serious.

Even if you are not *required* to submit a draft of part of your thesis, your supervisor's comments on such a draft can be invaluable. It is important to check that your style, level of analysis and use of academic sources is what is required by the institution. There may be simple ways in which major improvements can be made, and you should find out about these at an early stage in your drafting if at all possible.

If you start your drafting early, have developed your report-writing skills earlier in your course and are reasonably competent at word processing, producing your final dissertation or report can be one of the most satisfying parts of your whole course. You are creating a substantial piece of work based on your own findings, and are seeing this take shape before your eyes. Far from a chore, this can be enormously exciting.

SUMMARY

- Management research is usually directed, whether directly or indirectly, towards real organisational problems, although the relative emphasis on theory and practice may vary.

- You should start work on your initial planning months in advance of the official project start.
- Topic choice is critical, and should be an iterative process involving yourself, your project supervisor and, if relevant, your organisational client.
- A good topic is interesting to all parties, gives sufficient scope, exhibits symmetry of outcomes, is feasible and not too prone to catastrophe.
- It is important to consider your responsibilities to stakeholders in your research, and to ensure that you comply with your university's ethics policy.
- Diagnosis of complex organisational problems is both challenging and crucial.
- Normally you will be expected to show that you can make good use of literature and information sources beyond those introduced in earlier courses.
- You should take full advantage throughout your project of the support and expertise your supervisor can offer.
- Interviews, focus groups or questionnaires are often used to generate primary data, but care needs to be taken to ensure that these data are valid, and properly interpreted.
- Detailed project planning is essential, and cannot be undertaken until you have a clear idea of how you will proceed and the data that will be required.
- Networks and bar charts are invaluable for project control.
- Work should be as iterative as possible, with dummy analyses of data carried out and skeleton reports drafted well before data collection is complete.
- Analysis should be appropriate to the type of data collected.
- You should ensure that you avoid plagiarism by clearly identifying and attributing all text and diagrams that were originated by others.
- The final report should be clear, well presented and directed towards the right audience.

16

PROJECTS, THESES AND DISSERTATIONS

Further information

Bryman, A. (2012) *Social Research Methods (4th edn)*, Oxford University Press.

Bryman, A. and Bell, E. (2011) *Business Research Method* (3rd edn), Oxford University Press.

Bui, Y.N. (2009) *How to Write a Master's Thesis*. London: Sage.

Cameron, S. and Price, D. (2009) *Business Research Methods; A Practical Approach*, London: CIPD.

Coghlan, D. and Brannick, T. (2009) *Doing Action Research in Your Own Organization* (3rd edn), Sage.

Cook, C.R. (2005) *Just Enough Project Management*, McGraw-Hill. Although designed for those managing work projects, you may find the planning content particularly useful.

Glaser, B.G. and Strauss, A.L. (1967) *The Discovery of Grounded Theory, Strategies for Qualitative Research*, Weidenfeld & Nicolson. This is a classic text on qualitative approaches.

Howard, K. and Peters, J. (1990) 'Managing Management Research'. This is a special issue of *Management Decision* (Vol. 28, No. 5). Although now quite old, it provides a clear, fairly brief coverage of different types of management research, and what is involved.

Oliver, P. (2010) *The Student's Guide to Research Ethics* (3rd edn), Open University Press.

Rudestam, K.E. and Newton, R.R. (2015) *Surviving Your Dissertation* (4th edn), Sage.

Saunders, M., Lewis, P. and Thornhill, A. (2012) *Research Methods for Business Students* (6th edn), Pearson. This provides more detailed treatment particularly of data-collection methods and analysing both quantitative and qualitative data. It also includes a number of case studies.

Additional resources

For more on critical path analysis see

http://www.mindtools.com/critpath.html (accessed 16.1.15)

or

http://www.project-management-skills.com/critical-path-method.html (accessed 16.1.15) http://www.direct.gov.uk (accessed 24.11.10) Searches UK government and related websites.

http://scholar.google.co.uk (accessed 16.1.15). For academic references.

http://www.ukop.co.uk/help_boolean_search.aspx (accessed 16.1.15). For a clear explanation of Boolean search terms.

http://gethelp.library.upenn.edu/PORT/ (accessed 16.1.15). For an excellent set of tutorial resources from the University of Pennsylvania on finding and judging sources, as well as examples of how to paraphrase to avoid plagiarism – though note that the referencing styles covered are not likely to suit your university.

http://www.ethicsguidebook.ac.uk (accessed 16.1.15). For an interesting paper by the ESRC on research ethics. Although aimed at those applying for funding for rather larger projects, it is clearly written and includes a useful section on identifying risk in social science research.

Note

1. Boolean logic is a system within mathematical logic based on the algebra of sets, devised in the nineteenth century by George Boole.

17
MANAGING YOUR CAREER

Learning outcomes

By the end of this chapter you should have:

- a clearer idea of your career objectives for the next five years (and perhaps beyond)

- an initial plan for achieving these

- considered how to sustain your learning habit to develop relevant skills

- started to develop relevant networks

- begun to think about how best to find and obtain a better or different job if relevant.

Introduction

If you have now finished, or are about to finish, your Master's degree, congratulations on your considerable achievement. But this is not the end of your learning journey. Rather, you are now ready to learn more and take on greater challenges. Managing your studies was a considerable task. Managing your career is an even greater one, and will draw on all the skills you have developed thus far. These include the strategic thinking skills your course will have developed. If you are alert to developments in your organisation and outside that might offer interesting future job opportunities, and can develop skills they will need in anticipation, your career is likely to benefit. Organisations succeed by developing their resources and capabilities and exploiting them in the competitive environment. People do the same. In a rapidly changing world, lifelong learning is far more than a politician's slick phrase. It is the key to your continued career success, and the success of any organisation you set up or work for. Three elements are important here: clarity of objectives; reflective practice; and considering yourself as a 'brand' to be marketed in a changing but ever competitive market.

You considered your objectives at the start of the book. This chapter guides you through a reconsideration based on your current skills and thinking. These will have developed considerably since Chapter 1.

➤ Ch 6   If you worked through Chapter 6 you will already have started to develop a reflective learning habit. If you have been relying upon your formal studies to guide your learning thus far, now is the time to study that chapter, and think about how you can continue to learn after your degree. Reflective practice is a core component in continuing professional development. It helps you identify areas where thinking or practice may need to adapt to fit current demands.

In parallel with this you can usefully review your life and career objectives, and consider further steps you can now take to achieve them. You may already have been doing this at intervals during your programme. If not, this chapter offers a framework for doing so, and suggestions as to how to implement your chosen strategy. It explores a range of options that may now be open to you, and factors which may affect your choice between them. There is also guidance on researching job opportunities, preparing an application and making a good impression during an interview.

By this point your course studies should have included marketing and branding, and you can usefully draw on these ideas to look at consider how you might develop yourself as a brand.

Networking is important for your future. You will have made a number of useful contacts during your studies, particularly if you paid attention to developing your networking skills. You may already have joined one or more professional networks as a student member, and be ready to upgrade to full membership. A range of online networks are also available. Your success at work and in your career may well depend upon how you present yourself, and the contacts you make, outside your organisation.

In all these tasks you will, in a sense, be treating yourself as a live case study, and putting into immediate practice skills that your course will have developed. Furthermore, this will be in a context of obvious personal relevance and importance.

Lifelong learning

You may feel your brain has been stretched for too long, and by now you just want a rest. Or you may be 'addicted' to the excitement of learning, to the 'high' that comes on suddenly making sense of a situation in a new way because of a theory or concept, or of knowing that you have done something better than ever before because of improved skills. In either case, you need to continue to learn. In the latter case it will be easier: once you have developed the habit of reflective practice it will not feel like work. If you have yet to establish this habit, it is worth the effort of doing so now. You will learn much more easily and effectively if you do. And you cannot *afford* to stop learning if you want to progress in your career. (You will remember Maslow's highlighting of 'Growth' as an important need, so you are also likely to be unsatisfied as a person if you do not continue to develop.)

> **Lifelong learning**
>
> This requires continued, systematic:
>
> - reflection on experience
> - development of new concepts
> - testing of these against experience
> - practice of skills
> - seeking of new challenges.

As lifelong careers (*see* later in the chapter) have become less common, responsibility for management learning has tended to shift from the employer to the individual manager. Your future employability will depend on your continued learning, so it is very much in your interest to accept this responsibility.

The learning skills developed while studying may well be the most valuable benefit from the time and money you have invested. So think about how to exploit these skills when you no longer have the discipline of your course, and the goad of assignments and examinations. If you allow the pressure of everyday work to drive out all else you risk being trapped in the 'experience' part of the Kolb learning cycle. If you do not go through the other stages the model suggests you will stop learning.

➤ **Ch 6**

So find ways of continuing to reflect on your experience and develop your repertoire of useful concepts. Test these against the radically changing world in which you are likely to be working. The following elements are crucial to a sustained learning habit.

- **Having experiences.** This will be happening to you constantly at work and elsewhere: think about how you can extend the experiences you have (see the end of this list).

- **Reflection.** You need to schedule time to stand back and observe your experiences and your reactions to these. You could do this daily, weekly, at the end of each significant assignment or all of these. If you have been keeping a learning journal, as suggested earlier, continue this. If not, starting such a journal may go some way to replacing the course experience. Seek opportunities to reflect with colleagues. A key idea from the discipline of knowledge management is the need to make tacit knowledge explicit. Explicit knowledge can be stored and shared. For the tacit → explicit move to be achieved, the process needs to be recognised as important, and time scheduled for the necessary thinking and discussion.

- **Developing your thinking.** You then need to interpret/make sense of your experience. Your course will have introduced you to a wide range of theories and concepts. Try to continue the habit of applying these to your work experiences. Use them in new contexts as part of your process of making sense of what is happening in your organisation, and to assess responses to situations. Expand your repertoire by judicious reading, surfing, discussion with colleagues and attendance at professional meetings and conferences. (Remember to keep exercising your critical skills: many management books, papers and conference presentations are fairly superficial and/or based on inadequate evidence or dubious assumptions.)

- **Testing.** As you encounter new ideas, and develop your own, continue the process of deliberately testing them against your experience as a manager. Only thus can you develop an improved portfolio of conceptual tools.

- **Practice.** In the above you will be practising your learning skills, and some of your critical ones. There will be more concrete skills that you can continue to practise, too. There is probably still room to develop your communication skills in various contexts, for example, or expand your analytical skills.

- **Seeking new challenges.** Your job will probably throw up many new challenges – particularly if you now have the confidence to see situations as opportunities to put your competence to the test. If not, it is worth actively seeking such opportunities. Learning comes from stepping beyond what is 'safe', and stretching yourself.

It is worth taking time to think about skills you would still like to develop, as well as how to ensure that your 'reflective practitioner' skills are sustained. Use the following activity as the basis for doing this, deciding on targets and review dates, and noting the latter in your diary. Or you may like to use the Chapter 7 proformas.

➤ Ch 7

Activity 17.1

1. If you have not been keeping a learning journal as part of your personal development file, revisit the section in Chapter 6 on this. Decide on a form, and take any necessary steps to assemble a framework.

2. Identify suitable times for regular reflection, and those key events that should also prompt reflection. Identify occasions that would be suitable for group reflection. Take steps to ensure that such reflection takes place.

3. List skills that reflection suggests you could develop further, and make a plan (with actions and target dates) for this development. If you can, do this in discussion with your manager, perhaps in the context of an appraisal interview. (Remember the importance of feedback on performance in developing skills.)

4. List areas of interest, where you would like to find out more, and think about ways in which you can achieve this, again developing a plan with target dates. (Update this regularly, as new areas become important – reassessing your objectives may alter priorities.)

5. Whether or not you are keeping a learning journal, make sure that you schedule regular sessions (perhaps monthly) for consolidation of what you have learned, and further reflection on the effectiveness of your ongoing learning.

Reassessing objectives and options

Your life objectives, and the subset of your career objectives, have probably changed significantly as a result of your studies. Your perspective will have broadened, and you may realise that your earlier ambitions were unnecessarily limited. You will have made new contacts, and you will be aware of a wider range of options. Unless you actively revise your objectives in the light of your experiences, you are missing out on a significant potential benefit of study. It may be more interesting to work from a blank sheet, here, rather than consciously trying to develop objectives trees such as you constructed earlier. If you prefer a tabular format see the companion website.

Activity 17.2

Construct a new set of objectives trees showing your goals for the next five years. Do not restrict yourself at this point to career objectives. Start with the wider set of life objectives and nest your career objectives within these. When you have finished, you may like to compare your new trees with those you did at the start of your studies.

Exploring options

Your objectives trees should have clarified your medium-term objectives and the shorter-term goals needed to meet them: now you can think about ways of achieving these. Your options are likely to be highly personal and any discussion here will be necessarily general, but it may act as a prompt.

Talking to fellow students may have suggested a wider range of options. You may have heard about interesting jobs that you had not previously considered. Remember, it is important to generate as wide a range of options as possible before choosing. This chance suggestion of possibilities is a start. Try brainstorming to generate more options. As is so often the case, working with a small group of others can encourage creativity and produce more ideas.

When evaluating the options generated by your brainstorming, it may help to sort them into categories. Logically, the field of options can be divided into:

- making no change;
- staying with your present organisation but doing something different, either within your present job or in a different job;
- doing a similar job with a different organisation;
- doing a different job with a different organisation;
- doing something completely different.

If any category is 'empty', consider whether it might have potential in relation to your current or future objectives. Try brainstorming options within any missing category. Even if you are sure that you *know* your next step, broadening your options can be productive. Sometimes the obvious next step is not on the shortest path to where you ultimately want to be.

Staying with your own organisation

If your organisation funded your studies, you may have to refund your fees if you leave within a certain period. If your job is fully satisfying and continues to provide you with all the challenges that you need, staying may be a very positive course of action. Check that you have a good reason for staying, though, and that it is not merely inertia.

If you feel that you need more challenge, but would like to stay with your organisation, think carefully about how you might use your new skills and understanding. If you can, discuss this with relevant others – perhaps your mentor, a training manager, your own manager and/or a senior manager in an area that might suit your developing abilities. They may suggest other routes, or ways of achieving the move you would like. Keep initial discussions open. Your focus should be both on clarifying what *you* want to achieve, given the increased skills and altered perspective gained from your course and on how these might be taken advantage of by your organisation. Only then should you consider specific posts that might be suitable and how to position yourself for these.

If there are few job opportunities envisaged in the near future there might be other routes to job enhancement. Could you add additional roles to your current job? Might getting involved in management development as a trainer offers you scope for using and further enhancing your skills? Are there any attractive new projects starting up for which you could volunteer? Is there an ongoing issue that you could offer to tackle on an in-company consultancy basis? Are there opportunities for a short secondment to another part of your own organisation or even some other organisation?

Moving to a new organisation

If you think that you would like to move to another organisation, or have been studying full time and looking for a new job on graduation, use a similar approach. Think about what you want and can offer, and talk to others about the best route to meeting your needs and finding a job where your particular abilities will be an advantage to the organisation. In parallel, scan vacancies, both to broaden your understanding of possible options, and find ones that might suit you. You will recognise parallels with the diag-

➤ Chs 10, 16

nostic stage in case studies and project work covered in Chapters 10 and 16. It was argued there that it was important to look at objectives and measures of effectiveness *before* looking at possible options. Otherwise, a particular option might slant your thinking and limit your choice in consequence. What was important for a case study is even more so when your future is in question.

While your main sources of information about alternatives may be jobs pages in papers and relevant specialist publications and online recruitment sites, personal contacts can be important. Many jobs are still gained by this route, and for this reason there is a section on networking shortly.

It is not easy to assess the advantages and disadvantages of a potential job. Information gained through networking may be inaccurate. Job descriptions may be highly edited. The impression given at an interview may be carefully rose-tinted. Many organisations are concerned primarily with *selling* the vacancy to potential applicants, not realising that lack of honesty at recruitment can lead to expensive labour turnover soon after. You may need to be creative and devious in order to find out about what an organisation is like to work for. Are jobs frequently advertised? If so, is growth sufficient to account for this high rate? Do you know anyone who works there, or can you get to speak to someone who does? It is surprising how helpful switchboard operators can be in suggesting people you might like to talk to, and how informative these same people can be when you phone them up as a total stranger, explaining that you are considering applying for a job. The person vacating the advertised job is obviously an excellent source of information, if available for questioning. See what you can find out about the organisation in the role of a potential customer. Take advantage of any visits offered to potential candidates, and if none are formally offered ask if you might visit briefly. Does the job advertisement or further particulars invite you to contact a named individual? If so, take advantage of the offer.

Consider the economic strength of the sector in which the organisation is operating and the market position of the organisation. (Jobs have been advertised in organisations when preliminary discussions about redundancies were already taking place!) Is the organisation ripe for a takeover? Your studies should have put you in a position to assess the company much more effectively than before.

Doing something completely different

In thinking about the possibilities of doing something completely different, you should include consideration of as wide a range of potential areas as possible. The Graduate Management Administration Council (GMAT, 2013) gives examples of some MBA destinations which might prompt ideas. These include heading for Silicon Valley, for Wall Street. Your qualification may be more of an advantage in a country where there are few managers educated to that level. A different perspective may make finding creative solutions easier (this applies to shifts in specialism and industry, as well).

Research is a possible avenue if you loved your dissertation work and are eager to dig deeper. A PhD would give you this opportunity and qualify you to teach at university level, or develop specialist expertise that you could market as a consultant. Indeed, you might find that a pure research career without teaching or other commitments would meet your objectives. If you have studied part time for your Master's it is possible to continue part time to a PhD or a taught doctorate.

What about writing a book, or at least a series of articles for publication? You may have written a dissertation which is of potential interest to several audiences – if so consider what publications might be interested in an article based on some aspect of your work. (Publication in a relevant professional periodical is an excellent way of raising your profile with potential employers or clients, as well as strengthening your CV.) If you have practical experience in a particular area you may be able to write about the implications of particular theoretical ideas in that context. Consider what other possibilities there might be for using your knowledge in some way.

If you enjoyed working in groups and making presentations on your work, or found the academic side of the work really stimulating, what about starting to teach management studies? As with research, you do not need to give up your full-time job: given current academic salaries you might well not wish to. Part-time and distance management education programmes may well be seeking part-time teaching staff. Contact your local college(s) and the major distance learning institutions to see what opportunities are available. Your own recent study experience and your qualification should make you an attractive applicant. (You would of course need to check with your employer that such 'moonlighting' was not in breach of your contract, but many employers welcome the continued development opportunities offered by such leisure activities.)

If you already have extensive management experience and are still exploring options, taking on interim management roles allows you to broaden your experience, and can allow you to expand your network further. If you are considering yourself as a bundle of 'resources and capabilities', your network is a key resource, often referred to as social capital. If you are seeking rather than building on experience, working for a charity is one route. Pay may be lower, or you might work unpaid, but charities offer a range of opportunities up to, and including, Board membership.

Joining a management consultancy is another popular route to gaining experience and building a network, as well as a possible career in its own right. Again, your qualification would be highly relevant and working for a large consulting organisation would rapidly expose you to a wide variety of different organisations and their problems. This experience could stand you in excellent stead if you wished after a few years to take another managerial job.

Another way forward is to set up in business as a sole consultant or service provider. You may have skills which are in demand, and contacts who have expressed interest in those skills. If you like working with individuals at a personal level, then freelance training and development and/or executive coaching – a growth area in recent years – might be services you could consider offering. Attractions include being your own boss and demanding high fees. Barriers to entry are low – if you already have contacts you may not need to spend a great deal on marketing yourself. Writing and speaking may both generate income and raise your profile and lead to work. Business cards are relatively cheap.

Even if you plan a low-cost set up, minimising financial risk, the emotional investment can be high. Consider the potential negatives, as well the potential benefits. First, unless you have skills and experience in which demand exceeds supply, competition may be fierce. You will need to differentiate yourself from the competition, and market yourself effectively. Your relationship-building skills will be vital for success and you will need to meet, if not exceed, your client's expectations.

While some people are successful working on their own, and enjoy it, many do not find that it generates the income or other reward they expected. A one-person consultancy can be lonely. You may be able to ask high fees, but costs are high, too. You will need professional liability insurance, which may be expensive. You will need to constantly update yourself, and pay for this yourself. There will be no income when you take a holiday or are ill, or find yourself without work for a while. You will need to make your own pension arrangements. Many sole consultants (and trainers) complain that work is like buses: you wait for ages for a contract and then three come at once (and there is only one of you!). Networking with others in a similar position can help here. You can pass on the overload to someone you trust, which is better than simply turning it down and leaving the potential client to find someone else. And you may get work passed to you in turn.

The final area you might consider is setting up a company, or buying into a franchise. The growth of online business has removed some of the barriers to entry. Skills may be as important as capital, and your studies will have helped you see how capital might be raised. As with setting up as a consultant, you need a good product to offer, and running a business employing others may present a steep learning curve. A franchise will normally require financial investment and constrain your autonomy. But there may be valuable training and other support from the franchising company.

There are pluses and minuses for each option area: their relative strength will depend on what you have to offer and what you want in return. You may use an option from one area as a means to another, or combine options if this works for you. For example, working part time provides some regular income while setting up something where income may be more variable. Even if you choose one route, you may find yourself redirected by circumstances beyond your control. The fairly radical restructuring of organisations since the 1990s has forced many managers into a 'portfolio' lifestyle, at least for a part of their career. Such a portfolio might consist of a mix of activities from the above list. It can offer variety, opportunities for personal development and a more balanced risk than working in a single area.

Activity 17.3

Try to think of at least three further options that differ radically from those already suggested, to ensure that you are casting your net sufficiently broadly:

_____

_____

_____

Once you have decided upon the direction you wish to travel, you need to start thinking about how to increase your chances of success in pursuing that route. Two things will be helpful for most of the options you are likely to choose, presenting yourself effectively and using the 'social capital' you have developed through networking and other contacts.

Developing your 'brand'

At the start of the book you began to consider yourself as a product, and to assess your strengths and weaknesses in the light of a job market. By now you will have developed further strengths, and increased your awareness, both of yourself and of the potential employment market. It is therefore worth doing the exercise again.

> ➤ **Ch 2**

Activity 17.4

Revisit and update the self-assessment that you began in Activity 2.6 and may well have been updating ever since. Of course strengths and weaknesses exist in relation to a market, and the market you choose to address will see different things as strengths and weaknesses, but have a go at updating. You can revisit it later in the chapter.

The idea of thinking of yourself as if you were a product can be taken a step further to consider the way you would like to *brand* yourself. During your MBA you will have considered the value a brand can have in marketing a product. You will be stretching the analogy to apply branding ideas developed in the context of 'household names' to yourself, but analogies are aids to creative thinking so it is worth the effort.

A brand helps a customer distinguish one product from another: it comes with associated messages and/or values. So think about your own distinguishing features in the context of whichever options you want to pursue. What is it about your particular mix of skills, abilities, qualities and experience that might be of particular interest to a potential employer, client or other form of customer? Your strengths will provide a good starting point. Experiment with thinking of yourself in terms of a brand to see how this allows you to extend your list of strengths. From this perspective you might include things like reliability, professionalism, tolerance of ambiguity or a particular ethical stance that perhaps did not come to mind when thinking in terms purely of strengths. (If so, this is an example of how different frames for thinking can help you to gain a richer understanding.)

In branding it is important to signal the brand in a way that is consistent with its values. Think of all the ways in which you 'package' yourself, and consider how consistent they are with the values you wish to portray. Dress and personal grooming is one obvious form of packaging, but you give out a wide range of other signals. How professional (or creative) or whatever are emails and any letters you send that might reach a potential client or employer? What about your online presence? Is what you have posted for your friends open to potential clients or employers? If so, might this work against the 'brand' that you are trying to build? Would you want the major client Googling your name, only to find photos of you taken at a stag or hen night when the evening was well advanced? Note that, even if you post things to a closed circle of friends, they may circulate them more widely. Social media can provide an excellent medium for marketing yourself, but it needs to be done with care.

The above is not a lesson in brand management – this is not a marketing text. But it has tried to indicate the sort of thinking that might allow you to use what you have learned about brands to help your career after graduation.

Networking

A brand needs to be made visible. In the case of a product this will be by advertising or some other means of promotion. You need, similarly, to make yourself visible to potential employers (perhaps via head hunters) or to clients. There are several ways of becoming 'known'. Developing a particular line of recognised expertise so that journalists turn to you is one way. Writing in relevant professional magazines is another. Speaking at conferences is a third. But much of your self-promotion will come through your relationships with people who are likely to be interested in what you have to offer or to know others who are.

Networking refers to the process of developing and sustaining social relationships that have the potential to help you in your career. It is a key management skill. Luthans (1988) found it was highly associated with management *success* as measured by speed of promotion (though not with effectiveness as measured by degree of achievement of organisational objectives).

This book owes its existence to social capital and (accidental) networking. While working on an MBA course on HR, I went with one our professors to visit a potential author – someone I had worked with some 20 years previously. He was now a professor at Cranfield, and a key figure in the field of international HR. Unfortunately, he had many calls on his time, ones that were much more interesting, and more likely to advance his career than contributing to our course. But it was good to catch up with him.

A few weeks later I was approached to write this book. The publishers had originally asked the professor to write it. Again, he was working on other things, but he suggested they approached me . . . You are reading this book because (among other things) I had presumably made a reasonably favourable impression when we worked together, and reinforced this impression when we met. He could still remember this when the publishers approached him. Coincidence? Probably, but a lucky one. My involvement with this book has been personally (as well as financially) rewarding.

At the meeting about the HR course, as a very junior academic in the company of one of two distinguished professors I was not all that comfortable. My priority had always been teaching and learning the source of my 'brand values'. I could have pretended to be more of a 'real', i.e. research, academic in that meeting in order to fit in. I suspect that, if I had done this, I would not have been recommended to the publishers.

The fact that the publisher's request came shortly after the meeting was a fortunate coincidence. In one sense it was a one in a million chance. But networking can significantly increase the probability of such coincidences. Suppose you are actively networking, and in contact with perhaps 50 people – fellow alumni, professional association members and/or past colleagues and other contacts. If each of these has 50 contacts, that makes 2550 contacts, assuming no overlaps. Even with overlaps it will be a lot.

Activity 17.5

Think of all the people with whom you have had good working relationships, and those whom you know by other means, but who might have relevant contacts or information. Count up how many there are. Imagine that each has as many contacts as you do, and work out your potential network based on that assumption.

Of course this is only a useful network if the people in the first tier are likely to think of – and suggest – you when a suitable opportunity arises. This will happen only if they can easily remember you and know enough about you to know when something is relevant. They also need to be sufficiently favourably disposed towards you to make the effort.

During your studies you will have developed your interpersonal skills and be able to hold good networking conversations. By this I mean conversations that will establish for you and the other person areas of mutual interest and complementary expertise. Networking is about *mutual* benefit. Most people will not give you information or recommend you for work if it is likely to do them harm. They are much more likely to do it if they themselves will benefit. So, if they cannot take on a job themselves because they are too busy, or it is outside their expertise, it is in their interests to recommend someone who will do a good job. If they suggest someone dreadful they are diminishing their own social capital with a potential client. They need to believe in your ability to deliver. They also need to want to help you, to like you, and believe that you will not 'steal' a good client.

Sustaining and extending your network

You will already have at least the beginnings of a network made up of friends, fellow students and past and possibly present work colleagues. If you have been working on this it may already be quite extensive. Any network needs continual attention, both to existing relationships and to extending the number of people in your network.

Remember the characteristics of the relationship you are seeking. It is one of mutual respect and goodwill, combined with knowledge of each other's strengths and weaknesses, and objectives. As with all else, you can plan better once you are clear about your objectives. Knowing the sort of relationship you wish to build will guide your thinking about when, what and how to communicate with existing contacts, and how to make contact with new people with whom you could usefully form such relationships.

There are obvious and less obvious ways of identifying potential networkers. Fellow students are obvious candidates, as are alumni meetings and, for those qualified to join, AMBA (the Association of MBAs) meetings. There are various professional associations for both generalist and specialist managers. Consider the CIM, CIPD, CMI and other management-related professional institutes. All provide access to useful resources, as well as offering networking opportunities via local meetings. Where else might you meet people who would be particularly helpful in your chosen career path? Take time to think about this.

You can meet interesting people informally as well – many managers will have met some at least of their network members informally, whether socially, while travelling or at other times when conversations arise. Once you are in the habit of networking, and have the necessary talking – and in particular listening – skills, you will quickly see when there is potential. Conversations can easily and rapidly move to discovering areas of shared or complementary interest, and a networking relationship can begin.

While face-to-face meetings, with their rich non-verbal content, may make it easier to build relationship initially, social media can be excellent for sustaining them, and may provide some initial contacts too. Facebook groups and Twitter are popular ways of keeping in touch, and blogging can raise your profile and attract readers whose interests overlap with yours. In addition to sites that are also used for social contacts, there are now many more professionally-oriented sites. LinkedIn was one of the first, and is still popular, but you may find yourself bombarded with requests to 'link' to people you have never heard of, and receive 'updates' from people far more often, and less interestingly, than you would like.

Given the time and effort networking can take, both face to face and online, it is worth planning your approach, and reviewing its effectiveness at regular intervals. Building a network is a long-term investment. Ideally you start well before you need it, and any one member may be helpful only rarely. Allow for this in your evaluation. But if there is little benefit to what you are doing, either for you or your contacts, and future benefits look unlikely, see how you can change the quality of your interactions, or find different people to network with. The following guidelines may be helpful.

Guidelines for successful networking

Know yourself!	Be aware of your strengths, weaknesses, interests, wants.
Have a good introductory speech	Think of conversations as like speed-dating. You need to be able to convey, very briefly, your 'brand' and your interest in the other person's situation.
Be authentic/honest	Ensure that you reflect your self-awareness and your values in all you say and do.
Listen!	Listen well, and with networking potential in mind. Look for opportunities to help as much as be helped.
Follow up soon	Having made an initial contact, do or say something helpful to the person soon after.
Keep a record	Unless your memory is excellent, keep notes of each person's contact details together with relevant information – both personal as it can help build a relationship to remember family names etc., and information on areas of overlapping interest and potential help.

17

MANAGING YOUR CAREER

Stay positive	Interactions will be far more productive if you focus on positive aspects in any discussion.
Keep in contact	Find ways of remaining in contact that will be rewarding – rather than tedious – for the other person.
Review your approach regularly	Check at regular intervals that your network is in the shape you want, and change what you are doing if not.

Above all, think about your brand and about those with whom you are networking. If networking is a mutual benefit activity you need to be sure that you are meeting others' needs. If not, they will be less inclined to meet yours.

One person in my network sends around a regular 'newsletter' which is both interesting and informative. He shares his reading and the conclusions he has drawn, which is a great timesaver for those with less time to read. Another has a highly entertaining blog, which both amuses and conveys useful information. Others send me emails only very occasionally, but each is prompted by something they have found out that they know I will be interested in. All are valued contacts and I reciprocate with any information which would be helpful to them.

Less valued are those who send 'updates' that are about as welcome as the standard Christmas letter (. . . earlier this month little Johnny excelled himself in the school nativity play as a patient sheep, while Natasha did brilliantly in her music exams almost gaining a merit in her recorder Grade 2 . . .) and much more frequent. In Chapter 13 you learned to consider the perspective of your reader when constructing a written communication. It is equally important here. Ask yourself regularly 'Am I still making sure that whatever I send to members of my network is "brand compliant", of value to them, and likely to increase their chance of remembering me when a suitable opportunity arises?'

➤ Ch 13

Making an effective job application

Your network can give you access to key decision makers, and be a route to many opportunities, including imminent or current job vacancies. Recommendations from network members may increase your chances of being invited to interview. But for this you need to have made an effective job application. And if you are hoping to be noticed with no prior recommendation, it is even more important that you craft your application in a way that increases your chance of selection.

Whether you are looking for internal promotion, seeking a job in another organisation or aiming to work at something completely different but still as an employee, you are likely to need to make a job application. Your course may have covered this, but, if not, you should take this aspect seriously.

During my career I have dealt with hundreds of job applications from managers, many with MBAs or other Master's degrees. A significant number of these applications were rejected almost cursorily on the grounds that the applicant did not appear to be serious enough about the job to take a minimum amount of trouble over the application. Reasons for past rejections have included one or more of the following:

- The application form was full of errors and failed to address the person specification.

  Reaction: this is a person who can't be bothered.

- The required application form was not submitted – the applicant merely sent a CV that looked as if it was prepared some time previously, and was not tailored in any way to the job in question.

  Reaction: this person doesn't particularly want this job.

- The application came in after the deadline (and no reason was offered).

  Reaction: we have plenty of applications already that *were* in on time. Applicant probably lacks self-management skills.

- There was no supporting CV and no letter giving reasons for the application and high-lighting strengths in relation to this particular job.

  Reaction: this person misses opportunities.

- No references were given, or referees failed to respond (it is important to check that your referees are willing to give you a reference and will be in the country at the required time).

  Reaction: we don't interview/appoint without good references being received.

- A reference was unfavourable.

  Reaction: if even the referee thinks so poorly of this person . . .

  (This one is difficult, as people are often unwilling to say that the reference they are agreeing to write will be less than glowing – ask them outright if you have doubts.)

- The applicant did not seem to have fully understood the nature of the advertised job.

  Reaction: either this person has taken no trouble with their application or they are not very bright.

- The applicant seemed to have given no *thought* to what the organisation was looking for, and how they could deliver this.

  Reaction: this person has not taken their application seriously, or they are not good at analysing problems.

- The applicant was late for the interview.

  Reaction: if they can't manage to get to an interview on time . . . (Note: we did make an exception for a man who rang to say a large tree had fallen across the road right in front of his car– so ring to let the selectors know if something arises that you could not have foreseen.)

- The applicant was dressed inappropriately for the interview. (One person I interviewed for a job involving contacts with senior managers in client organisations showed up wearing not-very-clean jeans!)

  Reaction: this shows lack of judgement. Besides, the effect on clients/subordinates /superiors would be bad.

- The candidate gave one-word answers and did not look at the interviewers once.

  Reaction: this candidate lacks presence/communication skills/interpersonal skills.

- The candidate spent the interview talking incessantly without letting the interviewer get a word in edgeways. (You would be surprised how common this is.)

  Reaction: this person can't listen/understand what is required. They would be exhausting to work with.

- The candidate put all their energies into proving what a brilliant person they were rather than demonstrating how their skills matched job requirements.

  Reaction: may be good at selling themselves, but hasn't thought about the job or analysed what is required.

- When asked at the end of the interview if they had any questions, the only one was something like 'When will I hear?'

  Reaction: this person has not thought much about the job. Note: this would not lose you a job if you were well ahead in other respects but, if you are very close to another candidate, a penetrating question showing understanding of the likely challenges on taking the job might be a useful differentiator, showing you had really thought about the implications of working there.

> **To apply successfully:**
>
> - thoroughly research job and organisation
> - 'version' your application to the vacancy
> - highlight your strengths for *this* job
> - prepare carefully for interview
> - consider any potential weaknesses
> - behave professionally in the interview
> - listen carefully, and think before speaking.

I appreciate that it is bad practice to give advice in negative form, but these are all examples that have made a powerful impression on me when selecting. From the above it is fairly clear how you can increase your chances of making a successful application, provided you want the job sufficiently to put in the necessary homework beforehand.

First, it is essential to research the job and organisation as thoroughly as possible. You will have started this process when you were deciding whether or not you wished to apply. Once decided, it is necessary to take it further. Read any information sent you with extreme care. Find out everything you can from the organisation's website, and from recent press coverage of both organisation and industry. Once you *know* enough about the job and the organisation, you need to *think* about how you can use this knowledge to strengthen your application.

Considerable effort needs to be put into preparing your initial application. The impression created must be of a thoughtful, organised applicant, who really wants the job and who can argue for his or her strengths as a candidate succinctly and powerfully. It helps to say something somewhere that makes you stand out from what may be hundreds of other applicants. A slightly original turn of phrase in describing your leisure activities might catch the selector's eye. Or there might be something different in the way you argue why this is precisely the job to which you can make a significant contribution. An application checklist is available on the companion website.

Qualities needed in the application

All aspects of your application should show evidence of judgement and selectivity, with everything you write, whether on application form, CV or covering letter, tailored to the job in question.

You should 'version' your CV for each job application, emphasising your most relevant experience. Aim to go beyond merely listing jobs you have held, with key responsibilities that you had in each. It is far more impressive if your CV highlights the aspects of each job, and the skills that you exercised or developed in consequence, that are particularly important for *this* job. Always give more emphasis to more recent experience than to things you did a long time ago, unless early experience is singularly relevant.

Keep working at improving your CV if you are not being shortlisted. Although you may be aiming at unrealistic jobs (and it is worth asking if this is the case), it may be the way you are applying. (A friend made numerous unsuccessful applications before seeking advice on his CV. I made fairly minor changes in line with the above guidance and he got an interview – and the job – with his next application.)

Interview preparation

If you are invited for an interview, you will wish to find out even more about the job and the company. If you were making too many applications to do thorough research on each company before applying, make sure you do it for any who invite you to interview. Possible sources were listed above. You want to know as much as possible about the job, the organisation and the market in which it operates.

Before the interview you will obviously be thinking about your strengths in relation to the job. But consider, too, areas where you are less strong. You may well be asked about these, and will create a much better impression if you have clearly thought about them, and worked out a strategy for dealing with them as soon as you are in post. If you honestly think you are the perfect candidate, you can describe 'weaknesses' that interviewers may well interpret as strengths: 'I have a tendency to become *too* involved in my work.'

Research suggests that selection decisions are often taken within the first few minutes of an interview. At this point the selector has little to go on beyond appearance, so it is important that you take steps to ensure that your appearance works in your favour. Part of your research should cover the dress code within the organisation. You need to fit this 'model' and to look as if you have taken trouble with your appearance. Remember the importance of packaging in conveying brand values.

It is worth arriving early enough to repair any ravages of travel in the cloakroom. And to avoid carrying a lot of clutter into the interview, leave bags and coat at reception or in a secretary's office rather than dragging them into the interview room. Again, you will look far more professional without them. If you wish to take in examples of your work that you feel strengthens your application, pack materials in the order you would wish to present them in a neat case (but see the caution below).

If you are inexperienced at job interviews, or know that you tend either to clam up or to babble nervously, practise beforehand. Think of possible questions, and persuade someone to role-play the interviewer and feed you with the questions. Ask them to give you feedback on the impression you created. Record the interview and play it back. You should gain two benefits from this. First, you will be able to spot habits or weaknesses that impair your performance, and work on reducing these. Second, you should become less nervous with practice, and find that you have the courage to stop and think before replying, and that your replies become more coherent and fluent as well.

Interview techniques

During the interview it is important to listen very carefully to the questions asked, and to think about how to answer them before opening your mouth. If you are unclear as to what the interviewer wants, ask for clarification. If you want thinking time, ask for it. 'That's a really good/interesting/challenging question. May I think for a minute?' Try not to get bogged down in minutiae. If asked for an example of dealing with a discipline issue, don't go into what Fred was wearing and what Maisie had been saying for months, and where they were when you finally caught him at it. Instead, give only as much detail as is necessary to show that you acted appropriately and in accordance with sound principles and organisational policy.

In the sort of job you are likely to be seeking, interviewers are likely to be looking for the ability to think clearly, to select relevant factors from a situation and to take appropriate decisions in the light of available information. Getting into blow-by-blow discussions of things that have happened will not help you to convince them of your strategic ability!

In most managerial jobs interpersonal skills are important. You should have developed such skills during your studies, but remember to apply them in the interview. Eye contact with your interviewer is important, and occasional smiles can work wonders, though excessive smiling at inappropriate times can be off-putting. You need also to be aware of your body language. Remember the importance of first impressions and walk in confidently; smiling at any panel member whose eye you catch. Sit down in an 'open and interested' posture. Avoid leaning back, crossing your arms, or otherwise looking defensive and, of course, avoid nervous fidgeting. Watch the interviewers' body language too for cues that you may be talking too much, or otherwise not responding as they want.

Sometimes geography may mean that interviews are held by video-conference link or phone. If interviewed by standard video-conference, avoid rapid movements. Low bandwidth can make you look as jerky as an early movie star. Instead, sit in as relaxed a manner as possible, do not fidget or gesticulate, and look directly at the camera. Extremes of sound may be similarly exaggerated by the technology, so avoid these too.

Keep looking

There are likely to be many applicants for the jobs you want. If you are not immediately successful, try to obtain feedback on where you did not meet what the recruiters were looking for. Make sure that you regularly visit the main recruitment websites (see suggestions on the web), and those for any organisation you particularly wish to work for.

Check that your CV and application form are clear and focused and use relevant key words. The first sift may be electronic if large numbers of applications are expected, so ensure that the evidence of how you meet essential requirements is clearly signposted. Avoid 'padding'. If your CV is scanned by a human they are likely to spend a maximum of three minutes on the task. So your relevant strengths and experience need to make an impact on the selector well within that time.

Going forward

You should now have clarified your goals, at least for the next few years, and have thought about how to start moving towards them. You should be aware of your strengths and weaknesses as a potential candidate for a range of jobs, and have an idea of how to go about making yourself more marketable. The SWOT (strengths, weaknesses, opportunities, threats) framework, which you will probably by now know all too well, may be useful here. Pay particular attention to your strengths and how to exploit these – therein will lie your particular competitive advantage. Consider your 'brand' and how to promote it.

As with all other types of management, your career management will be helped if you schedule regular, if not necessarily frequent, reviews of your objectives and progress towards these. Only thus can you ensure that you are in control of your career, and are directing it towards the objectives that are of greatest importance to you, even when time or experience causes those objectives to change.

It remains only for me to wish you every success in travelling your chosen path. I hope that this handbook has been of help to you in gaining your qualification, and that the skills you have gained on your course will assist you in attaining your more important life objectives.

SUMMARY

- The skills and approaches you learned on your MBA are equally applicable to the 'case' of planning and managing your own career progression.
- Continuing to learn – from your experience, reading and other sources – will contribute to your success.

- Clarity about your objectives, and about how you will measure progress towards these, is also important.
- Think too about your strengths, weaknesses and brand values.
- Sustain and develop your networks, which can be a source of learning, valuable information, recommendations and sometimes contracts.
- Consider as wide a range of options as possible before choosing, including staying in your present job, which can be a positive choice.
- If you are seeking to change jobs, it is important to research possibilities thoroughly.
- Any job application needs to be carefully compiled, tailored to the particular job and crafted to make you stand out from perhaps hundreds of other applicants.
- In interviews your interpersonal skills are being assessed, as well as your other qualities relevant to the job. Again, careful preparation is important.
- Once you are in the job you want, continue to apply what you have learned on your Master's, not only to your job content, but to your own career management and achievement of your life objectives.

Further information

Bolles, R.N. (2011) *What Colour is Your Parachute? 2011: A Practical Manual for Job-Hunters and Career-Changers*, New York: Ten Speed Press.

Boldt, L.G. (2009) *Zen and the Art of Making a Living: a Practical Guide to Creative Career Design*, Penguin Arkana. This is very American, but has a wealth of useful activities, and includes self-assessment and interview preparation.

Bridges, W. (1997) *Creating You & Co: Be the Boss of Your Own Career*, Nicholas Brealey.

Bryon, M. (2013) *How to Pass Graduate Psychometric Tests* (4th edn), Kogan Page

Clutterbuck, D. and Dearlove, D. (1999) *The Interim Manager: A New Career Model for the Experienced Manager*, Financial Times/Pitman Publishing.

Comfort, M. (1997) *Portfolio People: How to Create a Workstyle as Individual as You Are*, Century.

Hopson, B. and Scally, M. (2014) *Build Your Own Rainbow: A Workbook for Career and Life Management* (5th edn), Management Books 2000. This is deservedly becoming a classic.

Hornby, M. (2012) *How to Get That Job: The Complete Guide to Getting Hired* (4th edn), Pearson.

Robinson, J. and McConnell, C. (2003) *Careers Un-ltd*, Pearson.

Rook, S. (2013) *The Graduate Career Handbook*, Palgrave Macmillan.

Additional resources

Online recruiting sites include https://targetjobs.co.uk/ (accessed 14.1.15). The MBA vacancies area on LinkedIn, http://www.indeed.co.uk/MBA-jobs (accessed 14.1.15). Many vacancies equally open to those with other management Master's degrees and a range of similar sites.

Practice your search skills to find those offering vacancies that look most suited to your needs.

Gottlieb (2015) https://www.linkedin.com/pulse/42-leading-social-networking-sites-business-you-may-know-gottlieb (accessed 14.1.15). For suggestions of appropriate professional networking sites to supplement LinkedIn (compiled April 2015) – this will give you some ideas of what is on offer (often at a price) but search for something more recent and more appropriate to your country.

http://www.mba.com/global/the-gmat-blog-hub/the-official-gmat-blog/2013/jan/unique-mba-career-transitions-stories-from-around-the-world.aspx (accessed 14.1.15).

http://humanresources.about.com/od/careernetworking/a/social_media.htm (accessed 14.1.15). For an interesting video aimed at recruiters to help them to do social network checks (this may strengthen your resolve to be careful what you post).

REFERENCES AND BIBLIOGRAPHY

Adair, J. and Allen, M. (2003) *The Concise Time Management and Personal Development*, Thorogood.

Allen, D. (2001) *Getting Things Done: The Art of Stress-Free Productivity* (New edn), Penguin.

Andreas, S. and Faulkner, C. (1996) *NLP: The New Technology of Achievement*, Nicholas Brealey.

Argyris, C. and Schön, D. (1974) *Theory in Practice: Increasing Professional Effectiveness*, San Francisco: Jossey-Bass.

Argyris, C. and Schön, D. (1978) *Organizational Learning: A Theory of Action Perspective*, Reading, MA: Addison Wesley.

Atkinson, I. (2011) *FT Essential Guide to Business Writing: How to Engage, Persuade, and Sell*, Pearson.

Back, K. and Back, K. (2005) *Assertiveness at Work* (3rd edn), London: McGraw-Hill.

Baguley, P. (1992) *Teams and Team-Working*, Teach Yourself Books, Hodder & Stoughton.

Barker, A. (2002) *How to Manage Meetings*, Sunday Times/Kogan Page.

Baumann, B. (1992) 'Master ohne Wert', *Forbes*, 10, pp. 68–72.

Baxter Magolda, M. B. (2001). *Making Their Own Way: Narratives for Transforming Higher Education to Promote Self-development*, Sterling, VA: Stylus.

Baxter Magolda, M.B. (2009). Promoting Self-Authorship to Promote Liberal Education. *Journal of College and Character*, 10 (3) pp. 1–5.

Belbin, R.M. (1981) *Management Teams*, Heinemann.

Belbin, R.M. (1993) *Team Roles at Work*, Butterworth-Heinemann.

Belbin, R.M. (2010) *Team Roles at Work* (2nd edn), Routledge.

Bickerstaff, G. (ed.) (2006) *Which MBA? A Critical Guide to Programmes in Europe and the USA* (18th edn), The Economist Publications/Pearson Education.

Bird, P. (1998) *Teach Yourself Time Management*, Hodder & Stoughton.

Bird, P. (2010) *Improve Your Time Management: Teach Yourself*, London: Hodder & Stoughton.

Bishop, S. (2010) *Creating Success: Develop Your Assertiveness* (2nd edn), London: The Sunday Times.

Blamires, H. (2000) *The Penguin Guide to Plain English*, Penguin.

Boldt, L.G. (2009) *Zen and the Art of Making a Living: A Practical Guide to Creative Career Design*, Penguin Arkana.

Bolles, R.N. (2011) *What Colour Is Your Parachute? 2011: A Practical Manual for Job-Hunters and Career-Changers*, New York: Ten Speed Press.

Bolton, G. (2014) *Reflective Practice: Writing and Professional Development* (4th edn), London: Sage.

Bowden, J. (2011) *Writing a Report* (9th edn), Oxford: How to Books.

Bradbury, A. (2010) *Creating Success: Successful Presentation Skills* (4th edn), Kogan Page.

Branson, R. (2008) *Business Stripped Bare: Adventures of a Global Entrepreneur*, London: Virgin Books.

Bridges, W. (1997) *Creating You & Co: Be the Boss of Your Own Career*, Nicholas Brealey.

Broughton, P.D. (2008) *What They Teach You at Harvard Business School*, London: Penguin.

Bryan, M., Cameron, J. and Allen, C. (1998) *The Artist's Way at Work: Twelve weeks to Creative Freedom*, Pan.

Bryman, A. (2012) *Social Research Methods* (4th edn), Oxford University Press.

Bryman, A. and Bell, E. (2007) *Business Research Method* (2nd edn), Oxford University Press.

Bryman, A. and Bell, E. (2011) *Business Research Method* (3rd edn), Oxford University Press.

Bryon, M. (2013) *How to Pass Graduate Psychometric Tests* (4th edn), Kogan Page.

Bryon, M. (2007) *How to Pass the GMAT*, Kogan Page.

Bryson, J.M., Ackermann, F., Eden, C. and Finn, C.B. (2004) *Visible Thinking*, John Wiley & Sons.

Bui, Y.N. (2009) *How to Write a Master's Thesis*, London: Sage.

Burchfield, R.W. (ed.) (2004) *Fowler's Modern English Usage* (3rd edn), Oxford University Press.

Butler, G. and Hope, T. (1995) *Manage Your Mind: The Mental Fitness Guide*, Oxford University Press.

Butler, G. and Hope, T. (2007) *Manage Your Mind: The Mental Fitness Guide* (2nd edn), Oxford University Press.

Butterworth, J. and Thwaites, G. (2005) *Thinking Skills*, Cambridge University Press.

Buzan, T. (2010a) *The Speed Reading Book*, Harlow: Pearson.

Buzan, T. (2010b) *Use Your Head,* Harlow: Pearson.

Buzan, T. and Buzan, B. (2010) *The Mind Map Book*, Harlow: Pearson.

Buzan, T. and Griffiths, C. (2014) *Mind Maps for Business: Using the Ultimate Thinking Tool to Revolutionise How You Think* (2nd edn), Pearson.

Cameron, S. (2010) 'The MBA: a system in need of rethinking?' in Proceedings of 17th EDINEB Conference: Crossing Borders in Education and Work-based Learning, available from http://www.fdewb.unimaas.nl/educ_v2/pdf/Proceedings_EDiNEB_2010_01_06_2010_final.pdf (accessed 18/11/10).

Cameron, S. and Price, D. (2009) *Business Research Methods: A Practical Approach*, London: CIPD.

Carter, R., Martin, J., Mayblin, B. and Munday, M. (1984) *Systems, Management and Change: a Graphic Guide*, Harper & Row, in association with the Open University.

Cashman, K. (1999) *Leadership from the Inside Out*, Minneapolis, MD: TCLG, LLC.

Caunt, J. (2000) *Organise Yourself*, Kogan Page.

Caunt, J. (2010) *Creating Success: Organise Yourself* (3rd edn), London: The Sunday Times.

Checkland, P. (1981) *Systems Thinking, Systems Practice*, John Wiley & Sons.

Clegg, B. (2000) *Instant Stress Management*, Kogan Page.

Clutterbuck, D. (1990) *The Phoenix Factor: Lessons for Success from Management Failure*, Weidenfeld & Nicholson.

Clutterbuck, D. and Dearlove, D. (1999) *The Interim Manager: A New Career Model for the Experienced Manager*, Financial Times Pitman Publishing.

Clutterbuck, D. and Kernaghan, S. (1990) *The Phoenix Factor*, Weidenfeld & Nicolson.

Coghlan, D. and Brannick, T. (2009) *Doing Action Research in Your Own Organization* (3rd edn), Sage.

Comfort, M. (1997) *Portfolio People: How to Create a Workstyle as Individual as You Are*, Century.

Conradi, M. and Hall, R. (2001) *That Presentation Sensation*, Financial Times Prentice Hall.

Cook, C.R. (2005) *Just Enough Project Management*, McGraw-Hill.

Cook, S.D.N. and Brown, J. (1999) 'Bridging Epistemologies: The Generative Dance Between Organizational Knowledge and Organizational Knowing', *Organization Science*, 10 (4), pp. 381–400.

Cramer, S. (2000) *The Ultimate Business Library: 75 Books That Made Management*, Capstone.

Damasio, A. (2006) *Descartes' Error,* Vintage Books.

Davies, G. (2010) *The Presentation Coach: Bare Knuckle Brilliance for Every Presenter,* Chichester: Capstone Publishing.

Deal, T. and Kennedy, A. (1982) *Corporate Cultures: The Rites and Rituals of Corporate Life,* Addison-Wesley.

Dewey, J. (1910) *How We Think,* Boston: D.C. Heath and Company (reissue from Lightning Source UK Ltd, Milton Keynes).

Easton, G. (1992) *Learning from Case Studies* (2nd edn), Prentice-Hall.

Entwistle, N. (1996) 'Recent Research on Student Learning and the Learning Environment', Tait, J. and Knight, P. (eds), *The Management of Independent Learning,* SEDA, Kogan Page.

Evans, C. (2008) *Time Management for Dummies,* Chichester: John Wiley & Sons.

Fayol, H. (1949) *General and Industrial Management,* Pitman (translated from the 1916 original in French).

Forster, M. (2006) *Do It Tomorrow: and Other Secrets of Time Management,* Hodder & Stoughton.

Forsyth, P. (2010) *Creating Success: How to Write Reports and Proposals,* London: The Sunday Times.

Fowler, A. (2006) *How to Write,* Oxford University Press.

Frost, V. (2006) 'Can Your Manager Manage?', *Guardian,* Work 2, pp. 1–2.

Gibson, R. (ed.) (1998) *Rethinking the Future,* Nicholas Brealey.

Giles, K. and Hedge, N. (1994) *The Manager's Good Study Guide,* The Open University.

Glaser, B.G. and Strauss, A.L. (1967) *The Discovery of Grounded Theory: Strategies for Qualitative Research,* Weidenfeld & Nicolson.

Glynn, J.J., Murphy, M.P. and Perrin, J. (1998) *Accounting for Managers* (2nd edn), International Thomson Business Press.

Goldsmith, W. and Clutterbuck, D. (1984) *The Winning Streak,* Penguin.

Goleman, D. (1998) *Working with Emotional Intelligence,* Bloomsbury.

Gowers, E. (1954) *The Complete Plain Words,* Penguin.

Gowers, E. (2014) *The Complete Plain Words,* HMSO - 232 Celsius, Kindle edition.

Graham, L. and Sargent, D. (1981) *Countdown to Mathematics,* Vol. 1, Addison-Wesley with Open University Press.

Grant, R.E. (1991) *Contemporary Strategy Analysis,* Oxford: Blackwell.

Gravett, S. (2003) *The Right Way to Write Reports,* Elliot Right Way Books.

Gray, J. (2010) *How Leaders Speak: Essential Rules for Engaging and Inspiring Others,* Toronto: Dundurn.

Greising, D. (1998) *I'd Like the World to Buy a Coke. The Life and Leadership of Roberto Gorzueta,* John Wiley & Sons.

Handy, C. (1999) *Inside Organisations,* Penguin.

Hardingham, A. (1995) *Working in Teams,* Institute of Personnel Development.

HBR's 10 Must Reads (2011), Harvard Business School Publishing Corp.

Harvard Business Review (2014) *Running Meetings,* HBR Press.

Herzberg, F. (1966) *Work and the Nature of Man,* World Publishing Company.

Honey, P. and Mumford, A. (1986) *The Manual of Learning Styles,* Peter Honey.

Hopson, B. and Scally, M. (2014) *Build Your Own Rainbow: A Workbook for Career and Life Management* (5th edn), Management Books 2000.

Hornby, M. (2000) *3 Easy Steps to the Job you Want* (2nd edn), Pearson Education.

Hornby, M. (2012) *How to Get That Job: The Complete Guide to Getting Hired* (4th edn), Pearson.

Hossenlopp, R. (ed.) (2010) *Organisational Project Management,* Vienna: Management Concepts.

Howard, K. and Peters, J. (1990) 'Managing Management Research', *Management Decision,* 28 (5).

Huczinski, A. (1996) *Management Gurus. What Makes Them and How to Become One*, International Thomson Business Press.

Huff, D. (1954) *How to Lie with Statistics*, Penguin.

Hussey, D.E. (1988) *Management Training and Corporate Strategy*, Pergamon Press.

Israel, R., Whitten, H. and Shaffran, C. (2000) *Your Mind at Work: Developing Self Knowledge for Business Success*, Kogan Page.

Jankovicz, A.D. (2005) *Business Research Projects* (4th edn), Thomson.

Jantsch, E. (1967) *Technological Forecasting in Perspective*, OECD.

Kakabadse, A., Ludlow, R. and Vinnicombe, S. (1987) *Working in Organisations*, Penguin.

Kellaway, L. (2000) *Sense and Nonsense in the Office*, Financial Times Prentice Hall.

Kelly, F.J. and Kelly, H.M. (1986) *What They Really Teach You at the Harvard Business School*, Grafton.

Kepner, C.H. and Tregoe, B.B. (1965) *The Rational Manager*, McGraw-Hill.

Kind, J. (1999) *Accounting and Finance for Managers*, Kogan Page.

Kline, N. (1999) *Time to Think*, Cassell Illustrated.

Kneeland, S. (2008) *Thinking Straight*, Pathways.

Kolb, D.A. (1976) *The Learning Style Inventory: Technical Manual*, Boston, MA: McBer.

Kolb, D.A. (1984) *Experiential Learning*, Englewood Cliffs, N.J.: Prentice Hall.

Kolb, D.A. and Fry, R. (1975) 'Towards an Applied Theory of Experimental Learning', Cooper, C.L. (ed.), *Theories of Group Processes*, New York: John Wiley & Sons.

Kolb, D.A., Rubin, I.M. and MacIntyre, J.M. (1984) *Organizational Psychology* (4th edn), Prentice-Hall.

Korzybski, A. (1931) 'A Non-Aristotelian System and Its Necessity for Rigour in Mathematics and Physics', Paper presented at the American Association for the Advancement of Science, 28 December 1931. Reprinted in *Science and Sanity*, 1933, pp. 747–61.

Lataif, L.E. (1992) 'MBA: Is the Traditional Model Doomed?', *Harvard Business Review*, Nov–Dec, pp. 128–140.

Lawler, E.E. and Porter, L. (1967) 'Antecedent Attitudes of Effective Managerial Performance', *Organizational Behaviour and Human Performance*, 2, pp. 22–42.

Lee, T.W. (1999) *Using Qualitative Methods in Organizational Research*, Sage.

Leech, T. (2001) *Say It Like Shakespeare*, McGraw-Hill.

Lepsinger, R. and DeRosa, D. (2010) *Virtual Team Success: A Practical Guide for Working and Leading from a Distance*, Hoboken, N: John Wiley & Sons.

Lewin, K. (ed. D. Cartwright) (1951) *Field Theory in Social Science: Selected Theoretical Papers*, New York: Harper Row.

Lifeskills International (1999) *Staying Healthy at Work*, Gower.

Lucas, B. (2001) *Power Up Your Mind*, Nicholas Brealey.

Luthans, F. (1988) 'Successful Versus Effective Real Managers', *Academy of Management Executive*, II (2).

Maginn, M. (2004) *Making Teams Work*, McGraw-Hill.

Mintzberg, H. (1973) *The Nature of Managerial Work*, Englewood Cliffs, N: Prentice Hall.

Mintzberg, H. (1992) Contribution to the debate in Lataif, L.E. 'MBA: Is the Traditional Model Doomed?' *Harvard Business Review*, 70 (6).

Mintzberg, H. (2004) *Managers not MBAs*, Harlow: FT Prentice Hall.

Mintzberg, H. (2009) *Management*, Harlow: FT Prentice Hall.

Moon, J.A. (2000, reprinted 2005) *Reflection in Learning and Professional Development*, RoutledgeFalmer.

Morgan, G. (1986) *Images of Organisation*, Sage.

Moroney, M.J. (1951) *Facts from Figures*, Penguin.

Morris, C. (2008) *Quantitative Approaches in Business Studies* (7th edn), FT Prentice Hall.

Morris, C. and Thanassoulis, E. (1994) *Essential Mathematics – A Refresher Course for Business and Social Studies*, Macmillan.

Morris, S. and Smith, J. (1998) *Understanding Mind Maps in a Week*, Institute of Management.

Morris, C. and Thanassoulis, E. (2007) *Essential Mathematics: For Business and Management*, Palgrave Macmillan.

Naughton, J. (2003) 'How PowerPoint Can Fatally Weaken Your Argument', *The Observer*, 21 December.

Neenan, M. and Dryden, W. (2004) *Cognitive Therapy: 100 Key Points and Techniques*, Routledge.

Nutz, K. and Freiberg, J. (1997) *Southwest Airlines Crazy Recipe for Business and Personal Success*, Orion Business Books.

Oakshott, L. (2009) *Essential Quantitative Methods for Business, Management and Finance*, Palgrave Macmillan.

The Official MBA Handbook 2003/2004 (19th edn) (2003), FT Prentice Hall with the Association of MBAs.

Oliver, P. (2010) *The Student's Guide to Research Ethics* (3rd edn), Open University Press.

Palmer, S. and Cooper, C. (2010) *How to Deal with Stress* (2nd edn), London: Kogan Page.

Parkinson, C.N. (1958) *Parkinson's Law: The Pursuit of Progress*, London: John Murray.

Pfeffer, J. and Fong, C.T. (2002) 'The End of Business Schools? Less success than meets the eye', *Academy of Management Learning & Education,* 1, pp. 78–95.

Pidd, M. (2009) *Tools for Thinking: Modelling in Management Science* (3rd edn), Chichester: John Wiley & Sons.

Pizzey, A. (1998) *Finance and Accounting for Non-Specialist Students*, Financial Times Pitman Publishing.

Porter, M.E. (1980) *Competitive Strategy*, Free Press.

Porter, M.E. (1985) *Competitive Advantage: Creating and Sustaining Performance*, New York: Simon and Schuster (Free Press imprint).

Powell, J. (1991) *Quantitative Decision Making*, Longman.

Revans, R. (1980) *Action Learning: New Techniques for Management.* London: Blond & Briggs Ltd.

Roberts, B. (1999) *Working Memory: Improving Your Memory for the Workplace*, London House.

Robinson, J. and McConnell, C. (2003) *Careers Un-ltd*, Pearson.

Robinson, P. (1994) *Snapshots from Hell: The Making of an MBA*, Nicholas Brealey.

Rook, S. (2013) *The Graduate Career Handbook*, Palgrave Macmillan.

Rose, C. and Nicholl, M.J. (1997) *Accelerated Learning for the 21st Century*, Piatkus.

Rowntree, D. (1987) *Statistics Without Tears: A Primer for Non-Mathematicians*, Penguin.

Rubin, R.S. and Dierdorff, E.C. (2009) 'How Relevant Is the MBA? Assessing the Alignment of Required Curricula and Required Managerial Competencies', *Academy of Management Learning & Education*, 8 (2), pp. 208–224.

Rudestam, K.E. and Newton, R.R. (2015) *Surviving Your Dissertation* (4th edn), Sage.

Russell, L. (1999) *The Accelerated Learning Field Book*, Jossey-Bass Pfeiffer.

Saunders, M., Lewis, P. and Thornhill, A. (2012) *Research Methods for Business Students* (6th edn), Financial Times Press.

Schein, E.H. (2013) *Humble Inquiry: The Gentle Art of Asking Instead of Telling*, San Francisco, CA: Berrett-Koehler.

Schön, D. (1983) *The Reflective Practitioner: How Professionals Think in Action*, New York: Basic Books Inc.

Senge, P.M. (1994) *The Fifth Discipline: The Art and Practice of the Learning Organization*, New York: Doubleday Currency.

Smith, H. and Bude, M. (2010) *Great at my Job but Crap at Numbers*. London: Teach Yourself.

Sofo, F., Yeo, R.K. and Villafane, J. (2010) 'Optimizing the Learning in Action Learning: Reflective Questions, Levels of Learning and Coaching', *Advances in Developing Human Resources,* 12: 205–224.

Sprent, P. (1991) *Management Mathematics*, Penguin.

Stutely, R. (2003) *The Definitive Guide to Managing the Numbers*, Pearson.

Thompson, G. (2005) *Stress Buster*, Summersdale Publishers.

Truss, L. (2003) *Eats, Shoots & Leaves: The Zero Tolerance Approach to Punctuation*, Profile Books.

Tuckman, B.W. (1965) 'Developmental sequence in Small Groups', *Psychological Bulletin*, 63, pp. 384–399.

Tufte, E. 'The Cognitive Style of PowerPoint', www.edwardtufte.com.

Tyler, S. (2004) *The Manager's Good Study Guide* (new edition), Open University.

West, M.A. (2012) *Effective Teamwork*, Blackwell.

White, B. (2005) *Dissertation Skills for Business and Management Students*, Thomson Learning.

Williams, J.S. (1995) *The Right Way to Make Effective Presentations*, Eliot Right Way Books.

Yankelovich, D. (1999) *The Magic of Dialogue*, London: Nicholas Brealey Publishing.

Young, T.L. (2010) *Creating Success: Successful Project Management* (3rd edn), London: The Sunday Times.

www.abs.ac.uk

UK Association of Business Schools.

www.acas.org.uk/media/pdf/q/c/Stress-at-work-advisory-booklet.pdf (accessed 27.7.15)

ACAS (2014) Stress at Work.

www.austhink.com/reason/tutorials

Explains argument mapping.

http://www.balancedscorecard.org/Portals/0/PDF/c-ediag.pdf (accessed 17.11.10)

For a tutorial on Ishikawa cause and effect diagrams.

http://www.bkconnection.com/static/Humble_Inquiry_EXCERPT.pdf (accessed 13.01.15)

For excerpt from Schein, E. H. (2013) *Humble Inquiry: The Gentle Art of Asking Instead of Telling*

http://www.bgfl.org/bgfl/custom/resources_ftp/client_ftp/ks3/ict/multiple_int/questions/questions.cfm (accessed 12.1.15)

For a test of multiple intelligences.

http://charteredabs.org/

The UK association of business schools. While mainly aimed at academics, you can find interesting topical material here on issues related to management teaching and learning.

www.cipd.co.uk/hr-resources/factsheets/stress-mental-health-at-work.aspx (accessed 27.7.15)

CIPD (2015) Stress in the workplace.

www.cipd.co.uk/subjects/health/stress/stress.htm

Site of the Chartered Institute for Personnel and Development.

http://www.clinteach.com.au/assets/LEARNING-STYLES-Kolb-QUESTIONNAIRE.pdf (accessed 8.7.15)

If you wish to test your own Kolb learning style.

http://www.colorado.edu/conflict/peace/example/fish7513.htm (accessed 13.1.15)

For a summary of Fisher and Ury's (1983) classic on negotiation.

http://www.crisp.se/henrik.kniberg/cause-effect-diagrams.pdf

For excellent examples and explanations of cause and effect diagrams more generally.

http://www.customshow.com/best-powerpoint-alternatives-presentation-programs/ (accessed 14.1.15).

For a review of alternatives to PowerPoint and explanation of how SlideDog works – but better still, look for a range of up-to-date alternatives to this (assuming you are reading the book a year or two after publication).

http://developmentalobserver.blog.com/2010/06/09/an-overview-of-constructive-developmental-theory-cdt/ (accessed 12.1.15)

For a clear and concise overview of Kegan's theory and self-authoring.

www.direct.gov.uk

UK government sites.

www.dogpile.com

A metasearch engine.

http://www.dummies.com/how-to/content/reduce-stress-and-anxiety-a-guided-relaxation-exercise.html (accessed 7.1.15)

For a 12-minute guided relaxation based on tensing then relaxing.

www.edwardtufte.com

On the cognitive style of PowerPoint.

http://www.ethicsguidebook.ac.uk (accessed 16.1.15)

For an interesting paper by the ESRC on research ethics.

www.ft.com/cms/s/2/2313a2f8-7c81-11e3-b514-00144feabdc0.html#axzz3eSDIgw7Q (accessed 29.6.15)

Pfeffer, J. (2014) quoted in 'Is an MBA worth the cost?' Financial Times, April 29.

www.ft.com/business-education

For regular updates on issues in business education and links to useful free non-credit bearing online courses - Massive Open Online Learning Courses (MOOCs).

http://www.gcflearnfree.org/word2010 (accessed 18.5.15)

For a series of tutorials on using Word 10.

http://gethelp.library.upenn.edu/PORT/ (accessed 16.1.15)

For an excellent set of tutorial resources from the University of Pennsylvania on finding and judging sources, as well as examples of how to paraphrase to avoid plagiarism.

www.google.com

A general search engine.

http://www.globaltrends.com/knowledge-center/features/shapers-and-influencers/190-corporate-clout-2013-time-for-responsible-capitalism (accessed 13.3.15). Global Trends (2013). *Corporate Clout 2013: Time for Responsible Capitalism.*

http://guides.nyu.edu/posters (accessed 14.1.15)

There are many useful websites but try this one.

http://gunning-fog-index.com/fog.cgi (accessed 18.5.15)

To calculate the fog index of any text.

www.helpself.com

Basic EQ test and material on leadership.

http://humanresources.about.com/od/careernetworking/a/social_media.htm (accessed 14.1.15)

For an interesting video aimed at recruiters to help them to do social network checks.

http://www.indeed.co.uk/MBA-jobs (accessed 14.1.15)

Many vacancies equally open to those with other management Master's degrees and a range of similar sites.

http://www.infospaceinc.com/onlineprod/Overlap-DifferentEnginesDifferentResults.pdf

For a (dogpile produced) comparison of search engines and argument in favour of metasearching.

https://intranet.birmingham.ac.uk/as/employability/careers/apply/assessment-centres/index.aspx (accessed 15.1.15)

For guidance Birmingham University offers its students on assessment centres.

www.intute.ac.uk

Resources for education and research.

http://www.kent.ac.uk/careers/cv/portfolios.htm (accessed 15.1.15)

For interesting ideas on multimedia portfolios geared towards impressing an employer.

http://learnonline.canberra.edu.au/mod/book/view.php?id=178430 (accessed 18.5.15)

For guidance on essays.

http://www.lib.berkeley.edu/TeachingLib/Guides/Internet/FindInfo.html (accessed 12.01.15)

For a good tutorial on online searching and assessing.

www.lights.com/publisher

Links to major publishers.

https://www.linkedin.com/pulse/42-leading-social-networking-sites-business-you-may-know-gottlieb (accessed 14.1.15) For suggestions of appropriate professional networking sites to supplement LinkedIn (compiled April 2015).

http://www.mba.com/global/the-gmat-blog-hub/the-official-gmat-blog/2013/jan/unique-mba-career-transitions-stories-from-around-the-world.aspx (accessed 14.1.15).

www.mba.hobsons.com

Information on various courses.

www.mbaworld.com

Site of the Association of MBAs.

http://www.mindtools.com/critpath.html (accessed 16.1.15)

For more on critical path analysis.

http://www.mmu.ac.uk/tips/reading/index.php (accessed 24.11.10)

Resource on critical reading and writing.

www.monmouth.edu/campus_life/counseling/questionnaires/stress.asp (accessed 2.7.15)

For a questionnaire designed to assess student stress from life events.

https://www.moresteam.com/toolbox/fishbone-diagram.cfm (accessed 10.01.15).

For a simple Ishikawa tutorial.

www.ncsu.edu/project/posters/NewSite/ (accessed 4.8.15)

On poster presentation.

www.netskills.ac.uk/TONIC

Online course in Internet-related skills.

www.nhs.uk/conditions/stress-anxiety-depression/pages/ways-relieve-stress.aspx (accessed 7.1.15)

For useful resources on stress reduction.

www.norvig.com/Gettysburg (accessed 14.1.15)

For the slide version of the Gettysburg address.

http://oli.cmu.edu/courses/free-open/argument-diagramming-course-details/
    (accessed 30.7.15)
For free courses on argument mapping and other useful approaches.
www.onenote.com (accessed 12.1.15)
For access to the OneNote free app and tutorials on how to use it.
http://www.open.edu/openlearn/education/english-skills-learning/content-section-overview
    (accessed 16.1.15)
For one of several free OpenLearn course in English for students.
http://www.open.edu/openlearn/education/extending-and-developing-your-thinking-skills/
    content-section-0 (accessed 14.1.15)
For a free course on thinking skills.
http://www.open.edu/openlearn/free-courses (accessed 17.1.15)
For a range of relevant (and other interesting) free short courses.
www.open.edu/openlearn/money-management/management/leadership-and-management/
    managing/systems-explained-diagramming (accessed 13.7.15)
For excellent resources on systems and diagrams.
http://www.open.edu/openlearn/money-management/management/guide-dia-
    grams?LKCAMPAIGN=Google_grant_GenericOU&MEDIA=olexplore&gclid=Cj0KE
    Qjww42tBRCO-sfEiO3DvYMBEiQAHeqMKPm6eefK2Jjy2vKRlARNNnSHictzfK_h_
    SX0bAurUqAaAmkQ8P8HAQ (accessed 13.07.2015)
For a series of excellent podcasts on diagramming, rich pictures, systems thinking and systems
    diagrams.
http://www.pon.harvard.edu/free-reports/thank-you/?freemium_id=15988&n=1
    (accessed 13.1.15)
For Harvard Negotiation report.
http://www.project-management-skills.com/critical-path-method.html (accessed 16.1.15)
For more on critical path analysis.
http://www.prospects.ac.uk/interview_tips_assessment_centres.htm (accessed 15.1.15)
For guidance on what to expect, and how to prepare for an assessment centre.
https://rapidbi.com/learningstyles/#honeymumfordlearningstyleslsq (accessed 12.1.15).
For a 'lite' version of the Honey and Mumford questionnaire.
http://scholar.google.co.uk/ for academic references (or)
www.scholar.google.com for US-based searches.
http://www.silverandclaret.com/wp-content/uploads/EI-Questionnaire.pdf (accessed 1.7.15)
For an emotional intelligence questionnaire
www.similarminds.com/personality_tests
Free personality tests.
http://www.spreeder.com/blog/speed-reading-methods-for-computer-screen/ (accessed 12.1.15)
For tips on speed reading from screen as well as paper.
www.surfwax.com
A metasearch engine.
https://targetjobs.co.uk/ (accessed 14.1.15)
The MBA vacancies area on LinkedIn
http://www.ted.com/talks/julian_treasure_5_ways_to_listen_better?language=en
    (accessed 13.1.15)

For how to listen better. In a more general sense.

http://the-abs.org.uk/

The UK Association of Business Schools.

http://www.ukop.co.uk/help_boolean_search.aspx (accessed 16.1.15)

For a clear explanation of Boolean search terms.

http://www.usingenglish.com/glossary/fog-index.html (accessed 18.5.15)

On fog index in general.

http://www.virtualschool.edu/mon/SocialConstruction/Logic.html (accessed 3.8.15)

Helpful for constructing arguments, and for spotting different examples of false logic.

http://www.vttutorials.ac.uk/detective/brief.html (accessed 12.1.15)

For a free tutorial on judging material found online.

http://www.williamury.com/books/getting-to-yes/ (accessed 13.1.15)

For an entertaining short video communicating the key points in Fisher and Ury's book.

http://www.writing.utoronto.ca/advice/reading-and-researching/critical-reading
(accessed 24.11.10)

This gives a concise overview of critical reading.

http://yourskillfulmeans.com/ (accessed 7.1.15)

For a wide range of resources and suggestions related to mindfulness, meditation and stress
reduction

www.youtube.com/watch?v=3nwwKbM_vJc (accessed 7.1.15)

For a video of a session at Google led by Jon Kabat-Zinn the originator of mindfulness.

www.youtube.com/watch?v=rSU8ftmmhmw (accessed 7.1.15)

For lecture by J K-Z 2007 at Google on mindfulness stress reduction and healing.

www.youtube.com/watch?v=upNONoxskiw (accessed 7.1.15)

For more on meditation.

https://www.youtube.com/watch?v=Xft5N5JWAr4 (accessed 12.1.15)

For a challenging approach to using ideas from sense-making to see how organisational
partnerships learn and respond to climate change, which is particularly interesting in
terms of risk and influence of disciplinary backgrounds – 20 fairly tough minutes viewing,
but on an important topic, and highlighting important aspects of arguments, and issues of
linking science to business issues.

https://www.youtube.com/watch?v=clNwWDEYr8Y (accessed 12.1.15)

For a University of Sydney discussion of work by Brenda Dervin: "From the Mind's Eye of the
User: The Sense-Making Qualitative-Quantitative Methodology".

https://www.youtube.com/watch?v=7RzXo_eD4Vk (accessed 12.1.15)

For a tutorial explaining how to use Evernote.

https://www.youtube.com/watch?v=cipckeeozBE (accessed 17.1.15)

For one of a whole series of very basic tutorials on mathematical operations.

https://www.youtube.com/watch?v=8L1OVkw2ZQ8 (accessed 17.1.15)

For good introduction to Excel spreadsheets (the first in a series).

https://www.youtube.com/watch?v=J4zq3R8b5dQ (accessed 17.1.15)

For an alternative series of tutorials.

https://www.youtube.com/playlist?list=PL09A34EF19596B7BB (accessed 14.1.15)

For a series of tutorials on using Prezi.

INDEX

THE GUINNESS
BOOK OF
BRITISH HIT
SINGLES

Jo and Tim Rice
Paul Gambaccini
and Mike Read

GRRR BOOKS
Editorial Associate: Steve Smith

Guinness Superlatives Ltd
2 Cecil Court, London Road, Enfield, Middlesex

ACKNOWLEDGEMENTS

The four authors would like to thank many of the artists featured in this book for their interest and cooperation and also to the following: BBC Photos, BBC Record Library, Graham Betts, Judy Craymer, Robert Duncan, Eileen Heinink, Karin Ilsen, Melanie Georgi, Sheila Goldsmith, Alan Groves, Keith Lambourne, London Features International, Jan Rice and John Timbers.

We also thank the *New Musical Express* and *Music Week* for the use of their charts and the many record company press offices for their patient help and for photographs.

Editor: Alex E Reid

Design and layout: David Roberts

Fourth edition 1983

© **GRRR Books Ltd. and Guinness Superlatives Ltd. 1983**

First edition 1977, reprinted three times
Second edition 1979, reprinted three times
Third edition 1981, reprinted three times

Published in Great Britain by
Guinness Superlatives Ltd.,
2 Cecil Court, London Road, Enfield, Middlesex
GRRR Books,
196 Shaftesbury Avenue, London WC2

British Library Cataloguing in Publication Data

The Guinness book of British hit singles.—4th ed
1. Music, Popular (Songs, etc.)—Great Britain—
Discography
I. Rice, Jo
016.7899'1245   ML156.4.P6

ISBN 0-85112-259-0

Typeset (Parts 1 and 2) by Bemrose Confidential and Information Products Ltd., Derby and Hazell Watson & Viney Ltd., Aylesbury.
Printed and bound in Great Britain by Hazell Watson & Viney Ltd., Aylesbury, Bucks